Sensation seeking is a trait describing the tendency to seek novel, varied, complex, and intense sensations and experiences and the willingness to take risks for the sake of such experience. The first sensation-seeking scale (SSS) was developed in the early 1960s and since that time the instrument and the theory of the trait have evolved as a function of continuing research around the world. More than 600 publications have appeared on this topic, of which more than 400 appeared after a book on the topic was published in 1979. The current book describes the research and theory on sensation seeking with emphasis on the new findings since this earlier book. The behavioral expressions of sensation seeking have been found in various kinds of risk-taking behaviors such as driving habits, health, gambling, financial activities, alcohol and drug use, sexual behavior, and sports. The trait is also involved in vocational preferences and choices, job satisfaction, social premarital and marital relationships, eating habits and food preferences, media and art preferences, humor, fantasy, creativity, and social attitudes. Its modes of assessment, behavioral expressions, and genetic and psychobiological bases are described by the leading researcher in the field. In the last chapter the author develops a biosocial model for the trait.

BEHAVIORAL EXPRESSIONS AND BIOSOCIAL BASES OF SENSATION SEEKING

BEHAVIORAL EXPRESSIONS AND BIOSOCIAL BASES OF SENSATION SEEKING

MARVIN ZUCKERMAN

University of Delaware

CAMBRIDGE
UNIVERSITY PRESS

Published by the Press Syndicate of the University of Cambridge
The Pitt Building, Trumpington Street, Cambridge CB2 1RP
40 West 20th Street, New York, NY 10011-4211, USA
10 Stamford Road, Oakleigh, Melbourne 3166, Australia

First published 1994

Library of Congress Cataloging-in-Publication Data
Zuckerman, Marvin.
   Behavioral expressions and biosocial bases of sensation seeking /
Marvin Zuckerman.
       p.   cm.
   Includes bibliographical references and index.
   ISBN 0-521-43200-6. – ISBN 0-521-43770-9 (pbk.)
   1. Sensation seeking.   2. Sensation seeking – Testing.
3. Psychobiology.   I. Title.
BF698.35.S45Z83   1994
155.2'32 – dc20   93-40276
                                                              CIP

A catalog record for this book is available from the British Library.

ISBN 0-521-43200-6 hardback
ISBN 0-521-43770-9 paperback

Transferred to digital printing 2004

to Mary

Contents

Preface

More than a decade has elapsed since the publication of my first book, *Sensation Seeking: Beyond the Optimal Level of Arousal*. It has been 30 years since the publication of the first Sensation Seeking Scale (SSS). Since the publication of the 1979 book publications on the topic have appeared with increasing frequency. Between the publication of the first SSS in 1964 and 1978 there were 246 citations in the psychological literature under the term *sensation seeking*. From the year of publication of the 1979 book to 1990 there were over 400 additional publications. This current book is primarily concerned with the new publications. The earlier literature, described in more detail in the 1979 book, will be summarized in the present volume.

The first extensive theoretical model for sensation seeking was presented in a chapter I wrote in a 1969 volume edited by John Zubek, *Sensory Deprivation: Fifteen Years of Research*. The psychobiological model was markedly changed as a consequence of the decade of research between 1969 and 1979. What began as an optimal level of cortical arousal theory was changed to one emphasizing limbic brain systems for reward and punishment. The model for the trait has evolved further and now attempts to encompass a wide variety of new findings on social behavior, cognition, activity, mood, and psychopathology. Historical antecedents of the sensation-seeking construct and the theoretical development between 1964 and 1979 are described in Chapter 1. New theoretical developments since 1979 are described in Chapter 14 after the presentation of the more recent literature in the intervening chapters.

The primary instrument for defining the sensation-seeking trait has been the SSS. This questionnaire has evolved in a series of forms over the years since 1964. The previous book described forms II, IV, and V and how they were developed from the intervening experimental forms. This book will also include newer forms that do not use the forced-choice format and have other interesting features. Copies of the now widely used form V and these new forms will be included in the appendix. Chapter 2 also describes forms developed for younger children and adolescents and translated forms developed in other countries. The four subscales of the SSS were derived from item factor analyses of experimental forms. Subsequent factor analyses by other investigators answered the question of replicability of the factor structure and will be discussed in this chapter. The intercorrelations of the scale scores from the factor analyses were used to justify the inclusion of a Total score in form V of the SSS. This score assumes the existence of a general sensation-seeking factor in all of the subscales in addition to some specific factor variance. This assumption has been challenged and the question will be addressed in terms of the newer analyses. The answer has implications for the fundamental definition of sensation seeking, but the questions of definition or construct validity must come primarily from the relationships between the SS scales and external criteria.

Chapter 3 attempts to answer the question of how sensation seeking fits into the broader dimensions of personality such as Eysenck's three-superfactor model and the currently popular five-dimensional model. Our own recent factor analyses of scales shows that sensation seeking together with impulsivity and asocial tendencies actually constitute the third dimension of personality that the Eysencks have called "psychoticism." In addition to factor analytic studies, correlations between the SSS and other scales are described to identify the nature of sensation seeking relative to the constructs described by other scales. New types of personality dimensions based on neo-Pavlovian theories have been developed in Eastern Europe. Comparisons between the SSS and the scales measuring these traits are also included in Chapter 3.

Since publication of the 1979 book, demographic data have been obtained from noncollege samples in the United States and elsewhere and these data will be presented in Chapter 4. Gender and age differences found in earlier college samples have generally been replicated in nearly all adequate-sized samples. Cross-national data are also presented along with educational, racial, regional, and socioeconomic comparisons on the SSS.

Risk taking for the sake of novel experience has been part of the definition of sensation seeking since the first scales were developed. At first the major emphasis was on physical risk taking, as embodied in the Thrill and Adventure Seeking (TAS) subscale. However, later research showed that other kinds of risk were involved in the broader trait, including legal, social, and financial ones. This led to a broader theory of risk taking in terms of conflict between positive and negative affects or outcome expectancies. New research on risk taking in terms of personality and cognitive traits, like generalized risk appraisal, is described in Chapter 5. Research on areas of risk taking like driving habits, health, gambling, and other kinds of financial risk taking are also included in this chapter.

Research on risk taking in sports has flourished since 1979 and now warrants a separate discussion. In Chapter 6, an attempt is made to explain the difference between the types of sports or exercise favored by high sensation seekers and those preferred by average and low sensation seekers. Vocational choice and work satisfaction relationships with sensation seeking are discussed in this chapter.

The 1979 book included research on the relation between sensation seeking and sexual attitudes and behavior, but not much on more complex social relationships between the sexes. The role of sensation seeking in premarital love relationships and marital adjustment is added to the topic of sexuality in Chapter 7.

Research on media preferences, including films, art, music, and humor, is described in Chapter 8. The use of fantasy and the fantasy content reported by high and low sensation seekers are also reviewed in this chapter.

Sensation seeking has been found to be the personality trait most predictive of early drug use. Sensation-seeking motivations are important in the early use of drugs and alcohol. This literature, along with that on eating habits and food preferences, is described in Chapter 9.

Sensation seeking is an essentially normal trait dimension; there is nothing intrinsically psychopathological, or even antisocial, in either high or low sensation seekers. Most high or low sensation seekers are not maladjusted or abnormal in the psychiatric sense. However, certain kinds of psychopathology are associated with high sensation seeking including antisocial personality, substance abuse, and bipolar disorder. Schizophrenia and some forms of anxiety disorder are associated with low sensation seeking (Chapter 10). The relation between normal sensation seeking and psychopathology also includes certain biological traits found in both. These shared biological correlates testify to the underlying biological variation affecting both normal personality variants and types of psychopathology. Stress can produce certain kinds of psychopathology as well as transient physical, social, and psychological disturbances. The role of sensation seeking as a mediator of stress is also discussed in this chapter.

Behavior genetical research suggests that genetic factors account for at least 30% of the variance in most broad personality traits. In sensation seeking, heritability is at the high end of the range, approaching 60% of the variance uncorrected for reliability. Because we do not inherit personality in the sense of specific behavior patterns, the differences due to heredity should be mediated by basic neuropsychological and psychopharmacological differences, more directly influenced by genes. Chapter 11 will deal both with the genetics and biochemistry of sensation seeking, including research on hormones, neurotransmitters and their metabolites, and enzymes controlling the production and disposal of neurotransmitters. Because most of the human research on the biochemistry of personality is correlational and uses indirect indicators of brain activity, the comparative research on other species will be examined to see if there are some common biological bases for sensation seeking and analogues of the trait in animal behavior.

Psychophysiology lies between the behavioral and biochemical levels of analysis, showing how high and low sensation seekers may differ in cortical and autonomic reactivity to stimuli varying in intensity, novelty, and meaning. Consistent differences between high and low sensation seekers have been found in heart rate indexes of orienting and defensive reflexes, and in cortical reactivity to high levels of stimulation. These and other topics in psychophysiology are reviewed in Chapter 12.

Differences in psychophysiology are related to different modes of information processing. Chapter 13 describes individual differences in sensation, perception, attention, problem solving, concept formation, and intelligence related to sensation seeking. These differences in information processing may be related to more basic differences in neuropsychology and biochemistry discussed in the preceding chapter.

Chapter 14 attempts to integrate the post-1979 research into a modified model that tries to explain many of the behavioral phenomena of sensation seeking in terms of the underlying psychobiology of the trait. Unfortunately, there is practically no developmental or even family history data on sensation seekers that might enable us to formulate the social-experimental determinants of the trait, but some speculations about this important aspect of personality will be attempted.

I hope this description of the book has made it clear that this is not simply a new edition of my previous book on sensation seeking, but one that is focused on the more recent theory and research. This book is written primarily for researchers, teachers, and graduate students. The 1979 book has been used as a text for advanced undergraduate courses and this book could be used for a similar purpose.

Some background in psychometrics and test construction would be useful for Chapter 2, and some knowledge of behavior genetics, psychobiology, and psychophysiology would be helpful for Chapters 11 and 12. A recent book, *Psychobiology of Personality* (Zuckerman, 1991a), offers a more detailed explanation of the methods and definitions in the biological areas, and these sections could be useful in reading the current book.

Figure P.1 High sensation-seeking granddaughter with a low sensation-seeking grandfather.

A comprehensive understanding of individual differences in personality must encompass many diverse areas from the biological to the sociological. This breadth of topics is what I find most challenging about personality. Broad behavioral theories have been deemphasized in psychology for the past 30 years or so. Personality theories remain the only redoubt of general theory.

Sensation seeking has been an exciting trait to study, which may explain why I have stuck to it for so long. The concept was not entirely a new one when I began to study it, but the trait had been neglected by most researchers who did recognize its importance in many diverse kinds of human behavior. This situation has changed, thanks to the many dedicated researchers who have used my scale or similar ones in their studies. I owe them all a special thanks for making this book possible. Another special debt is owed to my recent graduate students who have explored new areas of sensation seeking in their theses and dissertations: Sam Ball, James Black, Paula Horvath, and Mary Thornquist.

This book was largely written during my sabbatical year (1990–1991) as a fellow at the Netherlands Institute for Advanced Study where, thanks to the government of the Netherlands and the staff of the institute, I had the unusual opportunity to think and write in very congenial surroundings in the company of many distinguished international scholars. The University of Delaware also supported me during this sabbatical year, and my chairman Thomas Scott gave me some important released time during the semester preceding the sabbatical that allowed me to collect most of the reference materials I needed for the book prior to my arrival in the Netherlands. A grant from the University of Delaware covered the final costs of completing the manuscript.

Finally, a special acknowledgment of the most important support system, Mary Hazard, who, in spite of her own scholarly endeavors, gave generously in time and effort to the feeding, care, and love of a rather disorganized and slovenly brown bear.

1

Theory through 1979

Overview

The primary distinction between scientific theory and other types of explanation is that scientific theory is capable of disproof by empirical methods. Scientific theory cannot appeal to authority, intuition, or reason alone for proof or disproof, although all of these processes may play some role in the formulation of a theory. "God exists," says the believer. "What is your proof?" asks the skeptic. "His works are everywhere in the universe," replies the believer. This is proof of a sort, except that it allows for no other explanation; more important, there is no way to disprove the claim or prove the superiority of any other explanation, including a natural one.

Most theories described in standard texts of personality cannot meet this simple requirement of scientific explanation. Many appeal to positive evidence, usually of an anecdotal, historical, or clinical event, and in most cases the evidence is post hoc, and its relation to the theory is mediated by many unstated assumptions. There is usually no consideration of alternative explanations and no way to weigh the validity of competing explanations.

Some psychologists have a tendency to substitute description for explanation. We see a person act in a way judged to be aggressive and we explain his behavior by saying "He was angry." We see him do it twice and say "He is an aggressive person." States or traits are inferred from behavior with no independent confirmation and are then used to explain the behavior. These examples represent a misuse of state and trait theory. The observation of regularities in behavior in given situations is a necessary first step toward a theoretical explanation. Any theory of personality must demonstrate such regularities. If everyone's behavior is situation-specific, with no variation due to personality, we may have a social psychology but not a personality psychology. Giving these consistencies, trait labels are a necessary first step toward a causal theory because we must agree on what we are trying to explain, but the description of behavior, summarized in a label, does not explain the behavior. The classification of traits is the beginning and not the end of personality science.

What we decide to observe or study and how we go about studying our subject are essential parts of any scientific paradigm. Scientists who use radically different methods cannot even compare their constructs, let alone test one against another. To say that we study behavior or cognition is meaningless without further specifications of the "how"; it is like saying geologists study rocks. If I make a rock collection and sort my rocks by size or color alone, I am not practicing geology.

In order for psychologists to communicate, they must agree on what must be observed under what kinds of conditions. As Popper (1979) has pointed out, there is no such thing as a theory derived solely from unbiased empirical observation because preliminary theoretical notions determine what aspects of nature will be observed and how they will be observed. Some personality psychologists (Allport & Odbert, 1936) have attempted to develop a comprehensive description of personality traits by taking all the words with trait connotations out of the dictionary, eliminating redundancies or synonyms, and grouping them into trait dimensions by a combination of rational and statistical analyses. Is this a strictly empirical procedure? Granted that English is a rich language; however, we cannot assume that it exhausts the possibilities for trait description. Some traits may be underestimated because of a limited representation of adjectives. Soon after the definition of a sensation-seeking trait, we attempted to define it as a state using single adjectives. The few words we came up with, like "adventurous, daring, and playful," were not adequate to convey the trait in all its aspects. On the trait test we could use sentences to describe complex activities or attitudes that seemed to be prototypical for the trait.

No theoretical concept emerges without some intellectual ancestry. Theoretical antecedents of sensation seeking were described at some length in the previous volume (Zuckerman, 1979a) and will be more briefly summarized in this chapter. A more personal account of how my interest in the topic developed can be found elsewhere (Zuckerman, 1993a). The development of the sensation-seeking construct between 1964 and 1979 will be described next. Later developments of theory (e.g., Zuckerman, 1984a) are the subject of the final chapter of this book.

Instinct, drive, and need approaches

Humans and many other species engage in behavior that is not directly associated with satisfaction of primary biological needs, like food, water, sex, pain avoidance, and threats to survival. The goal of sensation-seeking behavior is the increase rather than the decrease of stimulation. Exploration of novel stimuli or situations by animals occurs even in the absence of hunger or thirst. Even behavior that is associated with "primary drives" and biological "needs" is influenced by novelty. A monotonous diet can incite prison riots even though the food provided to the prisoners meets all of their basic nutritional needs. Spices providing little nutritional value are commonly added to foods to make them more palatable. Sexual tensions are easily resolved by masturbation, but this mode of tension reduction is rarely satisfactory as the sole source of gratification once heterosexual or homosexual modes have been experienced. Monogamous relationships allow easy gratification of sexual needs but are often endangered by the pursuit of sexual variety in new partners. Many people needlessly engage in risky activities that threaten their survival and yet seem to enjoy these activities.

Instinct, drive, and need theorists have invoked various explanations for such phenomena. In his last formulation of "instinct" theory, Freud (1915/1957) grouped "instincts" into two major categories, those serving life and those with death as the ultimate aim. Life instincts included sex, hunger, thirst, and pain avoidance, all reducing tensions from cyclically arising needs or functioning to protect and prolong life. The death instinct represented a more constant tension-reduction need with its ultimate expression in the conscious or unconscious "wish to die." All activities not related to these kinds of needs (like sensation seeking) were regarded as displacements, sublimations, or attempts to deny fear by proving mastery or to build tensions to higher levels in order to increase the pleasure associated with tension reduction. The last explanation for the seeking of intense stimulation is like that of the simpleton who, when asked why he was banging his head against the wall, replied, "It feels so good when I stop."

Freud's concept of *Trieb,* translated as "instinct," has more in common with psychologists' concept of *drive* than with modern biologists' concept of instinct. Both Freud and the learning theorist Clark Hull (1943) believed that primary appetitive drives arose from innate physiological tensions, but that the objects required to reduce these tensions and the means of reducing them had to be learned. Because of his behaviorist strictures, Hull never used the term *pleasure,* but he believed that all primary reinforcement was reduction of a drive based on physiological needs. Exploration was simply regarded as a behavioral mechanism produced by other drives, such as sex or hunger, and characterized by general behavioral activity or restlessness produced by these other drives.

The observation that animals explored their environments, even when all primary drives were satisfied (Tolman, 1926), was inconsistent with Hull's concept of exploration. Sated animals should do little more than sleep or rest according to these theories. Sensory deprivation experiments showed that rodents (Kish, 1966), monkeys (Butler & Alexander, 1955), and humans (A. Jones, 1969) deprived of patterned or varied stimulation for any length of time developed a "drive for stimulation," as shown by their bar pressing for the reinforcement of external stimulation, even if that stimulation was meaningless and unrelated to primary drives. A. Jones's studies with humans demonstrated that the novelty or unpredictability of such stimuli was the quality most related to their reinforcement value. Experiments with several species have shown that the need for variation in sensory stimulation is as basic as the conventional "primary" drives and particularly strong in primates.

Sensation seeking as a primary drive

McDougall (1923) regarded curiosity as a basic instinct released by indistinct perception or identification of an object. Curiosity was not conceived of as an independent instinct but as one necessary for the operation of other instincts; it served only to identify potential satisfiers of these other instincts. This definition resembles Hull's concept of exploration as activity in the service of primary drives.

Similarly, post-Freudian analysts like Hartmann (1964) and Rapaport (1960) believed that activities like play and creative thinking could stem from natural functions of an "autonomous ego" rather than serving the instinctual functions of the id. However, these activities used id-related materials in "the service of the ego." Tolman (1926) included sensory needs along with food and sex as the basis of primary drives but, like McDougall, he conceived of curiosity as a drive in the service of other drives. However, he later expanded his concept of *sensory motor hungers* to include aesthetic and play needs (Tolman, 1932).

Henry Murray (1938), following the drive-reduction theories popular at the time, classified personality traits by the "needs" supposedly underlying them. Primary needs, like primary drives, were said to have their origins in specific physiological tensions. Whereas Murray regarded all needs as originating in "tensions in the brain," some of them were believed to begin in peripheral visceral tensions and were therefore called *viscerogenic*, while others were independent of visceral tensions and therefore called *psychogenic*. Psychogenic needs may have evolved from viscerogenic ones, but they eventually became "functionally autonomous" (Allport's term, 1937) from them.

Some of Murray's needs have been used as the basis for personality scales that have been correlated with the Sensation Seeking Scale SSS; (see Chapter 3). Two types of needs relevant to sensation seeking, *sex* and *sentience* (need for sensation), were classified as viscerogenic needs, whereas two others also related to sensation seeking, *exhibitionism* and *play*, were regarded as psychogenic. Other needs relevant to the sensation-seeking construct involve broad cognitive styles: *change* or *sameness, impulsion* or *deliberation, conjunctivity* (organized response) or *disjunctivity* (disorganized response). Murray did not attempt any higher-order classifications of his catalog of needs, although many appear to be interrelated in certain higher order trait constructs like extraversion and, possibly, sensation seeking.

Challenges to drive theories

The theories just discussed regarded sensation-seeking behavior as a function of a primary drive or need for stimulation. But the whole concept of drive as a state of tension arising from some internal physiological source did not describe the phenomenon very well. In the first place, sensation-seeking behavior often arises from a state of low arousal, produced by an invariant environment, and it is higher arousal, not reduction of arousal, that is the goal. This pattern is the opposite of that for classical primary drives, where arousal is conceived of as an unpleasant state of tension, and pleasure or reinforcement is produced by the reduction, not the increase, of arousal. However, many psychologists were beginning to question the entire concept of drive in all types of motivation.

Allport (1937) conceded that drive might be a useful construct with animals and young human infants and children, but he did not think that it was appropriate in explaining the motives of adult humans. Maslow (1954) also believed that more mature needs like love and self-actualization were the outcome of a maturational development of motivation that began with simple physiological needs but developed into autonomous needs like *self-actualization*. The latter need represents a search for growth and change rather than being directed at some kind of drive reduction. According to Maslow, self-actualizers seek and enjoy novel and "peak experiences" that are often quite arousing.

Harlow (1953a) rejected the idea of drive-reduction for nonhumans (mice and monkeys) as well as humans. He felt that complex learning is motivated for the most part by mildly arousing stimuli and disrupted by intense emotions. Concerning humans Harlow (1953b) said: "Learning efficiency is far better related to tensions in the brain than in the belly" (p. 25).

P. Young (1936, 1948) proposed that we return to a "factual hedonistic" theory of motivation. According to Young, pleasure is not simply a matter of drive or need reduction, but is intrinsic to certain qualities and *optimal intensities of stimulation*. Exploratory behavior is not elicited by internal tensions or tissue needs, but by a novel environment.

Optimal level of stimulation and arousal

Young's suggestion of a hedonically optimal intensity of stimulation is an old concept dating from the founder of experimental psychology Wilhelm Wundt. Wundt (1893) said that positive feeling was a function of an optimal level of stimulation producing an optimal level of sensation; intensities above or below this level were felt as either indifferent, less pleasurable, or unpleasant. However, Wundt's optimal level construct was not generalized across sensory modalities; it applied to senses of pressure, temperature, olfaction, and taste (the degree of bitterness in beer, for instance), but not to the "higher senses" of vision and audition.

Before Freud became a complete drive reduction theorist, he formulated an optimal level of arousal construct called the Constancy Principle (Breuer & Freud, 1895/1937). This principle states that there is a tendency to maintain a constant level of "intracerebral excitement." Levels of arousal above this optimal level become "burdensome and annoying" and create a need to reduce stimulation. Arousal below this level motivates attempts to increase stimulation. At the optimal level of excitement (arousal), the brain was said to be "accessible to all external stimuli" (p. 143). Later this homeostatic theory was replaced by a drive reduction one that conceived of the nervous system as an organ dedicated to the reduction of stimulation to a minimum (Freud, 1920/1955).

Wundt and Freud emphasized the effect of stimulation or arousal on feelings of pleasure or displeasure. Comparative psychologists like Yerkes and Dodson (1908) could not define feelings in rats, and therefore were more interested in the effects of stimulus intensity on behavioral performance. High levels of stimulation might facilitate learning involving easy tasks, but more complex and difficult learning was said to be most efficient at some intermediate level of stimulus intensity. For difficult learning the relationship between stimulus intensity and performance took the form of an inverted-U curve. The inverted-U was emblazoned on the banners of all subsequent optimal-level theorists.

Donald Hebb (1949) formulated an *optimal level of stimulation* (OLS) theory in a discussion of pain: "In most sensory modes there is an intensity limen [threshold] at which avoidance appears. Below this point the stimulation may be sought out – that is, it is 'pleasant'; above it, the same kind of stimulation produces avoidance and, if the avoidance is unsuccessful, behavioral disturbance" (p. 182).

Hebb translated the optimal-level theory into a behavioral-motivational construct; too little stimulation leads to sensation seeking and too much to sensation reducing (avoidance). But Hebb was a physiological psychologist and therefore needed a central neuropsychological explanation for the optimal level of stimulation. The explanation was provided when Moruzzi and Magoun (1949) discovered that the reticular formation (a pathway running through the brain-stem core and limbic system and innervating most parts of the cortex) had an activating effect on the cortex and that lesions in the pathway produced electroencephalogram (EEG) records characteristic of somnolence. Later studies showed that descending neural pathways from the cortex could inhibit the *reticular activating system* (RAS). The entire reticulocortical system operated like a homeostatic mechanism (Lindsley, 1961) maintaining an optimal level of brain arousal relative to the diurnal sleep–waking cycle.

Now Hebb had the physiological basis for an *optimal level of arousal* (OLA) regulated by the interaction between sensory stimulation and the physiological characteristics of the RAS including the cortex itself. He summarized the relationship in the chart shown in Figure 1.1.

Hebb (1955) distinguished two functions of sensory stimulation: The *cue* function guides behavior and the *arousal* function activates the whole behavioral system. Because the cue function cannot operate efficiently in an underaroused brain, the arousal function is necessary for the cue function. One cannot register or respond to stimuli while one is asleep, and one's attentiveness to cues is markedly reduced in drowsy states. However, the relationship between the cue function and arousal, which prepares and energizes it, is not a simple linear one (see Figure 1.1). Cue function is inefficient at low levels of arousal, reaches a peak at some OLA, but declines beyond this optimal level where further arousal is associated with negative emotions like anxiety.

Other theorists modified the OLA theory of emotions. Duffy (1951) and Schlosberg (1954) suggested that arousal was related to the intensity of emotions but not to the pleasantness–unpleasantness dimension. Their theories represent a change from the Wundt and Hebb notions suggesting an inverted-U-shaped relationship between stimulation or arousal and hedonic tone. The dissociation between emotional quality and arousal intensity is well

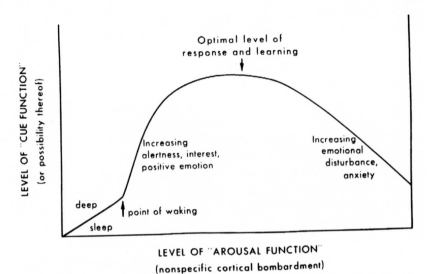

Figure 1.1 Relation between (cortical) arousal and cue functions. From "Drives and the C.N.S. (conceptual nervous system)," By D. O. Hebb, 1955. *Psychological Review, 62,* 243–254. Copyright 1955 by American Psychological Association.

taken. Very intense arousal, as in sexual excitement, is not usually unpleasant or anxious in quality, and low arousal, as in states of relaxation when there are no task demands, can be very pleasurable.

Arousal, as used by these theorists, refers to a general state of the organism rather than a momentary reaction to a stimulus. One may be in a low state of arousal, but a loud noise or a significant sound can quickly increase arousal to a high level. The pleasantness or unpleasantness of that change in arousal may be a function of the discrepancy between the basal level of arousal and that produced by the stimulus. Another group of theories propose that it is arousal change, rather than absolute level of arousal, that determines the hedonic effects of stimuli.

Stimulus change and arousability theories

Bain (1859/1875) suggested that pleasure or displeasure produced by stimulation depends on the relationship between the intensity of the stimulus and the general level of stimulation prior to the stimulus. If noise, for instance, is at a painful level, any reduction of the level is felt as positive; but if the basal level is very low, the same intensity of noise would be felt as unpleasant.

Freud (1930/1961) said that pleasure was in proportion to the extent and suddenness of tension reduction, but Baines stated that pleasure may be produced by sudden increases as well as decreases in stimulation.

The OLS and stimulus change theories discussed thus far have largely concerned the intensity of stimulation rather than the other qualities of stimuli. Novelty can be defined by either a change in intensity or general perceptual configuration of the stimulus. McClelland, Atkinson, Clark, and Lowell (1953) proposed that the pleasantness or unpleasantness of a change of sensory or perceptual event depends on the degree of discrepancy from an *adaptation level;* small discrepancies are associated with positive affect and large discrepancies with negative affect. A chimpanzee will react with positive interest to a whole model chimpanzee, even though it is different from a live chimpanzee, but the ape will be terrified by a model of a chimpanzee head (Hebb, 1946), even if it has never seen a horror movie. The whole model could be interpreted as a slight deviation from the perceptual adaptation level (engram of previous chimps seen) but a head alone represents a major deviation from the usual perceptual configuration.

Schneirla (1959) extended the stimulus change construct to a general postulate applicable to a broad range of comparative behavior patterns from the simple organisms to humans. His basic postulate was stated as follows: "For all organisms in early ontogenetic stages, low intensities of stimulation tend to evoke approach reactions, high intensities withdrawal reactions" (p. 3).

This seems at first like a simple OLS theory, but Schneirla emphasized the gradient of changing stimulation or deviations of the static stimulus from the general level of stimulation. A soft crooning voice or a light touch elicits positive reactions in a human infant; a sudden loud voice or heavy pressure usually produces emotional distress. The dimensions of the retinal image produced by an animal moving away tend to elicit approach, as in the pursuit reactions of predators. But when the image suddenly increases in size, as when one animal moves toward another, the sudden influx of stimulation may produce withdrawal or defensive reactions. Approach or Withdrawal (A or W) were terms used to describe reflexive or tropistic responses typical of behavior of less complex organisms and the young of more complex animals. For behavior in more evolved or mature organisms Schneirla used the terms *seeking* and *avoidance* to convey the goal oriented, more flexible nature of the response. Approach–Withdrawal has been identified as a basic dimension of temperament in human infants and is defined by the infant's reactions to novel stimuli and persons (Thomas & Chess, 1977). This tendency could be the first manifestation of a sensation-seeking trait in humans.

Berlyne (1960, 1971) extended the idea of the motivating properties of stimuli beyond the simple dimension of stimulus intensity. The *arousal potential* of stimuli represents their capacity to command attention, excite the nervous system, or influence behavior (Berlyne & Madsen, 1973). The qualities of stimuli that determine their arousal potentials are intensity, size, color, sensory modality, affective connotations, novelty, complexity, degree of change from preceding stimulation, suddenness of change, surprisingness, incongruity, and uncertainty. His optimal-level postulate was: "For an individual organism at a particular time there will be an optimal influx of arousal potential. Arousal potential that deviates in either an upward or downward direction from this optimum will be drive inducing or aversive" (Berlyne, 1960, p. 194). This definition emphasized aversive effects of deviations from an optimum level. Later, he conceded that both increases and decreases in arousal from the optimum level could still be pleasant rather than aversive.

Berlyne (1967) was the first of the optimal-level theorists to use the reward centers in the brain (Olds & Milner, 1954) to provide a physiological basis for the reward of arousing stimuli. He suggested that the arousal threshold for triggering reward systems was lower than the one for activating brain aversion systems. From this concept he could explain the inverted-U curve of Wundt and Hebb as shown in Figure 1.2. At low (L_a) to moderate (X_1) levels of arousal potential there is increasing activation of the primary reward system, but at higher levels of arousal potential the aversion system becomes activated and begins to reduce positive hedonic tone (pleasure) until a point is reached where aversion comes to predominate. The model assumes that the aversion system inhibits the effects of the reward system.

Fiske and Maddi (1961) also postulated that the discrepancy between current levels of brain activation and an optimal level or range of activation resulted in behavior that reduced the discrepancy. They also emphasized the *impact* of stimuli on the brain in terms of three qualities of stimulation: intensity, meaningfulness, and variation.

Both Berlyne and Fiske and Maddi suggested that there might be stable individual differences in optimal levels of stimulus arousal preference. Berlyne said that such differences might be based on physiological differences in tonic arousal, phasic arousability, or habituation of arousal. Fiske and Maddi speculated that individual differences might originate in the relative enrichment or limitation of stimulation in the early environment, but they did not further elaborate their ideas of optimal levels of arousability as the basis for a personality trait. The next group of theories have used the optimal-level constructs as the foundation for personality traits based on the physiological characteristics of brain systems.

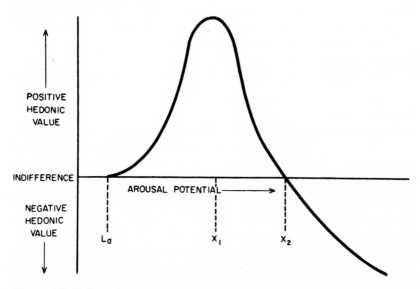

Figure 1.2. Relation between arousal potential of stimuli and their hedonic values. L_a = absolute threshold of stimulus; X_1 = point of maximal activation of the primary reward system; X_2 = intensity at which arousal of aversion system exceeds arousal of reward system. From *Aesthetics and Psychobiology*, p. 89, by D. E. Berlyne, 1971. New York: Appleton-Century-Crofts. Copyright 1991 by Appleton-Century-Crofts. Reprinted by permission.

Individual difference theories

Pavlov

Pavlov (1927/1960) defined temperament in dogs in terms of hypothetical differences in the properties of their nervous systems. The actual operational definitions of these properties were derived from conditioning, habituation and sensitization experiments in which the intensity of stimuli was a major variable. One of the primary characteristics defining temperament is the *strength* (of excitation) of the nervous system, defined as the capacity of brain neurons to continue to function under strong, prolonged, or recurrent stimulation without triggering protective inhibition mechanisms. *Balance* represents the equilibrium between processes of excitation and inhibition. *Mobility* is defined as the speed of switching from excitation to inhibition or vice versa.

Combinations of these basic properties define various types. Pavlov described a *sanguine* type of dog, who was curious, friendly, and active in natural behavioral situations, but was a poor conditioner because it fell asleep with the monotonous stimulation of the conditioned stimulus and movement-restraining conditioning apparatus. But Pavlov found that dogs could be conditioned if the conditioned stimuli were varied. In terms of the human trait of sensation seeking, one could say that they had high "boredom susceptibility." Sanguine dogs were described as having strong and balanced excitatory and inhibitory processes with a strong mobility of shift between processes. Repetitive or restricted stimulation tended to elict a rapid shift from excitatory to inhibitory processes. Their opposite was the *melancholic* type, including dogs who were restrained in activity and nonexploratory in natural environments, and fearful in social reactions to humans. This type of dog was easily conditioned because it remained awake and highly alert in the conditioning apparatus. It is not difficult to see the sanguine type as a sensation seeker in human terms because of its need for novel stimulation, although the melancholic type seems to be closest to an anxious introvert in H. Eysenck's terms. However, one must be wary of making these too easy generalizations from dogs to humans without further evidence of functional or biological links between the comparative behaviors. The extensions of Pavlovian·constructs to humans will be discussed in a later chapter. The relevance of the strong nervous system construct to sensation seeking will become more apparent in Chapter 12 on the psychophysiology of sensation seeking.

Eysenck

H. Eysenck's (1957) earlier theory incorporated Hull's and Pavlov's con-structs of drive and excitatory and inhibitory properties of the nervous system and their equilibrium into a theory of the major trait of introversion–extraver-sion. Extraverts were said to be characterized by greater strength of inhibition in reaction to repetitive stimulation, introverts by an excess of excitation. According to this theory, excitation of cortical neurons was associated with behavioral inhibition. Persons high on the independent trait of neuroticism (N), or emotionality, were thought to be characterized by high levels of autonomic system arousability.

Later, H. Eysenck (1967) shifted the focus of his theory to an optimal level of stimulation theory as shown in Figure 1.3. Eysenck took the Wundt and Hebb inverted-U curve for the population and divided it into two curves: The one for introverts is displaced to the lower end of the stimulation or arousal range and the one for extraverts is shifted to the high end of the continuum. This means that at low levels of stimulation (A) or arousal the

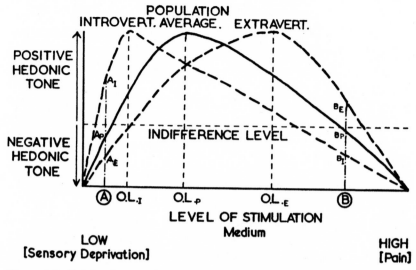

POPULATION
INTROVERT. AVERAGE. EXTRAVERT.

POSITIVE
HEDONIC
TONE

NEGATIVE
HEDONIC
TONE

INDIFFERENCE LEVEL

Ⓐ O.L.ᵢ   O.L.ₚ   O.L.ₑ   Ⓑ

LEVEL OF STIMULATION

LOW   Medium   HIGH
[Sensory Deprivation]   [Pain]

Figure 1.3. Relation between level of sensory input and hedonic tone for introverts and extraverts. From *The biological basis of personality*, p. 109, by H. J. Eysenck. 1967. Springfield, IL: Charles C. Thomas. Copyright 1967 by Charles C. Thomas. Reprinted by permission.

introvert feels better than the extravert, whereas at high levels (B) it is the extravert who feels better. Behavior should follow the same pattern with introverts reaching their optimal levels of performance at relatively lower levels of stimulation and arousal than extraverts. Because extraverts require higher levels of stimulation, not usually provided by routine environments, they would tend to be sensation seekers. But introverts are assumed to be usually at or closer to their optimal levels of stimulation and they would tend to be sensation reducers. This is why Eysenck regarded sensation seeking as a subtrait of extraversion (E). The actual relationship of sensation seeking within the Eysenckian dimensions is somewhat different than he postulated, as will be shown in Chapter 3.

The reason that optimal levels of stimulation and arousal are lower for introverts than for extraverts is that the extravert is hypothesized to have a low tonic level of arousal whereas the introvert is supposed to have a high level of arousal even in the nonstimulated state. These differences in cortical arousal were explained by differences in sensitivity of the reticulocortical system in response to general stimulation. The same intensity of stimulation would produce more activation of the RAS and cortex in an introvert than in an extravert up to some higher range of stimulus intensity. At high ranges of

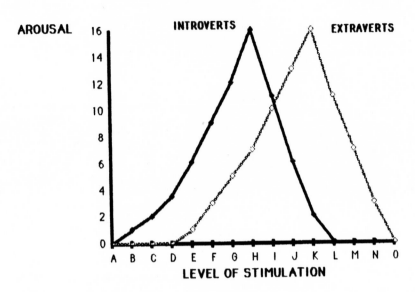

Figure 1.4. Theoretical relation between stimulus intensity and arousal for introverts and extraverts.

stimulus intensity, a mechanism of *transmarginal inhibition* is triggered at relatively lower intensities in the introvert than in the extravert. Figure 1.4 shows the theoretical relationship between stimulation and arousal in introverts and extraverts.

The theoretical formulations of H. Eysenck's (1967) optimal-level theory of extraversion seemed to make sensation seeking a central component of extraversion. However, there was a third dimension of personality lurking in the wings of Eysenck's theater of personality. Until the development of a scale to measure this third dimension, called psychoticism (P) by the Eysencks (H. Eysenck & Eysenck, 1976), the major efforts in Eysenck's research program centered around the traits of extraversion and neuroticism. In the earlier conception, extraversion was considered to be a blend of impulsivity and sociability (S. Eysenck & Eysenck, 1963), although the combination was questioned by others (Carrigan, 1960; Guilford, 1975); Guilford called it a "shot-gun marriage" of two unrelated traits. As research on the P dimension has developed it has become apparent that much of the impulsivity trait belongs more properly to the P rather than to the E dimension, and extraversion has become more of a measure of pure sociability. The position of sensation seeking in the three-dimensional system has also shifted to the P dimension (Zuckerman, Kuhlman, & Camac, 1988; Zuckerman, Kuhlman, Thornquist, & Kiers, 1991) where it seems to join with impulsivity in a congenial marriage, "made in biology" (Zuckerman, 1993b).

Gray

Most of the theories discussed until now used the arousal or arousability of the cortex or reticulocortical system as the biological basis for optimal levels of stimulation and the personality traits based on them. Berlyne (1967) was the first to suggest that arousal of limbic brain reward and aversion systems could account for the inverted-U-shaped relationship between stimulation and hedonic tone. Gray developed a personality theory based on the actual neurophysiological evidence connecting animal models for impulsivity, anxiety, and aggression with corresponding human traits. His model has evolved in a series of publications (Gray, 1973, 1982, 1987). A more detailed account of the theory can be found in these publications and in the book *Psychobiology of Personality* (Zuckerman, 1991a).

Gray defined three basic behavioral systems, identifiable in nonhuman species, with relevance to human personality. For each system he identified likely neurological and pharmacological substrates in the form of specific neural pathways whose functions were largely defined by experiments on nonhuman species, primarily rats. He also suggested where the corresponding dimensions of personality might be located within the three dimensions of Eysenck's system.

The approach system is defined by approach behavior based on a sensitivity to signals associated with reward or the cessation of punishment (relief). The system is based on responses to conditioned stimuli rather than responses to actual reward or punishment. At the human level the trait is identified with *impulsivity* and high levels of neuroticism (N), extraversion (E), and psychoticism (P) within Eysenck's dimensions. The biological bases of the disposition are dopaminergic pathways that have been shown to mediate brain self-stimulation in rats and may mediate the reinforcement of natural and learned rewards. They are also the pathways necessary for the euphoric effects of opiates, amphetamines, and cocaine.

The *behavioral-inhibition* system (BIS) is defined by inhibition of ongoing behavior programs in response to signals associated with punishment or nonreward (frustration), or novel stimuli. The BIS mechanism is described as one that continually scans the environment (the *checking mode*) for threatening, or unusual (novel) stimuli. If such stimuli appear, the BIS stops ongoing activity governed by other systems (the *control mode*), diverts attention toward the threatening or novel stimulus, and increases general arousal of the autonomic system.

In terms of human personality, the system is identified with the trait of anxiety at one pole and psychopathic (antisocial) personality at the opposite pole. Within Eysenck's dimensions, it is high N, low E (introversion), and low P at the anxiety pole, and low N, high E (extraversion), and high P at the psychopathy pole. Biologically, the core of the system is the reciprocal connections between the septal area and hippocampus, the associated Papez circuit, with inputs from ascending noradrenergic and serotonergic systems, and from descending prefrontal cortex via cingulate and entorhinal cortices.

Questions about the translation of some of these psychobiological systems, derived from comparative studies of nonhuman species, to human personality have been raised before (see commentaries following Gray, 1982, and Zuckerman, 1991a). The question of more immediate concern is how the human sensation-seeking trait would fit into the system. Gray suggests that novel stimuli are one of the types of inputs that move the BIS from the checking mode to the control mode. But other theorists, already discussed, have maintained that novel stimuli are unconditioned stimuli for approach behavior or for both approach and aversion systems. There is nothing intrinsically anxiety provoking in novel stimuli unless they are too intense, too discrepant from familiar stimulus configurations, too suddenly presented, and moving toward rather than away from the viewer.

Anxiety and psychopathy define the two ends of a bipolar dimension in Gray's model, but current clinical thinking and diagnostic criteria (*DSM-III*) do not regard the psychopath (now called "antisocial personality") as a person necessarily lacking in anxiety. Psychopaths are certainly high sensation seekers (Chapter 10), but sensation seeking in normals is not correlated at all with neuroticism or anxiety traits (Chapter 3). Sensation seeking has some relationship to E, and a higher one with P, but it has none with N.

A third dimension of Gray's model, *fight–flight*, seems to have little to do with sensation seeking. Aggression-hostility can be separated from the P dimension, forming its own factor in a five-factor solution (Zuckerman et al., 1991). Although some persons may use aggression as a mode of sensation seeking, aggression is not a high correlate of sensation seeking. If sensation seekers do not fight much, they also do not "flee" or actively avoid danger. Nor are they sensitive to unconditioned punishment, like pain, suggested by Gray to be the behavioral expression of fight–flight. In fact, high sensation seekers tend to have high thresholds for pain. The fight–flight dimension, as defined by Gray, is not a good match for either the broader P or the narrower sensation-seeking dimensions.

The approach or impulsivity dimension of Gray's model is a more likely candidate for identification with sensation seeking. Sensation seeking and impulsivity are highly related traits, and taken together, along with lack of socialization, they define the P dimension of personality (Chapter 3). But Gray also regards high N and E, in addition to high P, as correlates of the dimension. However, if we exclude N from the hypothesized relationship to impulsivity, then this dimension would be the best fit for sensation seeking among Gray's dimensions.

Zuckerman

Work on the first sensation-seeking scale (Zuckerman, Kolin, Price, & Zoob, 1964) began in the early 1960s based on the idea that there were consistent individual differences in optimal levels of stimulation and arousal and that these differences could be measured with a questionnaire. The first guiding hypotheses were modest, and postulated the existence of a reasonably general trait subsuming all sensory modalities (unlike Wundt's modality restricted construct) and involving all of the arousal-potential (Berlyne, 1971) qualities of stimulation. The finding of a general factor (Zuckerman et al., 1964) and the subsequent discovery of correlations among subfactors (Zuckerman, 1971a) suggested that the trait was not narrow or modality specific. Actually, the factors discovered through factor analyses of items were not modality specific but described different ways of seeking sensation and arousal – for example, through the mind and senses, through social interactions, or through risky sports and activities.

The first published theoretical statement on sensation seeking appeared in a chapter on an optimal level of stimulation and arousal theory of sensory deprivation during my last year of research on that topic (Zuckerman, 1969). Postulate III of this theory contained the hypotheses concerning a sensation-seeking personality trait: "Every individual has characteristic optimal levels of stimulation (OLS) and arousal (OLA) for cognitive activity, motoric activity, and positive affective tone" (p. 429).

The factors that might determine an individual's OLS or OLA state at a given time were listed:

1. *Constitutional factor:* strength of reactivity (excitatory) and satiability (inhibitory) processes in the central nervous system.
2. *Age:* Sensation seeking was suggested to increase between childhood and

adolescence, to peak in adolescence and decline with age thereafter. This hypothesis has been repeatedly confirmed in cross-sectional studies, although long-term longitudinal data are not yet available. In some studies the peak of sensation seeking occurred in the early 20s rather than the teenage years.

3. *Learning experiences:* Experiences of prolonged under- or overstimulation during life may raise or lower the OLS or OLA through adaptation, which results in raising or lowering the homeostatic level of cortical or autonomic system arousal.

4. *Recent levels of stimulation:* Shorter periods of under- or overstimulation, relative to the usual levels, may lead to sensation seeking or sensation avoidance until the general level of stimulation is returned to an optimal level.

5. *Task demands:* Optimal levels of stimulation and arousal vary with immediate task demands; lower levels are required for complex tasks requiring attention and cognitive effort and for fine perceptual discriminations, whereas higher levels are required for simpler tasks involving repetition, little cognition, and maximal effort.

6. *Diurnal cycles:* An obvious factor affecting momentary OLS and OLA is the state of the diurnal arousal cycle. Little stimulation is needed during the high points of wakefulness and arousal, and more stimulation is needed at low points in the cycle, excluding the period of sleep.

A second theoretical statement appeared in 1974 (Zuckerman, 1974). Most of the changes were based on biological data and new theoretical viewpoints of others. Based on a study of a limited sample of twins (Buchsbaum, 1974), the genetic influence (constitutional factor) was thought to vary with the subscales ranging from none for Experience Seeking (ES) to about 40% for Thrill and Adventure Seeking (TAS). A subsequent study (Fulker, Eysenck, & Zuckerman, 1980), based on much larger samples of twins and a more sophisticated biometric analysis, resulted in an upward revision of the genetic influence in sensation seeking, to 58% for the Total scale, with subscale genetic effects ranging from 34% to 58%, and ES now showing the highest heritability.

Another line of theoretical development emerged from psychophysiological studies. Some theories had suggested that the OLA was set by an individual's characteristic level of tonic arousal, but studies of the orienting reflex in response to novel stimuli showed that high and low sensation seekers differed in arousability, not arousal. The higher levels of arousal characteristically reached by high sensation seekers in response to a novel stimulus were presumed to *set* the OLA. Stimuli eliciting less arousal than the OLA (optimal level of *arousability*) were less preferred or liked than stimuli reaching or somewhat exceeding the OLA. Of course, if the characteristic level of stimulation sets the OLA, then a person's optimal level may be changed by adaptation and prolonged exposure to novel stimuli, according to postulate C of the theory (Zuckerman, 1969).

Another psychophysiological factor was more closely related to the disinhibitory type of sensation seeking and represented the capacity of the cortex to react to high levels of stimulation without overloading the cortex and eliciting protective inhibition. The reduction in cortical arousal in low sensation seekers responding to high-intensity stimulation was suggested to be a function of differential set-points in the reticulocortical ascending arousal and descending inhibition system (Zuckerman, Murtaugh, & Siegel, 1974). Because the Ascending Reticular Activating System of the high disinhibiters had a higher set-point they were thought to be more vulnerable to positive feedback, as in mania, where stimulation feeds on stimulation. Disinhibitors are more likely to use depressant drugs, like alcohol or opiates, to dampen cortical excitation produced by their own sensation-seeking activities. The physiological characteristics of sensation seeking may determine its relationship to disinhibitory forms of psychopathology.

The form of sensation seeking measured by the TAS scale might be more associated with the need for novel stimuli, whereas the kind assessed by the Disinhibition (Dis) subscale might be more closely related to the need for intense stimuli to reach a high OLA. The idea that there is more than one kind of sensation seeking reflected in the four subscales of the SSS might suggest different genetic and biochemical factors involved in each subfactor or it might reflect the interaction of a common heredity for a general factor with different environmental factors accounting for differences in the subfactors.

Environmental or interactional theories

Farley (1973, 1981) has noted that sensation seeking (or "thrill seeking" as he now calls it) is related to both delinquency and creativity but not necessarily in the same people. What determines which individual will become a creative innovator and which will become a delinquent? Farley points first to socioeconomic class as a determinant of choice of sensation-seeking activity. Both the creative youth and the delinquent start with the same biological source of the trait according to Farley: a deficit in physiological arousal from which a sensation-seeking need arises in order to raise arousal levels. But arousal may be increased by prosocial, neutral, or antisocial forms of behavior. The environment determines the forms sensation seeking will take. Families at high socioeconomic levels often provide socially acceptable outlets like sports, cars, travel, and so on, whereas in many low socioeconomic environments the only sensation-seeking activities are criminal or antisocial. The expression that "everything good is either illegal, immoral, or addictive" would apply to sensation-seeking reinforcement in a limited society.

Farley also points out the role of stultified educational methods in dampening the intellectual curiosity of young sensation seekers and increasing their delinquent expressions by default. A high sensation seeker needs a teacher with "high arousal potential" – that is, one who is loud, dramatic, extraverted, and uses interactive discussion (rather than lecture) with fast and variable pacing, color media, and an open-spaced classroom. A low sensation seeker, on the other side, benefits more from a more subdued teacher who uses quieter more traditional methods. Farley's formula for education according to personality recalls Pavlov's formula for conditioning the sanguine type of dogs – lots of stimulus variation.

Farley cites the success of stimulant drugs in calming behavior and increasing focused attention of hyperactive children in school as evidence for the low arousal basis of hyperactivity and the antisocial and even delinquency that develops in many of these children. But Farley would prefer to treat hyperactivity with an adjustment of the classroom rather than with drugs.

A major problem with Farley's underarousal theory is the lack of differences between high and low sensation seekers in tonic levels of arousal, as opposed to arousability. Differences are found in arousability but in opposite direction to an unarousability hypothesis (Zuckerman, 1990a). It is possible that the college students who served as subjects in most of these studies simply represented the group of high sensation seekers who were adequately stimulated by parents and schools. But Farley claims that intrinsic arousal levels do not vary by socioeconomic status, gender, culture, race, or generation, but are highly heritable. He claims that it is the modes of sensation seeking, not the trait itself, that vary as a function of social influences.

Farley also glosses over the problem with the concept of a generalized arousal across all biological systems and the consequent difficulty of measuring "arousal" with a single physiological channel. He himself has used rather crude measures of arousal like the two-flash threshold and the sweat-bottle technique instead of measures like EEG or skin conductance that are more direct measures of cortical arousal.

Zuckerman (1969) proposed that early differences in stimulation may also set the OLS before the infants are capable of doing much seeking of their own stimulation. Schaffer (1971) has made a similar argument, saying that "one of the essential functions of mothering is the administration of an adequate level of stimulation" (p. 156). He cited research showing a positive relationship between the amount of sensory-social stimulation received by infants and their own exploratory behavior and preferences for novel stimuli. Social class also affects mother–infant interactions. Middle-class mothers spend more time in face-to-face contact with infants, talking to them and entertaining them with play. This kind of stimulation could affect the development of the sensation-seeking trait in two ways: First, by maintaining arousal the mothers may prevent infants from developing a chronic underarousal; second, by providing social stimulation the child may learn to seek stimulation in normal social interactions rather than antisocial ways.

Schaffer (1971), however, also pointed to temperamental differences between infants; a level of stimulation that is optimal for one infant is suboptimal or overstimulating for others. The differences derived from Thomas, Chess, Birch, Hertz, and Korn (1964) included perceptual sensitivity, activity level, and approach–withdrawal (explorativeness). The last of these has already been described. Perceptual sensitivity is the threshold of stimulation required to elicit a response in an infant. Hypersensitive infants would not respond well to overenthusiastic parental stimulation. Infants with a high activity level do not need a lot of stimulation from parents; they make their own. Hypoactive infants need more stimulation. The outcome of the level of parental stimulation on adult sensation seeking may depend on the interaction of early levels of stimulation and the infant's innate reactivity to stimulation.

Kish (1973) suggested that both fear and exploratory tendencies are provoked by exposure to novel stimuli, thus putting the organism into an approach–avoidance conflict (potential reward versus fear). He proposed that the sensation-seeking trait represents the balance between the strengths of both components of the conflict. The strengths of approach and avoidance tendencies are partly genetically determined, but may also be influenced by child-rearing practices and role modeling. Fearful, overprotective parents may discourage exploration and make a child fearful of novel situations where outcomes are not predictable. Other parents may encourage a child's natural exploratory tendencies and avoid instilling fear more than is necessary.

One problem with Kish's theory of sensation seeking, as the balance between two tendencies, is that it would lead to the prediction of a negative relationship between trait anxiety and sensation seeking. Although specific fears of bodily harm are negatively related to thrill and adventure seeking, general trait anxiety is not. It would be more accurate to regard sensation seeking as the strength of the approach tendency independent of the anxiety trait. This is what we have done in our own theory of risk taking, as will be described at the end of the chapter.

Beyond the optimal level (of cortical arousal)

New research raised doubts about the usefulness of the OLA of the reticulo-cortical system as the basis of a sensation-seeking trait. Findings on the biochemical basis of sensation-seeking required explanation within a psycho-biological model (Zuckerman, 1979a).

First, there were no findings of underarousal in high sensation seekers or overarousal of low sensation seekers using either EEG or skin conductance measures of tonic arousal. There was a stronger physiological reaction to novel stimuli in high than in low sensation seekers. The usual optimal level of arousal theories predicted that high sensation seekers would be underaroused or underarousable, therefore requiring more variety and intensity of stimulation than low sensation seekers to reach the same level of arousal.

Second, although the use of stimulant drugs to increase arousal or hallucinogenic drugs to produce novel states was expected among high sensation seekers, the high sensation-seeking scores of those using depressant drugs like heroin, barbiturates, or alcohol were inexplicable from a simple arousal-seeking hypothesis.

Third, the fact that high and low sensation seekers did not react differently to stimulant and depressant drugs (the stimulant drug was optimal for both) did not support the hypothesis of an interaction between the arousal properties of the drug and its effect on high and low sensation seekers (Carrol, Zuckerman, & Vogel, 1982). High sensation seekers should have felt and functioned better after taking a stimulant, whereas low sensation seekers should have felt and performed better after taking a depressant.

Fourth, new findings on the biochemistry of sensation seeking required a place in the model and their connection with psychophysiological differences required explanation. Findings of a link between gonadal hormones in males and sensation seeking, particularly the Dis subscale, suggested a biological explanation for the sex differences and age decline on sensation seeking as well as the more active sexual behavior of high sensation seekers. But apart from more direct influences of gonadal hormones, they tend to reduce levels of an enzyme in the brain called monoamine oxidase (MAO). Reduced levels of MAO have been associated with increased motor activity in infants and social activity and antisocial tendencies in adult humans. Behavioral correlates of MAO in monkeys are also consistent with findings in humans.

MAO does not produce arousal directly but acts through its effects on the monoamine systems it regulates. The finding of significant negative correlations between MAO and sensation seeking required a new theoretical model involving the monoamine neurotransmitters. The revised model (shown in Figure 1.5) proposed that genetic factors affect this personality trait through their determination of levels of activity or sensitivity of systems regulated by the catecholamines dopamine and norepinephrine, as well as neuroregulators like MAO. Although the third monoamine, serotonin, the endorphins (endogenous morphinelike hormones), and gamma-aminobutyric acid (GABA) were likely to also be involved, they were not formally incorporated into the model.

On the basis of comparative experimental studies of the behavioral functions of these systems, the catecholamine pathways were said to control reward, the pursuit of reward, and readiness to approach novel stimuli and situations, all tendencies characteristic of human sensation seekers. The high arousability of the human sensation seeker was accounted for by direct pathways from the limbic reward system to cortex (now identified as noradrenergic tracts). Routtenberg (1968) noted that when this arousal system was activated it inhibited the ARAS arousal system through the medial septal-hippocampal-lateral septal projection that Gray identified as a system for detecting stimuli associated with punishment.

Are there differences in the type of arousal originating in limbic reward areas and ARAS pathways, or is neocortical arousal completely independent of its sources? It is interesting, in this regard, that the stimulation of the lateral septal area produces decreases in heart rate in contrast to both increases and decreases produced by medial septal stimulation. The decrease in heart rate in response to novel stimuli (orienting reflex) is characteristic of high sensation seekers (Chapter 12), whereas an increase in heart rate (defensive reflex) to the same stimulus is more generally seen in low sensation seekers. This differential heart rate response could represent the differing strengths of reward and punishment sensitivity systems that were described by Gray.

In my 1979 model, neocortical arousability was interpreted as an effect of activity in positive arousal limbic systems, particularly the noradrenergic and dopaminergic ones, and a lack of regulation of these systems by enzymes such as MAO. No longer was neocortical arousal itself interpreted as the physiological reward of sensation seeking. The arousing stimuli sought by

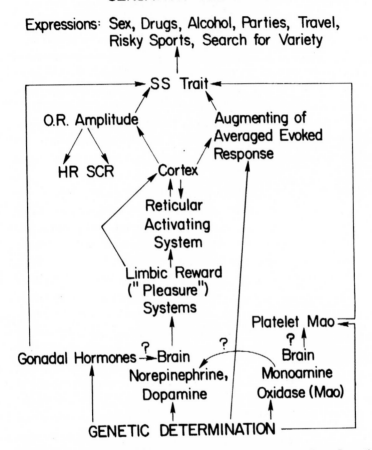

A BIOLOGICAL MODEL FOR SENSATION SEEKING

Expressions: Sex, Drugs, Alcohol, Parties, Travel, Risky Sports, Search for Variety

Figure 1.5. Revised biological model for sensation seeking. From *Sensation seeking: Beyond the optimal level of arousal*, p. 374, by M. Zuckerman, 1979. Hillsdale, NJ: Erlbaum. Copyright Lawrence Erlbaum Associates, 1979. Reprinted by permission.

sensation seekers produced release of catecholamines in the brain. At this time I believed that both norepinephrine and dopamine were involved in the reward mechanism. But increasing evidence in the intervening years showed that dopamine alone is essential to brain reward effects, while norepinephrine may serve as an arousal alerting mechanism. This did not preclude the possibility that norepinephrine may synergistically potentiate the reward effects of dopamine.

Environmental influences

The 1979 volume attempted to deal with potential environmental influences on sensation seeking. The role of the family environment in forming the sensation-seeking trait was cast into some doubt by the fact that the genetic study of sensation seeking (Fulker et al., 1980) showed no influence of shared environment on the trait. The environmental influence would have to consist of different factors acting on the various members of a family rather than the factors that affect them all in common. Farley's interpretation suggests a role for peer influence that is somewhat compatible with a specific environment effect, because siblings in a family may have different friends even though they have the same parents. Even though both members of a family come from the same social class, their particular influences by friends and nonparental role models may be quite different. One person may be more directed by environmental influences toward thrill and adventure seeking in the form of socially approved sports activities, whereas another youth may be more influenced in the direction of disinhibitory forms of sensation seeking like delinquency and drugs. The former may have had the good fortune to have an athletic coach take an interest in him, whereas the latter may have had the misfortune to have the guidance of a drug dealer or a drug-using peer. Genetic biological factors could be most influential in the latent trait, whereas environmental factors may predominate in determination of specific expressions of the trait.

There are two reservations about this hypothesis. One is that thrill and adventure and disinhibition forms of the trait could have some specific genetic determination and different biological factors mediating their influences on behavior. Chronic criminality and antisocial personality seem to have their own genetic and biological determinations that are different from those associated with sensation seeking. An antisocial personality has traits, such as lack of empathy, aggression, and callousness toward others, that are not related to the sensation-seeking trait. The second complication is that, although peers influence us, we also choose friends and models who fit our own personality needs. The similarity of friends in their personality traits is not usually accidental. The environmental factor also includes a genetic–environmental correlation.

The lack of influence of a shared environment does not mean that the family environment cannot have specific effects on siblings in the same family. A finding that firstborns and only children are higher on sensation seeking than later borns (Bone, Montgomery, & McAllister, personal communication, 1963) was explained by the tendency of parents to spend more time with firstborns (before subsequent births) and stimulate firstborns and only children more than those born later (Zuckerman, 1979a). Early and exclusive parental stimulation could influence later development of sensation seeking.

The biosocial model for sensation seeking was further modified and elaborated in view of the research evidence appearing after the publication of the 1979 book. But the plan of this current volume is to present the new research findings in the following chapters before discussing the latest theoretical advances in Chapter 14.

A working definition of sensation seeking

Some traits, such as sociability, seem to need little additional description in terms of behavioral definition, but sensation seeking is more ambiguous. The definition used in my first book (Zuckerman, 1979a) was "Sensation seeking is a trait defined by the need for varied, novel, and complex sensations and experiences and the willingness to take physical and social risks for the sake of such experience" (p. 10).

The definition was first derived from the types of items constituting the early forms of the SSS, and later from the research relating scores on the SSS to behavior, reported behavior, expectations, anticipations, and risk appraisals. A one-sentence definition cannot adequately summarize a complex construct. Certain modifications of the definition have been suggested. Perhaps *seeking* or *preference* should have been used instead of the less behavioral term *need*. The latter term implies compulsion, but the activity of sensation seekers does not seem to be characterized by the subjective quality of compulsion.

Perhaps the stimulus dimension of intensity should be added to those of variety, novelty, and complexity. It has also been suggested that the common denominator of the sensations attractive to sensation seekers is that they all produce transient spurts of physiological arousal. Is sensation seeking a form of "arousal seeking" (Apter, 1982; Farley, 1981)? This equivalence would have been quite satisfactory in terms of my 1969 theory, but the use of the subtitle "Beyond the optimal level of arousal" in my 1979 book indicated a theoretical shift away from *cortical* arousal as the hedonic object of sensation seeking. Cortical arousal theory could not account for the fact that many sensation-seeking drug users consumed depressant drugs (alcohol, barbiturates, opiates) instead of, or in addition to, stimulant drugs like amphetamine and cocaine. Actual reactions to the two classes of drugs showed no indication of a differential effect on high and low sensation seekers; both preferred the stimulant type of drug (Carrol et al. 1982). The idea that high sensation seekers have a higher optimal level of cortical arousal than low sensation seekers is now problematic.

Behavioral disinhibition is a common effect of most abused drugs at lower doses. Many of the biological correlates of sensation seeking are primarily related to the Dis subscale of the SSS. However, disinhibition cannot be used as the sole definition of sensation seeking because experience seeking, also central to the trait and equally related to drug use, involves the mind and senses and the seeking of novelty. Preferences for intensity, variety, novelty, and complexity may be involved in the search for varied sexual and social experiences, characterizing disinhibition, but they are also involved in other aspects of life that are not necessarily social, like preferences in art or music.

Current definition

For the present only a few minor changes (italicized) will be made in the 1979 definition as follows: Sensation seeking is a trait defined by the *seeking* of varied, novel, complex, and *intense* sensations and experiences, and the willingness to take physical, social, *legal,* and *financial* risks for the sake of such experience.

The latter two types of risk are added because of some results from recent factor analyses of risk appraisal categories (Horvath & Zuckerman, 1993). Many situations involve several types of risk. If some people drive very fast after heavy drinking and become involved in accidents, they may kill or injure themselves (physical risk); they may be arrested and jailed (legal risk); they may be fined or lose their jobs (financial risk); or they may be exposed in the newspapers and condemned by others as drunken drivers (social risk).

Risk-taking behavior is a correlate of sensation seeking but not an essential part of the definition. The sensation seeker underestimates or accepts risk as the price for the reward provided by the sensation or experience itself. But few sensation seekers, outside of the antisocial ones, seek to maximize risk for its own sake. Most accept the risk and attempt to minimize it. The low sensation seekers are not just risk aversive; they see no point or reward in the sensation-seeking activities that could justify what they regard as the high levels of risk involved. This is why high and low sensation seekers cannot understand each other, even if they are husband and wife, parent and child, or therapist and client.

Summary

One explanation of sensation seeking is that it is a primary drive in the service of other primary drives or one that operates independently from other drives. While other primary drives may originate in recurring bodily tensions or needs, sensation seeking was thought by some to originate in tensions in the brain. Since all feelings must be based on brain activity, this kind of distinction is not very useful.

Other theorists described these brain tensions as created by deviations of general levels of stimulation and arousal from an *optimal level of stimulation or arousal*. Whereas drive reduction theory suggested that only reduction of stimulation is positively reinforcing or pleasurable, optimal level theories proposed that either increases or decreases in stimulation may be rewarding, depending on the relation between current and optimal levels of stimulation and arousal. In the 1950s several theorists proposed that the reticulocortical activating system might be the basis for the optimal-level mechanism in view of its function in the regulation of cortical arousal. Most theories suggested a curvilinear (inverted-U) relationship between hedonic tone (pleasure–displeasure) and level of arousal. However, other theorists maintained that arousal and hedonic tone were separate and unrelated dimensions.

Another group of theorists suggested that reactions to a particular stimulus depend upon the deviation of that stimulus in quality as well as intensity from an adaptation level set by previous exposures to stimuli. Characteristics of stimuli such as novelty, incongruity, complexity, suddenness of presentation, and degree of change from an optimal level, or an adapted perceptual configuration, could produce either pleasure or displeasure depending on the degree of deviation. Berlyne was the first theorist to point to subcortical reward and aversion systems in the brain as a possible source of tensions produced by stimuli and the basis for the optimal level of arousability phenomena.

The final group of theories were explicitly individual difference theories, explaining differences in personality traits in term of differences in brain physiology. Pavlov explained temperaments on the basis of innate strengths of excitatory and inhibitory processes in the cortex, the balance between these two types of processes, and their mobility or ease of shift from one to the other. Eysenck developed a three-supertrait system and subsumed sensation seeking under extraversion, although much current evidence indicates a stronger relationship to the P (psychoticism or psychopathy) dimension of personality. Gray also has three basic behavioral mechanisms, based on comparative neuropsychological studies, but not identical with Eysenck's dimensions in a one-to-one fashion. Sensation seeking seems more closely related to Gray's approach dimension than either of the other two.

The theory of a sensation-seeking trait began with the hypothesis of consistent individual differences in optimal levels of stimulation and arousal, expressed in certain kinds of human activities and measurable with a self-report questionnaire. It was first proposed that differences in the balance of excitatory and inhibitory processes in the central nervous system influenced the optimal levels of arousal sought in sensation-seeking activities. Early or prolonged exposure to high or low levels of stimulation were also considered as determinants of sensation seeking along with more immediate influences on arousability like task demands and diurnal cycles. In the 1970s the model substituted the differential sensitivities of the reticulocortical activating system in place of equilibrium of central excitatory and inhibitory states as one of the determinants of sensation seeking. By 1979, however, it was proposed that genetic programs influencing the biochemistry of the central nervous system were the ultimate biological basis for the trait. Differences in activity of brain catecholamine systems influenced arousability of the higher cortical centers. Environment might determine the particular forms of expression of the trait, but the amount of variation in stimulation received during infancy and early childhood could also influence the developing trait. Risky sensation-seeking behavior can be seen as the outcome of a conflict between states of anxiety and sensation seeking that vary as a function of novelty and appraised risk.

Every paradigm incorporates an explicit or implicit methodology. The SSS has become the basic method of identifying high or low sensation seekers in the population in order to study their behavior and biology. The next chapter describes the definition of the factor structure of the sensation-seeking trait, advances in assessment of the trait, and the development of new forms of the SSS.

2

Test development

Forms of the sensation-seeking scales

The Sensation Seeking Scale (SSS) has evolved from the General SSS to a multiscale instrument. New forms have been developed differing in response format, scale coverage, and populations addressed. This chapter will describe these developments and their implications for the domain of content covered by the sensation-seeking construct. Because the four subscales used since 1971 were based on factor analyses of items, the issue of factor replicability will be discussed in terms of subsequent studies in other populations. The SSS has now been translated into many languages and sometimes revised in terms of the item content in order to be more usable in particular populations. The extent to which the factor structures have survived these translations will be discussed. The SSS was not appropriate for younger children (at least preadolescent) in the language used or the content of some of the items. New forms have been developed that are more suitable for children and these will be described. Beginning with the development of the SSS form IV, sensation seeking has been conceptualized in a hierarchal trait form with a general trait composed of narrower traits. The issue of whether there is a general factor of sensation seeking that is equivalent to the sum of the subfactors, or whether some of the subfactors assess unique traits, will be discussed. This issue will recur throughout the subsequent chapters as we look at the correlates of the subscales.

Forms II to IV

The development of forms prior to form V of the SSS has been described previously (Zuckerman, 1979a) and will be briefly summarized here. The initial experimental form (I) was developed from preliminary ideas about the likely expressions of a need for varied and intense stimulation and arousal in human activities and attitudes. Items were written in the forced-choice form in an attempt to minimize the factor of social desirability, once thought to be a major influence in personality tests. Form I was given to undergraduates and their responses to 50 items were intercorrelated and subjected to factor analyses and item–total correlations were calculated. Items for form II were selected on the basis of their factor loadings on the first unrotated factor and correlations with the arbitrary total score based on all items. At the time we were not interested in other possible factors so no further analyses were done to define factors beyond the first one. Items best defining the general factor in both men and women were used to make the General scale (form II, Zuckerman et al., 1964). In terms of the results of subsequent factor analyses, the General scale contained thrill and adventure–seeking, experience-seeking, and boredom-susceptibility items, but no items representing the fourth factor, disinhibition. Internal reliabilities of the General scale ranged from .68 to .80.

Subsequent analyses of forms I (Zuckerman & Link, 1968) and II (Farley, 1967) suggested that more than one factor could be identified among the items. Only the TAS factor seemed to have enough items for clear identification so a new experimental form (III) of 113 items was constructed for a more ambitious factor analysis. The first unrotated factor was quite similar to that found in the first factor analysis (Zuckerman et al., 1964) and so the General score was carried over into the new form IV (Zuckerman, 1971a). The rotations of the factors, in men and women separately, yielded four factors, three of which were very similar across gender. The fourth factor, boredom susceptibility, was not as similar in men and women but was retained in form IV anyway. The four factors may be described in terms of the types of items defining them.

Thrill and adventure seeking (TAS). These items express a desire to engage in sports or other physically risky activities that provide unusual sensations of speed or defiance of gravity, such as parachuting, scuba diving, or skiing. Because most of the activities are not common, most of the items are expressed as intention ("I would like . . .") rather than reports of experience. An attitude item that summarizes the factor is: "I sometimes like to do things that are a little frightening."

Experience seeking (ES). This factor seems to encompass seeking of novel sensations and experiences through the mind and senses, as in arousing music, art, and travel, and through social nonconformity, as in association with groups on the fringes of conventional society (e.g., artists, hippies, homosexuals).

Disinhibition (Dis). The items in this factor describe seeking sensation through social activities like parties, social drinking, and sex. An attitude item describing the factor is: "I like to have new and exciting experiences even if they are a little unconventional or illegal."

Boredom susceptibility (BS). This factor represents an intolerance for repetitive experience of any kind, including routine work, and boring people. An item expressing the attitude is: "The worst social sin is to be a bore" (versus the forced-choice alternative: "The worst social sin is to be rude.")

Form IV subscale internal reliabilities for TAS, ES, and Dis scales ranged from .68 to .84, but the four reliabilities obtained for the BS scale (.62 and .66 for males, .38 and .56 for females) were lower, particularly for women. Retest reliabilities for the General scale were high: .89 for periods up to 3 weeks and .75 for 6 to 8 months. Retest reliabilities for TAS, ES, and Dis were about the same for the 3-week interval, but all except TAS were lower for the longer interval (.47–.61).

Form V

There were several reasons for the development of a new form of the SSS. First, the General scale, carried over from form II, was not a satisfactory measure of the overall sensation-seeking factor as represented in the subscales because it lacked any of the items from the Dis subscale. We decided to develop a Total score, based on the sum of the four ten-item subscales to substitute for the General scale in forms II and IV. Second, we felt that some of the correlations between the subscales were too high because of the inclusion of items loading equally high on two or more factors. In the interests of discriminant validity, we wanted to reduce the correlations between subscales, although we still expected enough correlation remaining to justify a total score. Third, we wanted to be sure that the items in the scale had cross-cultural as well as cross-gender reliability so we factor analyzed the items in American and British populations, and selected items that had significant loadings on the same factor in both males and females in both populations (there was some relaxation of this criteria for the BS scale items). Finally, we wanted to reduce the length of the test from 72 items in form IV to 40 items (10 for each subscale), if this could be done without undue sacrifice in reliability. Shorter scales are more practical for many research projects.

The study was done in collaboration with Sybil and Hans Eysenck using a large sample of twins for the English sample (Zuckerman, Eysenck, & Eysenck, 1978). This provided a large, heterogeneous population and data for a later genetic analyses of the scales (see Chapter 11). Both British and American samples were given the 72 items of the form IV and these were intercorrelated and factor analyzed separately for males and females in both samples. The best items, in terms of highest loadings on the specific factors relative to loadings on other factors across all samples, were selected for the new scales comprising form V. The same four factors existing in form IV were found in all four samples in the study and a 40-item scale was formed with 10 items for each of the four factors. Some of the items in the original form used colloquial expressions (e.g., "swingers," "jet setters") no longer familiar to the current generation and these have been explained or reworded to make them understandable to current test takers. The current form V with scoring keys is given in Appendix Tables A and B. Standard (T) score conversions for the subscales, based on undergraduates (primarily sophmores) from personality psychology courses (1986–1992) at the University of Delaware, are given in Appendix C, and for the Total score in Appendix D.

Internal reliabilities of the Total score on form V ranged from .83 to .86; the ranges of reliability for the subscales were: TAS, .77–.82; ES, .61–.67, Dis., .74–.78, and BS, .56–65. ES was the only scale to show a drop in reliability as a function of the shorter scales. BS was neither better nor worse in reliability than the longer scale in form IV. Since its publication in 1978, form V has become the most widely used form of the SSS, although some researchers have continued to use forms II and IV.

A shorter sensation-seeking scale

Short versions of research scales are always in wide demand for researchers who want to give other scales or do experiments and testing on the same occasion. The General SSS of 22 items takes only 8 to 12 minutes, the 40-item form V takes about 12 to 25 minutes, and the 72-item form IV requires about 20 to 30 minutes. Madsen, Das, Bogen, and Grossman (1987) have developed a 10-item short form of the SSS useful for a ninth-grade junior high school population. They took items from form IV with content suitable for the population studied, eliminated all items pertaining to drug use, and included at least two items representing each of the four subscales. The short SSS was given to college undergraduates as well as junior high school subjects.

The test–retest reliability over a 2-month interval was .78, somewhat lower than the .94 retest reliability for form V over 3 weeks. However, the internal reliability for the scale was only .43 compared with the internal reliabilities of the Total score from form V of .83–.86., or the .68–.80 reliabilities of the General scale from forms II and IV. Although the authors did not give the two forms separately, they correlated the 7 short-form items appearing in form V with the Total score on this form and obtained a correlation of .78. The short scale correlated with drug use and sexual experience just as the long sensation-seeking scales do.

This short scale may be useful for research on sensation seeking when researchers are extremely pressed for time, but its low internal reliability limits its usefulness as a measure of a general trait of sensation seeking. If time permits, the slightly longer 22-item General SSS would be preferable.

Replicability of the factor structure of the SSS

The study in which the SSS V was developed (Zuckerman et al., 1978) was a replication of the factor structure found in the earlier study (Zuckerman, 1971a) from which form IV was constructed. Factor reliabilities (correlations of factor loadings) across four samples (American and British men and women) had ranges of .67–.90 for TAS, .51–.75 for ES, .60–.79 for Dis, and .01–.65 for BS. In all cases but those for BS, the correlations between factors were moderate and all convergent factor correlations were higher than the range of correlations between different factors. BS was the only factor that was difficult to replicate across samples. Items were selected for the SSS V scales on the basis of consistent loadings across British and American samples, but it was not certain how the item factor structure would hold up in other cultures, using translated scales, or in studies done in later times. Many of the items, particularly those on the TAS and ES scales, seemed too culture- and time-bound to retain their factorial classifications into the next generation. The items for form IV were written in the 1960s, a time of change and turmoil in Western countries. A number of studies done in the 1980s in countries outside of the United States have reexamined the factorial structure of the SSS V.

Ball, Farnhill, and Wangeman (1983) factored the items of the SSS V using large heterogeneous samples of Australian men and women and obtained good correspondence of a four-factor solution to the designated factors in form V. They also showed a high degree of similarity of factor structures in Australian men and women. As might be expected from the number of culture specific items in the ES scale, it showed the weakest replicability.

Rowland and Franken (1986) found even more impressive evidence of factor replication in male and female undergraduate Canadian students. A confirmatory factor analysis method showed that only two items for the males and three items for the females failed to load significantly on the expected factors.

Using a form V SSS translated into Hebrew, Birenbaum (1986) examined the structure of the scale in a sample of Israeli male applicants for security-related jobs. Instead of factor analysis, he used a nonmetric multidimensional scaling method. The data provided a very good fit to the four-dimensional structural model of the SSS V with 35 of the 40 items falling into the expected regions in a two dimensional space. As in other analyses, the TAS items were most tightly grouped together. Birenbaum and Montag (1987) also examined the factorial structure of the SSS using female applicants for a teaching certificate at a school of education in Israel. This time they used factor analysis in order to compare their results with those of Ball et al. (1983) and Rowland and Franken (1986). They found excellent replication for items assigned to the TAS (10 out of 10), BS (9 out of 10), and Dis (8 out of 10) scales, but only 3 of the 10 items on the ES scale loaded as expected on that factor. Comparing the results of all three studies, they noted that 24 of 40 SSS V items loaded as expected on the originally assigned factor in at least two of the three studies. ES was the least replicable factor.

Carton, Jouvent, and Widlöcher (1992) translated the SSS form IV into French and factor analyzed the items using a heterogeneous sample of men and women between the ages of 15 and 62. A principal components analysis with a varimax rotation yielded factors closely resembling those in the original SSS forms IV and V. The TAS factor contained 9 of the 10 items of TAS on form V; the ES factor included 7 of the 10 on the form V; the Dis factor had 7 of the 10 items from form V; and the BS factor contained 6 of 10 of the form V items. In light of the differences in languages, cultures, and subjects, the replication was encouraging.

Björck-Akesson (1990) used the SSS as a point of departure in writing forced-choice items for a Swedish version of the SSS for preadolescent children in Swedish schools. Most of the items were changed from the items in the original SSS to make them appropriate for children. LISREL (Linear Structural Relations, Jöreskog & Sörbom, 1988) methods were used to test various models that might account for the item intercorrelations. A one factor model was rejected. A model with four latent first-order factors and a second-order general sensation-seeking latent factor provided the best fit for the data. The model allowed for a hierarchal fit of four subscales to a broader sensation-seeking factor as we originally postulated. The four first-order factors were identified as thrill and adventure seeking (TAS); new experience seeking (NES); activity (Act); and outgoingness (Out). TAS was defined by items indicating a desire to engage in exciting and risky activities like lion taming and mountain climbing. NES items refer to participating in novel and varied activities versus routine ones and "being out of control." Act items refer to social, hedonistic, "wild" activity with friends. Out seems to contain both ES and Dis type items representing nonconformity in dress and a need to be the center of attention. No BS factor was found. Analyzing the communalities among the items in each scale, the author formulated broad interpretations of the factors:

TAS: "preference for extreme risk and challenge."

NES: "novelty, variation and a positive attitude towards being out of control."

Act: "preference for being an active part of the youth-culture and the preference for social interaction."

Out: "pertains to non-conformity with generally accepted norms, being the center of attention, preference for extreme appearance and emphasis on social feed-back."

Some new forms of the SSS have departed from the forced-choice item format. In constructing a Dutch translation of the SSS, Feij, van Zuilen, and Gazendam (1982) separated the choices in the items of the SSS form IV and used the separate alternatives to construct new items with a five-point Likert response format (agree–disagree). They factor analyzed the new items and found four factors very similar to those in the SSS. Nearly all of the items loaded significantly and had their highest loadings on the factors where they were originally assigned.

Zuckerman and Teta (1988) made up a 40-item scale consisting only of the sensation-seeking alternatives of the original forced-choice items. They gave this version in a "true–false" response format to a sample of undergraduate college students and a more hetergeneous sample of industrial employees at a plant in Delaware. The item responses were factor analyzed in both samples separately. The results strongly replicated the original factor assignment of items with 31 of the 40 items loading significantly and most highly on the appropriate factor in the undergraduate sample, and 33 of the 40 being correctly placed in the industrial sample. There were slightly more errors of placement for the ES and BS scale items than for the TAS and Dis items in both samples.

New forms of the SSS

The forced-choice format

The forced-choice format was originally used for the SSS in order to reduce or eliminate social desirability and acquiescence response sets. By forcing a choice between two alternate responses that were equivalent in social desirability, it was hoped that the effect of this response set could be reduced. Since the sensation-seeking choices were randomized, acquiescence (the general tendency to agree or answer "true" regardless of item content) could not influence scores. Occasionally, people who have taken the SSS will comment that they had trouble with the forced-choice form because in some items neither choice or both choices seemed appropriate to describe themselves. How widespread is this source of dissatisfaction with the forced-choice format of the test and how might it affect scores on the test?

Franken, Gibson, and Rowland (1989) asked subjects who had taken the test to rate the degree to which they found the forced-choice format to be "entertaining," "fun," "informative" (all positive affect), or "frustrating," "irritating," or "stressful" (negative affect). Ratings for positive-affect responses were much higher than those for negative-affect responses. There were no significant correlations between SSS Total scores and affect ratings of either type for men. For women SSS scores showed low correlations with both positive- and negative-affect scores; they found the test both frustrating *and* stressful, but also informative. Although significant, none of these correlations exceeded .16. Apparently, the negative effects of the forced-choice form have been exaggerated. There is a tendency for high sensation seeking women to be more exasperated (but interested) with the forced-choice form, but this does not mean that exasperation or interest affects scores on the test. However, a more crucial test of the influence of the forced-choice form is to assess correlations between versions with and without forced choice. This has been done with a new version of the SSS, form VI.

SSS form VI

Previous forms of the SSS contained some items expressing a desire or intention to engage in sensation-seeking activities (e.g., "I would like to learn to fly an airplane"), other items reporting preferences for activities already experienced (e.g., "I like 'wild,' uninhibited parties"), and other items reflecting general attitudes (e.g., "the worst social sin is to be a bore"). The TAS scale items were nearly all of the intention or desire type, because it was assumed that few young persons would have had the chance to engage in some of the more unusual thrill-seeking activities, like parachuting. Many of the Dis items, however, referred to preferences or aversions for activities already experienced. Intentions and experiences are different; intentions could be raised by inflated fantasies or reduced by depression or age. Experience, on the other hand, could be restricted by lack of environmental opportunity or financial resources. A scale was devised to contrast sensation-seeking tendencies judged from purely cognitive phenomena like intentions for future activities, with more behaviorally defined items based on reports of past experiences.

The SSS VI (Zuckerman, 1984b, 1984c) was limited to items drawn from previous versions and new items phrased in terms of specific activities (e.g., "scuba diving" or "using illegal drugs"). The entire list of activities is presented twice: The first section deals with actual experiences and the second part with intentions for the future. The response format was changed from the forced-choice to a three point scale of response. In the *Experience* section the choices are: A. I have never done this; B. I have done this once; and C. I have done this more than once. In the *Intentions* section the response choices are: A. I have no desire to do this; B. I have thought of doing this, but probably will not do it; and C. I have thought of doing this and will do it if I have the chance. The choices are weighted from 1 to 3 in scoring the items. Preliminary items were taken only from the TAS and Dis scales of the previous forms because these have proved to be more reliable than ES and BS scales and seem to cover the most diverse kinds of sensation seeking. The BS scale does not translate very well into activities.

The item responses were factor analyzed separately for men and women and separate analyses were done on the two parts of the test, *Experience* and *Intentions*. Factor analyses of the Intention part yielded two primary factors clearly identifiable as TAS and Dis in both men and women. Factor analyses of the Experience part, however, yielded the two factors in women but the factors tended to overlap in the first factor for men. Some items did not load highly on either factor because of the relative infrequency of experience reported for the particular activity. Because one of the goals of the test construction was to create comparable scales for experience and intention, it was decided to base the scales on the clearer and more consistent factors emerging from the analyses of the Intention part. Of the initial 80 items, 64 loaded over .3 on either TAS or Dis factors, and lower on the other factors for both men and women. The Intention Dis scale consists of 42 items, whereas the TAS scale has 22 items. The same items in the Experience part were also scored for TAS and Dis except for 7 items. The activities in these 7 items constituted a Lie or Infrequency scale, because a claim of having experienced them would almost certainly be false (e.g., "Taking a trip to the moon"). Thus, the test yields four content scores: Experience (E)-TAS, Experience(E)-Dis, Intention(I)-TAS, Intention(I)-Dis. The SSS VI is shown in Appendix E, the scoring key is in Appendix F, scale means and standard deviations for samples of undergraduate men and women are contained in Appendix G, and preliminary standardized T scores based on this sample is given in Appendix H.

Retest reliabilities of the scales over a 7-week period were .93 for the E-TAS, and E-Dis scales, .87 for the I-Dis and .84 for the I-TAS scales. Internal (alpha) reliabilities for the E-Dis, I-TAS, and I-Dis scales were all high ranging from .83 to .94. The alpha reliabilities for E-TAS were lower ranging from .62 to .66, probably because of the more restricted range of scores on this experience measure.

Because a large amount of research has been done on the SSS form V, the correlations between scores on forms V and VI are important. Higher correlations were expected between the corresponding TAS and Dis subscales on both forms than between the Form VI TAS and Dis scales and the form V ES and BS subscales. Form VI I-Dis correlated highly with form V Dis ($r = .60-.76$) as did form VI E-Dis ($r = .56-.80$). Form VI I-TAS also correlated highly with form V TAS ($r = .64-.79$), but form VI E-TAS and form V TAS correlated at a lower level ($r = .37-.53$). The lower correlations here were probably due to a greater discrepancy between the intention form used for most of the form V TAS items and the experiences actually reported in the form VI E-TAS. The form V Total score is also fairly highly correlated with form VI Dis scores (I-Dis $r = .56-.80$; E-Dis $r = .56-.72$). The results generally indicate a fair degree of correspondence between E-Dis and I-Dis scores on form VI and the Dis score on form V as well as the Total score on this form since the correlations between scales approach the limits set by the reliabilities of the scales.

How well do experience and intention correlate? For disinhibition scales the correlations were quite high ($r = .70-.88$). These young adults generally say that they intend to keep doing what they have already started to do. For thrill and adventure-seeking activities the correlations were only moderate ($r = .44-.58$), probably because they have not yet done many of the things they hope to do.

The discrepancy between past levels of sensation-seeking activity and intentions for the future might be considerably larger for a group of older adults, who are long past the peak years of sensation seeking, and younger adults. Persons who are currently depressed might show a large discrepancy between past experience and future expectations or intentions. Form VI might prove particularly useful with such populations. Form VI is not a substitute for Form V since it is missing the ES, BS, and Total scores from that form. It should only be used where the interest is solely in TAS and Dis scales and where the queries about specific types of experience (including sexual and drug experience) would be appropriate and acceptable to the population tested.

The influence of social desirability response set on the forms of the SSS

The forced-choice form of the SSS was originally chosen in an attempt to minimize the influence of social desirability (SD) on responses to the items of the test. Social desirability is the tendency to give responses that are regarded as more socially desirable rather than completely honest self-descriptive responses. A number of scales have been developed to measure the response set. The influence of SD in a particular scale is often assessed by the correlation between these scales and the scale in question. Studies using this method with forms II, IV, and V of the SSS (all of which use the forced-choice item form) were discussed in the previous volume (Zuckerman, 1979a, pp. 178–181). It was concluded that SD or defensiveness played only a minimal role in these forms of the SSS. Among the subscales the TAS showed the least relationship with SD, whereas the other scales had some low negative relationships with some SD scales.

Because the SSS form VI does not use the forced-choice format and asks subjects about their actual behavior, in addition to what they might like to do, SD might be expected to influence scores on this form more than on previous forms. Table 2.1 compares the correlations between the TAS and Dis scales in forms IV, V, and VI and three social desirability scales: the Eysenck Personality Questionnaire (EPQ) Lie (L) scale, Jackson's (1964) Personality Research Form (PRF) Social Desirability scale, and the Crowne and Marlowe (1960) Social Desirability scale.

TAS scales from both SSS forms V and VI showed only low correlations with the EPQ Lie scale, and although three of the four correlations were significant for form V scales, only one of the four was even significant for form VI. All of the correlations of the Dis scales with SD were significant for both forms of the SSS, but there was little difference between the two forms in the magnitudes of the correlations between Dis and SD. The only corrlation higher than $-.30$ for either form was the one between form V Dis and SD for one of the two female samples.

Table 2.1. *Correlations of social desirability and sensation seeking scales*

		Male	Female		Male	Female
EPQ Lie scale	S. Eysenck & Zuckerman (1978)[a]			Zuckerman (1984)[b]		
	TAS	−.18**	−.21**	E-TAS	−.11	−.07
	TAS	−.16	−.24**	I-TAS	−.04	−.12*
	Dis	−.13*	−.31**	E-Dis	−.27*	−.30**
	Dis	−.22*	−.47**	I-Dis	−.30**	−.28**
Jackson PRF SD	Zuckerman (1979a)[c]			Zuckerman (1984c)		
	TAS	−.05	−.03	E-TAS	−.17	−.12
				I-TAS	.06	−.23*
	Dis	−.06	−.16	E-Dis	−.10	−.09
				I-Dis	−.13	−.09
Crowne-Marlowe SD scale	Khavari et al. (1977)[d]			Zuckerman (1984c)		
	TAS		−.13*	E-TAS	−.13	−.02
				I-TAS	−.06	.06
	Dis		−.26*	E-Dis	−.40**	−.13*
				I-Dis	−.40**	−.10

Note: TAS = Thrill and Adventure Seeking scale; Dis = Disinhibition scale; E = Experience scales (SSS form VI); I = Intention scales (SSS form IV); SD = Social Desirability scale.
[a] Subjects = 97 male, 122 female American undergraduates; 254 male, 625 female English twins.
[b] Subjects = 74 male, 191 female undergraduates.
[c] Subjects = 82 male, 71 female undergraduates.
[d] Subjects = 298 male and female labor union members.
*$p < .05$.
**$p < .01$.

With one minor exception, *none* of the correlations of TAS or Dis scales from either SSS form with the PRF SD scale was significant. In the study by Khavari, Humes, and Mabry (1977), using a sample of labor union members, scales from form IV of the SSS correlated low but significantly with the Crowne-Marlowe SD scale. Form VI E-Dis and I-Dis scales of the SSS correlated substantially with SD in men, but only slightly in women.

The relationship between SD and SSS seems to depend on the particular SD scale used; it is practically zero with the Jackson SD scale, low but significant with the EPQ Lie scale, and significant only for the Dis scales with the Crowne-Marlowe scale. The more consistent correlations with the EPQ Lie scale may have something to do with the fact that it correlates negatively with scales of psychopathology, whereas the Jackson and Crowne-

Marlowe scales were designed to be uncorrelated with measures of psychopathology like neuroticism scales.

In general, there is little difference between SD influences in forms V and VI of the SSS, or between Experience and Intention scales of form VI. When differences are found between subscales in either SSS V or VI, SD influence is greater for Dis than for TAS.

Another method for assessing the SD influence is to give a scale using normal instructions, and then to contrast the results with those obtained when subjects are told to answer the test items in a manner designed to give a "good impression" or a "bad impression" to others. Farley and Haubrich (1974) used this method for form IV of the SSS. Each of three groups of subjects was given the SSS under one of three sets: honest self-description, best impression, and worst impression. As in most studies using this method, the persons on whom the impression was to be made were not specified. They found no differences between the three groups on any of the subscales of the SSS and concluded that there was little influence of social desirability on the SSS.

Rowland and Heatherton (1987) gave the SSS form V to the same group twice, once under instructions to respond by describing themselves honestly, and a second time under instructions to answer the test as if they wanted to present "the best possible image" of themselves to someone they had just met whom they found very attractive. Scores under the two conditions were not significantly correlated. Both men and women had higher sensation-seeking scores under the "best impression" instructions. The differences were significant for all scales for women, but only for the TAS and BS scales for men. It is interesting that the Dis scores were lower for men but increased significantly for women trying to create a good impression on an attractive stranger.

The results of these investigators differ from Farley and Haubrich's findings, probably because Rowland and Heatherton were so specific in their definition of "good impression." If they had asked these young college students to create a good impression on parents, teachers, or even a peer whom they did *not* find attractive, the results would probably have been different. Their results also suggest that high sensation seeking is socially desirable, which is opposite to the direction of the correlations found between SSS and SD scales. The difference in their results on the Dis scale indicated that women would want to appear *more* disinhibited to an attractive man, whereas men would want to appear somewhat *less* disinhibited to an attractive woman. Disinhibition usually shows strong gender differences with men scoring higher than women. Women seem to believe that most men would prefer a highly disinhibited woman to a more constrained one, at least on first meeting. Men, on the other hand, seem to think that it would be better not to exaggerate their disinhibition tendencies.

The results suggest that there might be some interaction of gender of subject and target in the value placed on sensation seeking as a trait. Women, for instance, might value sensation seeking more in men than in women. This hypothesis was tested (Zuckerman, 1978) by writing fictitious descriptions of high and low sensation seekers, one set based on TAS types of behavior and the other on Dis kinds of behavior. Each of these four persons (high TAS person, low TAS person, high Dis person, low Dis person) was given a man's name in one set and a woman's name in another. Except for the names and appropriate pronouns (he or she) the two sets of descriptions were exactly alike. All portraits were rated on evaluative attitude scales by separate groups of male and female undergraduate subjects. Each subject rated only one type of person.

There were no differences as a function of the gender of the person described or any interaction of the gender of the subject with that of the described person. However, women tended to judge the Dis type of sensation seeker less favorably than the men did regardless of the gender of the person being described. Men regard sensation seeking of the Dis type as more socially desirable than women do, but there is no evidence of a "double standard" in the application of judgments of the trait in men and women.

Experimental true–false forms

If social desirability is of little more importance in SSS form VI than in the forced-choice forms of the SSS, then a true–false form of the items in forms IV and V is possible. In a previous section the factor analysis of the sensation-seeking choices in the 40 items from form V was described (Zuckerman & Teta, 1988). The items loading highest and significantly on their respective factors in both the industrial employees and undergraduates are listed in Table 2.2. As yet, no further work has been done on this scale, and questions of reliability and validity remain to be answered. One problem is that there are too few items in the subscales with only 9 items for TAS, 7 for Dis, 6 for ES, and 7 for BS. The reliabilities of such short scales are likely to be low. But perhaps the balanced Total score based on all of these items might achieve a higher reliability. Another problem could be the use of only true-scored items. Acquiescence response set could influence scores and should be investigated as a possible methodological flaw.

Another true–false format scale has been developed as part of a broader

Table 2.2. *Factor loadings on primary factor for items in true–false form of the Sensation Seeking Scale*

Item	Factor	Employees	Students
I: Thrill and Adventure Seeking			
3	I often wish I could be a mountain climber.	.37	.49
16	I would like to take up the sport of water skiing.	.76	.60
17	I would like to try surfboard riding.	.70	.50
20	I would like to learn to fly an airplane.	.60	.64
21	I would like to go scuba diving.	.70	.61
23	I would like to try parachute jumping.	.52	.66
28	I like to dive off the high board.	.43	.50
38	I would like to sail a long distance in a small but seaworthy sailing craft.	.45	.39
40	I think I would enjoy the sensations of skiing very fast down a high mountain slope.	.54	.54
II. Disinhibition			
1	I like "wild" uninhibited parties.	.54	.62
9	I have tried marijuana or would like to.	.49	.52
12	I enjoy the company of people who are free and easy about sex.	.58	.51
13	I often like to get high (drinking liquor or smoking marijuana).	.49	.52
30	Keeping the drinks full is the key to a good party.	.33	.66
32	A person should have considerable sexual experience before marriage.	.55	.54
35	I enjoy watching many of the "sexy" scenes in movies.	.46	.48
III: Experience Seeking			
14	I like to try new foods that I have never tasted before.	.48	.38
18	I would like to take off on a trip with no preplanned or definite routes or timetable.	.40	.35
19	I would like to make friends in some of the "far out" groups like artists or "punks."	.68	.61
22	I would like to meet some persons who are homosexual (men or women).	.54	.33
26	I often find beauty in the bright colors and irregular forms of modern painting.	.39	.39
37	People should dress in unusual ways even if the effects are sometimes strange.	.27	.53

Table 2.2. *(cont.)*

Item	Factor	Employees	Students
IV: Boredom Susceptibility			
2	I can't stand watching a movie that I have seen before.	.31	.49
5	I get bored seeing the same old faces.	.53	.47
7	When you can predict almost every- thing a person will do and say he or she must be a bore.	.42	.53
8	I usually don't enjoy a movie or play where I can predict what will happen in advance.	.42	.53
27	I get very restless if I have to stay around home for any length of time.	.49	.38
31	The worst social sin is to be a bore.	.64	.35
39	I have no patience with dull or boring persons.	.66	.54

five-factor personality test: the Zuckerman-Kuhlman Personality Question-naire (ZKPQ; Zuckerman, Kuhlman, Joireman, Teta, and Kraft, 1993). Using true–false versions of SSS items along with items from many other personality scales, Zuckerman et al. (1993) did a factor analysis of the items. A five-factor solution seemed optimal. One of the five factors consisted entirely of impulsivity and sensation-seeking items and was therefore called impulsive sensation seeking (ImpSS). The close connection between sensa-tion-seeking and impulsivity scales has been noted before (Zuckerman, 1979a; Zuckerman, 1994a) and their combination seems to constitute the core of the P dimension of personality (Zuckerman et al., 1988, 1991, discussed in Chapter 3). The two traits have many common behavioral and biological correlates (Zuckerman, 1993b). The ImpSS scale items are given in Table 2.3. One advantage of this scale is that all items are of a general type and do not specify particular activities like drinking, drug use, or sex that might be objectionable in some settings, or specific sports that might be very uncommon or even unfamiliar in certain cultures. Such items are a confounding influence when sensation seeking is related to these types of activities. These types of items were deliberately removed from the initial item pool. Of the 11 sensation-seeking items, 8 actually came from the SSS V; 4 were from the ES, 2 from the Dis, 1 from the TAS, and 1 from the BS subscales. The TAS items had lower loadings on the factor and we only selected those items with the highest loadings.

The ImpSS scale has thus far been used within the context of the broader

Table 2.3. *Impulsive Sensation Seeking Scale (ImpSS) from Zuckerman-Kuhlman Personality Questionnaire (ZKPQ)*

DIRECTIONS: If you agree with a statement or decide that it describes you, answer TRUE. If you disagree with a statement or feel that it is not descriptive of you, answer FALSE. Answer every statement either True or False even if you are not entirely sure of your answer.

  1. (I) I tend to begin a new job without much advance planning on how I will do it.
  6. (I*) I usually think about what I am going to do before doing it.
14. (I) I often do things on impulse.
19. (I) I very seldom spend much time on the details of planning ahead.
24. (SS) I like to have new and exciting experiences and sensations even if they are a little frightening.
29. (I) Before I begin a complicated job, I make careful plans.
34. (SS) I would like to take off on a trip with no preplanned or definite routes or timetable.
39. (I) I enjoy getting into new situations where you can't predict how things will turn out.
45. (SS) I like doing things just for the thrill of it.
50. (SS) I tend to change interests frequently.
55. (SS) I sometimes like to do things that are a little frightening.
60. (SS) I'll try anything once.
65. (SS) I would like the kind of life where one is on the move and traveling a lot, with lots of change and excitement.
70. (SS) I sometimes do "crazy" things just for fun.
75. (SS) I like to explore a strange city or section of town by myself, even if it means getting lost.
79. (SS) I prefer friends who are excitingly unpredictable.
84. (I) I often get so carried away by new and exciting things and ideas that I never think of possible complications.
89. (I) I am an impulsive person.
95. (SS) I like "wild" uninhibited parties.

Note: Item numbers are those in the ZKPQ. An "I" in parentheses before an item indicates it is an impulsivity item; a "SS" indicates a sensation seeking item. In the usual scoring of the scale no distinction is made between I and SS items; all are scored on the single ImpSS scale. However, investigators may be interested in analyzing the two scales separately so the original content is distinguished. All items are scored 1 for the "True" response except for item 6, where the asterisk indicates a score for the "False" response.

questionnaire, which also includes scales for sociability, neuroticism-anxiety, aggression-hostility, and activity. The ImpSS scale has internal reliability coefficients of .77 in one study and .82 in another. ImpSS correlated highly with the SSS form V Total score ($r = .66$), and moderately with the TAS, ES, and Dis subscales of the SSS ($r = .43–.45$), and slightly lower with the BS subscale ($r = .37$). ImpSS appears to measure the general sensation-seeking tendency. It is encouraging that it correlates about equally with the SSS subscales indicating that it is not biased toward one subtype of sensation seeking. ImpSS correlated close to zero with the Crowne-Marlowe and Jackson SD scales, and had a low, but significant, correlation with the EPQ Lie scale ($r = -.30$). It did not correlate at all with an acquiescence scale. Correlations with other personality scales will be discussed in the next chapter. Although the scale also includes impulsivity items, it is the most promising short, true–false form for the general sensation-seeking trait.

Translations of the SSS

The SSS (forms II–VI) has been translated into many languages including: Arabic (Torki, 1993) Chinese (Yuching, 1988), Dutch (Feij & van Zuilen, 1984; Feij et al., 1982), Finnish (S. Eysenck & Haapasalo, 1989), French (Carton, Lacour, Jouvent, & Widlöcher, 1992), German (Andresen, 1986), Hebrew (Birenbaum, 1986), Italian (Magaro, Smith, Cionini, & Velicogna, 1979), Japanese (Terasaki, Shioni, Kishimoto, & Hiraoka, 1987), Hungarian (Kulcsár, Kutor, & Arató, 1984), Norwegian (Pederson, Clausen, & Lavik, 1989), Oriyan (Mahanta, 1983), Polish (Oleszkiewicz, 1985), Spanish (adult version: Perez & Torrubia, 1986; child version: Perez, Ortet, Pla, & Simo, 1986), and Swedish (adult version, Schalling et al., 1981; child-adolescent version, Björck-Akesson, 1990). Some of these studies have simply translated the SSS V into the other language, others have eliminated or rephrased some of the original items or substituted others felt to be more appropriate to the culture or age of subjects, and some have recomposed the scales based on factor analyses of items. The scales and some of the reliability results are described briefly in Appendix I.

Forms for children

Forms IV and V contain many items that would be inappropriate for preadolescent children including questions about drinking, drugs, and sex. The items in form II are more general and innocuous in content (except for one concerning a desire to try hallucinogenic drugs), although the wording might be a problem for younger children. It is important to extend the studies of sensation seeking to younger ages, but until recently this has not been possible because of the lack of an appropriate child version of the SSS.

Kafry (1982) simplified the items in form II and had them read to children of ages 6 to 10 years for their responses to the forced-choice items. The internal reliabilities were .57 for the total sample, .39 for 6-year-old kindergarten children, .57 for 8-year-old second graders, and .74 for 10-year-old fourth graders. The reliability for parents, who filled out the forms as they thought their children would, was .64. While the reliability of the kindergarten children was too low to consider use of the scale for children this young, that for the 8- and 10-year-olds was high enough compared with adult reliabilities (.68–.75). The score level of children was lower than that found for 14 to 17-year-olds by Farley and Cox (1971) and for adults by Zuckerman (1971a). Parents tended to overestimate the scores of their own children, but the correlation between parents estimated scores and the actual scores of their children was .40. As a further test of the validity of the General SSS for children, Kafry correlated the children's sensation-seeking scores with various measures of preferences for activities, puzzles, pictures, responses in a maze with alternate correct routes, foods, mazes varying in complexity, and behaviors. Sensation seeking correlated positively with preferences for risky physical activities and negative social behaviors, and complex puzzles and visual stimuli. Activity and behavioral preferences were assessed by showing the children pictures of these activities and asking "Which is most like you?" or "Which things do you do?" Most of the significant correlations were only around .3, but the correlation with preference for complex visual stimuli reached .54. Preferences for complexity are also found to be related to sensation seeking in the adult studies (Zuckerman, 1979a).

Russo et al. (1991) developed a children's form of the SSS (SSS-C) using the adult form V as a point of departure for constructing items. Twelve items were immediately excluded as inappropriate for children, and the remaining 28 items were simplified in expression for children between 7 and 12 years of age. Scale items were read aloud to all children who were unable to read proficiently. The 3-week retest reliability of the Total score was .71, the split-half reliability was .62, but the alpha index of internal reliability was only .49. A factor analysis of the items yielded two clear factors with item loadings above .40, which were identified as TAS and BS.

The SSS-C was developed further by Russo et al. (1993) using children 9 to 14 years of age. More of the items were modified to be appropriate for children. This time a factor analysis of items yielded three interpretable factors: thrill and adventure seeking (TAS), drug and alcohol attitudes (DAA), and social disinhibition (SD). Internal reliabilities for the scales based on these factors were .83 for a Total score, .81 for TAS, .72 for DAA, and .67 for SD. Retest reliabilities were moderate in one sample and low in another. This improved version with higher reliabilities and a disinhibition factor with items suitable for children is the best form now available for children.

State forms of the SSS

Traits are relatively enduring dispositions while states may be defined as "the arousal of an affect or motive at a particular point in time or for a delimited period of time (from a minute to a day)" (Zuckerman, 1979a, p. 114). Although the state concept has usually been applied to affects, it can also be used to describe motives (Patrick, Zuckerman, & Masterson, 1974). Because the state just preceding behavior is generally more predictive of behavior than the trait (Zuckerman, 1979b), a measure of sensation seeking as a state could be useful in experiments. What kinds of words might be used to assess a sensation-seeking state? Presumably they would be words expressing a kind of positive affect associated with the motivation to explore a novel situation. The description of the development of such a state scale by Neary (1975) is described in detail in the previous sensation-seeking book (Zuckerman, 1979a, pp. 114–121).

Neary drew adjectives from various checklist scales of theoretical relevance to sensation seeking. He also included items from the Zuckerman (1960) Affect Adjective Check List anxiety scale because the relation of state anxiety to the hypothetical sensation-seeking state was not known. The initial list of adjectives was given to persons high or low on trait sensation seeking, as measured by the General scale of form IV. Subjects were asked to imagine their reactions to four hypothetical situations and check the adjectives describing these reactions. The four situations, intended to correspond to the four factors in the SSS, including parachute jumping, hypnosis, taking a drug, and listening to a boring lecture. Adjectives checked significantly more by either high or low sensation seekers in at least two of the four situations were chosen for further analyses.

The high-trait sensation seekers checked positive affect words like *daring, elated, enthusiastic, adventurous,* and *playful,* indicating enjoyment of the situation and a kind of positive arousal. Low-trait sensation seekers primarily checked anxiety words like *frightened, panicky, upset,* and *worrying* and did not check the positive affect words checked by the high sensation seekers. Since the empirical method of item selection often results in multifactorial scales, a factor analysis was done on the 36 items differentiating the responses of high and low sensation seekers to the hypothetical situations. A two-factor solution showed a clear separation between the sensation-seeking positive-affect items and the anxiety negative-affect items. On the basis of this two-stage analysis the Sensation Seeking (SS) and Anxiety (A) states scale (or SSAST) was constructed. The actual scale and scoring keys are shown in Appendix J.

The items comprising the SS state scale are *enthusiastic, playful, pleased, adventurous, elated, imaginative, daring, zany, lucky, mischievous, interested, amused, curious, confident,* and *cooperative.* They are a mixture of arousal and positive affect (e.g., elated), surgency (adventurous), and heightened attention (interested, curious).

Internal reliability of the SS state scale ranges from .87 to .93, and that of the A state scale varies between .87 and .92. Unlike trait scales, state scales are not expected to have high retest reliabilities (Zuckerman, 1976b, 1983a) because states are expected to change from day to day, hour to hour, or moment to moment. Retest reliabilities of the SS state ranged from .38 to .57, and those for the A state ranged from .32 to .48 showing that they are not merely trait scales in a different form. Neary gave the state SS and A scales to subjects in class on five occasions a week apart (neutral baseline), and just prior to two experiments. In one experiment they thought they would be given an unknown drug "that could produce some strange effects" and in another they expected to be hypnotized. A trait is not expected to predict a single state on neutral days, when the state is not likely to be aroused. But if states over a number of occasions are aggregated, the trait is expected to predict the average of states. On occasions when the state is aroused the trait should predict the level of arousal. In this study, the SS General scale (trait) correlated low with the SS state measure on the first baseline state assessment day, but the SS trait scale correlated substantially with the means of five baseline SS state measures. The trait measure also correlated significantly with the SS state measure taken while the subject was expecting to be given an unknown drug, but it did not correlate significantly with the SS state taken while waiting to be hypnotized. The lower correlation in the latter situation could have been due to the fact that it was group hypnosis, and low sensation seekers may have felt more reassured by the presence of others. The SS trait scale correlated negatively with the A state in the drug experiment, but did not correlate with the A state on baseline or hypnosis experimental days.

A second state measure of sensation seeking has been developed from factor analyses of items used to develop the revised form of the Multiple Affect Adjective Check List (MAACL-R, Zuckerman & Lubin, 1985). In this case we had not expected to find a sensation-seeking factor. The old MAACL (Zuckerman & Lubin, 1965) contained scales for negative affects only: anxiety, depression, and hostility. Positive affect responses were scored in a reverse direction on the negative affect scales. Years later factor analyses showed that such bipolar scales were not justified because positive and negative affects constitute relatively independent dimensions, even in state tests. Factor analyses of item responses in two groups on two testing occasions yielded five fairly reliable factors: anxiety, depression, hostility, a large positive affect factor, and a smaller factor that we decided to call "sensation seeking" on the basis of its similarity to the empirically developed scale constructed by Neary. The actual words loading on this factor were (scored if checked) *active, adventurous, aggressive, daring, energetic, enthusiastic, merry, wild,* and (scored if not checked) *bored, mild, quiet, tame.* Actually there were only two words in common with the Neary scale because the initial pool of 132 MAACL adjectives did not include most of the ones we had used in the pool for the SSAST. We had not expected an SSS factor to emerge and so did not expand the pool of items beyond those in the old MAACL. However, the contrast between the words in the larger positive affect factor and those in the SS factor was striking. The larger factor had words like *glad, good, happy, peaceful,* and *pleasant,* which did not suggest a state of arousal or eagerness to act as did the SS scale items. In retrospect, we could have just as well called the factor "surgency." The two positive affect scales, developed from the factors, correlated moderately (about .40), and the three negative affect scales correlated among themselves. The alpha reliability of the SS state scale was .74.

The model for a sensation-seeking trait: one, four, or one plus four?

The addition of subscales to the General SSS (Zuckerman, 1971a) raised certain questions about the nature of the trait and how to measure it. Farley (1967) suggested that there were additional factors in the SSS, and his theory (Farley, 1973, 1981) implied that these factors might represent alternative modes of sensation seeking dependent on the interaction of the latent trait with specific environmental circumstances.

Zuckerman (1979a, 1984a) proposed a hierarchal model of the trait with a broad latent factor composed of four narrower subfactors. Björk-Akesson (1990) presented a thoughtful analysis of the evolving concepts of the sensation-seeking trait. She suggests that the use of a total score, composed of the sum of the four balanced subscales, to measure a broad sensation-seeking trait represents a *component model.* The component model is one form of the hierarchal model in which the general factor is identical with the subfactors, and everything contained in the subfactors is part of the general trait. Each subfactor represents a different aspect or expression of the trait. According to this model there is nothing in the subfactors that does not come from the general factor. The *factor model,* in contrast to the component model, as-

Table 2.4. *Median correlations of*
among the four subscales on Sensation
Seeking Scale (SSS) forms IV and V

	SSS forms	
Subscales correlated	IV	V
TAS × Dis	.30	.27
TAS × ES	.41	.33
TAS × BS	.28	.14
ES × BS	.58	.28
ES × Dis	.54	.36
Dis × BS	.45	.41

Note: Each median is based on correlations
among scales in four samples: men and women
in English and American samples. Form IV
n's included 254 English males and 693 females, and 160 American males and 170 females. Form V *n*'s included 254 English males
and 693 females, and 97 American males and
122 females. TAS = Thrill and Adventure
Seeking; ES = Experience Seeking; Dis = Disinhibition; BS = Boredom Susceptibility.

sumes that the general factor does influence all of the subfactors, but each
subfactor also contains some unique variance. The relative amounts of broad
and narrow factor variance may vary among the subfactors, so that the use of
a total score may actually misrepresent the general factor by weighting each
subscale equally.

Both H. Eysenck (1984; H. Eysenck & Eysenck, 1985, pp. 70–72) and
Royce (1984) questioned the unitary nature of the sensation-seeking trait,
suggesting that the trait, or *behavior complex* to use Royce's term, is a
complex combination of higher- or lower-order traits. Eysenck pointed to the
low order of correlation between subscales in form V, and the higher correlation of some subscales with E or P scores on the EPQ. In reply (Zuckerman,
1984a, pp. 456–457) it was pointed out that the lower correlations among
the subscales in form V than in form IV were the result of a deliberate
attempt to increase discriminant validity of the subscales by making them
more homogeneous.

Table 2.4 shows the median correlations from four samples (British and
American men and women) of the subscales on forms IV and V. The

greatest changes were in the correlations between ES and the other subscales, probably as a function of the lower reliability of the 10-item version of this scale, compared to the 18-item scale in form IV. Four of the six correlations among the scales in form IV were above .4, but in form V only one of the correlations reaches this level. The results on form V are a function of the way the scales were developed rather than any intrinsically low correlations between the types of sensation seeking. Even so, the four subscales of the SSS V remain significantly intercorrelated suggesting a higher-order factor participating to some degree in each of the subscales. The degree of correlation required for summing subscales is an arguable question. State scales given on single occasions rarely correlate much above .3 from one occasion to another, and yet their summed scores reach a highly reliable level, characteristic of most trait score reliabilities (Zuckerman, 1976a).

The position of the four subscales of the SSS in relation to higher order factors like, E, N, and P, and other narrower factors, like impulsivity, will be discussed in the next chapter. Rather than the complex picture suggested by Eysenck and Royce, the SS subscales cluster fairly closely together with other scales within a single major dimension of personality.

Björk-Akesson (1990) tested the models for sensation seeking more directly using the LISREL method. Eysenck's criticism suggested a model in which all of the subscales represent unique first-order factors with no need to postulate a latent second-order factor of general sensation seeking. This model did not fit the data in the study and the fit was significantly improved by a model providing a second-order broad factor of general sensation seeking. This general factor accounted for 55% of the total variance among the four subscales while the four narrower factors accounted for 26%. The remaining variance of 19% represented error of measurement. Björk-Akesson's data show a robust influence of a general sensation-seeking factor that accounts for an amount of variance comparable to what has been found for the influence of a broad dimension of general intelligence (g) among intelligence test subscales. The factor model does allow for variation of influence of the general factor among the subscales and Björk-Akesson's data show that her ''New Experience Seeking'' and ''Outgoingness'' subscales partake of relatively more of the general factor than the TAS and social ''Activity'' (Dis) subscales.

LISREL was applied to the SSS V scales in a study of risk taking by Horvath and Zuckerman (1993). Factor analyses of a risk appraisal scale yielded four categories of risk appraisal: criminal risk taking, minor violations risk, financial risk, and physical risk (sports). The question was posed as to whether the four subscales of the SSS V composed one latent factor and the four subscales of risk appraisal another factor. Another possibility was that certain SS subscales formed latent factors with certain risk appraisal scales in contrast to their relations with other SS or risk scales. LISREL analyses showed that the assumption of a separate sensation-seeking factor, composed of the four SS subscales, and a risk appraisal factor, made up from the four risk appraisal scales, was fully justified and superior to other models.

Fulker et al. (1980) reported that about 60% of the genetic covariance in sensation seeking was due to a general factor loading positively on all four subscales. H. Eysenck (1983) did some additional analyses of the SSS subscales and found that the ES scale had the highest and the BS scale the lowest genetic contribution. Nearly all of the genetic contribution of the ES scale was on the general factor, while a greater part of the genetic contribution of the other subscales was on specific factors. What this suggests is that both general and narrow factors have some genetic bases; therefore, variations in the subscale scores cannot be attributed solely to environmental determination of the mode of sensation seeking. These genetic analyses also support the hypothesis of a general factor of sensation seeking.

Summary

The SSS has evolved from a General scale to a Total score made up of the sum of four subscales: Thrill and Adventure Seeking (TAS), Experience Seeking (ES), Disinhibition (Dis), and Boredom Susceptibility (BS). Three of the four factors from which the subscales were developed have shown good cross-gender and cross-cultural replicability. The BS scale has not been as reproducible as the other scales across populations. The ES scale has also shown some problems in factor replications, probably because of the culture-specific nature of some of its items. TAS and Dis factors also hold up better than ES and BS factors in factor analyses of a true–false version of the SSS.

A recent version of the SSS (form VI) uses only TAS and ES scales and divides each type of scale into two sets: experienced activities (E) and intended or desired activities (I). The response format was changed to a three-point Likert-type weighted response scale. Reliabilities were high for these scales. E and I scales correlate highly for Dis and moderately for TAS. The scale is intended to assess sensation seeking in persons where current levels may have changed from past levels due to age, depression, or other factors.

The forced-choice format for the SSS was used in forms I to V in order to control the response sets of social desirability and acquiescence. Social desirability has little influence in sensation-seeking scales whether those of the forced-choice or true–false forms, as judged from correlations of SSS and SD scales. Because social desirability is not a strong and consistent influence in the SSS, the original reasons for using the forced-choice form are no longer compelling, and true–false forms have been developed.

The SSS has been translated from English into 15 other languages. Those who have retained most of the original items, or only slightly altered them to fit the culture, have generally found factors similar to those in the English version of the SSS. Special forms have been developed for children in the United States, Spain, and Sweden, eliminating nonappropriate items and simplifying the language in other items. The factors in children are somewhat different from those found in adults, probably because of the exclusion of many items from the ES and Dis scales. State versions of the SSS have been developed in order to assess sensation seeking as a current emotional-motivational state rather than as an enduring trait disposition based on retrospective reports.

Since the development of the subscales, some have questioned whether there is a unitary trait of sensation seeking or only distinct factors related to more than one major dimension of personality. The correlations among the subscales were lowered somewhat by deliberate enhancement of scale homogeneity going from form IV to V, but all scales remain intercorrelated. LISREL studies show that a hierarchal factor model, with a broad general factor contributing to the variance in all of the subscales, together with narrower more specific factors in the subscales, best explains the relations among the subscales. A genetic analysis suggests a similar conclusion. The issue of the place of sensation seeking among the dimensions defined by other measures is addressed in the next chapter.

3

Sensation seeking in relation to other dimensions of personality

Personality traits and tests tend to proliferate like rabbits and it is often difficult to trace their ancestry or relationships with other dimensions of personality. Sensation seeking began as a special kind of trait concept and its relationships with other major dimensions of personality have gradually emerged from studies over the years. This chapter will attempt to define the relationship of sensation seeking to conceptually similar trait dimensions and its position within multitrait systems claiming to encompass the entire personality domain. Comparisons will be confined to traits for which a standard questionnaire or rating measure has been developed and correlated with the SS scales.

Personality constructs with different names are often very similar. It is rare for test makers to use another test constructor's name for their tests. The only way to determine the equivalence of two tests is to calculate the correlation between them. We would not expect two tests to correlate perfectly because the correlation between them is limited by the reliabilities of both tests. There is no strict rule one can apply to all test correlations, but when two tests correlate .6 or higher they are approaching equivalence. Correlations in the .4–.6 range suggest moderate to strong relationships between the traits measured by the tests but not strict equivalence. Significant correlations of less than .4 indicate minor relationships between the traits.

Generally, personality trait tests correlate to the extent that their items are similar in content. There is a time-hallowed custom of borrowing slightly modified forms of items from other personality tests to use in one's own test. Items originally appearing in one of the forms of the SSS frequently show up in other tests with different names. Some tests have borrowed only one type of sensation-seeking item, most often of the thrill and adventure–seeking type. Generalizations made about "sensation seeking" from such tests are limited by the scope of the items in the tests.

Sensation seeking and conceptually related narrow traits

Need for novelty and change

The definition of sensation seeking given in the first chapter emphasizes the seeking of "varied, novel, and complex sensations and experiences." The definition does not include cognition. Even though novel ideas are a primary source of interest for some persons, they are generally not as arousing as novel sensations. P. H. Pearson (1970) developed a set of four Novelty Experiencing scales (NES) measuring External Sensation Seeking (ESS; thrill-seeking activities); Internal Sensation Seeking (ISS; fantasy, feelings, dreams); External Cognitive (solving tangible problems as in puzzles, constructions, games); and Internal Cognitive (solving conceptual problems). Correlations among subscales within the NES show that the cognitive and sensation dimensions are relatively independent (C. Waters, 1974).

In my previous book (Zuckerman, 1979a) three studies were presented on the relationships between the SSS and NES scales in three groups of men and two groups of women. Substantial correlations were found between the NES ESS scale and the General SSS in four of the five groups ($r = .51-.62$), but even higher correlations were found between this NES subscale and the SSS TAS scale in these groups ($r = .64-.73$). The latter finding is not surprising in view of the item similarities in the ESS and TAS subscales. In the women the General SSS also correlated significantly with the other subscales of the NES but the correlations were at a lower level ($.2-.4$) and only the ISS scale also showed consistent correlations with the SSS General and subscales. Sensation seeking was primarily related to the seeking of novelty through the senses rather than through cognition.

New data (from Kohn, Hunt, & Hoffman, 1982) showing the relationships between the NES and SSS are shown in Table 3.1. Only the NES ESS and ISS scales were related to any degree with sensation-seeking scales. Only the sensation-seeking (primarily the external type) part of novelty seeking is nearly equivalent to general sensation seeking as measured by the SSS.

Novelty and change are obviously related, but are not the same. Change can be expressed in alternation between familiar activities or things, while novelty requires something not experienced previously. All novelty is change but not all change is novel. A person may do a variety of things during a day, changing from one activity to another, but may do the same things each day. Garlington and Shimona (1964) developed a test called the Change Seeker Index, which correlated very highly with the General SSS; the correlations exceeded .60 in five of seven samples (studies presented in Zucker-

Table 3.1. *Correlations between the Novelty Experiencing scales (NES) and the SSS form IV General and subscales*

	SSS				
	Gen	TAS	ES	Dis	BS
NES: Men (n = 117)					
External Sensation	.58**	.54**	.33**	.15	.13
Internal Sensation	.25**	.32**	.20*	−.01	.07
External Cognition	.23*	.14	.17	−.18	.05
Internal Cognition	.21*	.17	.24**	−.15	.17
NES: Women (n = 161)					
External Sensation	.66**	.50**	.40**	.34**	.15
Internal Sensation	.45**	.06	.40**	.35**	.27**
External Cognition	.17*	.07	.12	−.06	−.07
Internal Cognition	.25**	.04	.28**	−.04	.17*

Note: NES = Novelty Experiencing Scales; SSS = Sensation Seeking Scales; Gen = General; TAS = Thrill and Adventure Seeking; ES = Experience Seeking; Dis = Disinhibition; BS = Boredom Susceptibility.
*$p < .05$.
**$p < .01$.
Source: Part of table 1, p. 17, from "Aspects of experience seeking," by P. M. Kohn, R. W. Hunt, & F. M. Hoffman, 1982, *Canadian Journal of Behavioral Science, 14,* 13–23. Copyright 1982 by Canadian Psychological Association. Reprinted by permission.

man, 1979a). Not surprisingly, the item contents of both tests are quite similar despite the difference in names. Similarly, the General SSS was highly related to the Penney and Reinehr (1966) Stimulus Variation Seeking scale ($r = .60, .66$). However, various measures of the need for change, developed from Murray's (1938) construct, correlated only moderately with the SSS ($r = .39-.60$) as reported previously (Zuckerman, 1979a). Seeking of change is a vital part of sensation seeking but not the whole of it.

Openness to experience

McCrae and Costa (1985, 1987, in press) developed the construct of *openness to experience* as one of their "big five" factors of personality. Other five factor theorists use the terms *culture,* or *intellect* to describe this factor, but McCrae and Costa do not agree that these are appropriate labels; they maintain that this factor is not simply a function of education or intelligence. They use the creative artist as an exemplar for the concept. Peer ratings that defined the openness factor included original, imaginative, creative, broad interests, complex, curious, daring, prefer variety, independent, analytic, liberal, untraditional, and artistic (McCrae, 1987). Costa and McCrae (1985) measure openness in six areas corresponding to modes of expression: fantasy, aesthetics, feelings, actions, ideas, and values. Five of these represent internal types of experience seeking, and only actions represents an external type. Both internal sensation and cognitive modes are represented. According to McCrae (1987) what all these elements have in common are "an interest in varied experience for its own sake" (p. 1259).

Zuckerman et al. (1993) found that only the ES subscale of the SSS correlated with the NEO Openness scale. The ZKPQ ImpSS scale did not correlate with the Openness scale, although it showed a low but significant correlation with the Fantasy and Actions subscales of Openness. These would correspond to what Pearson calls internal and external sensation seeking. There is no relation of sensation seeking to the cognitive aspects of the openness construct.

As part of the validation of the dimension, McCrae (1987) related the Openness scale to performance measures of divergent thinking (originality) and sensation seeking. Openness was significantly related to the SSS Total score and all of the subscales except BS. The highest correlation was with the ES scale, as we would expect from the definition of that factor as "the seeking of arousal through the mind and senses" (Chapter 2). However, ES also includes a predilection for a nonconforming life-style, which is not necessarily part of Openness. Both Openness and the SS scales were moderately related to the total score on divergent thinking tests (Openness $r = .39$, SSS Total $r = .31$).

Curiosity

Berlyne (1971) distinguished two kinds of curiosity and exploration: *epistemic curiosity* stems from uncertainty from perceptual or symbolic stimulation and the need to resolve it; *diversive curiosity* involves the seeking of stimulation with appealing collative properties (e.g., novelty, complexity) and may be driven by a state of boredom. Obviously, the construct of diversive curiosity is more closely related to sensation seeking.

A number of trait and state curiosity scales have been developed. Olson and Camp (1984) factor analyzed several of these curiosity scales along with the SSS form V, and measures of intellectual abilities. Using the Total scores they found four factors: general curiosity, emotionality, intellectual ability, and experience seeking. The latter factor included the SSS Total score and only one of the measures of curiosity: diversive curiosity. This scale is described by Day as "a general condition which may be analogous to . . . the need to seek new experiences or to extend one's knowledge into the unknown, and which may elicit what Berlyne has called 'diversive explora- tion' '' (Day, 1968, p. 37). Diversive curiosity actually correlated .45 with the SSS Total. Another factor analysis involving the SSS subscales showed that ES, Dis, and BS scales loaded on the factor that included diversive curiosity. The TAS subscale of the SSS defined another factor that included the Proverbs test, a test of divergent thinking unrelated to curiosity trait scales and only weakly related to intelligence.

Cacioppo and Petty (1982) developed a questionnaire measure of the *need for cognition* by contrasting responses of university faculty and assembly line workers to items about the need or desire to engage in abstract, or complex thinking. Olson, Camp, and Fuller (1984) found strong correlations between this scale and various measures of trait and state curiosity. In view of what has been said about sensation seeking not being related to novelty seeking in the cognitive mode, one would not expect correlations between the SSS and the Need for Cognition (NC) scale. Olson et al. did find low but significant correlations between NC and the SSS V Total score (.25) and TAS (.31), and a higher one with the ES scale (.41), but these did not approach the high correlation found between the NC and Spielberger's Trait Curiosity scale (.67). The correlation between the SSS and NC may be due to the fact that a number of items in the NC refer to the desire to solve complex as opposed to simple problems. The need for complexity in perceptual stimuli and cognitive problems is a salient feature of the sensation-seeking trait (see Chapters 8 and 13).

Telic Dominance

The concept of telic (vs. paratelic) dominance comes from Apter's (1982) phenomenological theory of motivation. A *telic* state is one in which an individual is concentrated on a goal and concerned with the means of reach- ing that goal. The opposite state is *paratelic* in which the individual is concerned with the enjoyment of immediate sensations, is playful and sponta- neous, and is concerned only with present and not with the future. Low intensity of stimulation and arousal is preferred in the telic state, whereas high levels of stimulation and arousal are preferred in the paratelic state. Essentially, the theory describes a contrast between achievement and hedo- nistic orientations, or between work and play, as if these were incompatible states at any given moment of time. Murgatroyd, Rushton, Apter, and Ray

(1978) developed a Telic Dominance scale (TDS) based on the idea that there are stable individual differences in the relative amount of time an individual spends in one state or the other during an extended period of life. Given the description of the two states one would expect that sensation seekers would be low on telic dominance and high on paratelic dominance.

Each item in the scale requires an individual to chose between two alternatives respresenting either telic or paratelic dominance, thus building the dichotomy into the scale in the same way that high and low sensation seeking are built into the forced-choice form of the versions of the SSS through form V. The authors of the scale divided the items among three subscales described by Murgatroyd (1985):

(a) *Seriousmindedness* – the frequency with which an individual is seen to be oriented toward goals which they regard as important, rather than goals that are merely excuses or end-points for ongoing activities enjoyed in themselves; (b) *planning orientation* – the frequency with which an individual tends to plan ahead in the pursuit of goals rather than taking things as they come; (c) *arousal avoidance* – the frequency with which an individual tends to avoid situations which generate high arousal. (p. 22)

Murgatroyd (1985) presents data from an unpublished study by Cowles and Davis on the correlations between the SSS Total score and each of the three TDS subscales. The Seriousmindedness scale did not correlate at all with the SSS in either males or females or the total group and Planning Orientation correlated negatively with the SSS in females only. Arousal Avoidance correlated significantly and negatively with sensation seeking in both males ($r = -.43$), females ($r = .58$), and the total group ($r = -.54$). Apparently, arousal seeking – avoidance is the primary type of telic trait that is associated with sensation seeking.

Monotony avoidance

Schalling, Edman, and Åsberg (1983) initially used a translated version of the SSS form IV but, finding difficulties with the content of some of the items for their Swedish population, they decided to construct their own measure of sensation seeking. After some analyses of items from the SSS and another questionnaire, they developed the Monotony Avoidance (MA) scale. The items describe the need for change, action, and excitement, and the avoidance of routine activities. Although the title of the scale suggests an aversive reaction to boredom, the terms *bored, boring,* or *boredom* do not appear in the items. The correlation between the MA scale and the General SSS from form IV was .50. The correlations of MA with the SSS subscales

Table 3.2. *Correlations between SSS form VI and other sensation-seeking type scales*

Other scales	Women (n = 191)				Men (n = 74)			
	E-TAS	E-Dis	I-TAS	I-Dis	E-TAS	E-Dis	I-TAS	I-Dis
KSP Monotony Avoidance	.41	.39	.52	.40	.35	.53	.44	.59
JPI Risk Taking	.44	.36	.49	.36	.30	.47	.35	.49
EASI Sensation Seeking	.40	.47	.44	.40	.33	.46	.42	.51

Note: All correlations in table are significant, $p < .01$. E = Experience scale; I = Intention scale; TAS = Thrill and Adventure Seeking; Dis = Disinhibition; KSP = Karolinska Scales of Personality; JPI = Jackson Personality Inventory; EASI = Buss–Plomin Temperament scales.

were: TAS .23, ES .31, Dis .41, and BS .51. All of these correlations were significant except for the one with TAS. The highest correlation with BS is congruent with the name Schalling et al. give to their scale. Dis is also correlated with it, but MA is not as good at measuring the TAS and ES aspects of sensation seeking.

Zuckerman (1984c) correlated the scales of the SSS VI (Chapter 2) with the MA scale. These correlations are shown in Table 3.2 along with correlations between SSS VI and other variables to be discussed. The MA scale correlated highly with E-Dis ($r = .53$) and I-Dis ($r = .59$) in males; in females the corresponding correlations were also highly significant but somewhat lower (.39 and .40). The correlations with MA were higher for the Dis scales in the males and the TAS scales in the females.

Risk taking

The definition of sensation seeking (Chapter 1) includes "the willingness to take risks" and some related scales have emphasized this aspect of sensation seeking. There are different kinds of risk as will be described in Chapter 5. Physical risk taking is mainly involved in the TAS scale, whereas social and legal risks are more important in the ES and Dis scales. The second row in Table 3.2 shows correlations between the Risk Taking scale from the Jackson (1976) Personality Inventory and the SSS form VI scales. These are all significant and moderate ($r = .36 - .49$).

S. Eysenck and Eysenck (1977) regard sensation seeking as a component of impulsivity. In their first Impulsivity scale, one of the four factors was called risk taking, but later these items were merged with TAS type items in a broader factor called venturesomeness (S. Eysenck & Eysenck, 1978). Risk taking correlated highest with the SSS TAS subscale ($r = .46$ for females, $.42$ for males), and somewhat lower but more significantly with the other subscales of the SSS form V (Zuckerman, 1983b, Table 3.3, p. 118). In a factor analysis of the these data, the sensation-seeking subscales and risk taking formed one factor (Zuckerman, 1984a, table 1, p. 457). Impulsivity and nonplanning loaded on a second factor.

Pearson, Francis, and Lightbown (1986) decomposed the Venturesomeness scale of the Junior Impulsiveness Inventory into two subscales: Risk Taking and Sensation Seeking (mainly of the TAS type). The two subscales of Venturesomeness were moderately correlated ($r = .47$) but showed a different pattern of correlation with empathy and religiosity scales. High risk takers showed low empathy and religiosity, but sensation seeking was not related to empathy and was only minimally correlated with religiosity.

A. Buss and Plomin (1975) also view sensation seeking as a component of impulsivity. Impulsivity was regarded as one of four basic temperaments, but later (A. Buss & Plomin, 1984) they eliminated it from the list of temperaments. Table 3.2 shows the moderate correlations ($r = .40–.50$) between their sensation-seeking scale and the SSS form VI scales.

Impulsivity

Both S. Eysenck and Eysenck (1977) and A. Buss and Plomin (1975) regard Impulsivity as a multivariate trait. Eysenck and Eysenck (1977) describe narrow Impulsivity (acting quickly without much forethought), Risk Taking, and NonPlanning as subtraits. Buss and Plomin (1975) define impulsivity in terms of Decision Time (corresponding to the Eysencks' narrow impulsivity), Inhibitory Control, and Persistence. The correlations between subscales in both tests are low, but significant. Barratt and Patton (1983) analyzed their impulsivity test into cognitive, motor, nonplanning, and sensation-seeking subscales. Like Eysenck and Buss, they also see sensation seeking as part of a broad impulsivity factor.

Schalling et al. (1983) treat impulsivity and sensation seeking (monotony avoidance) as distinct traits rather than one being subsumed under the other. Their Impulsivity scale describes the fast decision-making aspect of impulsivity together with a carefree attitude toward life. They report that the two scales are generally correlated between .30 and .40 in all samples. In a factor analysis, Monotony Avoidance and Eysenck's Venturesomeness scale form one factor, while the Karolinska Scales of Personality (KSP) Impulsivity and Eysenck's broad Impulsivity scale form another. Jackson's (1976) Personality Research Form (PRF) also contains an impulsivity scale stressing fast, impulsive reactions and emotional volatility. The PRF Cognitive Structure scale is kind of a nonplanning scale scored in the reverse direction.

Relationships between the SSS and Impulsivity scales were previously summarized (Zuckerman, 1979a, table 6.8, p. 149). Eysenck's narrow Impulsivity scale was not highly related to sensation seeking, but nonplanning was more highly related. The Jackson PRF Impulsivity scale showed moderately high correlations with the SSS ($r = .51$ in men, $.42$ in women with General or Total scales). The PRF Cognitive Structure scale showed even higher correlations with sensation seeking ($r = -.64$ for men, $-.45$ for women) with the General SSS.

Corulla (1989) analyzed the relationships between the Eysencks' Venturesomeness, Impulsivity, and Empathy scales and the SSS form V. The SSS Total score correlated low but significantly with Venturesomeness, but not at all with Impulsivity. Campbell and Palus (1987) found a remarkably high relationship between the SSS Total score and Venturesomeness ($r = .77$) and a significant if somewhat lower one with Impulsivity ($r = .38$). Much of the correlation between the Total score and Venturesomeness was accounted for by the $.84$ correlation with the TAS subscale, but substantial correlations ($.45$, $.49$) were also found with Dis and ES. They also found a high correlation ($.52$) between the SSS Total and the Barratt and Patton's (1983) Impulsivity scale.

Gerbing, Ahadi, and Patton (1987) did a massive factor analysis on items from the Barratt, Eysenck, and Jackson impulsivity scales together with some items from the MMPI and the SSS ES scale. They also included behavioral measures of impulsivity: simple reaction time, time perception, and Kagan, Rosman, Day, Albert, and Phillips's (1964) Matching Familiar Figures Test (MFFT). A narrow sensation-seeking factor called thrill seeking (primarily risk taking) emerged and scores on this factor correlated highly ($r = .59$) with a narrow impulsivity factor (reacting quickly on impulse). Lower, but significant, correlations were found with other factors: quick decisions (cognitive impulsivity), nonplanning, energetic, impulse buying, unreflectiveness, and restlessness. Thrill seeking, however, was the only impulsivity factor besides unreflectiveness that correlated significantly with behavioral indicators. Thrill seekers had faster simple reaction times and made fewer errors on the MFFT. Unreflective persons made more errors on the MFFT.

The SSS form VI was correlated with a number of impulsivity scales as

Table 3.3. *Correlations between SSS form VI and impulsivity scales*

Impulsivity scales	Women (n = 191)				Men (n = 74)			
	E-TAS	E-Dis	I-TAS	I-Dis	E-TAS	E-Dis	I-TAS	I-Dis
KSP Impulsivity	.31**	.15*	.32**	.19**	.34**	.31**	.20*	.36**
EASI Inhibitory Control	.13	.17**	.17**	.27**	.13	.30**	.20*	.36**
EASI Decision Time	.25**	.26**	.31**	.19**	.16	.20	.02	.23*
EASI Persistence (lack)	−.02	.17**	.02	.17**	.18	.05	−.09	.03
JPI Restraint	−.11	−.26**	−.02	−.31**	−.15	−.52**	.27**	−.60**
PRF Cognitive Structure	−.10	−.30**	−.33**	−.29*	−.32**	.38**	−.29**	−.44**

Note: E = Experience scale; I = Intention scale; TAS = Thrill and Adventure Seeking; Dis = Disinhibition; KSP = Karolinska Scales of Personality; EASI = Buss-Plomin Temperament scales; JPI = Jackson Personality Inventory; PRF = Personality Research Form; Cognitive Structure = Need for Cognitive Structure.
*$p < .05$.
**$p < .01$.

shown in Table 3.3. In general, the Schalling Impulsivity, and the Buss and Plomin measures of inhibitory control and decision time tended to correlate positively and the Jackson (1976) Restraint and Cognitive Structure scales tended to correlate negatively and significantly with at least some of the SSS VI subscales in one or both sexes. Most of these correlations are in the low range of .2 to .4. One outstanding exception is the Jackson Personality Inventory (JPI) Restraint scale, which correlated −.52 with E-Dis and −.60 with I-Dis in males, but the correlations were much lower in women.

Personality styles (psychopathology)

Individuals with tendencies toward certain types of psychopathology can be found in any "normal population." Some of these individuals are diagnosable as "personality disorders," but many function adequately if not optimally. Some have a lack of behavioral control that suggests diagnostic terms like mania or psychopathy. The Minnesota Multiphasic Personality Inventory (MMPI) scales are defined by types of psychopathology such as depression, hypochondriasis, and psychasthenia. Studies relating the MMPI to SSS were discussed previously (Zuckerman, 1979a, pp. 156–159). The most consistent correlations in normal, prisoner, and patient samples were between the

MMPI Hypomania (Ma) scale and the General SSS. In the college student normal groups the SSS Dis and ES subscales also correlated with the MMPI Psychopathic Deviate (Pd) scale:

Miller and Magaro (1977) developed a method of typing normal subjects in terms of personality styles using their factor scores based on personality tests including hysteric, compulsive, character disorder (antisocial personality), manic, and depressive styles. Before they had defined the manic style, they found that high sensation seekers tended to fall into the cluster of persons with a character disorder style. Those persons falling into the compulsive or depressive groups tended to be low on sensation seeking (Miller & Magaro, 1977). Later studies including the manic style have found that males scoring high on SSS General and Dis scales tend to fall into groups designated as "manic style" (Magaro & Smith, 1981; Pederson & Magaro, 1982). Females scoring high on Dis tend to fall into the character disorder or hysteric style groups.

Measures of specific psychopathological correlates of sensation seeking in normals show that hypomanic and psychopathic (antisocial personality) tendencies tend to be associated with sensation seeking. In patients it is mainly the manic tendencies that are associated with sensation seeking. As will be seen in Chapter 10, there is substantial evidence that persons with clinical disorders like antisocial personality and bipolar disorder (manic-depressive) tend to score higher on sensation-seeking scales than control groups. In Chapters 11 and 12, we will see that these disorders have some biological correlates in common with the sensation-seeking trait. This suggests continuity of deviations in the normal range of personality with clinical disorders characterized by disinhibition of behavior.

Hedonism and play

An intrinsic pleasure from sensations and activities seems to motivate sensation seeking. Are sensation seekers hedonists, and conversely are low sensation seekers anhedonic? Or perhaps high and low sensation seekers differ only in the sources of their pleasures rather than the generalized capacity to feel pleasure.

Play may be the first expression of sensation seeking in children and the adult delight in games and fantasy may represent an extension of this source of pleasure into later years. As noted previously (Zuckerman, 1979a), the need for Play scale from the Jackson PRF correlated significantly with the General and nearly all of the subscales of the SSS form IV, but the strongest correlations were with the Dis scale ($r = .55$ for men, and .64 for women).

Dis represents an adult type of play in the form of parties and sex. Correlations between the Play scale and Dis scales in form VI (Zuckerman, 1984b) were also higher than those with TAS scales, suggesting that the games of adult life are more social than physical.

Bailey's (1987) sociobiological theory suggests that more "primitive" types of pleasures stem from subcortical brain mechanisms, whereas more "advanced" pleasures originate in the neocortex. Characteristics of primitive pleasures include an emphasis on concrete bodily feelings and sensations, concreteness involving little or no concentration or verbalization, or "gut-level experiencing." More advanced pleasures are abstract, do not involve bodily feelings, have a high degree of verbal mediation, and involve sustained mental concentration. As previously noted, sensation seeking is more related to sensation than cognition and it is clear that many of the pleasures sought by sensation seekers involve unusual body sensations.

Bailey, Burns, and Bazan (1982) developed rating scales to evaluate primitive and advanced mechanisms in pleasures and aversions in reality and fantasy. Sensation seeking correlated with "primitiveness" of actual pleasures for men. The strongest relationship was with the Dis scale as expected. For women, however, the relationship was just the opposite; more advanced types of pleasure were related to sensation seeking, and among the subscales this was true mainly for TAS. No relationships were found between the SSS and aversive types of activities or fantasies. Bailey et al. consider the data evidence for the proposition that men are more ruled by their "basic drives" (i.e., sexuality and aggression) than women. This hypothesis fits the gender differences found in the Dis scale as described in Chapter 4. However, another possibility is that the gender differences are in control mechanisms rather than "drive strengths."

At the opposite extreme of hedonism lies the condition of *anhedonia,* or the incapacity to experience or seek pleasure. Anhedonia is one of the primary traits associated with schizotypic personality and schizophrenia (Meehl, 1962) as well as major depressive episodes. Schizophrenics, particularly those of the withdrawn and inactive type, do score low on the SSS (Kish, 1970a), and hospitalized depressives also score low on sensation seeking even after treatment (Carton, Jouvent, Bungener, & Widlöcher, 1992).

Chapman, Chapman, and Raulin (1976) devised questionnaire scales for the measurement of anhedonic tendencies. There are two subscales, one for physical anhedonia, or incapacity to enjoy physical pleasures, and the other for social anhedonia, or the lack of pleasure in social relationships. Watson (1972) developed an interview method for assessing anhedonia.

Watson and Jacobs (1977) found moderate relationships between their interview measure of anhedonia and the General SSS in schizophrenics $(r = -.41)$. They also found significant relationships between the SSS and Chapman's Physical Anhedonia $(r = -.43)$ and the Social Anhedonia $(r = -.50)$ scales. Carton, Jouvent, Bungener, and Widlöcher (1992) reported that their own scales for anhedonia and "global indifference" correlated negatively with the General SSS and the TAS, ES, and Dis subscales in younger female depressed patients, but positively with these sensation-seeking scales in younger male depressives. In older patients none of the correlations were significant. In all patients, however, significant increases in general sensation seeking from admission to discharge were associated with decreases in anhedonia and increases in emotional expressiveness.

The Carton et al. findings suggest that in younger depressed patients both sensation-seeking levels and anhedonia are inversely related states produced by depression rather than long-standing personality traits. In normal controls only a low negative relationship has been found between sensation seeking and the scale for social anhedonia (McCann, Mueller, Hays, Scheuler, & Marsella, 1990).

If the strong relationship between anhedonia and sensation seeking is limited to patients with psychopathology, anhedonia may not be on a continuum with the strength of normal pleasure seeking. Low sensation seekers may simply derive their pleasures from less arousing activities than high sensation seekers. Hamilton, Haier, and Buchsbaum (1984) developed a scale to measure *intrinsic enjoyment*. Intrinsic enjoyment is defined as the capacity for intense involvement, interest, and absorption, even in routine kinds of activities and work. To the extent one has the capacity for this type of pleasure, one cannot easily become bored. They also developed another scale called *boredom coping* intended to reflect the specific capacity to restructure perceptions so that potentially boring activities are not experienced as aversive. Both of these scales were correlated with the boredom susceptibility scale (BS) from the SSS form IV. Only the intrinsic enjoyment scale correlated with the BS scale $(r = -.39)$. Apparently sensation seekers may become bored even if they have the capacity to cope with boredom. What they lack is the capacity to become involved in routine kinds of activities.

Conservatism versus liberalism

Conservatives want to preserve the past and liberals want change in society. This basic distinction in social attitudes generalizes across many areas of attitude and may represent a general personality trait sometimes called "authoritarianism" (Adorno, Frenkel-Brunswick, Levinson, & Sanford, 1950). As reported previously (Zuckerman, 1979a), sensation seeking is directly related to liberal permissive attitudes and negatively related to conservative attitudes in political, religious, and sexual areas, and to authoritarianism measured as a trait. A study by Pearson and Sheffield (1975), using the Wilson-Patterson (1968) Conservatism Test, found that the General SSS was highly and negatively related to general conservatism as well as to specific attitudes of militarism-punitiveness, ethnocentrism, religious puritanism, and antihedonism. The last type of attitude is relevant to the discussion on hedonism in the preceding section.

Rokeach (1960) proposed that dogmatism, as a style of thought, might characterize ideologues of both right and left regardless of the particular content of their dogma, but this dimension also proved to be related to convervatism (Brand, 1981). The low internal reliability of the Rokeach Dogmatism (D) scale suggested that it is multifactorial. Schmitz (1985) factor analyzed the D scale and found seven factors: belief in one truth, belief in one cause, future orientation, self-proselytization, isolation, alienation, virtuous self-denial. He correlated the SSS form IV with the D scale and found that the General SSS and all the subscales were significantly and negatively related to the Total D score, and the subscale *belief in one truth.* The General SSS correlated −.46 with belief in one truth and the ES scale reached the high correlation of −.64 with this subscale. The correlation may explain why sensation-seeking scores of atheists and agnostics are higher than those of followers of traditional religions (Zuckerman & Neeb, 1980). The only other subscale of D showing any correlation with sensation seeking was *virtuous self-denial,* which correlated only with the General SSS and more highly with Dis (−.48) and ES (−.30). Not surprisingly, high disinhibiters do not regard self-denial as a virtue.

Masculinity–femininity and sex role concept

Sex differences are commonly found on the SSS (Chapter 4) and these differences are particularly strong on the scales measuring physical risk taking (TAS), and permissive attitudes toward sex (Dis). Sensation seeking may be related to a stereotypical type of masculinity. Traditionally, masculinity–femininity was measured by selecting items of attitudes, vocational and avocational interests, and behavior on which men and women differed. Items scored for masculinity usually reflect interests in sports and "tough-minded" attitudes, whereas items scored for femininity show an interest in art, literature, and culture and more "tender-minded" attitudes. These older scales are bipolar, ranging from extreme masculine to extreme feminine scores. Recent scales, like the Bem (1974) Sex-role Inventory, conceptualize masculinity and femininity as two independent dimensions derived from trait ratings rather than expressions of interest in activities. All the traits included are socially desirable but are ones on which the sexes differ in their self-characterizations. For instance, aggressive, ambitious, and assertive are traits on the masculine scale, and affectionate, compassionate, and gentle are contained in the feminine scale. It is possible for a person to score high on both dimensions and such persons are called "androgynous" (used in a positive sense of not being role stereotyped).

The SSS has never shown much correlation with the traditional masculinity–femininity scales like the one on the MMPI. Although there appears to be some relationship between stereotypic masculinity–femininity scales and sensation seeking, it is a weak one (Kish, 1971). Using the Bem scale, with its independent masculinity and femininity scales, both men and women show negative correlations between femininity and sensation seeking (Tobacyk & Thomas, 1980; C. Waters & Pincus, 1976) and low positive correlations with masculinity (Tobacyk & Thomas, 1980).

Anxiety, anger and aggressiveness, emotionality

Anxiety. Since sensation seekers seem ready to take all kinds of risks, it has been suggested that the dimension is relevant to anxiety. Are low sensation seekers just anxious persons and are high sensation seekers characterized by an extreme lack of anxiety? Or are high sensation seekers "counterphobic" (to use an esoteric psychoanalytic concept) individuals who compulsively do the things they are afraid of in order to deny their anxiety? Either way one would expect negative correlations between self-report anxiety scales and sensation seeking, since counterphobics would never admit they were anxious. It must be pointed out that most anxiety trait scales are social anxiety scales, and not scales for fear of physical harm. Generalized human anxiety seems to be shown more in social situations than in physically dangerous situations.

A previous survey (Zuckerman, 1979a, pp. 165–172) of correlations between anxiety and sensation-seeking trait scales showed that there was generally no relationship between sensation seeking and anxiety of the type measured by broad trait scales or fear in social situations. There was a low negative relationship between the SSS TAS subscale and specific trait fears

Table 3.4. *Correlations between SSS form VI and tests for trait anxiety*

Anxiety scales	Women (n = 191)				Men (n = 74)			
	E-TAS	E-Dis	I-TAS	I-Dis	E-TAS	E-Dis	I-TAS	I-Dis
JPI Anxiety	−.09	−.06	−.18**	−.09	−.05	.09	−.06	.16
KSP Psychasthenia	−.20**	−.13	−.28**	−.18**	−.08	−.02	−.08	.00
KSP Anxiety	−.10	−.07	−.15*	−.07	.01	−.01	−.05	.01
EASI General Emotionality	.01	−.05	−.08	−.05	.06	.18	.11	.19
EASI Fear	−.28**	−.19**	−.37**	−.11	−.23*	−.16	−.21*	−.11

Note: E = Experience scale; I = Intention scale; TAS = Thrill and Adventure Seeking; Dis = Disinhibition; JPI = Jackson Personality Inventory; KSP = Karolinska Scales of Personality; EASI = Buss–Plomin Temperament scales.
*$p < .05$.
**$p < .01$.

of physical harm and state anxiety in situations where physical harm is a theoretical possibility.

Table 3.4 shows the relationships between four measures of anxiety trait and one of general emotionality and the SSS VI scales (Zuckerman, 1984c). Only 2 of the 20 correlations were significant for the males; both of these were between A. Buss and Plomin's (1975) EASI fear scale and the two TAS subscales. Many more were significant for the women but most of these were with the TAS subscales and, with one exception, none exceeded −.30 in magnitude. The results with form VI reinforce the conclusions based on earlier forms of the SSS. To the extent there is any relationship between anxiety and sensation seeking, it is a low one between thrill and adventure seeking and fear. Anxiety has little or nothing to do with other forms of sensation seeking.

Anger and Aggression. The capacity to express anger and act aggressively could be construed as a form of sensation seeking. Some men seem to enjoy fights as a kind of sensation seeking. These "heroes" can serve a useful function during wartime. Is aggressiveness related to sensation seeking? Studies correlating the aggression scale of the Jackson PRF with the SSS in students, reported in Zuckerman (1979a), show a relationship between aggression and the Dis scale in females, and the Dis, ES, BS, and General scales in males. The relationship with Dis ($r = .43$) was the highest one.

Table 3.5 shows the correlations between scales of aggression, anger, and

Table 3.5. *Correlations between SSS form VI scales and aggression-hostility-anger scales*

Aggression-hostility scales	Women (n = 191)				Men (n = 74)			
	E-TAS	E-Dis	I-TAS	I-Dis	E-TAS	E-Dis	I-TAS	I-Dis
PRF Aggression	.10	.20**	−.02	.17**	.06	.37**	.15	.43**
Buss Hostility	.02	.13*	−.02	.10	.18	.49**	.20*	.55**
EASI Anger	.06	.13*	.03	.13*	.09	.28**	.06	.32**
KSP Inhibition of Aggression	−.21**	−.24**	−.21**	−.25**	−.21*	−.34**	−.29**	−.39**

Note: E = Experience scale; I = Intention scale; TAS = Thrill and Adventure Seeking; Dis = Disinhibition; PRF = Personality Research Form; EASI = Buss–Plomin Temperament scales; KSP Karolinska Scales of Personality.
*$p < .05$.
**$p < .01$.

inhibition of aggression and the SSS form VI subscales (Zuckerman, 1984c). Aggression and anger are related almost entirely to Dis subscales and not related to TAS subscales in men and women. The correlations are very low in women but higher in men. Inhibition of Aggression from the KSP scales is negatively related about equally to both TAS and Dis subscales in both men and women. Apparently, aggression and anger are related to the Dis type of sensation seeking, particularly in men.

General emotionality or emotional expressiveness. General emotionality is often equated with negative emotions like anxiety or anger, but there is a dimension of emotional intensity that is orthogonal to the type of emotions typically expressed in these scales (Diener, Larsen, Levine, & Emmons, 1985). Allen and Hamsher (1974) developed a Test of Emotional Styles. Using this test, Allen (1976) found relationships between value placed on emotional expression and reported frequency and intensity of emotional expression and sensation seeking in males (but not in females). High sensation-seeking males were characterized by enjoyment of emotional expression and the ability to express emotions freely and intensely. Goreman and Wesman (1974) had subjects keep records of their emotional states over a 4-week period and found that high sensation seeking was associated with levels of *positive moods* over the period.

Other evidence of association between freedom of emotional expression and sensation seeking comes from data discussed in the earlier volume

(Zuckerman, 1979a) relating the Shostrom (1966) Personal Orientation Inventory (supposedly a measure of self-actualization). A number of the subscales refer to the capacity to express emotions freely: Feeling Reactivity, Spontaneity, Acceptance of Aggression, and Capacity for Intimacy. Feeling Reactivity and Spontaneity were related to all of the SS scales in women; lower correlations were found in men and primarily with the ES scale. Acceptance of Aggression and Capacity for Intimacy were related to sensation seeking in both sexes.

Autonomy and Narcissism

Sensation seekers tend to be nonconformists. They dance to the beat of a different drummer. In their search for novel experience, they seek out that which is different. In the previous book (Zuckerman, 1979a) fairly substantial correlations were reported between the General SSS and *need for autonomy*, as measured by several multiphasic personality inventories. Snyder and Fromkin (1977) developed a scale for measuring *"Uniqueness"* defined as "a sense of independence, anticonformity, inventiveness, achievement and self-esteem." Baird (1981) correlated this scale with the SSS form IV and found a substantial correlation with the General scale ($r = .64$) and significant correlations with all the subscales. Raskin and Hall (1979) devised a scale to measure *Narcissism,* a trait sharing some features with sensation seeking like autonomy, dominance, exhibitionism, sense of self-importance, and easy boredom with sex partners. Emmons (1981) found that Raskin and Hall's Narcissism scale correlated primarily with the Dis scale of the SSS form IV ($r = .48$ for men, .51 for women), unlike Autonomy and Uniqueness, which tended to correlate about equally with all of the SSS scales. Dis seems to represent a more antisocial type of nonconformity than that found in general sensation seeking.

Tests based on stimulus and arousal modulation theories

Reducer–augmenter scale. A number of theories discussed in Chapter 1 are based on the idea that a primary dimension of personality depends on how the organism modulates the intensity of stimuli, or how much arousal is produced by given levels of stimulation. Eysenck's extraversion, Strelau's reactivity (based on Pavlovian models) constructs, and sensation-seeking theory describe individual differences in sensitivities to stimulation and arousal effects of stimulation as a source of behavioral differences. Petrie (1967) provided a typology based on regulation of stimulus intensity. *Aug-*

menters are sensitive to pain and other kinds of stimulation, and *reducers* have a type of nervous system that suppresses the effects of incoming stimuli and are therefore more resistant to pain and other forms of intense stimulation. According to the theory, reducers suffer from lack of stimulation and are more prone to seek stimulation, whereas augmenters are sensitive to stimulation and avoid intense stimuli. Petrie also provided a psychophysical laboratory test intended to measure the trait without resorting to painful levels of stimulation. The Kinesthetic Figural Aftereffect (KFA) test has subjects: (1) estimate the size of a block of wood by running their fingers down a tapered wedge until they reach a width that they think is equivalent to the first block (the subject is blindfolded), (2) vigorously rub another wider or smaller block, and (3) immediately make a second estimate of size on the tapered wedge. Augmenters are those who make judgments of increased width after the interpolated stimulation, and reducers are defined as those who show a decrease in estimated block width.

Petrie showed relationships between this test and pain tolerance, drug preferences, and other measures. Problems with the instrument, including an embarrassing lack of retest reliability, have led many investigators in recent years to use pain or noise tolerance tests in place of the KFA technique. Furthermore, a more direct measure of cortical augmenting-reducing effects was developed by Buchsbaum and Silverman (1968) based on the relation between the amplitude of the cortical evoked potential and stimulus intensity within individuals. This measure has identified high sensation seekers as augmenters and low sensation seekers as reducers in many studies (Zuckerman, 1990a), which will be discussed in Chapter 12. But according to the theory developed from Petrie's work based on her psychophysical method, sensation seekers should be reducers, not augmenters. This seeming paradox in findings is undoubtedly a function of the different methods used to assess the same hypothetical physiological trait (Davis, Cowles, & Kohn, 1983; Zuckerman, 1986a). In personality psychology, things called by the same name are not necessarily the same thing, and things called by different names are not necessarily different.

To complicate matters even further, Vando (1974) developed a questionnaire called the Reducing–Augmenting scale (RAS) and designed to identify augmenters and reducers without having to resort to laboratory measurements. Although intended as a substitute for the KFA test, it has shown no relationship to that test (Davis, Cowles, & Kohn, 1984). A perusal of the forced-choice type items on the 54-item version shows that 21 of the 54 items are either slightly altered forms of items from the SSS or similar to those found on the SSS.

Kohn, Hunt, Cowles, and Davis (1986) factor analyzed the RAS and found three factors describing the items. The first was called musical augmenting–reducing; seven of the eight items refer to preferences for loud, rock-type music in contrast to quiet, popular, ballad type music. The factor is almost entirely specific to the one sensory modality of sound, even though the augmenting–reducing construct is also based on kinesthetic and pain senses as well. Factor 2 is called general life-style augmenting–reducing and refers to a variety of preferences for people, pets, politics, occupations, and body odors. It seems closest to the Dis and ES scales of the SSS. Factor 3 is called physical thrill seeking and resembles the TAS subscale of the SSS. Dragutinovich (1987a) replicated the factor analysis in Australia and found factors very close to those of Kohn et al. Dragutinovich calls the Music factor "auditory modality," the Thrill Seeking factor "kinesthetic activity," and the general life-style factor "sensation seeking," noting that most of the items for this last factor are quite similar to those in the SSS.

Table 3.6 shows the correlations obtained between the RAS Total score and SSS form IV or V scales in the studies by Dragutinovich (1987a), Kohn, Hunt, and Hoffman (1982), and Kohn et al. (1986). The last study also included correlations between the factor-derived subscales of the RAS and all of the scales of the SSS form IV. The General SSS and all the subscales were significantly correlated with the full-scale RAS in all three studies; the correlations with the Total or General scales were all very high, ranging from .60 to .71. The correlations of the RAS Total with the subscales varied more from study to study, but in two of the studies the highest correlations were with the Dis scale. However, the correlations between RAS and the SSS subscales were all high in the studies by Dragutinovich (1987b) and Kohn, Hunt, and Hoffman (1982). An examination of the correlations with the three-factor subscales of the RAS (Kohn et al., 1986) shows that the correlation between the General SSS and full-scale RAS is largely produced by the .72 correlation with the general life-style factor, secondarily by the .43 correlation with the thrill seeking factor, and least by the low .27 correlation with the musical reducing–augmenting factor. However, the patterning of the subscale correlations is interesting. The Dis scale correlates most highly with the musical factor, ES and BS scales with the general life-style score, and the TAS with the Thrill Seeking subscale of the RAS. Each factor of the RAS seems to best measure a specific aspect of sensation seeking.

It is apparent that the SSS and RAS are nearly equivalent in what they measure. To a large extent this communality is a function of the similarity in the content of the items for at least two of the three factors in the test. The other factor refers mainly to sound intensity in preferred music. When the

Table 3.6. *Correlations between the Sensation Seeking Scale (SSS) and the Vando Reducing–Augmenting scale (RAS)*

SSS	Dragutinovich (1987b) ($n = 211$)	Kohn et al. (1982)[a]	
		Males ($n = 117$)	Females ($n = 161$)
Total/General	.71**	.60**	.62**
TAS	.46**	.20*	.23*
ES	.38*	.27**	.41**
Dis	.59**	.46**	.42**
BS	.55**	.19*	.26**

Note: TAS = Thrill and Adventure Seeking; ES = Experience Seeking; Dis = Disinhibition; BS = Boredom Susceptibility.
[a] Correlations involving the TAS, ES, and BS subscales of the SS form IV are partial correlations corrected for item overlap of these scales with the General scale in this form.
*p < .05.
**p < .01.
Source: Data from study by Dragutinovich from table 1, p. 696, from "Stimulus intensity reducers: Are they sensation seekers, extraverts, and strong nervous types," by S. Dragutinovich, 1987, *Personality and Individual Differences, 8,* 693–704. Copyright 1987 by Pergamon Press. Reprinted by permission. Data from study by Kohn et al. from table 1, p. 17, from "Aspects of experience seeking," by P. M. Kohn, R. W. Hunt, & F. M. Hoffman, 1982, *Canadian Journal of Behavioral Science, 14,* 13–23. Copyright 1982 by Canadian Journal of Behavioral Science. Reprinted by permission.

first SSS was developed we had tried some stimulus intensity items of the type in the Musical factor, but most of these did not find their way into the final forms of the SSS because of a lack of general or specific factor correlation. But at that time we did not have the Dis scale, which seems to be the one most related to the intensity factor. As will be seen (Chapter 12), it is the Dis factor that is related to augmenting or reducing the cortical evoked potential, but in a direction opposite to the theory behind the Vando scale.

Sensitivity. The Vando RAS seems to measure reported reactions to high-intensity stimuli, mostly auditory and musical. According to the concept of *reactivity* (Strelau, 1983), tolerance for high-intensity stimuli is directly related to *insensitivity* to low intensities of stimulation. K. White (1984) developed a Sensitivity scale for the low-intensity type of stimulation that includes various stimulus modalities: somesthetic, temperature, olfactory, auditory, pain, and visual stimuli. Dragutinovich (1987b) correlated this scale with the SSS form V scales and found low but significant correlations ($r = -.18--.25$) with the Total score and all of the subscales except ES. The weakness of the relationship is consistent with the weak and inconsistent data relating sensation seeking to sensory thresholds (Chapter 13).

Arousal seeking. The RAS is a mixture of stimulus modulation and arousal-seeking types of items. The only basis for grouping the two types of items in a single scale is the theory behind the test that claims that persons who reduce are more likely to seek stimulation and arousal, whereas those who augment are more likely to be low sensation seekers. Mehrabian (1978) separated these concepts and developed separate scales for each: The Stimulus Screening scale is designed to measure arousability in response to stimulation, whereas the scale for Arousal Seeking Tendency (AST) is intended to measure the behavioral tendency to seek novel stimuli or situations and the need for change in friends and surroundings. Despite the theoretical relationships between the two constructs, Mehrabian (1978) reported that the two scales are essentially uncorrelated ($r = -.08$). Only one study has come to light correlating the Stimulus Screening scale with the SSS. Kohn (1987) reported a weak but significant correlation ($-.26$) between the Stimulus Screening scale and the General SSS.

The AST consists of a 32-item, 9-point Likert-type response scale. As with the RAS, many of the items are similar to those on the SSS. For instance AST item 17 seems to combine the low sensation-seeking choice from three items of the SSS TAS scale: "I wouldn't enjoy dangerous sports such as mountain climbing, airplane flying or sky diving." Table 3.7 shows the correlations between the SSS forms IV and V and the AST in studies by Kohn, Hunt, and Hoffman (1982) and Furnham (1984). The General or Total SSS were highly related to the AST in both studies (r's $= .56-.71$). In the Kohn et al. study the SSS-ES scale shows the highest relationships of the subscales with the AST, but in the Furnham study all the subscales except BS were about equally related to the AST. As noted previously, the SSS is negatively correlated with the *arousal avoidance* subscale of the Murgatroyd et al. (1978) Telic Dominance Scale. Sensation seeking is moderately related to arousal seeking but not to sensitivity to stimulation traits.

Reactivity. The concept of reactivity (Strelau) includes both sensitivity to low intensities of stimulation and lack of tolerance or endurance for high intensities of stimulation. Kohn (1987) constructed a scale designed to measure this trait. The Reactivity scale correlated moderately with the General SSS ($r = -.44$) and RAS ($r = -.46$), but not at all with the Stimulus Screening scale. Although lower than the correlations found between the General SSS

Table 3.7. *Correlations between the Sensation Seeking Scale (SSS) and the Mehrabian and Russell Arousal-Seeking Tendency (AST) scale*

SSS	Kohn et al. (1982)		Furnham (1984) ($n = 196$)
	Men ($n = 117$)	Women ($n = 161$)	
General/Total	.61*	.71*	.56*
TAS	.13	.21*	.29*
ES	.42*	.52*	.28*
Dis	.13	.44*	.32*
BS	.36*	.40*	.11

Note: TAS = Thrill and Adventure Seeking; ES = Experience Seeking; Dis = Disinhibition; BS = Boredom Susceptibility.
*$p < .01$.
Source: Kohn et al. data from table 1, p. 17, from "Aspects of experiences seeking," by P. M. Kohn, R. W. Hunt, & F. M. Hoffman, 1982, *Canadian Journal of Behavioral Science, 14,* 13–23. Copyright 1982 by Canadian Journal of Behavioral Science. Reprinted by permission. Furnham data from table 2, p. 138, from "Extraversion, sensation seeking, stimulus screening and type "A" behaviour pattern: The relationship between measures of arousal," by A. F. Furnham, 1984, *Personality and Individual Differences, 5,* 133–140. Copyright 1984 by Pergamon Press. Reprinted by permission.

and RAS, the correlations with the reactivity scale are important because the items of this scale were designed to assess the experiencing of sensation rather than the seeking of sensation.

A large program of research has developed around Strelau's questionnaire measure of reactivity, as assessed by his Strength of Excitation subscale. As would be predicted, Kohn's reactivity scale correlated negatively ($r = -.45$) with Strelau's Strength of Excitation scale. The relationships between all of Strelau's dimensions and the SSS will be discussed next.

The position of sensation seeking within broader dimensions of personality

Pavlovian dimensions (Strelau)

Strelau (1983) was the first to translate Pavlovian dimensions of temperament into a questionnaire form. The Strelau Temperament Inventory (STI) contains three rationally developed scales, Strength of Excitation (SE), Strength of Inhibition (SI), Mobility (M), and a ratio of SE to SI called Balance (B). Translating the Pavlovian concepts into questionnaire items required an interpretation of what the conditioning phenomena, previously used to define these terms, would mean in human behavioral terms. The SE scale was defined by items indicating a capacity for action in very stimulating situations, sometimes for prolonged periods, and being able to persist in work or other goal-appropriate behavior in such situations without loss of efficiency or manifestation of emotional disturbance. Persons who are high in SE are also regarded as nonreactives, whereas persons who have weak SE are termed reactive types. The definition implies a mixture of extraversion and low emotionality, and the SE scale does correlate positively with Eysenck's E scale and negatively with the N scale (Strelau, Angleitner, & Ruch, 1989). The SI scale items include behavioral restraint and the ability to delay or interrupt action where inhibition is required. SI sounds like the converse of impulsivity. The M scale items describe the ability to react quickly and effectively to changing circumstances, sometimes calling for inhibition and sometimes for action. Some of the items also describe lability, or arousability.

There are a number of problems with the first version of the STI, as admitted by Strelau et al. (1989). First is that the three subscales, which should be reasonably independent, are highly intercorrelated, almost as if there were only one or two dimensions rather than three being measured by the test. Strelau et al. report that the median correlation between SE and SI in 16 studies was .42, .54 between SE and M, and .26 between SI and M. Factor analyses also suggested that SE and M may form a single dimension with SI somewhat distinguishable from the other two. Despite the fact that SE and SI are supposed to be independent dimensions, there is a positive correlation between the two scales. Strength of the Nervous System means strength of both excitatory and inhibitory characteristics, and thus might account for the positive relationship between the scales. Strelau et al. (1989) have pointed out other problems with the STI scales, including an item content too restricted to work activities, many items with poor correlations with the scales they are placed in and higher correlations with other scales, a high correlation of the scales with social desirability responding, and an imbalance of true and false items within scales. Ruch, Angleitner, and Strelau (1991) described the first validity studies on a revised STI in which some of the psychometric problems have been dealt with.

Strelau (1983) and Zuckerman (1979a) both suggested that sensation seeking has much in common with the concept of the strong nervous system,

Table 3.8. *Correlations between Sensation Seeking Scale (SSS) and Strelau Temperament Inventory (STI) scales*

Study	SSS	Subjects Sex/n	STI study			
			SE	SI	M	B
Gilliland (1985)	Total	M&F/58	.21	.11	.26	.11
Corulla (1989)	Total	M/312	−.07	−.29**	.12*	.23*
	Total	F/2	.15*	−.21**	.23**	.31**
Strelau et al. (1989)	Total	M/51	.29*	−.57**	.10	.62**
	Total	F/34	−.03	−.63**	.48**	.51**
Dragutinovich (1987b)	Total	M&F/212	.13	−.18**	.20**	—
Strelau et al. (1989)	General	M/62	.24	−.12	.27*	.33**
	General	F/72	.31**	−.22	.42**	.49**
Daum et al. (1988)	General	M/58	.28*	−.26*	.63**	—
Oleszkiewicz (1982)	General	M/171	.25**	—	—	—
Median correlations			.23	−.22	.26	.33

Note: M = male; F = female; n = number of subjects; SE = Strength of Excitation; SI = Strength of Inhibition; M = Mobility; B = Balance (SE/SI); General = General SSS from form IV; Total = Total score (sum of subscales) from form V.
*$p < .05$.
**$p < .01$.

equated by Strelau with strength of excitation and nonreactivity. However, given the correlations between sensation seeking and impulsivity, we might also expect the SSS to correlate negatively with strength of inhibition. Furthermore, considering the relation between sensation seeking and need for change, the mobility dimension should correlate positively with sensation seeking. The correlations between the SSS and the STI scales in 10 studies surveyed by Strelau et al. (1989), plus one additional study (Dragutinovich, 1987b) missed by them, are listed in Table 3.8. There is much variability in the correlations from one study to another, perhaps because of the use of different translated scales, forms of the SSS, and gender and population differences.

The median results are given for an appraisal of general relationships across studies. There is evidence of a weak relationship between the SSS and all of the STI scales; the Total or General SSS correlates about .24 with SE, −.26 with SI, .26 with M, and .33 with the balance between SE and SI (in the direction of SE). In terms of the constructs behind the STI scales, high sensation seekers may be described as having strong strength of excitation, weak strength of inhibition, and a high degree of mobility in nervous processes. Excitation process is relatively stronger than inhibition process.

Examination of correlations among the subscales shows some evidence of different patterns for the STI dimensions. SE correlates primarily with the SSS TAS subscale, and very little with the other subscales. This is not surprising, in view of the physical stamina element in many of the SE scale items and the emphasis on physical activities in the TAS. SI correlates primarily with BS and Dis subscales and very little with TAS. Dis, of course, represents a lack of behavioral inhibition. The BS and Dis scales are the ones most related to impulsivity and BS represents an intolerance for monotonous tasks that require inhibition of competing activities in order to be able to persist in the prolonged task. TAS also correlates with M, perhaps reflecting the athlete's ability suddenly to mobilize excitation for demands of an athletic task, and to relax between events. The most general relationship between the SSS Total and all of its component subscales is found with the balance score between excitation and inhibition. This finding recalls the earliest formulation of a biological model for sensation seeking (Zuckerman, 1969a) in which it was suggested that the strengths of excitatory and inhibitory centers in the central nervous system might determine the optimal levels of stimulation for individuals. The concept of overall excitability or inhibitory strengths of the total nervous systems has been abandoned in favor of specific neural pathways governed by particular neurotransmitters (Zuckerman, 1979a), but there is evidence that sensation seekers are excited or aroused by novel stimuli (Chapter 12) and at the same time are somewhat disinhibited in behavior.

Because there are some questions about the STI, particularly the lack of discriminant validity indicated in the correlations among the subscales, the relationship of the new revised STI-R to the SSS is of interest. Many of the psychometric problems of the old STI have been reduced by more careful item analyses and selections of items for revised scales. Table 3.9 shows the first results relating the SSS V to the STI-R in two heterogeneous, mixed-gender samples (Ruch, Angleitner, & Strelau, 1991). Correlations were higher and more of them were significant in the larger sample than in the smaller one. In the smaller group the SSS Total score correlated positively with SE and negatively with SI at a low level of correlation similar to the median values in Table 3.8. Also similar was the finding that TAS was primarily associated with SE and Dis with SI, although in this study ES also related negatively to SI. However, in the larger sample SE was substantially, positively correlated with the SSS Total and all of the subscales, and M was also generally correlated with the SSS, a result seen with the old STI. SI negative relationships with the SSS were limited to the Total, Dis, and ES subscales, as in the smaller sample. Even though the correlations between the STI subscales have been reduced by the revised form, even greater

Table 3.9. *Correlations between the SSS form V and the Strelau Temperament Inventory – Revised*

SSS	STI-R Study I: 85 M & F subjects			STI-R Study II: 159 M & F subjects		
	SE	SI	M	SE	SI	M
Total	.29*	−.28*	—	.50**	−.34**	.40**
TAS	.36**	—	—	.45**	—	.36*
ES	—	−.29*	.25*	.46**	−.35**	.43**
Dis	—	−.35*	—	.36**	−.35**	.22**
BS	.26*	—	—	.31**	—	.23*

Note: Correlations not significant at $p = <.05$ or less are not listed in the table.
*$p < .05$.
**$p < .01$.
Source: Table 2, from "The Strelau Temperament Inventory – Revised (STI-R). validity studies," by W. Ruch, A. Angleitner, & J. Strelau, 1991, *European Journal of Personality, 5*, 287–308. Copyright 1991 by John Wiley & Sons, Ltd., Chichester. Reprinted by permission.

generality of relationships with the SSS subscales is evident and the relationships are more robust. The implications of the relationships in terms of constructs of stimulus regulation and arousal, common to both the Pavlovian and sensation-seeking models, will be explored in subsequent chapters.

Western dimensions

H. Eysenck (1984), Royce (1984), and others have raised the question of the location of sensation seeking in the multidimensional personality space. Is sensation seeking a unitary trait or do the subtraits align themselves with different dimensions of personality? In this section, factor analytic studies of sensation-seeking subscales, along with other markers for major dimensions of personality, will be described.

Sensation seeking, Eysenck's, and Strelau's dimensions

In response to the commentaries by Eysenck and Royce, Zuckerman (1984a, table 1, p. 457) presented the results of a factor analysis of the SSS form V subscales, E, N, P, and L scales from the EPQ, and Impulsivity-Narrow (Imp$_n$), Nonplanning (Non-Plan), and Risk-Taking (Risk) scales from the S. Eysenck and Eysenck (1977) Impulsivity Questionnaire. In this and all of the factor analyses to be presented, only the results of the principal components–varimax rotations will be presented because the oblimin results are nearly identical and the varimax offers a clearer definition of factors.

In the analyses of both male and female data a sensation seeking–risk taking factor appeared, containing all of the SSS subscales and the Risk scale from the Impulsivity test. In the women only, the P scale from the EPQ had a lower loading on the factor. The other factors were a Imp_n combined with N and P in the males; Non-Planning and P in the females; and a third factor, which was different in men and women.

Corulla (1988) factor analyzed the SSS subscales along with the EPQ-R scales and S. Eysenck and Eysenck's (1978) Impulsivity-7 questionnaire, which contains scales for broad impulsiveness, venturesomeness, and empathy. Varimax and oblimin rotations yielded practically identical results. A sensation-seeking factor was clearly defined, with loadings from all of the SSS subscales in females, and all subscales but the ES scale in males. Other factors were extraversion-impulsivity, psychoticism combined with lack of empathy in males and Lie scale in females, and neuroticism.

A second factor analysis by Corulla (1989) used the SSS subscales, the EPQ-R scales, and Strelau's STI scales. The results showed a sensation-seeking factor involving Dis, ES, and BS plus the P scale in females, but only BS and Dis in the males. In both men and women, TAS and Venturesomeness formed a separate thrill-seeking factor along with ES in the males and L in the females. As in the previous analysis by Corulla, there was an extraversion-impulsivity factor, and a neuroticism-empathy factor. The remaining factor was one defined by all three scales from the STI, strength of excitation, strength of inhibition, and mobility, reflecting the high correlations among these subscales relative to their correlations with scales from other tests. From the analysis it would appear that the STI measures a unidimensional method trait. Of course, this result is due to the lack of attention to the selection of items in the construction of the first STI.

A cohesive sensation-seeking factor, composed of at least three of the four SSS subscales, appeared in five of the six analyses presented in this section. In the Corrula (1989) male sample, the SSS was split, with Venturesomeness, TAS, and ES in one factor and BS and Dis in another. From these studies it appears that there is some justification for speaking of a general or total sensation-seeking factor rather than regarding sensation seeking as multifactorial or a subtrait of impulsivity. One caveat to this conclusion is that these analyses included mainly markers for sensation seeking and impulsiveness and only single scales for the higher order dimensions defined by the EPQ E, N, and P scales. Two larger factorial studies, which included

a number of markers for these major dimensions of personality, will be
described later in this chapter.

Cattell's 16 factors

For many years, Cattell's (1950) system for classification of personality traits
has been regarded as the major alternative to Eysenck's simpler 3-factor
model. Cattell regarded the narrower traits in the 16 Personality Factor (PF)
test as first-order factors. Broader personality traits like extraversion can be
scored from the primaries, but as H. Eysenck and Eysenck (1985) point out,
"although many investigators have tried to replicate Cattell's results [factor
analyses of 16PF items] none outside of his own circle has ever succeeded"
(p. 125). Despite the questions about Cattell's primary-trait scales, they are
so widely used that their relationship to sensation seeking is worth examining.

In the previous volume (Zuckerman, 1979a, table 6.10, p. 154), simple
bivariate correlations between the 16PF scales and SSS form IV scales
from four samples were listed. The General SSS correlated *positively* and
significantly with dominance, surgency, adventurous, bohemian, and radicalism scales, and *negatively* with the superego strength scale in all four groups.
The highest correlations were with the dominance scale. As expected, there
were no correlations with the Cyclothymia scale. Dominance, adventurous,
and surgency represent an active, impulsive, energetic type of extraversion,
whereas cyclothymia simply represents a quieter type of sociability. The
patterns among the subscales of the two tests revealed some interesting
distinctions among the SSS subscales. Superego, paranoid, bohemian, and
control 16PF scales correlated with Dis, ES, and BS but not with the TAS
scale. Apparently the TAS scale represents the socially acceptable form of
sensation seeking, whereas the other scales represent the nonconformist,
impulsive type.

Birenbaum and Montag (1986) analyzed the relationships among 16PF and
SSS scales using a Hebrew translation of SSS form V given to 765 adult
male Israelis. The bivariate correlations resembled those found with American samples except that most of the correlations were lower in the Israeli
study. Dominance was significantly related to all four subscales and the SSS
Total score, and superego, sophisticated, radicalism, and control were related
to the total score and three of the subscales. A factor analysis of the 16PF
with the SSS Total score showed that the SSS loaded on only one of the
higher-order factors, independence (dominance, radicalism, and low sophisti-
cation). A similar factor analysis using the subscales of the SSS showed

some diversity of loadings. BS and Dis loaded primarily on the independence factor and Dis showed a negative loading on the superego factor as well. None of the SS scales loaded on the extraversion factor. The ES scale loaded most highly on the sensitive-bohemian factor. The TAS scale did not load highly on any of the factors, suggesting that perhaps this scale represents a specific kind of trait that is more peripheral to the major dimensions of personality.

Royce (1984) hypothesized that sensation seeking is related to emotional independence and extraversion at the higher order of traits, and to surgency, dominance, and gregariousness (cyclothymia) at the first-order trait level. He was right about emotional independence, surgency, and dominance, and wrong about extraversion and gregariousness. This latter conclusion from analyses of the 16PF test seems to contradict previous findings (Zuckerman, 1979a) of relationships between extraversion and sensation seeking found in many studies, and the conclusion that sensation seeking is equally related to both E and P dimensions of personality.

Costa and McCrae (1985) developed the NEO Personality Inventory (NEO-PI) designed around the five-factor model for personality. The five primary factors measured by the scales are extraversion, neuroticism, openness to experience, agreeableness, and conscientiousness. Each of the major factor scales is composed of six "facet scales," or measures of narrower factors making up each of the five supertraits. Like Eysenck's model, this is a hierarchal one. The relationship of the SSS to the Openness scale was discussed in an earlier section of this chapter.

P. T. Costa, Jr., and R. R. McCrae (personal communication, 1990) provided data relating the SSS form V scales to all of the five revised major scales, and the facet scales comprising them. Details about the sample of 217 men and women and the measures are contained in Costa, McCrae, and Dye (1990). The SSS and NEO-PI (revised form) were given a year apart and therefore the correlations are likely to be somewhat attenuated by the lower reliabilities of the two tests over time. The correlations between the SSS and the five major scales are given in Table 3.10.

Neuroticism correlated low, but significantly and positively with Dis and BS subscales but not at all with the Total SSS score. These SSS subscales and the Total score correlated with only two of the six subscales making up the Neuroticism score: Hostility and Impulsiveness. There was hardly any correlation between the SSS and Anxiety, Depression, Self-Consciousness, or Vulnerability subscales. It is unusual for impulsivity to be regarded only as a subtrait of neuroticism. In Eysenck's current hierarchal model it is regarded as a subtrait of the P dimension. At any rate, since the correlations

Table 3.10. *Correlations between SSS form V and Costa and McCrae NEO scales*

NEO scales	Sensation Seeking Scale				
	TAS	ES	Dis	BS	Total
Neuroticism	.01	−.07	.19**	.22**	.10
Extraversion	.13	.17*	.19**	.16*	.22**
Openness to Experience	.30**	.54**	.25**	.17*	.45**
Agreeableness	−.16*	−.07	−.37**	−.32**	−.31**
Conscientiousness	−.10	−.11	−.24**	−.20**	−.21**

Note: Number of subjects = 217 men and women. TAS = Thrill and Adventure Seeking; ES = Experience Seeking; Dis = Disinhibition; BS = Boredom Susceptibility.
$*p < .05.$
$**p < .01.$
Source: Personal communication: R. R. McCrae & P. T. Costa, Jr. (1990).

of the SSS with neuroticism are based on these two subscales, it is consistent with previous findings that there is no relationship between sensation-seeking and anxiety traits, but there are positive relationships between the SSS and aggression and impulsivity.

There is a low but significant correlation (.22) between the SSS Total and Extraversion based on very low but significant correlations between Extraversion and the SSS subscales ES, Dis, and BS. These correlations are largely a function of correlations of the SSS with three of the six subscales of Extraversion: Activity, Excitement Seeking, and Positive Emotions. Hardly any significant correlations were found with warmth, gregariousness, or assertiveness. Excitement seeking is, of course, a construct close to that for sensation seeking, and activity resembles the manic factor found to be related to sensation seeking in other studies.

The highest correlation between the SSS Total score and NEO scales is that with Openness to Experience ($r = .45$). All of the SSS subscales were significantly correlated with Openness, but the correlation with ES ($r = .54$) was clearly higher than those with the other sensation-seeking scales. The SSS Total correlated significantly with all six subscales of Openness: Fantasy, Aesthetics, Feelings, and Actions and Ideas. The highest correlation was with Values ($r = .45$), followed by those with Fantasy and Actions (.34, .31). Those with Aesthetics and Ideas were lower (.20, .19).

The second highest correlation between the SSS Total score and NEO scales was a negative one with Agreeableness (−.31). Unlike Openness,

Agreeableness correlated most with the Dis and BS subscales, minimally with TAS, and not at all with ES. Among the six subscales of Agreeableness, sensation seeking correlated negatively with Straightforwardness, Altruism, Compliance, and Modesty, and there was very little correlation with Trust or tendermindedness.

The SSS Total score correlated low ($-.21$) but significantly with the conscientiousness factor of the NEO. As with Agreeableness, the highest negative correlations were with the Dis and BS subscales of the SSS. Only two of the Conscientiousness subscales correlated to any degree with the SSS Total: Dutifulness and Deliberation. Dutifulness concerns the degree to which one follows strict standards of conduct. In Cattell's terms it represents superego strength. Deliberation represents planning, caution, and thoughtfulness. The opposite pole resembles the nonplanning facet of impulsivity.

Although the Openness to Experience factor is the strongest correlate of sensation among the "big five," McCrae and Costa (in press) claim that "Zuckerman's construct is multidimensional, because his scales are also related to low Agreeableness and Conscientiousness." But if we examine which of the subscales of agreeableness and conscientiousness correlate with sensation seeking, particularly Dis and BS, it is apparent that these facets, like Noncompliance, Immodesty, Lack of Standards, and Lack of Planning, as well as Impulsivity located by them in the N dimension, are part of the broader P dimension traits in Eysenck's system. Sensation seeking is also a powerful marker for this higher-order dimension. This point will be made clearer in the next section dealing with factor analyses of sensation-seeking scales along with other trait measures of personality.

Analyses of the particular NEO subscales correlated with sensation seeking confirms many previous findings from other studies using other scales measuring similar constructs. High sensation seekers can be described as people who are open to new experiences, particularly in terms of values, actions, and fantasies. They tend to have a high activity level, are impulsive and excitement seeking, and tend to experience and easily express positive emotions and anger. Those sensation seekers who are socially disinhibited and susceptible to boredom tend to be devious, noncompliant, immodest (narcissistic), nonaltruistic (egocentric): They are not constrained by conventional moral standards and do not plan their lives very carefully.

In order to define the precise position of the sensation-seeking subscales within the larger framework of personality, we decided to undertake large-scale factor analyses including an adequate number of markers for each of the first-order traits considered of importance in the Eysenckian hierarchal model.

Broad factor analyses of personality traits

Zuckerman, Kuhlman, & Camac (1988) selected 46 scales from eight personality tests to provide at least three markers for each of nine hypothesized factors: activity, sociability, impulsivity, socialization, sensation seeking, general emotionality, anxiety, hostility, and social desirability. These scales were given to two large classes of undergraduates over a number of class meetings during a semester. Both varimax and oblimin rotations were done for seven-, five-, and three-factor solutions.

In this study, the three-factor analysis yielded the most replicable factors, comparing men and women. The three factors were sociability, emotionality, and what we ended by calling impulsive unsocialized sensation seeking (ImpUSS). Eysenck's three EPQ scales provided excellent markers for all three dimensions: E for sociability, N for emotionality, and P for ImpUSS. As the name for the ImpUSS dimension implies, it contained most of the scales for impulsivity, socialization, and sensation seeking. However, some of the sensation-seeking scales had secondary loadings on the sociability or extraversion dimension and two had equal or nearly equal loadings on P-ImpUSS and E-Sociability (E-Sy) dimensions as shown in Figure 3.1.

The SSS BS scale actually had the highest loading on the P-ImpUSS factor, followed closely by the PRF autonomy and the EPQ P scale. All of the sensation-seeking scales fell in the quadrant defined by P and E dimensions, but most fell closer to the P axis than to the E one, including SSS BS, ES, and Dis scales; JPI risk taking; and EASI sensation seeking. The SSS TAS scale loaded exactly equally on both E and P dimensions, and the KSP Monotony Avoidance and PRF Play scales fell slightly more into the E half of the quadrant. Only the JPI Risk Taking scale had a secondary loading of any significant magnitude on the N dimension. The results place sensation seeking primarily in the P dimension of personality. In fact, sensation seeking forms the core of this dimension, along with impulsivity and lack of socialization.

Zuckerman et al. (1991) did a second study, using 33 scales that were good markers for the personality factors found in the previous study. This time only the four SSS subscales and the KSP Monotony Avoidance scale were used to assess sensation seeking. A large sample of 525 subjects was used. Six-, five-, four-, and three-factor rotations were done. Simultaneous component analysis and correlations of factor loadings were used to test the similarity of factors found in four groups (males and females in two semesters). These methods, particularly the last one, indicated that the five- and

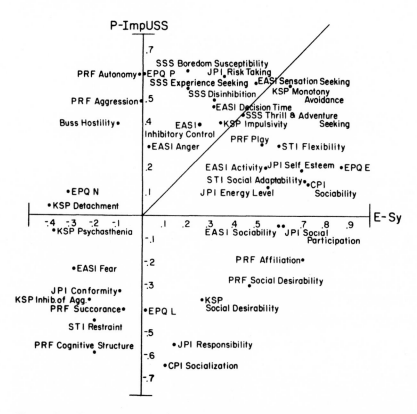

Figure 3.1. Factor plots of personality scales on factor dimensions of Impulsive Unsocialized Sensation Seeking (P-ImpUSS) and Sociability (E-Sy). Based on data from Zuckerman et al. (1988).

three-factor solutions were both robust and superior to the four- and six-factor ones.

In this study the results were much sharper, probably due to the selection of clear markers from the last study and the larger number of subjects. *All of the sensation-seeking scales,* including the four SSS subscales and the Monotony Avoidance scale, loaded primarily on one factor, which was also defined by the EPQ P and PRF Autonomy scales at the six-factor level. Impulsivity scales formed a separate factor at this level. At the five-factor level, the sensation-seeking scales were merged with the impulsivity scales to form the familiar P-ImpUSS factor. This factor persisted with little change through the four- and three-factor levels. The other factors at the five-

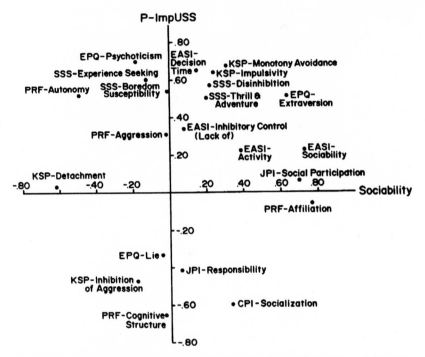

Figure 3.2. Factor plots of personality scales on factor dimensions of Impulsive Unsocialized Sensation Seeking (P-ImpUSS) and Sociability (Sy). Based on data from Zuckerman et al. (1991).

factor level were N-Anxiety, Aggression-Hostility, Sociability, and Activity. Figure 3.2 shows the plot of the P-ImpUSS versus Sociability factors at the three factor level. Since there was practically no scale overlap of these two dimensions with the N-Emotionality dimension, the scales loading primarily on the latter dimension are not shown in this plot except for the few that had secondary loadings higher than .3 on either P-ImpUSS or Sociability.

All the sensation-seeking scales, including TAS and Monotony Avoidance, clearly fall nearer to the P dimension axis than to the E dimension axis. Eysenck's P scale provides the best marker for this dimension. At least in these American samples, the SSS, with all of its subscales, is most closely aligned with the P dimension of personality, even when this dimension first emerges in the six-factor analysis. Impulsivity is closely related to sensation seeking from the five-dimensional analysis up to the three.

Table 3.11. *Four-Factor Analysis*

Test scale	Factor loadings			
	Factor 1	Factor 2	Factor 3	Factor 4
NEO: E	.88	−.14	−.05	.17
EPQ: E	.79	−.32	.17	−.08
ZKPQ: Sy	.76	−.16	.10	−.07
ZKPQ: Activity	.60	.01	−.18	.02
ZKPQ: N-Anx	−.13	.92	−.01	.08
NEO: N	−.15	.90	.10	−.11
EPQ: N	−.16	.91	−.04	−.08
NEO: Conscientiousness	.15	−.07	−.86	−.02
EPQ: P	−.09	−.08	.80	−.28
ZKPQ: ImpSS	.48	.08	.74	−.02
NEO: Agreeableness	−.04	−.07	−.31	.81
ZKPQ: Agg-Host	.35	.34	.24	−.72
NEO: Openness	.27	.14	.18	.67

Note: Four factors account for 74% of the variance. E = Extraversion; N = Neuroticism; Anx = Anxiety; P = Psychoticism; ImpSS = Impulsive Sensation Seeking; Agg-Host = Aggression–Hostility.
Source: "A comparison of three structural models for personality: The big three, the big five, and the alternative five," by M. Zuckerman, D. M. Kuhlman, J. Joireman, P. Teta, & M. Kraft, 1993, *Journal of Personality and Social Psychology, 65,* 757–768. Copyright 1993 by American Psychological Association.

The placement of ImpSS within factor dimensions defined by ZKPQ, EPQ, and NEO scales

The development of a personality questionnaire reflecting the five robust factors found in the Zuckerman et al. (1991) factor analyses was described in Chapter 2. A factor analysis was done using the five scales of the ZKPQ (Zuckerman, Kuhlman, Joireman, Teta, & Kraft, 1993), the five major factor scales of the NEO-PI-R (Costa & McCrae, 1992), and the three scales of the EPQ-R (S. Eysenck, Eysenck, & Barrett, 1985). A four-factor solution accounted for 74% of the variance and extraction of further factors produced only single variable factors with eigenvalues of less than one. Table 3.11 shows the results of this analysis.

The ImpSS scale loaded highly on factor 3, also defined by the Eysenck P and Costa and McCrea Conscientiousness scales. An Openness to Experience factor was identified when the NEO facet scales were used in a factor analysis but ImpSS and the other ZKPQ and EPQ scales showed little correlation with this factor. Apparently the earlier results showing relationships between sensation seeking and openness were primarily due to the experience-seeking subscale of the SSS.

Correlations were computed with other scales in this study, although these were not included in the factor analyses. Other than the expected correlation with the SSS ($r = .66$), the ImpSS scale also correlated highly with the A. Buss-Plomin (1975) EASI Impulsivity scale ($r = .70$), and the Block and Block (1980) Ego [Under] Control scale ($r = .63$). These correlations are consistent with the negative relationship between ImpSS and Conscientiousness.

Summary

The relationships of sensation seeking to other scales and to factor dimensions of personality are summarized in Table 3.12. The particular relationships with specific subscales as well as the General or Total SSS scores are indicated. The table is divided into three columns: the first consists of scales that correlate with the SSS or one of its subscales to a degree of near equivalance as defined at the beginning of this chapter; the second consists of scales that are strongly correlated with at least one or more of the SSS; and the third consists of scales that are only weakly, if significantly, correlated with the SSS. The relationships of the SSS to factors in Eysenck's and Cattell's systems are also listed in the table.

A limited number of measures are near equivalent to the SSS in what they measure. The Garlington and Shimona (1964) Change Seeker Index and the Penney and Reinehr (1966) Stimulus Variation Seeking Scale are two measures of a similar construct to the need for "varied" sensations and experience described in the definition of sensation seeking (Zuckerman, 1979a). The need for change, defined in terms of Murray's construct and embodied in tests like Jackson's PRF, is strongly related to general sensation seeking and the experience-seeking subscale, but only weakly related to the other subscales. The seeking of novel experiences is another part of the definition of sensation seeking, but only the external sensation-seeking subscale of P. H. Pearson's (1970) Novelty Seeking questionnaire was nearly equivalent to general sensation seeking, primarily because of its strong relationship with the thrill and adventure–type of sensation seeking. Relationships with other subscales were lower. Relationships between the seeking of novel cognitive experiences and sensation seeking were weaker and inconsistent.

Openness to experience (McCrae & Costa, 1987) describes an interest in varied sensory and cognitive experiences, similar to the idea of experience

Table 3.12. *Summary of relationships between sensation seeking scale (SSS) and other tests*

Near equivalent	Strong relationship	Minor relationship
Change Seeker Index-SSS Gen	Need Change-SSS Total, ES	Need Change-SSS TAS, Dis, BS
Novelty Seeking ES-SSS TAS	Novelty Seeking ES-SSS Gen Internal Sensation-SSS ES	Novelty Seeking ES-SSS ES, . . Dis, BS
Stimulus Variation Seeking-SSS-Gen	Openness (to Experience)-SSS ES Diversive Curiosity-SSS Total Need Cognition-SSS ES	Need Cognition-SSS Total, TAS
Venturesomeness-SSS TAS	Vent.-SSS Gen, Dis, BS Monotony Avoidance-SSS Gen, Dis, BS	Monotony Avoidance-SSS TAS, ES
RA-SS Gen	RA-Musical Auditory-SSS Dis RA-Gen, Life-Style-SSS ES, Dis	Sensitivity-SSS (–)Total, TAS Stimulus Screening-SSS(–) Gen
Arousal Seeking-SSS Gen, Total	Reactivity-SSS (–) Gen Impulsivity-SSS Gen, Dis, BS Cognitive Structure (–)SSS Gen Risk Taking-SSS Total, TAS	Impulsivity-SSS TAS, ES Cognitive Structure (–) SSS Dis, BS Risk-Taking-SSS Dis, BS, ES Hypomanic-SSS Gen Need Play-SSS TAS, ES Anhedonia (–) SS Gen(normals)
	Need Play-SSS Gen, Dis Anhedonia (–) SS Gen (patients) Conservatism (–) SSS Gen Aggression-SSS Dis (males) Positive Emotion Exp.-SSS Gen Autonomy, Uniqueness-SSS Gen	Aggression-SSS Dis (females) Fear of physical harm-SSS TAS Narcissism-SSS Dis

Table 3.12. *(cont.)*

Multitrait systems	Strong relationship	Minor relationship
Pavlovian (Strelau)		Strength of Excitation-SSS (+) Gen, TAS
		Strength of Inhibition (−) Gen, Dis, BS
		Mobility (+) SSS Gen, TAS
		Balance (+) SSS Gen, TAS, BS, ES
		Supergo (−) SSS Dis
Cattell	Independence-SSS Gen, Dis, BS	
Costa & McCrae*	Openness-SSS ES	Openness-SS TAS, Dis, BS
	Agreeableness (−) SS Dis, BS	Agreeableness (−) SS Total
	Conscientiousness (−) SS Total, BS	Conscientious (−) SS TAS, ES, BS
		Extraversion-SS Total, TAS
Eysenck	Psychoticism (P)-SSS Total, ES, Dis, TAS, BS	

Note: A minus sign in parentheses before SS indicates that the relationship between the scale or factor and the sensation-seeking scales correlated with it is a negative one; a plus sign in parentheses or the absence of parentheses before SS indicates that the relationship between the scale and the sensation-seeking scales is a positive one. Subscales of the SSS: Gen = General; TAS = Thrill and Adventure Seeking; ES = Experience Seeking; Dis = Disinhibition; BS = Boredom Susceptibility; RA = reducer–augmenter.
* Based on results of Zuckerman, Kuhlman, Joireman, Teta, & Kraft (1993)

seeking in both Pearson's scales and the experience-seeking subscale of the SSS. McCrae and Costa's scale based on this construct correlates moderately with the SS Experience Seeking subscale, but more weakly or not at all (Zuckerman et al., 1993) with the other subscales. Diversive curiosity (Day, 1968) has a moderate relationship with sensation seeking, but trait and state curiosity scales measuring the epistemic type of curiosity do not correlate much with sensation seeking. A test measuring the need for complex cognition (Cacioppo & Petty, 1982) correlates more highly with these epistemic types of curiosity measure but weakly with sensation seeking. Sensation seeking seems to be limited to sensation and does not include the need for cognitive experience to the same degree. Immediate sensations, whether from external or internal sources, are generally more arousing than cognitions.

S. Eysenck and Eysenck's (1978) Venturesomeness scale is a near equivalent of the TAS subscale of the SSS and is strongly related, but not equivalent, to the other subscales of the SSS. The S. Eysenck and Eysenck (1977) Risk Taking scale is strongly related to the TAS part of the SSS, but only weakly related to other SS subscales. There is a tendency to equate such subscales with "sensation seeking," but in fact they only sample a limited part of the broader construct. This is an example of the dangers of assuming equivalence where only some correlation exists. The seeking of unusual physical sensations from sports or other activities and the willingness to take physical risks represent only one part of the broader sensation-seeking construct.

Similarly, a special susceptibility to boredom when there is no change or variety in stimulation represents a part of sensation seeking. Schalling's Monotony Avoidance scale shows a strong relationship to general sensation seeking, and boredom susceptibility and disinhibition subscales of the SSS, but the relationships with experience seeking and thrill and adventure seeking are weaker.

The sensation-seeking scale was first based on the idea of arousal seeking, and innate differences in reactivity to different intensities of stimulation. Two scales developed from such theories have shown near equivalent correlations with the General or Total SSS: the Vando (1974) Reducing–Augmenting and the Mehrabian (1978) Arousal Seeking Tendency scales. A third scale, the Arousal/Avoidant subscale of the Telic Dominance scale, also shows a strong relationship to sensation seeking. However, only part of the items in the RAS have to do with reactions to intensity of stimulation, and these almost all deal with stimulation in the auditory modality as expressed by musical preferences. The other two factors in the test are like the general life-style sensation-seeking kinds of items in the SSS and the thrill and adventure ones.

Most of the high correlations between the Vando RAS and general sensation seeking are produced by the general life-style factor of the RAS, and least by the auditory reducing–augmenting items. K. White's (1984) Sensitivity and Kohn's (1987) Reactivity scales are purer measures of reactions to the intensity property of stimulation. The former shows only low relationships with the SSS, but the latter has a stronger negative correlation with general sensation seeking, perhaps because of its more specific content dealing to a large extent with motion and sea sickness and reactions to extremes of temperature. Strelau uses a Strength of Excitation of nervous processes scale to measure reactivity (inversely). The relations between the earlier form of this scale and sensation seeking were rather weak (although a new form shows a moderate relationship). Similarly, Mehrabian's (1978) Stimulus Screening scale, measuring reported arousal in response to stimulation, is only weakly related to sensation seeking.

In contrast to the generally weak results linking stimulus sensitivity and reactivity to sensation seeking, Mehrabian's (1978) measure of AST is nearly equivalent to general sensation seeking. A perusal of the items makes the reasons for this obvious; many are similar to those in the SSS.

Impulsivity, while not an equivalent or supraordinate of sensation seeking, is a highly related trait, particularly in its nonplanning and risk-taking aspects. In factor analyses of traits, sensation seeking and impulsivity are essential parts of the major dimension of personality identified as psychoticism by Eysenck. A lack of social restraint, as exemplied by a manic style in normal subjects, and actual hypomania in patients, is weakly related to sensation seeking. Playfulness, as a trait, is related strongly to the disinhibition type of sensation seeking, but only weakly to the TAS type. A need for play as opposed to work seems to characterize disinhibiters; they seem to be "hedonists." However, the opposite extreme of anhedonia seems strongly related to low sensation seeking only in patients. The implication is that among normal subjects, high and low sensation seekers are not differentiated by the capacity for pleasure but by the types of things that give them pleasure. For sensation seekers pleasure comes from highly arousing sensations or activities, whereas for low sensation seekers the sources of their pleasure are quieter, more familiar things or people.

Work prior to 1979 found that sensation seeking was strongly related to liberal (and negatively related to conservative) attitudes in social, political, religious, and sexual areas, as well as to authoritarianism. Research on dogmatism had yielded inconsistent results. A recent study, however, found that sensation seeking correlated with only two of the seven factors in the D scale: belief in one truth and virtuous self-denial. Sensation seekers seem to be more open-minded and skeptical of one-truth types of belief and they do not see any virtue in self-denial.

In previous studies, need for aggression was not a strong correlate of sensation seeking. In recent studies with SSS form VI, moderate relationships were found between aggression scales and disinhibition scales in men, and weaker relationships between these scales were found in women. A scale measuring "inhibition of aggression" was negatively but weakly related to sensation seeking in both men and women. Weak relationships were also found between masculinity and femininity scores on the Bem Sex-role Inventory and sensation seeking.

Previous studies had shown that sensation was unrelated to trait tests of anxiety or neuroticism, except for weak negative relationships between specific fear of physical harm and the TAS subscale. None of the new research contradicts this conclusion. Sensation seeking, however, does relate to emotional expressiveness, primarily for positive emotions but also for anger expression.

In the pre-1979 research, sensation seeking was found to be positively related to the need for autonomy, or emotional independence from others, on a number of tests measuring this trait. A similar trait called uniqueness (Snyder & Fromkin, 1977) has recently been found to be very strongly correlated with general sensation seeking. However, a trait called narcissism is primarily correlated with the Dis subscale of sensation seeking.

Sensation seeking is weakly related to all three of the Pavlovian dimensions as measured by the subscales of the Strelau Temperament Inventory (STI), positively with strength of excitation and mobility, and negatively with strength of inhibition. There is a problem in that the STI subscales are themselves intercorrelated.

Within the dimensions of personality defined by the higher-order factors derived from the Cattell 16 PF, general sensation seeking is related to just one of the supertrait dimensions: independence. The subscales of the SSS are also related to independence, but the Dis subscale is also negatively related to the super-ego strength factor.

Among the "big five" supertraits defined in the NEO test developed by Costa and McCrae, openness to experience emerges as the strongest correlate of the experience-seeking part of sensation seeking, but the other sensation-seeking factors, particularly Dis, are related to conscientiousness. Conscientiousness and agreeableness are negative correlates of sensation seeking. There is a slight positive correlation with extraversion, due to very low correlations with all of the SSS subscales, but clearly there is little in common between sensation seeking and neuroticism or extraversion dimensions of the "big five." The low correlations between E and N and sensation seeking are probably a function of some particular inclusions of variables under the major scales, like impulsivity as a component of neuroticism and excitement seeking as a subscale of extraversion. Sensation seeking correlates highly with these types of scales as shown in previous studies, but not with the scales that are usually central to the definitions of N (anxiety) and E (sociability or gregariousness).

Factor analyses of scales relevant to Eysenck's hierarchal model show that all of the SSS scales, plus sensation-seeking scales from other tests, load primarily on the psychoticism dimension of personality and, in fact, actually comprise the core of this dimension along with impulsivity and socialization scales. For this reason the dimension has been called impulsive unsocialized sensation seeking (ImpUSS). Eysenck's P scale still provides one of the best markers for the dimension.

The scales that correlate most highly with sensation seeking are those sharing at least part of a similar kind of item content, regardless of the label given to the scales. Some of the scales are derived from other theories, but the correlation between two tests with similar kinds of item content does not validate the theories behind either of them. Tests must be validated with other kinds of data from peer ratings, self or others' reports of behavior or life experiences, and laboratory measures theoretically related to the behaviors. The chapters that follow will carry us beyond a mere consistency in self-description.

4

Demographic data

Demographic differences can be fascinating, but by themselves they tell us little or nothing about the sources of the differences between populations. Few would interpret differences between French and English samples as evidence of genetic-evolutionary differences. Yet we find differences between "races" interpreted on this basis (Rushton, 1988) despite the fact that the genetic diversity within such broad groupings is just as great, if not greater, than that within nations (Zuckerman, 1990b). Sex differences are also interpreted as either due mostly to biology or social influences, with little evidence other than popular stereotypes or ideology to justify either type of causal interpretation. Most people believe that the restraint that comes with age is a matter of increments in wisdom, but other data suggest that it may have something to do with the age changes in our biology. Demographic differences may suggest hypotheses but they cannot be used alone to test them.

Sex differences

The use of the term *sex* in place of the currently popular term *gender* should not be taken as a political statement or an assumption of the biological basis of such differences. It is appropriate, however, for a book on psychobiology to consider the contribution of biology to the trait differences between men and women, particularly when such differences appear to be cross-cultural. In this chapter I will attempt simply to present the demographic differences. Interpretation will be reserved for later chapters, with the exception of a few hypotheses for social explanations.

The previous volume (Zuckerman, 1979a) presented data on SSS differences between male and female undergraduates at colleges in America, England, Scotland, Japan, and Thailand. The Japanese and Thai samples

Table 4.1. *Means (M) and standard deviations (SD) of SSS form V scores from four countries*

	Males					Females				
	TAS	ES	Dis	BS	Total	TAS	ES	Dis	BS	Total
Australia										
M	7.7^a	6.1^a	5.9^a	4.2^a	23.9^a	6.7^a	5.5^a	5.1^a	3.2^a	20.6^a
SD	2.2	2.2	2.6	2.3	5.9	2.4	2.4	2.8	2.4	7.1
Canada										
M	7.8^a	5.6^a	5.8^a	3.9^a	23.1^a	6.6^a	4.4^b	4.7^b	3.2^a	19.9^a
SD	2.0	2.0	2.5	2.1	5.6	2.5	2.0	2.5	1.2	6.0
United States										
M	7.7^a	5.2^b	6.5^b	3.6^a	23.0^a	6.4^a	4.8^c	5.1^a	2.6^b	19.0^b
SD	2.2	2.4	2.6	2.1	5.6	2.7	2.1	2.3	2.0	5.7
Spain										
M	6.8^b	5.7^a	5.1^c	3.6^a	21.4^b	6.2^a	5.5^a	3.0^c	3.0^a	17.8^c
SD	2.6	2.1	2.5	2.3	6.5	2.4	2.0	2.0	2.0	5.4

Note: Means with the same superscript (*a, b,* or *c*) are *not* significantly different between countries ($p > .05$). TAS = Thrill and Adventure Seeking; ES = Experience Seeking; Dis = Disinhibition; BS = Boredom Susceptibility; Total = Total score on SSS form V.
Sources: Australia: Ball, Farnhill, & Wangeman (1984); Canada: Ridgeway & Russell (1980); United States: Zuckerman, Kuhlman, Thornquist, & Kiers (1991); and Spain: Perez & Torrubia (1986).

had used the General SSS only while the American, English, and Scottish comparisons used the four subscales and total score on the SSS form V. In all five groups men scored significantly higher than women on the General or Total scores. Men scored significantly higher than the women on TAS, Dis, and BS in all the countries where form V, containing the subscales, was used. There were no sex differences on ES in any of the three countries.

Table 4.1 shows comparisons of male and female undergraduates from four countries, where the same form (V) of the SSS was used without modification of the items. All of these data were collected in the mid-1980s. Three of these are English-speaking, while the fourth is a Spanish-speaking sample given a translated form of the SSS V. Men scored significantly higher than women on the Total, TAS, and BS scales in all four countries and on Dis in the United States, Canada, and Spain, but the last difference was short of significance in Australia. As in earlier sex comparisons, there were no sex differences of any magnitude or significance on ES, except in Canada where the men scored significantly higher than women on this scale.

Some other sex comparisons on SSS or similar scales are shown in Table 4.2. Seven studies were done on children and early adolescents in the 1980s, five using special adaptations of the SSS and two using the Venturesomeness subscale of the Eysenck Impulsivity scale (Björk-Akesson, 1990; S. Eysenck, Easting, & Pearson, 1984; Kafry, 1982; Perez et al., 1986; Russo et al., 1991; Russo et al., in press; Randhawa, deLacey, & Saklofske, 1986). In all four studies using an SSS Total score, boys scored significantly higher than girls. In five of the seven group comparisons using TAS or Venturesomeness scales, boys scored higher than girls. In four of the five comparisons using General or Total scores, boys scored were higher than girls. Other scales were used in only one or two groups.

Ten studies (Carton, Jouvent, & Widlöcher, 1992; S. Eysenck & Haapasalo, 1989; S. Eysenck, Pearson, Easting, & Allsopp, 1985; Giambra, Camp, & Grodsky, 1992; Kurtz & Zuckerman, 1978; Magaro et al., 1979; Perez & Torrubia, 1986; Terasaki, Shimi, Kishimoto, & Hiroaok, 1987; Zuckerman, 1984c; Zuckerman & Neeb, 1980) of normal adults, not including the groups shown in Table 4.1, are listed in Table 4.2. In seven of eight studies using the TAS or a similar kind of scale, such as Venturesomeness, men scored significantly higher than women on the scale. Men generally scored higher than women on Dis, and results on BS were mixed. But in all the studies where the ES scale was used, with the exception of the Japanese study by Terasaki et al. (1987), the differences between men and women were not significant.

With few exceptions, men score higher than women on TAS and Dis scales and no sex differences are found on ES. The lack of difference on ES suggests that while men are high on the more active forms of sensation seeking, women are just as open to novel experiences through the senses and life-style as men. Could this mean that different biological or social factors control the development of experience seeking as opposed to thrill seeking and disinhibition? ES is particularly vulnerable to generational differences. The greater openness in Western society would affect particular generations of women and men, but particularly women who reached maturity in the 1970s or later. The ES type of items probably reflects this more than the Dis items. TAS and Dis also tend to show more steady and stronger age changes than ES.

Table 4.2. Sex differences on sensation seeking

Authors/study	Ages	M = n	F = n	Nationality	Difference	Scales on which sexes differ
Bjork-Akesson (1990)	12, 14	715	756	Swedish	M>F	Total, TAS, ES
S. Eysenck et al. (1984)	8–15	633	872	English	M>F	Venturesomeness (from Imp. scale)
Kafry (1982)	6–10	36	32	American	NS	(Gen scale only)
Perez et al. (1986)	14–15	123	149	Spanish	M>F	Total, Dis ($p < .10$ on ES, BS)
Randhawa et al. (1986)	11, 14	87	139	Australian	M>F	Venturesomeness
Russo et al. (1991)	7–12	65	61	American	M>F	Total, TAS, BS (only 2 scales used)
Russo et al. (1993)	9–14	302	358	American	M>F	Total, Dis (not TAS)
Carton, Jouvent & Widlöcher (1992)	15–62	46	56	French	M>F	TAS, Dis
S. Eysenck et al. (1985)	16–89	383	206	English	M>F	Venturesomeness
S. Eysenck & Haapsola (1989)	18–70	501	448	Finnish	M>F	TAS, Dis
Giambria et al. (1992)	17–92	1356	1080	American	M>F	Boredom, n External stimulation
Kurtz & Zuckerman (1978)	18–21	100	100	American	M>F	TAS, Dis, BS
Magaro et al. (1979)	15–72	101	110	Italian	NS	Only Gen scale used
Perez & Torrubia (1986)	17–21	50	83	Spanish	M>F	Total, Dis
Terasaki et al. (1987)	18–21	458	431	Japanese	M>F	Total, TAS, ES, BS
Zuckerman & Neeb (1980)	18–69	859	1218	American	M>F	Total, TAS, Dis, BS
Zuckerman (1984a)	18–21	74	192	American	M>F	TAS, Dis (experience and intention scales from SSS VI, no Total, ES, BS)

Note: M = males; F = females; M > F = males scored significantly higher than females on indicated scales; NS = nonsignificant differences between males and females on the scales used; Total = Total score on the SSS form V; TAS = Thrill and Adventure Seeking; ES = Experience Seeking; Dis = Disinhibition; BS = Boredom Susceptibility.

National differences

In order to make comparisons between nations, subjects must be drawn from comparable social class, education, and age groups. The way this is usually done is to limit comparisons to undergraduate college students. While these subjects are not representative of the larger populations from which they are drawn, they are more likely to be comparable in age and education. In the previous volume (Zuckerman, 1979a), American, Japanese, and Thai students from three studies were compared on the General SSS. The two Asian groups scored significantly lower than the American group. Comparisons of three English-speaking groups of students, American, English, and Scots, on the SSS form V revealed significant differences among the three nations for women on the Total score, but none for men. The Scottish women scored higher than the American and English women, and the Americans scored higher than the English. On the Dis scale there were no differences among the male national groups, but the Scottish women scored higher than both American and English women. Although there were some differences in the pattern among the subscales (Americans scored higher on TAS), men from the three countries were more alike than were women from the three nations on sensation seeking.

Although the SSS scales have been translated and used in many countries, most of these cannot be compared with the results in English-speaking countries because researchers modified the scales by deleting some of the original items and adding new ones. Comparable samples of young adults tested on the SSS form V in the 1980s in four countries, the United States, Canada, Australia, and Spain, are shown in Table 4.1. Only the Spanish sample used a translated scale. Australian, American, and Canadian males did not differ among themselves on the Total score, but all three national groups scored significantly higher than Spanish males. Australian and Canadian women scored higher than American women, who in turn scored higher than Spanish women. American males scored higher than all other groups on Dis, whereas Canadian and Australian males scored higher than Spanish males. Spanish females were particularly low on this subscale compared with the other three groups.

Differences between Spain and other Western countries might reflect the greater influence of Catholicism in Spain, particularly among the women. Men at a Catholic university in America scored lower than men at a state university. However, conclusions about national differences are further limited by the fact that the students from each country are generally drawn from only one university. Different universities within a country may attract different types of students. Differences on the SSS among students from different colleges in the United States have been found (Zuckerman, 1979a). Apart from the difference between Catholic and other universities already mentioned, women at the state universities were higher on the SSS than women at a finishing school type of college.

Age and sex

Figure 4.1a shows the declines in Total SSS scores with age in the English sample tested by Zuckerman, Eysenck, and Eysenck (1978), and Figure 4.1b shows a heterogeneous sample of Australians tested by Ball, Farnhill, and Wangeman (1984). The scores of men and women in the English group declined at a similar rate from the earliest age group (16–19 years) to the oldest group (60 and older) in both sexes and the sex differences were significant at each age. In the Australian group, however, there was a significant age-by-sex interaction, caused by the steeper decline of the men at ages 30 to 39 with the result that the mean for females was slightly higher at this age. Analyses of the subscales (Figures 4.2 to 4.5) showed that the interaction between age and sex in Australians is produced primarily by the ES and Dis subscales, particularly the former. All subscales showed a significant decline with age, but only the ES scale had a significant age-by-sex interaction. The Australian females actually show an increase in ES until ages 40–49. Ball et al. speculate that the differences are generational rather than age-related because the women aged 30–39 years were the first group to be exposed to the postwar feminist movement. It must be remembered that the ES scale is the only SS scale that does not show sex differences, and is the one most influenced by educational and cultural changes. However, a similar kind of finding on the SSS General scale was reported in an Italian population in which women had a lower mean score than men in the youngest age group (15–19 years) but not at subsequent ages (Magaro et al., 1979). The question is to what extent the other age differences represent generational changes in these cross-sectional data.

Table 4.3 shows the mean scores of undergraduates from introductory psychology courses at the University of Delaware tested in the mid to late 1970s contrasted with the mean scores of undergraduates at the same school tested in the mid to late 1980s. The type of students attending the university did not change much during this period so these comparisons may give

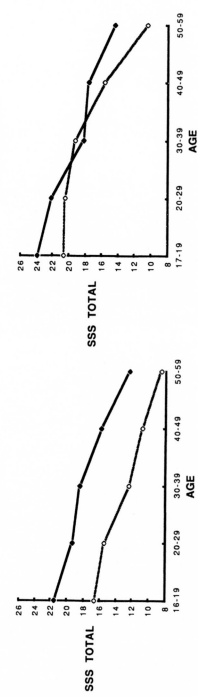

Figure 4.1a. (left) Sensation Seeking Scale (SSS) Total score (form V) as a function of age in English men and women. Solid line and filled-in circles are plots of means for men and hatched line and open circles are plots of means for women. From "Sensation seeking in England and America: Cross cultural, age, and sex comparisons," by M. Zuckerman, S. B. G. Eysenck, & H. J. Eysenck, 1978, *Journal of Consulting and Clinical Psychology*, *46*, 143. Copyright American Psychological Association.

Figure 4.1b. (right) Sensation Seeking Scale (SSS) Total score (form V) as a function of age in Australian men and women. Constructed from data in "Sex and age differences in sensation seeking: Some natural comparisons," by I. Ball et al., 1984, *British Journal of Psychology*, *75*, 257–265.

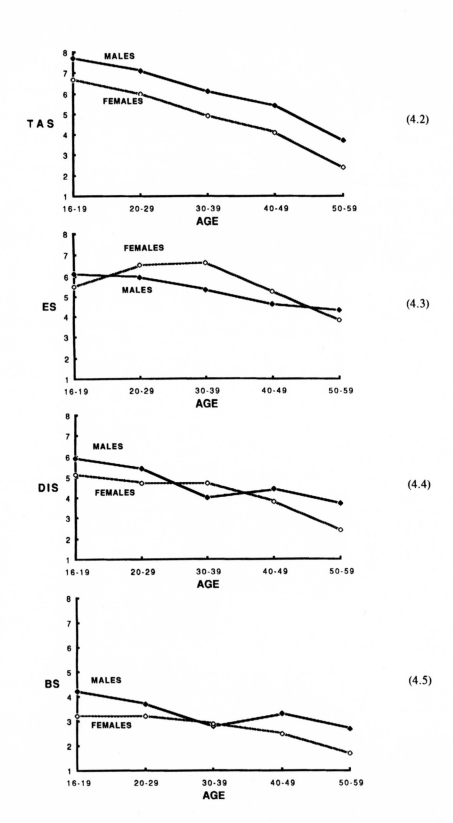

Table 4.3. *Comparisons of two generations of students at the University of Delaware on the Sensation Seeking Scale*

Years	Males					Females				
	TAS	ES	Dis	BS	Total	TAS	ES	Dis	BS	Total
1978–1979	7.8	4.7	5.5	3.1	21.2	7.1	4.7	4.3	2.4	18.5
1988–1989	7.7	5.2	6.5	3.6	23.0	6.4	4.8	5.1	2.6	19.0
t	−.6	2.4*	4.2*	2.7*	3.5*	−4.1*	.7	5.2*	1.6	1.3

Note: TAS = Thrill and Adventure Seeking; ES = Experience Seeking; Dis = Disinhibition; BS = Boredom Susceptibility.
*$p<.05$.

some insight into generational changes. Men from the later period showed significantly higher scores on ES, Dis, BS, and Total score; womens' scores decreased on TAS and increased on Dis, with no significant change on Total score. The increase in Dis during this decade may have reflected the increasing sexual permissiveness in American society, or at least among college students at the University of Delaware.

Longitudinal data provide the best way to see if the age declines noted in cross-sectional age comparisons represent real age changes in sensation seeking. Giambra et al. (1992) did both cross-sectional and longitudinal studies of two scales, closely resembling two of the sensation-seeking subscales: Need for External Stimulation, resembling the TAS, and Boredom, close to the BS scale from the SSS. The longitudinal sample first took the scales in the mid 1970s and were tested again 6 to 8 years later. The cross-sectional data showed a significant decline in both scales for both men and women. The longitudinal data for men also showed a significant decline in need for external stimulation, but not in boredom; the women demonstrated a significant decline in boredom with age, but not in need for external stimulation.

Figure 4.2 (top). SSS Thrill and Adventure Seeking scale (TAS) scores as a function of age in Australian men and women. Constructed from data in I. Ball et al. (1984).
Figure 4.3. SSS Experience Seeking scale (ES) scores as a function of age in Australian men and women. Constructed from data in I. Ball et al. (1984).
Figure 4.4. SSS Disinhibition scale (Dis) scores as a function of age in Australian men and women. Constructed from data in I. Ball et al. (1984).
Figure 4.5 (bottom). SSS Boredom Susceptibility scale (BS) scores as a function of age in Australian men and women. Constructed from data in I. Ball et al. (1984).

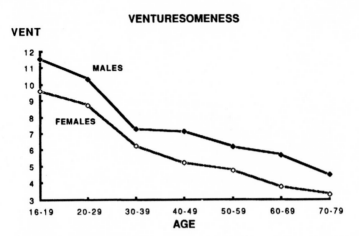

Figure 4.6. Relation between venturesomeness (VENT) and age. Based on data from S. Eysenck et al. (1985).

Other studies have also found age differences using cross-sectional data. Figure 4.6 shows the relationship between age and Venturesomeness, a scale equivalent to the SSS TAS, and with strong relationships to the General SSS (S. Eysenck et al. 1985). Venturesomeness steadily declines from ages 16 to 79 in both men and women, and men are higher than women at all ages. Using a special sample of readers of *Psychology Today,* Zuckerman and Neeb (1980) found a highly significant age decline on the SSS form V Total score over the age range 15 to 60+ for both men and women. Unlike the English and Australian studies, Total scores increased from the 15–19 period to the 20–29 one, peaked in the 20s rather than adolescence, and then declined with each decade of age; the increase from adolescent years to the twenties was significant for the men and approached significance for the women. Men were higher than women at all ages, and the differences were significant for all but the youngest (15–19) and oldest (60+) groups. Carton, Jouvent, Bungener, & Widlöcher (1992), using a French translation of the SSS form IV, compared subjects over 30 years of age with those under 30 and found that the younger subjects were significantly higher on the General SSS.

Are the scales differentially susceptible to the age changes? In the Zuckerman et al. (1978) study, the age declines were significant for all the subscales for the women, but only for the TAS and Dis, and not for the ES and BS subscales in men. Zuckerman and Neeb (1980) found a significant age decline on all the subscales except BS. Carton, Jouvent, Bungener, & Wid-löcher (1992) found that subjects under 30 years of age scored significantly higher than those over 30 on every subscale of the SSS, but they did not compare age by sex.

Thus far we have looked at the age changes from late adolescence to older age. Are there changes over the years of childhood? The early theory of sensation seeking (Zuckerman, 1969a) suggested that sensation seeking increases from infancy and early childhood to adolescence and declines thereafter. The decline has been well documented by the cross-sectional studies, although more longitudinal studies are needed. The hypothesis of increasing sensation seeking up to adolescence is based on observations of animals and humans, which tend to show a greater tolerance for novel stimulation in older children than in younger ones, and a greater tolerance for repetition and routine in younger children. This kind of developmental research has been hampered until recently by the lack of sensation-seeking scales for younger children.

Farley and Cox (1971) found no increases in the General SSS between ages 14 and 17 in male and female adolescents. The scores tended to peak at 16 but the differences between age groups were not significant. Kafry (1982) slightly modified the items of the General SSS to adapt them to children and tested groups between the ages of 8 and 10. Items were read to the children. Parents were asked to fill out the forms as they thought their children would answer them. Boys scored higher than girls and there was a tendency for scores to increase from the youngest to the older age groups, but neither sex nor age proved to be significant, possibly because of the small numbers of subjects. Kafry compared her data with Farley's and noted that her oldest group (10 years) scored considerably lower than his youngest group (14 years). Parents' estimates of their children's sensation seeking correlated modestly with the SSS scores of their children ($r = .40$), but the parents significantly overestimated their children's absolute levels of the trait.

Russo et al. (1991) developed a children's version of the SSS containing only TAS and BS subscales and a Total score. Only the TAS subscale increased over the ages 7 to 12. Russo et al. (1993) then revised the test to include three subscales: Thrill and Adventure Seeking (TAS), Social Disinhibition (Dis), and Drug and Alcohol Attitudes (DAA). TAS, Dis, DAA and Total Score significantly increased as a function of age in groups between 9 and 14 years of age. Figure 4.7 shows the changes for the Total score and Figure 4.8 shows the change for Social Disinhibition.

Findings of a decline in general sensation seeking, and in its forms of

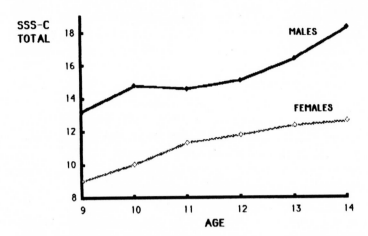

Figure 4.7. Relation between children's version of the Sensation Seeking Scale (SSS-C, Russo et al., 1993) Total score and age in boys and girls. Based on data from Russo et al. (1993).

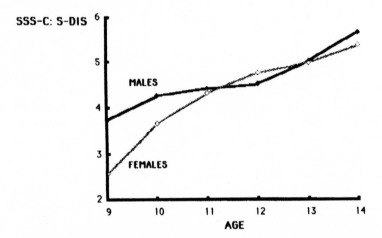

Figure 4.8. Relation between children's version of the Sensation Seeking Scale (SSS-C) Social Disinhibition subscale (S-Dis) and age. Based on data from Russo et al. (1993).

disinhibition and thrill and adventure seeking or venturesomeness, from late adolescence or the early 20s are well established by cross-sectional studies. In some populations there seems to be some interaction of sex and age, particularly for the experience-seeking subscale. This could represent a confounding of generational and real age changes. Changes in mean scores at one university over a period of 10 years suggest a strong possibility of generation changes. The one longitudinal study suggests that at least some of changes can be found in the same adults followed over seven years, but even here there is some indication of an interaction between age and sex. Age changes over the adult years are not typical for most personality traits (Costa & McCrae, 1988). One of the few scales to show consistent declines in longitudinal and cross-sectional analyses was *openness to experience as expressed in actions*. Openness in fantasy showed a decline in the cross-sectional data but an increase in the longitudinal study. Perhaps as some individuals grow older they substitute fantasy sensation seeking for a more active type.

Increases in sensation seeking from 7 years to adolescence seem probable from three different studies, but no one study has measured sensation seeking over the entire age range using the same instrument, and changes are small within limited segments of the range. Parental ratings may not be satisfactory as estimates of children's sensation seeking since they only correlate modestly with the children's self-reports and tend to overestimate their levels of the trait. Further research is needed in order to study the developmental aspects of sensation seeking. The scale developed by Russo et al. should be particularly useful in this work.

"Racial" differences

The concept of race as some kind of population distinction based on biology (in contrast to ethnic differences) is a dubious assumption (Zuckerman, 1990b). Races are supposedly distinguished by certain features such as skin color and physiognomy, but even these distinctions are blurry and in practice the basic criteria for distinguishing groups are ethnic identifications. Researchers don't use a colorimeter to distinguish races, and even if they did, they would run into problems of distinction between sun-tanned whites and light-skinned blacks.

Table 4.4 shows the results of comparisons of blacks and whites on forms of the SSS in 11 groups in 10 studies (Carrol & Zuckerman, 1977; Galizio & Stein, 1983; Jaffe & Archer, 1987; Kaestner, Rosen, & Apel, 1977; Karoly, 1975; Kurtz & Zuckerman, 1978; Russo et al., 1991, 1993; Sutker, Archer, & Allain, 1978; Zuckerman & Neeb, 1980), 5 of which used drug-abuser or

Table 4.4. *Studies comparing blacks and whites on the sensation seeking scale*

Study	Population	Total	TAS	ES	Dis	BS
Russo et al. (1991)	Normal children	NS	W	—	—	NS
Russo et al. (1993)	Normal children	W	W	—	NS	—
Kurtz & Zuckerman (1978)	College students	W	W	NS	NS	W
Zuckerman & Neeb (1980)	Gen. pop. males	W	W	W	NS	NS
	Gen. pop. females	NS	W	NS	NS	NS
Carrol & Zuckerman (1977)	Drug abusers	W	W	W	NS	W
Kaestner et al. (1977)	Drug abusers	W	W	W	W	W
Sutker et al. (1978)	Drug abusers	W	W	—	—	—
Karoly (1975)	Female delinquents	W	—	—	—	—
Jaffe & Archer (1987)	College students	W	—	—	—	—
Galizio & Stein (1983)	Drug abusers	W	W	W	—	—

Note: TAS = Thrill and Adventure Seeking; ES = Experience Seeking; Dis = Disinhibition; BS = Boredom Susceptibility; W = whites significantly higher than blacks on the scale; NS = difference between whites and blacks not significant; dash indicates subscale not used in study.

delinquent groups. Whites scored significantly higher than blacks on the SSS Total in 9 of the 11 groups, and whites were higher on the TAS in all 7 groups where this scale was used. Whites also scored significantly higher than blacks on the ES scale in 4 of the 6 groups, on BS in 2 out of 6 groups, and on Dis in only 1 of the 6 groups given these scales. The General and TAS scales yield the greatest, and the BS and Dis scales the least, difference between races.

Randhawa et al. (1986) compared groups of Australian Anglocelt and Aboriginal children on the S. Eysenck and Eysenck (1978) Impulsivity scales. The Anglocelts tended to score higher on the Venturesomeness scale, but the difference between groups was not significant. Although Australian Aborigines are dark in skin color, their racial origins are unknown; some anthropologists regard them as Caucasoid and others class them as a separate race from the "big three" races.

The racial differences occur most consistently on the TAS subscale. The items in this scale ask subjects if they would like to engage in a variety of sensation-seeking sports or activities, many of which (e.g., skiing, scuba diving) are not common forms of recreation in the cultures in which most blacks are raised. The Dis scale, on which racial differences are seldom found, represents a universal kind of sensation seeking in partying, drinking, and sex. It is also the scale most consistently related to certain kinds of biological markers to be discussed later in the book. Racial differences on the SSS are probably due to differences in cultural background.

Ethnicity

The Kaestner et al. (1977) study compared whites and blacks with a group of Hispanic drug abusers as well as with each other. Hispanic is, of course, not a race but an ethnically defined category. Whites scored higher than Hispanics on all the scales, and blacks and Hispanics differed on only one scale; Hispanics scored higher on TAS. Zuckerman and Neeb (1980) classified their subjects into ethnic categories excluding blacks and Asiatics from this comparison. About half of the subjects listed Anglo-Saxon as their ethnic identify while the others were primarily divided among Irish, Italian, Jewish, Polish, and Slavic. Differences were significant only among males, and were largely produced by higher scores in the Slavic group; however this was the smallest group, consisting of only 15 subjects so that not much can be inferred from the finding.

Educational and socioeconomic differences

The racial differences raise the question of the influence of educational and socioeconomic background factors on sensation seeking. Farley and Farley (1967) compared a male sample composed mostly of English industrial apprentices with a male sample of college students from a small American university on the General SSS and found no difference despite the national and educational differences between the samples. However, the American university used in that study had lower General SSS scores than at the University of Delaware, the source of most of the American normative data. Kish and Busse (1968) tested a more heterogeneous sample of American men and compared educational groups with grade school, high school, and college education. Only the difference between SSS scores of grade school and college groups was significant suggesting only a weak influence of education on sensation seeking, at least in men. Magaro et al. (1979) found that education was a significant determinant of sensation seeking in Italian women, even more important than age, but for men age was more important and the influence of education was negligible.

Table 4.5. *Analyses of variance results (F ratios) for demographic variables on SSS form V Total score*

Variables	Males		Females	
	df	F	df	F
Education	7/853	2.8**	7/1214	3.1**
Fathers' education	7/839	1.5	1/1187	2.7**
Mothers' education	7/854	1.1	7/1193	2.5*
Current student	1/849	0.7	1/1210	10.8*
Occupation[a]	4/658	1.9	4/934	2.9*
Fathers' occupation	4/763	1.7	4/1045	1.4
Mothers' occupation[b]	4/797	1.1	4/585	2.6*
Region-U.S.A.	9/799	0.8	9/1178	1.2
Race	3/850	3.4*	3/1187	1.1
Ethnicity	8/808	2.3*	8/1141	0.6
Religion	6/809	7.2***	6/1155	10.6***
Marital status	3/849	5.5***	3/1218	4.5**

Note: Results for sex: $df = 1/2065$, $F = 55.7***$; for age, $df = 5/2065$, $F = 9.1.***$
[a]Persons listing "student" as primary occupation not included.
[b]"Housewife" not included in occupational analysis.
*$p < .05$.
**$p < .01$.
***$p < .001$.
Source: Table 3, p. 199, from "Demographic influences in sensation seeking and expressions of sensation seeking in religion, smoking, and driving habits," by M. Zuckerman & M. Neeb, 1980, *Personality and Individual Differences 1*, 197–206. Copyright by Pergamon Press. Reprinted with permission.

A substantial body of demographic information was obtained in the study by Zuckerman and Neeb (1980) involving a heterogeneous sample of more than 2,000 subjects. These subjects were self-selected from readers of the periodical *Psychology Today*, who volunteered to take the SSS form V and fill in a personal data sheet on their backgrounds. They were clearly not a random sample of the population and their SSS scores were higher than samples tested previously. Despite the nonrepresentativeness of the sample, data obtained on demographic variables were useful in a relative sense, since the selective nature of the sample was common to all of the subjects and therefore a constant in comparisons between demographic classifications.

The first analysis was by sex and age. As shown in the *F* values listed in Table 4.5, these proved to be the most powerful demographic variables for the Total SSS score, and, of the two, sex of subjects was the most powerful.

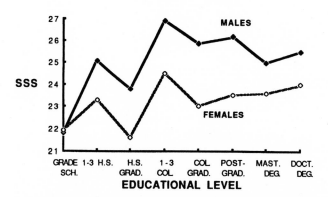

Figure 4.9. Relation between subjects' own education and Total score on the Sensation Seeking Scale (SSS). Based on data from Zuckerman & Neeb (1980).

The next set of variables included the subjects' own educations, their fathers' and mothers' educations, their status as current students or nonstudents, their occupation if nonstudents, and their fathers' and mothers' occupations. For the men only one of these seven indicators of socioeconomic class (own educational level) was even a weakly significant influence on the Total score. By contrast , six of the seven socioeconomic variables were significant for women although only one, student status, was of major significance as judged by the size of the *F* value. This is an interesting finding that suggests that college men may be more representative of the general population in their country than college women. The results also suggest that the sex differences found in the college samples may be an underestimate of those in the general population since women students tend to be higher on sensation seeking than nonstudents. This last difference is confounded with age, since students tend to be younger than nonstudents, but this did not influence the variable for men.

Figure 4.9 shows the relationships between subjects' own education and their scores on the SSS Total. The relationships between education and sensation seeking are not simple linear ones. In general, college groups are higher on sensation seeking than noncollege groups. But in both sexes there is an increase from grade school to partial high school (1–3 years) and then a lower score for high school graduates. A similar phenomenon can be seen for those with 1–3 years of college as opposed to college graduates, and (for men) partial graduate school as contrasted with a graduate degree. These breaks in the linear trend suggest that school "drop-outs" at any of the stages

EDUCATION OF PARENTS

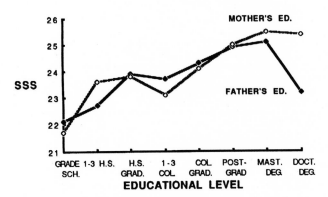

Figure 4.10. Relation between education of parents and Total scores on the Sensation Seeking Scale (SSS). Based on data from Zuckerman & Neeb (1980).

of education tend to have somewhat higher sensation-seeking scores than those who complete a degree. As will be shown in Chapter 13, high sensation seekers are at greater risk for school failure than low sensation seekers.

The relationship between social class of rearing, as indicated by fathers' and mothers' educational levels, and SSS Total scores for women is shown in Figure 4.10. Male subjects are not included because their results were not significant. There is a generally linear trend between these women's SSS scores and their fathers' and mothers' educations except for a marked drop in scores for women whose fathers reached the doctoral level. These are weak relationships with the major difference between those whose parents had less than a high school education and those whose parents were college graduates.

Occupational levels are even more central to the socioeconomic distinction than education. However, it is usually the father's occupation that is used because so many women are classified as "housewife," a category that is indeterminant for social class. However, we classified occupations for self (excluding those with current student status), father, and mother (excluding those listing "housewife" as their sole occupation). Occupational levels were scaled according to an index that rates specific occupations from 1 (unskilled) to 5 (major professionals and positions requiring high education and responsibility). None of these ratings influenced sensation-seeking scores in male subjects; own occupation and mother's occupation were related to

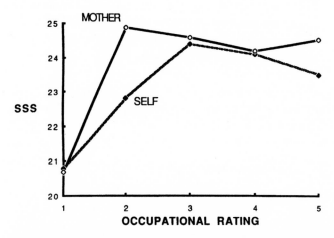

Figure 4.11. Relation between occupational levels of mother and self for female subjects. Occupational levels from 1 (unskilled) to 5 (major professional and high educational/responsibility positions). Based on data from Zuckerman & Neeb (1980).

sensation seeking in female subjects. The relations between SSS Total scores and occupation of self and mother for women is shown in Figure 4.11. The major difference in own occupational level is between levels 2 (semiskilled) and 3 (skilled occupation) – for instance, between a clerk or secretary and a store manager or insurance agent. After the skilled occupation category, further increments in occupational level make little difference in SSS scores. For mother's occupation we had to exclude about half of the sample where respondents listed "housewife" as their occupation. Among the remaining women there was a significant relationship between mother's occupations and their own sensation-seeking scores. As Figure 4.11 shows, however, the relationship was produced almost entirely by the difference between those whose mothers were in the lowest occupational category and the others. Beyond the unskilled category, increments in maternal occupational level made little difference in sensation seeking.

Social class, as defined by one's own or one's parents' education and occupations, seems to be a more important determinant of sensation seeking for women than for men. If cultural sex-role polarizations express more approval of sensation seeking in men than in women and such restrictions are more common in those who are lower in social class, then there would more encouragement of these tendencies by more educated parents and more attempt to inhibit these tendencies by less educated parents. But being older than their children, most parents would be less sensation seeking and might therefore try to restrict sensation seeking, particularly when it peaks in their children during adolescence. While these restrictions may be more intensive for girls than for boys, it is also possible that it is more difficult to inhibit sensation-seeking tendencies in boys than in girls. Some recently collected data show a correlation between parental punishment and impulsive sensation seeking for male, but not for female, college students. Study of the direct effects of sensation-seeking modeling or reinforcement in young boys and girls would be useful.

Religion

Zuckerman and Neeb classified their subjects by self-reported religious preference into seven categories: atheist, agnostic, Protestant, Catholic, Jewish, Unitarian, and Other (unconventional religions in the United States). As shown in Table 4.5, religion was a highly significant source of variance for both men and women. However, the differences were primarily between the categories of atheist and agnostic and all the conventional religions with the exception of Unitarians. The "Other" category also was high in sensation seeking.

Many people identify themselves as members of a particular religious faith but in practice do not often enter a church or synagogue. Subjects were asked about their church attendance and classified into categories of none, occasional, frequent, and regular attendance. Analyses of these groups yielded more powerful differences than those of religion itself as shown in Figure 4.12. There is a linear relationship between reported church attendance and sensation seeking, with nonattenders highest and regular churchgoers the lowest in sensation seeking. Of course, the atheists and agnostics make up many of the nonattenders, but the relationship is apparent even between the occasional, frequent, and regular attenders.

Sex, age, nationality, social class of rearing, and birth order are demographic variables involving no choice. Religion and marital status, however, depend on choice. Relationships with sensation seeking must therefore be regarded as correlative rather than causative. Most persons in America are brought up in homes with at least some nominal religion. Persons who become atheists or agnostics are usually making a choice that puts them in ideological disagreement with their parents. The more religious the parents,

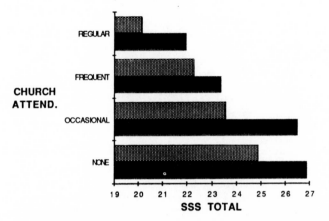

Figure 4.12. Relation between church attendance and Sensation Seeking Scale (SSS) Total score for men (solid bars) and women (stipled bars). Based on data from Zuckerman & Neeb (1980).

the more conflict this may engender. Not surprisingly, given their antidogmatic and liberal attitudes, many high sensation seekers tend to be atheists or agnostics. High sensation seekers who do have a nominal identification with a religion tend not to go to church very much. This could be because of underlying theological doubts or because they find the services rather boring and prefer to worship in private.

Marital status

As indicated in Table 4.5, marital status was a significant source of variance for both men and women. Table 4.6 shows the mean SSS Total scores for single, married, divorced, and widowed subjects. The widowed constituted a small group with means close to those for the married subjects. The divorced men scored significantly higher than the single and married men on the Total score and all of the SSS subscales. Among the female groups, the single and divorced subjects did not differ from each other on the Total score, but both were higher than the married women. All three groups differed significantly on Dis, with the divorced group highest, the married group the lowest, and the single group intermediate. On ES the divorced were higher than the marrieds and singles. Apparently, divorced persons of both sexes are high sensation seekers, disinhibited and searching for new experiences. Is this

Table 4.6. *Mean SSS Total scores by sex and marital status*

Marital status	n's		SSS Total, means	
	Men	Women	Men	Women
Single	421	601	25.8	23.7
Married	309	402	25.0	22.6
Divorced	116	204	28.0	24.7
Widowed	7	15	25.2	22.0

Source: Table 5, p. 200, from "Demographic influences in sensation seeking and expressions of sensation seeking in religion, smoking, and driving habits," by M. Zuckerman & M. Neeb, 1980, *Personality and Individual Differences, 1,* 197–206. Copyright 1980 by Pergamon Press. Reprinted by permission.

effect because divorce leads to resurgence of a need for new experiences that may have been frustrated during marriage, or are high sensation seekers more likely to get divorced? Demographic data cannot answer these questions. We would have to do a prospective study of those newly married and use the SSS to predict which marriages will end in divorce.

There is some evidence (Chapter 7) suggesting that lack of congruence of marital partners on sensation seeking may be an important predictor of marital dissatisfaction. Studies have shown that assortative mating tends to be the rule for most couples; high sensation seekers tend to marry other highs, and lows tend to marry lows. However, this could be due to the tendency to marry persons of similar age and education, variables influencing sensation seeking. Lesnik-Oberstein and Cohen (1984) correlated the SSS scores of couples, controlling for age and education of both partners with the use of partial correlations. They found that the assortative mating effect was significant for the Total, ES, and Dis scores even when age and education of both partners were controlled. Another possibility for explaining the similarity of sensation seeking in marital couples is that the partners tend to become more alike as a function of how long they have lived together. The authors found that this was not the case; the resemblance was ʾhere in the first years of marriage and after 21 to 40 years of marriage, even though scores of both partners tend to drop as a function of years of marriage, and undoubtedly age itself.

Regional residence (United States)

Regional differences in sensation seeking are unlikely given the diversity of populations in all parts of the country. However, popular stereotypes would suggest that Californians, New Yorkers, and perhaps Texans might differ from Midwesterners and Southerners (the "Bible Belt") on sensation seeking. Zuckerman and Neeb (1980) divided their subjects according to the postal codes of their return addresses and divided them into the 10 major regions of the United States indicated by the codes. The proportions participating in the survey did not differ grossly from the population distribution in the United States except for a slight overrepresentation from the western states, including California, and a slight underrepresentation from the southeastern part of the country. There were no significant differences between regions on the SSS Total score. However, on the ES scale the differences were significant for both men and women. Midwesterners (from Illinois, Kansas, Montana, Missouri, and Nebraska) of both sexes tended to be low experience seekers. Women from the western area (not including the Pacific coastal states) and men from the north-central states tended to be high experience seekers. The ES data confirm the popular stereotypes about conservative Midwesterners, and perhaps the "Wild West" women, but the experience seeking of north-central men is a surprise, unless it is the influence of New York City alone.

Birth order

Bone, Montgomery, and McAllister (1973) reported higher SSS General scores in firstborns and only children of both sexes and lower scores for later borns. Earlier studies using other kinds of measures had suggested that firstborns were less likely than later borns to be risk takers. However, Eisenman (1987) found that firstborns were more risk taking on a laboratory experimental task than later borns. The risk conflict involved the possibility of winning large sums of money at the risk of receiving painful electric shock. The option was the chance to win small sums with no risk of shock. About half of the firstborns, as contrasted with only about a quarter of the later borns, chose the risky option. The firstborns also scored higher on a questionnaire measuring creative attitudes and performed better than later borns on the Unusual Uses test, a measure of creative verbal performance that has been related to sensation seeking (see Zuckerman, 1979a, p. 239). A hypothesis that might explain the higher sensation seeking in firstborns (and only children) is that they have the exclusive attention of their parents, until the birth of a second child, and may receive more varied stimulation from parents. This greater stimulation may "set" the optimal level of stimulation at a high level. When later borns arrive, parents must divide their attention. Perhaps the experience of interacting with children has lost some of its novelty, and there is proportionally more time given to routine care activities and less to providing novel experiences.

Summary

Age and sex are the most powerful demographic influences on sensation seeking. Sensation seeking is higher in men than in women, rises between ages 9 and 14, peaks in late adolescence or early 20s, and declines steadily with age thereafter. Longitudinal studies suggest that these changes seen in cross-sectional studies are real age changes rather than generational differences, although the latter may affect some of the SS scales.

National differences are found on the SSS. Students in Asiatic countries score lower than students in Western countries on the General SSS. More recent analyses show young Australians, Americans, and Canadians to be high on sensation seeking relative to Spanish students. Racial comparisons in college and among drug abusers and delinquents generally show blacks scoring lower than whites on the SSS General and TAS scales, but differences are less commonly found on the Dis scale. Socioeconomic status, as assessed by education and occupation of parents, seems to exert more influence on sensation seeking among women than among men.

Birth order data on sensation seeking are limited, and what there are suggests that it is firstborns who are the higher sensation seekers. High sensation seekers are more prone to atheism or agnosticism than the practice of any of the conventional religions, and those who are affiliated with a church attend church services less often than low sensation seekers.

High sensation seekers seem to be more likely to divorce, and divorced men rank higher on sensation seeking than the younger singles as well as married men. Among women both single and divorced subjects were higher on sensation seeking than married women. Regional differences in the United States in sensation seeking are more a matter of stereotype than actuality, although Midwesterners as a group seem to be low on the specific scale of experience seeking.

Demographic differences suggest alternative hypotheses of explanation, some to do with social learning and some with biological-developmental tendencies. I have stated the more obvious social hypotheses, but there is as yet little research on these in longitudinal or laboratory studies.

Demographic data on sensation seeking are consistent with known sex and age risk factors pertaining to driving accidents, criminal violations, and other phenomena on which young males are usually the group at highest risk. The next chapter looks at the relation of risk taking to sensation seeking.

5

Risk taking

Risk taking is part of the definition of sensation seeking as discussed in Chapter 1. However, the last phrase of the definition, ". . . and the willingness to take . . . risks for the sake of such experience," implies that the risk itself is not an essential motivation for the behavior. Risk may be defined as the appraised likelihood of a negative outcome for behavior. Risks may be physical, legal, financial, or social, as described in Chapter 1 after the definition of sensation seeking. Sensation seekers, particularly experienced seekers, engage in much behavior that is not risky at all. But in those situations that do entail risk, high sensation seekers find the sensations or experiences worth the risk, whereas the low sensation seekers either do not value the sensations of the activity, or do not think they are worth the risk.

An opportunity for sensation seeking often puts the person in an approach–avoidance conflict where the rewards are positive sensations and experiences, and the possible punishments are of several kinds including physical, social, legal, or financial harm. Various types of risk taking will be discussed in this chapter. More thorough discussions of the topics of substance abuse, sex, and sports will be reserved for other chapters in this book, but studies concerning the risk-taking issue in these activities will be included in this chapter.

Towards a theory of sensation seeking and risk taking

Like most behavior, risk taking depends more on the motivational and emotional states at the instant of decision rather than general motivational or emotional traits. Traits summarize the long-term consistencies of states likely to be activated in certain classes of situations. Figure 5.1 portrays a model for the interactions of sensation-seeking and anxiety states and the cognitive appraisal of risk, in determining approach or withdrawal from a risky situation. A state has been defined as "a person's self-perceived affects, impulses,

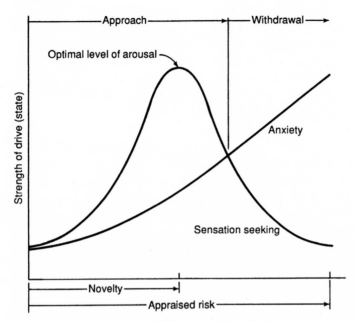

Figure 5.1. Theoretical model for the relationship between sensation seeking and anxiety states as a function of novelty and appraised risk. From "Sensation seeking and anxiety, traits and states, as determinants of behavior in novel situations." by M. Zuckerman, 1976. In I. G. Sarason & C. D. Spielberger (Eds.), *Stress and anxiety,* Vol. 3, pp. 141–170. Washington, DC: Hemisphere, 1976. Copyright Hemisphere Publishers, 1976. Reprinted by permission.

and physiology for a short period of time ranging from a given instant to as long as a day" (Zuckerman, 1991a, p. 47). Neary (1975) developed state scales for sensation seeking and anxiety, described in Chapter 3. The sensation-seeking state is a kind of surgent, positive arousal as described by words like *daring, elated, enthusiastic, adventurous,* and *playful.* Anxiety state is conveyed by words like *frightened, upset,* and *worrying.*

According to the model, anxiety state varies directly with degree of appraised risk. Sensation-seeking state varies directly with novelty of the situation and appraised risk up to some maximal point (the optimal level of arousal) beyond which it declines. Approach and withdrawal tendencies are a function of the differential strength of sensation seeking and anxiety states. At the optimal level of arousal approach tendencies are strongest. Beyond this point they begin to weaken. At the point where the anxiety state becomes stronger than the sensation-seeking state, withdrawal tendencies begin to dominate and increase in strength as a function of increasing anxiety state and decreasing sensation-seeking state. High and low sensation seekers are hypothesized to differ in the gradients of the two states. Low sensation seekers should have a steeper avoidance gradient and the peak of sensation-seeking arousal should occur sooner than in high sensation seekers.

Before we could test these predictions about high and low sensation seekers it was necessary to examine the relationships between: (1) novelty and appraised risk of situations; (2) sensation-seeking trait and appraised risk. Sensation seekers might have lower risk appraisals simply because they have already tried the risky activities and thereby reduced their appraisal of risk. Diverse situations were rated for risk, and subjects were also asked how many times they had experienced the situations (Zuckerman, 1979c). The correlation between appraised risk and experience was high ($r = -.56$), but an examination of the scatterplot showed that the relationship was produced by the low novelty (high experience) end of the scale. Frequently experienced situations were seldom rated as even moderately risky, but novel or rarely experienced situations were quite variable in risk ratings; some were judged as quite risky and others as not risky at all. The risk appraisal of novel situations is determined by other factors affecting judgment of degree of threat in the situation. Thus, novelty alone cannot be presumed to produce anxiety as suggested by Gray's (1982) theory of anxiety.

The second question concerned the relationship between risk appraisal and the sensation-seeking trait. The 50 most novel situations (those which most college students had not or rarely experienced) from the preceding study were chosen and presented to subjects who had taken the SSS form V and the EPQ. Subjects were asked to rate each situation for three kinds of risk: physical, mental, and punishment risk. A total risk appraisal score was obtained by summing the three kinds of risk appraisals. The correlations between the SSS Total and the total risk appraisal was $-.42$ for men and $-.40$ for women. Correlations between the SSS Total and different kinds of risk were all significant and negative ranging from $-.27$ to $-.40$. Except for the BS scale the subscales of the SSS all correlated significantly with the three kinds of risk and there was no particular pattern of relation between SSS subscales and the type of risk. There were no significant correlations between E, N, or P scores from the EPQ and any of the risk appraisal scores. Unlike sensation seeking, these three broad dimensions of personality were not relevant to risk appraisal. Franken, Gibson, and Rowland (1992) constructed a danger (risk) assessment scale consisting of activities described in the SSS. Not surprisingly, danger estimation showed a high and negative correlation with sensation seeking. Low sensation seekers see these situations as more risky than high sensation seekers and therefore are less willing to take risks they see no reason to take.

Given that high sensation seekers tend to appraise many situations as less risky than do low sensation seekers, it was necessary to select situations for which there was little or no difference in their risk appraisals in order to test their reactions as a function of common risk values. Two sets of situations were found meeting this criterion, at least for males. One involved travel situations and the other involved participating in psychological experiments. The latter was particularly interesting since it has been found that high sensation seekers tend to volunteer more than low sensation seekers for certain types of experiments, such as those involving sensory deprivation, hypnosis, and being given a drug (R. N. Bone, L. W. Cowling, & M. C. Choban, personal communication, 1974; Zuckerman, Schultz , & Hopkins, 1967). On the other hand, sensation seeking is unrelated to volunteering for other types of experiments, such as learning or social psychology experiments. In the risk appraisal study we found that both high and low sensation seekers regarded participation in a drug experiment as quite risky; a hypnosis experiment was judged to be of moderate riskiness; and a social psychology experiment was seen as low in risk. As a baseline we used the current state while they were taking the paper-and-pencil tests, presumably perceived as a very low risk situation.

Subjects used an abbreviated form of the Neary (1975) state scales for sensation seeking and anxiety, imagining that they were in each situation and describing anticipations of their affective reactions. Their current state was also taken at this time of assessment prior to the imaginal tasks. Figure 5.2 shows the relations between risk appraisal and anxiety and sensation-seeking states for high- and low-trait sensation seekers. As predicted, anxiety state varied directly with the appraised riskiness of the situations and sensation-seeking state showed evidence of an inverted-U-shaped relationship. High sensation seekers showed higher sensation-seeking and lower anxiety states than low sensation seekers over all situations. However, the interactions were also significant; high and low sensation seekers did not differ at the lowest-risk situation, but did at higher levels of risk. There was also a sex interaction produced by the contrast in sensation-seeking state in the riskiest situation where the females showed a decrease in sensation-seeking state while the males did not.

Figure 5.3 shows the contrast in the anxiety and sensation-seeking state reactions of low and high sensation-seeking males. The low sensation-seeking males show the conflict effect predicted by the model with the anxiety gradient crossing the sensation-seeking gradient at a relatively low

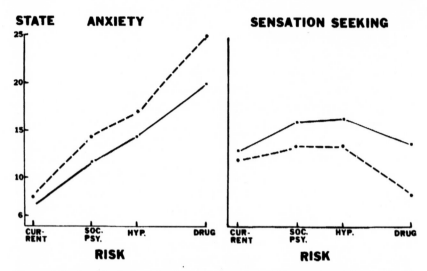

Figure 5.2. Actual relationships between appraised riskiness of participation in different types of experiments and anticipations of affective reactions (sensation-seeking and anxiety states) in high and low sensation seekers. Solid line = high sensation seekers, dashed line = low sensation seekers. From "Sensation seeking and risk taking." by M. Zuckerman, 1979. In C. E. Izard (Ed.), *Emotions in personality and psychopathology,* p. 178. New York: Plenum. Copyright Plenum Press. Reprinted by permission.

level of risk and a significant reduction in sensation-seeking state at the highest level of risk. Although the gradients tend to converge for the high sensation seekers, the sensation-seeking state remains higher than the anxiety state even at the highest level of risk. These data would explain why more high sensation seekers than lows volunteer for hypnosis and drug experiments, whereas there is no difference in the rate of volunteering for less unusual types of experiments.

Of course, these were imagined reactions rather than actual reactions to real situations. Neary (1975; also see Zuckerman, 1979a) used the sensation-seeking and anxiety state scales to see if they could predict whether subjects would volunteer to take an unknown drug in a psychology experiment. After arrival for an unspecified experiment, subjects were told that the experiment concerned the effects of a drug that might "produce some strange effects, possibly hallucinations." They were shown the pill and the physiological recording equipment to enhance the credibility of the situation. At this time they were given the state scales. After they completed them, they were assured that their participation was entirely voluntary and that taking the drug

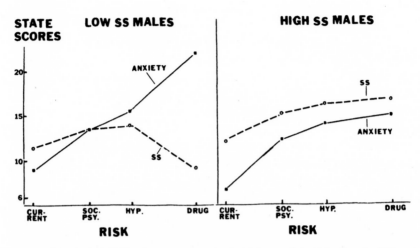

Figure 5.3. Relationships between appraised riskiness of participation in different types of experiments and anticipated anxiety and sensation-seeking states in male high and low sensation seekers. From "Sensation seeking and risk taking," by M. Zuckerman, 1979. In C. E. Izard (Ed.), *Emotions in personality and psychopathology*, p. 178. New York: Plenum. Copyright Plenum Press, 1979. Reprinted by permission.

was their choice. Finally they were given an informed consent form on which to indicate their decision.

Sensation-seeking trait predicted the levels of sensation-seeking states on baseline measures, obtained class days prior to the experiment, and on the state measure taken while anticipating the experiment. The correlations of sensation-seeking trait with anxiety states on baseline days were not significant for either sex, but were significant and negative for females in the experimental situation. Interestingly, there was no correlation between sensation-seeking and anxiety states in men just prior to making the drug-taking decision, although the negative correlation was significant for women. Trait and baseline states of sensation seeking did not predict the decision to take the drug, but both sensation-seeking and anxiety states just prior to the drug decision did correlate with the actual decision. The maximal contrast was between a high sensation-seeking and low anxiety state group, in which 71% of the subjects volunteered, and a low sensation-seeking and high anxiety state group, in which only 41% volunteered. However, anxiety state only made a difference in those subjects with a low sensation-seeking state. Anxiety state made practically no difference in the volunteering rate among those in a high sensation-seeking state.

Why didn't sensation-seeking trait predict the actual volunteering, but only correlated with sensation-seeking states prior to volunteering? Many high sensation seekers at this time were experimenting with LSD and other hallucinogenic drugs. However, the situational factor of taking a drug in a laboratory, rather than at a party with friends, could have attenuated the relationship. Also, as a general rule, the state just prior to entering a situation is usually more predictive of behavior in the situation than is the general trait (Zuckerman, 1979b).

The subjects in this experiment were not asked how risky they thought participation in the experiment would be. Does appraised risk actually mediate the relationship between sensation-seeking trait and risky behavior, or is it a consequence of actual experience with such behavior? Horvath and Zuckerman (1993) attempted to answer this question by using the model testing methods of Linear Structural Relations.

A General Risk Appraisal Scale (GRAS) was developed by factor analyzing responses to a variety of risky situations. Subjects indicated in four separate ratings for each activity how risky the activity would be for themselves and for their peers, and to what extent they and their peers had actually engaged in such behaviors. Factor analyses for both risk and behavioral experience scales showed that the risk items grouped into four distinctive factors: (1) criminal risk, such as shoplifting, selling drugs, vandalism; (2) financial risk, such as gambling, risky business ventures; (3) minor violations, such as traffic offenses, violation of club rules ; (4) sports risk, such as scuba diving, sailing.

The GRAS was given to a new group of subjects who had also taken the SSS form V and the Eysenck narrow (fast decision time) Impulsivity scale. The first analyses were addressed to the question of whether there is a general risk appraisal tendency, or if risk appraisal is entirely specific to certain types of risk. Similarly, is there a general risk-taking tendency or is risk taking specific to the area of risk? Table 5.1 shows the correlations between appraised risk in the four areas of the GRAS and Table 5.2 gives the correlations between the same four areas applied to the subjects' own behaviors. For both appraised risk and risk-taking behavior there were generally low but significant correlations among all four areas of risk. Only the correlations between the areas of criminal risk and minor violations were relatively high ($r = .50$ and $.51$). The results suggest that there are generalized risk appraisal and risky behavioral tendencies, but there is also a great deal of specificity in risk appraisal and behavior. Further analyses within the four areas were done using a LISREL analysis to see if a model could incorporate the higher-order factor levels.

Table 5.1. *Correlations among the four risk appraisal scales in the General Risk Appraisal scale (GRAS)*

| | Type of risk estimated for self | | |
	Financial risk	Minor violations risk	Sports risk
Criminal risk	.34**	.50**	.29**
Financial risk		.29**	.12*
Minor violations risk			.29**

*p<.01.
**p<.001.

Table 5.2. *Correlations among four areas of self-reported risky behavior*

| | Risky behaviors | | |
	Financial	Minor violations	Sports
Criminal	.22**	.51**	.20**
Financial		.26**	.15*
Minor violations			.22**

*p<.01.
**p<.001.

The next question concerned the extent to which risky behavior could be predicted from peer behavior, one's own risk appraisal, and sensation-seeking and impulsivity traits. Exploratory multiple regressions were done using one's own risky behavior as the dependent variable and the four other factors as the predictor variables. Table 5.3 shows the results of the analyses. The beta weights represent the independent contributions of each of the variables to the prediction of risky behavior in the particular area of risk, controlling for the effects of the other variables. The best predictions were in the areas of criminal behavior and minor violations where the four predictors were able to account for about half of the variance in the reported behaviors. For financial risk, taking the predictors accounted for about a third of the variance, and for sports, only about a fifth of the variance. Higher prediction for sports might have been obtained had we used the TAS subscale, but all of these analyses used only the SSS Total score.

Peer behavior made the strongest independent contribution to the predic-

Table 5.3. *Predictors of self-reported risky behaviors: Multiple regression beta weights*

	Crime	Violations	Finance	Sports
Peer behavior	.43	.54	.49	.39
Sensation seeking	.27	.23	.15	.15
Impulsivity	.13	.11	—[a]	—[a]
Risk appraisal	−.15	−.14	−.18	−.14
Multipler	.71	.72	.59	.47
r^2	.50	.51	.34	.21

[a] Did not enter multiple regression equation.
Source: Table 4, p. 46, from "Sensation seeking, risk appraisal and risky behavior," by P. Horvath & M. Zuckerman, 1993, *Personality and Individual Differences, 14,* 41–52. Copyright 1993 by Pergamon Press. Reprinted by permission.

tion of the subjects' risky behaviors in all four areas with beta's ranging from .39 for sports to .54 for minor violations. Sensation-seeking trait was the second strongest predictor with significant betas in all areas, ranging from .15 for sports and financial risk taking to .27 for criminal risk taking. Risk appraisal also showed significant prediction in all areas although somewhat lower beta weights than sensation-seeking trait in the areas of crime and minor violations. The trait of impulsivity was the poorest predictor of risky behavior with nonsignificant contributions to two of the areas and only weak contributions to the other two.

The strong predictive value of peer behavior on the subjects' own risky behaviors could be interpreted as evidence of social influence. But one must remember that these are self-report estimates and subjects may tend to exaggerate the similarity between themselves and their peers. Even if their estimates were accurate, the correlation of own behavior with peer behavior is not necessary evidence of a social influence alone. Adolescents and adults tend to choose their peer groups from among those that are available. The choice of friends may be strongly influenced by the similarity of their values and behaviors to one's own.

The strongest prediction of risky behavior from sensation seeking was in the area of criminal risk taking ($r = .53$, $p < .001$). However, all of the variables significantly predicted criminal risk-taking behavior to some degree and all of the variables were significantly intercorrelated as shown in Figure 5.4. The existence of a matrix of correlations does not indicate which variables are direct influences and which are mediators or consequences of behavior. For this purpose we used LISREL.

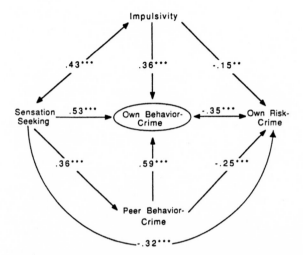

Figure 5.4. Correlations among sensation seeking, impulsivity, reported peer criminal behavior, appraised riskiness of criminal behavior, and subjects' own criminal behavior in a college student population. From "Sensation seeking, risk appraisal, and risky behavior," by P. Horvath & M. Zuckerman, 1993, *Personality and Individual Differences, 14,* 47. Copyright Pergamon Press, 1982. Reprinted by permission.

Several competing models involving sensation seeking, impulsivity, peer behavior, own behavior, and own risk appraisal were initially examined. These preliminary analyses suggested that all four subscales of the SSS and impulsivity constituted one latent factor, all four types of risk constituted one risk appraisal factor, and another risky behavior factor. Peer behavior, however, could not be distinguished from own behavior so the analysis focused on a test between two simplified models. In one model sensation-seeking trait leads to low risk appraisal, a kind of cognitive trait, which in turn leads to risky behavior. The second model suggests that sensation-seeking trait leads directly to risky behavior and risky behavioral experience results in lowered risk appraisal. These two models are shown in Figure 5.5. All four goodness-of-fit tests showed that model 2 was clearly superior to model 1 in describing the correlations among the variables. Figure 5.5 shows the results for model 2. Risk appraisal did not seem to be a mediator between sensation-seeking trait and risky behavior, but was more likely to be a consequence of such behavior, or the lack of it in the case of low sensation seekers.

The SSS form V contains a mixture of items expressing an interest in engaging in risky activities, expressing general sensation-seeking orientation

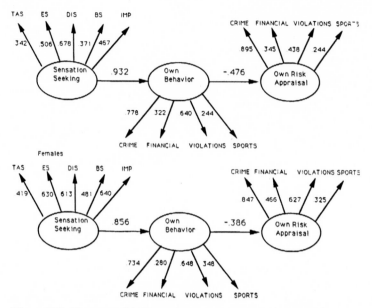

Figure 5.5. Outcome of LISREL analysis in terms of standardized measurement and structural parameters for model 2, males and females. From ''Sensation seeking, risk appraisal, and risky behavior,'' by P. Horvath & M. Zuckerman, 1993, *Personality and Individual Differences, 14,* 49. Copyright Pergamon Press, 1982, reprinted by permission.

values, or actually reporting sensation-seeking behavior, some of which is risky. In the TAS scale of the SSS V 8 of the 10 items indicate an interest in physically risky sports or activities, and only 2 items inquire about actual experience. Half of the items in the ES scale indicate desire or intention to engage in sensation-seeking behavior, and many of the others indicate art or music preferences not entailing any risk. The Dis scale, however, contains only 2 items expressing mere desire, whereas most of the rest indicate actual activities that entail some risk, at least social risk.

The study by Horvath and Zuckerman showed that sensation-seeking trait, as measured by the SSS V was correlated with risky behavior, but to what extent is this because the SSS is partly a behavioral scale itself? In the SSS VI, described in Chapter 2, behavioral experience scales for TAS and Dis are separate from scales for desire or intention. The items of the scales consist entirely of activities that are the same for experience and intention scales. Correlations between the two types of scales are therefore an unconfounded indication of the extent to which sensation seeking reflects mere fantasy or is related to actual risky experience. The correlations between intention and experience scales are very high for Dis ($r = .70–.88$) and fairly high for TAS also (.44–.58). The correlations between TAS on SSS form V and the TAS experience scale on SSS VI range from .37 to .53. The correlations of the Dis scales from both forms range from .56 to .80. What these data show is that high scorers on the SSS do engage in much risky behavior, or at least report that they do. The next sections will examine risky behaviors and sensation seeking in a number of areas. In most of these studies there is more substantial evidence for the risky behaviors of high sensation seekers.

Volunteering

Experimenters are usually unconcerned about the possibility that volunteers for experiments may not be a random sample of the population from which they are drawing subjects. This confidence in random selection may not be warranted. While running experiments on sensory deprivation and hypnosis at a research institute in Philadelphia in the 1960s, we noticed that our volunteers, who responded to advertisements in the student newspapers in the area, were not a typical group of undergraduates. The term "hippie" was coming into use at the time to describe those who dressed unconventionally, wore their hair long, used drugs, and had a different life-style than most others. Superficially, many of our subjects seemed to warrant this label. Many of our concepts of "experience seeking" were derived from this group. To test this assumption, we gave the SSS to groups of students at three universities in the area and then asked them if they wished to volunteer for experiments in sensory deprivation or hypnosis being conducted at the medical center (Zuckerman et al., 1967). Volunteers for both types of experiments scored higher on the SSS form II General scale than nonvolunteers. The question not answered was: Do sensation seekers volunteer just for unusual kinds of experiments that offer some novel kind of experience, or are they highly represented in volunteers for all kinds of psychological experiments?

Bone et al. (1974; also see Zuckerman, 1976a) asked students if they would volunteer for experiments in learning, social psychology, sleep research, sensory deprivation, extrasensory perception (ESP), hypnosis, and drug effects. The General SSS correlated significantly with volunteering for hypnosis and drug experiments in both men and women, and with volunteering for sensory deprivation and ESP studies in men, but not with learning or social psychology experiments in either sex. Apparently, the relation between sensation seeking and volunteering is limited to experiments promising some novel and unusual kinds of experience. Learning nonsense syllables does not attract any more high than low sensation seekers.

Other studies showed that high sensation seekers tended to volunteer more than low sensation seekers for gambling studies, sensitivity training, and alpha brain wave control (Zuckerman, 1974), transcendental meditation (Myers & Eisner, 1974), and encounter groups (Stanton, 1976). Some of these activities, including encounter groups, hypnosis, and sensory deprivation, are considered risky by nonpsychologists whereas others, such as sensitivity training and meditation, are not generally regarded as risky. Myers and Eisner (1974) found no differences in sensation seeking between volunteers and nonvolunteers for karate training even though such activity is considerably more risky than meditation. Sensation seekers volunteer for activities that promise a new kind of experience whether or not it entails risk. If the activity is risky, they are still more likely to volunteer than low sensation seekers.

The perceived riskiness of an experiment depends on more than a mere description of the experiment itself. The use of informed consent forms, now required to warn subjects of any conceivable negative effects of an experiment and their rights to confidentiality, may make experiments seem more risky than they actually are. Trice and Ogden (1986) investigated the effect of such forms on volunteering for: (1) a study in problem solving; (2) a muscle strength and stress test; (3) a shock-assisted learning study; (4) completion of a "life-style" questionnaire. The liability waiver waived the right to legal action in the case of physical or emotional harm, and the confidentiality waiver (most relevant to the life-style questionnaire) waived the right to confidentiality should the legal authorities press for disclosure of information (like illegal drug use). The Thrill and Adventure Seeking subscale from the SSS form IV was used as a predictor. Volunteers for the learning-shock experiment and the life-style questionnaire scored significantly higher on the TAS than nonvolunteers, but no differences in sensation seeking were related to volunteering for the problem-solving or physical education experiments. As expected, the liability waiver considerably reduced volunteering for the shock experiment and the confidentiality waiver more than halved the percentage of volunteers for the life-style interview. When both waivers were used, those who still volunteered were higher TAS sensation seekers than the nonvolunteers, again indicating the willingness to take risks among high sensation seekers.

Kohn, Hunt, Davis, and Cowles (1982) asked for volunteers for unspecified psychological research instead of describing particular kinds of studies. They found that volunteers scored higher than nonvolunteers on the General,

TAS, and ES scales from the SSS IV, as well as the Internal Sensation Seeking scale from the Pearson (1970) NES and the Mehrabian (1978) Arousal Seeking Tendency scale. About 84% of those who volunteered in principle showed up for the experiments when asked to. The authors question the assumption that sensation seekers only volunteer for novel or exciting research topics. By not specifying a topic, however, they created an ambiguous situation, which is particularly threatening to low sensation seekers. The low sensation seeker is not likely to volunteer for something unknown and possibly dangerous. One has to offer a choice of possible experiments as Bone et al. (1974) and Trice and Ogden (1986) did in order to see if there is a preference for unusual types of experiments.

Soldiers of many armies have repeated a maxim that embodies an age old wisdom: "Never volunteer!" Volunteers in a wartime army do not enjoy a long life-expectancy. However, sensation seekers may be the ones who violate this maxim, sometimes more from boredom than altruism. The following quote from an autobiographical account of a Vietnam soldier-author expresses the sensation-seeking motivation for war:

I had no illusions, but I volunteered for a line company anyway. There were a number of reasons, of which the paramount was boredom. . . . I cannot deny that the front still held a fascination for me. The rights or wrongs of the war aside, there was a magnetism about combat. You seemed to live more intensely under fire. Every sense was sharper, the mind worked clearer and faster. . . . You found yourself on a precarious emotional edge, experiencing a headiness that no drink or drug could match. (Caputo, 1977, p. 218)

Jobe, Holgate, and Sorapansky (1983) asked for U.S. Army volunteers for a hazardous combat simulation task involving the setting off of dynamite charges nearby simulating artillery fire. Of 60 soldiers receiving the request for volunteers, 38 actually volunteered. The volunteers were significantly higher on a risk-taking personality scale and lower on an anxiety scale than nonvolunteers. In a second experiment the investigators asked for volunteers for a psychological study involving nothing more than the filling out of personality tests during an afternoon. Only 28 of 69 soldiers volunteered for this one, and volunteers and nonvolunteers did not differ on either of the personality tests. Like most of the college student studies, this study shows a specificity of the volunteering–sensation seeking effect. Unlike the study by Kohn, Hunt, Davis, & Cowles (1982), which did not specify the nature of the psychological experiment, Jobe et al. described a test-taking session that did not promise much novelty or excitement.

Hobfoll, Rom, and Segal (1989) studied a group of Israeli former soldiers who had completed their army service and were currently university students. The authors tested subjects with the Interest and Preference Inventory, which they claim is analogous to the SSS, and Spielberger's Trait Anxiety scale. Correlations indicated that high sensation seekers had volunteered to be in a combat unit, participated in actions with combat forces, and engaged in scuba diving as recreation. Anxiety was unrelated to any of these voluntary activities. On the other hand, sensation seeking was not related to drug use as it usually is in American settings (see Chapter 9). Anxiety was positively related to drug use among Israelis, a finding that is not common in America. The study illustrates the cultural differences in the phenomenal forms of sensation seeking. In a country often engaged in war, a voluntary exposure to combat is enough sensation seeking for anyone, and it is the more anxious and neurotic, rather than sensation-seeking, types who use drugs. Of course, many American soldiers used drugs in Vietnam, but from all accounts drugs were used more to alleviate boredom than to reduce anxiety, and a surprisingly high percentage gave up drug use on returning to civilian life.

The research on volunteering confirms the definition of sensation seeking as the seeking of novel and intense experiences, and the willingness to accept risks for the sake of such experiences rather than as an end in itself. It also suggests that boredom is a negative emotional state for the high sensation seeker (boredom susceptibility) that leads to volunteering for activities that could be dangerous, but also could be very interesting or arousing.

Driving behavior

Driving probably represents the most common form of sensation seeking in young men. Insurance companies know that the highest accident rate is among men 16 to 20 years old, and this is why insurance rates are higher for this group in the United States. It is not coincidental that this group also shows the highest scores on the SSS (see Chapter 4). As cars and roads are made safer, people tend to drive faster, pushing the limits of risk to their maximum. For the high sensation seeker, a car is more than a way of getting from one place to another. Their thrill and adventure seeking can be fatal to themselves as well as others. Driving at high speeds and passing other cars in areas of limited visibility and driving after heavy drinking entail physical, legal, and social risks. Although most young drivers have good reflexes and can handle their cars well, they often drive at the limits of their control, particularly when their judgment and driving behavior are disinhibited by alcohol.

Zuckerman and Neeb (1980) asked subjects how fast they usually drive on

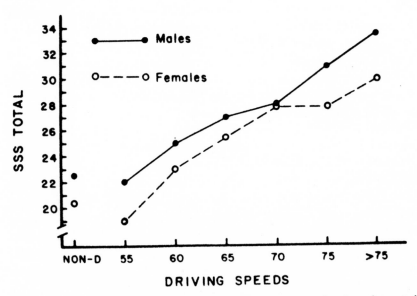

Figure 5.6. Mean Sensation Seeking Scale (SSS) scores as a function of reported driving speeds (miles per hour). From "Demographic influences in sensation seeking and expressions of sensation seeking in religion, smoking, and driving habits," by M. Zuckerman & M. Neeb, 1980. *Personality and Individual Differences, 1,* 204. Copyright Pergamon Press, 1980. Reprinted by permission.

a clear road with a 55 mile per hour (mph) speed limit and plotted their SSS Total scores as a function of their reported driving speeds. Figure 5.6 shows the relationships between SSS and speed. SSS levels increase linearly as a function of driving speed for both men and women and the relationship was highly significant for both sexes, even when age was statistically controlled. The lowest sensation-seeking scores were found in nondrivers and those who reported driving at the speed limit or lower. The highest scores were found in those who said they typically drove at 75 mph or higher. Significant results were found with all of the SSS subscales as well as the Total score.

Clement and Jonah (1984) also found significant correlations between SSS Total and reported speed in Canadian drivers responding to the same question used by Zuckerman and Neeb, and the correlations were significant even when age and driving experience were controlled. Arnett (1991), Heino, van den Molen, and Wilde (1992), and Furnham and Saipe (1993) also reported significant correlations between sensation seeking and reported speeding.

The literature strongly suggests that high sensation-seeking drivers are more likely to have driving accidents and convictions for driving offenses than low sensation seekers. Sensation seeking correlated significantly with alcohol-related accidents. In a group of convicted second offenders for driving offenses (Mann et al., 1987), and in the study by Furnham and Saipe (1993), nonalcohol related driving convictions were significantly correlated with thrill-seeking and boredom susceptibility scales (the only ones used in the study), although driving accidents were not. Heino et al. (1992) found that 52% of high sensation seekers had one or more accidents, whereas only 24% of low sensation seekers reported any accidents. Hartman and Rawson (1992) reported that both Dis and TAS subscales of the SSS VI correlated with automobile accidents as well as suspensions and arrests for alcohol related offenses. Loo (1979) reexamined previous findings relating extraversion to traffic convictions and accidents. He found that a sensation-seeking component of the extraversion scale was responsible for the relationship of the total scale to traffic convictions, and Narrow Impulsivity (fast decision times) accounted for the relationship of extraversion to accidents.

V. Johnson and White (1989) developed a risk-taking and impulsivity measure combining the Dis and ES subscales of the SSS V with four PRF subscales including Play, Impulsivity, Harm Avoidance, and Cognitive Structure, all correlates of the SSS as described in Chapter 3. They applied this measure in a longitudinal study of alcohol use and driving among a population sample of young drivers in New Jersey. It is indeed sobering to note that 57% of the sample had driven while drunk, 50% consumed alcohol while driving, and 50% smoked marijuana while driving and drove while "stoned." Risk-taking trait contributed significantly to the prediction of these intoxicated driving behaviors in a longitudinal study. "Coping" with problems by using alcohol or drugs was the strongest predictor of intoxicated driving. Path analysis showed that a risk-taking personality predicted alcohol intoxicated driving both directly and through the substance-coping mechanism, but for marijuana the effects were mediated entirely through the coping mechanism. Stacy, Newcomb, and Bentler (1991) also found that a short form of the SSS (excluding items with drug or alcohol content) directly predicted driving while intoxicated among men, and predicted this behavior indirectly, through its association with alcohol use, in women.

Given these associations between intoxicated driving and sensation seeking–impulsivity in the younger general population it is not surprising to find that individuals arrested for driving while intoxicated (DWI) are higher sensation seekers than drivers in the general population. Donovan, Queisser, Salzberg, and Umlauf (1985) compared a DWI group, a high-risk driver group (HRD), who had at least four traffic violation convictions within a year but without intoxication, and a group of men selected from the general driving population in the state of Washington. The three groups of men were given a battery of tests assessing driving attitudes and personality traits, including sensation seeking, assertiveness, emotional adjustment, internality, externality, and hostility. The high-risk drivers differed from the other two groups on driver attitudes such as driving aggression and competitive speeding. But both DWI and HRD groups were higher than the normal driver group on sensation seeking, aggression and hostility, and depression, and perceived themselves as having less personal control over the outcome of significant life events.

Donovan and Marlatt (1982) identified five personality subtypes among men arrested for driving while intoxicated. One of these types contained individuals high on both sensation seeking and aggression-hostility. Individuals of this last type had more accidents per year than those of the other types. The hostile, sensation-seeking types also had more speeding and general traffic violations than adjusted, moderately adjusted, anxious, and depressed types in a longitudinal prediction study (Donovan, Queisser, Umlauf, & Salzberg, 1986). The lack of significant differences on alcohol related violations suggests that even if the intoxicated driving is controlled, hostile sensation-seekers continue to accumulate traffic offenses.

Heino et al. (1992) actually observed the driving behavior of subjects in a semicontrolled road situation. The task was to follow a lead car, at first choosing their own distance behind the car and then at prescribed distances behind the car. Subjects rated their risk feelings at various points in time and heart rates were recorded. High sensation seekers followed the lead car at much closer distances than the low sensation seekers, but did not perceive their "tailgating" as more risky. During the prescribed following period, the low sensation seekers showed a greater increase in perceived risk and a threefold greater increase in heart rate variability than high sensation seekers. The same absolute distance in following was perceived as more risky by low sensation seekers over the entire range of following distances. Similar differences in appraised risk were seen in the laboratory using photographs of cars at different distances apart. Both high and low sensation seeking groups accepted the same amount of risk, but for high sensation seekers the critical risk was at shorter following distance than for the low sensation seekers.

These results suggest that a general difference in risk appraisal may account for the different driving habits of high and low sensation seekers. Furnham and Saipe (1993) found that TAS and BS sensation-seeking scales correlated substantially with a scale assessing attitudes toward driving risks and reasons for taking these risks. Subscales of the risk scale reflect a lack of regard for the driving laws; feelings of confidence despite illegal, risky, or fast driving; enjoyment of the sensation of speed; impulsivity; a generalized risk taking as expressed in gambling; and aggressiveness expressed in driving. TAS and BS scales correlated with all of these except the last one, aggressive driving. High sensation seekers seem to have remarkable confidence in their abilities to survive risky driving and escape legal punishment.

Injury proneness

Given that high sensation seekers are more willing to accept risk in the pursuit of novel and intense sensations, it might be expected that they would be more injury-prone than lower sensation seekers. This assumption led Ditunno and McCauley (1985) to predict that persons who had sustained spinal-cord injuries would be drawn from the high sensation-seeking part of the population. High-risk activities such as reckless driving, motorcycle riding, gun shooting, diving, and some sports are frequent sources of spinal-cord injuries. Patients undergoing physical rehabilitation after such injuries were compared with the normative population on the SSS V. No significant differences were found. Nor were differences found between patients injured by ''imprudent'' and ''prudent'' behavior. But there are two problems with the comparison of a spinal-cord group with the normative group. One is that the nature of some of the items of the SSS, particularly the TAS scales, ask about future desires to engage in physical thrill-seeking activities. The spinal-injured group would be incapable of engaging in most of these activities even if they wanted to and so would be less likely to say they would like to do so. Examination of the subscale means of the male spinal-injured group shows lower scores on the TAS scale, but practically no difference in their scores on the other subscales of the SSS. A second problem is that a severe injury like the spinal-cord severance is likely to change one's outlook on physical sensation seeking. The theory developed in the first section of this chapter suggests that sensation seekers have lowered their risk appraisals as a function of engaging in risky behavior without serious negative consequences, like permanent physical damage. Perhaps if those in the injured group were given form VI of the SSS, which separates experience from mere intentions, it would be shown that they score high on TAS and Dis experience, but low on TAS and Dis intentions scales.

Connolly (1981) compared less experienced skiers, ski instructors, and nonskiers recruited from a health spa, on the SSS V. Skiers scored higher than nonskiers on the Total and TAS scales but lower than more experienced ski instructors. Skiers who reported past injuries while skiing had higher scores than the other skiers (excluding the ski instructors) on Total, TAS, and Dis scales. This might indicate that they took more risks accounting for their higher accident rate. However, risk is always relative to skill. The ski instructors were the highest sensation seekers and they usually have few accidents because they know the limits of risk and observe them. Another problem is that lower sensation seekers who may have quit skiing after their accidents may not be represented in the sample.

Bouter, Knipsfeld, Feij, and Volovics (1988) obtained their injured sample from those filing medical insurance claims as a result of ski injuries and therefore did not exclude those who may have quit skiing. The controls were selected from among skiers filing nonmedical claims, like loss or theft, from the same company. The subjects were given the Dutch translation of the SSS. As in the American study, all skiers were higher than the normative population on the TAS scale. But in this study the skiers who sustained injuries while skiing were lower on TAS than the control group skiers. The authors explain their results by suggesting that high TAS skiers may be more skillful whereas lower (average) TAS skiers may unknowingly take risks because of their inferior skills. This is a reasonable hypothesis in view of the high scores of ski instructors in the Connolly study and in another study by Calhoon (1988).

Sensation seeking was unrelated to injuries sustained by Dutch construction workers on the job (Landeweerd, Urlings, & DeJong, 1990), and was not predictive of athletic injuries among school athletes at an American university (Smith, Ptacek, & Smoll, 1992). However, in the latter study the investigators found that low sensation seekers who had injuries were more stressed by them as indicated by the number of days they failed to participate in athletics after the injury. This finding gives more credence to the idea that low sensation seekers are more likely to avoid an activity in which they have sustained an injury. This selective effect could explain Connolly's findings, if low sensation-seeking skiers who had injuries failed to return to the ski resort where the study was done, while the high sensation seekers followed the old adage about "getting right back on the horse [or skis in this case] that threw you."

A final example from sports illustrates the possible dissociation between sensation seeking and risky behavior (Heyman & Rose, 1979). The subjects were novice scuba divers on their first open-water dive. As with skiers, scuba divers tend to score higher than the general population on sensation seeking and this group of learners also scored lower on trait anxiety. Sensation seeking was positively related to the time length of the dive and negatively related to the depth of the dive. Because deeper dives are more risky than shallower dives, this last finding seems paradoxical, since it is the lower (average) sensation seekers who are taking the greater risks. However, an understanding of the physics of diving is necessary to interpret the result. The deeper one dives, the more pressure exerted by the water, the more air from the tank is used, and the less time can be spent underwater. Furthermore, visibility is better at shallower than at deeper depths. The high sensation seekers were probably curious and wanted to spend more time exploring this new world under the water, while the lower sensation seekers were more task-oriented; they went down and came up as instructed but did not explore the novel environment. Risk may be necessary for some sensation seeking, but it is not the point of the activity for most sensation seekers.

Sexual behavior

High sensation seekers tend to engage in a greater variety of sexual behaviors with a greater number of partners than low sensation seekers, as will be described in more detail in Chapter 7. Variety in partners and certain forms of sexual activity in the absence of protection by the use of condoms put persons at risk for various kinds of sexually transmitted diseases (STDs) as well as pregnancy and various social risks. The current litany of STDs is depressing: crab lice, chlamydia, genital warts, herpes, gonorrhea, syphilis, and acquired immune deficiency disease (AIDS). The last is the most serious since it is presently incurable and the outcome is eventually fatal. Apart from disease, another risk of unprotected sex is unwanted pregnancy.

Horvath and Zuckerman (1993) developed scales to assess general and personal AIDS risk appraisal. The general scale is a kind of information scale since it asks subjects to estimate AIDS risk for a number of activities that differ in actual riskiness for AIDS. The personal risk scale consists of a single item asking the subjects to estimate their own risk for AIDS, and a relative personal risk item asks them to estimate their risk relative to that of their peers. A risky (for AIDS) sex behavior scale was developed from selecting items from a more general sex behavior scale taken by all subjects. For males it consisted of the following items: lifetime number of heterosexual partners, lifetime number of homosexual partners, frequency of receptive anal intercourse, and nonuse of condoms. The relations between sensation seeking, impulsivity, risk appraisal, and risky behavior were assessed as in the analysis of other areas of risk previously discussed, but peer behavior and risk variables were not included in this part of the study. Only sexually active subjects were used for this part of the study.

None of the variables predicted risky sex behavior in females. Sensation seeking, impulsivity, and personal (absolute) and relative AIDS risk estimates were both significantly related to risky sex behavior in males. Unlike the results with the other kinds of risk, the correlation between AIDS risk and risky behavior was positive in direction; those who engaged in risky sex behavior appraised their personal risk, particularly relative to peers, as high. Multiple regression analysis showed an equal contribution of sensation seeking and risk appraisal to risky behavior in males; however, the amount of variance in risky behavior accounted for by all variables (11%) was much lower than the variance accounted for by personality and risk appraisal variables for other kinds of risk (22%–52%).

The contrast in the relation of AIDS personal risk appraisal to risky behavior and that for the other kinds of risk is interesting. It was suggested that risky behavior tends to reduce appraisals of personal risk for other kinds of risk. However, AIDS poses a particular kind of risk that is different. The subjects' risk ratings on the general AIDS risk scale, itemizing specific sex behaviors, placed most of the items in the order of their known risk. If one engages in other kinds of risk taking, one knows whether the outcome is negative or not soon after the behavior. One commits a crime or goes through a red light and is caught or not; one gambles and wins or loses; one parachutes and is injured or not, and is frightened or made euphoric by the experience. But in the case of AIDS one does not know if one has caught the virus unless one takes a regular HIV blood test (and few do). Those who do engage in risky sex behavior know this and therefore judge themselves to be at risk for AIDS, particularly relative to their peers' risk.

We have seen with other kinds of risk taking that sensation seekers may attempt to reduce the risk, not by abstaining but by taking the proper precautions. Male sensation seekers who speed, for instance, are not less prone than low sensation-seeking men to use their seat belts (Clement & Jonah, 1984). Impulsivity combined with sensation seeking might, however, push the limits of risk too far. H. White and Johnson (1988) investigated the use of contraception and the method of contraception in subjects given the ES and Dis subscales from the SSS V and a measure of impulsivity. Both Dis and impulsivity were related to the absolute "virginity" status of the adolescents and young adults in the study, and Dis predicted subsequent frequency of intercourse; but Dis, ES, and impulsivity were unrelated to the consistency of use of any birth control methods, or the reliability of the methods used. Thus sexually active high and lower sensation seekers do not differ in their use of contraception, like condoms or spermicidal jellies, that might reduce the risk of pregnancy or AIDS and other STDs.

Criminal risk taking

Studies in Chapter 10 show a strong sensation-seeking tendency in persons diagnosed as antisocial personalities and some relationship with delinquency and adult criminality as well. Much criminal behavior involves risk of punishment, but the professional criminal weighs the risks against the gains and decides on whether the potential gain justifies the risk. The antisocial personality does the same, but the gains for him are excitement and arousal in addition to or even instead of money.

Stewart and Hemsley (1984) used a questionnaire asking about perceptions of risk (expectancy of gain) and their likelihood of taking the criminal action in a series of hypothetical situations of temptation. The test was given to small groups of criminal offenders and controls along with the EPQ scales and the General SSS. P correlated positively with expectancy of gain in both groups, and N correlated negatively with expectancy of gain and likelihood of action in the offender group only. Sensation seeking did not correlate with either measure in either group. However, the authors used the General scale only, and it is the Dis scale in particular that should relate to criminal behavior and thinking. Furthermore, these data relate only to "likelihood of action" in hypothetical situations. In the Horvath and Zuckerman (1993) study the SSS Total score correlated highly ($r = .53$) with reports of actual criminal behavior in college students, although for the most part these were not serious crimes.

Kafry (1982) showed young children (6–10 years old) pictures of children doing negative behaviors (playing with matches, hitting peers or adults, shoplifting, playing truant, etc.) and asked them to indicate which of those things they did or did not do. The author's children form of the SSS correlated significantly with the number of antisocial behaviors that the children reported doing themselves. The relationship between criminal risky behavior and sensation seeking appears to begin quite early.

Dahlback (1990) found a very high correlation ($r = .62$) between self-reports of similar kinds of crimes in college students and risk taking in a laboratory gambling situation. The subjects used their own money in the gambling. Individuals who took greater risks in their betting were generally those who reported having commited more crimes. This study shows the generality of risk taking from criminal to gambling behavior and suggests that gambling may be a good way to test sensation seeking in the laboratory.

Gambling

Comparisons of pathological gamblers and others will be reserved for Chapter 10, on psychopathology. This section is limited to laboratory studies of risk taking in gambling. As noted in the section on volunteering, students who volunteered for a gambling course were higher on the Dis scale than the normative group at the same university (Zuckerman, 1974). In this course students made "bets" in various games, competing for a prize for those with the highest "paper money" winnings. Since they were not gambling with their own money, much of the risk element was lacking, but some relationships between the Dis scale and bet size in hypothetical betting, and actual amount bet in the game of blackjack (or "21") were found. No relationships were found in the other two games, roulette and craps, possibly because blackjack allows some degree of control over the outcome. Long odds do not necessarily discourage high sensation seekers. In another laboratory study with college students it was found that students with higher sensation-seeking scores chose to make bets at higher odds (with greater risk of losing) than low sensation seekers in a game betting on the outcome of a card draw (Waters & Kirk, 1968). But Zuckerman and Kuhlman (1978) found that high sensation seekers were more sensitive to the "expected value" of bets in their betting in hypothetical situations. In the latter type of situation the high sensation seekers were probably calmer and more likely to use their gambling experience in making appropriate cognitive choices. In real gambling, gamblers may have the "illusion of control" (Langer, 1975), even in situations where the outcome is due to pure chance.

Hayes (1988) investigated the interaction between sensation seeking and the illusion of control using a Desirability of Control (DC) scale. The control measured by this scale is not self-control, but refers to a desire to control the events in one's life. Hayes reasoned that the combination of high sensation seeking and a desire for control leads to the illusion of control in gambling situations, reduced perceptions of risk, and increased bet size as a consequence. Students were given the SSS and DC scales and asked if they would like to participate in a dice game where they would have the chance to win one of four cash prizes. As in Kuhlman's "gambling casino" at the University of Delaware, high sensation seekers were more prone to volunteer for such gambling activity. The highest proportion of volunteers came from the high SSS–high DC group (72%) and the lowest proportion from the low SSS–high DC group (44%).

Subjects were selected from the four groups formed by combinations of high and low SSS and DC scores. They were brought into the laboratory and asked to bet on a series of dice throws under one of two conditions. In the illusion-of-control condition, they chose the group of numbers to bet on and bet size before tossing the dice in order to foster the illusion of control. In the other condition, the experimenter threw the dice and kept them covered before the subject chose the numbers and made the bets. As expected, subjects bet more in the illusion-of-control condition and high sensation seekers bet more overall. However, only the high SSS–high DC trait group showed a significant differential susceptibility to the illusion-of-control condition. The study suggests the interaction of a cognitive trait and sensation seeking in susceptibility to pathological gambling.

Money is not necessarily the primary motivation for gambling since most compulsive gamblers end up losing large sums of it. Anderson and Brown (1984) asked gamblers why they gambled. Only 8% of gamblers said they gambled to win money compared to 50% who said they did it for enjoyment or excitement. R. I. Brown (1986) postulates that arousal is the primary reinforcer for betting. Hypothetical or low-stakes betting has little appeal for real gamblers. L. Brown, Ruder, Ruder, and Young (1974) found a higher correlation between the Change Seeker Index (CSI; very highly correlated with the SSS) and reported gambling for money than between the CSI and nonmonetary gambling. Nadler (1985) reported that the most highly discriminating items in a compulsive gambling scale were:

"When playing a game I prefer to play for money."
"The higher the stakes, the more I enjoy the bet."
"When gambling, I would 'go for broke' rather than play it safe. "

Why does the gambler need high stakes to enjoy betting? Obviously more is involved than a cognitive challenge. Arousal theory suggests that the arousal during anticipation of the outcome of a high-stake bet is reinforcing to high sensation seekers who may have low states of tonic arousal when not stimulated (Zuckerman, 1984a). Betting does increase heart rate markedly, particularly in real gambling situations where the gamblers are playing with their own money (Anderson & Brown, 1984; Blaszczynski, Winter, & McConaghy, 1986). In the Anderson and Brown study, gamblers showed more heart rate increase (+25 bpm) in a real casino gambling situation than in the laboratory simulation condition (+8 bpm).

There was no significant correlation between SSS Total score and bet size in the laboratory betting situation, but the correlation rose to a significant one ($r = .57$) in the real casino. The correlation between the mean bet size and the heart rate increase for the gamblers was insignificant in the laboratory, but highly significant ($r = .74$) in the real casino. The SSS also correlated significantly with the heart rate increase of the gamblers in the real casino. None of these correlations were significant for students, who were only studied in the laboratory (for ethical considerations). This study shows that high sensation-seeking gamblers in real gambling situations make larger bets and have larger heart rate increases than lower sensation seekers, and suggests that the arousal produced by high-stakes betting is rewarding to the high sensation seeker. The question of why sensation seekers should find cardiovascular arousal reinforcing goes to the ''heart'' of the matter in the physiological differences between high and low sensation seekers to be discussed in Chapters 11 and 12.

Financial risk taking

Business investment is a form of gambling where there is a large risk range from very secure investments, as in government bonds, to very speculative investments, as in ''junk bonds'' or stock in new companies. Economic researchers have noted individual differences in risk aversiveness in investors (Harlow & Brown, 1990). Risk aversiveness varies with age and sex in the same way that sensation seeking does (Chapter 4). Males are more willing to accept financial risk than females and risk aversiveness increases with age. Harlow and Brown suggest that risk aversiveness versus risk acceptance is a trait that is related to sensation seeking, extraversion, and biological markers for these personality traits.

They brought students to the laboratory where they participated in competitive bidding against three computerized opponents. Various measures of relative risk aversion were derived from this game. The SSS V Total score and the Social Introversion scale (Si) from the MMPI were administered to subjects, and on another occasion blood was drawn in order to measure monoamine oxidase (MAO), a biochemical correlate of sensation seeking and extraversion that will be discussed in Chapter 11. A lottery procedure, more like ordinary gambling, was added to the end of the experiment and risk-taking measures based on a choice of bets were obtained from it. Sensation seeking and extraversion (Si scale reversed) were positively related to riskiness of auction and lottery strategies for men but not for women. Women were more risk aversive than men. MAO was negatively related to risk taking, a result consistent with the negative relationship between MAO and sensation seeking and extraversion (Chapter 11). The significant results were much stronger for sensation seeking than for extraversion or MAO. These findings extend the concept of individual differences in risk acceptance into an everyday area of life. Without any hint of irony, the authors note that it is psychologists [situationists?] who usually argue that choices are determined by factors unique to the particular decision setting, whereas economists assume there are also some individual specific mechanisms playing a role in all economic decisions.

Sciortino, Huston, and Spencer (1987) related a sensation-seeking scale developed by themselves to the concept of the "precautionary demand for money," defined as "those held in order to meet contingencies which are not expected to occur in the normal (or most likely) course of events, but which if they occur, would call for cash payments." In the financial world this translates into how much money is kept in fluid accounts, where it is immediately available for expected and unexpected contingencies. But with the college students studied the concept referred to how much money they carry around, controlling for their wealth (amount in the checking account) and income (the amount spent in a week). The theory is that low risk takers carry more ready cash around than high risk takers. Their results show that high sensation seekers do carry around less money than low sensation seekers for unforseen contingencies. A high risk aversive, low sensation seeker carried around about a third more cash than the average person. Of course, these findings might be reversed in cities where there is a perceived high risk of being robbed in the streets.

Travel and migration

Low sensation seekers like the comfortable familiarity of their usual environment. When they have to travel they like to plan their trips very carefully or have it planned for them so that there will be no unexpected events. When they vacation they often go to the same place every year. High sensation seekers like to travel to exotic places and do not worry much about booking all of their reservations in advance. They may change their itinerary on impulse as they travel.

As this chapter was being written there was a war crisis in the Mideast, with threats of terrorism. Many Americans canceled plans to fly to Europe, or even domestically, because of what was perceived to be a major risk. Presumably the higher rates of cancellation were among the lower sensation seekers. Risk is partly a subjective matter along the sensation seeking dimension.

Zuckerman (1979b) had subjects rate hypothetical travel destinations for their riskiness. Europe and the United States were rated as relatively low risk, Asia was higher, the Antarctica was even higher, and travel to the moon was rated as the most risky. Subjects were asked to anticipate how they would feel if about to embark on a trip to these destinations, using Neary's (1975) scale for sensation-seeking and anxiety states. As predicted from our model (Figure 5.1), anxiety increased directly in proportion to riskiness of the destinations, whereas sensation-seeking state showed a curvilinear relationship to riskiness. High- and low-trait sensation seekers did not differ on anxiety for the two low-risk destinations, but low sensation seekers expected more anxiety on departure to the three high-risk places (Asia, Antarctica, and the moon). High sensation seekers anticipated more positive sensation-seeking affect for all situations of travel, and the differences between high and low sensation seekers were larger for the higher-risk destinations.

While there is some risk in travel there is even more risk in migration because the change in environment is relatively permanent. Some have speculated that throughout history it is the more adventurous who choose to migrate, even when economic and political conditions are bad in one's native country. The following lines from Hamlet's soliloquy probably reflect the feelings of low sensation seekers who refuse to migrate:

> The undiscover'd country from whose bourn
> No traveller returns, puzzles the will,
> And makes us rather bear those ills we have,
> Than fly to others that we know not of.

Jacobs and Koeppel (1974) asked undergraduates at a university in southern Mississippi about their future plans to stay in Mississippi or to move out of the state. Sensation seeking correlated significantly with the intention to move out of the state. Winchie and Carment (1988) compared males living in India who had applied for immigrant visas to Canada with controls who indicated that they have never considered migrating from India. Sensation seeking was among the variables most strongly discriminating between migrants and nonmigrants; migrants had higher scores. Although limitation of opportunity and consequent occupational dissatisfaction obviously played their roles in migration intention, sensation seeking, as indicated by the scores on the external sensation seeking scale of Pearson's (1970) NES and a desire to meet new people, also played an important role in migration. However, risk taking itself, as measured by the JPI (Jackson, 1976), was only weakly predictive of migration in one analysis, and not predictive at all in a second analysis. Apparently risk itself is not the motivator for migration, but as with other sensation-seeking activities, it is tolerated for the sake of the potential rewards of the activity.

Fear of physical harm (phobic)

The conscious fear in many simple phobias is fear of physical harm, even if the phobic understands the low risk in the situation. Statistics on the low mortality rates of airline accidents will not reassure someone who has developed a fear of flying. Even agoraphobics are not convinced that they won't die during panic attacks if they venture outside of their homes. Short of clinical phobias, many persons have some degree of anxiety in certain situations, such as looking down from a height, or confronting a snake. These have been called "biologically prepared" fears because, in contrast to other stimuli, they are so easy to condition. Although sensation seeking has no relationship to general anxiety trait measures (see Chapter 3), the TAS component of the SSS does have a negative relationship with fear of physical harm, and therefore might be expected to predict phobic reactions in the normal range.

Mellstrom, Cicala, and Zuckerman (1976) assessed behavior and emotional reactions in three situations where some people have developed phobias: approaching a snake, looking down from a high place, and being confined in darkness. The last is a more ambiguous type of threat, but many people associate it with vague possibilities for physical harm. Subjects were actually exposed to these situations in natural and laboratory settings. The SSS TAS subscale was used as a predictor along with general and specific scales of anxiety. The TAS correlated significantly and negatively with five of the six indexes of anxiety in the snake situation including self-report and observer ratings of anxiety, and behavioral latency in approaching the snake. TAS predicted better than the general anxiety scale, but not as highly as the specific anxiety scale, in this situation. The TAS also significantly predicted five of the six anxiety measures in the heights situation, and five of the six in the darkness situation. In all three of these situations low sensation seekers showed more self-report and behavioral evidence of anxiety than high sensation seekers even though the general scale of anxiety and the TAS trait were not correlated. The results show that sensation seeking is inversely related to anxiety in specific physical harm threatening situations rather than to generalized anxiety.

Many persons are blood-phobic and are uncomfortable when blood must be drawn from them or in situations where they might cut themselves. Farnhill and Ball (1982) questioned female college students who had not yet donated blood on their willingness to donate blood in the immediate future. Women who were willing to donate blood were significantly higher than adamant nondonors on the SSS Total, TAS, and ES scales. According to the authors, "The findings suggest that a substantial percentage of nondonors may be deterred because they perceive donation among the class of risky and unknown experiences which they prefer to avoid" (p. 126).

Smoking and health risk

Zuckerman, Ball, and Black (1990) investigated the smoking habits of college students at the University of Delaware in the mid 1980s and compared the results with data from the same university collected in the early 1970s. In both eras there was a significant relationship between smoking and sensation seeking, although the proportion of high sensation-seeking males smoking in the 1980s was nearly half the proportion seen in the 1970s. Most students felt that smoking was at least a moderate to great health risk and about half of the smokers actually overestimated the risk of developing lung cancer from heavy smoking. Smokers who quit smoking estimated the general health risk of smoking as greater than current smokers did. Even though high sensation seekers tended to be more likely to smoke than low sensation seekers, sensation seeking was not related to smoking risk appraisal in either past or current smokers. Differential risk appraisal cannot explain the stronger smoking tendency in the higher sensation seeker.

Summary

Risk taking is sometimes necessary in order to enjoy some types of sensations and experiences but it is not the essential goal of sensation seeking. High and low sensation seekers differ in their willingness to take risks for desired sensations, but the low sensation seeker does not value the sensations as much as the high sensation seeker.

A model for sensation-seeking behavior has been presented. Novelty, per se, elicits positive interest and sensation-seeking affect up to some maximal degree of novelty, after which the effect of further novelty is unpredictable, depending on the degree of threat in the situation. However, anxiety state varies directly with the appraised threat or risk. Sensation-seeking state first increases with appraised risk in the lower range, but beyond some optimal level of arousal it is diminished by further increases in risk. High sensation seekers have lower anxiety gradients and higher sensation-seeking affect gradients in response to increasing degrees of novelty and appraised risk. Data on anticipated affective reactions to hypothetical situations generally are in accordance with this model.

Experience with any activity that does not lead to punishment reduces the risk appraisal of that activity. High sensation seekers tend to appraise many situations as less risky than low sensation seekers. But many of these activities are ones in which they are already experienced. Has experience lowered their risk appraisal or do they engage in risky behavior because of a cognitive trait or disposition to underestimate risk? Conversely, do low sensation seekers avoid risky behavior because of a tendency to overestimate risk? Correlational research subjected to LISREL analysis to test causal models suggests that the strong link between sensation seeking and certain kinds of risky behavior does not require the mediation of a generalized risk appraisal trait. Rather, the lower risk appraisal of high sensation seekers seems to be a function of their behavioral experience.

Sensation-seeking students are more likely than low sensation seekers to volunteer for unusual types of experiments, even those considered risky. Sensation-seeking soldiers are more likely than lower sensation seekers to volunteer for combat assignments or risky combat simulation. Sensation-seeking drivers drive faster than low sensation seekers, and are more likely to be among those who drive while intoxicated and/or have frequent accidents. However, it is a combination of hostile aggressiveness and sensation seeking that predicts intoxicated and reckless driving rather than sensation seeking alone. There is no necessary relationship between accidents among construction workers or skiers and their sensation-seeking scores.

Sensation seekers engage in much risky behavior but they do not generally seek to maximize the risk. Although male sensation seekers tend to drive at fast speeds, they do not neglect fastening their seat belts anymore than low sensation seekers do. Similarly, although high sensation seekers are more likely to be sexually active than low sensation seekers, they are not less likely to use contraception and condom protection against infection.

Gambling is a kind of sensation seeking in which the major reinforcement for gamblers is the anticipatory arousal during the betting. One study showed correlations among sensation seeking, bet size, and heart rate increases in gamblers while gambling in a real casino setting. These relationships are often not seen among the gamblers or in students gambling in laboratory settings where the stakes are small. However, there is some evidence that even in these less exciting settings with minimal kinds of real risk taking, sensation seeking may predict bet size and preferred odds in some games. Other studies have extended the concept of risk taking from ordinary gambling to the kind we call financial strategies. Sensation seekers tend to choose more risky strategies in laboratory investment games, and feel less need to have ready cash on hand in their daily lives ("precautionary demand for money").

Sensation seekers like to travel and are more willing to accept uncertainty and risk in travel to less familiar kinds of places. They anticipate more pleasurable arousal and less anxiety in travel than low sensation seekers. They are more likely to migrate when faced with dissatisfactions about jobs and economic conditions.

Low sensation seekers are more likely to show higher levels of state anxiety than high sensation seekers when confronting situations related to simple phobias, like fear of snakes, heights, darkness, and blood. Low sensation seekers among young college students are also less likely to smoke than high sensation seekers even though high and low sensation seekers have an equal estimation of the health risk in smoking.

Sensation seekers are attracted to activities and situations offering novel or intense experiences, and they are willing to accept the risks involved, although they do not seek to maximize them. Low sensation seekers are less attracted to these kinds of experiences, regard them as more risky, and anticipate more unpleasant, anxious reactions if they engaged in such activities. Even though low sensation seekers anticipate anxiety in what they regard as risky situations or activities, they are not generally anxious or neurotic people. They are just cautious and conservative with a preference for a world that is predictable and safe.

The next chapter will discuss sensation seeking in a particular area, sports. The issues of sensation and risk and their balance will again appear in relation to the type of sports or athletic activities preferred by high and low sensation seekers.

6

Sports and vocations

Sports

The young and adolescents of many mammalian species spend a great deal of their time in play, or activity where the reward seems to lie in the "game" itself. Kittens stalk inanimate objects as well as each other. Dogs chase each other and have an indefatigable love of chasing and retrieving balls, sticks, or frisbees.

Primates have an even more advanced taste for play. Young male chimpanzees and humans frequently engage in rough-and-tumble play. Such behavior may occur in the females of both species but less commonly. War games are popular among boys, even those who are discouraged by pacifist parents. Later games become more organized and eventually become formal sports with established rules and strategies. With increasing age fewer adults actively engage in sports on a frequent or regular basis but many continue to have an intense interest in college and professional sports, going to the games or watching them on television, reading about them in their newspapers and magazines, and spending a great deal of time discussing them with others. Some do continue to play at sports like swimming, running, golf, tennis, and bowling. Most of these are relatively risk-free sports compared with body contact sports like football or soccer, or flying and water sports like hang gliding and scuba diving.

Sports seem to provide a relatively prosocial form of sensation seeking in that they stimulate arousal, require skills, and sometimes provide a competitive-aggressive outlet that only rarely results in serious injury to oneself or others. Watching sports is practically risk-free but less arousing than actual participation. But for millions of people the excitement of watching their teams compete is the greatest thrill they have except for sex (and, for some poor souls, it may be even greater).

The TAS subscale of the SSS forms IV and V includes items asking people if they would like to engage in various sports that provide unusual sensations or experiences, like parachuting or scuba diving. To what extent is participation in a particular sport indicative of a more general sensation-seeking trait that would be reflected in at least some of the other sensation-seeking subscales that do not mention sports? Another question to be addressed in this chapter is: Are all types of athletes high sensation seekers, or is high sensation-seeking trait specific to certain kinds of sports?

General participation in sports

Morgan (1980) attempted to answer those who questioned whether personality has any relevance to sports participation. Despite the wide use of nonrelevant theories or completely atheoretical approaches noted by Morgan, he claims that "various personality traits have consistently been observed to account for 20% to 45% of the variance in sport performance" (p. 72). H. Eysenck, Nias, and Cox (1982), in an extensive review of the role of personality in sports, concluded that those who engage in sports tend to be more extraverted than nonparticipants. The relation between extraversion and sports is said to be mediated by narrower traits like sensation seeking, assertiveness, competitiveness, impulsivity, and high pain thresholds. Psychoticism (P) is also associated with sports participation mediated by the aggressiveness and high competitiveness among those high on this dimension. Neuroticism (N) is said to be more weakly related to sports, although researchers note a tendency for N to be low among particularly outstanding athletes. However, state anxiety, as well as energy and competitiveness, may vary markedly before, during, and after the actual involvement in the athletic competition.

Gundersheim (1987) compared college team athletes and nonparticipants in organized high school and college athletics on the SSS form IV. Male athletes could not be distinguished from nonathletes on the SSS, but female athletes did score higher on sensation seeking than nonathletes, particularly on the General, TAS, and BS subscales. The SSS did not discriminate among the four female athletic teams, and among the male teams it only differentiated between baseball and lacrosse and wrestling teams; baseball players were lower than the other two groups of athletes on General and TAS scales. Gundersheim feels that these differences are produced by the contact–noncontact sports dichotomy, a conclusion substantiated by other studies, such as Potgieter and Bisschoff's (1990) comparisons of rugby players and marathon runners. Contact sports are usually more aggressive and arousing than noncontact sports, which may account for their greater association with sensation seeking. However, there are other aspects of sports that could account for their differential association with sensation seeking, such as their riskiness, the novelty of sensations produced by the activity, and degree of regular training required in the particular sport.

In contrast to these results, Hartman and Rawson (1992) found that male and female college students participating in mainly noncontact sports were still higher than their general college controls on experience and intention Dis scales of the SSS VI, but not on the more relevant TAS scales.

Rowland, Franken, and Harrison (1986) found that high sensation seekers among college students had tried a greater number of sports (males) or were currently engaged in a greater number of sports (females). These relationships were significant even when they left the TAS subscale out of the analyses and summed the remaining three nonsports-related subscales of the SSS. Rowland et al. found that high and low sensation-seeking groups could not be distinguished on the basis of the most popular sports, such as bicycle riding or swimming. However, low sensation-seeking males listed running or jogging, weight lifting, and hiking, and low sensation-seeking females listed golf and tennis among the top ten most popular activities, but these did not make the top ten for the high sensation seekers. Babbitt, Rowland, and Franken (1990a) reported that women who were active in aerobic exercise classes were much lower than the general population on the total SSS. Except for tennis, all of these sports that were relatively more popular among low than high sensation seekers are sports that can be engaged in alone and without competition. Competition may provide the kind of arousal necessary for sensation seekers.

Fletcher and Dowell (1971) found that freshmen reporting a history of athletic participation in high school scored higher than nonathletes on dominance and aggression, whereas the nonathletes scored higher on need for order, a trait associated with low sensation seeking. However, different results were found for college females by Stoner and Bandy (1977); nonparticipants in sports scored higher than team sport participants on needs for change and heterosexuality, and lower on deference, a pattern suggestive of higher sensation seeking.

The personality characteristics of participants in sports may be different at the high school and college levels. Schiendel (1964) found that participants among 9th and 12th grade students scored higher on scales of sociability and conformity than nonparticipants, but in college the nonparticipants had more socially desirable traits, like conscientiousness, responsibility, tolerance, and intellectual efficiency. One characteristic was similar across the educational and age levels: Athletes were more conventional in their responses to social situations.

Selective sports participation

A review of the literature on sensation seeking and sports identified riskiness as a major factor in sports showing a positive relationship with sensation seeking (Zuckerman, 1983c). High-risk sports, like parachuting, hang gliding, auto racing, scuba diving, mountain climbing, and skiing were reported to be associated with high sensation seeking in various studies. Medium risk sports, such as body-contact ones, were also associated with sensation seeking. Lower-risk sports requiring intensive training and practice, such as running and gymnastics, were not associated with sensation seeking, and in the case of running were actually more common among low sensation seekers (McCutcheon, 1980); male runners were lower on Dis and female runners were lower on Total and TAS scales than nonrunners.

Rowland et al. (1986) found that the athletes who were currently active in risky sports, such as climbing, skiing, and parachuting, were generally above the mean on sensation seeking. But high sensation seekers also were attracted to some low-risk sports like playing pool, snooker, target shooting, and modern dancing(!). Kerr and Svebak (1989) used the risk classifications of Zuckerman (1983c) and Rowland et al. to compare those engaging in risky and nonrisky sports on impulsivity (Barratt & Patton, 1983) and the traits of arousal avoidance, planning orientation, and seriousmindedness assessed by the Telic Dominance Scale (TDS; Murgatroyd et al., 1978). The only consistently significant difference between those engaging in risky and safe sports was on the arousal avoidance scale. Those practicing safe sports were higher on arousal avoidance. Arousal avoidance is the TDS most similar to sensation seeking (low arousal avoidance = high sensation seeking), and the results confirm the greater tendency of high sensation seekers to engage in more risky sports (like canoeing, downhill skiing, and motor racing) whereas the low sensation seekers choose the less risky sports (like archery, golf, and bowling). However, risk is not the only thing differentiating high- and low-risk sports. Most of the high-risk sports provide arousing sensations like speed, suspension of gravity (as in free fall), and novel views (like the underwater one).

Svebak and Kerr (1989) classified sports as "endurance" (requiring strenuous and persistent activity) and "explosive" (requiring intense concentration and activity for relatively short periods of time). Cricket, soccer, hockey, baseball, and surfing are given as examples of explosive sports, whereas long-distance running, rowing, and jogging are regarded as endurance sports. In one study long-distance runners were compared with tennis and field hockey players on the Barratt Impulsivity scale and the TDS. The

long distance runners were more planning-oriented and arousal-avoidant than
the tennis and hockey players. This is consistent with other data showing that
long-distance runners tend to be lower sensation seekers (McCutcheon, 1981)
and more introverted (H. Eysenck et al., 1982). Potgieter and Bisschoff
(1990) found marathon runners (low-risk, endurance sport) to be lower
sensation seekers (Total and TAS scales) than rugby players (medium-risk,
explosive sport). Both rugby players and marathon runners rated rugby as a
higher-risk sport than marathon running, but the rugby players rated both of
these sports as less risky than the marathon runners did.

Svebak and Kerr (1989) also reported that students who engaged regularly
in "paratelic" sports (baseball, cricket, touch football, surfing, wind surfing)
were compared with students who engaged in nonparatelic sports (long
distance running, rowing, etc.). Those engaging in paratelic or "explosive"
sports were lower on planning, seriousminded, and arousal avoidance scales,
and higher on nonplanning and total impulsivity scores.

Comparisons of selected sports groups

Mountain climbing. Freixanet (1991) compared four groups: (1) experienced
mountain climbers (Alpinists) who had participated in several expeditions to
the Himalayas; (2) mountaineers, both climbers and mountain skiers; (3)
sportsmen engaging in a variety of other risky sports including parachuting,
scuba diving, water skiing, gliding, hang gliding, ballooning, racing of cars,
motorcycles, or boats, and adventuring; (4) a control group not engaging in
any risky sports. In addition to the usual SSS V scales, groups were compared on a total score not including the TAS scale. All three groups engaging
in risky sports were significantly higher than the control group on TAS, ES,
and SSS Total scales, and the mountaineering-related sportsmen scored
higher than the other sportsmen on the same scales. Mountaineers and sportsmen also scored higher than controls on a Total score which did not include
the TAS subscale, showing that the differences on sensation seeking were
general and not due solely to the one scale that includes sports activities.
Dis and BS did not yield overall differences between groups, although
the mountaineers were higher than controls on the Dis scale. None of the
differences between the Alpinists and the other risky sport groups were significant.

The study shows that the primary difference in sensation seeking tends to
be between all risky sports and any other kinds of sports, rather than among
the different types of risky sports. Experience in mountaineering also did not
make a difference as judged from comparisons between the Alpinist and

the other mountaineering group. Disinhibition was not very discriminating although mountaineers and sportsmen tended to score higher than controls. Perhaps the kind of drinking and social risk taking characteristic of Dis are inimical to the careful planning necessary for risky sports. However, Zaleski (1984a) compared a risky sports group in Poland (racing drivers, mountain climbers, glider pilots, and parachutists) with controls and found that the sports group was significantly higher on TAS *and* Dis.

Fowler, von Knorring, and Oreland (1980) found that a group consisting of experienced mountaineers, or those with an interest in mountaineering, were higher on the SSS General, TAS, monotony avoidance, impulsive extraversion, and plain impulsivity scales than students not even interested in mountaineering. The mountaineering group was also lower on monoamine oxidase (MAO), an enzyme shown to be lower in high sensation seekers in the general population (Chapter 11). Cronin (1991) also found that experienced mountain climbers scored high on Total, TAS, and ES scales of the SSS V. D. W. Robinson (1985) compared elite rock climbers with the normative American SSS data and reported that the rock climbers were significantly higher on Total, TAS, and ES scales. It is interesting that mountaineering groups differ on ES as well as TAS. This suggests that thrills and adventure are not the only goal of such risky activity, but that the climber is looking for some more general kinds of experiences "through the mind and the senses."

Skiing. Downhill skiing involves both speed and heights and has been associated with high sensation seeking in America (Calhoon, 1988; Connolly, 1981) and in the Netherlands (Bouter et al., 1988; Landeweerd, Urlings, & DeJong, 1990). In the Connolly study, skiers scored higher than nonskiing controls on the Total and TAS scales only, but ski instructors scored higher than ordinary skiers on Total, TAS, and ES. Calhoon's skiers were all ski instructors and ski patrolmen, and they scored much higher than college student nonskiers on the Total and all of the subscales of the SSS form V, as well as the TAS and Dis experience and intention scales of SSS VI. Skiers in the Netherlands scored higher than controls on TAS, BS, and Total scores of the Dutch SSS (Bouter et al.). But in the study by Landerweerd et al., where skiers were compared with a high-risk vocational group of construction workers, the skiers scored significantly higher on TAS, but lower on Dis than the construction workers. People who make their living at skiing (at least during the season) seem to be more generalized sensation seekers, whereas for less experienced, recreational skiers sensation seeking is limited to TAS and either ES or BS forms.

Other high-risk sports. Straub (1982) compared groups of hang gliders, auto racers, and bowlers. Two-thirds of the hang glider group and half of the automobile racers considered their sport to be a "high-risk activity"; none of the bowlers considered their sport to be risky. The three groups differed significantly on the Total, TAS, ES, and BS scales; the Dis scale did not differentiate the groups. Both risk-taking groups were higher on all scales than the bowlers. The hang gliders were highest on TAS and ES, whereas the auto racers were highest on Dis and BS, the more antisocial SS scales.

Novice scuba divers were compared with the SSS norms for the Total score on form V but the subscales were not analyzed (Heyman & Rose, 1979). Female divers were higher than the female norms on the SSS, but the difference for males was only of borderline significance ($p < .10$). Males scored higher than women on the SSS in the normative and most other samples in the SSS norms, but these female divers had scores that were even a little higher than those for the male divers. This may be an example of a phenomenon observed in other areas. On an activity where most of the volunteer participants tend to be men, the women who do participate are much higher on the relevant trait than other women, and the differences are larger than those found between male participants and the male norms.

At the extremes of the SSS we find skydivers scoring higher on the scale than controls (Hymbaugh & Garrett, 1974); and female participants in aerobic exercise classes scoring much lower than Australian female norms at every age decade from adolescence to the 30s (Babbitt, Rowland, & Franken, 1990a). The aerobics participants were quite dedicated to this activity, attending every week and not participating in many other sports or activities. Their main motives were health, appearance, and weight control. As with regular running or jogging, the low sensation seeker is the most persistent and regular practicioner of this physical activity. High sensation seekers sometimes try these kinds of activities but they rarely persist or practice.

The broadest comparisons of participants in various sports have been done by Breivik (1991a) in Norway. Table 6.1 shows mean scores on the SSS form V of three groups of elite performers in risky sports and control groups of sports students and military recruits. All groups were male. Significant differences were found between groups on TAS, ES, and Total SSS scales. The three elite risk sport groups scored higher than the control groups on these scales and did not differ much among themselves. The control groups of sports students and military recruits did not differ on the SSS. Two years later Breivik, (personal communication, 1993) replicated these comparisons on four of the groups (climbers, sky divers, physical education students, and military groups), and there was little difference in the findings. The two

Table 6.1. *Mean Sensation Seeking Scale (SSS) scores of Norwegian elite sportsmen, sports students, and military recruits*

	Climbers (n = 40)	Canoeists (n = 32)	Parachutists (n = 20)	Students (n = 43)	Recruits (n = 28)	F-value
TAS	8.33	8.78	8.75	7.79	6.61	8.48*
ES	7.73	6.44	6.85	5.44	4.75	10.60*
Dis	5.95	5.59	6.50	5.37	5.82	1.32
BS	3.73	4.03	4.55	3.49	3.71	1.92
Total	25.73	24.78	26.65	22.09	20.89	6.41*

Note: n = number of subjects; TAS = Thrill and Adventure Seeking; ES = Experience Seeking; Dis = Disinhibition; BS = Boredom Susceptibility; Total = Total score of SSS form V.
*$p < .01$.
Source: Breivik (1991a), with permission.

high-risk sports groups were higher sensation seekers than the ordinary physical education students or soldiers. The second sky diver group showed a rise in Total, TAS, and ES scales compared with the earlier group. They were informally characterized as a "wilder" group.

In the later study, comparisons of the groups were also made on the SSS VI scales. Sky divers scored higher than all groups, including climbers, on all four TAS and Dis experience and intention scales. Climbers were higher than students and recruits on TAS and Dis experience scales, but *not* on TAS and Dis intention scales. The distinction between experience and intention was important here. The climbers were actively seeking sensations in both areas, whereas the students and recruits were not as currently active in sensation seeking, but their intentions were at the same level as those of the climbers. The sky divers, however showed even higher sensation-seeking ambitions than any of the groups, as well as higher current sensation-seeking activity.

Table 6.2 lists the scores of these elite groups along with other less-risky sports, participants, physical education students, military recruits, and male and female teachers, and Figure 6.1 compares some of the male groups on the SSS Total score. Four of the elite climber group who had participated in an expedition (fatal to two other climbers) were combined with six climbers from the successful Everest expedition in 1985 to form an elite expedition group. This latter group had the highest mean SSS Total, ES, and BS scores of all the groups presented. The parachutists, elite mountain climbers, and white-water canoeists were next highest on the SSS Total and ES scores. The

Table 6.2. *Mean Sensation Seeking Scale (SSS) scores of Norwegian elite athletes, national teams in selected sports, physical education students, teachers, and military recruits*

		SSS				
Groups	*n*	TAS	ES	Dis	BS	Total SSS
Expedition climbers	9	9.11	8.55	5.88	5.11	28.66
Parachutists	20	8.75	6.85	6.50	4.55	26.65
Elite climbers	36	8.25	7.58	5.91	3.55	25.30
White water canoeists	32	8.78	6.44	5.59	4.03	24.78
Karate, males	17	8.00	4.82	5.65	3.82	22.29
Karate, females	14	7.50	5.64	5.29	3.79	22.22
Phys ed students, males	43	7.79	5.44	5.37	3.49	22.09
North Sea divers	5	7.80	5.00	4.40	4.80	22.00
Ice hockey players	19	7.11	4.58	5.68	4.58	21.95
Teachers, males	12	4.83	6.50	6.25	3.83	21.41
Tennis players, males	5	7.60	5.20	6.40	1.80	21.00
Military recruits	28	6.61	4.75	5.82	3.71	20.89
Volleyball players, males	13	5.15	4.00	4.92	4.38	18.46
Volleyball players, females	16	5.44	5.31	4.00	2.44	17.19
Teachers, females	17	3.88	5.25	2.50	2.75	14.38

Note: Groups are arrayed in order of mean scores on the Total SSS. TAS = Thrill and Adventure Seeking; ES = Experience Seeking; Dis = Disinhibition; BS = Boredom Susceptibility.
Source: Breivik (1991a), with permission.

parachutists had the highest score of all groups on the Dis scale, but did not differ much from male teachers (!) or tennis players on this scale. The next lower groups are both male and female karate teams (no sex difference), male sports and physical education students, North Sea divers, ice hockey players, male tennis players, male teachers, and military recruits. The risky-sports groups are clearly higher than these other sports and control groups. Volleyball players of both sexes and female teachers were the lowest groups on the SSS.

These data on elite sports participants, as well as much of the other literature, shows that participants in risky sports tend to be higher overall sensation seekers than participants in less risky sports involving fewer unique kinds of experiences. The difference in the Total scores is produced primarily by high scores on TAS and ES subscales. High scores on Dis and BS can be found in other groups not practicing risky sports. TAS may represent the physical risk-taking element, whereas ES suggests the reward in novel sensation and experience from the risky activities. Their own evaluations of risk bear out the sug-

SSS-T

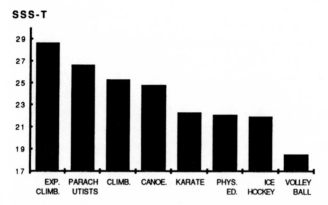

Figure 6.1. Comparisons of various sports groups on the Sensation Seeking Scale Total score (SSS-T). From unpublished data by Breivik (1991a). With permission from author.

gestion that maximizing risk is not the goal of their activities. On a risk scale elite performers in risk sports say that they would take only a medium physical risk, only slightly higher than what military recruits rate. They think that the objective risk in their sport is high, but not "very high." They think that their friends regard them as bolder than they actually are. Although they are above average in risk in achievement-competitive situations, they are about the same as students and military recruits in economic risks.

The elite performers were mostly in their late 20s, had a high educational background, and their fathers often had jobs that required physical or social risks, whereas their mothers had jobs with lower risks than those of recruits. The author does not mention the jobs of the sportsmen but notes that a third of them felt their sport was more important than their job, and regarded their fellow participants as a special subculture. One can speculate that among those whose jobs fully satisfy their sensation-seeking needs there is less need for extracurricular sensation seeking through risky sports. The next part of this chapter will explore the possible self-selection of high and low sensation seekers in specific vocations according to the possibilities for variety, excitement, change, and adventure in the vocations.

Vocations, vocational interests, and job satisfaction

Many factors may determine the choice of a vocation. One's intelligence and education put certain limits on the jobs that are possible. Unfortunately for poorly educated high sensation seekers, most of the unskilled jobs available for them are monotonous and uninteresting. Having no job is rather boring too unless one finds something else exciting to do. Very often the only exciting things in lower socioeconomic class neighborhoods are crime and drugs. Employment opportunities, financial need, and salaries play a role in vocational choice in the middle class. While in school, adult role models may be important in vocational choice. For most jobs there are different motivations influencing their attractiveness for different individuals. One person might become a policeman because of the adventure and excitement in the job, and another might be attracted by the civil service security. High sensation seekers might choose boring jobs in banking or accountancy in order to earn a lot of money, buy expensive sports cars, and travel to exotic places in their leisure time.

Personality is just one of the factors influencing our choice of vocations. However, it can be a crucial one in determining job satisfaction. The low sensation seeker who takes a risky job calling for many changes and unpredictability of circumstances from one day to the next may experience a great deal of stress on the job and perform suboptimally while under stress. The high sensation seeker who, lured by the salary, takes a monotonous, routine job is unlikely to be satisfied in his or her work. People who choose a vocation strictly on economic grounds sometimes underestimate how long an eight hour day can be when there is no challenge or interest in the activities they must perform during those hours.

Drug abusers who had formerly worked on an automobile assembly line, and were now in a therapeutic community, told me that they started by getting high on weekends, and then progressed to taking drugs as soon as they got off work in the afternoon. Finally, they had to get high in the parking lot before going in to work, simply in order to face a day on the line. Eventually they found a more stimulating line of work, full of excitement and adventure and with excellent wages. They bought and sold drugs.

Risky vocations

Musolino and Hershenson (1977) asked personnel specialists to rank 10 occupations according to the amount of risk taking involved in the job, with risk taking defined as placing the safety of oneself or others in jeopardy. The listing in order of judged riskiness is given in Table 6.3. Test pilot was judged to be the riskiest followed by air traffic controller in second place and policeman and fireman in third and fourth ranks for riskiness. The least risky occupation was judged to be librarian, the next least risky was civil service–clerical, and the next was accountant.

Table 6.3. *Rank order classification of occupational risk taking*

Occupation	Mean rating	Rank for riskiness
Test pilot	1.92	1
Air traffic controller	2.50	2
Policeman	2.58	3
Fireman	3.00	4
Psychologist	5.33	5
College professor	6.75	6
College student	7.42	7
Accountant	7.50	8
Civil service – Clerical	8.75	9
Librarian	9.08	10

Source: Table 1, p. 360, from "Avocational sensation seeking in high and low risk taking occupations," by R. F. Musolino & D. B. Hershenson, 1977, *Journal of Vocational Behavior, 10,* 358–365. Copyright 1977 by Academic Press. Reprinted by permission.

Air traffic controllers. The investigators then compared two groups: male air traffic controllers, a vocation near the top of the risk scale, and male civil servants and college students, both groups at the low end of the risk scale. The air traffic controllers scored significantly higher than the civil servants and college students on the General and all of the subscales of the SSS IV. The risks taken by air controllers on their jobs are, of course, physical risks for others rather than themselves. However, the job is reported to be highly stressful. Apparently, those who work at it do take risks for themselves outside of the job. One would expect that someone in a risky job would avoid additional risks outside of the job and try to restore an "optimal level of arousal" by doing nonrisky relaxing things. However, one of the largest differences between the controllers and the civil servants is on the TAS scale, suggesting involvement in physical risk-taking activities.

Military and paramilitary jobs. Sport parachutists and sky divers are generally high sensation seekers, as reported in the previous section on sports. Parachutists in the military are usually a select group of volunteers. Are these professionals also high sensation seekers? Breivik (1991a) compared Norwegian paratroopers with civilian sport parachutists and ordinary military recruits. The paratroopers scored higher than the ordinary recruits on TAS, Dis, BS, and Total SSS, but did not differ from the sports parachutists except on ES, on which the sports parachutists scored higher.

Montag and Birenbaum (1986) compared male applicants for risky security-related jobs in Israel with applicants for less dangerous jobs on the Hebrew version of the SSS. Those seeking the more dangerous job scored significantly higher on the Total SSS, and on three of the four subscales, TAS, ES, and BS. Air force recruits in the Swedish air force were compared with randomly selected conscripts by Hallman, Klintberg, Oreland, et al. (1990). The pilots were significantly higher than the conscripts on the SSS IV TAS and Dis subscales, the KSP Monotony Avoidance and Impulsivity scales. Somewhat different results were reported for American preflight naval students beginning their training. Compared with male college students, they were significantly higher on TAS, like the Swedish pilots, but *lower* on ES, Dis, and BS. However, the authors suggest that the lower scores of the fliers on the latter scales may have been influenced by a social desirability response set, a measure of which correlated negatively with Dis and ES.

Biersner and LaRocco (1983) reported similar findings for American navy divers. Compared with the American norm group of college students, the divers scored significantly higher on TAS but lower on the more social and less socially desirable forms of sensation seeking, Dis and ES. However in this case the risk-taking group was older (mean age = 30) than the college student norm group. Since SSS scores drop with age, the divers may not have differed from the students on the Dis and ES scales, and the difference on TAS may have been larger than it was if the groups had been equated for age.

Firemen, policemen, and other risky occupations. Zaleski (1984a) found that a group of Polish men working in risky occupations (firemen, mountain rescue men, and mine rescue men) scored higher than controls only on the Dis scale. They scored lower than men engaging in risky sports on the TAS subscale. These results suggest that civilians who have physically risky jobs are not attracted to these jobs because of the physical risk but are disinhibited types of sensation seekers. Differences in social class and education might also affect these forms of sensation seeking, because the TAS scale is loaded with middle-class activities like skiing, whereas the working class may be more likely to use social drinking, fighting, and casual sex as their forms of sensation seeking. But an exception to this interpretation is found in the results of Goma, Perez, and Torrubia (1988) comparing firemen and students on a Spanish version of the SSS. The firemen were significantly higher on the Total, TAS, and ES scales of the SSS, but did not differ from students on the Dis scale.

Much police work consists of monotonous routine duties, despite the dramatizations of more exciting events in the media. The patrolman walks his beat or cruises in his patrol car with only an occasional chase or encounter to liven his days or put him at risk. Many are in administrative jobs where there is nothing but desk work. Others spend long hours in stakeouts or sitting along the highway in patrol cars. Levin and Brown (1975) compared a group of patrolmen from semirural areas of Virgina with jailers. The patrolmen were significantly higher than the jailers on General and TAS scales of the SSS IV. But the group of jailers was older than the patrolmen and when an age correction was applied to the data, the jailers were higher than the patrolmen on boredom susceptibility and apparently no differences were found on the other scales.

Carlson and Lester (1980) devised a thrill and adventure–seeking scale designed specifically for policemen with items asking about preferences in risk taking, such as whether they would prefer to wear bullet-proof jackets or carry guns off-duty. State police officers had higher scores on this scale than municipal police officers, and officers in the suburbs had higher scores than city police officers. However, these differences could reflect differences in appraised risk. Because crime rates in the city are generally higher than those in the suburbs or country, the city officer probably feels more need to avoid unnecessary risks in his or her work. Although well-controlled studies done under conditions where social desirability would not affect scores (e.g., anonymity while taking the test) have not been done, the results thus far do not suggest that policemen are uniformly high sensation seekers. In view of the military studies (Hallman, Klintberg, Oreland, et al., 1990; Mongtag & Birenbaum, 1986) it would be interesting to compare police who volunteer for special units engaging in risky operations with those who prefer desk or routine patrol jobs.

Some insights into the background, personal motivations, and personality of those who choose very risky occupations can be gleaned from an interview study by Piet (1987) of six of the world's highest ranking "stunt men" (actually one of these was a woman). "All subjects evidence an early search for varied and risky experience and for vigorous activity, a low boredom threshold, and weak inhibitory effects of possible aversive consequences of one's own actions" (p. 209). However, all said that the actual risks of their jobs were "relatively small" because of their skill and planning. They felt capable of reducing the risks to a minimum through their careful preparations, skills, and concentration at the time of the stunt. Some said they were more afraid of risks they couldn't control like the hazards of everyday life (e.g., driving on the expressway). Piet suggests that their ability to concentrate and control fear when under stress suggests a "strong nervous system" (Strelau, 1983). Arousal or excitement was not the reward of the risky activity. Rather the reward was the sense of mastery and competence in handling the challenge.

Nonrisky but stimulating occupations

Many occupations are not risky in the physical sense of risk but may attract high sensation seekers because they offer varied and interesting activities, although in the case of journalists they are sometimes in situations where they are close to those actually taking physical risks. Hirschowitz and Nell (1983) found that South African journalists scored higher than other types of professionals on the Total, ES, Dis, and BS scales of the SSS V. Umapathy and Suvarna (1988) compared Indian journalists to controls matched for age and sex. The journalists scored higher on the Total, TAS, and ES scales. Taking the two studies together, journalists seem to have a high level of general sensation seeking, with an emphasis on experience seeking in both studies.

Medicine is an area that may offer varied and interesting activities with some risk taking on the behalf of others. Golding and Cornish (1987), however, found that English medical students scored lower than arts and sciences and agriculture students on the General SSS. However, sensation seeking may determine what type of medical activities physicians prefer. Irey (1974) compared professionals and paraprofessionals, including physicians and psychologists, who performed voluntary work in crisis intervention centers with those who limited themselves to professional practice or teaching. The traditional physicians were lower on sensation seeking than the emergency room physicians and psychologists. A similar kind of finding emerged from a study comparing female rape crisis counselors with pediatric nurses. The rape crisis counselors scored higher on Dis and ES scales of the SSS IV (Irey, 1974). Irey describes the rape crisis counselors as "open-minded . . . nonanxious, relatively assertive, profeminist, and whose mood of vigor and activity leads them to seek out and enjoy new experiences" (p. 1133).

Psychotherapist's styles, particularly in regard to their activity in interactions with patients, could be affected by their sensation-seeking trait. Berzins and others have studied the characteristics differentiating therapists who are relatively more successful with schizophrenics (A type) from those who are more successful with neurotics (B type). Berzins, Dove, and Ross (1972) found that B types tend to be risk takers with strong needs for change and new sensations and weak needs for harm avoidance. Kuhlberg and Franco (1976) correlated a personality scale developed to differentiate the two types and found that the B tendency was significantly and positively correlated with the SSS General scale in both men and women. The authors speculate that the B type therapist may become impatient with schizophrenics because of the patients' wariness and low verbal output, and because the therapists are bored, they may push the patient too fast before a basic trust has been built up. Schizophrenics tend to be low sensation seekers and can be overwhelmed with too much emotional intensity or confrontation.

Vocational interests

Interest patterns among students who are not yet specialized in a specific vocational field may not predict their eventual vocation but may indicate what they would like to do in terms of their personalities. Pemberton (1971) correlated the General SSS with a scale of academic temperaments. He found that sensation seeking correlated positively with interests in the humanities and social sciences (including psychology) and negatively with interest in the biological sciences. An interest in economics (business administration) was not correlated with the SSS. However, Farley and Dionne (1972) related the SSS to a scale of values and found that the SSS correlated positively with aesthetic values and negatively with economic values.

The Strong Vocational Interest test measures the extent to which subjects' responses on the test compare with scales empirically derived by comparing test item responses of people actually in specific occupations. Each scale is named after the occupation of the particular vocational group used in its development. For male college students the SSS correlated positively with scales derived from the "helping professions," including psychologist, physician, psychiatrist, and social worker. The SSS correlated negatively with many vocations in the area of business, including banker, purchasing agent, and accountant (Kish & Donnenwerth, 1969, 1972). Of course, the helping professions involve more variety and stimulating social interactions than the usual routine transactions of business. But to some extent the association between sensation seeking and vocational interests may be influenced by the times. In the period (during the Vietnam War) when these studies were done, college students were less vocationally oriented and business was regarded by many as something very "straight" and associated with conformist and conservative political attitudes. They may have been right, but students today seem to have many of these same business values. The media have created an image of the adventurous, sexy, risk-taking businessperson. Even more important, there are fewer jobs for straight liberal arts graduates and what jobs there are require graduate training and pay little in comparison with careers in business. The sensation-seeking students today may be more focused on the activities they can pursue in their leisure time with the money they will make in business jobs.

The results for female students in the same study were quite different. Only one Strong scale correlated positively with the SSS: lawyer. At this time very few women went into the law. Negative correlations with sensation seeking included most of the occupations then regarded as conventional occupational choices for women: housewife, elementary school teacher, teacher of home economics, and dietician. All of these revolve around the home or children. Modern feminism was in its infancy when these data were collected, but the higher sensation seeking women were obviously beginning to defy the gender stereotypes of work.

Oleszkiewicz (1982) studied the vocational preferences of male Polish students in their last year of high school, about the time when they had to make vocational decisions. In many countries in Europe, specialization occurs quite early in college, because students applying for higher education must apply for a specific vocationally related area of study. A list of 44 vocations was drawn up and the subjects were asked to choose the three most preferred and the three least preferred occupations. All of the occupations on the list were rated along four dimensions according to the degree to which they provided intellectual-cognitive stimulation, social responsibility, physical danger (vs. safer jobs), and "new sensations and experiences." The latter dimension, of obvious relevance to sensation seeking, included vocations requiring traveling or changes of work place, in contrast with desk jobs. Job preferences in this dimension were positively related to scores on the Polish SSS General, TAS, and BS scales. Rejection of vocations requiring change was related to low scores on the same sensation-seeking scales and on ES and Dis scales as well. A preference for dangerous occupations was positively related to TAS only, and a rejection of such vocations was related to low scores on TAS and ES. These data obtained from students closer to actual vocational choices than the American students described earlier show that a sensation-seeking trait plays a role in job choice, even in a society where choice is much more limited by governmental quotas.

The study by van den Berg and Feij (1988) takes the vocational interest one step closer to the actual vocation by studying people applying for specific types of jobs at a commercial placement office in the Netherlands. None of these job types involved risky work. Two of the four subscales of Feij et al.'s (1982) Dutch SSS differentiated among the applicants for 12 types of jobs. On the risk-taking or TAS scale the highest-scoring groups were those applying for technical and organizational sales work; the lowest-scoring groups were those interested in medical-social record keeping and business bookkeeping. Obviously the former pair involves more variety, social stimulation, and a greater outlet for extraversion than the latter pair. The other scale differentiating all groups was BS. The highest two groups on this scale were the commercial salespersons and accountants. The latter is difficult to understand in view of previous findings. It would seem that a boredom-susceptible accountant would have to be a misfit unless he or she was keeping the books for the Mafia. The lowest two group on BS were the same as for the TAS scale, the medical-social record keepers and the business book-keepers.

Little research has been done on the characteristics of job applicants who are successful in getting a job compared with those who are not. Cellini and Lorenz (1983) studied former prisoners who were attempting to find employment with the help of the Safer Foundation Job Club, which prepares the ex-offenders for productive employment and trains them in job application methods. The group studied consisted entirely of ex-offender, black males from the inner city of Chicago. One month after completing the program, the clients were contacted to see if they had found a job. About half of the group had done so. This employed group was compared with the still-unemployed group on the SSS form V. The difference on a vocabulary test was not significant, indicating that verbal skills were not the crucial factor determining employability. The employed group was significantly higher than the unemployed group on the Total and Dis scales of the SSS. This finding is surprising since one might think that more disinhibited ex-offenders might not be the best bet for employment. However, disinhibition may be related to certain social skills that are important in making an impression on prospective employers. The subsequent employment history, however, was not studied. One might predict subsequent job problems in this group, depending on the nature of their jobs and consequent job satisfaction.

Job satisfaction

What happens when high sensation seekers have a monotonous job? Anecdotal evidence suggests that they become highly dissatisfied and may cope with their boredom by using alcohol and drugs. Perone, DeWaard, and Baron (1979) actually investigated the relationship between sensation seeking and work satisfaction in a group of young adult male industrial workers. The group of workers was recruited from their local union offices. Drug use was determined by a survey. Job satisfaction was determined by two kinds of surveys concerning their real job, and by response to a simulated job consisting of a monotonous signal detection task. They worked 10 4-hour days

on this job and were paid a base rate plus a bonus for correct detections of
movement on a meter. The job somewhat resembles that of people in atomic
plants whose work consists only of monitoring meters. Not surprisingly,
given the lack of stimulation in the work, there were increases in tension,
depression, anger, and fatigue states as the day progressed. The General SSS
and ES scale were negatively and significantly related to both the indexes of
satisfaction with their real job, and two of the three indexes of satisfaction on
the simulated job. The Dis scale related negatively to satisfaction in their real
jobs, but not significantly with satisfaction in the simulated job. Job satisfaction was inversely related to negative moods, particularly fatigue, on the
jobs. Surprisingly, there was no relationship between job satisfaction and
drug use. If drug use is related to job satisfaction, as was found in some
other studies, the relationship may be mediated through sensation seeking
since sensation seekers are more likely to use drugs (Chapter 9). Although
high sensation seekers are likely to be dissatisfied with monotonous jobs, it
is not a foregone conclusion that they will attempt to cope through the use of
drugs. They may find activities outside of work that compensate for the
tedious hours on the job. But a more likely outcome is that they will
eventually quit the job. The next study attempted to predict the intention to
leave the job.

Van den Berg and Feij (1991) used personality tests, including the Dutch
SSS, measures of job characteristics, and measures of work stress and job
satisfaction to predict the intention to leave the job among employees of a
Dutch organization. The subjects were tested as job applicants and, 1.5 years
after starting the job, they were sent the measures of work, stress, job
satisfaction, and intent to leave. The results were analyzed with a LISREL
path model. After some initial modification a model was developed that fit
the data better than other models (Figure 6.2). Sensation seeking, work
stress, and job satisfaction directly predicted the intent to leave, with the
latter showing the most powerful prediction. High sensation seekers who
were under work stress and dissatisfied with the job were most likely to
intend leaving it. Work stress was related to personality traits of anxiety and
achievement motivation, and negatively related to job satisfaction. Jobs
characterized as dynamic, autonomous, and structured were most likely to be
satisfying. The model shows, however, that sensation seeking predicts the
intent to leave independently of job satisfaction. This may reflect the need
for change in sensation seekers, regardless of satisfaction with the current
job.

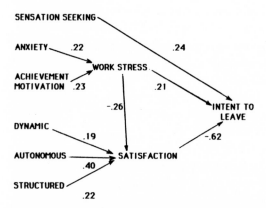

Figure 6.2. Structural parameters for LISREL model predicting work stress, job satisfaction, and intent to leave job. From "Selection and work redesign in an attempt to retain information technology professionals," by P. T. van den Berg & J. A. Feij, 1991. In H. Schuler & W. Stehle (Eds.), *Eignungs diagnostik in Forschung und Praxis: Psychologische Information für Auswahl, Beratung und Förderung von Mitarbeiten*, pp. 350–353.

Summary

Those who participate in athletics in general tend to be higher sensation seekers than those who do not participate, but the results vary unpredictably as a function of gender, level of school grade, type of school, and extent of athletic participation. High-risk sports attract more high than low sensation seekers, and medium-risk sports like body contact sports also attract high sensation seekers. Sensation seeking is not related to low-risk sports requiring intense effort and constant training and practice, and some of these, such as long-distance running, are more attractive to low sensation seekers. Generally, the participants in risky sports differ from others on the General, Total, and ES scales, but rarely on the Dis scale. There are exceptions, such as expert skiers who, in contrast to less experienced skiers, are high on all sensation-seeking scales. The results suggest that those who engage in risky sports are interested in a broad range of thrill-seeking outdoor activities that provide novel and stimulating experiences, but they are not necessarily social sensation seekers nor are they necessarily boredom susceptible. Interview data suggests that the risk is not an attraction, and is reduced as much as possible by developing the skills required for the activity, careful planning for the activity, and intense concentration at the time of the activity. Although observers regard their activities as very risky, elite performers in risky activities tend to feel that the risk is minimized by their skills and preparations.

Sensation seeking is only one of many motives and traits involved in vocational selection. Risky vocations do tend to attract higher sensation seekers, but sometimes the difference is confined to the General, Total, TAS, or ES scales. High sensation seekers who have risky jobs often seek additional sensations involving risk taking in their off-job hours. Even some professions that provide interesting activities without much risk, like journalism, seem to attract high sensation seekers. Male students interested in the "helping professions," and male and female students interested in the social sciences and humanities in general, are higher sensation seekers than those interested in business and economics in general. Persons working in the helping professions, like psychiatry and clinical psychology, are not necessarily sensation seekers, but the type of work or style of psychotherapy they prefer may depend on their sensation seeking needs. Sensation seekers among women tend to be the ones interested in traditionally male occupations like law, and the low sensation-seeking women were more interested in jobs that are more traditional, including housewife. These data were collected in the 1970s and there have been some changes in attitude in regard to business and some newer studies are needed here. Polish studies suggest that persons who prefer occupations requiring travel or frequent changes of work tend to be higher sensation seekers than those who prefer a desk job in one location.

Sensation seeking is inversely related to job satisfaction in jobs where the work itself is monotonous and does not require much skill or decision making. Persons who are dissatisfied are more likely to quit their jobs, but one study showed the sensations seekers were more likely to quit regardless of job satisfaction. High sensation seekers are best suited for jobs where there are varied activities and challenges. Low sensation seekers probably function best on jobs where the work problems are predictable and routine. Jobs like those in the helping professions, saleswork, and journalism, where there are constantly changing interpersonal challenges, are good for high sensation seekers. Thrill and adventure seekers are, of course, best suited to work in the physically risky vocations like pilots, police, and fireman. However, within any group such as the military, the high sensation seekers may seek the more challenging and risky assignments, like parachutist or commando units.

While there are moments of stress and risk in most of these fields most of the time the duties can be quite monotonous. It is somewhat paradoxical that high sensation seekers are involved in work where they must cruise for hours looking at nothing but clouds or dark sky and instrument panels, or sit at a desk watching a computer screen, or sit in a patrol car watching people go by, or in a police office filling out forms, or in a fire station polishing the fire engine. It is the rarer moments when action is demanded and danger threatens that the high sensation seekers come into their natural element. At such times the low sensation seeker is probably less effective because the high arousal is more aversive and inhibiting to them. Sensation seekers who combine TAS and Dis may react to boredom by engaging in more antisocial activities. The high sensation-seeking soldier stuck in routine garrison activities during peacetime may get into trouble and be court-martialed because of arousal-seeking behavior arising from a chronic state of boredom.

Sports and work are major sources of sensation for only a minority. Sadly, most work, particularly for those with less education, is monotonous and unarousing. The primary source of stimulation for most persons is other people. Sociability is characteristic of our species. Apart from serving attachment needs and instrumental purposes, social interaction provides stimulation and arousal. Sexuality is a type of social interaction in which high and pleasurable arousal may be experienced. For many people, particularly among young adults, it is a major mode of sensation seeking. But novelty is a major factor in arousal and habituation applies to interpersonal relationships as well as simpler stimuli. The next chapter will examine the role of sensation seeking in sex, love, and pre- and postmarital relationships.

7

Social, sexual, and marital relationships

Social relationships are a major source of stimulation and arousal for most people but the arousal can be positive or negative depending on the other people involved. An extravert enjoys the company of a wider variety of people than an introvert and parties are more enjoyable for extraverts than introverts. However, a boring person can reduce arousal or increase irritation. Sensation seekers value stimulating people, but are susceptible to boredom and therefore the stimulation value of the other person is crucial in their relationships. This chapter will explore the social interactions of sensation seekers from reactions to strangers to marital relations.

General sociability and social reactions

Sensation seeking is positively related to extraversion (E), as measured by Eysenck's scales, but only to a low degree. A survey of 14 studies found a median correlation between General or Total SSS and E of only .25 (Zuckerman, 1979a). Sensation seeking is more closely aligned with the P than the E dimension in multifactorial comparisons (Chapter 3).

The first SSS was developed to predict reactions to sensory deprivation on the assumption that persons with strong needs for varied sensations would become more uncomfortable and anxious in invariant environments. Sensation seekers developed more motoric restlessness than low sensation seekers in either sensory deprivation or social isolation conditions in which they were confined and socially isolated but with some variation in visual and auditory stimulation (Zuckerman, Persky, Hopkins, et al., 1966). Another experiment was designed to test the factor of social isolation contrasted with a confinement condition that included another person in the room (Zuckerman, Persky, Link, & Basu, 1968). Subjects in different groups were confined in sensory deprivation, social isolation, or social confinement conditions. The latter condition consisted of confinement in a small experiment-cubicle for 8 hours with another person with whom they could converse. All subjects were also studied on another day when they were not confined to the laboratory during the 8 hour period.

As expected, the social confinement condition was less stressful than the other conditions, particularly the full sensory deprivation one. However, there were some negative reactions in some subjects, particularly hostility, impatience, and depression. Surprisingly, it made little difference if friends or strangers were confined together.

Correlations between the General SSS and reactions to sensory deprivation and social isolation conditions were not significant, but the SSS correlated negatively with six of the nine indexes of stress in the social confinement condition. Low sensation seekers tended to be more stressed than high sensation seekers, as indicated by depression, hostility, and somatic symptom change scores, measures of tedium and unreality stress, and levels of adreno-cortical activity.

What were the sources of stress for low sensation seekers in this kind of close confinement? Experimenters noticed that the high sensation seekers paired with a low sensation seeker seemed to dominate the situation by talking more. Unfortunately, no systematic observation of behaviors during confinement was made. However, other research suggests typical social reactions in high sensation seekers that might account for the negative reactions of low sensation seekers to confinement with another person.

Subjects in one study were asked to describe their usual modes of conflict resolution in reaction to a friend, a professor, and a parent using an inventory designed to assess conflict resolution (Pilkington, Richardson, & Utley, 1988). No effects due to sensation seeking were found for males, but high sensation-seeking females dominated more and obliged less in conflict situations than low sensation seekers. It is interesting that need for dominance, as measured by a questionnaire, tends to correlate significantly with sensation seeking in women, but not in men (Zuckerman, 1979a, table 6.9, p. 151). If high sensation-seeking women attempted to dominate the other person in the experiment, this could have produced the hostility and stress reported by the low sensation seekers.

Some people like to engage in self-disclosure when they have to spend a lot of time with someone. Such self-disclosure, particularly from strangers, can be upsetting to other people. Demands for self-disclosure can be even more discomfiting. High sensation seekers engage in more self-disclosure and encourage self-disclosure in both casual and close friends (Franken, Gibson, & Mohan, 1990). If someone insists on self-disclosure and the other person is made uncomfortable, they can usually find some pretext to escape the situation. But in a situation of close confinement for 8 hours such escape is difficult and low sensation seekers would have to listen to what they didn't care to hear and be asked questions they didn't want to answer.

Most people feel more attracted to people who think like themselves than to people who are drastically different in outlook, since this reduces the possibility of conflict and enhances communication. Although most people may want to associate with people who are similar to themselves, high sensation seekers are relatively more attracted to persons perceived as dissimilar to themselves (Thornton, Ryckman, & Gold, 1981; Williams, Ryckman, Gold, & Lenney, 1982). Mehrabian (1975) found that low-arousal seekers preferred to affiliate with persons just like themselves, whereas high-arousal seekers liked to associate with persons of an intermediate level of difference from themselves. High sensation seekers are more likely than low sensation seekers to pick a topic for discussion on which they know they will disagree with the other person than a topic on which they think there will be agreement (Thornton et al., 1981). High sensation seekers value difference and conflict as a source of positive arousal, whereas low sensation seekers tend to avoid differences and controversies with others.

Behavior in nonintimate interactions

High sensation seekers are attracted to each other, but how quickly can people recognize the sensation-seeking qualities of the other person, and can people involved in a relationship correctly estimate the sensation-seeking levels of their partners? Student experimenters working with selected samples of high and low sensation seekers have told me that they can recognize a high or a low within a few moments of the time they enter the experimental room. Experimenters are "blind" as to the sensation-seeking status of the subject, but checking their impressions after the experiment is over, they are almost invariably right. They say that high sensation seekers look around and examine the room and apparatus, ask questions, interact with the experimenter, and are generally curious. Low sensation seekers are more passive. They do not look around much, do not ask questions, and do what they are told. They are "good subjects" in that they follow instructions to the letter and do not make problems. Of course, these are impressions that we have never checked out in an empirical study.

A former student swore that high and low sensation seekers looked different and actually did a study using shoulder and head photographs of subjects (Daitzman, unpublished). He gave the photographs to judges and, after describing the trait of sensation seeking, he asked them to try to pick out the high and low sensation seekers from the photos. Judges were successful in this task well beyond chance levels. Poring over the photographs it was difficult to see any one characteristic that explained their success. Highs seemed to have a little more expressiveness in their faces, and for some unfathomable reason low sensation-seeking males seemed to favor plaid sport shirts!

Cappella and Green (1984) studied nonverbal behavior of sensation seekers during an interview. There were two conditions, one involving a normal distance between interviewer and the subject and the other a close distance. It was hypothesized that high sensation seekers have "wider acceptance regions" and therefore would be less disturbed by the interviewer's intrusion into their "personal space" than low sensation seekers. High sensation seekers exhibited more eye gaze, posture oriented toward (rather than away from) the interviewer, more vocalization with fewer pauses and shorter latencies to respond, and more smiles and laughter. High sensation seekers showed more of the behavior associated with affiliation and approach and less of the behavior associated with hesitancy and self-monitoring. This spontaneity and openness in the behavior of high sensation seekers may be what makes them distinguishable from low sensation seekers.

Rowland, Franken, Williams, and Heatherton (1988) showed subjects 20-minute segments of the films *Arthur, Rocky, Night Shift,* and *Odd Couple* and asked judges to take the SSS for themselves and then as they thought one of the characters in the films would answer it. There was a high degree of agreement on the sensation-seeking qualities of the film characters: Arthur in *Arthur,* Bill in *Night Shift,* and Oscar in *Odd Couple* were judged to be high sensation seekers; Chuck in *Night Shift,* and Felix in *Odd Couple* were at the extreme low end of the scale; and Rocky was judged to be a middle-range sensation seeker. There was no projection based on the sensation-seeking qualities of the subjects themselves since there was no correlation between their own scores and those they assigned to the film characters. Of course, these film characters were broadly drawn, but how well can people rate real people they know?

The authors recruited 20 heterosexual couples from undergraduate classes and asked each partner in a pair to take the SSS for themselves, and again as they thought their partner would answer it. Subjects were highly successful in predicting the scores of their partners. Women's estimates of their male partners responses correlated .66 with the partners' scores and mens' predictions of their female partners' responses correlated .59 with the womens' actual scores. High sensation-seeking women tended to overestimate their partners' scores and low sensation-seeking women tended to underestimate their partners' scores. Women, but not men, seem to want to believe that their partners' levels of sensation seeking are closer to their own than they actually are. One might expect that increased duration of the relationship would increase knowledge about the partner and accuracy of prediction. However, duration of the relationship made no difference for males and accuracy *decreased* for women with increased length of the relationship. Perhaps women in relationships for a longer time expected their partners to change more in their direction on sensation seeking. Sensation seeking may be a trait where congruence is more important for women than for men.

Love relationships: premarital

Poets and songwriters seem to feel that love is undefinable, but undaunted psychologists have not only defined it but attempted to measure it. Two widely used tests are Rubin's (1970) Loving and Liking scales and the Love Attitudes Scale (C. Hendrick & Hendrick, 1986). Rubin's scale is a general measure of love, in the sense of absorption in and emotional dependence on the other, and liking, in the sense of esteem for the other. Hendrick and Hendrick classify love into six different "styles" of loving:

Eros is passionate, focused, and commited love, or romantic love in the traditional sense like the feelings of the lovers in *Romeo and Juliet.*
Ludus represents a more playful, less commited type of love with more autonomy for partners. Love is a game for ludic lovers.
Storge identifies love more closely with friendship than with passion.
Pragma is a selection of a mate based on appraisal of the mate's potentials for a long-term relationship. It is love from the head rather than the heart.
Agape is a selfless devotion to the loved one. It is idealized Christian love.
Manic love is a misnomer; it should be called "anxious" love, since it is an obsessive, dependent, emotionally tense, possessive type of relationship.

Given the variety and novelty-seeking characteristic of Ludic love, Richardson, Medvin, and Hammock (1988) predicted that it would relate more strongly than other love styles to sensation seeking. Table 7.1 shows the correlations between sensation seeking and love styles. As expected, Ludus correlated significantly and positively with the Total and all of the SSS subscales, although somewhat more highly with Dis and BS than with ES and TAS. High sensation seekers tend to play at love and have less commitment to their relationships. At a weaker level, Total sensation seeking, Dis, and TAS correlated negatively with Pragma. High sensation seekers are not very pragmatic and do not appraise partners in terms of their long-term

Table 7.1. *Correlations between Sensation Seeking Scales (SSS)*
and love styles

Love styles	SSS				
	Total	TAS	ES	Dis	BS
Eros	.08	−.02	.09	.14	.02
Ludus	.35*	.16*	.19**	.39**	.30**
Storge	−.10	−.02	−.11	−.06	−.15*
Pragma	−.19**	−.16*	−.05	−.18**	−.14
Manic	.02	.06	−.03	−.01	.03
Agape	−.11	.02	−.18*	−.15*	−.03

Note: TAS Thrill and Adventure Seeking; ES = Experience Seeking; Dis = Disinhibition; BS = Boredom Susceptibility.
*$p<.05$.
**$p<.01$.
Source: Part of table 4, p. 649, from "Love styles, relationship experience, and sensation seeking: A test of validity," by D. R. Richardson, N. Medvin, & G. Hammock, 1988, *Personality and Individual Differences, 9,* 645–651. Copyright 1988 by Pergamon Press.

marriage potentials. They are probably more interested in the immediate gratifications than in future prospects. S. Hendrick and Hendrick (1987a) also correlated the SSS with these love scales. The Total, Dis, and BS scales were significantly related to Ludus, but in this study TAS and ES were not related at all to the Ludic style.

Richardson et al. did not report the relationships between sensation seeking and the Rubin scales. However, Thornquist, Zuckerman, and Exline (1991) used these scales in a study of relationships between college students. They combined the loving and liking scores, and global ratings of loving and liking, together with ratings of satisfaction in the relationship into a single Relationship Satisfaction Index (RSI).

The sensation seeking scores on the SSS Total, ES, and Dis scales of the partners correlated significantly, even when ages of both partners and the length of their relationship were controlled ($r = .39$, .34, and .42 for Total, ES, and Dis respectively). There was evidence for homogamy in these as yet unmarried and noncohabiting couples, although the correlations were not as high as those that have been found in married couples. It could be that the couples most discordant in sensation seeking are the ones who break up before they get married. If this is the case we would expect to find lower satisfaction with their relationships in those who are most discordant on

Table 7.2. *Correlations between Relationship Satisfaction Indexes (RSI)*
and Sensation Seeking Scores (SSS)

SS scale	Own RSI		Other's RSI	
	M SSS/M RSI	F SSS/F RSI	M SSS/F RSI	F SSS/M RSI
Total	−.33**	−.40**	−.28*	−.29*
	(−.24*)	(−.33**)	(−.15)	(−.19)
TAS	−.15	.01	.02	−.19
	(−.12)	(.01)	(.02)	(−.17)
ES	−.23*	−.30*	−.14	−.31*
	(−.15)	(−.27*)	(−.05)	(−.26*)
Dis	−.25*	−.41**	−.11	−.32**
	(−.15)	(−.40**)	(.05)	(−.25*)
BS	−.15	−.53***	−.12	−.04
	(−.14)	(−.52***)	(.01)	(−.01)

Note: Partial correlations (correcting for partner's sensation seeking) are in parentheses. TAS = Thrill and Adventure Seeking; ES = Experience Seeking; Dis = Disinhibition; BS = Boredom Susceptibility; M = Male; F = Female.
*$p<.05$.
**$p<.01$.
***$p<.001$.
Source: "Loving, liking, looking and sensation seeking in unmarried college couples," by M. H. Thornquist, M. Zuckerman, & R. V. Exline, 1991, *Personality and
Individual Differences, 12*, 1283–1242. Copyright 1991 by Pergamon Press. Reprinted by permission.

sensation seeking. The absolute differences in sensation seeking scores were
translated into standard scores. There was a low but significant negative
correlation between the size of the difference and relationship satisfaction for
the women ($r = -.31$) but not for the men. Apparently a difference in
sensation seeking between themselves and their partners is more dissatisfying
to women than to men.

Table 7.2 shows the correlations between each partners' own SSS scores
and their own and their partners' relationship satisfaction indexes (RSIs).
Corrections were also made for the partners' sensation-seeking score levels
using partial correlation. For both men and women, their own SSS Total
score correlated negatively with their own RSIs. High sensation seekers
liked and loved their partners less, were less satisfied and happy in their
relationships, and saw more alternatives for themselves outside of the relationship than low sensation seekers. These relationships with total sensation-
seeking scores were independent of the sensation-seeking scores of their

partners. However, for the men the relationships with the subscales were not significant after controlling for their partners' scores. For women the relationships between RSI and ES, Dis, and BS were significant regardless of their partners scores. Furthermore, the women's ES and Dis scores correlated significantly and negatively with their partners' RSIs, but this was not true for the men. The male partners of high experience-seeking and disinhibiting women were not as satisfied in the relationship as the partners of low sensation seekers, regardless of their own levels of sensation seeking. Once again, the women's sensation seeking seemed to have more effect on the relationship than the mens' levels of the trait. Men do score higher than women on Total score and all subscales except ES (Chapter 4). However, in this study it was the absolute difference rather than the directional difference between male and female partners that related to dissatisfaction in the women. Women were less satisfied regardless of whether their partner was much higher or lower than themselves. Either discrepancy poses particular kinds of problems for the woman. But for both sexes, and for men in particular, high sensation seeking in their partners was associated with dissatisfaction in the relationship.

The effect of individual partners' SSS scores in this study was more powerful than the discrepancy in scores. Given this fact, it would follow that the combination of two high sensation seekers in a relationship would be additively detrimental to their satisfaction, whereas two low sensation seekers should be the most satisfied and commited to each other. The group where one is high and the other is low should be worst for satisfaction from a lack of congruence standpoint, but intermediate in satisfaction based on the idea that the individual SSS scores affect satisfaction more than the discrepancy in scores. Several of the indexes of satisfaction, considered separately, supported the latter interpretation as shown in Table 7.3.

For all of the relationship satisfaction scores shown in Table 7.3, the combination of two low sensation seekers was related to greater satisfaction in both partners and the combination of two high sensation seekers was most detrimental to relationship satisfaction. The group where one was high and the other was low was intermediate for all of the variables except the women's comparison level for alternatives to a woman's present partner. Analyses of the high–low group showed that which partner was the higher made no difference on any of these variables.

Thornquist et al. (1991) also studied eye-gaze and speech patterns of the couples in an interaction situation where they were supposed to arrive at a solution to a problem. Couples sat across a table from each other and periods of mutual and nonmutual eye gaze and speech were recorded by observers

Table 7.3. *Means of three sensation-seeking groups on loving and liking measures*

Groups	n	Male's liking score	Female's alternatives	Male + female liking scores	Sum all scores
High-high	17	86.53^a	3.71^{ab}	179^a	425^a
High-low	22	93.68^b	4.64^a	187^a	440^{ab}
Low-low	15	97.93^b	3.13^b	200^b	458^b

Note: Groups that share at least one superscript (a, b) are not significantly different. Groups that do not share a common superscript are significantly different ($p<.05$). High-High: Both partners scored above the mean on the SSS. High-Low: One partner scored above the mean and the other one below the mean on the SSS. Low-Low: Both partners scored below the mean on the SSS.

from behind a one-way window. Eye gaze was not related to sensation seeking for men, but was related to their belief in how much their partners loved them. The *more* men felt they were loved, the *less* they gazed at their partners. The women's SSS scores were related to many of the eye-gaze and speech patterns. High sensation-seeking women tended to look more at their partners and speak more to them, and this tended to elicit more mutual gaze and speech from their partners. It is interesting that mutual gaze while the female was speaking was correlated with her sensation-seeking score, but mutual gaze when the male was speaking was not correlated with her SSS. Men with high sensation-seeking partners tended to break off a mutual gaze with their partner more than those with lower sensation-seeking partners.

Mutual gaze results in high levels of cortical arousal, and gaze aversion reduces this arousal (Gale, Kingsley, Brookes, & Smith, 1978). The high sensation-seeking woman gazes at a partner as a means of eliciting mutual gaze and speech, thereby increasing her own arousal. This nonverbal demand of the female high sensation seeker does produce reciprocation from her male partner, but his frequent gaze aversion suggests that her gaze stimulant may become too intense for him.

Whereas gaze may serve as an erotic arousal mechanism for women, it seems to be more of a power assertion or even threat mechanism for men. Dominant men tend not to look at subordinates while talking (Exline, Ellyson, & Long, 1975). Among nonhuman primates, a prolonged direct eye stare may elicit either aggression or fear in the recipient of a stare. People living in cities such as New York learn to avoid eye contact with strangers. Many men construe eye contact from a woman as an erotic invitation and eye contact from a man as an aggressive challenge. The low eye contact in the men who felt strongly confident about the love of their partners may have been a reflection of their enhanced power and confidence, whereas the frequent glances of the men who were unsure of the love of their partners may have been a symptom of insecurity.

Premarital sexual attitudes and relationships

Sexuality is a primary form of sensation seeking for many people. Given the needs of high sensation seekers for change and variety, the prediction that they would have greater variety in their sex lives is obvious. Dis contains some items reflecting attitudes toward sexual permissiveness, and BS has items indicating a preference for exciting people. These two scales would be expected to relate most highly to sexual attitudes and activities.

Studies done on college students in the early 1970s showed strong relationships between sensation seeking and both sexual attitudes and behavior. This period represented the onset of the "sexual revolution" in Delaware. Changes in attitudes and behaviors were taking place, particularly among college women. Many women were taking contraceptive pills, thus removing the fear of pregnancy. Gender mixed dorms were instituted. A "task force" on sex was set up and this group started a course in human sexuality for undergraduates, using explicit visual teaching materials and informal lecture formats. The course was oversubscribed for many semesters after its inception, although recent years have seen some falling off in its popularity, perhaps because of recent emphases on AIDS and other venereal disease risks in the course.

Zuckerman, Tushup, and Finner (1976) studied the relationship between sexual attitudes and the SSS in students in the sex course and in other groups from general psychology courses. Two scales for sexual permissiveness were used: One asked about what kind of social relationships made various kinds of sexual activities permissible, and the other asked about what kind of emotional involvement was necessary for the individual to do various sexual things. At one extreme the scale rating said the particular form of sex was all right even if you just met the partner and didn't even know if you liked him or her. At the other extreme the particular activity was rated as only permissible among married people, or if you were deeply in love with the person, or wasn't permissible under any circumstances. Marked sex differences were found on these scales. Female students generally required higher degrees of social and/or emotional relationships to make the more advanced sexual activities permissible. The SSS IV General and all of the subscales except BS were highly correlated with permissiveness of sexuality in terms of both social and emotional relationship criteria, and for both men and women. Although Dis tended to correlate slightly more highly with sexual attitudes than the other SSS subscales, the differences in correlations among the subscales were not great. Even the TAS subscale, whose items have absolutely no relevance to relations between the sexes, correlated highly with sexual attitudes in the males. During the same period, Kish and Donnenwerth (1972) found similarly high correlations between the General SSS and a scale of sexual permissiveness in both male and female students.

Recent studies done in the late 1980s continue to find these relationships between the SSS V and sexual attitudes. The relationship between the Ludic love style and sensation seeking suggested that high sensation seekers would have more permissive sexual attitudes than low sensation seekers. S. Hendrick and Hendrick (1987b) developed multidimensional scales of sexual attitudes and related these to both their love scales and to the SSS V. Their sexual attitude scales included permissiveness (e.g., sex is recreational, and need not be associated with love or even liking); sexual practices (stressing responsibility of both partners for birth control and need for sex education); communion (acceptance of sex within the context of a close love relationship); and instrumentality (egocentric, sex is for one's own pleasure, it is a natural physical function). Ludus love style combined with permissiveness and instrumentality is one of the three factors emerging from a factor analysis. SSS Total, Dis, ES, and BS scales were associated with permissiveness and instrumentality. The correlation ($r = .62$) between Dis and sexual permissiveness was quite high.

All of these studies found associations among a ludus love style, sensation seeking, and sexually permissive attitudes. Like Zuckerman et al. (1976), C. Hendrick and Hendrick (1988) found very large gender differences in ludus and sexual permissiveness. It is interesting that these differences in attitudes toward sex have persisted from the early 1970s to the late 1980s, even though a much higher percentage of the undergraduate female population is currently sexually active. What has happened is that many women have lowered their social and emotional standards for sex (e.g., long acquaintance instead of engagement or marriage, and "liking very much" instead of being "in love") but they still have less permissive attitudes toward sex than men of their own age. The explanation may be either cultural or sociobiological (Gangstead & Simpson, 1990). These persisting sex differences in attitudes toward love and sex may account for part of the sex difference on sensation seeking itself.

Attitudes are often highly related to experience because they set the stage for choices as they become available, or sometimes change after the behavioral events because of the necessity to reduce cognitive dissonance. Zuckerman et al. (1976) found that sexual attitudes of women were related to their

Table 7.4. *Correlations between SSS form IV scales and heterosexual experience*

SSS	Heterosexual activities[a]				No. of heterosexual partners[b]	
	Males (n = 38)	Females (n = 60)	Males (n = 82)	Females (n = 71)	Males (n = 120)	Females (n = 131)
General	.51**	.15	.39**	.29*	.40**	.27
TAS	.44**	.16	.42**	.35**	.47**	.20
ES	.37*	.32*	.45**	.37**	.35**	.28*
Dis	.33*	.43**	.39**	.33*	.42**	.29*
BS	.36*	.29**	.23*	.20	.25*	.20

Note: TAS = Thrill and Adventure Seeking; ES = Experience Seeking; Dis = Disinhibition; BS = Boredom susceptibility.
[a] Data from Zuckerman et al. (1972) and Zuckerman et al. (1976).
[b] Data from both studies.
*p < .05.
**p < .01.
Source: Shortened version of a table from "Sensation seeking," by M. Zuckerman, 1978. In H. London & J. Exner (Eds.), *Dimensions of Personality.* New York: Wiley. Copyright 1978 by John Wiley & Sons, Ltd., Chichester. Reprinted by permission.

sexual activities but the relationships for men were generally not significant. Many of these young men may have had permissive attitudes, but they had not had the opportunity to translate their attitudes into behavior for various reasons, foremost of which may have been the lack of a willing partner.

Scales were developed to measure extent and variety of heterosexual and homosexual activities, and one-item experience scales asked about the number of partners one had sexual experience with. Two studies (Zuckerman, Bone, Neary, Mangelsdorff, & Brustman, 1972; Zuckerman et al., 1976) done in the 1970s found correlations between the SSS IV scales and both variety of heterosexual activities and number of heterosexual partners as shown in Table 7.4. All of the SS scales correlated significantly with a measure combining number and frequency of specific sexual activities and the number of heterosexual partners. Dis was not the subscale correlating most highly with sexual activity as might have been expected from the item content of the subscales. In fact, the TAS scale correlated more highly with sexual activities than the Dis scale, although the differences in correlation were small. For males, at least, sexual experience is related to the broad sensation-seeking tendency rather than to the specific scale (Dis) of greatest relevance. For the women the correlations in the 1972 study were limited to

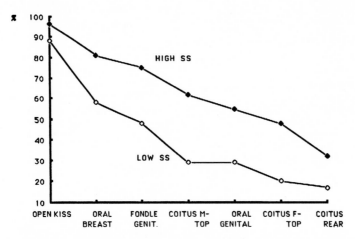

Figure 7.1. Percentages of high and low sensation seekers engaging in specific sexual activities. Based on data from Zuckerman, Neary, & Brustman, 1970, and Zuckerman et al., 1972.

the ES, Dis, and BS scales and Dis was the highest correlate of sexual experience. However, in the 1976 study, using data collected a few years after the start of the sexual revolution, heterosexual activities correlated significantly with a broader range of SS scales in women, including the General, TAS, ES, and Dis scales and Dis was only the third in size of correlation. With the prevalence of sexual activity in the female college population increasing, such activity seems to have become even more of an expression of the broader sensation-seeking tendency.

Heterosexual experience tends to proceed in stages from kissing to manual stimulation, to oral and coital activity, and to varieties in coital positions. All of these activities were tabulated for groups of high and low sensation seekers (General scale) using data from two studies of university students (Zuckermam, Neary, & Brustman, 1970; Zuckerman et al., 1972). Figure 7.1 shows the percentages of high and low sensation seekers engaging in each of 10 sexual activities from kissing to coital entry from the rear position. The two groups did not differ for the more common activities like kissing since even most low sensation seekers had this much experience. But genital stimulation and coitus in various positions were more characteristic of highs than lows. Sexual experience is a function of age and development. For this group in the first years of college during the beginning of the sexual revolution, the differences in practices between high and low sensation seekers were in the middle of the scale. However, virginity became less common among college students in the 1980s so that the curves of both high and low sensation seekers might be moving toward the higher end of the scale, and the scale might have to be extended with more esoteric sexual practices at the higher end.

Masturbation

Masturbation experience was not related to sensation seeking in these studies, but Daitzman and Zuckerman (1980) found that males scoring in the high and low ranges on the Dis scale did differ in the *proportions* of current orgasmic outlet from masturbation and heterosexual coitus. The high sensation seekers were obtaining orgasm relatively more from coitus and less from masturbation than the low sensation seekers. Differences among males' masturbation experience would be hard to find because nearly all males have some masturbatory experience. Differences might be found between female masturbators and nonmasturbators in sensation seeking since their incidence of experience is not as high as it is for males. Differences were not found among college women but were found among married women. In Fisher's (1973) study of young married women, a positive relationship was found between masturbation and sensation seeking in three separate samples. Unlike the male college students who were using masturbation in lieu of coitus, most of these married women were using masturbation to supplement marital coitus.

Homosexual relations

Sensation seeking was not related to homosexual experience or numbers of homosexual partners in these studies, except for a low significant correlation between ES and homosexual activities in the males. However, these groups contained only a small number of subjects with any great degree of homosexual experience. Actually, 24% of the high sensation seekers as compared with 15% of the low sensation seekers reported any kind of homosexual experience (chi-square not significant), but for most it was incidental kinds of experience and not their primary form of sexual activity. In contrast, 62% of the high and 29% of the low sensation seekers had experienced heterosexual coitus, and this difference in frequency was highly significant. Zuckerman and Myers (1983) compared "gay" and nongay male student groups on sensation seeking. The two groups did not differ significantly on any of the SSS V scales. Thus far, it would appear that homosexual and heterosexual males do not differ in sensation seeking, but these conclusions are limited to the college populations. Sensation seeking is probably related to the variety of homosexual activity and the number of homosexual partners within the gay community, just as it is to the variety of heterosexual activity in the heterosexual population. If this is true, it is of great significance for the AIDS epidemic. Whereas variety in some forms of sexual behavior may be the spice of life for those who practice them, it may also be the poison of life for some of them. The study of risky behavior by Horvath and Zuckerman (1993), described in Chapter 5, showed that risky sexual behavior in the general male university student population was related to sensation seeking and impulsivity, and impulsive sensation seekers seemed aware that they are at higher risk for AIDS than their less promiscuous peers.

H. White and Johnson (1988) found that the SSS Dis scale and an impulsivity measure were related to the sexual experience (vs. nonexperience) of both adolescent males and females. This was a longitudinal study and it was also found that the subjects who were still virgins but who scored high on Dis and impulsivity at the first assessment were more likely to engage in sexual relations by the second time of assessment three years later. Thus, Dis was shown to have predictive as well as concurrent validity for sexual activity. However, Dis and impulsivity were not related to consistency or reliability of contraceptive use among the sexually active part of the sample.

Marital relations

Fisher (1973) used the SS General scale in his studies of sexual behavior in young married women. Although some of these data are contained in his book, much of it was reported to me in a personal communication. The SSS correlated with self-ratings of sexual responsiveness in two out of three samples of women, but it did not correlate with relative preference for vaginal or clitoral stimulation or the number of different positions used in marital intercourse. The high sensation-seeking women prefered a higher frequency of intercourse, reported more frequent multiple orgasms, more copious vaginal lubrication during sex, more continued interest in sex during pregnancies, and even reported more sexual arousal during a laboratory session involving no explicit sexual stimulation than the low sensation seekers. The high sensation-seeking married women in this study seemed to be more sexually hyperarousable.

A more recent study of married women (Apt & Hurlbert, 1992) found that high sensation seekers reported more sexual desire, more arousability, and more "erotophilic" attitudes toward sex, but there were no differences between high and low sensation seekers in frequency of sexual intercourse and sexual assertiveness. Despite the stronger sexual desire and arousability of the high sensation seekers, the low sensation-seeking women reported higher marital *and* sexual satisfaction. The paradox of more sexual desire and arousability with less sexual satisfaction in the high sensation-seeking women might have been due to a lower level of desire and arousability in their husbands. Unfortunately, husbands were not assessed in the study.

When there is a discrepancy in sensation seeking between marital partners, it may be that the higher sensation seeker is more likely to be dissatisfied in the relationship and more likely to seek extramarital sources of gratification. When both partners are low in sensation seeking, they are more likely to be satisfied because they both do not have high needs for variety in sexual activities or partners. But if both partners are high sensation seekers, they may both need extramarital sources of stimulation. Covert relationships are often disruptive when discovered. One solution advocated by some couples is comarital sex or ''wife swapping.''

It might be predicted that married persons engaging in comarital sex are higher sensation seekers than more traditionally monogamous or covert extramarital types because of their willingness to take risks for the sake of sexual variety. However, it must be recognized that for many of these couples the comarital arrangement is an attempt to reduce the risks of secret extramarital affairs that can end in divorce, by satisfying their own and their spouses' needs for variety in sexual partners in groups of people with similar needs. Wheeler and Kilmann (1983) solicited comarital couples from clubs devoted to sexual exchanges and compared them with married persons recruited from other kinds of clubs in the area. The comarital couples did not differ from the controls on the SSS II General scale. Unfortunately, the authors did not use the forms of the SSS containing the subscales, and therefore they could not test the more likely association of Dis with comarital sex. Surprisingly, the comarital couples scored higher than the controls on a SD scale, supposedly measuring need for social approval. But then the purpose of these groups is to be able to hide their activities from the general community they live in. They do feel a need to be accepted and a high proportion of them are conservatives and vote Republican.

Assortative mating for sensation seeking

Most people believe that like tends to marry like. In behavioral genetics this homogamous tendency is called *assortative mating*. Although there is good evidence of assortative mating for intelligence, and an even greater degree of assortative mating based on social attitudes, this kind of mate selection does not seem to hold for most personality variables (H. Eysenck, 1990). Ahern, Johnson, Wilson, McClern, and Vandenberg (1982), for instance, give husband–wife correlations for a variety of personality traits and the typical correlations are close to zero. Sensation seeking is an exception. Investigators have found high correlations between SSS scores of spouses in the United States, Germany, and the Netherlands (Farley & Davis, 1977; Farley & Mueller, 1978; Ficher, Zuckerman, & Neeb, 1981; Ficher, Zuckerman, & Steinberg, 1988; Lesnik-Oberstein & Cohen, 1984).

D. Buss et al. (1990) did a study of preferences for mate selection in 37 cultures. The first three highest-ranking traits for both men and women in the entire cross-cultural sample were: (1) kind and understanding; (2) intelligent; (3) exciting personality. It is not clear what an "exciting personality" means to subjects but I suspect it is something like an extraverted high sensation seeker. Because these are all highly desirable traits in a potential mate and there are a limited supply of persons high on these traits, then the highs are attracted to each other and the lows have to make do with each other. Much as the lows would prefer a mate with an exciting personality, providing he or she is also kind and understanding, it is probably just as well that they end up with someone closer to their own low levels of sensation seeking since there is evidence that a lack of congruence on sensation seeking can be a source of marital dissatisfaction.

Congruence in sensation seeking and marital adjustment

Ficher et al. (1981, 1988) found that the correlations between the SSS scores of satisfied couples were higher than the correlations found in couples requesting marital therapy. In the first study (Ficher et al., 1981), the correlations on the Total SSS were .43 for the therapy couples and .76 for the control couples; in the second study the correlations were .12 for the therapy couples and .51 for the controls. The difference between the groups in the first set of correlations was clearly significant, whereas the difference in the second study was only marginally significant. The correlations were significantly higher in the control couples for the BS scale than in the marital therapy couples in both studies. A lack of congruence on boredom susceptibility seems particularly characteristic in dysfunctional couples.

Generally the male partner scores higher than the female on sensation seeking and this was the case in 83% of the control couples. However, in the therapy couples the male partner scored higher than the female partner in only 53% of the couples, and the difference in frequency and the male-minus-female difference scores were significant. In the couples where the male scored higher than the female, it was almost always the female who initiated the contact with the marital therapy clinic, but when the female was higher on the SSS it was more often the male partner who initiated the contact. In the cases where the female was the higher sensation seeker, there were more frequent complaints of impotence and hypertension in the male partners.

In the second study (Ficher et al., 1988) the results were somewhat different, perhaps because of a change in the marital therapy population in the seven year interval (male impotence was less of a problem than lack of sexual desire in either or both partners). The difference between groups on the male-minus-female SSS was not significant, although the difference was in the same direction as in the previous study. In this study it was the males' SSS scores alone that seemed to affect who initiated therapy and the sexual problems, if any. When the male partner was high on the SSS, the female partner initiated the request for therapy in 87% of the cases, but when the male partner was low on sensation seeking, he initiated the request for therapy in 67% of the cases. In couples where the male partner was a low sensation seeker, a preponderance of both partners reported that sexual relations between them were only "tolerable" or "distasteful." In the cases where the male partner was high on the SSS, they both tended to describe their sex lives as "enjoyable" and they came to marital therapy for other reasons. Although there were differences in results in the two studies, it would appear that the partner who is lower in sensation seeking is more likely to be the one who initiates marital therapy, probably because of a dissatisfaction with the behavior of the higher sensation seeker. Sexual problems, like impotence, low sexual desire, or negative sexual attitudes, occur more in the male low sensation seeker than in the high sensation seeker.

Donaldson (1989) studied college couples involved in "intimate dating" or marriage for at least 3 months. He found that congruence in sensation seeking, as measured by the absolute difference between the partners' standardized SSS scores, was highly and positively related to their sexual satisfaction and relationship contentment. For those together for more than a year, the measure of congruence on sensation seeking correlated significantly with all of the SSS IV scales; however, for those married less than a year, only scores on the TAS subscale correlated with sexual satisfaction and contentment in the relationship. Sensation-seeking congruence may become more important in a relationship over time. A discrepancy in sensation-seeking needs may be less important during the initial period of the relationship for the high sensation seeker because there are enough novel things about the partner to keep him or her interested. But if the partner is a low sensation seeker with little changeability, his or her low sensation-seeking tastes and preferences may become more frustrating for the high sensation seeker, and the unpredictable behavior of the higher sensation seeker may become equally bothersome to the low sensation seeking partner. The fact that divorced persons are higher on sensation seeking than married persons, and singles as well in the case of men, suggests that sensation seeking is a risky trait for marriage even among those couples where both partners are high sensation seekers (Zuckerman & Neeb, 1980).

Gibson, Franken, and Rowland (1989) studied the effect of sensation seeking on marital adjustment in married couples at a Canadian university. Marital adjustment was correlated negatively with sensation seeking for the female, but the correlation for males was not significant. High sensation-seeking females had lower marital satisfaction indexes than low sensation seekers, and this difference did not depend on the level of sensation seeking in their husbands. This result is congruent with the findings in the first Ficher et al. (1981) study showing a greater number of higher sensation-seeking women in the marital therapy group, but it is somewhat at odds with the Ficher et al. (1988) findings that the males' sensation seeking was more determinant of who initiated therapy, a putative measure of relative marital dissatisfaction. However, a group requesting marital therapy may be different than persons in the normal population who are merely dissatisfied. Actually, Ficher et al. could find no relationship between relative marital satisfaction (using the same scale of satisfaction used by Gibson et al.) in their control couples and their sensation-seeking scores. The college married couples may be more like the close relationship of nonmarried college couples studied by Thornquist et al. (1991). In these couples, it was also primarily the female partners' SSS score that was negatively related to relationship satisfaction.

High sensation-seeking females tend to be more dominant, assertive, and autonomous in their relationships and therefore they are going counter to the cultural stereotype of ''proper'' female behavior. This may not bother and may even attract a high sensation-seeking male. But if the mate of the high sensation-seeking woman is a low or even a moderate sensation seeker, he may find it difficult to tolerate the unconventional, independent behavior of his partner. Even high sensation-seeking males may have a problem if they are ideologically opposed to a feminist outlook. In marriage and long-term relationships, the need for variety and the high boredom susceptibility of the high sensation seeker may lead to increased exploration of sources of stimulation outside of the primary relationship. As the novelty of the initial sexual relationship diminishes, the lower sensation seeker may not be in sympathy with the higher sensation seeker's desire for sexual experimentation within the marital relationship. It may be somewhat easier for low sensation-seeking women to adjust to high sensation-seeking men than the reverse because of their acceptance of the cultural stereotypes ("that's the way men are").

The restrictions of child rearing may be difficult for some high sensation-seeking women who find the routine of the traditional housewife role too monotonous and unstimulating. However, many women who do not have outside work and who care for children may find exciting aspects to the job. Breast feeding a baby is not normally thought of as a sensation-seeking experience, but apart from the bonding experience some women describe a sensory-emotional "high" from it (Berg-Cross, Berg-Cross, & McGeehan, 1979). One of the mothers interviewed by Berg-Cross et al. is quoted as follows: "Nursing produces a flood of feeling in me – I have such intense rapport. It's second only to intercourse" (p. 352). Breast-feeding mothers in their sample scored significantly higher than bottle-feeding mothers on the General SSS. Apart from the more routine activities of shopping, cooking, cleaning, and diaper changing, some women find stimulation from their children who are interesting, complex, spontaneous, active, and often unpredictable creatures.

Summary

High sensation seekers seem to enjoy social interactions and it reduces the stress of confinement for them. Low sensation seekers are more likely to be stressed by close confinement with another person of the same sex for an extended period of time. High sensation seekers tend to dominate social situations and engage in a great deal of self-disclosure, even with strangers, and encourage self-disclosure from others.

High sensation seekers are more affiliative in their nonverbal responses, such as eye gaze, posture, and pattern of vocalization, and more spontaneous and emotionally expressive. High sensation-seeking women among couples tend to gaze more at their partners than low sensation seekers, thereby eliciting gaze and speech from their partners. People are very accurate in their estimations of sensation seeking in "significant others."

Among the various styles of loving, high sensation seekers tend to favor the "Ludus" style, which sees love as a game without strong commitment. Low sensation seekers favor the "Pragma" style, which considers the long-term potentialities of a partner more than his or her current arousing values. Unmarried couples tend to have correlated levels of sensation seeking, although not as highly correlated as in married couples. Congruence on sensation seeking is more important to relationship satisfaction in women than in men. High sensation seekers exhibit less relationship satisfaction in terms of loving and liking than low sensation seekers. However, for men this relationship is dependent on their partners' sensation seeking, whereas for women it depends only on their own levels of sensation seeking. Two low sensation seekers are more compatible than two high sensation seekers among unmarried couples.

High sensation seekers of both sexes have more permissive attitudes toward sex and more varied types of sexual experience with more partners than low sensation seekers. Young married women who are high sensation seekers are more sexually desirous and hyperarousable than low sensation seekers, but the low sensation seekers report more marital and sexual satisfaction. Sensation seekers' attitudes toward sex are similar to their style of love. Male homosexuals as a group do not differ from heterosexuals and couples engaging in comarital heterosexual relations do not differ from controls in sensation seeking. Social deviance in sexuality per se does not seem to be related to sensation seeking. Nor is risk taking in sexuality (use of contraception) related to sensation seeking among the young who are already sexually active.

Unlike most other personality traits, there is a high level of assortative mating based on sensation-seeking trait. A lack of relationship between levels of sensation seeking is found in couples in marital therapy. The degree of congruence on sensation seeking among college couples is related to their relationship satisfaction, particularly for the women. However, whereas some congruence is desirable for the relationship, pairs of high sensation seekers are less satisfied than low sensation-seeking couples and high sensation seekers of both sexes are at higher risk for divorce.

Although compatibility in sexual needs and social preferences is part of what makes sensation seeking an important trait in mate selection, other kinds of likes and preferences are also important. Couples may share sensations and vicarious experiences from the media, music, art, humor and fantasy. Different tastes in these areas could lead to boredom in the higher sensation-seeking partner and everyday kinds of conflict between both partners. The next chapter will present some of the contrasts between high and low sensation seekers in their tastes for stimulation of the senses and fantasy.

8

Vicarious experience: art, media, music, fantasy, and humor

Long before radio, film, television, or books, stories and myths were orally transmitted from one generation to the next. The children sitting in the dark around a campfire telling frightening ghost stories are probably reenacting an ageless scene. Why do grim fairy tales still appeal more to children than bland "Bobsey twin" stories? Why do older children, adolescents, and adults enjoy gruesome horror films?

All news and media experts know that people like to watch and read about bad news more than happy events. When there are no wars, television news programs in America turn to the reliable nightly images of crimes, fires, traffic accidents, and natural disasters. Despite this nearly universal fascination with morbid events happening to other people, there are marked individual differences in the taste for vicarious violence (Zuckerman & Litle, 1986). This chapter will explore the role of sensation seeking in preferences and tastes in art, television, films, reading, music, fantasy, and humor.

Optimal level of arousal

The optimal level of arousal (OLA) theories discussed in Chapter 2 have been widely used to account for the interest in stimuli that can elicit anxiety, depression, anger, and disgust. According to OLA theories, even arousal of negative emotions can be positively reinforcing because it takes us up to a level of arousal that is optimal or just a little beyond that level. Positive hedonic tone does not lie at either extreme of arousal but at some intermediate level. Vicariously aroused emotions are never too intense because we are always aware that the events are not really happening and there is no objective threat to our well-being. The emotions stimulated depend on empathic identification with the characters or real persons portrayed in the text or images. Young children, who have not yet established a clear distinction between fantasy and reality, or psychotics, who have lost that discriminative capacity, may be terrified by media images or their own fantasies. During the Gulf War there were reports of young children in America who were disturbed by the threats and images of war on television. Even though they were thousands of miles from where these events were occurring, the children experienced them as a personal threat. Why aren't these children equally disturbed by the violence that permeates most cartoons? The mouse leads the cat over cliffs, blows him up, chops him up, and commits an endless series of atrocities against him. However, the cat never bleeds, cries in pain, or is permanently killed or mutilated. Like Lazarus, he rises from the mayhem and all loose body parts magically reassemble themselves. Children can vicariously release some negative feelings toward bigger persons who dominate their lives without being frightened by threats of retaliation or the fantasy of destroying their primary sources of love. While the news and horror films may be too realistic for young children, adult viewers know that the missles cannot reach them and the monster cannot come off the screen and kill them.

Arousal potential

Stimuli vary in their capacity to increase arousal or their *arousal potential*. This term was used by Berlyne (1971) to describe the capacity of a stimulus to command attention, increase physiological arousal, and influence interest and behavior. The stimulus qualities influencing arousal potential are intensity, novelty, complexity, change and suddenness of change, surprisingness, incongruity, uncertainty, size, color, sensory modality, emotional significance of the content, and associations with basic rewards or punishments. Everyone has experienced pain and its anticipation, therefore watching the image of a knife approaching a victim elicits a conditioned empathic response. From the time we first experience sexual arousal, certain images, such as nude bodies, become associated with that arousal and capable of eliciting it when presented in visual, auditory, or textual form.

Repetition of an arousing stimulus reduces arousal through the basic form of learning called *habituation*. When one is exposed repeatedly to a stimulus, that stimulus loses its arousal potential and ceases to interest or arouse. At that point a novel stimulus or a change in the familiar stimulus can result in *dishabituation*, or the revival of arousal. During the Vietnam War, when scenes of killing and destruction appeared nightly on television, it was said that the American public was becoming habituated to the scenes of violence. Habituation to violence in the media leads to demands for novel and more extravagant depictions of violence. Similar habituation to portrayals of sex in films, and increased permissiveness in Western society, led from the passionate kiss and fadeout in the movies before the 1960s to the explicit portrayals of sex from the first kiss to simulated sex and orgasm in the films of the 1970s and 1980s. Only the direct image of the genitals in action now separates the pornographic from the art film.

Preferences in the static image and art

One of the determinants of arousal potential is complexity. A simple way of varying complexity is the generation of polygons with different numbers of random turns in the outlines. Sensation seeking was significantly correlated with the degree of complexity of preferred polygons in two studies (S. R. Griffin, personal communication, 1972; Looft & Baranowski, 1971). The Barron-Welsh Art Scale of the Welsh (1959) Figure Preference test measures the preference for complexity in designs. Zuckerman et al. (1970) found that high sensation seekers scored higher than low sensation seekers on their preferences for complex designs. This scale was developed using creative artists as a criterion group, and the results suggest an association between creativity and sensation seeking that will be discussed in Chapter 14.

Zuckerman et al. (1972) selected the designs showing the best discrimination between high and low sensation seekers and gave them as a preference test to new groups of subjects. The designs preferred more by high sensation seekers are shown in Figure 8.1 and those preferred relatively more by low sensation seekers are given in Figure 8.2. The contrasts in the two sets of designs are striking. The designs preferred by the low sensation seekers are simple and symmetrical; those liked more by the high sensation seekers are complex, asymmetrical, and suggest movement, and some have symbolically suggestive forms. The scale of figure preferences derived from the previous study was given to a new group. The relative preferences for the type of figure shown in Figure 8.1 as opposed to the simple figures shown in Figure 8.2 correlated significantly with the General and all of the subscales from the SSS IV; the highest correlation between the figure preference score and the subscales was with the ES scale.

The ES scale is the one specifically measuring the seeking of sensation through the mind and the senses, rather than in risky activities, and therefore would be expected to correlate most highly with visual preferences. In the field of art preferences, the dimensions of the stimuli are even more complicated than for simple designs since color, composition, and style confound the simple idea of complexity. Osborne and Farley (1970) failed to find a

Figure 8.1. Designs liked more by high sensation seekers. From "What is the sensation seeker? Personality trait and experience correlates of the Sensation Seeking Scales," by M. Zuckerman et al., 1972, *Journal of Consulting and Clinical Psychology, 39,* 317. Copyright American Psychological Association, 1972.

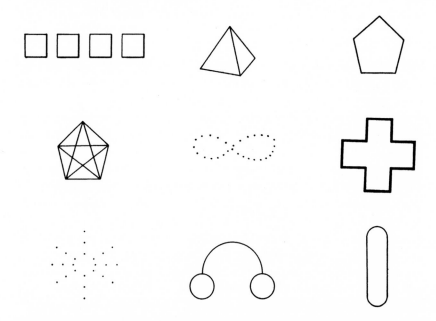

Figure 8.2. Designs liked more by low sensation seekers. From "What is the sensation seeker? Personality trait and experience correlates of the Sensation Seeking Scales," by M. Zuckerman et al., 1972, *Journal of Consulting and Clinical Psychology, 39,* 318. Copyright American Psychological Association, 1972.

relationship between the General SSS and preferences for complexity in paintings. However, they used a limited range of painting styles representing only four modern artists. The study by Furnham and Bunyan (1988) grouped paintings into four categories based on a factor analysis: simple-representational, complex-representational, simple-abstract, and complex-abstract. The SSS V Total score correlated positively with liking for the complex-abstract paintings and negatively with liking for the complex-representational paintings. Apparently the representative or abstract quality of the paintings was more important than the dimension of complexity. Tobacyk, Myers, and Bailey (1981) factor analyzed responses to 40 paintings and found seven factors including an aggression content one and others associated with particular artists. The investigators predicted that sensation seeking would be associated with greater preferences for paintings by three abstract painters, Olitski, Boccioni, and Pollock, and paintings containing aggressive themes. Their hypotheses were supported for the complex abstract paintings of Pollack, the futurist-cubist paintings of Boccioni, and for paintings with aggressive content. The stronger association of sensation seeking with the paintings of Pollack supports the finding of a preference for complex-abstract paintings in the study by Furnham and Bunyan.

Zuckerman, Ulrich, and McLaughlin (1993) examined the relationship between sensation seeking and liking for 19th-century nature paintings with a variety of artists and styles represented. Two studies were done; the second was a replication. First, the SSS V was related to the ratings of all paintings on the dimensions of complexity and tension. There was no interaction between sensation seeking and complexity in the ratings of liking. There was an interaction for the tension dimension: There was no difference between high and low sensation seekers for the low tension paintings, but the high sensation seekers liked the medium- and high-tension paintings more than the low sensation seekers. Next the paintings were factor analyzed revealing a grouping into five factors: (1) a hazy, semiabstract category of paintings mostly by Turner in his later style; (2) realistic-turbulent scenes rated high on both tension and complexity; (3) romantic, fantasylike landscapes; (4) placid-realistic pastoral landscapes; and (5) expressionist but nonabstract and complex paintings. Most subjects liked the paintings in factors 3 and 4 more than those in factors 1 and 5 (less representational), but the high sensation seekers (Total score) liked the paintings in category 5 more than did lows, and high sensation seekers on the ES scale liked the paintings in both factors 1 and 5 more than lows in both studies. Again, the quality of abstractness versus representation was the one most relevant to sensation seeking. Abstract-complex paintings have the arousal producing quality of uncertainty or ambiguity, in contrast to representational paintings, even complex ones, where everything is obvious. Figures 8.3 and 8.4, show reproductions of two paintings, one (Figure 8.3) a placid, pastoral scene by Bierstadt liked more by low sensation seekers, and the other (Figure 8.4) a hazy and tension-producing painting of a seascape by Constable, liked more by the high sensation seekers.

The art preferences of sensation seekers have more to do with the form of the art, representational or abstract and complex or simple, than the content. Arousal value and positivity or negativity of hedonic tone may be independent dimensions. Although the simpler versions of optimal-level theory suggest a curvilear relationship between hedonic tone and arousal, the relationship between the two depends on other factors, like the context of the stimulus and its reality. The vicarious enjoyment of negative themes, as in horror films and torture museums, has to do more with the arousal value of the stimulus than its significance for the person.

Zaleski (1984b) used pictures that had been rated on an emotionality scale from very negatively arousing to those rated as very positively arousing.

Figure 8.3. Bierstadt painting liked more by low sensation seekers: "Autumn Woods." Reprinted courtesy of the New York Historical Society, New York City.

Figure 8.4. Constable painting liked more by high sensation seekers: "Seascape with clouds." Reprinted by permission of Royal Academy of Arts, London.

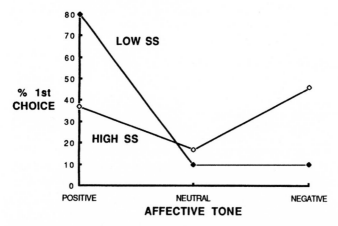

Figure 8.5. Percentages of first choices of pictures by high and low sensation seekers as a function of affective tone of pictures. Based on data from Zaleski (1984b).

Emotionally positive scenes included themes of celebration and "mild lovemaking"; emotionally negative images included scenes of torture, hanging, and corpses. Seven pictures were selected for each of the three ranges: the most positive, the most negative, and those in the neutral range. Polish university students were asked to pick out the picture they liked the most, ignoring its artistic value. High and low sensation seekers were contrasted in their choices. The distribution of the first-choice picture was significantly different in its distribution among positive, negative, and neutral affective tone categories for both male and female high and low sensation seekers on the General and ES scales of the SSS V. Men also showed significant differences between high and low sensation seeking when the Dis and TAS subscales were used as criteria. Figure 8.5 shows the frequency of choices for men and women combined as a function of the affective tone of the stimuli and sensation seeking as defined by the ES scale. For the low experience seekers there is a clear preference for the stimuli that have a positive arousal value, but for the high sensation seekers the distribution of choices was a U-shaped one with both positively and negatively arousing pictures preferred to the neutral ones. Actually there was also a strong sex difference. In women there were hardly any low sensation seekers expressing a liking for the negative pictures and among the highs there were still more who liked the positive than the negative pictures. Among the men a clear majority of the high sensation seekers preferred the negative as compared to the positive pictures. However, for high sensation seekers of both sexes the neutral pictures had the lowest frequencies of choice. Arousal value seems to be more salient than the positivity or negativity of the pictures' themes for preferences of high sensation seekers. Probably the negative themes were actually more arousing than the positive ones, since Zaleski did not use the strongest positively arousing stimuli, explicit sexual ones.

General preferences among the media

Brown et al. (1974) found that the Change Seeker Index correlated significantly with movie attendance, reading, and listening to music, but not at all with television watching. Sensation seeking was even more highly related to attendance of movies with explicit depictions of sexual activity ("X-rated") than to less sexually explicit films or those with more general themes.

Schierman and Rowland (1985) also examined media and activity choices in relation to sensation seeking. The SSS was positively correlated with reading of X-rated magazines and going to X-rated movies for both men and women. For men sensation seeking was positively related to reading news magazines and nonfiction books and watching television news reports. The low sensation-seeking men tended to like musical movies and read romantic fiction. Apart from a liking for X-rated magazines and movies and listening to popular music, the high sensation-seeking women liked "live" entertainment in pubs and lounges, rock concerts, and nightclubs. Negative correlations showed that the low sensation seekers liked theater comedies and dramas. For the women in this study sensation seeking in the real world was more important than vicarious experience. What preferences they had in the media centered around sex.

Rowland, Fouts, and Heatherton (1989) compared the extent of television watching during various times of the week and enjoyment of different types of programs among Canadian college students. Male high sensation seekers watched television less than those medium or low on the scale. For females, however, the medium group watched television more than either the high or low sensation-seeking groups. One could speculate that the low group spent more time studying while the high sensation-seeking group devoted more time to partying, but there were no data presented that could be used to test this hypothesis. However, it was noted that difference in television watching between high and low male sensation-seekers was greatest for the period of Friday afternoon and evening, the traditional "pub and party" time at this university. Although there were marked sex differences in preferred program types (males like sports and situation comedies, females like soap operas) preferred program content was not related to sensation seeking. However, low sensation seekers tended to avoid programs with sexual, "offensive," or frightening material. Low sensation seekers preferred to concentrate on watching the programs, whereas highs often left the television on while they did other things like read, converse, eat dinner, engage in their hobbies, play the stereo, or "cuddle" with a boy- or girlfriend. Clearly, television is of lesser interest than other life activities to high sensation seekers. High sensation seekers also reported changing back and forth between two or more programs on different channels while watching. Channel switching was behaviorally tested in another study described next.

Schierman and Rowland (1985) allowed subjects a choice of watching 30-minute segments of five movies on video cassettes, including *48 Hours* (action), *Halloween* (horror), *Caddyshack* (comedy), *Ordinary People* (drama), and *Endless Love* (romance). Subjects were free to switch back and forth between movies. The number of such channel changes correlated highly with the SSS for males ($r = .69$) and females ($r = .54$). The high sensation seekers spent a relatively greater proportion of their time watching the movie *48 Hours*, whereas the low sensation seekers spent more of their viewing time watching *Caddyschack*. The first segment of *48 Hours* contains four graphically depicted shootings, some female nudity, and a lot of profanity. The comedy *Caddyshack* is totally nonviolent and nonerotic. The comedy is predictable and rather banal (at least to this critic). The primary finding is that sensation seekers like to switch programs. This probably reflects their boredom susceptibility when there is nothing else they can do but watch television. As things get dull on one channel they switch to another. This finding may be emblematic of their general attitudes toward work and relationships (Chapters 6, 7).

Zuckerman and Litle (1986) studied the relationships between sensation seeking, extraversion, neuroticism, and psychoticism and "curiosity about morbid and sexual events." They developed two scales for this purpose, one for curiosity about morbid events (CAME) and the other for curiosity about sexual events (CASE). The CAME scale included a variety of likes and desires, such as violence shown on television and movies and described in newspapers, a desire to see an autopsy, execution, bullfight, or the enjoyment of watching violent sports like prizefighting. The CASE scale items indicated likes or dislikes for portrayals of sex in movies, novels, stories, looking at nude pictures of persons of the opposite sex. Two additional questions asked about frequency of attendance of X-rated movies and gory-type horror movies.

Table 8.1 shows the bivariate and multiple correlations between the SSS, the general CAME and CASE scales, and reported movie attendance. The

Table 8.1. *Correlations between Sensation Seeking Scale (SSS), curiosity about morbid and sexual events, and horror and sex film attendance*

	SSS				
	Total	TAS	ES	Dis	BS
CAME Males	.44**	.33**	.25*	.50**	.17
CAME Females	.36**	.29**	.18*	.29**	.21**
CASE Males	.41**	.09	.23*	.58**	.25*
CASE Females	.39**	.11	.26**	.48**	.19**
Horror Males	.23**	.21*	.14	.26*	.06
Horror Females	.27**	.18**	.11	.31**	.14*
Sex Males	.37**	.30**	.15	.38**	.25*
Sex Females	.22**	.09	.24**	.21**	.10

Note: n: males = 89, females = 213. TAS = Thrill and Adventure Seeking; ES = Experience Seeking; Dis = Disinhibition; BS = Boredom Susceptibility; CAME = Curiosity about Morbid Events scale; CASE = Curiosity about Sexual Events Scale; Horror = frequency of attendance of horror movies; Sex = frequency of attendance of X-rated sex movies.
*$p < .05$.
**$p < .01$.
Source: Part of Table 3, p. 53, from "Personality and curiosity about morbid and sexual events," by M. Zuckerman & P. Litle, 1986, *Personality and Individual Differences, 7,* 47–56. Copyright 1986 by Pergamon Press Ltd. Reprinted by permission.

Total and all of the SSS subscales except BS for the males were significantly related to CAME. For males the Dis scale had the highest correlation with CAME. Among the EPQ scales only the P scale was significantly related to CAME in the males, but E was also related to CAME in the females. Curiosity about morbid events seems to be most strongly related to the more psychopathic scales (P and Dis), but there is a relationship with general sensation seeking as shown by the relationship of CAME to the Total score and TAS and ES subscales in addition to Dis.

The SSS Total and all of the subscales except TAS also predicted the interest in vicarious sex. The Dis scale had the highest correlation of the subscales with CASE for both men and women. The EPQ P scale also correlated with CASE. Attendance of horror and sex films was less strongly predicted by the personality scales, but the SSS Total and Dis scales correlated with attendance of both types of films by men and women. Dis also accounted for most of the variance in the multiple regression, and the EPQ scales contributed little.

In the Zuckerman et al. (1976) study of sexual attitudes and behavior, an item was added asking subjects if they would be interested in participating in an experiment where they would be shown an "erotic film" and asked to rate their reactions to it. Among the unmarried students more men than women volunteered to make their "contribution to science." Sex differences in the taste for visual erotica have been well documented (Kinsey, Pomeroy, Martin, & Gebhard, 1953). However, among married persons, mostly from those students taking the sex course, there was no sex difference in volunteering. The ES and Dis scales were significantly correlated with the desire to view the sex film for both sexes (Zuckerman, 1976c). The General scale correlated with the desire in men only.

The association between sensation seeking and interests in vicarious experience of morbid and sexual events has sometimes been theorized to be an indication of suppressed aggressive or sexual needs. However, for sex at least we know that high sensation seekers are more sexually permissive and active than low sensation seekers. The fact that high sensation seekers also like to view erotic activities suggests that this media interest is simply another indication of their general sexual interest and activity rather than an expression of frustrated sexual drive.

Tamborini and Stiff (1987) described two unpublished studies relating the SSS to horror film exposure. In a study by Edwards (1984) the General and all four subscales of the SSS IV were significantly correlated with horror film exposure. The correlations were highest for the General ($r = .32$) and the Dis ($r = .36$) scales. Sparks (1984) developed a 20-item scale to measure enjoyment of frightening films, and this scale correlated at a low but significant level with sensation seeking for males ($r = .22$) and females ($r = .28$). Tamborini and Stiff also developed a model for predicting frequency of horror film attendance directly from a generalized "like for fright" (liking of horror films because they are exciting and "scary") and an indirect prediction from sensation seeking as mediated by like for fright. The sample was a rather restricted one of people who had just emerged from seeing the movie *Halloween II;* most were probably horror movie aficianados. The effects of emotional states produced by the movie might have affected their responses to the SSS and other measures. Sensation seeking predicted like for fright which in turn predicted frequency of actual horror film attendance.

Further studies by Tamborini, Stiff, and Zillman (1987) in more neutral settings showed that ES and BS scales and enjoyment of pornography were significantly correlated with preference for graphic horror for males but not for females. Boredom susceptibility (BS) was a good predictor of men's preferences for graphic horror scenes in film versions featuring male and female victims, whereas a liking for pornography predicted only for the versions with female victims. For female subjects both Dis and BS predicted their preferences for horror scenes with male victims, but for female victims only BS predicted and in a negative direction – namely, the high sensation seekers did not like the scenes in which females were being victimized.

One explanation of the tastes of high sensation seekers for gruesome, morbid pictures could be that they are either less arousable or habituate more rapidly as a function of repeated exposure to such stimuli. As suggested previously, the carnage in Vietnam depicted on the nightly news on television may have habituated the American public to scenes of violence. Mangelsdorf and Zuckerman (1975) exposed students to a slide made from a photograph of the American massacre at My Lai in Vietnam. All subjects habituated, as shown by a reduced level of skin conductance response with each successive presentation of the slide, but students in the Reserve Officers Training Corps (ROTC) habituated more quickly than nonmilitary students. The ROTC students may be habituated by the films they watch or their actual military training, or the difference could be a cognitive one based on attitudes toward the war. Another possibility was that these students were higher sensation seekers than ordinary students and high sensation seekers could be less arousable in response to negative stimuli.

Litle (1986; described in Zuckerman, 1991b) measured the electrodermal responses of students to a 20 minute segment of a horror movie *Friday the Thirteenth*. Figure 8.6 shows the skin conductance reactions during the movie sequence. Each of the peaks in rate of spontaneous skin conductance reactions represents a period of the movie when some startling thing happened, like the discovery of dead bodies and attempted assaults. Up until the last moment of the movie, the reactions of high and low sensation seekers were fairly similar. During the last scene, the hero decapitates the mad killer and his head goes flying off with blood spurting in all directions. The low sensation seekers showed a particularly strong increase in skin conductance arousal in response to this scene whereas the high sensation seekers hardly responded at all. The reason could be that during all of the earlier scenes the highs were habituating so that by the time the real "shocker" came along they were not arousable. Differences in habituation between high and low sensation seekers in response to neutral stimuli have not been found. Although the highs tend to have a strong response to any novel stimulus, the difference in response usually disappears on subsequent presentations of the stimulus (Chapter 12). However, stimuli of interest to high sensation seekers require moire trials for them to habituate to the level of the low sensation seekers (Smith, Perlstein, Davidson, & Michael, 1986). Although high sen-

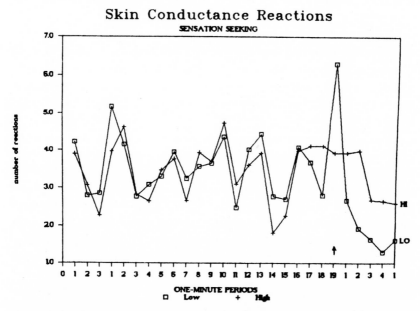

Figure 8.6. Spontaneous skin conductance reactions of high and low sensation seekers per minute during a 20-minute segment of the horror movie *Friday the Thirteenth.* From Little (1986), figure published in "One person's stress is another person's pleasure" by M. Zuckerman, 1991. In C. D. Spielberger, S. Kulczár, & Hicks (Eds.), *Stress and emotion,* Vol. 14, p. 39. Washington, DC: Hemisphere. Copyright, 1991 by Hemisphere Publishing Corp. Reprinted by permission.

sation seekers may be pleasantly aroused by the initial scenes of a horror or a pornographic movie, they probably habituate to the repeated scenes of slaughter or sex before the film is over. When showing pornographic films to college students (for educational or experimental purposes), there is usually total silence during the first scenes of sexual activity, but after the third, fourth, or fifth sexual encounter the audience begins to make jokes and laugh, indicating some diminishment of empathic involvement in the action on the screen. This detachment may occur sooner for high sensation seekers than for lows.

Targeting of sensation seekers in media messages

Advertisers sometimes study the populations using particular products and tailor their advertisements to appeal to these groups. Some years ago when

men were the major consumers of cigarettes, advertisements showed cow-
boys smoking, appealing to the macho ideal in some men. Now that more
women have taken up smoking and more men are quitting, the image is often
that of a high-achieving woman carrying a briefcase. Some advertisements
showing motorcyclists and sports car drivers suggest a use of sensation-
seeking models for smokers, perhaps in an attempt to counteract the manda-
tory health warning that must now be included in large letters in the adver-
tisement.

Although the attempt to persuade people to use a product that may injure
their health is ethically questionable, the media can also be used to present
antismoking advertisements to counteract the influence of the tobacco advertisers. Dealers in illegal drugs like marijuana and cocaine cannot, as yet, use
media advertising to sell their products, but unfortunately they are quite
successful with mere word-of-mouth and live demonstration methods. A
massive effort is being made through drug education and media presentations
to dissuade nonusers from drug use and to persuade users to give up drug use
and seek treatment.

Donohew and his colleages at the University of Kentucky are engaged in a
program of research to design communications that will be effective in
reaching the goals of the antidrug campaigns. They are particularly interested
in the interaction of the message form with individual differences in sensation-seeking trait, predicting that different kinds of message presentation
will be effective with high and low sensation seekers.

Donohew, Helm, Lawrence, and Shatzer (1990) used the SSS V and a
drug use survey to select four groups of subjects: (1) nonuser low sensation
seekers, (2) nonuser high sensation seekers, (3) moderate-user low sensation
seekers, and (4) moderate-user high sensation seekers. Subjects were brought
to the laboratory and exposed to different kinds of messages against the use
of marijuana. Exposure preference was measured by their choice of continued exposure to the message during an interval in which they were asked if
they wanted to hear and see more. Their exposure preferences and attitudes
toward drug use, before and after exposure to the messages, were measured.

Overall, high sensation seekers showed greater comprehension of the
message than the low sensation seekers. The two groups showing the greatest
preference for the antidrug presentations were the low sensation-seeking
users and the high sensation-seeking nonusers. Both of these groups expressed a greater interest in seeing and hearing more of the message and
somewhat greater attitude changes after the message. The other two groups
were probably not interested because their attitudes were already so anti- or
promarijuana use: 83% of the high sensation-seeking users held promarijuana

attitudes and 96% of the low sensation-seeking nonusers held antimarijuana attitudes. Although a majority of users held promarijuana attitudes before the message, there was more dissonance between attitude and behavior in the low sensation-seeking users than in the highs, with 32% of the lows as opposed to 17% of the highs holding antimarijuana attitudes despite the fact that they were using it. Among the nonusers only 4% of the low sensation seekers held pro-use attitudes compared with 21% of the high sensation-seeking nonusers. In other words, the groups most interested in the messages were the high sensation-seeking nonusers, who were probably more at risk than low sensation seekers to become users because of a lack of ideological opposition to use, and the low sensation-seeking users in whom use was most dissonant with their attitudes.

In the next study, Donohew, Lorch, and Palmgreen (1991) tested messages specifically designed to target high and low sensation seekers. Pretesting was done to get the reactions and preferences of high and low sensation seekers for different types of video formats. Although both groups liked rock music backgrounds, high sensation seekers preferred the more "intense hard-edged music," novel formats involving extreme close-ups and heavy use of sound-effects in the absence of music, higher levels of suspense, tension, and emotional impact than low sensation seekers. Most of these features incorporate arousal-producing qualities of narratives. The low sensation seekers liked closure at the end of a story with a "tag line" summing up the message. The high sensation seekers regarded a summing up as "preaching" and preferred to reach their own conclusions. This result reflects the greater need for autonomy in high sensation seekers.

On the basis of these studies two video formats were designed, one to appeal to low sensation seekers and the other to high sensation seekers. The low SS message suggested social activities as alternatives to drug use and resistance to peer-group pressures; the high SS format showed exciting alternatives to drug use, like risky sports. More of the low sensation seekers indicated an intention to call a drug "hotline" after exposure to the message designed to appeal to them than after the high-intensity message, whereas relatively more high sensation-seeking users were moved to call by the message designed to arouse and interest them. It had been anticipated that high sensation-seeking users would be relatively more resistant to any of the antidrug messages than the lows, but in fact the highs were more receptive to the message than the low sensation-seeking users as indicated by their intention to call the hotline. The high-intensity message was particularly effective, but the high sensation seekers showed some positive response to the low-intensity message as well. The authors speculate that even high sensation seekers may have a problem with peer-group drug influence, stressed in the low SS message. If your peers are all drug users, then autonomy would be manifested in not using drugs. However, the specific effects of messages designed for high and low sensation seekers suggest that the media formats should be tailored to the personality targets. But given the fact that there are many more high than low sensation seekers among the drug-using population (Chapter 9), if one format is to be used in antidrug media appeals it should be an exciting one designed for the high sensation seekers.

Music preferences

Given the definition of sensation seeking, high sensation seekers should prefer music that is intense, complex, novel, and dissonant. In an experiment where music was provided as positive reinforcement in a sensory deprivation situation, the subjects had a choice of three kinds of music that they could listen to on demand: classical, jazz, or a bland and simple type of popular music (Zuckerman et al., 1966). Most high sensation seekers chose either classical or jazz, whereas most of the lows picked bland popular music. Both classical and jazz music are complex, compared to the simple melodies of popular music, so complexity might be the crucial factor in the choices of the highs. However, Glascow, Cartier, and Wilson (1985) compared high and low sensation seekers' responses to short selections of classical music rated for familiarity and complexity and found no relation of SSS scores to musical preference along these dimensions. Litle and Zuckerman (1986) criticized this study because Glascow et al. used only classical music selections. Many students today seem to have little experience in listening to classical music. Furthermore, the study ignored other possible dimensions like intensity that could have affected choices. They also used only a summary score rather than examining relationships of the subscales with musical preferences. Scales like ES seem to have particular relevance to art and may also be the salient ones to look at in relation to music.

Watson, Anderson, and Schulte (1977) used five music selections that were rated along the dimensions of "grating" (atonality?), exciting, or bland. High sensation seekers in their sample of psychiatric patients liked all kinds of music more than lows, but the difference was particularly marked for the music judged to be grating.

All of these studies examined only a narrow range of musical styles. Litle and Zuckerman (1986) devised a questionnaire for musical preferences, using ratings of types of music on scales of liking from dislike, to indifference, to three degrees of liking. The areas of music included different subtypes of rock, classical, electronic, jazz, soul and rhythm and blues, popular (easy listening), country and western, folk and ethnic, religious, and soundtracks from Broadway, movies, and television. The questionnaire also contained questions about musical training and education, time spent and involvement while listening to music, and attendance at live musical performances. The Total SSS correlated positively with all three kinds of rock music (hard, soft, and classic) but somewhat more highly with hard and soft rock than with classical rock, and sensation seeking correlated negatively with liking of movie soundtrack music. Except for the TAS scale, which correlated only with soft rock, the other SSS subscales tended to correlate more highly with hard than with soft rock. The TAS and ES subscales also correlated with a liking for folk music, but only the ES scale was related to a liking for classical music. Subjects who were high on Dis tended to like both hard and soft rock and dislike religious and soundtrack-type music. Musical education did not correlate with the SSS, but intensity of involvement in listening to music correlated with Total, TAS, and ES scales, particularly the latter. Experience seekers seem to have a broader range of musical likes, including folk and classical as well as rock, whereas disinhibiters just like rock. The ES scale also correlates most strongly with involvement in the experience of music. These differences in preference are compatible with the definitions of the subscales. ES represents the seeking of sensation through the mind and the senses. It is the scale that is most similar to the Costa and McCrae scale of Openness to Experience. Disinhibition, however, is more closely linked with the need for intensity of experience rather than novelty of experience. Rock provides an intense experience sometimes linked with sex in the reported effects. One fan of rock told me "you listen with your whole body, not just your ears."

Fantasy

Fantasy is what we imagine doing rather than actually doing. What we do has limits set by our circumstances and personal limitations, but fantasy has no limits. Most types of daydreaming and absorption in daydreaming decline with age, as does sensation seeking, but particularly strong declines are seen for sexual, hostile, heroic, and achievement-oriented daydreams (Giambra, 1977). Is this decline in daydreaming a function of changing motivations with age or an existential realization of the reduced chances of realizing one's daydreams?

To the extent that sensation seekers engage in active behavior, we would expect that they spend relatively less time in daydream fantasies than low sensation seekers just as they watch less television than low sensation seekers. Windholz (1970) found a low but significant negative correlation between the General SSS and the general daydreaming scale of the Imaginal Process Inventory (IPT, Singer & Antrobus, 1972). Segal and Singer (1976) factor analyzed the scales of the SSS IV along with the scales of the IPT. There was little relationship between the SSS and daydreaming scales; the SSS formed one factor, along with marijuana use, and none of the daydreaming scales loaded on this factor. Bailey et al. (1982) studied "primitive" and "advanced" pleasures and aversions in behavior and fantasies. Primitive, as opposed to advanced, is defined as concerned with bodily sensations, subcortical, nonverbal, and involving little mental concentration. Sensation-seeking males were found to engage in many primitive pleasure-seeking activities (presumably including sex) in reality but there was no correlation between sensation seeking and primitive pleasure or aversion types of fantasy.

Franken and Rowland (1990) attempted to stimulate fantasy by asking subjects what they would buy and what they would do if they suddenly won a million dollars. Presumably this is the type of fantasy that prompts people to buy lottery tickets. The differences in fantasies reported by highs and lows suggest the fulfillment of sensation-seeking needs. In contrast to lows, more high sensation seekers of both sexes would buy exotic sports cars and large sailboats, move around a lot, pursue a series of short-term sexual relationships, buy drugs, try new sports, and travel abroad, making frequent trips with minimal planning and spending more money than lows. Not surprisingly, considering their expensive tastes, the highs said that they would need more money than the lows to satisfy their fantasies.

Daydreaming and fantasy do not seem to be strongly related to sensation seeking. To the extent that high sensation seekers daydream, their fantasies are concerned with extravagant fulfillment of their hedonistic goals. Many of the things they fantasize about when they are younger are likely to be fulfilled as they get older and have more money to devote to the cause of pleasure and variety seeking. In contrast, low sensation seekers dream of the more conventional rewards like buying a good home and nice things for their families rather than Walter Mitty type daydreams of power and pleasure. Low sensation seekers are not simply frustrated or inhibited high sensation seekers; their goals and values are basically different from those of high sensation seekers.

Humor

The analysis of humor is perhaps the most humorless area of psychological investigation. If you have to explain why something is funny, it destroys the humor. However, it does provide a chance to present some good jokes, as Freud (1905) did in his book on *Wit and Its Relation to the Unconscious*. Freud believed that jokes provide a release of repressed impulses from the unconscious, explaining the quantity of jokes with sexual and aggressive content. Yet there are many jokes in which the humor seems to depend more on incongruity and paradox rather than the content. On the basis of Freudian theory, one might expect to find that persons who are most repressed or inhibited in the area of sexuality enjoy sexual jokes, whereas those who are more repressed in aggressiveness should enjoy jokes in which the victim is attacked, ridiculed, or demeaned. Ruch and Hehl (1988) investigated the repression hypothesis, using their own humor test and scales measuring sexual attitudes and behavior. Their results are in the opposite direction to those which would be predicted from Freud's theory. Permissive attitudes toward sex and enjoyable sexual experience were positively related to rated funniness of sexual jokes and cartoons. Prudishness and a lack of sexual satisfaction were related to ratings of aversiveness of such humor. As in previously discussed studies of sexuality in the media, a taste for vicarious experience in this area is positively, not negatively, related to permissive attitudes and life experience.

Cattell and Luborsky (1947) devised a humor test based on reactions to jokes, and correlated humor factors with personality. Ruch (1992) comments: "Although the humor test was used in several studies . . . its overall impact is low and it now seems obsolete." Ruch devised a new test of individual differences in responses to different types of humor. His humor categories are based on factor analytic studies of overlapping sets of jokes and cartoons. Three basic humor factors have emerged; two are factors depending on the structure of the joke or cartoon and the other (sex) is a content factor.

The first category is called *incongruity-resolution*. All jokes begin with some kind of incongruity, but jokes or cartoons in this group have a "punch-line" that completely resolves the surprising incongruity. An example joke is: " 'Do you believe in the Easter Bunny?' Margie asked her new friend in Kindergarten. 'Why not?' he answered. 'With today's technology anything is possible.' "

The second type is labeled *nonsense* humor. In this type the punchline may provide no resolution at all, may provide a partial resolution leaving part of the incongruity unresolved, or may create new incongruities or absurdities. The first frame of a cartoon shows two men sitting outside of a house. The smoke from the chimney is strongly blowing toward the right. One man says to the other: "You know why the wind always comes from that direction [left]? Because Eagles never fly backwards." The second frame of the cartoon shows an enlargement of the scene with the men and house on the back of a huge eagle flying in the leftward direction. The second man asks: "How am I to understand that?"

The third type, *sexual humor*, has obvious sexual content, but may be secondarily classified by one of the two structural types just described or may have little relevance to the two types. This example of sexual humor is based on incongruity-resolution: " 'So how was Scotland?' the father asked his daughter, who had just returned from vacation. 'Is it true they all have bagpipes?' 'Oh, that's just one of those silly stereotypes. All the ones I met had quite a normal one.' " A second example of sexual humor is based on nonsense: A cartoon shows a hen lying on its back with its legs up in air facing a rooster poised above it. The hen says: "Just once . . . for a change."

Subjects taking the test are asked to make two ratings on seven-point scales: *funniness*, from not funny at all to very funny; and *aversiveness:* not aversive at all (no rejection) to very aversive (strong rejection.) While the two scales correlate negatively for scores in the three categories of humor, the correlations are low for the two structural types of humor and moderate for the sexual humor. Moderate correlations between the three funniness scores and the three aversiveness scores suggest that general sense of humor and humor aversiveness scores could be derived from the subscales, but Ruch does not use such scores. However, he does use subtractive scores and partial correlations to define the specific factors affecting correlations with personality traits.

Ruch (1988) described four studies relating the Ruch 3 W-D Humor test to a German translation of the SSS form V scales. The total sample consisted of German university students, but with one sample of Austrian teachers. Table 8.2 shows the correlations between sensation seeking and the six humor scales (funniness and aversiveness scores for each of three content scales), and two Structure Preference Indices (SPI).

High sensation seekers, particularly experience seekers and boredom susceptible types, liked incongruous humor that is unresolved or nonsense humor more than low sensation seekers. Low sensation seekers tend to find

Table 8.2. *Correlations between the Sensation Seeking Scale (SSS) and funniness (F) and aversiveness (A) ratings for incongruity–resolution (Inc-Res), nonsense, and sex humor, and structure preference indexes (SPI)*

	SSS				
Humor type	TAS	ES	Dis	BS	Total
Inc-Res F	.02	−.24**	−.18**	−.23**	−.20**
Nonsense F	.09	.20**	.07	.15^b	.17**
Sex F	.11	−.03	.20^a**	−.02	.08
Inc-Res A	−.09	.01	−.11	.01	−.06
Nonsense A	−.13*	−.22**	−.20**	−.22**	−.25**
Sex	−.17**	−.15*	−.36**	−.15*	−.28**
SPI F	.06	.40**	.23**	.35**	.34**
SPI A	−.05	−.27**	−.11	−.24**	−.22**

Note: TAS = Thrill and Adventure Seeking; ES = Experience Seeking; Dis = Disinhibition; BS = Boredom Susceptibility.
^{a}Partialing out Inc-Res F, r = .39, p < .001.
*p < .01.
**p < .001.
Source: Parts of tables 1 and 5, pp. 866, 868, from "Sensation seeking and the enjoyment of structure and content of humor: stability of findings across four samples," by W. Ruch, 1988, *Personality and Individual Differences, 9*, 861–871. Copyright 1988 by Pergamon Press. Reprinted by permission.

nonsense and sexual humor aversive, but they liked nonsexual humor where incongruity is resolved by the punchline. Those low on the Dis scale had an especially aversive response to sex humor.

The preferences of high sensation seekers for unresolved incongruity can be related to their tolerance of ambiguity, preference for complex designs, and liking for nonrepresentational forms of art. Related personality traits like impulsivity, venturesomeness, surgency, superego strength, radicalism, and psychoticism are also related to the liking of, or lack of aversion to, nonsense humor (Hehl & Ruch, 1985). Liking for incongruity resolution and dislike of nonsense humor are related to conservative attitudes, and a liking for nonsense humor is related to the liberal side of the dimension (Ruch & Hehl, 1986). Enjoyment of sexual humor is related to tough-mindedness which can be either liberal or conservative. Age trends in the types of humor appreciation or aversion are also consistent with the age decline in sensation seeking (Ruch, McGhee, & Hehl).

Some examples of the jokes that were most successful in differentiating high and low sensation seekers can give a better idea of their preferred types of humor. Those rated funnier by high sensation seekers and more aversive by low include:

1. The eagle cartoon. (See example given previously for *nonsense humor*.)
2. Cartoon: first frame: Little girl holding an ice-cream cone approaching a man in a raincoat; second frame: Man opens rain coat exhibiting his genitals; third frame: Man is standing with a chagrined expression, the ice cream cone is impaled on his genitals.
3. Cartoon: Nude man and woman in bed, man is crouched over the pubic hair of the woman saying: "For God's sake, don't move – My contact lens!"

Those rated funnier by low sensation seekers include:

1. Joke: " 'A writer sent his latest novel to a publisher. At the meeting the publisher said: 'Your novel is excellent, but we only take work from authors with well-known names.' 'Wonderful,' beamed the writer, 'my name is Smith.' "
2. Joke: "The telegram delivery boy rings the doorbell at Professor Duffey's house. 'Here's a telegram for you, Professor.' 'Thank you,' nodded the professor in his typical friendly but absentminded way, 'I don't need any today,' and he was quickly back at his work."
3. Cartoon: A tourist is being boiled in a large pot by cannibals. The cannibal says to the man: "Can't you cheer up a little? The chief can't stand sad dinners!"

The situational sense of Humour Test (SHRQ) asks subjects to indicate the likelihood that they would laugh in actual life situations which might be more annoying than funny to many people, for example a waiter in a restaurant accidentally spilling a drink on the subject. The SHRQ correlated highly with the total SSS in Indiana ($r = .52$) and Germany ($r = .43$) and moderately with all of the SS subscales (Deckers & Ruch, 1992).

Summary

Optimal-level theories suggest that the arousal potential of stimuli provides their motivating value for high sensation seekers. Arousal potential of any stimulus is reduced by repetition so that high sensation seekers seek novel experiences and activities in order to avoid the inevitable decline in arousal produced by familiarity. Complexity and ambiguity are two qualities of visual stimuli that produce arousal. Liking for designs, art, and music shows the high sensation seekers' interests in complex and ambiguous (as in complex abstract art) and intense (as in rock music) stimuli, and the low sensation seekers' preferences for calming, low-tension art and music. Although these types of preference difference are usually related to the General, Total, and several or all of the subscales of the SSS, the ES subscale usually shows the strongest correlation with preference. ES seems to measure "openness to experience" through the senses and is therefore most relevant to broad tastes in art and music.

Real life experience is generally more arousing than vicarious experience. It is more exciting to play a game than to watch others playing it, to do something risky rather than see others doing it, and to have sexual experiences rather than watching them in films or reading about them. However, for many low sensation seekers vicarious experience may provide just the level of arousal they desire. Actual experience would push them beyond their optimal levels of arousals into the range of unpleasantness. High sensation seekers prefer to listen to "live music" in exciting surroundings whereas lows prefer to see and listen to it on television. High sensation seekers will watch television for the news reports, or use it as background while they are doing other things, but their interest is only peripheral. Based on their own reports and observed in an experiment, the high sensation seekers like to switch channels a lot keeping track of two or more programs simultaneously. Low sensation seekers become more absorbed in a single program. On traditional drinking nights, only the low sensation seekers are found in front of the television set.

In photographs, television, films, and reading, the high sensation seekers show a greater interest than the lows in morbid and sexual themes, whereas low sensation seekers find these themes distasteful and avoid them. High sensation seekers are more likely to be found among those attending sexually explicit (X-rated) movies and horror films. There is some evidence that the high sensation seekers may habituate more rapidly than lows to scenes in horror films. An awareness of the different kinds of media preferences in high and low sensation seekers has proved valuable in the design of media messages designed to discourage drug abuse.

Daydreaming and fantasy are not strongly related to sensation seeking and there is even some evidence of a negative relationship between daydreaming and sensation seeking. When high sensation seekers do daydream, they are likely to have fantasies of more extravagant hedonic fulfillment in the areas they are already active, like sex, travel, and fast driving. Humor preferences reflect the cognitive styles of sensation seekers as well as their enjoyment of sex. High sensation seekers like nonsense humor, in which the resolutions are still incongruous or absurd, whereas lows like humor in which the punchline neatly ties things up, as in misunderstandings of words or intentions. Low sensation seekers tend to find sexual and nonsense humor aversive, and the rejection of sexual humor is particularly strong in those who are low on disinhibition.

Sensation seekers generally prefer active to passive experience, or real life involvement to spectator status. Their preferences in art, media, and humor reflect a liking for stimuli that arouse strong emotions, demand a suspension of reality and an acceptance of ambiguity or absurdity, or that vicariously involve spectators in activities that they find particularly rewarding in life, such as sex. Low sensation seekers prefer a predictable, understandable, rational, and unemotional world where there are few surprises and where everything is clear.

The next topic concerns internal sensation seeking through the use of alcohol and drugs. Drugs may be used to alter our inner experiences, create euphoric moods, increase energy, facilitate social disinhibition, as well as to reduce negative moods. Whatever the motive for their use, they entail some severe risks, particularly the hard, illegal drugs. An understanding of the role of this trait in drug use, as well as in other kinds of ingestive preferences, is important in helping those who go too far beyond the optimal level of arousal.

9

Smoking, drinking, drugs, and eating

There are many interesting links between drugs that are abused and the hypothesized biological bases of sensation seeking. In this chapter the phenomenal relationships of substance use and abuse to sensation seeking and related traits will be described without going into the psychobiology of drug abuse, a topic reserved for Chapter 11. The chapter also deals with other addictions. There is considerable evidence for the existence of an "addictive personality"; cross-addictions are quite common. Carpenter (1992) found that recovering alcoholics engage in coffee drinking, cigarette smoking, overeating, and gambling to a greater degree than people who never abuse alcohol. Personality factors such as sensation seeking could be the common denominator of these cross-addictions.

Certain basic questions must be asked in this chapter. Does a relationship between sensation seeking and drug abuse indicate a common causal effect or is sensation seeking a result of involvement in the drug-using population? The same question may be asked of other traits like anxiety and depression, which may be "causes" or "consequences" of drug abuse. A second question, relevant to the optimal level of arousal theory, is whether sensation seekers are more attracted to stimulant drugs, like amphetamine and cocaine, than to depressant drugs, like alcohol, opiates, and barbiturates. A final question, which cannot yet be fully answered because of the paucity of studies of treatment is: If sensation seeking is a motive involved in drug abuse, can we find substitutes for drug use in noninjurious sensation-seeking activities?

Smoking

Many do not regard cigarette smoking as a drug addiction because tobacco is a legal substance. However, smoking is maintained in part by a dependence on the drug nicotine, a central nervous system stimulant. Smoking produces cortical activation, as directly reflected in the electroencephalographic (EEG) changes (Knott, 1988). Many people report that they smoke, even when alone, to increase their alertness and concentration on difficult or complex tasks (Frith, 1971; O'Connor, 1980; Zuckerman, Ball, & Black, 1990). But other persons smoke when they are emotionally upset or in stressful situations, claiming that smoking "calms" them. The latter effect seems paradoxical but there are explanations other than purely cognitive ones for such effects. The activation effects of nicotine may depend upon differences between individuals in their cortical reactivities. Using an EEG-derived measure of arousal, O'Connor (1982) found that smoking increased cortical arousal in extraverts but reduced it in introverts. This could explain why introverts are more likely to smoke in situations requiring concentrated attention on a task, whereas extraverts are more likely to smoke in either boring or social situations where an increase in arousal is pleasant.

Since the first reports linking cigarette smoking to lung cancer in the 1950s, the health risks of smoking have been increasingly publicized. Even before these findings, the health risks were appreciated. Cigarettes used to be referred to as "coffin nails," an earthy label that the surgeon general might put on cigarette packages in place of the more problematical: "may be injurious to your health." Most people are more aware of the risks of smoking today than they were 20 years ago. How does this awareness of risk affect smoking as a sensation-seeking mode in high and low sensation seekers?

Smoking was studied in relation to sensation seeking at the University of Delaware in the early 1970s and again in the 1980s, providing a comparison of changes in the relationship between the habit and the trait in the intervening decade and a half (Zuckerman et al., 1990). In the early 1970s 45% of the male and 40% of the female students were smokers and there was no significant sex difference. In the 1980s only 24% of the men and 37% of the women were smokers; a significantly higher proportion of the women were current smokers. If smoking was once associated with the "macho" quality, it no longer seems to be so. In the early 1970s sensation seeking was found to be more strongly associated with smoking in male than in female students. The proportions of smokers in the high, medium, and low sensation-seeking groups of males were 67%, 47%, and 18% respectively (Zuckerman et al., 1972).

Table 9.1 shows the relationship between sensation seeking and past or current smoking in students at the University of Delaware in the 1980s. The relationship is a highly significant one with current smokers constituting 20% of the high SS group, 12% of the medium SS group, and 9% of the low SS

Table 9.1. *Smoking status and sensation seeking*

Sensation seeking	n	Smoking (%)		
		Never	Past	Current
High	360	57	23	20
Medium	349	68	20	12
Low	362	78	13	9

Note: chi-square = 40.10 ($df=4$), $p<.001$.
Source: Table 3, p. 214, from "Influences of sensation seeking, gender, risk appraisal, and situational motivation on smoking," by M. Zuckerman, S. Ball, & J. Black, 1990, *Addictive Behaviors, 15,* 209–220. Copyright 1990 by Pergamon Press. Reprinted by permission.

group. Combining past and current smokers, the corresponding percentages are 43%, 32%, and 22%. Despite the fact that sensation seeking is still significantly related to smoking in the male students, less than half the proportion of high sensation-seeking males are smoking in the 1980s as compared with the 1970s (Zuckerman, 1988b). The small proportion of smokers in the low sensation-seeking group hardly changed, but given the change in the total number of males smoking, it is becoming increasingly difficult to find any low sensation-seeking male smokers. The studies show how the relationship between a particular behavioral phenomenon and sensation seeking can change in a given population at a certain time as a function of risk information and its effects on changing habits. The change is slower in the female students for reasons that we do not fully understand.

The relationship between smoking and sensation seeking has also been found for a general American population (Zuckerman & Neeb, 1980), American high school students (Andrucci, Archer, Pancoast, & Gordon, 1989), British male college students (Golding, Harpur, & Brent-Smith, 1983), a Swiss male general population (Sieber & Angst, 1977), young Norwegian Army recruits (von Knorring & Oreland, 1985), Norwegian high school students (Pederson et al., 1989), a Dutch general population (Feij & van Zuilen, 1984), and Israeli adolescents (Teichman, Barnea, & Rahav, 1989a, 1989b). In most studies the General or Total, ES and Dis scales discriminated between smokers and nonsmokers.

Zuckerman and Neeb (1980) found that past smoking was related to sensation seeking in both men and women, but current smoking was related to sensation seeking only in women. Sensation seeking was not linearly related to amount of past smoking but was higher in those who smoked to

Table 9.2. *Differences in Sensation Seeking Scale (SSS) between nonsmokers (n = 229), ex-smokers (n = 252), and regular smokers (n = 213)*

Smoking	Mean SSS scores			
	BS	TAS	mES	mTotSS
Never	3.3	5.0	2.8	11.2
Former	3.7	5.9	3.0	12.6
Irregular	4.0	5.8	2.9	12.7
Regular	4.2	5.6	3.0	12.7
F	10.65*	5.78*	0.74	10.36*

Note: BS = Boredom Susceptibility, TAS = Thrill and Adventure Seeking, mES = modified Experience Seeking, mTotSS = modified Total Sensation Seeking.
*$p < .001$.
Source: Table 2, p. 330, from "Personality traits and platelet monoamine oxidase in tobacco smoker," by L. von Knorring & L. Oreland, 1985, *Psychological Medicine, 15*, 327–334. Copyright 1985 Cambridge University Press.

any degree compared to nonsmokers. Among the current female smokers there was also an increment in SSS scores between nonsmoking and any smoking, and little difference between occasional and one- to two-pack-a-day smokers. However, the very heavy female current smokers, smoking two packs a day or more, were as *low* as nonsmokers on the SSS. In these heavy-smoking women, smoking may be more related to anxiety than to sensation seeking.

Von Knorring and Oreland (1985) compared nonsmokers, ex-smokers, irregular smokers, and regular smokers using a modified form of the translated SSS with no Dis scale and a shortened ES scale (excluding drug relevant items). Their results are shown in Table 9.2. As in the Zuckerman and Neeb (1980) study the major difference in sensation seeking was between those who never smoked and those who smoked to any degree. The strongest relationship was with the BS scale. Feij and van Zuilen (1984) also found that the General and BS scales were the only ones related to extent of smoking among smokers in a Dutch population, although all the subscales except TAS differentiated between smokers and nonsmokers. Teichman et al. (1989a) found that those who started at a younger age had the highest scores, followed by those who started later, and the constant abstainers had the lowest scores.

Recent results suggest that the relationship between sensation seeking and smoking is an all-or-none phenomenon. Low sensation seekers do not smoke at all. High sensation seekers are more likely to smoke, but are not necessarily heavy smokers. In the heaviest smoking group the reasons for smoking may be quite different for men and women. The men may smoke heavily because of boredom and because the nicotine keeps them aroused. The women who smoke excessively may be those who are anxious or depressed and who smoke to decrease arousal rather than increase it. A similar kind of difference between male and female alcoholics will be discussed in the next section.

If nicotine is the addictive ingredient in cigarettes, then those who inhale more deeply are getting higher doses and are more likely to become smoking dependent. Zuckerman et al. (1990) found that 46% of those who were able to quit smoking reported that they had inhaled very little, whereas only 6% of current smokers said this. Conversely, 62% of current smokers as compared with 22% of past smokers reported that they inhaled on almost every puff. Those who persist in smoking are probably more nicotine-dependent as indicated by their style of smoking. Sensation seeking was related to inhaling of smoke among past smokers but not among current smokers. The lack of relationship between inhaling and sensation seeking among current smokers is probably because so many of them (94%) inhale on most or almost every puff. Among past smokers 68% of the high, 41% of the middle, and 43% of the low sensation seekers said that they had inhaled on most or every puff when they smoked.

Since nicotine seems to be the element of cigarettes most strongly related to smoking for high sensation seekers, we would expect them to report smoking more in situations where increased arousal is desirable, such as tasks requiring concentrated attention or social situations. Zuckerman et al. (1990) factor analyzed the items in a Smoking Questionnaire (SQ) and found five situational factors for smoking: (1) attentive-coping, (2) negative emotionality, (3) alone-relaxed, (4) social situations, (5) heavy smoking (generalized across all situations). Sensation seeking correlated significantly with smoking in social situations in both men and women and with attentive-coping situations for men only. Smoking tends to be related to arousal seeking in men more than in women. However, whereas men had higher scores on the attentive-coping smoking factor, women actually scored higher on smoking in social situations, as well as negative-emotionality (arousal reduction need), and heavy smoking.

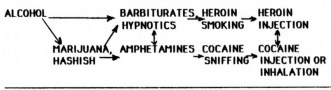

PATHWAYS TO DRUG DEPENDENCE

PERCEIVED RISK (Legal, Social, Physical Harm) ⟶
BIOLOGICAL REWARD (Potency, Speed to Peak Effect) ⟶

Figure 9.1. Pathways to drug addiction as a function of perceived risk and reward (pleasure).

Alcohol and drug use

The reasons for starting to drink and use drugs are not necessarily the same as the reasons for continuing to use them after one is dependent on them. Sensation seeking is probably more important in the early stages of alcohol and drug use than in the later stages where the drug is needed to maintain normal mood and function (Zuckerman, 1983d). The drug abuser is first motivated by curiosity, then by pleasure, and finally by the need to avoid pain and feel normal (Zuckerman, 1987a, 1987b). There is typically a progression in the use of substances from alcohol to marijuana or hashish and then to stimulant or suppressant drugs, first taken orally and then, with more potent forms, injected or smoked (Windle, Barnes, & Welte, 1989). The order varies in different cultures and at different times in our own society, depending on fads and the availability of different kinds of drugs.

Sensation seekers are looking for variety and intensity of experiences and therefore are more likely to be polydrug users, at least in their younger years. Later the polydrug user may become dependent on one particular drug and use that one exclusively. However, many users go back and forth from drugs to alcohol depending on the availability of the former. Alcohol is, of course, readily available in most countries and is cheaper than hard drugs. Even though laws restrict its consumption by children, it is not difficult for preadolescents and adolescents to find alcohol when they want it. This is why alcohol is usually the first drug of experimentation (see Figure 9.1). After alcohol one may take the suppressant or stimulant drug route, although the polydrug user may take both. As one moves to other drugs, and other ways of ingesting the drugs in search of stronger biological rewards, the risks increase. The risks include legal, social, and physical ones. Drug abusers may get arrested for the things they do to support their habits, they may be alienated from their families and friends, and they may be more willing to accept the physical risks of accidental overdose, or arrest. In terms of the risk–reward conflict (Chapter 5), sensation seeking is related to the tendency to move further along the risk continuum in anticipation of greater sensation reward without much increase in anxiety.

Because sensation seeking may play a different role in drug use during the stages of life, the chapter will be organized by developmental periods. The question of whether the sensation-seeking tendency is an antecedent or a consequence of drug use can be best answered by predictive studies starting before substance abuse or when it is in its early experimental phase.

Preadolescence and early adolescence

Using data from the Oakland growth study, Jones investigated childhood personality antecedents of alcoholism in men (M. Jones, 1968) and women (M. Jones, 1971) who 30 years later had became heavy drinkers or alcoholics. The children were first studied at the age of 10 while they were in junior high school. At this time the men who were destined to become problem drinkers were described by observers as more rebellious, undercontrolled, hostile, manipulative, self-indulgent, sensuous, negativistic, expressive, assertive, talkative, humorous, and "other-directed" than their peers who became moderate drinkers or abstainers. The total picture is one of impulsive, extraverted, and sensation-seeking boys. During high school and in early adult life, most of the same differences were found and the future problem drinkers were rated low on dependability, objectivity, calmness, productivity, and acceptance of dependency.

The girls who were to become problem drinkers showed many of the same prealcoholic traits as the boys indicating an unstable, impulsive personality. However, they also resembled the total abstainers in depressive, self-negating, and distrustful personality traits. They were submissive when young but rebellious as adults. The female heavy drinkers showed the traits of disinhibiting sensation seekers when younger, but those who were to become problem drinkers demonstrated neurotic traits in addition to impulsive ones.

Cloninger, Sigvardsson, and Bohman (1988) used the behavioral observations made of boys at 11 years of age to predict alcoholism at the age of 27 years. High novelty-seeking (sensation seeking) and *low* harm-avoidance traits were strongly predictive of later alcohol abuse. Teichman, Barnea, and Rahav (1989b) assessed alcohol and drug use in a large sample of Israeli young adolescents at two time periods a year apart. A Hebrew translation of the SSS was used with the items referring to alcohol or drugs deleted from the scores used in the analyses. Sensation seeking significantly predicted overall lifetime and current substance use, but trait and state anxiety and depressive mood did not. The same results were found at every age from 14 to 17 with the exception of a weak but significant *negative* relationship between depressive mood and substance use at age 14. Sensation seeking was higher in early users of wine, beer, hard liquor, hashish, and depressant drugs, but trait and state anxiety and depressive mood were related only to use of depressant drugs. Users scored higher on dysphoric affect than nonusers. Earlier use was a strong predictor of later use, and drug availability was a weaker predictor and only significant for the 15- and 18-year-old groups. After these two variables were extracted from the multiple regression, only sensation seeking added significantly to the prediction of drug use at ages 15, 16, and 17.

A second large-scale prediction study was conducted by Bates, Lambourie, and White (1985) on 584 American adolescents aged 15 or 18 at the first time of assessment and 18 or 21 at the second assessment three years later. Subjects were randomly selected from the New Jersey population. Only the Dis scale from SSS form V was used, and two items related to alcohol or drug use were deleted. The Dis scale and drug use inventories were given at both times of assessment. Mean Dis scores did not change over the three year interval between assessments in either age group but alcohol and marijuana use and number of illicit drugs used increased, mostly in the group going from 15 to 18 years of age.

Although there was no mean change in Dis, some individual subjects showed increases or decreases over the 3-year interval. Alcohol and drug use was related to disinhibition sensation seeking at a given time in adolescence, and changes in Dis were related to future changes in level, quantity, and effects of alcohol and drug use. Those who rose in Dis from an initially low level tended to increase alcohol and drug usage, whereas the high Dis subjects whose Dis scores dropped tended to level off in substance abuse. Although the relationship of change scores in Dis to change scores in drug usage is suggestive of causation it is still basically correlational. Changes in drug use could result in changes in Dis rather than the other way around. One would have to know the precise time of change of both to make stronger causal inferences.

Concurrent correlational studies of large groups of adolescents have been done in Scandinavia. Pederson et al. (1989) studied a sample of more than 1,000 Norwegian students aged 16 to 19 from seven senior high schools. They compared the reported uses of specific drugs with a shortened 18-item

Table 9.3. *Significant correlations between drug use and SSS*
Disinhibition and Experience Seeking scales for male (n = 466) and female
(n = 501) Norwegian high school students

	Disinhibition		Experience seeking	
	Males	Females	Males	Females
Tobacco	.28	.34	—	—
Alcohol	.46	.40	.19	.15
Cannabis	.18	—	.22	.17
Inhalants	.27	.15	—	—
Tranquilizers	—	—	.19	—

Note: The correlations listed have $p < .01$.
Source: Table 2, p. 388, from "Patterns of drug use and sensation seeking among adolescents in Norway," by W. Pederson, S. E. Clausen, & N. J. Lavik, 1989, *Acta Psychiatrica Scandinavica, 79,* 386–390. Copyright Acta Psychiatrica Scandinavica 1989. Reprinted with permission.

translation of the SSS that excluded all items mentioning drugs, and included scales for TAS, Dis, and ES but not BS. Table 9.3 shows the correlations between the use of tobacco, alcohol, cannabis, inhalants, and tranquilizers and the Dis and ES scales in boys and girls. No correlations were found with the TAS subscale. Tobacco, alcohol, and inhalant use correlated primarily with Dis for both sexes. Extent of alcohol use also correlated with ES but the correlations were much lower than those with Dis. Cannabis use correlated about equally with Dis and ES in males, but only with ES in females. Tranquilizer use correlated only with ES.

Von Knorring, Oreland, and von Knorring (1987) used a total population of over 1,200 18-year-old Swedish male military draftees. Subjects took a translated SSS that excluded the entire Dis scale and items in the ES scale that alluded to an interest in drug use. Alcohol and mixed drug and alcohol abuse groups both showed signs of incipient alcoholism in reports of increased alcohol tolerance, blackouts, inability to abstain, and loss of control during alcohol consumption. There was little difference between the two abuser groups on the SSS scales but both groups were higher than abstainer and infrequent user groups on Total, TAS, ES, and BS scales, as well as Impulsivity and Monotony Avoidance scales.

Victor, Grossman, and Eisenman (1973) studied marijuana use in nearly 1,000 American high school students between the 8th and 12th grades in a middle-income, predominantly white neighborhood in Philadelphia. They used a scale of adventuresomeness (resembling TAS), P. H. Pearson's (1970) Internal Sensation Seeking scale (resembling ES), a scale of creativity (also resembling ES), and scales of authoritarianism and manifest anxiety. Both creativity and internal sensation seeking were highly related to the extent of marijuana use (frequent users highest, nonusers lowest) and adventure-someness was also related positively to usage. Authoritarianism was nega-tively related to marijuana use. Manifest anxiety was totally unrelated to usage. In another study done with Canadian high school students in the politically turbulent 1970s, Kohn and Annis (1978) found that both internal sensation seeking and sociopolitical outlooks predicted attitudes toward mari-juana, which in turn predicted marijuana use. These findings, however, could be limited to those times in which drug use and attitudes toward the Vietnam war were closely identified. More current studies are needed on the relation of conservatism–radicalism to drug use.

Victor et al. (1973) found that level of marijuana use was related to use of other drugs including amphetamines, barbiturates, LSD, opium, and heroin. This tendency has been shown in modern path analyses studies (see Figure 9.1). This does not mean that all those who use marijuana go on to use harder drugs, because most do not. However, the openness to experience and the willingness to take risks involved in sensation seeking can easily lead one beyond marijuana into the use of more potent and risky drugs.

Huba, Newcomb, and Bentler (1981) studied the relationships between abbreviated sensation-seeking scales and alcohol and drug use in a sample of over 1,000 high school students between the 10th and 12th grades. The data were analyzed using canonical correlation, which attempts to align factors found in two sets of data. One SSS factor was highly identified with Dis and was more closely associated with a substance abuse factor of beer, wine, hard liquor, marijuana, and hashish. The second SSS factor was dominated by ES and secondarily by BS. The correlating factor in the drug set included the marijuana and hashish, and other drugs in addition including barbiturates, sedatives, amphetamines, cocaine, LSD, and other psychedelics. A third SSS dimension composed of TAS correlated positively with the use of alcohol and marijuana but negatively with use of cigarettes and hard drugs.

All of the sensation-seeking scales correlated significantly with both licit (alcohol and tobacco) and illicit (marijuana and hard drugs) drug use in females, but only Dis was associated with illicit drug use for males (New-comb & McGee, 1991). In all cases Dis was clearly the strongest correlate of both licit and illicit drug use.

Newcomb and McGee followed this group over the period of one year. For females a general sensation-seeking factor predicted increased alcohol use one year later, but for males only Dis predicted alcohol use and only one aspect of alcohol use: quantity.

Andrucci et al. (1989) compared users and nonusers of a variety of drugs in an adolescent high school population using both the MMPI and the SSS V as predictors of drug use. The Total SSS "was the most effective and powerful predictor of use versus nonuse" (p. 263) of any drug and of most specific drugs. The SSS Total, ES, and Dis scales significantly differentiated users from nonusers for alcohol, amphetamines, barbiturates, cocaine, hallucinogens, marijuana, and narcotics; users of all of these substances scored higher than nonusers. Note that the drugs include a mixture of stimulant, suppressant, and psychedelic types. There is no type of drug that is used more by low sensation seekers than by highs. Furthermore, all of the SSS subscales differentiated users from nonusers of amphetamines, barbiturates, cocaine, and marijuana. The general sensation-seeking tendency in users is not confined to scales relevant to a particular style of sensation seeking. Anxiety and depression scales predicted little except barbiturate use (perhaps self-medication). When the Pd, Ma, and MacAndrew Alcoholism Scale were combined with the SSS Total score as predictors in a discriminant function, the SSS had the highest weighting for each class of drugs, and for alcohol it was the sole significant predictor. Within the drug-using group, polydrug users were higher on Total SSS than single-drug users and removal of SSS relevant items in the ES and Dis scales did not change the results. The Total SSS was the sole predictor in the multivariate discriminant function.

In all of these studies of youthful drug use, sensation seeking is strongly implicated whereas anxiety and depression seem to have little or no predictive value. At the ages studied most drug use is still experimental and only a small percentage have even tried the harder drugs. Of Victor et al.'s (1973) high school students, only 2% had tried heroin and hardly any of the Israeli or Scandinavian samples had used opiates. In the Andrucci et al. (1989) study, 4% of the students had tried narcotics and 12% had used cocaine. However, many more were beginning to experiment with amphetamines, barbiturates, and hallucinogens. Alcohol use was the most common form of substance abuse in these adolescent subjects and some were already showing early symptoms of alcoholism. As alcohol becomes more commonly used, many take up its use because of peer pressure rather than any kind of experience-seeking tendencies. These types are not likely to become alcoholics or even heavy drinkers.

There is little support for the idea that anxiety is a primary trait associated with youthful drinking and drug use. Only the use of depressants in the Israeli sample was associated with anxiety and depression. Israeli high school seniors have more to be anxious about since they must begin their military service right after graduation even if they plan to go on to college later. However, depressants may be used to cope with the anxiety developing out of drug use in older drug users. Those who use stimulant drugs may need depressants just to "come down" from the extreme states of arousal produced by amphetamine and cocaine and in order to sleep.

Young adults

When discussing drug and alcohol use in college or other populations of young adults one must consider the time of the study since drugs wax and wane in popularity over time. Our first studies of sensation seeking and drugs were done in the early 1970s (Zuckerman et al., 1970; Zuckerman et al., 1972). At that time marijuana, hashish, amphetamines, LSD, and barbiturates were the most popular drugs on campus. The heavy-drinking group was a different one from the group using drugs. Drugs were a political statement as well as a path to self-discovery. In both studies high sensation seekers were more likely to use any drug than low sensation seekers (74% vs. 23% in Zuckerman et al., 1970; 67% vs. 31% in the Zuckerman et al., 1972). A recent study done at a nearby university (Kumar, Pekala, & Cummings, 1993) shows considerable stability over a 20-year interval with 71% of high male and 66% of high female sensation seekers now reporting having tried drugs contrasted with 17% of low males and 21% of low female sensation seekers. On the other hand the significant difference in regular drinking (six drinks per week or more) found in the 1970 University of Delaware study (53% of highs vs. 13% of lows) was not found in the 1972 study because of a decrease in the percent of high (42%) and an increase in the percent of low (38%) sensation seekers drinking regularly. Substances that are popular with high and low sensation seekers do change with time.

An analysis of individual drugs used by college students (Zuckerman, 1979a, table 10.8, p. 286) showed significant differences in use between high and low sensation seekers for nearly every popular drug, including marijuana, hashish, amphetamines, and LSD. Actually every drug listed was used more by high than by low sensation seekers, although the difference was not significant for the less popular drugs because of the low numbers of users in both groups. Cocaine use, for instance, was found in only 6% of the subjects in one study and 9% in the other, but all of them were from the high sensation-seeking groups in both studies. The only drug used to any significant extent by low sensation seekers was tranquilizers, but more high than low sensation seekers had used them as well.

Zuckerman et al. (1972) correlated total drug and alcohol use with the SSS IV scales and a questionnaire measuring sex experience. Drug use correlated significantly with the General and all of the SSS subscales for female college students and all but the Dis scale for males. The highest correlation was with the ES scale, as we might expect, but the correlations with the other subscales were not much lower. Drug and sex experience correlated highly in both the men and women. The pattern of correlation for alcohol use was more delimited, correlating only with TAS and Dis in men (perhaps the hard-drinking athletic types or "jocks") and with ES and Dis in women. Alcohol use in men was not correlated with either sexual experience or drug use, but in women it correlated with both of these. The data for men showed a separation of groups using drugs from those using alcohol. In later studies this distinction is not as clear, and the same men tend to drink *and* use drugs.

Segal and Singer (1976; Segal, Huba, & Singer, 1980) did a large-scale survey of personality and drug use among college students at two universities and among naval personnel. They asked college students their reasons for using particular drugs. The main reasons given for use of marijuana, hallucinogens, depressants, and even narcotics were to experience something new and "curiosity." Thus an internal sensation- or experience-seeking motive seems primary with early use of most drugs among college students. The most frequently given reason for drinking was "just to be sociable." More specifically, students say that alcohol "makes get-togethers more fun," "makes you less shy," and "makes you feel happier." The responses suggest a social disinhibitory motive plus mood elevation as primary reasons for drinking. However other reasons given suggest that alcohol may be used by some when feeling stressed, bored, or depressed.

Segal et al. (1980) divided users into four major categories: nonusers (neither alcohol or drug use), alcohol only users, marijuana only (but not excluding alcohol) users, and multidrug users. All drug and drinking items were removed from the SSS scales before analyses. Significant differences among the four groups on all of the SSS scales were found, and the SSS scales, particularly ES and Dis, proved to be the primary personality predictors of drug and alcohol use in multivariate analyses. Locus of control, personality need scales from the PRF, and daydreaming-style scales had little predictive value for drug use and little discriminative value in comparisons of the four groups. Figure 9.2 shows the mean scores on ES and Figure 9.3 on Dis of male and female college students and naval personnel divided into the four types of nonusers and users. Among the college students significant increases in ES and Dis are seen going from nonusers to alcohol only users and from alcohol only users to marijuana users, but there was only a

EXPERIENCE SEEKING SCALE

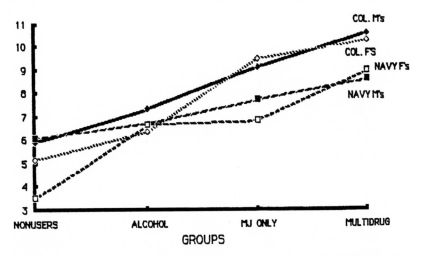

Figure 9.2. SSS Experience Seeking (ES) mean scores of substance nonusers, alcohol only users, marijuana only users, and multidrug users. Based on data from Segal et al. (1980).

nonsignificant increment going from marijuana users to polydrug users. The big step seems to be from legal (alcohol) to illegal (marijuana) drugs rather than from marijuana to other drugs. However, in the naval men and women there was less difference between alcohol only and marijuana only users. For them the largest differences in sensation seeking, apart from that between nonusers and drinkers, is the difference between marijuana only and polydrug users.

Galizio, Rosenthal, and Stein (1983) also classified their college student population into nonusers (of drugs), marijuana only users, and polydrug users. For the General, TAS, and BS scales of the SSS IV the polydrug and marijuana only users scored higher than the nonusers with no difference between the two types of users. However, for the ES and Dis scales all three groups differed significantly with the highest scores in the polydrug users, the lowest in the nonusers, and the marijuana users intermediate. More polydrug users (42%) liked to do high sensation-seeking activities, such as meeting people, dancing, and engaging in sexual activity, than low drug users (24%), and marijuana users were intermediate (37%). The SSS Total score correlated significantly ($r = .40$) with the percentage of high-stimulation

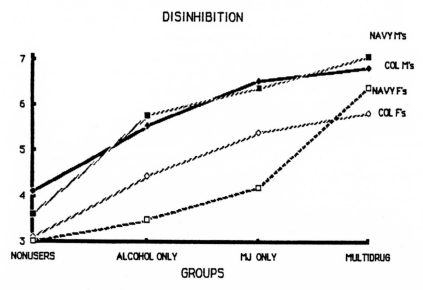

Figure 9.3. SSS Disinhibition (Dis) mean scores of substance nonusers, alcohol only users, marijuana only users, and multidrug users. Based on data from Segal et al. (1980).

activities in their lists. A drug preference index was developed that measured reported preferences for stimulant and depressant drugs. Marijuana was a third category kept separate from the first two classes. An index of stimulant minus depressant drug choices was also calculated. The SS scales did not correlate with any of these measures of drug preferences, but the percentage of high sensation-seeking activities in the reinforcer list correlated with the drug choice index. Subjects who liked many stimulating activities had a tendency to prefer stimulants and hallucinogens to alcohol, opiates, and bar-biturates.

Jaffe and Archer (1987) compared the SSS, MMPI, and drug and alcohol abuse scales as predictors of use of various drugs in a college population. The SSS was the most effective and powerful predictor of use in 7 out of 10 classes of drugs, even more powerful than personality scales specifically developed to predict alcohol and drug abuse. The SSS was also strongly predictive of polydrug abuse. Douglass and Khavari (1978) found that all subscales of the SSS correlated significantly with a summary drug use index composed of many different drugs; the highest correlation was with the ES scale.

Anxiety and depression have been regarded as major causes of drinking and drug use, largely based on reports from those with serious drinking and drug problems who are willing to admit that they have a problem. However, much of the stress and depression in drug and alcohol abusers is a direct consequence of substance abuse, including legal, vocational, and relationship problems and the withdrawal effects of alcohol and drugs.

The longitudinal studies of future alcoholics previously discussed (Cloninger et al., 1988; M. Jones, 1968, 1971) suggest that in boys who were to become alcoholic, neurotic problems were not apparent. In fact, impulsivity was their main problem and, if anything, they had too little anxiety rather than too much. Loper, Kammeier, and Hoffman (1973) examined the MMPI records of men taken when they were entering college, to their status as alcoholics 13 years later. The college men who were to become alcoholic had higher scores on the Psychopathic Deviate and Hypomania scales of the MMPI (the latter scale is consistently correlated with the SSS), but did not differ from their classmates on the anxiety and depression scales of the MMPI, and actually scored lower on a Social Maladjustment (neuroticism) scale.

Concurrent personality and drinking studies of young men in college also suggest a major role for sensation seeking and little influence of anxiety at this stage in their lives. Schwartz, Burkhart, and Green (1978) compared extent of drinking in college students with sensation-seeking and anxiety scales. Sensation seeking accounted for 33% of the variance in drinking while anxiety scales only added an additional 1% to the prediction provided by the SSS scales. All of the SSS scales correlated with drinking, but the correlations with all but one of the anxiety scales were insignificant. The exception was a small but significant negative correlation ($r = .15$) between a physical danger scale and the drinking index. This is the same kind of measure used by Cloninger et al. (1988) that was related to future alcoholism in boys. In both studies present or future alcohol abuse was related to low fear of physical harm. This is also the only type of anxiety scale that is related (negatively) to sensation seeking (Chapter 3).

Similar results are found in a study comparing heavy and light alcohol use in another college population. Ratliff and Burkhardt (1984) compared these groups on measures of sensation seeking (SSS form V), depression, self-esteem, and anxiety. Large and significant differences were found on all of the sensation seeking scales, particularly disinhibition. There was no relation between anxiety of any type and drinking in women. In men the heavy drinkers reported less anxiety in dangerous situations than the light drinkers and there was also less anxiety in interactions with the opposite sex. The authors had expected the women to show more neurotic trends associated with drinking, but the heavy drinking women reported no more anxiety or depression and actually fewer problems resulting from drinking than the male drinkers. Women expressed less state anxiety than men when drinking in daily routine situations, but more anxiety than men when drinking in physically dangerous situations.

Forsyth and Hundleby (1987) also investigated the situational factor in drinking in college students. Reported frequency of drinking correlated significantly with all of the SSS V scales and the Total score. The correlation was highest with Dis, even though the items in the Dis scale referring to drinking had been removed. The EPI extraversion scale also correlated positively with cross-situational frequency of drinking but neuroticism did not correlate at all with drinking. Analyses of the interactions of classes of situations with personality showed that high sensation seekers were relatively more desirous of drinking than lows in boring situations compared with neutral ones. Persons high on neuroticism reported relatively more desire to drink than more stable persons in stress and social situations.

The lack of relationship between anxiety and alcohol use is also found for marijuana use. Brill, Crumpton, and Grayson (1971) found that sensation-seeking and psychopathic-deviate scales were related to frequency of marijuana use in a college population, whereas MMPI scales of depression, manifest anxiety, and ego strength were not. Khavari et al. (1977) used a more general population sample consisting of semiskilled Midwestern industrial plant workers recruited from labor unions. Degree of use of marijuana, hashish, LSD, and other psychedelics all correlated significantly with the General and all of the subscales from the SSS IV; the correlations in each case were highest with the ES scale. The correlation between ES and the use of marijuana was .59. In a later analysis of the same group using other personality scales in addition to the SSS, they found that the ES scale accounted for the greatest amount of criterion variance; Dis and BS from the SSS, and measures of social alienation and traditionalism in social values also contributed to prediction. Measures of extraversion, neuroticism, and manifest anxiety were not able to predict any class of drug abuse.

Other recent studies just using sensation seeking–type scales have continued to find strong relationships between the trait and marijuana use in college students. Satinder and Black (1984) found that marijuana users scored significantly higher than nonusers on all of the scales of the SSS V with the strongest findings on the Dis subscale and the Total score. Eisenman, Grossman, and Goldstein (1980) used the Pearson Novelty Seeking scales, and other scales for creativity, desire for novelty and adventuresomeness. College

students in the Philadelphia area were classified according to level of marijuana use. Internal sensation seeking, adventuresomeness, creativity, and
external sensation seeking all related significantly to marijuana use.

Physicians are at special risk for drug abuse because of their easy access to
drugs. Golding and Cornish (1987) factor analyzed drugs used and personality scales including the General SSS using 2-year medical students as subjects. Sensation seeking and the P scale loaded on a factor most highly
identified by usage of drugs and alcohol, and smoking. Use of tranquilizers
loaded on a second factor related to neuroticism. Forney, Ripley, and Forney
(1988) found that heavy drinkers among medical students were more involved in sensation-seeking sports and other sensation-seeking types of activities than abstainers or light drinkers. However sensation seeking was not
predictive of amount of drinking in physicians (McAuliffe, Rohman, &
Wechsler, 1984). Carrol et al. (1982) selected subjects from the top and
bottom deciles of the SSS distribution in a class of medical students. A drug
history revealed that 87% of the highs and only 12% of the lows reported
having smoked marijuana. Use of other psychoactive drugs was reported by
almost half of the high sensation seekers and none of the lows. Conversely,
about a third of the low sensation seekers reported being total abstainers from
tobacco, alcohol, and drugs, whereas none of the highs were such abstainers.

McAuliffe et al. (1984) investigated drug use among randomly selected
physicians and medical students using a special 20-item adaptation of the
SSS. They also studied the relation of life and job stress, emotional problems, psychopathology, and other variables to drug use. Among both the
physicians and the medical students, sensation seeking was the highest correlate of recreational drug use, although a history of life stress and emotional
problems also correlated with drug use. However, the number of repeated
episodes of recreational drug use correlated as highly or more highly with
life stress and emotional problems. Sensation seeking correlated low or not
at all with the use of drugs for self-treatment for physical or emotional
problems. The drugs used for recreation by the high sensation-seeking physicians are the same as those used by college students: marijuana, cocaine,
hallucinogens, and amphetamines. Opiates and sedatives were less commonly used. The main drugs used for self-treatment were tranquilizers.

Choice and effects of drugs in experimental settings

The factors determining choice of drugs among drug abusers will be discussed later. There are two studies that have used the SSS in exploring the
choice of drugs among normals actually given the drugs in experimental

settings. These studies are interesting in answering the question of whether high sensation seekers have a preference for stimulant drugs that increase arousal and low sensation seekers have a preference for suppressant drugs that reduce arousal. The optimal level of arousal hypothesis for sensation seeking would predict these results. Both of these studies have used amphetamine as a stimulant drug, diazepam (valium) as the suppressant drug, and a reaction to a placebo as a standard of comparison.

De Wit, Uhlenhuth, and Johanson (1986) found that two-thirds of subjects comparing placebo and amphetamine indicated a preference for amphetamine. In contrast only about a third of subjects chose diazepam in preference to placebo. These results reflect the difference in drug preferences in the streets where amphetamines are sought much more than tranquilizers. In the diazepam experiment the mean SSS scores of the nonchoosers and choosers (18.9 and 20.0) were not significantly different. The two groups also did not differ on locus of control or manifest anxiety scores. In the amphetamine experiment the choosers mean SSS score of 20.7 was about 3 points higher than the mean score (17.8) of the nonchoosers. Ordinarily a three point difference on the Total score of the SSS would be significant with a moderately large sample size, but the sample size in this experiment was only 11 in one group and 20 in the other. As it stands, neither outcome is supportive of the optimal level of arousal hypothesis. The problem with diazepam is that it only sedates and does not usually give the kind of "high" that other depressants, like alcohol and heroin, provide at lower doses.

Carrol et al. (1982) compared the effects of amphetamine, diazepam, and a placebo, given to medical students selected from the high and low ranges of the SSS. Each drug was given on a different occasion and both subjects and experimenters were blind as to which drug the subject was taking on a given day. Contrary to the optimal level of arousal hypothesis, both high *and* low sensation seekers liked amphetamine better than placebo or diazepam and showed more positive mood changes and performance improvement after taking amphetamine. There were only drug effects and no interaction of sensation seeking with drug type.

Perhaps our mistake was in using diazepam as a suppressant drug rather than some other type that reduces arousal but also produces some euphoric effects. Euphoria is not a necessary consequence of either high or low arousal. Arousal and hedonic tone are independent dimensions. Amphetamine produces both euphoria and arousal, whereas diazepam produces only lowered arousal. Weinstein (1978) found that a personality trait described as "sensual hedonism" correlated significantly with use of alcohol, marijuana, hallucinogens, and amphetamines but not with use of barbiturates or tranquil-

izers. There are other drugs like lactate and yohimbine that increase arousal
with only negative mood changes, primarily anxiety.

Schwarz, Burkhart, and Green (1982) followed up their previous correlational work (Schwarz et al., 1978), showing that sensation seeking, but not
anxiety, correlated with reported extent of alcohol use in college students, by
doing an experimental study in which students were allowed free access to
an alcoholic beverage. The General SSS was significantly related to the
amount drunk in the experiment but anxiety was not, thus confirming the
relevance of sensation seeking and the irrelevance of anxiety to drinking in
the previous correlational study.

Alcoholics and drug abusers

Exactly where one crosses the line from heavy drinking to alcoholism, or
from recreational drug use to drug abuse, or from drug abuse to drug
dependence is not clear even with the help of standards in the DSM III. For
the purposes of this section alcoholics and drug abusers will be identified by
whatever criteria were used in particular studies to define them. Some alcoholics use nothing but alcohol, whereas others use a variety of illegal drugs
in addition to alcohol. After experimenting with a variety of drugs, some
drug users come to favor a particular drug and use it almost exclusively while
others continue polydrug use, ingesting whatever is available or suits their
mood at particular times. Taking only a single type of drug suggests a lack
of boredom susceptibility and low experience seeking. However, the abuser
may become tolerant to the effects of the drug and dependent on it to avoid
negative feelings and painful somatic states. Sensation seeking at this stage
is irrelevant, the drug is needed for self-medication.

Kilpatrick, Sutker, and Smith (1976) compared groups of young veterans,
most in their 20s, from substance abuse and general medical wards of a
Veterans' Administration hospital on the SSS and other personality measures.
The groups consisted of (1) regular drug users including users of heroin and
barbiturates, or polydrug users who usually use both stimulants and depressants; (2) problem drinkers (alcoholics); (3) occasional drug and alcohol
users (the modal group in this population); and (4) nonusers of either.
Significant differences were found among the four groups on all of the SSS
IV scales. Occasional drug and alcohol users scored higher than the nonuser
group on all SSS scales. Problem drinkers were higher than occasional users
on only one scale, BS. The regular drug users scored higher than the problem
drinkers on all of the scales except BS. The general conclusion is that the

nonuser group is abnormally low and the regular drug user group is abnormally high on sensation seeking. The only type of sensation seeking characteristic in the alcoholics was their susceptibility to boredom, a trait they share with regular drug users.

On measures of neuroticism and anxiety there were no differences between occasional users and nonusers, but both of these groups were lower than problem drinkers and regular drug user groups on these measures. The anxiety found in the alcoholics and regular drug abusers is in contrast to the lack of anxiety found in young drug users and heavy drinkers, and the absence of signs of neuroticism or anxiety in future alcoholics when they were young (from longitudinal studies). The current anxiety found in many alcoholics probably developed after they became alcoholic and in reaction to their life stress. Signs of neuroticism and anxiety in drug abusers are often seen in drug abusers just after entering a treatment program, but tend to decrease after 6 to 8 months in treatment (Zuckerman, Sola, Masterson, & Angelone, 1975). Their initial scores on scales of depression and anxiety were higher than those of a comparable population of drug abusers in prison (Skolnick & Zuckerman, 1979), suggesting that their anxiety was reactive to the current stresses of their indeterminant legal outcome and the program itself, which was of a tough confrontational type. In contrast, scores on the SSS in drug program and prison groups of drug abusers were not different in the pretest and the only difference on the second testing was a lower BS score in the prisoners, perhaps due to habituation to the monotonous prison conditions.

Alcoholics

One would not think that chronic alcoholics would still be high sensation seekers after years of heavy drinking. However, a group of chronic alcoholics at a veteran's administration center who were over 55 years of age were higher on BS and Dis scales of the SSS than a group of comparable age veterans from the same hospital (Kipatrick, McAlhany, McCurdy, Shaw, & Roitzsch, 1982). They also scored higher on anxiety scales of various types. The differences found between this older group of alcoholics and controls were essentially the same as those found between young alcoholics and controls at the same hospital in the earlier study (Kilpatrick et al., 1976).

The diagnosis of alcoholism covers a heterogeneous range of personality types (Nerviano, 1976). Some attempts have been made to distinguish two major types based on patterns of drinking, age of onset, and antisocial behavior. Two studies classified alcoholics by their scores on standardized alcohol screening tests (Mookherjee, 1986; O'Neil et al., 1983). O'Neil et al. used the MacAndrew (1979) scale from the MMPI to distinguish a group (called "nonalcoholic") carrying a diagnosis of alcoholism but scoring in the nonalcoholic range of the test, from groups scoring in the low, middle, and high range of alcoholism on the scale. The nonalcoholic group began drinking at a later age than those scoring in the alcoholic range on the test, but groups did not differ on duration of drinking or of heavy drinking. Higher scores on the alcoholism scale were associated with a history of drug abuse in addition to alcohol abuse. Drinking-related arrests and convictions were low in the nonalcoholic group and highest in those in the high range of the scale. Although the SSS was not actually used in the study, the authors state that the men in the high range of alcoholism were "uninhibited, energetic, outgoing (including more drinking in bars), self-confident, and given to the use of substances for psychotropic effect without regard for subsequent legal or personal consequences. The recurring theme over all of these groups of descriptions is that of sensation seeking (Zuckerman, 1979a), the striving to maintain an optimal level of arousal through engaging in a variety of exciting, risky, stimulating, and/or uninhibited behaviors" (O'Neill et al., 1983).

Mookherjee (1986) used the Michigan Alcoholism Screening test to classify a group of men from rural Tennessee who were convicted of drunken driving. Based on the test they were classified into alcoholic, probable alcoholic, and nonalcoholic groups. The groups differed significantly on an unspecified scale of sensation seeking with the alcoholic group scoring highest and the nonalcoholic group scoring the lowest on the scale. Malatesta, Sutker, and Treiber (1981) compared subgroups of men differentiated on the basis of arrests for public drunkenness. The chronics had a history of 20 or more involuntary admissions to the detoxification center over a 3-year period, whereas the acutes had 5 or fewer admissions during the same period. Chronics scored significantly higher than acutes on the General and all the subscales of the SSS IV. The mean score of the chronics on the General scale was nearly twice that of the acutes. The authors conclude that "chronic offenders can be seen as similar to life style illicit drug abusers, whose antisocial cognitions and behavior bring them into repeated conflict with societal norms" (p. 293).

Von Knorring, Palm, and Andersson (1985) have developed a method for classifying alcoholics based on age of onset and social complications such as alcohol-related job loss or arrest, drunken driving, criminality, and illegal drug use. Alcoholics with a late onset and few social problems are called type I and those with early onset and many social problems are classified as type II. Type II alcoholics show more evidence of heredity in adoption studies and a stronger relationship to biological markers like low levels of the enzyme MAO. They scored higher on the Swedish SSS than those labeled type I (Oreland, Hallman, von Knorring, & Edman, 1988).

Most of these results suggest that the chronic, antisocial type of alcoholic is more sensation seeking and aggressive, whereas the less chronic, more socialized type is low sensation seeking and more inhibited in normal assert-iveness as well as aggression. Sturgis, Calhoun, and Best (1979) classified alcoholics admitted to the alcoholic ward of a veterans' hospital on the basis of the Rathus (1973) Assertiveness Schedule (RAS). The high assertive group of alcoholics scored significantly higher than the low assertive group on the General and BS scales of the SSS IV. The low assertives also scored higher on scales of deviancy, depression, paranoia, anxiety, neuroticism, and extraversion.

Galizio, Gerstenhaber, and Friedensen (1985) classified alcoholics in a treatment program into extreme high and low sensation-seeking groups on the basis of their scores on the SSS IV. The high sensation-seeking group was younger and used many other drugs in addition to alcohol. The low sensation group reported virtually no other drug use beside prescribed tran-quilizers. They drank to avoid or escape from physical withdrawal symp-toms. They were clearly drug-dependent. The high sensation-seeking group said that they drank along with taking drugs to heighten the effects of both.

The studies of male alcoholics suggest that high sensation seeking is specifically associated with an early onset, more chronic, and aggressive antisocial type of alcoholic who also uses other drugs, whereas low sensation seeking is more typical in a late onset type of alcoholism characterized by neurotic problems such as anxiety and inhibition. The first type seems to be more weighted by genetic and biological predisposition factors and, as will be seen in later chapters, it shares these markers with sensation-seeking trait.

Drug abusers

In the 1970s heroin users constituted the main type of hard drug users, and cocaine was not as widely used. The soft drug users took suppressant drug pills and amphetamine by pill or injection, as well as psychedelics. Craig (1982, 1986) reviewed personality studies of heroin addicts and concluded that most studies show them to be high sensation seekers despite their preference for a depressant drug. He also noted that there is no relation between heroin addiction and extraversion. Although there is some elevation on depression, this subsides with treatment. Platt and Labate (1976) found that prisoners in a youth detention center with a history of heroin use scored higher than non–heroin user prisoners on General and ES scales. Skolnick and Zuckerman (1979) compared hard drug users (mainly heroin addicts) with soft drug users (mainly amphetamine) from a treatment center and found that the soft drug users were higher on the SS General and BS scales. Carrol and Zuckerman (1977) rated drug histories for depressant drug use (mainly heroin) and stimulant drug use. Those with relatively higher stimulant than depressant use scored higher on the ES scale and depressant drug use correlated negatively with ES. The Dis scale correlated positively with both stimulant and hallucinogenic drug uses; the correlations were significant but low. These studies do not suggest very broad sensation-seeking differences between different types of drug abusers within the drug-abusing population. The differences between all types of drug abusers and nonabusers on sensation seeking are much greater than the differences, if any, between stimulant and depressant drug users.

Kaestner et al. (1977) correlated sensation seeking with the number of drugs used by clients in three ethnic groups in a drug treatment center. The range of drugs used was more restrictive in the black and Hispanic groups and, perhaps because of this, there was little correlation of number of drugs with sensation seeking (only ES correlated with polydrug use in the black group). In the white drug abusers, TAS, Dis, and ES all correlated with number of drugs used.

Sutker et al. (1978) also reported that blacks used fewer drugs than whites and tended to prefer opiates and depressants more than white drug abusers. This difference is consistent with the lower scores of blacks on the General SSS and ES in particular. High sensation seekers reported earlier and more varied drug use than low sensation seekers, but the groups did not differ in drug preference. High and low sensation seekers did not differ in the reasons they gave for using drugs. For the first use of alcohol, 62% of the lows said they were motivated by social influences, whereas 67% of the high sensation seekers said that they first used alcohol out of curiosity or the desire for pleasure. Kern, Kenkel, Templer, and Newell (1986) compared drug preferences and sensation seeking in a prison population. Although those who said that they felt best after taking opiates, stimulants, or hallucinogens scored higher on the SSS than those who only used alcohol, there were no differences among the three drug preference groups. Gali..io et al. (1983) compared depressant drug abusers (almost all heroin users) with polydrug users among clients in a drug program. The polydrug users were significantly higher than the opiate users on the TAS, ES, and General scales of the SSS IV, and this was true for blacks as well as whites even though whites scored higher than blacks on TAS, ES, and General scales.

Moorman, deCocq, van Delwünen, Wessel, and Bauer (1989) used the Dutch version of the SSS with drug abusers in methadone, detoxification, and therapeutic community programs. The majority of the group comprised heroin addicts but many had also used other drugs like cocaine and amphetamines. University students were used as a control group. The drug abusers scored significantly higher on the Total and all the subscales of the SSS. Kohn, Barnes, and Hoffman (1979) used the Pearson Novelty Experiencing scales with a large sample of young male inmates of a correctional center. Both the External Sensation Seeking and Internal Sensation Seeking scales correlated significantly with all uses of all four categories of drugs: psychedelics, narcotics, amphetamines, and barbiturates. Internal sensation seeking was the most important predictor of drug use accounting for about half of the explained variance.

Thus far, all of the studies indicate little or only weak relationships between sensation seeking and different types of drug use or preferences within the general drug-abusing group. However, almost all of these studies had subjects who used many different kinds of drugs and the measures of drug use or preference were only relative ones. Another problem with most studies is that the subjects were either in treatment programs or prison where there are many kinds of pressures that might distort reporting on sensation-seeking needs. Spotts and Shontz (1984, 1986) took a different approach. They screened over 1,000 candidates who were not in programs or incarceration, but were currently in the community leading independent (but not necessarily legal) lives and still using drugs. Each subject selected was a relatively pure user with a heavy commitment to one particular drug. Although they had experimented with different drugs in earlier years they had decided on one particular drug of choice and had been using it for anywhere from 2 to 27 years. There were only nine of these pure types in each type of drug group as well as a control group but all groups were closely matched for age, sex, IQ, and socioeconomic background. Education was closely matched in the drug abuser groups but was higher in the controls. Table 9.4 shows the mean SSS scores in the five groups.

An optimal level of arousal theory of sensation seeking predicts that the two stimulant user groups (cocaine and amphetamine) would score higher than the normal controls, whereas the two depressant drug user groups (opiate and barbiturate) would score lower than the controls. Although the overall differences between groups were significant, the pattern of change shown in Table 9.4 does not conform to the theoretical expectations. On all scales the amphetamine group scored the highest and the cocaine group scored the lowest. The differences between the opiate, barbiturate, and

Table 9.4. *Mean Sensation Seeking Scale (SSS) scores of specific drug chronic user groups*

Groups[a]	SSS				
	General	TAS	ES	Dis	BS
Amphetamine users	14.11	11.67	13.11	9.44	8.00
Barbiturate/sedative users	13.11	10.00	11.00	7.33	7.22
Nonusers	12.78	9.67	11.44	7.78	7.00
Opiate users	11.89	9.67	9.78	7.22	7.56
Cocaine users	10.22	7.67	9.78	6.78	4.89

Note: TAS = Thrill and Adventure Seeking; ES = Experience Seeking; Dis = Disinhibition; BS = Boredom Susceptibility.
[a] $n = 9$ in each group.
Source: Table 3, p. 371, from "Drugs and personality: Dependence of findings on method," by J. V. Spotts & F. C. Shontz, 1986, *American Journal of Drug and Alcohol Abuse, 12,* 355–382. Copyright 1986. Reprinted by permission.

nonuser groups were all small and fell between the amphetamine and cocaine groups' scores.

It is the low scores of the cocaine group that are most out of line with the OLA theory. If both amphetamine and cocaine users had shown higher SSS scores than the other groups, it would have been a partial confirmation of the theory, even though the depressant drug users were not lower sensation seekers than the nonusers. Cocaine users scored very low on extraversion compared with all of the other groups, while the mean score of the amphetamine users was higher than the nonuser controls. Cocaine is known to have an introverting effect on chronic users. Amphetamine may also have this effect, but it clearly did not do so for this group. The introverting effect of the stimulant drug in chronic users is accompanied by a constriction of activity and interests. Thus the personality differences could be a result rather than a cause of the preference for cocaine. Another difference is in the drug histories of the groups before they specialized. The chronic cocaine users had on average tried fewer than half the number of drugs used in the other groups. They were clearly a less experimenting group than the other chronic users. Other studies show that sensation seeking is related to the absolute number of drugs used. As the authors point out, these chronic users of a specific drug were not looking for novel or varied sensations and experiences from their drug of choice because after 6 years of daily use they were totally familiar with the drug's effects. They persisted because they liked or *needed* the particular effects of the drug. Chronic drug-dependent individuals may not be the ideal subjects on which to test the OLA theory. But it must be conceded that studies of younger drug abusers and those first experimenting with drugs do not lend any more support than Spotts and Shontz's study to the theory. As with other phenomena, it seems that the need for variety and novelty of experiences is more important in determining the drug history of sensation seekers than the particular direction of arousal produced by the drugs.

Treatment of drug abusers

This author was personally involved in the treatment of drug abusers in a therapeutic community. Part of the difficulty with these programs is that they offer few prospects for a life that is interesting and potentially stimulating for a high sensation seeker after successful completion of the program. Because of their lack of education, due to dropping out of school early, they have poor job prospects, and what jobs they can get are often monotonous and boring. This could be why the major predictor of long-term outcome in our therapeutic community was intelligence level. Theoretically, former drug abusers could find some excitement in their recreational hours after work. But the program continually emphasized that they cannot associate with current drug users or even go to parties where drugs are being used. This restriction almost limits their social life to church groups in the communities they come from. It is as difficult for them to enjoy a party where there are no drugs as it is for social drinkers to enjoy parties where no alcohol is served. The only stimulating people they know of their own age are still using drugs. Among those who can stay off illegal drugs, many develop alcoholic problems.

Given these problems it is not surprising that the success rates for treatment programs are low. Simpson and Sells (1982) reported on follow-ups of over 44,000 clients admitted to 52 treatment programs. Four years after termination from the programs show only 35% of the clients had a favorable outcome in either outpatient drug-free or therapeutic communities, provided they stayed in these programs at least 3 months. Methadone maintenance did as well if clients stayed in the program over a year. But at least half the clients do not stay in the programs this long. Comparable rates of good outcome for nontreatment other than detoxification are lower, only 15%.

If predictors of outcome could be found to select clients for the programs, a better success rate might result. Better yet, if the personality studies show an essential need, like that for novel experience and sensation, programs and subsequent care might be better designed to insure improved outcome rates. Does treatment in therapeutic communities reduce the need for sensation?

Skolnick and Zuckerman (1979) compared SSS scores before and after treatment of drug abusers in a therapeutic community compared with a control group spending an equivalent amount of time in prison. The treatment group decreased significantly more than the prison group on only one scale, ES. This result must be regarded with caution because items referring to a desire to try drugs were not removed from that scale. Apparently, treatment does not reduce the general need for excitement and novel experiences. In our studies sensation seeking did not predict outcome of drug treatment. However, Bradley and Redfering (1978) found that high sensation seekers on the General and all of the subscales took less time to complete a drug rehabilitation program for male airmen in the U.S. Air Force. However differences on the counselors' reports for groups of high and low sensation seekers were only significant for the ES scale. Although sensation seeking clearly predicted success in completion of the program, the lack of a generalized relationship of the SSS to counselor's reports suggests some caution. In our therapeutic community, the more psychopathic types, as indicated by MMPI profiles, had an excellent prognosis for completing the first phase of the program but were among the first to relapse in the second phase of the program when they were allowed out of the house during the daytime to work (Zuckerman et al., 1975). Sensation seekers are not afraid of confrontation groups such as those used in these programs (Stanton, 1976), and they have no problem expressing emotions (Allen, 1976), but they may have problems if alternate sources of sensation are not available to them after completion of a drug program. Some programs in California have taken up sky diving. Former heroin users compared the free-fall experience to the "rush" produced by heroin. But one cannot go sky diving every day and the best substitute for the sensation-seeking life of the drug abuser may be an interesting and varied job, perhaps one dealing with people rather than products. This is why many of the successes from these programs become paraprofessional counselors.

Food preferences and eating and dieting habits

The psychoanalytic theory of alcoholism stresses the oral-passive character of the alcoholic. Like young infants, alcoholics find their major gratification in the bottle. Wolowitz (1964) developed a Food Preference Inventory (FPI) specifically designed to assess the distinction between "oral-passive" and "oral-sadistic" through the types of foods preferred. A preference for bland, sweet, and soft foods is supposed to reflect the oral-passive, whereas a preference for spicy, sour, and crunchy foods indicates oral-sadism. Kish (1970b) gave the FPI to alcoholics but was unable to confirm the predicted association between alcoholism and oral-passive needs. However, he did find that males show more oral-sadism than females, and that oral-sadism (as opposite to oral-passivity) is related to less socialization, conformity, authoritarianism, and concern over making a good impression on other people. Without using the questionable theoretical labels, the more unconventional, nonconforming, and undersocialized people prefer foods that are spicy, sour, and crunchy, whereas their opposites prefer foods that are bland, sweet, and soft. This suggested the hypothesis that sensation seekers might prefer foods that are less bland and more stimulating.

Kish and Donnenwerth (1972) correlated the FPI and General SSS in groups of male alcoholic, male and female college students, and male psychiatric patients. The three qualities of food cannot be distinguished in the FPI score so that a high score indicates a relative preference for foods that have any or all three stimulating properties, spicy, sour, and crunchy. Significant but low and negative correlations ($-.26$ to $-.36$) were obtained in all three groups confirming the hypothesis that high sensation seekers prefer stimulating qualities of food.

Logue and Smith (1986) correlated the SSS form V with a variety of classes of foods and drinks. The largest number of significant correlations (23 of 55 foods) were with the ES subscale. The SSS Total correlated positively with preferences for alcoholic beverages in all forms, but particularly hard liquor and beer, and negatively with preferences for soda and carbonated beverages. Among foods the Total score correlated positively with preferences for Japanese food, chili peppers, Middle Eastern food, French food, and shell fish, and negatively with preferences for bread and cereals, corn, candy, nuts and seeds, fruit, and reconstituted meats. ES in particular also correlated positively with a liking for Mexican food, black pepper, spices other than salt and pepper, tea, and Chinese foods. The results generally confirm the Kish and Donnenwerth findings of preferences for spicy and sour foods among high sensation seekers, but also indicate a generalized liking for foreign foods that are different from ordinary American cuisine. The low sensation seekers do like soft, sweet, and bland foods, but they also like crunchy foods (i.e., nuts).

Terasaki and Imada (1988) studied food preferences and sensation seeking in Japan using a Japanese translation of the SSS. The Total SSS correlated with preferences for alcoholic beverages (excluding sweet ones), spicy foods, and meats. It also correlated with a liking for foreign cuisines, Middle Eastern, Italian, and Mexican foods. The SSS also was related to the number of "unusual foods" they had eaten from a list of food oddities, such as locust, larva of the bee, bullfrog, snake, slug, lizard, newt, gecko, snail, and Japanese diving beetle. Not on this list but listed under "Other foods" was the category "insect"; a preference for insects as food also correlated with sensation seeking. Like American sensation seekers, the Japanese share a taste for alcoholic drinks, foreign food, and spicy food. They also have an amazing willingness to try and like a variety of food sources that most Americans would regard as "disgusting" and be unlikely to eat except on a dare. The main national difference concerns the preference for meat in high sensation-seeking Japanese. The authors explain that eating meat was considered "abominable" in Japan until this century and even now much less meat is eaten there than in America.

Disgust is recognized as one of the primary emotions and a major source of food revulsions (Rozin & Fallon, 1987). Haidt, McCauley, and Rozin (1992) developed a scale to measure disgust as an emotional trait. The SS Total score correlated negatively with the total Disgust scale and the specific food disgust scale. Both TAS and ES subscales contributed most to these correlations with the disgust scales. Low sensation seekers are disgusted by a wider variety of foods than highs.

High sensation seekers like food that is unusual, novel, and/or stimulating in taste. Foreign foods provide novelty of taste even if they are not spicy. Back (1981) compared those interested in gourmet food with vegetarians and found that the former were higher on sensation seeking than the latter. Gourmets, of course, like a wider variety of foods than vegetarians who exclude an entire class of food from their diet. Otis (1984) gave the SSS V, excluding the Dis scale, to Canadian students. She then showed them some samples of bite-sized foods including octopus, hearts of palm, seaweed, blood sausage, pickled watermelon rind, raw fish, quail egg, star fruit, sheep milk cheese, and black beans. Subjects were led to believe that they would be asked to taste the foods and then given the SS and A state scale. Next they were asked to rate how their willingness to try each of the 12 foods shown them and their familiarity, if any, with the foods. Familiarity did not correlate highly with willingness to try the foods. Of the three SSS trait scales only the ES scale correlated significantly with the willingess to taste various foods ($r = .32$). The SS state scale taken just before indicating willingess to try foods was not correlated with ratings of willingness, but the anxiety state scale was negatively correlated with willingness. Age was highly and positively correlated with willingness to try the foods. Since sensation seeking falls with age, the correlation between sensation seeking and willingness to try the foods may have been higher if age were controlled through partial correlation.

Sensation seekers may be gourmets in their taste for novel or unusually prepared foods, but are they also gourmands, preferring large amounts of foods and therefore subject to food "binging"? Anorexics might be low sensation seekers since they often give up two major sources of sensual gratification, food and sex. While no study was found dealing with anorexia, Schumaker, Groth-Marnat, Small, and Macaruso (1986) studied bulimics who are characterized by bouts of impulsive binge eating followed by self-induced vomiting to avoid the weight gain. The authors predicted that bulimics would be high sensation seekers, but they turned out to be no different than controls on the SSS V.

Women who are preoccupied with their weight, diet frequently, and are subject to weight fluctuations have been compared with controls in two studies (Babbitt, Rowland, & Franken, 1990b; Jansen, Klaver, Merckelback, & van den Hout, 1989). The subjects in the Babbit et al. study were all female participants in an aerobic exercise class. A subgroup of the sample was designated as a preoccupied (with weight)/regimented (exercise) group and compared with the others in the classes who were primarily interested in physical fitness. The preoccupied/regimented (P/R) group scored higher on the SSS Total score than the other exercisers and even higher than the Canadian female college norm group. A problem with the study was the fact that the P/R group was significantly younger in age than the aerobic control group, but this would not explain why they were higher on the SSS than the norm group as well. Jansen et al. also found that a group of Dutch university women who were restrained eaters scored higher than controls on a short form of the SSS. The authors predicted this result on the basis that the restrained eaters, who typically go through binge and diet cycles, are analogous to drug addicts in their impulsivity and lack of control over the impulse to consume their favored substances. One might add that the desire to maintain optimal weight may be related to a desire to be sexually attractive, probably characteristic of high sensation-seeking young women. Whether the effort is made to control weight by compulsive exercise or diet or both, this kind of concern about weight (excluding the abnormal obsessive preoccupation of anorexics) may be more characteristic in high sensation seekers than in lows. The low sensation seeker is either better able to control daily eating or less concerned about weight and appearance that the high sensation seeker. While the highs are out drinking and dancing at the disco, the lows are curled up in front of the television set with a bowl of ice cream (soft, bland, and sweet).

Summary

Tobacco is often the first drug of abuse. Although many fewer male college students smoke now than 2 decades earlier, the relationship between smoking and sensation seeking first reported in the 1970s is still a significant one; more high sensation seekers of both sexes smoke than low sensation seekers. The relationship has been found in many countries.

Sensation seeking is related to alcohol and drug use in adolescence and preadolescence, and early adolescent sensation-seeking trait predicts later substance use. Young problem drinkers score higher than nonusers of alcohol or drugs, but not as high as drug users, particularly those who use drugs beyond marijuana. Marijuana tends to be the first illegal drug used and is favored by the higher sensation seekers among the young.

In contrast to sensation seeking, impulsivity, and antisocial tendencies, anxiety has little to do with drinking in men. While little anxiety is found in young male drinkers or users of drugs, anxiety and depression are seen in alcoholics and chronic drug abusers. Alcoholics may be divided into two types, one with an early onset and pattern of antisocial behavior associated with drinking, and the other with a later onset and little or no antisocial behavior, but a lack of assertiveness and more neurotic problems. The former type is associated with higher sensation seeking than the latter type of alcoholic.

The fact that anxious and neurotic patterns diminish rapidly in those drug abusers who are abstinent and in a treatment program for several months suggests that anxiety is reactive to the physiological, social, or legal stresses produced by chronic drug abuse, rather than a long-standing part of the substance abuser's personality. Sensation seeking and impulsivity, however, are part of the substance abuser's personality and do not go away after the abuser discontinues drinking or drugs. These latter traits pose special problems for rehabilitation since almost all of the sensation seekers' excitement revolved around drugs and the drug life itself.

The earlier optimal level of arousal theory of sensation seeking predicted that sensation seeking would be positively related to use of stimulant drugs and negatively related to use of depressant drugs, but the cumulative evidence suggests that sensation seeking is related to the extent of illegal drug use and the variety of drugs used (polydrug use) rather than to the use of specific classes of drugs.

Sensation seekers seem to be motivated to use all types of drugs by their need for novel experiences and curiosity. In the next stage they use the drugs to get the "high" or for the pleasure produced by the drug itself. They also enjoy the excitement and disinhibition of the drug life in association with other drug users of a similar disposition. But after tolerance for the drug and consequent dependence on it develops, sensation seeking is probably irrelevant to continued use of the drug. Sensation-seeking drug users start by seeking positive arousal but end by using the drug to reduce negative arousal (withdrawal effects) and maintain an optimal level of arousal that may be considerably lower than where they started.

Sensation seekers in both the United States and Japan enjoy foods that are spicy and novel for their own culture. Sensation seekers tend to be gourmets with a special taste for spicy and ethnic varieties of food as opposed to bland, customary foods but they are not gourmands. Low sensation seekers' food preferences for bland, sweet foods resemble those of younger children who are also resistant to trying novel foods. Sensation seekers are more willing to try new foods, even those that are very unusual and which lower sensation seekers would regard as inedible or "disgusting."

Some high sensation seekers may find a conflict between their passion for food and their desire to keep a trim figure and be sexually attractive to others. Consequently, binge eating may be combined with strenuous exercise regimes and dieting. There is no evidence that people who binge or fast, as in bulimia and anorexia, are higher or lower on sensation seeking than others.

In this chapter we have looked at the involvement of sensation seeking in types of disorders that involve substance abuse. However, substance abuse is a clinical disorder that often develops in a long-standing antisocial personality disorder. In the next chapter we will examine the role of sensation seeking in antisocial personality and pathological gambling, as well as other types of psychopathology, including bipolar disorders, hyperactivity in children, anxiety disorders, and schizophrenia.

10

Psychopathology and stress

The *Diagnostic and Statistical Manual* (*DSM-III*, 1987) of the American Psychiatric Association distinguishes between episodic clinical disorders and long-standing personality disorders. Alcohol and drug abuse and dependence, discussed in the previous chapter, are listed as clinical disorders. They may exist at some periods of a person's life but not at others. These particular forms are not commonly seen in childhood but develop in or after adolescence and may abate later in life. Personality disorders, in contrast, develop slowly during childhood and usually persist for a long period thereafter. Clinical disorders are distinguished from personality disorders in terms of their duration, their severity, specific symptoms, and functional disability. Personality disorders, in turn, differ from extremes of normal personality traits by their inflexibility, maladaptability, and functional impairment. Persons with an antisocial personality disorder, for instance, may be distinguished from persons who have strong traits of disinhibitory sensation seeking and impulsivity by the pervasiveness of their behavior and its long-term maladaptiveness. Antisocial personality disorders usually end up in social, financial, vocational, and/or legal trouble, if not in jail. But as Cleckley's (1976) case studies of middle-class, educated professionals show, many psychopaths can lead quite "successful" lives (in terms of wealth and position) and manage to stay out of jail. The difference between those who end up in jail and those who rise to high positions in society may have to do with intelligence more than degree of psychopathy. Those who develop chronic alcoholism and drug dependence rarely can maintain the success that they may have achieved before the acute phase of substance abuse.

Although many forms of psychopathology, such as neuroses, frequently occur without a preexisting personality disorder (Tyrer, Casey, & Gall, 1983), there are strong links between the clinical disorders of alcoholism and drug dependence and a preexisting personality type called *antisocial personality* (the older terms *sociopathic* and *psychopathic* are used synonymously with antisocial personality). The relationships between alcoholism,

258

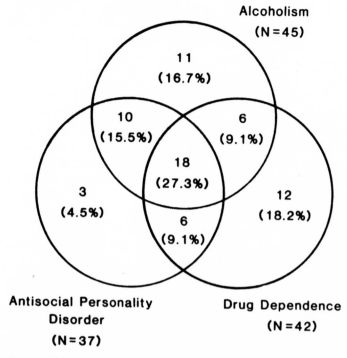

Figure 10.1. Overlap of antisocial personality disorder, drug dependence, and alcoholism diagnoses. From "Associations among major psychiatric disorders," by A. W. Wolf et al., 1988, *Journal of Consulting and Clinical Psychology, 56,* 293. Copyright American Psychological Association, 1988. Reprinted with permission of author.

drug dependence, and antisocial personality disorder in a study by Wolf et al. (1988) are shown in Figure 10.1: 43% of alcoholic patients and 36% of the drug-dependent patients also received a diagnosis of antisocial personality, and 52% of patients with antisocial personality also received a diagnosis of alcoholism or drug dependence or both. Given the association between alcoholic and drug disorders and sensation seeking, shown in Chapter 9, we would expect to find an even stronger association between sensation seeking and the personality disorder that antedates the development of the clinical disorders in a majority of substance dependents.

Childhood antecedents of antisocial disorders

There has been little work on childhood disorders because child sensation-seeking scales have been only recently developed. According to current psychiatric criteria in the *DSM-III*, one cannot be diagnosed as an antisocial personality until 18 years of age. However, in order to receive this diagnosis as an adult one must have a history of conduct disorder before the age of 15. Conduct disorder is defined in terms of the typical childhood expressions of antisocial behavior, including truancy, running away from home, starting fights and using weapons, forcing sexual relations on others, cruelty to people and/or animals, vandalism, fire setting, lying, and stealing.

The diagnosis of hyperactivity in children is associated with a later adult criminality in a third (Robins, 1966) to half (Satterfield, 1987) of this population. Given these findings from longitudinal studies, and assuming an association between adult antisocial personality and sensation seeking, we would expect to find high sensation seeking in hyperactive as well as conduct-disorder children.

The concept of a high optimal-level of stimulation, used with sensation seeking (Zuckerman, 1969a, 1979a), has also been used to explain hyperactivity (Zentall & Zentall, 1983). Hyperactive children are highly boredom susceptible in nonstimulating environments, like ordinary classrooms, and under these circumstances they become restless and impulsive. Adult sensation seekers also become easily bored and restless in invariant environments (Zuckerman et al., 1966), also suggesting a connection with childhood hyperactivity.

At the time of the previous sensation-seeking book (Zuckerman, 1979a), little work had been done with neurotics of any kind. Sensation seeking is not correlated with anxiety measured as a trait in normals (Chapter 3). Although the SSS subscale TAS does predict anxiety reactions to phobic types of situations in normals (Mellstrom et al., 1976), it is not clear if this would extend to the characteristics of clinically phobic children or adults. The normal college students were responding to situations related to simple phobias, such as exposure to small animals, high open places, and darkness. General sensation seeking could be more related to syndromes like agoraphobia where the patients give up all external stimulation and confine themselves to their homes. In children this kind of anxiety reaction is usually seen in school phobias.

Russo et al. (1991) tested a group of male clinic children and nonclinic controls using their own child version of the SSS. This test only contains a Total score and subscales for TAS and BS. The clinic children were initially divided into three groups: conduct disorder (CD), attention deficit with hyperactivity disorder (ADHD), and anxiety disorders (ANX). The CD group tended to have higher scores than the other groups on the Total scale. The CD group scored highest and the hyperactive group the lowest on the BS scale. The authors concluded that anxiety exerts a moderating effect on the stimulation seeking of conduct disorder boys because those who were both conduct disorder and anxious were not higher than controls in contrast to the simple, nonanxious conduct disorders. Russo et al. (1993) further revised their children's SSS now including three scales: Thrill and Adventure Seeking, Drug and Alcohol Attitudes, and Social Disinhibition. Conduct disorder boys scored higher than all non-CD clinic cases on all three scales, but did not differ from normal boys on any of the scales. The non-CD cases (attention deficit and anxiety disorders) were lower than normals on the three scales.

The finding of low SSS scores in hyperactives was contrary to prediction, but a similar finding was reported by Salkind (1981) using another children's sensation-seeking scale. However, Shaw and Brown (1990), using their own children's SSS, found that hyperactive children scored higher than controls. Their scale sounds more like the adult SSS than Salkind's, because it uses forced-choice items directly adapted from the Zuckerman SSS. However, given the two negative findings regarding hyperactives on self-report scales of sensation seeking, we cannot say that the group is high on this trait.

Behavioral measures of sensation or stimulation seeking may be more appropriate for children of this age who often have reading problems. Lambert and Levy (1972) showed that adult sensation seekers responded more than low sensation seekers in order to view slides in a short-term sensory deprivation situation. However, the work of Hocking and Robertson (1969) showed that the activity factor in button pressing must be controlled in order to test the stimulation-seeking hypothesis. Brimer and Levine (1983) used the operant response method with auditory and visual reinforcement in a study of hyperactive children. The hyperactives responded to turn on the auditory stimuli more than the controls, but there was no difference in responses to turn off the stimuli. The two groups did not differ in response to visual stimuli, possibly because of a ceiling effect; the visual stimuli were highly attractive and preferred to the auditory by both groups.

Zentall and Meyer (1987) contrasted the responses of attention deficit–hyperactive children in two experimental situations: a high-stimulation, active response situation and a low-stimulation, passive response one. In the high-stimulation condition, the children could view slides activated by a button press while waiting for the auditory stimulus that was the target one in a signal detection task. The hyperactive children made fewer errors and talked less in the high-stimulation, active condition than in the passive one. They showed a deficit compared to controls in the low-stimulation, passive condition but not in the high-stimulation, active condition. The results suggest support for an optimal level of stimulation (and activity) theory of hyperactivity. Given sufficient variation in stimulation, even stimulation that is irrelevant to the task, they can maintain better attention and they show less extraneous verbal activity.

Adult disorders

Most studies of personality in persons with diagnosed behavior disorders occur in hospitals or clinics and the tests are administered on admission or soon after admission when the patients are in an acute phase of their disorder. While this timing of assessment may be useful for diagnosis, it can be quite misleading in assessment of the premorbid personality. Trait measures of neuroticism and anxiety typically are elevated in the acute phase of the disorder but diminish as symptoms subside. In the previous chapter I discussed how this kind of assessment of substance abusers entering a therapeutic program can be misleading. Zuckerman and Neeb (1979) were able to test persons from the population who reported a history of a particular diagnosed disorder, but were at home, and probably in remission, at the time they took the SSS. Other information in the survey was used to cross-check the reported diagnoses. The sample was collected for normative comparisons and the questions about previous diagnoses were part of a larger demographic background survey, so that the former patients and controls did not think they were being singled out because they had a particular disorder or were to be compared with those who did. Over 2,000 people responded to a request in a magazine article to take the SSS and provide additional information about themselves. On the basis of their answers to a series of questions concerning serious past "psychological problems," the respondents indicating a particular diagnosis were classified into six broad groups: manic-depressive (bipolar disorder), unipolar major depression, sociopathic (antisocial personality disorder), schizophrenic, neurotic (primarily dysthymic and anxiety disorders), and personality trait disorders (exclusive of sociopathy). Since the diagnosed groups varied in age, gender, education, and socioeconomic background, subjects in each group were individually matched with members of the same population of respondents to the magazine article who were as close as possible on all of the demographic characteristics, but who reported no history of psychological problems of any severity. The judges who did the matching were blind as to the SSS scores of both clinical and

Table 10.1. *Comparisons of diagnostic groups and matched control groups*

Groups	n	Age	TAS	ES	Dis	BS	Total
Bipolars	19	30.3	8.2**	7.6*	6.7	5.4	27.8***
Controls	19	30.5	5.6	6.1	5.2	2.0	21.0
Major depressives	39	31.0	6.5	7.1	5.9	4.5	24.0
Controls	39	31.5	7.2	7.1	6.1	4.2	24.6
Antisocials	17	30.8	9.0*	8.4**	7.2*	4.7	29.2*
Controls	17	29.7	7.7	6.2	5.4	3.7	22.7
Neurotics	100	35.8	6.2	7.2	6.1	5.0	25.1
Controls	100	35.7	6.8	7.1	5.6	4.5	24.1
Personality Disorders	15	33.8	7.4	7.7	5.9	5.3	26.3
Controls	15	34.0	7.1	6.6	5.8	4.0	23.5
Schizophrenics	20	28.5	6.7	7.0	5.0	4.8	23.4
Controls	20	27.8	6.6	6.9	5.9	4.0	23.3

Note: TAS = Thrill and Adventure Seeking; ES = Experience Seeking; Dis = Disinhibition; BS = Boredom Susceptibility.
* Significantly higher than control mean, $p < .05$.
** Significantly higher than control mean, $p < .01$.
*** Significantly higher than control mean, $p < .001$.
Source: "Sensation seeking and psychopathology," by M. Zuckerman & M. Neeb, 1979, *Psychiatry Research, 1,* 255–264. Copyright Elsevier/North-Holland Biomedical Press. Reprinted by permission.

nonclinical subjects, having access to the demographic data only. The results of the comparisons of the diagnosed groups and their matched control groups are given in Table 10.1.

About 1% of our sample reported a history of manic or manic-depressive (bipolar) disorder, which is about the incidence of the disorder in the general population. More than half of the group said that they had received drugs that are often used in the treatment of this disorder. The group was significantly higher than its control group on the Total and TAS scales and marginally higher on the ES scale as well. The results were essentially the same when comparisons were confined to the bipolars taking lithium, a drug used specifically for the treatment of the disorder.

The group classified as major depressives was distinguished from dysthymic (neurotic) depressions by their reports of receiving antidepressive medications, hospitalization for the disorder, and/or receiving shock treatments. None of the differences between depressive and matched control groups were significant.

The sociopathy label was used as a loose classification for persons reporting a diagnosis of sociopathic personality, alcoholism, drug abuse, or criminality. This group was higher on the Total and all of the SSS subscales except BS.

The percentage of schizophrenics in our group also closely approximated the figure in the general American population (about 1%). More than half of the group reported having received antipsychotic medications. Their scores did not differ from that of the general population. It is very likely that this was a group of acute schizophrenics in remission, given the complexity of the procedures in responding to the survey.

In selecting a group of diagnosed neurotics, we were careful to rule out reports of what seemed to be transient, situation-related, or minor symptom problems. Most of them were anxiety or dysthymic disorders. The group did not differ from the controls on any of the SSS subscales. The personality disorder group contained passive-aggressive, hysterical, obsessive-compulsive, and narcissistic disorders. This group also did not differ from controls on the SSS. In sum, the only groups scoring higher than controls on the SSS were bipolar and sociopathic disorders. None of the groups were found to score lower than their controls on the SSS. Results from formally diagnosed groups, in prison or hospitals will be reported next.

Antisocial personality (psychopathy)

Whereas previous psychiatric definitions of antisocial personality included many trait terms like "grossly selfish, callous, irresponsible, impulsive," the *DSM III* (1987) stresses the behavioral history: "The essential feature of this disorder is a pattern of irresponsible and antisocial behavior beginning in childhood or early adolescence and continuing into adulthood." The significant kinds of behavior that are used to identify the disorder include inability to hold a job and perform it well, arrests for unlawful behavior, fighting, spouse and child abuse, failure to honor financial obligations, impulsive lifestyle (wandering from place to place), lying, reckless or drunken driving and recurring speeding, child neglect, and "inability to maintain a monogamous relationship for more than one year." Quay (1965) described the psychopathic personality as a "pathological stimulation seeker" who seeks intense or unusual stimulation in order to counteract an unpleasant low level of arousal.

Hare and Cox (1978) used some of these behavioral definitions combined with some of the personality trait definitions listed by Cleckley (1976). They use an extensive review of the case and an intensive interview with the prisoner to rate them on 22 characteristics in their list. Their Psychopathy

Check List (PCL) correlates highly with the diagnosis of antisocial personality disorder made from the *DSM III*. Harpur, Hakstian, and Hare (1988) factor analyzed the items of the PCL and found two highly replicable factors. Factor 1 reflects the unusual egocentricity and lack of strong emotions and empathy with others said to be the essential personality defect in the psychopath. Factor 2 depends more on objective records of antisocial behavior and less on inferential data like the depth of feelings and sincerity.

Not unexpectedly, objective diagnosis and records of institutional behavior and postrelease violations correlate more highly with the score on the factor 2 variables (Harpur, Hare, & Hakstian, 1989). More surprising is the fact that nearly all of the personality scores, including sensation seeking and socialization, also correlated more highly with factor 2 than with factor 1. The SSS V Total correlated .39 with factor 2 but only .12 (not significant) with factor 1. Trait anxiety and neuroticism scales correlated with both factors, negatively with factor 1 and positively with factor 2, but these correlations were weak ($<.20$). Socialization and sensation seeking in this study were the highest questionnaire single-scale predictors of factor 2 psychopathy. In contrast to these results, Thornquist (1993) found that the PCL factor 1 ratings of a prison drug rehabilitation group correlated with the ZKPQ Impulsive Sensation Seeking scale but the PCL factor 2 scores did not. The difference between the results of the two studies may have to do with the different populations used.

Blackburn (1978) and T. Emmons and Webb (1974) classified prisoners into three groups on the basis of psychometric criteria: primary and secondary psychopaths and nonpsychopaths. However different criteria were used in the two studies, which could account for some of the differences in their results. Both used the MMPI Psychopathy scale with other scales to distinguish psychopaths from nonpsychopaths in a prison population, but Emmons and Webb used an anxiety scale while Blackburn used a sociability scale to further divide the psychopaths into primary and secondary types. The Dis scale showed the best overall discrimination between the three groups in both studies as judged from the size of the *F* ratios, although other subscales also differentiated the three groups in both studies. Later studies by Blackburn (1987) also show the best discrimination of primary and secondary psychopaths by the Dis scale as well as the SSS Total score. Deforest and Johnson (1981) also found that psychopathic types among prisoners had a higher SSS Total score than nonpsychopaths, but they did not report the results for subscales of the SSS.

Most of the studies of antisocial personality types have used incarcerated criminals but these may not be a representative sample of psychopaths in the community. Sutker and Allain (1983) have studied the "adaptive psychopath," or antisocial personality who is at least temporarily successful in the community. They selected such a group from a class of medical students using MMPI criteria followed by interviews. The group designated as adaptive psychopaths did report a greater history of norm-violating behaviors before age 15 and since age 18, and 88% of the group reported being arrested at least once as compared with 25% of the normal controls. The psychopathic group scored higher than the controls on the ES subscale of the SSS, but the differences on other scales were not significant. The results suggest that the ES scale may be more discriminating than the Dis scale in higher socioeconomic and more educated types of antisocial personalities.

Delinquency

These last studies compared subgroups within the criminal population. Other studies have not attempted to diagnose psychopathy within the criminal population but have simply contrasted criminals, as an antisocial group, with noncriminals. Thorne gave the SSS form I, containing only a General scale, to groups of male and female felóns, delinquents, and mentally ill persons. After the results were corrected for age differences between groups, only the female felons and delinquents scored higher than the mentally ill patients on the SSS. However, the mentally ill (schizophrenics) tend to score lower than normals on the SSS (Brownfield, 1966; Kish, 1970a) so the differences in this study could be a function of the lower-than-normal scores of the mentally ill rather than abnormally high scores of the female felons and delinquents.

Ono and Murayama (1986) found that a group of Japanese incarcerated male delinquents scored higher than university students on the ES scale alone, although the Dis scale difference also approached significance. However, when Berman and Paisey (1984) compared American male juvenile offenders whose crimes involved assault with a nonassaultive group of delinquent prisoners, they found that the aggressive group scored higher on General, Dis, ES, and TAS scales than the controls. Shoham, Askenasy, Rahav, Chard, and Addi (1989) found similar differences between violent and nonviolent adult prisoners.

Karoly (1975) found no significant differences between SSS General scores of female delinquents and normal high school students, suggesting that unclassified delinquents of either sex are not higher than normals on sensation seeking. However, Farley and Farley (1972) compared incarcerated female delinquents 14 to 17 years of age who scored high on the SSS with those who scored low and found that the high sensation seekers made more escape attempts, were punished more for disobeying the warders, and engaged in more fighting than the low sensation seekers. It appears that the higher sensation seekers within the delinquent population are more psychopathic than the low sensation seekers. Farley (1973) reported similar results for incarcerated male delinquents. English and Jones (1972) found that high sensation seekers among narcotic addicts in a treatment center were more likely to "elope" from the center than lower sensation seekers. The SSS seems to predict rebellious behavior within the incarcerated delinquent population rather than distinguishing it from the broader adolescent population.

Much delinquency occurs without arrest records. Simo and Perez (1991) studied self-reported delinquency and sensation seeking in a Spanish junior high school. The anonymously administered delinquency scale correlated substantially with Dis, ES, and SSS Total scores in both males and females. Wallbank (1985) found that American high school students reporting a great deal of delinquent behavior had higher SSS scores on the Total and all subscales except TAS than nondelinquents. Delinquents who used drugs other than alcohol were even higher on the SSS than other delinquents. Wasson (1981) used only the BS subscale and found that it was positively correlated with deviant behavior at school reported by high school students. Perez and Torrubia (1985) used a self-report delinquency scale on college students and found that such behavior correlated significantly with all of the SSS V subscales and the Total score in both males and females. The correlations with ES and Dis were much higher than those with TAS and BS.

Two studies used the SSS to predict delinquent behavior. Newcomb and McGee (1991) conducted one of the rare predictive studies of delinquency. The subjects were high school students first assessed at ages 15 to 18, subsequently during late adolescence, and finally four years later when subjects were in their early 20s. A short version of the SSS was given during the first period of assessment. Among the other scales were measures of law abidance, or the stated williness to commit minor kinds of dishonest acts, drug and alcohol abuse, and deviant behaviors scales. The latter included different kinds of antisocial activities such as theft, fighting, use of weapons, vandalism, and arson. The concurrent correlational data during the first period showed that TAS, Dis, and BS scales were negatively related to law abidance attitudes, and positively related to drug and alcohol use, sexual activity, and deviant behaviors. For most of these variables the Dis scale showed the strongest relationship and the ES scale was unrelated or only minimally related to law abidance and alcohol and drug abuse and deviant behaviors like fighting, stealing, and property damage.

Predictive analyses were done using Structural Model Analyses (LISREL).

The path analyses showed that the general sensation-seeking factor measured during early and middle adolescence was correlated with the general deviant behavior factor during subsequent periods, but the effects of sensation seeking on specific deviant behaviors were generally mediated through law abidance attitudes and the general deviancy factor. As an example, disinhibition predicted lower law abidance both 1 and 5 years later and these negative values concerning honesty led to increased criminal activities.

White, La Bouvie, and Bates (1985) used Dis and ES subscales of the SSS in concurrent and predictive studies of delinquency over 3-year periods of adolescence (15–18 and 18–21 years). Both scales were related to concurrent reports of delinquency, but only Dis predicted future delinquency. In subjects who became delinquent by the second assessment, Dis scores rose significantly during the interval.

Criminality

Stewart and Hemsley (1984) found no differences between adult male prisoners and controls on the General SSS. Goma et al. (1988) compared male prisoners with two normal groups, firemen and students. Means of the three groups on the Spanish version of the SSS V are shown in Table 10.2 along with means on the EPQ scales. Prisoners were higher than students on the Dis, BS, and Total SSS scores, but they did not differ from the firemen on these scales and were lower than the firemen on TAS. While the prisoners seem to be a high sensation-seeking group compared with students they are not when compared with a group of more normal sensation seekers working in a dangerous job. Perhaps fire fighting might be a good placement for high sensation-seeking ex-convicts who are trying to find a legitimate vocation.

Goma and Grau (1989) compared another group of Spanish prison inmates, who were imprisoned for more serious offenses (armed robbery), with a group of adventurous sportsmen. Both groups of subjects had engaged in very risky behavior. The sportsmen and prisoners did not differ on the SSS. G. Breivik (personal communications, April 1991; March 1993) found that Norwegian prisoners were not high sensation seekers, but those convicted for robbery, murder, or other violent or drug-related crimes had higher SSS scores than prisoners convicted for sexual or economic crimes and at about the level of noncriminal sportsmen.

The results so far suggest that prisoners do not differ from high sensation-seeking groups in the general population, but the question remains as to whether they are higher than normal population groups. It is necessary to compare criminals with a control group more similar in education, age, and

Table 10.2. *Personality scores of prisoners, firemen, and students*

Scales	Prisoners ($n = 40$)	Firemen ($n = 54$)	Students ($n = 170$)
SSS			
TAS	6.67[a]	8.35[b]	6.89[a]
ES	6.40[ab]	6.72[b]	5.71[a]
Dis	6.18[a]	5.57[ab]	5.19[b]
BS	4.56[a]	4.05[ab]	3.64[b]
Total score	23.75[a]	24.68[a]	21.49[b]
EPQ			
Extraversion	13.00[ab]	14.35[b]	12.39[a]
Neuroticism	14.30[a]	7.24[b]	9.99[c]
Psychoticism	6.80[a]	4.20[b]	5.03[c]
Lie (reverse scored)	11.70[a]	11.70[a]	12.48[a]

Note: Means followed by common superscripts (*a, b, c*) are not significantly different. SSS = Sensation Seeking Scale; TAS = Thrill and Adventure Seeking; ES = Experience Seeking; BS = Boredom Susceptibility; EPQ = Eysenck Personality Questionnaire.
Source: Adapted from table 1, p. 216, from "Personality variables in antisocial and prosocial disinhibitory behavior," by M. Goma, J. Perez, & R. Torrubia, 1988. In T. E. Moffitt & S. A. Mednick (Eds.), *Biological contributions to crime causation.* Dordrecht, the Netherlands: Martinus Nijhoff Publishers. Copyright 1988. Reprinted by permission.

socioeconomic status, but not engaged in sensation-seeking vocations or avocations. Haapasalo (1990) compared a group of Finnish offenders, convicted for property offenses like theft and fraud and driving offenses like drunken or reckless driving, with a large normal population sample of men. The prisoners scored higher than the normative sample on the Total, ES, and Dis scales (a BS scale was not included) but lower than the normal sample on TAS.

Pathological gambling

In Chapter 5, I described studies of the relation between gambling behavior and sensation seeking in normal controls. Gambling, like drinking, is a common form of recreation that can become pathological in some persons when the level and frequency of betting relative to income is out of control and the gambling disrupts or damages family, personal, and vocational pursuits. Pathological gambling is included in the *DSM-III* as a "mental illness." Cross-addictions to alcohol and drugs are not uncommon (Lesieur, Blume, & Zoppa, 1986).

Custer and Milt (1985) have described the compulsive gambler as someone who craves stimulation, loves risk, challenge, and adventure, needs change stimulation and excitement, and is bored when he or she cannot find these fulfillments in the routine of everyday life. This description of the gambler is very like that for high sensation seekers. However, the pathological gambler is preoccupied with one narrow type of sensation seeking and may not have the characteristics of a broad experience seeker. Unlike most sensation seekers where the risk is secondary to the rewarding sensations, the risk (amount of money bet) seems to be the main source of the arousal that provides the thrill for the pathological gambler (Anderson & Brown, 1984). The pathological gambler finds no pleasure in low-stakes gambling.

R. Brown (1986) discussed three major theories of gambling behavior: the psychoanalytic (Freud, 1929/1950; Lindner, 1958), the operant (Dickerson, 1979; Skinner, 1953), and arousal and sensation seeking (Anderson & Brown, 1984; Zuckerman, 1979a). Anderson and Brown (1984) found that gamblers experience substantial arousal while waiting for the outcome of bets in real gambling situations, and the amount bet correlated with the heart rate increases. According to the arousal–sensation seeking theory, the arousal is the reinforcement as much as or even more than the money. Gamblers themselves describe "excitement" as the attraction of gambling. According to R. Brown (1986), the regular gamblers lead ordinary lives that do not provide enough excitement to maintain their optimal levels of arousal. Social and cultural circumstances lead to the discovery of gambling as an exciting activity. Gamblers become addicted for the usual reasons of tolerance and withdrawal stress. As gambling becomes habitual, they need to place bigger and riskier bets to achieve the level of arousal once reached by smaller and safer bets. Withdrawal symptoms occur when they are not gambling and are due to underarousal. Life then seems boring and empty. Increased arousal while gambling can explain the narrowed focus of the gambler on the game to the exclusion of all other concerns and the irrational, confused, and superstitious thinking that leads to reckless betting.

Although Brown's theory suggests that pathological gamblers as arousal seekers should be high on sensation-seeking trait, it also suggests that under certain circumstances even moderate level sensation seekers could become addicted to gambling. If the moderate sensation seeker's work and personal life are incredibly dull, gambling can offer a highly reinforcing mode of arousal.

The optimal level of arousal in Brown's theory is autonomic arousal not cortical arousal as in most optimal-level theories. Persons who start with low levels of autonomic arousal have the greater chance to become addicted according to this theory, since they have more range of possible increase when they are betting. Persons with high autonomic arousal should find further increases in arousal disturbing. Zuckerman's more recent theory (1984a) suggests that catecholamine system arousal rather than cortical arousal is the basis for sensation seeking and that sensation seekers are in states of less than optimal catecholamine system activity when unstimulated. This would tie in with Brown's theory since central noradrenergic arousal is related to peripheral autonomic arousal. This aspect of the theory and its application to gamblers will be discussed further in the next chapter. For now, I will present the findings on sensation-seeking levels in regular or pathological gamblers.

Most of the studies comparing pathologic gamblers or habitual gamblers with controls have suffered from several sources of bias, such as the lack of controls for age and gender, and small sample sizes. Most studies used gamblers who were entering or were in treatment programs. Only a minority of gamblers seek treatment and they are likely to be the less sensation-seeking ones. It is not surprising that the results have been mixed across studies.

Blaszczynski et al. (1986) studied a group of pathological gamblers seeking treatment for their self-admitted problem. The gamblers were tested before treatment started and their test scores were compared with general Australian population norms for males (from Ball et al., 1984) rather than with their own relevant age group. The gamblers scored significantly lower than the general norms on TAS, ES, and Total scales of the SSS V. The low sensation-seeking scores of this group might reflect a revaluation of excitement seeking prior to treatment.

In a more recent study of pathological gamblers involved in therapy, Blaszczynski, McConaghy, and Frankova (1990) gave the SSS, the Beck (1967) Depression Inventory, and a new scale of Boredom Proneness (Farmer & Sundberg, 1986) to these subjects and to a group of medical outpatients without gambling or addiction problems. The two groups were similar in age. The gamblers were higher on the Depression Inventory and the Boredom Proneness score but did not differ from the controls on the SSS. The differences found in the gamblers in treatment may reflect their depressed and bored withdrawal states. Unlike the earlier study by these authors the scores of gamblers in this one were not different from the same-age control group. In a final report, the authors reported that the SSS scores prior to or after treatment did not differentiate groups who stopped gambling from those who were still gambling at follow-up (Blaszczynski, McCongaghy, & Frankova, 1991).

Allcock and Grace (1988) compared pathological gamblers entering a treatment program with groups of alcoholics, drug addicts, and controls. The drug addicts were higher and the alcoholics were lower than the controls but the gamblers were only slightly and nonsignificantly higher than the controls on the SSS V Total score.

Anderson and Brown (1984) found no differences on an SSS score between their small samples of regular gamblers and students even though the gamblers were probably older. Dickerson, Hinchy, and Fabre (1987) studied off-course betting agency customers first interviewed and recruited in the betting agency. This was a somewhat older sample than those in previously mentioned studies with mean ages of 42 for males and 53 for females. Not surprisingly they scored lower on the SSS than the population norms for Australia on every scale but the BS scale, the only one not correlated with age. Since this was not a group of diagnosed pathological gamblers, the relationship of the SSS to the characteristics of their betting is of more interest than the overall scores of the group. Correlations of the SSS with patterns of betting, controlling for age, showed that the ES and Dis scales correlated with the "chasing" pattern of betting, characteristic of pathological gamblers, in which gamblers increase their bets when they are losing. The BS scale correlated with reported arousal during betting, and Total, TAS, and ES scales correlated positively with the level of betting. Thus within the group the gamblers showing the signs of pathological gambling were the highest on the SSS.

Kusyszyn and Rutter (1985) solicited people in various public areas including racetracks to answer a questionnaire containing personality tests and some demographic questions and items referring to gambling. On the basis of returned questionnaires, they composed groups of heavy gamblers (who gambled more frequently and bet more money), light gamblers, nongamblers, and exclusively lottery players. The heavy gamblers scored highest and the lottery players scored lowest on a scale of risk taking, reflecting the need and liking for exciting activities. The combined group of gamblers scored significantly higher than the combined nongamblers and lottery players. Years of gambling in the heavy-gambling group (possibly a sign of pathological gambling) correlated positively with risk taking and negatively with anxiety scales. In all groups the risk-taking scale correlated with measures of hostility and aggression.

The final study (Kuley & Jacobs, 1988) is one of pathological gamblers who were not in a treatment program. Subjects were recruited from responders to advertisements in newspapers, and notices placed in liquor stores where race forms were posted, and local card rooms, and handed to persons boarding buses for the racetracks. The notice offered payment for those willing to spend a half hour filling out questionnaires. On the basis of their responses to 20 questions formulated by Gamblers Anonymous to identify problem gambling, the subjects were classified into "problem gamblers" and "social gamblers." Age and education were matched for the two groups. The problem gamblers scored significantly higher than the social gamblers on the Total, Dis, ES, and BS scores of the SSS. The Total, Dis, and BS scores correlated significantly with the score on the 20-question test, and the percentage of their incomes spent on betting reported by subjects correlated significantly with the Dis and BS scales. This is the only study of pathological gamblers outside of a treatment program and it shows that they are higher on the SSS than a well-matched group of social gamblers. The correlations of the SSS with amount bet in this study and the study by Dickerson et al. (1987) also suggest that the "high rollers" among gamblers are the most sensation seeking.

Bipolar (manic-depressive) disorder

There are a number of reasons to expect that manic-depressives are high sensation seekers even when they are not in a manic state. The manic state is itself a caricature of sensation-seeking behavior with high levels of activity, fast speech, impulsive traveling, euphoria or anger, little sleep, drinking, sexual sensation seeking, and impulsive spending or gambling of large sums of money. Mania is sensation seeking out of control. But manic states are episodic, so the question is what are bipolars like when they are not high? The higher SSS scores of the manic-depressives in the study by Zuckerman and Neeb (1979) suggest that they are still high sensation seekers when they are in a normal state, since the respondents to that survey were unlikely to have been in either clinical state when they took the time at home to fill out the forms.

The Hypomania scale of the MMPI is the most consistent and highest correlate of the SSS among normal subjects (Zuckerman et al., 1972), as well as prisoners (Blackburn, 1969; Thorne, 1971) and psychiatric patients (Daitzman & Tumilty, 1974). The Hypomania scale was developed by comparing the MMPI item responses of hypomanics to those of normals and selecting the most differentiating items. Persons who score high on this scale resemble manics in their self-descriptions even though they may not have the actual clinical disorder.

Cronin and Zuckerman (1992) studied a group of diagnosed bipolars in a hospital setting. Even though nearly half of the group were in the depressed state of the illness, the group as a whole scored higher than normal controls on the Dis and BS scales of the SSS V, and there were no significant differences between those in the manic and depressed states. The results suggest that the sensation seeking in bipolars is not dependent on the clinical state because the scores are elevated in manic, depressed, and probably normal states. The "at risk" offspring of parents with bipolar disorder scored higher than offspring of controls on the Dis and Total SSS, suggesting a genetic link between sensation seeking and bipolar disorder (Nurnberger et al., 1988). There are other biological links between sensation seeking and bipolar disorder (Zuckerman, 1985) that will be discussed in Chapters 11 and 12 on biological correlates of sensation seeking.

Major depressive disorder

The unipolar major depressive disorder was not found to differ from controls on sensation seeking in the study by Zuckerman and Neeb (1979), but these were not clinically diagnosed patients. Carton, Jouvent, Bungener, & Widlöcher (1992) tested 108 patients diagnosed as having major depressive disorders using DSM III criteria. These patients scored significantly lower than controls from the general French population on the General and four subscales of the SSS form IV both before and at the end of treatment and hospitalization. The fact that SSS scores of the patients did not change after treatment suggests that they were not mood dependent. However, a relationship was found between changes in anhedonia and emotional expressiveness and sensation-seeking scores: The more the emotional expressiveness increased and anhedonia decreased, the more the sensation-seeking scores increased. This suggests that while there was no change overall in sensation seeking in the depressive group, the sensation-seeking scores did vary with degree of mood change in individuals.

Schizophrenia

Many schizophrenics can be characterized as stimulus aversive, particularly for intense, complex, and novel stimulation. Their withdrawal or schizoid reactions seem to reflect a need to avoid the arousal produced by social stimulation. Normal subjects who posed as psychiatric patients in order to study what goes on in hospitals reported tremendous personal boredom (Rosenhan, 1973) in contrast to the real schizophrenic patients who appeared merely apathetic. Schizophrenics, in contrast to most normals, tend to enjoy a sensory-deprivation situation (Harris, 1959) and some researchers have found it to be therapeutic for them (Azima & Cramer-Azima, 1956; Reitman & Cleveland, 1964).

The *input-dysfunction* theory of schizophrenia (McGhie & Chapman, 1961; Payne, Matussek, & George, 1959; Venables, 1964) proposes that certain types of schizophrenic symptoms represent a disorder of the selective and inhibitory mechanisms required for focused attention. Instead of concentrating on one aspect of the stimulus environment and ignoring others some schizophrenics seem to be responding to all stimuli, relevant as well as irrelevant, producing confusion. Intensities of stimuli may also seem amplified. Normal low sensation seekers also have poor focused attention, particularly under conditions of distraction (Ball & Zuckerman, 1992).

Other theories of schizophrenia (Broen, 1968; Epstein, 1970; Mednick, 1958) suggest that schizophrenics are in a hyperaroused state and therefore seek to reduce stimulation in order to reduce arousal. Meehl (1962) says that *anhedonia*, or the lack of capacity to feel pleasure, is a nuclear symptom of schizophrenia. This deficit would explain the narrow interests and apathy characteristic of some schizophrenics. All of these theories would lead to the prediction that schizophrenics are low sensation seekers. However, recent distinctions between positive and negative types of symptoms must be considered before generalizing about sensation seeking in schizophrenia. Positive symptoms represent the presence of abnormal behavior, like delusions and hallucinations, whereas negative symptoms are the absence of normal behavior, like activity, pleasure seeking, work motivation, and emotional expression. It is the apathetic schizophrenic with primarily negative types of symptoms who is most likely to be a low sensation seeker.

Brownfield (1966), Kish (1970b), and Thorne (1971) found that schizophrenics scored lower than normal controls on General or Total SSS. Brownfield did not find differences between schizophrenic and other types of patients, but age was not controlled. Kish (1970a) and Tumilty and Daitzman (1977) controlled for age and reported that chronic schizophrenics scored lower than other psychiatric and medical groups as well as normals. When the high and low scorers among the schizophrenics in the Kish study were compared, it was found that the low-SSS schizophrenics were rated by nurses as more behaviorally retarded, suggesting that it is the more apathetic and inactive schizophrenics who are the lowest sensation seekers. The last studies certainly suggest that chronic hospitalized schizophrenics are low sensation seekers, but the lack of differences between younger schizophrenics, who were probably in remission, and controls (Zuckerman & Neeb, 1979) makes one wonder if the low sensation seeking is associated with the disorder itself, the drugs used to treat the disorder, or the apathy and anhedonia that often develop in the chronic patient. A study of the SSS differences between acute schizophrenics with a predominance of negative symptoms and those with positive symptoms might help answer this question.

Behavioral measures of stimulation and variety seeking have been used to test the sensation avoidance hypothesis of schizophrenia. McReynolds (1963) gave schizophrenics the choice of looking at novel slides they had not seen before and familiar slides that they had previously looked at. The more withdrawn schizophrenics preferred the familiar slides and the less withdrawn ones favored the novel slides.

Sidle, Acker, and McReynolds (1963) compared schizophrenics, non-schizophrenic patients, and normal controls on the Howard (1961) maze test. The test measures the extent to which subjects vary their paths to the same goal in a maze, where alternate paths are equally effective. The test does not correlate with SSS in normals (Zuckerman et al., 1964). The maze test may measure something more akin to rigidity than to sensation seeking. However, schizophrenics scored lower than the other two groups, meaning that they showed less variation in paths to the goal. Harrison and Nichols (1984) compared chronic male schizophrenics and normal controls on the maze test before and after being exposed to novel associations. The schizophrenics had lower scores on the maze test both before and after stimulation although significance of the difference was marginal. After exposure to novel stimuli, however, the maze variation scores decreased in the schizophrenics and increased in the controls. The results suggest a lower optimal level of stimulation in schizophrenics, assuming that the novel stimuli overexcited them, resulting in a need to reduce variation in their behavior.

Neurosis (anxiety disorders)

Theoretically one might expect anxiety to reduce sensation seeking since anxious persons are already overaroused and would avoid the kind of stimulation that further increases arousal. But, as discussed previously, measures of trait anxiety and neuroticism do not correlate at all with sensation seeking. Zuckerman and Neeb (1979) found no significant differences on the SSS between persons who reported a history of neurosis and normal controls. These were, of course, persons who may no longer have been anxious or neurotic at the time they took the SSS. Thorne (1971) found that a group of hospitalized neurotics (not otherwise classified) scored lower than patients with personality disorders and as low as schizophrenics on the General SSS. Faravelli, Degl'Innocenti, Sessarego, and Cabras (1987) tested groups of patients with panic disorder and agoraphobia with panic attacks during the follow-up period after a course of drug treatment when the patients were supposed to be either symptom-free or with symptoms at a minimum (actually anxiety scales of the MMPI were still quite high). The agoraphobics, who demonstrate sensation avoidance by seldom leaving their house, were expected to have lower sensation-seeking scores than controls. The two anxiety groups, panic disorder and agoraphobia with panic disorder, did not differ very much on the SSS and were combined into one panic disorder group for comparison with a normal control group. The patients scored significantly lower than controls on the TAS, ES, and Total SSS. The SSS did not correlate with duration of illness, age of onset, or rated symptom severity scores at either the time of administration or during the peak of the symptoms, suggesting that scores on the SSS were not influenced by the clinical state. This would suggest that panic disorder patients, with or without agoraphobia, are low sensation seekers even when they are not subject to panic attacks. One problem with the study is that there were relatively more males in the control group (43%) as compared with the panic disorder group (25%). Since males tend to score higher than females on most of the SSS, this may have accounted for part of the difference between the SSS scores in the two groups.

Posttraumatic Stress Disorder (PSD) is a form of anxiety disorder that manifests itself in recurrent anxiety, depression, and persisting general life maladjustment, supposedly as a result of traumatic events that occurred some time in the past. Orr et al. (1990) compared a group of male Vietnam veterans diagnosed as PSD with a smaller group of veterans with anxiety disorders that did not have PSD characteristics and a group of veterans screened for absence of disorders. The PSD group differed from the normal group on only one SSS subscale: They were *higher* than the controls and those with anxiety disorders on BS. They were also higher than those with anxiety disorders, but not the controls, on the ES subscale. The anxiety patients were lower than the controls on TAS. None of the groups differed on the General SSS. Apparently PSDs are fairly normal on the SSS. The one scale, BS, on which they are higher than controls is the same one that differentiated alcoholic veterans from normal subjects in the study by Kilpatrick et al. (1976). This suggests that the PSD group is more similar to groups with disinhibitory disorders than to other types of anxiety patients. In some cases PSD can be a post hoc attribution for socially undesirable behavior that develops in a survivor of severe stress.

Stress

The impact of life stress on an individual depends on factors of individual resiliency and coping ability. The same stress can disable one person and hardly upset another, and one person's stress can be another person's pleasure (Zuckerman, 1991b). Sensation seekers are often the instruments of their own stress since the stress is often a consequence of their sensation-seeking activities (Cohen, 1982). A person who reacts more negatively and severely to stress does not generally do things where the consequences may produce stress. But some stress is inevitable in life simply because change is inevitable and major life changes are an important source of stress.

Life stress has been conceptualized as a function of major life changes. In this sense, getting married may be as stressful as getting divorced. However, the same kind of change may be experienced as positive or negative depending on its meaning to an individual and whether the change was desired or forced on the person. If divorce, for instance, represents the reluctant loss of a highly valued relationship, the event will be stressful; but if divorce represents the termination of a conflictual relationship and the beginning or possibility of a new and loving one, it is generally not at all stressful. Low sensation seekers tend to appraise more imagined life events as stressful and anticipate a longer time to recover from them than do high sensation seekers (Jorgensen & Johnson, 1990). Smith, Johnson, and Sarason (1978) found that only those life changes that are regarded as negative contribute to the psychological distress of an individual. They found that such negative events caused more distress in low than in high sensation seekers. There was essentially no correlation between negative life events and psychological distress in the high sensation seekers. In another study, J. Johnson, Sarason, and Siegel (1979) found that negative life changes correlated with heightened anxiety and hostility in persons scoring low on Mehrabian's (1975) Arousal Seeking scale.

Siegel, Johnson, and Sarason (1979) tested the hypothesis that immediate mood might affect the positivity or negativity of scores on the life events scale. They used the Velten (1967) method for the self-induction of mood states. Mood states were effectively manipulated, as judged by responses on the MAACL (Zuckerman & Lubin, 1965). Although there were some weak but significant relationships between general mood states and life change scores, there were no significant effects of induced mood states on life change scores. Low sensation seekers were initially more anxious than highs, but high sensation seekers responded more to the depression induction procedure with greater increases in depression and hostility. Despite the effect of sensation seeking on mood manipulation, there was no interaction between sensation seeking and induced mood in effects on life stress scores. The results suggest that life stress scores and the mediating effect of sensation seeking are not due to the effects of immediate mood on life events evaluations.

In contrast to the results of these studies by the Sarason group, Cohen (1982) did not find a mediating effect of sensation seeking on the relationship between negative life stress and psychological discomfort. He did find that negative life stresses of high sensation seekers were largely a result of their own activities, such as going to jail for violations of the law, trouble with their employers, and sexual difficulties. But the impact of negative events did not differ as a function of sensation-seeking levels.

Life events are usually regarded as environmental influences rather than a function of personality itself. Plomin and Bergeman (1991) have shown that many putative measures of environment have some significant genetic determination. Life events themselves have a considerable degree of genetic determination that is as high as that seen for many personality traits. Monozygotic twins reared apart, in whom similarity is entirely a function of genetic influences, correlate .49 on a life events scale and the correlation is the same for undesirable and desirable events. As might be expected though, the correlation is much higher for controllable events, which are in part a consequence of the individual's own behavior, than for uncontrollable events (Plomin, Lichtenstein, Pederson, McClearn, & Nesselroade, 1990). It would be interesting to know how much the impact of such events on the person is also genetically determined.

Clarke and Innes (1983) actually found a difference in the opposite direction in the relations between life stress and emotional distress or physical illness in Australian firemen; it was the high sensation seekers in this study who showed greater response to stress. Social support buffered the effect of stress but only for the low sensation seekers. Innes and Clarke (1986) repeated this study using the Venturesomeness scale as the sensation-seeking measure. They found that social support, but not venturesomeness, affected psychological symptoms in the firemen, but venturesomeness mediated the relationship between work station stress and physical and somatic symptoms, whereas social support played no role in this. High sensation seekers showed higher relationships between symptoms and work stress than low sensation seekers. The results suggest that while high sensation-seeking firemen do not differ in strain and tension from lows, they are more likely to relate their symptoms to job stress. It might be that high sensation seekers are more vulnerable to the boredom of fire station life between fire calls.

Cooley and Keesey (1981) found that the number of life change events correlated significantly with physical disorders in low but not in high sensation seekers, but the differences between the two groups in magnitudes of the correlations were not significant. Feij, Doorn, van Kampen, van de Berg, and Resing (1992) used a larger and more representative sample and they looked at all of the subtypes of sensation seeking as possible mediators of stress in a Dutch population. They found that one of the SSS subscales, TAS, mediated the relationship between unpleasant life events and psychological and somatic symptoms, particularly for those events called "jointly controllable" (as in relationship problems). Social support also affected the relationships between stress and negative reactions; the group who were low on both thrill and adventure seeking and social support showed the greatest degree of negative reaction to stress.

"Burn-out" reaction has been defined as reduced expectations for work rewards together with a sense of physical and emotional exhaustion. Meier and Schmeck (1985) studied the "burn out" reaction in college students and found that those showing the symptoms were lower on General, ES and BS scales than controls. High sensation seekers may find ways of varying their college experiences and seeking variety in courses and other aspects of college life that make it meaningful to students.

Smith et al. (1992) focused their study on the relationship between general life events and sports-related events in a large group of high school students who were active participants on various sports teams. This was a predictive study since the sensation-seeking and stress measures were taken at the beginning of a season and studied in relation to subsequent athletic injuries. High and low sensation seekers who sustained athletic injuries were compared on the time lost as a consequence of their injuries. Sensation seeking did not moderate the relationship between general life stress and loss of time due to injuries, but it did moderate the relationships between previous major negative sports experiences and reactions to injuries as shown in Figure 10.2. There was no relationship between negative athletic experience and vulnerability to injury in the high sensation seekers, but the relationship was positive and significant in the low sensation seekers.

The high sensation seekers scored higher on an athletic coping skills inventory designed by the authors. Specifically, the high sensation seekers were higher on subscales measuring freedom from worry, concentration, stress management, and peaking under pressure. All of these variables sug-

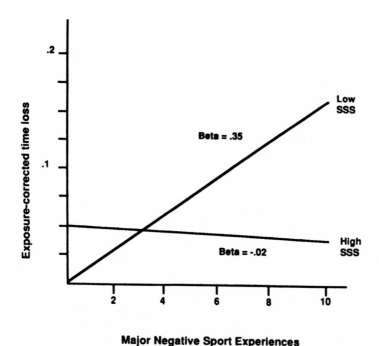

Major Negative Sport Experiences

Figure 10.2. Sensation seeking as a moderator between life stress and time lost due to athletic injuries. From "Sensation seeking, stress, and adolescent injuries, a test of stress buffering, risk-taking, and coping skills hypotheses," by R. E. Smith, V. T. Ptacek, & F. L. Smoll, 1992, *Journal of Personality and Social Psychology, 62,* 1021. Copyright American Psychological Association, 1992. Reprinted by permission of author.

gest the ability to control and even use high levels of arousal to facilitate performance. Despite the fact that high sensation seekers had better ways of coping with stress in athletic competition, their coping skills could not be shown to be responsible for the relationship between stress and injury vulnerability in the low sensation seekers.

The need for prospective studies like the one by Smith et al. is illustrated by the results of Davidson and Baum (1986), investigating the reactions of people living close to the Three Mile Island nuclear plant where an accident in 1979 resulted in radioactive leakage and widespread fear and depression in the community. A control group was taken from another community at a safe distance from the nuclear accident. Studies showed considerable evidence of PSD in both psychological and physiological measures of stress in the group from the exposed community. However, an unexpected result was that the exposed group scored *lower* than the control group on the SSS Total, ES, and BS scales. Since there was no reason why one community should have differed from the other on basal levels of sensation seeking, the inference would be that the stress of the nuclear accident lowered sensation-seeking trait. If this is indeed the case, then it is imperative that sensation-seeking measures be taken before stress rather than after. At a minimum, it must be shown that sensation seeking is unrelated to life stresses themselves as reported in retrospective measures like life stress inventories.

Stress related psychophysiological disorders

If low sensation seekers are more vulnerable to stress they may be more prone to stress related psychophysiological disorders. Headache sufferers had lower scores on the Total score and all of the subscales of the SSS V compared with controls (Ginsberg & Pollack-Fels, 1991). Arque and Torrubia (1988), however, found no significant differences between SSS scores of headache sufferers and controls, although the headache patients were about three points lower on the Total score.

Johansson (1982) found no significant differences on the SSS between patients with chronic pain diagnosed as of organic and psychogenic origins, but von Knorring, Almay, and Johannson (1987), using larger groups of subjects, found that idiopathic (psychogenic) pain patients were significantly lower than controls on the KSP Monotony Avoidance scale while a group of neurogenic (organic) pain patients had scores that were slightly above the controls. Psychogenic patients have been shown to have higher levels of endorphins than organic pain patients and endorphins have been shown to be negatively related to sensation seeking (Johansson, Almay, von Knorring, Terrenius, & Aston, 1979).

During a physical examination by a physician screening medical students for a study on effects of drugs, Carrol et al. (1982) discovered that low sensation seekers had higher systolic blood pressures (BP) than high sensation seekers, whose blood pressures were essentially normal. Curiously, these BP differences disappeared in readings taken by a nurse on six separate occasions during the subsequent experiments. Although this seemed like a simple stimulus–person interaction effect, the medical histories of the subjects revealed that 56% of the high sensation seekers had a family history of cardiovascular disease in contrast to only 19% of the controls. A similar kind of finding emerged from a study by von Knorring, Oreland, and Winblad (1984) where BPs were taken by physicians on over 1,000 Swedish Army recruits who were also tested on the SSS.

The relationship between systolic BP and the SSS score was significant even though the range of mean BPs was not large. Average to high sensation seekers all had BPs at or below average levels for the population. Only the lowest 9% of sensation seekers (scores 0 to 6) had mean levels of systolic BP that exceeded the normal range, but even these were not in the borderline clinical range.

Thus, while there is some evidence of a weak inverse relationship between blood pressure and sensation seeking, there is as yet no evidence that clinical hypertensives are low sensation seekers. Since there is some suggestion that low sensation seekers have a family history of hypertension, a prospective health study incorporating the SSS as a predictor is needed.

Summary

Sensation seeking is a normal trait of personality. Unlike neuroticism, there is no necessary association with behavior disorder at either extreme of the trait. However, when combined with certain other traits, the result can be a personality disorder or a clinical condition. Unless high sensation-seeking trait is combined with a lack of socialization, an antisocial personality is not inevitable. Criminals have about the same SSS scores as noncriminals who engage in risky sports like parachuting or risky vocations like fire fighting. Sensation seeking seems to be a necessary but not sufficient ingredient of an antisocial personality.

Among childhood disorders, sensation seeking is higher in the conduct disorders than in attention deficit or anxiety disorders. Laboratory behavioral measures of stimulation seeking show more consistent evidence of differences between hyperactives and normals, but findings on child versions of the SSS are mixed.

The results on children are consistent with those found in adults. Criminals with antisocial personalities score higher than other criminals or normals on the SSS, particularly on the ES, Dis, and BS subscales. Most studies show little difference on sensation seeking between neurotics and normals, although panic disorders are lower than controls on TAS and ES subscales.

Neither delinquent nor criminal groups differ from normals of an equivalent age on sensation seeking, but the more aggressive and generally psychopathic criminals are higher on sensation seeking than other delinquents or criminals. Among delinquents or normals, sensation seeking differentiates those who are relatively more socially deviant, more likely to use drugs, and more likely to engage in generally deviant behavior in school or in the community. Sensation seeking in adolescence predicts lack of law-abiding attitudes and deviant social behavior in later adolescence and early adult life. The Dis scale is usually the subscale most related to delinquent behavior.

Pathological gamblers seem like a behavioral prototype for arousal seeking since they seem to find their major source of pleasure in the arousal produced by high-stakes betting. Although studies of pathological gamblers in treatment groups do not show them to be high sensation seekers, studies of currently active heavy gamblers recruited at racetracks and other facilities (Kuley & Jacobs, 1988; Kusyszyn & Rutter, 1985) do show them to be high sensation seekers, particularly on Dis and BS subscales.

Persons with bipolar disorder (manic-depressives) show an extreme of sensation-seeking behavior and self-reports when they are in a manic state, but they have high SSS scores even in normal and depressed states. Hypomanic tendencies in the normal population are also correlated with sensation seeking. Major depressive disorders are low on sensation seeking even after treatment, but there is some evidence of a relationship with mood changes in treatment. Chronic schizophrenics who are withdrawn and inactive tend to be sensation avoiders, both behaviorally and on the SSS.

Some studies have reported that low sensation seekers are more vulnerable and reactive to life stress. However, other studies have been unable to confirm these results, and still others have found the opposite results, with more relationship between stress and distress in high sensation seekers. The controllable types of stress, in which the individual plays some role, seem to be the ones that account for the relationship with sensation seeking.

There are some studies linking low sensation seeking to chronic headaches, chronic pain of a psychogenic origin, and signs of heightened blood pressure, but the evidence is mixed for all of these and the latter seems situation-specific. High sensation seekers are certainly not vulnerable to psychophysiological disorders even though they are more likely than low sensation seekers to do unhealthy things that are implicated in these disorders, like smoking, drinking, and using drugs.

11

Biological bases

The biological correlates of sensation seeking are drawn from four disciplines: behavior genetics, neuropsychology, biological psychiatry, and psychophysiology (Zuckerman, Buchsbaum, & Murphy, 1980). Behavior genetics has developed methods for estimating the genetic and environmental contributions to human traits and animal behavior. Neuropsychology, including psychopharmacology, experimentally explores the structural and biochemical bases for behavior, mostly in nonhuman species. Biological psychiatry extends the findings from animals to human psychopathology in order to discover the causes of mental illnesses and devise new and better treatments for them. There has also been an increasing interest in the personality disorders and normal personality. Psychophysiology uses data gathered from skin surface recordings of activity in the brain, cardiovasculatory and respiratory systems, muscles, and sweat glands to study the reactivity of these systems to various kinds of stimuli or characteristic tonic levels of activity in unstimulated resting conditions. The first three areas will be discussed in this chapter and psychophysiology in the next one.

Genetics

Evolutionary speculations

A trait that has some basis in the genetic code for building the nervous system must have an evolutionary history. Much of what is called *sociobiology* as applied to extant human traits represents little more than "Just So" stories based on studies of the behavior of other living species and flights of fancy back to the past of our own prehistoric ancestors. Adaptation may explain the origin but not necessarily the persistence of a behavioral trait that is general to a species. A trait that has lost its adaptive value, if it ever had one, may hang on simply because nothing better has come along to replace it. Nature is conservative in that once something works it is preserved even if it is irrelevant to current adaptation. The adaptation shaping some traits was in reaction to some environments existing during the distant past of our species. It is difficult to reconstruct those environments and the selection that may have occurred in response to them.

Some forms of sociobiology suggest there are universal characteristics of our species. We share with other species certain broad behavior patterns like foraging and exploration, defense of territory, competitive and defensive aggression, courtship and mating, and at least a rudimentary kind of interest in novel stimuli. But the cultural and technological changes in our species have changed the phenomenal nature of these tendencies to the point where their identity with earlier evolved traits is problematic. Are trips to the supermarket "foraging" and is vacation travel "exploration"? The tremendous variation in behavior patterns within and between cultures defies simplistic generalizations about "human nature" or differences between broad classes of humans like "races" (Zuckerman, 1990b). There is equal diversity among species of animals from which generalizations about our species are drawn. Do we generalize about human sexuality from the harem-dominant gorilla or the opportunistic mating of the promiscuous chimpanzee? Among primates, only gibbons engage in the semimonogamous pair bonding characteristic of humans (Symons, 1979). Regardless of which we choose, we must recognize that while their species' specific patterns of behavior have not changed much in millions of years, ours most certainly have, sometimes within a few generations.

Given these caveats, it may seem hypocritical to speculate about the past adaptiveness of a trait of sensation seeking and its role in natural selection. But this exercise has a scientifically useful purpose in the search for appropriate animal models for a comparative approach to human personality. If we can speculate that human patterns of behavior are based on underlying structural and physiological bases that have evolved from mammalian and primate ancestors, we can observe the descendants of these ancestors for analogous behaviors. If we stopped at this point we would still have nothing but an anthropomorphic metaphor. But if we can identify common biological markers of analogous behaviors in two species, using experimental methods with other species and primarily correlational methods with our own, we may learn much about the biological bases of our own trait variations (Zuckerman, 1991a). A comparative approach to personality (Zuckerman, 1984a; Zuckerman, Ballenger, & Post, 1984) is important because biological experimentation with humans is limited by ethical constraints.

Schneirla's (1959) theory (Chapter 1) lends itself to a comparative approach to sensation seeking. Recall that he described two basic behavioral dimensions found across all species, approach (A) and withdrawal (W). The terms *seeking* for approach and *avoidance* for withdrawal were used to describe the behavior in more complex organisms where behavior is more modifiable and flexible. A-type behavior includes things like foraging for food and seeking mates, whereas W-type behavior consists of defensive adjustments like behavioral freezing, huddling, and flight. Schneirla said that high-intensity stimulation tends to produce W-type responses, whereas low to moderate intensity stimuli elicit A-type reactions.

Novelty is another aspect of stimulation that may produce either approach or avoidance. Sensation seeking is essentially a greater disposition to approach novel and intense stimuli, people, or situations, whereas low sensation seeking is the tendency to avoid such stimuli. The advantages of high sensation seeking in other animals, and perhaps in our own hominid ancestors, are increased access to new potential food sources and mates but the advantages are somewhat offset by the risks. Exploring unknown territory means increased risk of being killed by wild animals or other humanoid groups. Jane Goodall (1986) describes the murderous reactions of chimpanzees to members of other groups who are found in the territory of the proprietary group. Low sensation seekers stay in their own territory and "stick to their own kind," but an aversion to exploration may result in the exhaustion of the food resources in a small, restricted area and a reproductive rate depleted by the limited supply of available females. Humans have often reacted to reduced resources in an area by migration, but low sensation seekers are the most reluctant to migrate (Jacobs & Koeppel, 1974; Winchie & Carment, 1988).

A successful adaptation to the Pleistocene environment probably required the addition of meat to the homanoid diet; therefore, hunting large as well as small animals became an important group activity for males. Women may have participated to some degree, but nursing mothers would not be an asset on a hunt and the greater muscle strength of men was quite important. A successful hunter must take some risks and even enjoy predation. Because of the risks, a moderate but not too high level of the trait was probably optimal for survival, reproduction, and insuring the survival of one's offspring.

Specialization is another way that species who dwell in colonies may increase their survival. Bees and termites have evolved different types of members built for different functions: workers, soldiers, and reproducers. Human types are not so biologically differentiated, but a society may accommodate high sensation seekers in one role, such as warriors and explorers, and low sensation seekers in another, like diplomats, priests, and record keepers. The balance between the adventurous and the more cautious members of society may determine the fate of everyone in the society. There are short-term risks incurred by revolutionary change and longer-term risks of stagnation in a static society. As long as evolution was not directional toward one extreme of the trait or the other, natural selection would stabilize for the middle, optimal range, and enough at both extremes of the trait to balance the two kinds of risk or choose between them according to the circumstances.

If natural selection persists for many generations, there can be directional change. Could this affect a trait like sensation seeking? Studies showing assortative mating for sensation seeking were discussed in Chapter 7. Assortative mating would increase the variability in the trait, but would not necessarily give it a directional basis unless one extreme or the other were universally preferred and resulted in more pair-bonding and reproduction at that end of the trait distribution. D. Buss et al.'s (1990) study of trait preferences for mate selection in 37 cultures found a remarkable degree of agreement across genders and cultures in the three highest-rank attributes for a mate: kind and understanding, intelligent, and "exciting personality." While it is not clear what "exciting personality" means, it sounds like extraversion and sensation seeking. If these preferences were around for many generations in societies that permitted choice of marital partners, we might see an increase in the desirable traits. There is evidence of an increase in measured intelligence over the past half century (Flynn, 1987), but this increase may be due to improved nutrition rather than directional genetic change (Lynn, 1990). In fact, the relationship between intelligence and fertility is a negative one; more intelligent people have fewer children (Van Court & Bean, 1985). If anything, this tendency would result in a decline in intelligence rather than the increase that has occurred. There are no intergenerational data in regard to kindness and understanding or "empathy." In Chapter 4, I noted an increase in SSS scores, particularly Dis, over a decade at one university, but a decade is too short a time for a genetic change and the increase in Dis probably reflects the cultural changes in permissiveness over that period. The question of the effect of selection for sensation seeking over a long period of time is difficult to answer. Cultural changes probably account for most of the changes that we see now in the phenomenal forms of sensation seeking. These changes can go both ways depending on changes in values, the fads in expressions of sensation seeking, and the amount of environmental stress. Sensation-seeking behavior probably decreases during times of stress, danger, and uncertainty, as during war or following natural disasters (Davidson & Baum, 1986). One does not need extra risks for stimulation when risks are part of everyday life. However, in periods of safety and security, persons with high sensation-seeking needs may voluntarily engage in moderately risky activities to relieve the boredom of everyday life. There is a strong possibility that the fundamental trait of sensation seeking has not changed since the Pleistocene period when it may have had an adaptive value at moderate levels. Assortative mating may have maintained variability in the trait. Of course, the phenomenal expressions have changed from activities like hunting to reckless driving.

Genetic studies of other species

These essentially untestable speculations about the evolution of sensation-seeking trait, or high and low sensation-seeking types within the human population, depend on the assumption of a genetic source for the trait, since heredity is the biological mechanism of evolution. Experimental approaches to establishing heredity depend on experimental models used with other species. Primates are too slow breeding and too expensive and fruit flies are too evolutionarily distant from humans, so that most investigators have used mice and rats for experimental behavior genetics. Inbred strains of rodents often show marked differences in behavioral traits. Behavioral differences within a population may be magnified by experimental inbreeding of successive generations between members of the strain showing both extremes of response. If the trait is genetic to some degree, one may eventually produce two populations differing on the response selected for and sometimes responses to other situations and certain physical traits as well.

Most rodents have some fear of open places, which is not too difficult to understand from an evolutionary point of view. A mouse running into an open field is exposed to aerial and ground predators, but field mice must come out of their burrows to forage or they will starve. When a mouse is put into an open arena in the laboratory, the situation seems to produce a conflict between the innate fear of an open field and a natural explorative reaction to novel environments. On the first trials, some mice will freeze and show signs of emotional arousal including defecation. Others will show little emotional arousal and, after a short pause, will run around and explore the field, and still others may show mixtures of the two tendencies. As fear habituates, activity increases and the two tendencies become negatively correlated (Whimbey & Denenberg, 1967).

Inbred strains are genetically quite homogeneous, almost the equivalent of colonies of identical twins. Two such strains of mice, the BALBs (B-Albinos) and the C57BLs differ markedly on open-field behavior. The BALBs show strong fear (much defecation and behavioral inhibition) when first exposed to the open field whereas the C57BLs are fearless, active, and exploratory in this novel situation (DeFries, Gervais, & Thomas, 1978). Cross-strains between BALBs and C57BLs show intermediate levels of the two traits depending on the proportion of genes from the two strains. Starting with an intermediate cross-bred strain, DeFries et al. selectively bred separate high and low open-field activity strains for 30 generations. The final generation showed no overlap in response to the open field. Essentially they had reproduced the original strains. From a population with a normal distribution they created two distinct populations or types. The study also showed the genetic covariance between open-field activity and defecation; although the mice were bred for activity, the final generations differed in emotionality as well.

Explorativeness in the open field might be analogous to the adventure-seeking type in the human, but there are problems with this kind of comparison. For one thing, although exploration in the open field is genetically linked with low levels of fearfulness, the human sensation-seeking trait seems to be uncorrelated with general anxiety. For another, some forms of human sensation seeking, like disinhibition, involve social reactions, and the open-field situation does not assess social reactions. Finally, the behavior in the open field can be markedly affected by the specifics of the situation, such as the levels of light and sound and the height of the roof of the field (Walsh & Cummins, 1976). The BALB is adapted to dark, closed-in spaces, and the more the environment varies from this ideal the more the BALB is at a disadvantage. It must be shown that the open-field reactions are good markers for traits of explorativeness and fearfulness in other situations before we could regard the open field as an appropriate model for a relatively broad trait like sensation seeking. McClearn (1959) did find consistent rankings of six strains of mice across six different situations, including the open field, and concluded that explorativeness was not a situation-specific trait. However, Simmel (1984) has argued that the open field is a test of exploration of empty spaces, whereas sensation seeking is supposed to be based on reactions to novel stimuli, situations, and people. The File and Hyde (1978) model for fear might also be used as a model for sensation seeking since it tests reactions to novel social and physical stimuli in environments of different degrees of familiarity.

Genetic studies of humans

Since we have no pure strains of humans and cannot selectively breed them, human behavior genetics relies on natural variations in genetic relatedness and comparisons between genetically related and unrelated individuals within a common family environment. Identical twins have all of their genes in common, whereas fraternal twins have about 50% of their genes in common. If there is additive polygenetic determination of most complex human traits, identical twins should be twice as much alike as fraternal twins. Identical twins are usually compared with fraternal twins because both types of twins are born at the same time into the same families and therefore presumed to share a common environment to a similar degree. But because identical twins tend to be treated more alike, this assumption of behavior genetics has been questioned. Separated identical twins raised in different families and social environments constitute a purer case for genetic influence. If there is no selective placement, these twins can only be alike to the extent that genetic influences determine outcome. Biologically unrelated individuals growing up in a shared family environment are the pure case for environmental influence. These individuals can only be alike to the extent that a shared environment influences outcome. This still leaves another source of environmental influence on traits and behavior, namely the environment that is not shared but is specific for each member of a family. Even if parents are consistent in their child-rearing methods with different children, children in the same family may react differently to them and may have different friends, teachers, and other social influences outside of the family. A surprising but consistent finding emerging from behavior genetics is that this latter type of nonshared environment is of much greater importance in shaping personality than the shared family influences (Bouchard, Lykken, McGue, Segal, & Tellegen, 1990). This may explain why children in the same family often end up with such different personalities.

Genetics of sensation seeking

Fulker et al. (1980) analyzed the genetic and environmental contributions to the trait of sensation seeking, using a large sample of twins (442 pairs) from the Maudsley twin register. Age and sex differences in means were statistically controlled before the genetic analyses were performed. The correlations for identical and fraternal male twins were .63 and .21 respectively; those for identical and fraternal female twins were .56 and .21 respectively. Applying the Jinks and Fulker (1970) biometric method of analysis to the data on identical and fraternal same-sex twins, and a sample of fraternal opposite-sex twins, the results showed that *58% of the general sensation-seeking trait is heritable*. The remaining variation (42%) is due to specific or nonshared environmental influences and error of the trait measurement. If the unreliabil-

Table 11.1. *Relative contributions of common and specific genetic and environmental effects to the total variation in each of the components of sensation seeking*

SSS	P due to genetic effects			P due to environmental effects		
	Common	Specific	Total	Common	Specific	Total[a]
Female						
Dis	.15	.27	.41	.59	.00	.59
TAS	.18	.26	.44	.02	.54	.56
ES	.53	.04	.57	.03	.40	.43
BS	.08	.27	.34	.13	.53	.66
Male						
Dis	.12	.39	.51	.49	.00	.49
TAS	.18	.27	.45	.02	.53	.55
ES	.52	.06	.58	.03	.39	.42
BS	.07	.34	.41	.11	.48	.59

Note: Dis = Disinhibition; TAS = Thrill and Adventure Seeking; ES = Experience Seeking; BS = Boredom Susceptibility.
[a] Error variation has not been deducted from the contribution of specific environmental factors.
Source: Table 1.5, p. 18, from "A biometrical–genetical analysis of impulsive and sensation seeking behavior," by H. J. Eysenck, 1983. In M. Zuckerman (Ed.), *Biological bases of sensation seeking, impulsivity and anxiety.* Hillsdale, NJ: Erlbaum. Copyright 1983 by Lawrence Erlbaum Associates. Reprinted by permission.

ity component is taken into account, the heritability of sensation seeking increases to 69%. As with most other personality traits, there was no evidence of a shared family environmental influence.

The range of heritability calculated for most personality traits of any breadth is 40%–60%, with the typical heritability around 50% (Zuckerman, 1991a, chap. 2). Thus the uncorrected figure of 58% for general sensation seeking is at the high end of the range for personality traits and close to the range for cognitive abilities. H. Eysenck (1983) took the analysis of the data from this study a step further by analyzing the proportions of common (among scales) and specific (to the subtest itself) variance of the four subscales that were due to genetic and environmental effects (Table 11.1).

The results were quite similar for men and women. The genetic variance for the subscales was relatively high, particularly for ES (57%–58%) in both sexes. Nearly all of the genetic effects of ES were for the common genetic factor. Moderate genetic effects (41%–51%) were seen for Dis and TAS but these came more from specific genetic factors. The BS scale showed the weakest genetic influences, possibly because of its lower reliability. Error variation was not subtracted from the specific environmental variance. Eysenck applied the same kind of analyses to the same population using subscales of the S. Eysenck and Eysenck (1977) Impulsivity questionnaire. The total genetic effects had a range of 15%–40% compared with 34%–58% for the SSS subscales.

Because the EPQ P, E, N, and L scales, the impulsivity scales, and the SSS had all been given to the same twins from the Maudsley twin register during the same year, Martin, Eaves, and Fulker (1979) decided to do a joint genetical and environmental analyses of the 12 subscales in the three questionnaires. The genetical analysis of covariance structures was adapted from confirmatory factor analytic methods. The model that was tested assumed that Eysenck's four dimensions of personality (L was regarded here as a fourth dimension rather than a response set scale) can account for the genetical and environmental variance in the other scales. The proportional contributions of each variable within each of the four arbitrarily designed P, E, N, and L dimensions for females is presented in Table 11.2. The percentages were similar in the male data except in the specific genetic contributions for risk (0%), nonplanning (2%), liveliness (24%), and disinhibition (18%).

The heritabilities, which are the sums of the genetic factors and specific genes for each variable, were rather low for impulsivity, E, and L scales. The highest heritabilities were found for the SS scales. The greater proportions of genetical variance for the Dis and BS scales fell in the designated E factor while ES and TAS were related inversely to social desirability (the Lie scale factor). Error accounted for a large part of the specific environmental variance for most of the variables, which is not surprising considering the abbreviated length of the scales.

Martin et al. (1979) concluded that "it is also apparent that the attempt to fit the variables within the straightjacket of P, E, N, and L is far from satisfactory" (p. 206). One of the major mistakes was insisting on a special dimension for L when there were significant negative correlations between L and P. A greater contribution of Dis to the P factor may have been found if the a priori definition of the dimensions by the Eysenck factors had not been done (see Zuckerman, 1984a, p. 457). All of the sensation-seeking subscales are subsumed in the P factor in a three-factor analysis (Zuckerman, Kuhlman, Thornquist, & Kiers, 1988) or a five-factor one (Zuckerman et al., 1991), and the Lie scale loaded negatively on this factor.

Comparisons of adopted identical twins separated at or near birth and reared in different families with no contact during their formative years constitute the pure case for heredity and the correlation between the pairs of

Table 11.2. *Percentage contributions of individual environmental (E₁) and additive genetic (D_R) factor and specific components to total variation for each character in females*

	Individual environments (E₁)						Additive genes (1/2 D_R)					
	I	II	III	IV	Specific	Error[a]	I(P)	II(E)	III(N)	(L)	Specific	Total[b]
Im	16	11	49	2	0	(26)	5	2	3	2	10	22
Risk	54	3	0	15	7	(28)	1	6	0	1	13	21
NonP	9	0	3	0	49	(41)	13	6	4	2	14	39
Live	4	10	2	0	58	(34)	0	6	6	0	14	26
P	8	—	—	—	50	(36)	42	—	—	—	—	42
E	—	80	—	—	0	(15)	—	20	—	—	—	20
N	—	—	4	—	54	(15)	—	—	42	—	—	42
L	—	—	—	2	78	(26)	—	—	—	20	—	20
Dis	23	0	6	20	3	(23)	1	24	7	6	10	48
TAS	12	1	0	3	47	(20)	0	2	5	18	12	37
ES	3	0	1	1	41	(39)	4	8	2	25	15	54
BS	8	0	0	1	50	(34)	6	14	1	0	20	41

Note: Im = (narrow) Impulsivity; Risk = Risk Taking; NonP = Nonplanning; Live = Liveliness; P = Psychoticism; E = Extraversion; N = Neuroticism; L = Lie; Dis = Disinhibition; TAS = Thrill and Adventure Seeking; ES = Experience Seeking; BS = Boredom Susceptibility.
[a]Expected measurement error is calculated as 1/4n.
[b]Total additive genetic variance. This was not in original table but was added.
Source: Table 4, p. 205, from "The genetical relationship of impulsiveness and sensation seeking to Eysenck's personality dimensions," by N. G. Martin, L. J. Eaves, & D. W. Fulker, 1979, *Acta Genetica Medica Gemellol, 28*, 197–210. Copyright 1979 by Alan R. Liss, Inc. Reprinted by permission.

twins is a direct expression of the proportion of variance due to broad heritability. A comparison of the correlations between identical twins reared apart and those reared together provides a measure of the influence of a shared family environment, including the mutual influence of the twins on each other. If this is an important influence, we would expect that the correlations would be lower in separated twins as contrasted with identical twins reared together.

The Minnesota study of separated twins (Tellegen et al., 1988) found a .54 correlation between Total SSS scores of identical twins and .32 between fraternal twins *reared in different environments* (D. Lykken, personal communication, 1992). This means a heritability of 54% based on identicals and 64% based on fraternals (2 × .32). If the heritability is somewhere between these two figures, it can be estimated at 59%, almost exactly the same as the heritability of 58% from the Fulker et al. (1980) study of twins reared together. Comparing the correlations between identicals reared together (.58) and those reared apart (.54) shows no influence of shared family environment on sensation seeking. The remaining third of the variance in the trait (after correction for reliability) must be due to nonshared environmental influences, or those affecting identical twins reared separately.

Both studies suggest that general sensation seeking has a substantial heritability for a personality trait. The ES scale has a high genetic influence compared with TAS and BS in both studies. ES is also the scale that shows the highest degree of assortative mating (Lesnik-Oberstein & Cohen, 1984). Assortative mating has the effect of increasing the phenotypic variance of a heritable trait above that of a randomly mating population. It could have the effect of inflating the estimate of the shared environment in twins, but that does not seem to be the case for these studies in which there is no evidence of a shared environmental influence.

Personality traits are not inherited as such; only the biological structures coded in the DNA are inherited. Genes are chemical templates that control the production and regulation of proteins, which form the structures of cells, act as neurotransmitters and hormones, and form enzymes that determine the chemical reactions in the cells. This suggests that we look to the biochemistry of personality in order to find out what is being inherited. One such enzyme has been identified as a biological trait marker for sensation seeking and some related traits.

Monoamine oxidase

Monoamine oxidase (MAO) is an enzyme that is involved in the metabolic breakdown of the monoamine neurotransmitters in the brain. MAO regulates these systems, keeping a balance between production and disposal, and catabolizing the neurotransmitter in the synaptic space or in the presynaptic neuron after reuptake (see Figure 11.1 showing the noradrengergic synapse). Most assays of MAO in living humans obtain the MAO from blood platelets. There are two types of MAO in the brain, designated A and B, but platelets contain only the B type. Human brain also contains a predominance of B type MAO. The A type is mainly involved in the regulation of the monoamines norepinephrine and serotonin, but dopamine deamination is primarily effected by MAO-B in the human brain (Murphy, Aulakh, Garrick, & Sunderland, 1987). However, it has been suggested that platelet MAO activity is determined by the same set of genes that regulate levels of serotonin turnover (Oreland, Wiberg, & Fowler, 1981). MAO correlates highly across different

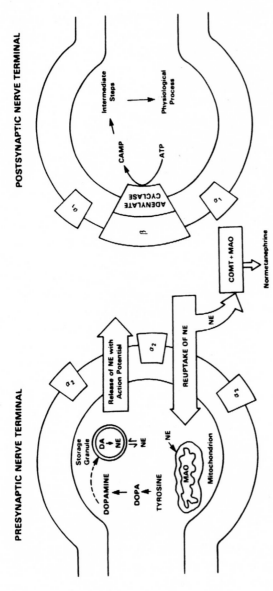

Figure 11.1. Illustration of a noradrenergic synapse. DA, dopamine; NE, norepinephrine; dihydroxyphenylalanine (dopa) is a precursor of the transmitters DA and NE. The enzymes monoamine oxidase (MAO) and catechol-O-methyltransferase (COMT) are involved in the degradation of NE: 3-methoxy-4-hydroxyphenylglycol (MHPG) and vanillymandelic acid (VMA) are metabolites from the breakdown of NE. Alpha₁, Alpha₂, and beta are receptor sites on the cell membrane. Andenosine triphosphate (ATP) is an energy source for the cell and a precursor to the "second messenger," cyclic adenosine monophosphate (cAMP). From "Antidepressants and biochemical theories of depression," by E. T. McNeal & P. Cimbolic, 1986, *Psychological Bulletin, 99,* 363. Copyright 1986 by American Psychological Association. Reprinted by permission of author.

brain areas (Adolfsson, Gottfries, Oreland, Roos, & Winblad, 1978) and correlates positively with serotonin in these areas. However, investigators have failed to find correlations between platelet MAO-B activity and activity in brain MAO using brain material obtained from postmortem or in surgery (Winblad, Gottfries, Oreland, & Wilberg, 1979; Young, Laws, Sharbrough, & Weinshilbaum, 1986), although Bench et al. (1991) did find a high relationship between inhibition of MAO-B in platelets and brain.

Despite the unresolved question of the relationship between brain MAO and platelet MAO, platelet MAO is a reliable biological marker related to many behavioral and personality traits in humans and other primates. MAO is quite reliable and stable over periods of 2 months or more and variations within subjects are small compared with variations between subjects (Murphy et al., 1976). However, MAO gradually increases with age in human brain, platelets, and plasma (Robinson, Davis, Nies, Revaris, & Sylvester, 1971). Women have higher MAO levels than men.

A summary of twin studies of platelet MAO (Zuckerman, 1991a, pp. 199–201) shows that MAO is under near-total genetic control. Analyses of MAO distributions have led some to conclude that MAO is determined by one or two major gene loci. A study using MAO obtained from the umbilical cord at birth has shown that platelet MAO and plasma amine oxidase (AO) are related to behavioral differences between infants in the first 3 days of life (Sostek, Sostek, Murphy, Martin, & Born, 1981). Low MAO or AO babies were more aroused, more active, cried more, and were rated as "less cuddly." But the low MAO babies showed more optimal motor behavior reactions and motor maturity. In general they were more reactive while the high MAO infants were more passive. The low plasma AO infants showed better orienting responses to visual and auditory stimuli.

Table 11.3 summarizes the findings relating MAO to the SSS. In studies using both male and female subjects in which the data are presented for the combined group, the combined data are listed instead of the data from the separate sex groups in order to maximize the power of the correlational tests. The first studies by Murphy et al. (1977) and Schooler, Zahn, Murphy, and Buchsbaum (1978) were conducted at the research laboratories of the National Institute of Mental Health in Bethesda, Maryland. They showed moderate and significant negative correlations between the General SSS and platelet MAO in two male samples and one of two female samples. High sensation seekers tend to have lower levels of MAO than low sensation seekers. The correlations in subsequent studies tended to be lower but almost always negative in sign (11 of 13 correlations). For the Total or General

Table 11.3. *Correlations between the Sensation Seeking Scale (SSS) and platelet MAO*

Study	Sex	*n*	Total/General	TAS	ES	Dis	BS
Murphy et al. (1977)	F	65	.17	.16	.09	.22	.08
	M	30	−.45***	−.16	−.26	−.51***	−.34*
Schooler et al. (1978)	M & F	93	−.47***	−.25**	−.43***	−.24**	−.33**
Harlow & Brown (1990)	M & F	125	−.18**	−.23***	−.03	−.09	−.15
Ballenger et al. (1983)	M & F	36	−.13	−.28	−.15	−.09	−.11
Arque et al. (1988)	M & F	13	−.66***	−.65***	−.54**	−.71***	−.07
	M & F Pts	44	−.25*	−.11	−.26**	−.34**	−.04
Schalling et al. (1987)	M	40	−.25*	.03	−.20	−.26**	−.11
Shekim et al. (1989)	M	58	−.23**	−.23**	−.27**	−.19*	−.19*
Ward et al. (1987)	M	57	−.24**	−.14	−.14	−.28**	.06
	F	30	−.15	−.10	−.14	−.05	.24
Reist et al. (1990)	M	10	.18	.19	−.11	.00	.08
	M Pts.	13	−.74***	−.76***	−.60**	−.42	−.53*
Significant (*p* < .10) *r*'s/13			9	5	5	7	4
Median correlations			−.24	−.16	−.20	−.24	−.11

Note: One tailed tests used for all studies beyond initial ones by Murphy et al. (1977) and Schooler et al. (1978), in which two tailed tests were used. TAS = Thrill and Adventure Seeking; ES = Experience Seeking; Dis = Disinhibition; BS = Boredom Susceptibility.
*p < .10.
**p < .05.
***p < .01.

SSS, 9 of 13 correlations were significant. Even though the typical (median) correlation is only −.25, the aggregated results are clearly beyond chance.

The largest study done comparing MAO with sensation seeking was one of over 1,000 army recruits in Sweden (von Knorring et al., 1984). Unfortunately, these investigators were compelled to use an abbreviated Swedish version of the SSS that did not contain the Dis scale, the one most strongly related to MAO, and half the items in the ES scale. The upper and lower 10% of the distribution on MAO were compared on selected scales from the SSS, EPI, and KSP. The low MAO soldiers were higher than the high MAO subjects on BS and the modified Total SSS score, and the Impulsivity and Monotony Avoidance scales of the KSP. The MAO groups did not differ on Extraversion from the EPI, Guilt from the KSP, or a special neuroticism-type scale. The Total SSS was the only personality measure that contributed to the discrimination between high and low MAO groups in a discriminant function analysis and the BS scale was the most powerful predictor of MAO level in a multiple regression equation. Similar results relating low MAO to impulsivity were obtained in a general Swedish population (blood doners) by Schalling, Edman, Åsberg, and Oreland (1988) but these investigators found no relationships between MAO and Monotony Avoidance.

Low MAO subjects were heavier drinkers and more of them showed signs of alcohol dependence, but low MAO men with high intellectual capacities were less likely to show these signs than those of low to average ability. Low MAO subjects also were more likely to use marijuana and to be regular tobacco smokers. Alcohol, marijuana, and tobacco use were also related to sensation seeking as discussed in Chapter 9.

Many other studies also link low MAO levels with tobacco, drug, and alcohol use (Arque & Torrubia, 1987; Coursey, Buchsbaum & Murphy, 1979; Kuperman, Kramer, & Loney, 1988; von Knorring & Oreland, 1985) and abuse (Hallman, von Knorring, von Knorring, & Oreland, 1990; Major & Murphy, 1978, Pandey, Fawcett, Gibbons, Clark, & Davis, 1988; Stillman, Wyatt, Murphy, & Rausher, 1978; von Knorring, Oreland, & von Knorring, 1987). Among male alcoholics, low MAO is especially associated with the type II alcoholic characterized by a younger onset, more antisocial behavior when intoxicated, and a family history of alcoholism (Hallman et al., 1990; Pandey et al., 1988; von Knorring et al., 1985).

Given the association between antisocial personality and substance abuse (Chapter 10), it is not surprising to find low MAO associated with antisocial personality. Coursey et al. (1979) found that 37% of a "normal" sample of male college students selected from the lowest decile of the MAO distribution reported previous convictions for offenses other than traffic violations, as compared with 6% in the high MAO group. Studies contrasting questionnaire-item responses of those with low and high MAO found discriminating items, such as "during one period when I was a youngster, I engaged in petty thievery" (Donnelly, Murphy, Waldman, Buchsbaum, & Coursey, 1979) and "I have never been in trouble with the law" (Schalling et al., 1983). Low MAO types generally answered "true" to the first and "false" to the second.

Patients with borderline personality disorder have lower MAO levels and higher sensation-seeking scores than controls and nonimpulsive types with other personality disorders (Reist, Haier, DeMet, & Chicz-DeMet, 1990). MAO correlated significantly and negatively with the General SSS in patients but not in controls.

The association of sensation seeking with tendencies toward mania (bipolar disorder) were discussed in Chapter 10. Those with bipolar disorder do tend to have low levels of MAO that do not change with their clinical states (Murphy & Weiss, 1972). Leckman, Gershon, Nichols, and Murphy (1977) found that the well relatives of bipolar patients also tend to have low MAO levels, indicating that MAO is a marker for a broader genetic disposition associated with bipolar disorder rather than a specific marker for the disorder.

Low MAO levels have also been reported in chronic schizophrenics, which would seem to contradict the association of low MAO with high sensation seeking since schizophrenics as a group tend to be sensation avoiders rather than seekers. However, in a meta-analysis of studies of MAO in schizophrenia, Zureik and Meltzer (1990) found that paranoid and hallucinating schizophrenics had lower levels of MAO than controls, whereas other types of schizophrenics had higher than normal levels. The studies of sensation seeking in schizophrenia (Chapter 11) found that it was the withdrawn, behaviorally retarded type of schizophrenic who was low on sensation seeking, and this may be the type who is high rather than low on MAO. A comparison of MAO and sensation seeking in subgroups of schizophrenics showing positive and negative types of symptoms is needed to clarify this issue.

A study contrasting low and high MAO monkeys living in a natural environment found that low MAO monkeys were more active, social, and spent more time in play than high MAO monkeys of both sexes (Redmond, Murphy, & Baulu, 1979). The low MAO male monkeys were also more aggressive, dominant, and sexually active than the high MAO monkeys. The differences in sociability among monkeys suggest that low MAO might also be associated with extraversion in humans, but the findings relating MAO to the trait scales are quite mixed (Zuckerman, 1991a, p. 201). However, Coursey et al. (1979) did find that low MAO males and females among college students reported spending more hours socializing on an average weekday and weekend than high MAO types. The low MAO males also reported belonging to more clubs and organizations than the high MAO males. The results on behavioral measures in both species do suggest an association between MAO and sociability even though the studies of the measured trait are inconclusive.

Laboratory studies of performance tasks showed negative relationships between MAO and number of failed inhibitions in a motor disinhibition task and reaction times, suggesting to the authors a connection with disinhibitory disorders and serotonergic deficiency (Klinteberg et al., 1985; Klinteberg et al., 1991).

The monoamines

The interesting results linking MAO to sensation seeking suggest that the monoamine neurotransmitters themselves might provide the biological basis of the psychological trait because MAO regulates these systems in the brain. There are three primary monoamine systems in the brain whose pathways are shown in Figure 11.2. The major catecholamine systems in the brain are mediated by dopamine and norepinephrine. Dopamine (DA) is the immediate precursor of norepinephrine (NE) in the noradrenergic neurons (see Figure 11.1) as well as the neurotransmitter in the dopamine neurons. The other monoamine is the indoleamine, serotonin. There are many brain locations, such as the septum and hypothalamus, where two or three systems converge and we might expect interactions between them. The systems have synergistic or antagonistic effects on many behavioral functions such as activity and sexuality.

Animal studies and theories of monoamine function derived from them

Comparative studies of the roles of the monoamines in animal behavior as relevant to sensation seeking have been reviewed elsewhere (Zuckerman, 1984a; Zuckerman et al., 1984). Dopamine systems are the basis for activity in general and motivated activity directed toward significant rewards such as food and sex. Dopamine also plays a role in aggressive behavior. Social and sexual interactions are enhanced by dopamine and reduced by dopamine depletion. Dopamine controlled pathways are necessary for the intrinsic reward effects produced by intracranial self-stimulation in rats (Stellar & Stellar, 1985). Most of the findings support the general theory of Crow (1977) and Stein (1978) that dopamine energizes or activates behavior directed toward primary biological rewards and activates search and exploration for such rewards. By analogy with human behavior, this description would make dopamine a prime candidate for a primary role in sensation seeking. But analogy is not a sufficient basis to link findings on other species with human behavior. We must also find empirical evidence, even if only correlational, associating the human trait with the biological marker found in animals.

There is more disagreement about the role of noradrenergic (or NE) systems in personality. The theories of Redmond (1977) and Gray (1982) suggest that the ascending NE system, originating in the locus coeruleus, plays an essential role in the anxiety or fear response to stimuli associated with punishment or intrinsically threatening types of stimuli. Other theories

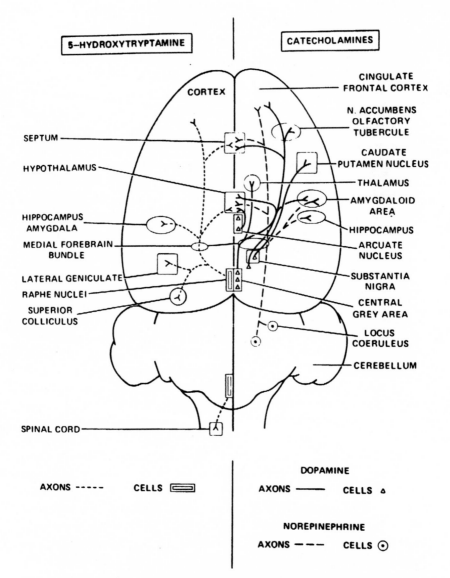

Figure 11.2. Three primary monoamine systems in the brain. Schematic representation of serotonin (5-hydroxytryptamine), dopamine, and norepinephrine pathways in the rat brain. From "Indoleamines and other neuroregulators," by G. E. Elliot, A. M. Edelman, J. F. Renson, & P. A. Berger, 1977. In J. D. Barchas, P. A. Berger, R. D. Ciaranello, and G. R. Elliot (Eds.), *Psychopharmacology,* p. 38. New York: Oxford University Press. Reprinted with permission.

suggest that this NE system is involved in cortical and behavioral arousal in response to external stimulation of biological significance, whether positive or negative (Aston-Jones & Bloom, 1981), although the system may be biased toward high-intensity or threatening types of novel stimuli rather than novel stimuli per se (Grant, Aston-Jones, & Redmond, 1988). Panksepp (1982) hypothesizes that NE is involved in general arousal of all emotional systems, those associated with approach and foraging as well as those associated with fear and avoidance.

Most theories are in agreement that serotonergic systems are involved in the inhibition of behavior in response to signals of danger. In animal studies, depleted levels of serotonin are associated with general activity, aggressivity, sexuality, and insensitivity to signals of punishment. However, low levels are also associated with enhanced startle response suggesting that serotonin may inhibit emotional systems as well as behavioral approach tendencies, as Panksepp (1982) suggests. In many areas the behavioral responses associated with serotonin activity seem to be antagonistic to tendencies related to dopamine, suggesting an interaction between the two neurotransmitters in the regulation of behavior.

Assessment of monoamines in humans and relationships to sensation seeking and psychopathology

Studies of activity of brain neurotransmitters in humans usually rely on measures of their metabolites obtained from cerebrospinal fluid (CSF), plasma, or urine (see Figure 11.3). The primary metabolite of brain dopamine is homovanillic acid (HVA), norepinephrine's is 3-methoxy-4-hydroxy-phenylglycol (MHPG), and that for serotonin is 5-hydroxytryptophan (5-HIAA). Whereas NE may be assayed in the CSF and blood, the NE and dopamine in blood have their origins in the peripheral catecholamine systems. Even the metabolites MHPG, HVA, and 5-HIAA have some part of their origin in peripheral sources in spinal neurons and the peripheral autonomic system, but they are better indicators of the activity of the central systems or those systems most directly under their control, such as those in the spinal cord.

Reliabilities of the monoamine metabolites in plasma and CSF are fair but they do show variations with clinical mood states, such as mania and depression, suggesting that they might be influenced by mood and physical activity as well as stress (Zuckerman, 1991a, p. 196). Urinary measures are influenced by stress, diurnal variation, and changes of activity but aggregated 24-hour samples yield reliable measures over periods as long as 3 months. CSF

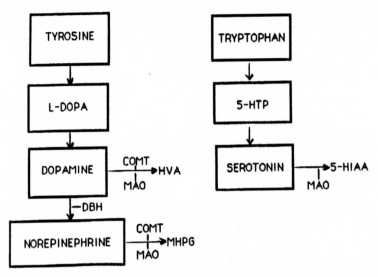

Figure 11.3. Biosynthesis and breakdown of monoamine systems and enzymes and metabolites. DBH = dopamine-beta-hydroxylase, MAO = monoamine oxidase, COMT = catechol-O-methyltransferase, HVA = homovanyllic acid, MHPG = 3-methoxy-4-hydroxyphenylglycol, 5-HIAA = 5-hydroxyindoleacetic acid. From *Psychobiology of personality*, p. 177, by M. Zuckerman, 1991. Cambridge: Cambridge University Press. Copyright 1991, Cambridge University Press.

MHPG and NE, plasma MHPG and NE, and CSF and plasma MHPG are highly intercorrelated, suggesting that there is a common system affecting all noradrenergic measures (Zuckerman, 1991a, pps. 197–199). CSF and plasma MHPG show a high degree of heritability in twin studies (Jimerson, Nurnberger, Post, Gershon, & Kopin, 1981; Oxenstierna et al., 1986), but CSF 5-HIAA shows only little to moderate heritability (Oxenstierna et al., 1986).

There have been only a few studies in humans of the relationships of the monoamines or their metabolites to sensation seeking. Ballenger et al. (1983) studied the relationships between personality traits and CSF, plasma, and urinary measures of monoamines and their related enzymes in a group of normal subjects. The CSF measures of NE and plasma dopamine-beta-hydroxlase (DBH) were both negatively correlated with the General SSS in the total group and the relationships were significant in both males and females, as shown in Table 11.4. The scatterplot for the relationship between the General SSS and CSF NE is shown in Figure 11.4.

Since DBH is the enzyme that converts dopamine to NE in the noradrener-

Table 11.4. *Correlations between the Sensation Seeking Scale (SSS) General scale and cerebrospinal fluid (CSF) norepinephrine (NE) and plasma dopamine-beta-hydroxylase (DBH)*

	Total group		Males	Females
	r_p	r	r	r
SSS with				
CSF NE	$-.49^c$	$-.51^c$	$-.40^a$	$-.72^b$
Pl.DBH	$-.60^b$	$-.44^a$	$-.60^a$	$-.72^a$

Note: r_p = partial correlations controlling for the effects of age, height, and weight.
*$p < .10$.
**$p < .05$.
***$p < .01$.
Note: CSF = cerebrospinal fluid; NE = norepinephrine; Pl = plasma; DBH = dopamine-beta-hydroxylase.
Source: Adapted from table 7.2, p. 238, from *Biological bases of sensation seeking, impulsivity and anxiety,* by M. Zuckerman, 1983. Hillsdale, NJ: Erlbaum. Copyright 1983 by Lawrence Erlbaum Associates. Reprinted by permission.

gic neuron (Figures 11.1 and 11.3), a depletion of DBH may result in a low level of NE, and if one correlates negatively with sensation seeking, the other should as well. It is not clear why plasma DBH, and not CSF DBH, correlated with sensation seeking, except that plasma DBH correlated more highly than CSF NE than did CSF DBH. A crucial question is whether the results were a function of state or trait sensation seeking on the morning when the lumbar puncture and plasma measures were obtained. A lumbar puncture can be a threatening procedure and perhaps low sensation seekers were more threatened by it than highs. A measure of state anxiety was taken on the morning of the procedures. Neither sensation seeking or CSF NE were correlated with state anxiety but both CSF and plasma DBH were positively correlated with state anxiety. Anxiety state, therefore, cannot explain the NE–sensation seeking relationship, and given the total lack of correlation between the SSS and state anxiety, it cannot explain the SSS–DBH relationship either unless low sensation seekers were denying their anxiety states on the test.

No one has attempted to replicate the CSF NE and SSS relationship but there have been a number of tests of the relationship between plasma DBH and sensation seeking. The negative relationship between the two measures

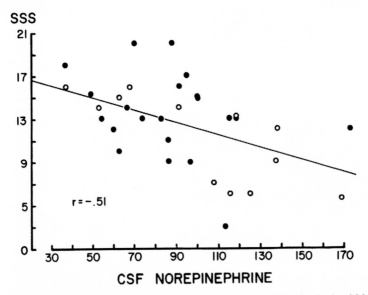

Figure 11.4. Relation between the General Sensation Seeking Scale (SSS) and nor-epinephrine (NE) in the cerebrospinal fluid (CSF) in normals. From "Biochemical correlates of personality traits in normals: An exploratory study," by J. C. Ballenger et al., 1983, *Personality and Individual Differences, 4,* 621. Copyright 1992 by Pergamon Press. Reprinted by permission.

was replicated by Umberkoman-Wiita, Vogel, and Wiita (1981) and Kulcsár, Kutor, and Arató (1984). However, Kuperman et al. (1988) found a *positive* correlation between the SSS and serum DBH in a sample of young men who had been diagnosed as hyperactive children in years previous. Perris, Jacobssen, Oreland, Perris, and Ross (1980) also found a positive correlation between plasma DBH and the KSP Monotony Avoidance scale in hospital-ized depressive patients.

Calhoon (1988) compared a group of high sensation-seeking skiers and a control group of nonskiing students. The skiers had higher levels of DBH than the controls and DBH correlated positively with sensation seeking in the combined group, but DBH did not correlate at all with sensation seeking within the separate skiing and nonskiing groups. Because the blood had been sampled from skiers just after a period of skiing, there was a possibility that the exercise of skiing elevated their DBH levels. Calhoon (1991) did a follow-up study with students and took blood samples before and after exercise consisting of a 1-mile run. Exercise did not affect DBH levels very much, although it raised them about 10% in females and in subjects over 30 years of age. The overall correlations between DBH and SSS were insignificant for males and females and the total group.

There are many significant correlational results relating DBH to sensation seeking, but unfortunately the direction of the relationship is not consistent, with about an equal number of studies showing positive and negative correlations. The crucial factor determining the direction of the results is not apparent.

Clinical studies are more uniform in outcome, suggesting a negative relationship between DBH and disinhibitory psychopathology. CSF levels of DBH are low in bipolar disorders when they are in a manic state and high when they are in a depressed state (Lerner et al, 1978; Post et al., 1984). Like the Ballenger et al. (1983) correlations between DBH and state anxiety, these mood-associated changes show the state-dependent nature of DBH. Major et al. (1980) found that patients in an alcoholic rehabilitation center with low levels of CSF DBH were high on MMPI indicators of psychopathy, paranoia, and schizophrenia. Rogeness et al. (1984) reported that a group of emotionally disturbed boys with low levels of plasma DBH were characterized by symptoms of an undersocialized conduct disorder and borderline personalities. Their previous behavior involved setting fires, cruelty to animals, homicidal threats, and other problems of impulse control. These studies using deviant clinical groups suggest that an antisocial type of sensation seeking is associated with low rather than high levels of DBH. The low levels of DBH in bipolars in the manic state suggest a similar conclusion, although it is not clear which comes first, the mania with its feverish activity or the lowered DBH levels.

Urinary MHPG, the NE metabolite, is lower in all depressed patients, but is particularly low in bipolar depressives (Muscettola, Potter, Pickar, & Goodwin, 1984). Urinary MHPG varies with the clinical state in bipolar disorders, rising in the manic state and falling during depressive episodes relative to normal levels during periods of remission (Schildkraut, Orsulak, Schatzberg, & Rosenbaum, 1984). Buchsbaum, Muscettola, and Goodwin (1981) found that sensation seeking was positively correlated with urinary MHPG during both stress and resting periods in a group of normal controls, but no correlations were found in a patient group. Post et al. (1984) found elevations of CSF NE in bipolars during manic states that were 400% above NE in normals. Because sensation seekers had low levels of CSF NE, this seems inconsistent with the high levels found in manic episodes. Perhaps when sensation seekers are unstimulated their tonic levels of NE are low, as are the urinary metabolite measures of NE in manics when they are in normal or depressed states. When sensation seekers are highly stimulated, however, their NE systems may be overactivated as they are in bipolar mood disorders in the early manic phase of their disorder. A moderate level of catecholamine system activity may be associated with euphoria, very low levels with depression, and higher levels with clinical mania (Zuckerman, 1984a). A low tonic level of noradrenergic activity and a highly reactive system could explain the behavioral and psychological trait connection between sensation seeking and bipolar disorder.

Plasma MHPG correlated negatively with sensation seeking (Total, ES, and Dis scales) in a group of healthy normals, but not in a group of psychosomatic disorders in the study by Arque, Unzeta, & Torrubia (1988). The same correlations were not significant in the normals tested by Ballenger et al. (1983). A group of gamblers in treatment had lower levels of plasma MHPG than controls, but higher levels of CSF MHPG than controls (Roy et al., 1988)! The anomaly of different directions for the plasma and CSF MHPG differences between gamblers and controls may have had something to do with the fact that the gamblers were in treatment and many were depressed at the time of the study. The depressed gamblers tended to have higher levels of both forms of MHPG, although the differences were not significant.

Serotonin and dopamine metabolites (5-HIAA and HVA) did not correlate with the SSS in the Ballenger et al. (1983) study. In a study by Schalling, Åsberg, and Edman (1984), both 5-HIAA and HVA correlated negatively with the KSP Monotony Avoidance scale in depressed and nondepressed patient groups but not in a normal group. CSF MHPG also correlated negatively with the Monotony Avoidance scale, but the correlations were not significant.

Correlational studies like the ones cited thus far are bound to be somewhat inconclusive due to variations in the types of populations studied, the influences of trait and state emotions that are not related to the sensation-seeking trait, the unreliability of peripheral indexes of brain monoamine activity, and the small samples of subjects used in many of the studies.

Experimental studies that give drugs that stimulate the systems and observe their effects may offer more answers. Amphetamine is a stimulant that increases activity in the catecholamine systems in the brain (DA and NE) by increased release and decreased uptake of the neurotransmitters. Low doses of amphetamine given to normals typically increase arousal, alertness, performance, activity, euphoric mood, and sociability (Zuckerman, 1991a, pp. 214–215). The increase in euphoria depends on the stimulation of dopamine receptors. When these are blocked by the drug Pimozide euphoric effects are reduced, but when an NE receptor blocking drug is used there is no effect on mood enhancement (Jönsson, Anggard, & Gunne, 1971). The increased cortical arousal and consequent performance enhancement are probably produced by the NE stimulation effects.

All drug abusers tend to be higher than normal sensation seekers, but those favoring amphetamine tend to be high even among drug abusers (Carrol & Zuckerman, 1977; Spotts & Shontz, 1986). There seems to be something about amphetamine that attracts high sensation seekers, although Carrol et al. (1982) could find no different reactions of high and low sensation seekers to the drug. If sensation seekers have low activity in NE and/or dopamine systems, as suggested by some of the previously cited correlational studies, they may have a special susceptibility to the drug that brings them closer to an optimal level of positive arousal.

L-dopa is the immediate precursor of dopamine in the production of that neurotransmitter. Giving L-dopa, thereby increasing dopamine activity, may temporarily improve the mood of depressed patients, but if they have bipolar tendencies L-dopa can precipitate a manic state. The famous treatment experiment by Sacks (1983) giving L-dopa to Parkinsonism patients (suffering from low dopamine levels) who had been "frozen" and unresponsive to their environments since they were young adults, resulted in a dramatic "awakening." Initially they showed euphoria, interest in their environments, heightened sexual interest, and other signs of increased sensation seeking. But as the renewed dopamine output began to act on supersensitive receptors, many of the patients developed manic psychoses followed by depressive "crashes." Perhaps mania is produced by unstable dopaminergic systems that do not have sufficient regulation by their own enzymes or other systems. Mania is like a speeding car in which the accelerator is jammed and the brakes are defective.

Netter and Rammsayer (1991) gave L-dopa on one occasion and placebo and halperidol (a dopamaine antagonist) on other occasions to normal subjects. The subjects high in boredom susceptibility showed little change in performance, reaction time, and time discrimination in reaction to either active drug. They also had less depression of arousal and felt more relaxed after halperidol than the low boredom susceptible subjects. Those low in boredom susceptibility increased performance after L-dopa but showed decreased performance and felt less relaxed after taking halperidol. Similar results were obtained when the TAS subscale of the SSS was used to classify subjects. The results suggest that high sensation seekers do have a highly active but well-regulated dopaminergic system, whereas low sensation seekers suffer from a dopaminergic deficit and therefore benefit more from L-dopa and less from halperidol than the high sensation seekers.

Another study by the same authors concerned effects of a serotonin agonist (fluoxetine) and antagonist (ritanserin) on sensory and motor responses (Netter & Rammsayer, 1989). High and low experience seekers (ES subscale of the SSS) did not differ in reaction time performance after taking the agonist, but the serotonin blocker, ritanserin, improved performance in the low experience seekers but slowed performance of the high experience seekers. The results could suggest that low sensation seekers have *overactive* serotonergic systems that are inhibited by a serotonergic blocker. High sensation seekers may have *underactive* serotonergic systems and further inhibition of serotonergic activity may interfere with performance.

What keeps normal sensation seekers from running out of control like hypomanic sensation seekers? The dorsal ascending noradrenergic system serves an arousal function that may increase both dopaminergic and serotonergic functions. The noradrenergic neurons (see Figure 11.1) contain a homeostatic feedback system for regulating production. The alpha$_2$ receptors on the presynaptic neuron control the production and release of NE. When there is too much NE activity, they tend to shut the system down in a negative feedback fashion. Shekim et al. (1990) examined the alpha$_2$ receptors in blood platelets. High values on their measure indicate a high density of these receptors which control the release of NE. They found that the density of alpha$_2$ receptors was positively correlated with the Total SSS and scales measuring needs for autonomy and play, and negatively correlated with the Hypomania scale of the MMPI. The low levels of NE found in the CSF of high sensation seekers (Ballenger et al., 1983) are consistent with the existence of an abundance of the receptors that reduce activity in the system. Conversely, the negative correlation with the Hypomania scale suggests that persons with hypomanic tendencies might have a low density of alpha$_2$ receptors and therefore lack the protection against a positive feedback overstimulation effect.

Endogenous opiates

The discovery of endogenous morphinelike peptides or *endorphins* in the brain was exciting because it suggested a possible biological basis for individual differences in pain sensitivity, susceptibility to opiate addiction, emotionality, and personality traits like sensation seeking. A group of Swedish investigators (Johansson, Almay, von Knorring, Terrenius, & Astrom, 1979), including one of the discoverers of endorphins (Terenius), studied the relationship between endorphins and sensation seeking in a group of chronic pain patients. The patients with low levels of endorphins were significantly higher on all subscales of the SSS than the patients with high endorphin levels. The scales showing the strongest negative relationships between endorphins and sensation seeking were the Dis and BS scales. The subjects with high levels of neuroticism and the subgroup of patients with psychogenic pain syndromes had high levels of endorphins. The results suggest that stable high sensation seekers have low levels of endorphins, whereas neurotic low sensation seekers tend to have high levels of endorphins. However, interpretation of these isolated results must be cautious until they can be replicated in a larger sample of a normal population. Ballenger et al. (1983) found no relationships between beta-endorphins and sensation seeking in normals.

Hormones

Hormones are biochemical substances that may affect distant cells of the body by traveling through the bloodstream. They are chemically regulated by centers in the hypothalamus. Releasing hormones from the hypothalamus discharge tropic hormones from the pituitary gland. Tropic hormones travel to their respective target glands to effect release of hormones with specific effects on the body. The hormone systems (Figure 11.5) also have a feedback mechanism so that high circulating levels of a hormone may be detected in the brain resulting in a shutdown of releasing hormones.

Cortisol. One pathway mediating stress effects begins in the hypothalamus. Stimulated by reactions in higher brain centers or sensory receptors in the body, the hypothalamus secretes corticotropin-releasing factor (CRF). CRF travels to the pituitary gland at the base of the brain where it releases adrenocorticotropic hormone (ACTH). ACTH travels through the bloodstream to the adrenal cortex where it releases a variety of adrenocortical hormones including cortisol. Cortisol's function in stress response is the release of glycogen from the liver into the bloodstream. It also influences fat metabolism, muscle strength, blood pressure, and antiinflammatory effects. Cortisol is found in the CSF and urine as well as in the blood plasma.

Cortisol tends to be elevated in severe types of depression, but it tends to be lower in bipolar disorders in the manic state. Low levels of urinary cortisol have been found in habitually psychopathic and violent prisoners (Virkkunen, 1985). Consistent with this clinical finding, Ballenger et al. (1983) found that CSF cortisol correlated negatively with markers for a P (disinhibitory) factor, including the EPQ P scale, the SSS Dis scale, the MMPI Hypomania scale, and a life history item, the number of reported sexual partners. A factor analyses of the variables in the Ballenger et al.

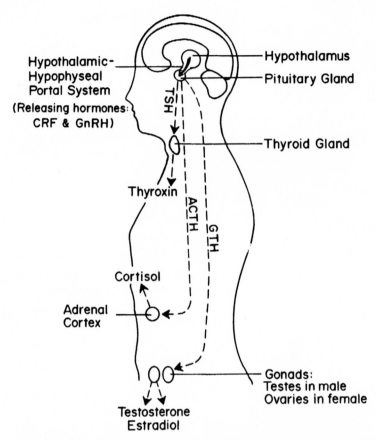

Figure 11.5. Hypothalamic-pituitary controlled hormone systems. From *Psychobiology of personality*, p. 182, by M. Zuckerman, 1991. Cambridge: Cambridge University Press. Copyright 1991 by Cambridge University Press.

study yielded three factors corresponding to Eysenck's primary three. Figure 11.6 shows a plot of the variables along the neuroticism and P dimensions. The P dimension is defined by sensation seeking, hypomania, and the P scale at the positive end and by CSF cortisol and CSF norepinephrine at the negative pole. Plasma DBH, serum cortisol, and plasma amine oxidase have weaker negative loadings on this dimension. Since CS.ʾ cortisol did correlate with anxiety state on the morning of the lumbar puncture, we cannot be sure if this is a state or trait relationship with sensation seeking. However, the low cortisol levels of high sensation seekers might also have something to do with their modulation of stress as discussed in Chapter 10.

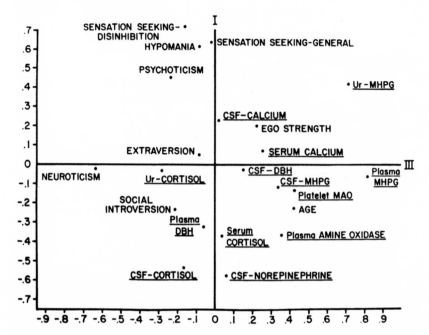

Figure 11.6. Factor plot of personality, neurotransmitter metabolite, and hormonal variables in dimensions of P-ImpUSS (I) and neuroticism (III). From "The neurobiology of some dimensions of personality," by M. Zuckerman et al., 1984. J. R. Smythies & R. J. Bradley (Eds.), In *International review of neurobiology*, Vol. 25, p. 424. New York: Academic Press. Reprinted by permission.

Thyroid hormones. The thyroid gland secretes thyroxin, a hormone involved in metabolic processes. Excess production may cause states of anxiety and depression. The hypothalamus secretes thyrotropin-releasing hormone (TRH), which releases thyroid-stimulating hormone (TSH) from the pituitary gland, which in turn releases thyroxine (T4) from the thyroid gland. The noradrenergic (NE) system plays a role in activating TSH secretion. A blunted TSH secretion in response to TRH has been reported in depression.

Arque, Segura, and Torrubia (1987) investigated the relationships between the SSS and T4 and TSH in groups of psychosomatic patients and normal controls. The Total score on the Spanish sensation seeking scale correlated negatively with TSH in both groups, but the correlation reached significance only in the normal group. Because of the role of NE in TSH release, the lower level of TSH in high sensation seekers could be a function of their low levels of NE (Ballenger et al., 1983), and the lower levels of plasma MHPG in this same group of normals in which TSH was measured (Arque, Beltri, & Torrubia, 1988).

Gonadal hormones. Androgens are produced by the testes in males and the adrenal cortex in females. Androgen production in males is regulated by gonadotropins from the pituitary gland, primarily luteinizing hormone (LH). Pituitary LH release is in turn controlled by luteinizing hormone releasing hormones secreted by the hypothalamus. The same kind of hormonal negative feedback system exists as that for cortisol.

The sex and age differences on sensation seeking suggested that gonadal hormones might be related to the trait. In particular, it was hypothesized that testosterone might account for the types of sensation seeking (TAS and Dis) in which men are higher than women and which show the most pronounced age declines. Testosterone in the human male declines with age at a constant rate from the early 20s on. Testosterone affects sexual arousability in both sexes (Zuckerman, 1971b; 1983e). Experimental studies in other species show that testosterone is related to competitive aggressiveness and dominance. Prenatal exposure to androgens affects girls' subsequent interests and play patterns resulting in more "rough and tumble" and other play more typically seen in boys, and a lack of interest in "dolls" and "house" play compared with other girls of their age and their own female siblings (Ehrhardt, Epstein, & Money, 1968). Levels of circulating testosterone are moderately heritable (Turner, Ford, West, & Meible, 1986). There is diurnal variation in androgen and estrogen measures but the values tend to be stable and reliable if obtained from blood samples drawn at the same time of day in the same individuals (Daitzman, Zuckerman, Sammelwitz, & Ganjam, 1978; Kreuz & Rose, 1972). Despite the reliability of individual differences, the levels of gonadal hormones may reflect environmental events as well as a biological trait. Stress can lower testosterone levels and sexual stimulation can increase them.

Daitzman et al. (1978) found significant correlations between the Dis scale of the SSS and androgens and estrogens in college males. Another study by Daitzman and Zuckerman (1980), using more specific assays for gonadal hormones, found that male subjects who score in the upper range of the Dis scale were significantly higher than those from the lower Dis range on testosterone, 17-beta-estradiol, and estrone. High and low Dis groups did not differ on progesterone. The low sensation seekers (disinhibiters) had average testosterone levels for their age, but the high sensation seekers had unusually high levels of the hormone.

The differences on testosterone confirmed our hypotheses and, if taken alone, suggested one biological source for the sex and age differences on sensation seeking. But the differences between high and low sensation-seeking males on estrogen was not predicted and seemed to argue against the hormonal interpretation of the sex difference in sensation seeking. However, there is a difference in the sources of estrogen in men and women. Estrogen in women is produced by the ovaries, but in men it is primarily produced by the conversion of androstenedione and testosterone to estrone and 17-beta-estradiol. The aromatization hypothesis (Brain, 1983) suggests that androgens in males have their major motivational effects after conversion to estrogenic metabolites. Aromatizable (convertible to estrogens) androgens are all effective in maintaining fighting in castrated male rats but, with one exception, the nonaromatizable androgens cannot do this.

Daitzman and Zuckerman (1980) also gave subjects other personality and sex experience and attitude questionnaires in order to look at a broader range of hormone–personality correlates. Testosterone and estradiol were correlated with many other variables, but estrone and progesterone were not. There was no correlation between testosterone and estradiol but both were significantly and positively correlated with socialization and self-control scales. Testosterone also correlated with extraversion, sociability, dominance, and activity scales, while estradiol correlated with scales of deviancy and psychopathology from the MMPI, including Schizophrenia, Hypomania, Psychopathic Deviate, and the F scale of general deviancy of response. Testosterone correlated negatively with scales measuring depression, psychasthenia, introversion, and femininity. Estradiol correlated negatively with Responsibility, Good Impression, Well-Being, Tolerance, and Achievement. While both hormones seem to be related to impulsivity, unsocialized tendencies, and heterosexual experience, high testosterone is found in a normal kind of extraverted, assertive, masculine, and sensation-seeking types, whereas the males low in testosterone seem to be introverted and anxious as well as low in sensation seeking. Estradiol in males is related to a more deviant kind of sensation seeking associated with antisocial personality and hypomania.

The scales and hormones were factor analyzed substituting the General SSS for the Dis subscale on which the subjects were selected. Two major factors incorporating both psychological and hormone variables were found (Figure 11.7). The first, including Extraversion, Sensation Seeking, Sociability, and Masculinity scales at the positive pole and Introversion, Depression, Psychasthenia, and Androgyny scales at the negative pole, was called *stable extraversion versus neurotic introversion*. Testosterone loaded positively on this factor. The second factor, with MMPI Schizophrenia, Psychopathic

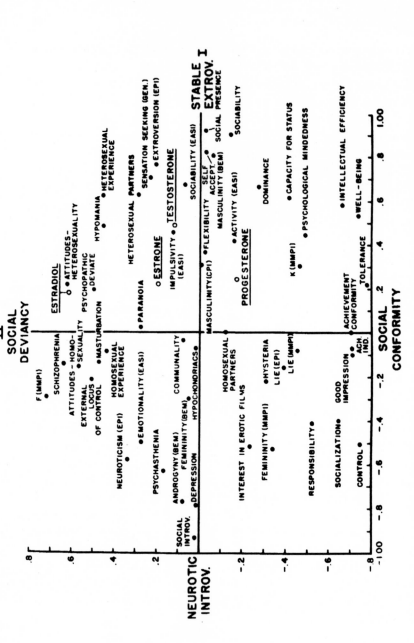

Figure 11.7. Factor plot of personality, sexual experience, and gonadal hormone variables on the dimensions of stable extraversion versus neurotic introversion and social deviancy versus social conformity. From ''Disinhibitory sensation seeking, personality, and gonadal hormones,'' by R. Daitzman & M. Zuckerman, 1980, *Personality and Individual Differences, 1,* 221. Copyright 1980 by Pergamon Press. Reprinted by permission.

Deviate, and Hypomania scales at the positive pole and Self-Control, Socialization, Achievement need, Responsibility, and Good Impression at the negative pole, was labeled *social deviancy versus social conformity.* Estradiol loaded positively on this factor.

O'Carroll (1984) compared a group of hypogonadal men with a group of men who had normal testosterone levels but had complaints of erectile sexual dysfunction or loss of sexual interest. Despite the fact that the men in the normal testosterone group were older in age and were suffering from sexual problems, they had significantly higher scores on the General and Dis scales of the SSS than the hypogonadal males. The two groups did not differ on P, E, or N scores from the EPQ. Both groups received testosterone injections over a period of months and then were retested. There were no changes in the personality scores of the hypogonadal men after receiving testosterone. The sensation-seeking scores of the testosterone-normal men after receiving testosterone were not different from their scores after a placebo period. The results show that long-term effects of testosterone insufficiency may result in lower sensation seeking, but there is no evidence that raising testosterone increases sensation seeking.

Dabbs, Hopper, and Jurkovic (1990) found a small positive but nonsignificant correlation between testosterone measured from saliva and the Dis scale in a small group of college males. Saliva testosterone related negatively with neuroticism in men and daily hassles (stress) in both men and women. A subsequent study of a much larger group of males showed no relationship between this measure and any of the personality measures used (SSS scales were not included). A study measuring serum testosterone in a very large sample of over 5,000 male military veterans revealed many small, significant correlations with MMPI and diagnostic measures. The highest correlations were with symptoms of antisocial personality and drug abuse, disorders associated with high sensation seeking (Chapters 9 and 10). Mattson, Schalling, Olweus, Low, and Svennsson (1980) found that plasma testosterone correlated positively with Aggressiveness, Sociability, and Monotony Avoidance (the KSP sensation-seeking scale) and a preference for physical sports in delinquent boys.

Summary

A comparative approach to personality is unusual but necessary for a psychobiological understanding of personality. This chapter has emphasized the scattered psychobiological findings from studies of humans, but an understanding of these results can only come from experimental studies of other species. The problem is in connecting meanings across the evolutionary gap between nonhuman and human species. Sociobiology has filled this biological niche in science. The generalizations of this field are based on analogies with behavior of other species, a cross-cultural search for uniformities in human behavior, and a speculative reconstruction of the evolutionary history of homanoids living in hunter–gatherer groups. Commenting on the more simpleminded of these efforts, Symons (1979) says:

It is not clear how meaningful comparisons are to be made between humans and other animals, and seemingly straightforward comparisons may mislead more often than they enlighten; many times biology not only fails to increase our understanding of human beings but seems to have the magical power to make us forget what we already know. . . . There is no harm in such borrowings [anthropomorphic ones] unless they are taken seriously and imagined to reveal deep biological truths. (pp. 128–9)

Hard evidence must come from biological data from living organisms. Showing that ''similar'' behavior exists in rats and humans is not evidence of a common biological basis for that behavior; we must be able to show that the behavior is dependent on similar biological characteristics in both species. Exploratory tendencies (open-field behavior) have been selectively bred in rodents, but the relevance of this animal model to human sensation seeking is not obvious. Biometric analyses of human traits is used to determine the contributions of heredity and environment to these traits. Twin studies of sensation seeking have shown a relatively high heritability for a personality trait.

An enzyme (MAO) with a strong genetic determination is related to sensation seeking. MAO from blood platelets is negatively related to sensation seeking; high sensation seekers have low MAO levels. The correlation is a well-replicated one and, although the correlation is not high, it is significant in a majority of studies. Another type of confirmation comes from the other associations of MAO with sex and age differences and behaviors, disorders, and traits that are related to sensation seeking. MAO is the kind of biological marker that carries behavioral trait cross-species comparisons beyond mere analogy.

Since the function of MAO in the brain is to regulate monoamine neurotransmitter systems, these seemed a good place to look for biological bases for sensation seeking. Comparative studies of the functions of noradrenergic, dopaminergic, and serotonergic systems suggested that dopamine systems might be related to the approach tendencies and the search for biological reward that seems to characterize human sensation seeking. Serotonergic activity, vital in behavior inhibition in animal studies, should be negatively related to sensation seeking. Correlational studies of humans showed no relationship between sensation seeking and dopamine or serotonin metabolites in normals, but negative correlations were found between norepinephrine from cerebrospinal fluid and sensation seeking. Correlational results relating the enzyme dopamine-beta-hydroxylase (DBH) from plasma to sensation seeking were mixed, but clinical findings of low DBH in manics and conduct disordered children suggest that it might have a negative relationship with disinhibitory sensation seeking. Perhaps the inconsistencies in the findings are due to the influence of current emotional states on DBH. Experimental studies using drugs that increase or block dopaminergic and serotonergic effects give some support to the hypothesis that dopaminergic activity is high and serotonergic activity is low in high sensation seekers.

Cortisol, a stress responsive hormone, is negatively related to sensation seeking, suggesting that low cortisol activity may explain the tendency for sensation seekers to have fewer deleterious symptomatic effects of stress. Gonadal hormones in males are positively related to sensation seeking, particularly disinhibition. Gonadal hormones are also related to heterosexual experience, which is more extensive in high than in low sensation seekers. Gonadal hormones are inversely related to socialization and self-control, traits more characteristic of low sensation seekers.

Most of the biological variables other than MAO are only moderately reliable and can be influenced by stress; therefore, the causal implications of the purely correlational data are questionable. A correlation between sensation seeking and one of these variables might indicate that the biological *trait* is produced by the genotype for sensation seeking, *or* that high sensation seekers are more stress resistant than lows and show this in the biological *state*. Genetic studies examining the genetic covariance between the psychological trait and biological markers and experimental studies of the effects of stress on sensation seeking and biological states might help distinguish cause and effect in these relationships.

The biochemical factors discussed in this chapter are important because they determine how the brain will react to stimulation from the environment. The salient features of stimulation for sensation seeking are novelty, intensity, and other properties that determine arousal potential of the stimuli. Psychophysiology provides methods for assessing the impact of these qualities of stimulation at the biological level. These methods use recordings from the surface of the body and therefore have enabled us to gather more data from humans, although an animal model for at least one type of physiological response will be presented in the next chapter.

12

Psychophysiology

The earlier psychobiological theory of sensation seeking proposed that the trait was based in part on "A constitutional factor, possibly reactivity and 'satiability' of the central and autonomic nervous systems to specific classes of stimulation, or the strength of excitatory and inhibitory centers in the central nervous system" (Zuckerman, 1969a, p. 429). The sensation seeker was seen as someone seeking arousal through external stimuli and activities. The qualities of stimulation appealing to high sensation seekers included stimulus intensity, complexity, unexpectedness, incongruency, and emotional connotation. Stimulus repetition, constancy, and familiarity were arousal reducing and therefore aversive to the high sensation seeker. Stimulus effects on arousal are testable by psychophysiological methods, but the theory was not very specific in whether sensation seeking was related to cortical or autonomic arousal, whether sensation seekers were generally underaroused, were less or more reactive in response to intense or novel stimuli, or habituated more quickly in response to intense or novel stimuli. High sensation seekers were characterized as having a high optimal level of cortical arousal (Zuckerman et al., 1964), but the definition of an optimal level of arousal in psychophysiological terms was unspecified.

Individual differences in arousal and arousability are a basis for H. Eysenck's (1967) theory of introversion–extraversion, Gray's (1964) interpretation of the Pavlovian concept of a "strong nervous system," Strelau's (1983) theory of reactivity, as well as the earlier theory of sensation seeking (Zuckerman, 1969a). But the translation of the construct of arousal into psychophysiology has encountered major methodological obstacles (Zuckerman & Como, 1983).

Duffy (1951, 1972) defined arousal in terms of a generalized activation in cortical and peripheral autonomic activity, including cardiovascular, respiratory, electrodermal, and muscle systems. Hebb's (1955) "arousal function" was more specific, referring only to cortical arousal as indexed by the EEG during states ranging from deep sleep to intense negative emotional arousal.

The generalized construct of arousal assumes a high degree of relationship between the central and peripheral nervous systems, and among the various peripheral systems, in states of rest or in reaction to stimulation from the environment. In actual fact, the relationships between physiological systems are low and often nonexistent. Different kinds of stimuli elicit different kinds and degrees of response in different individuals (Engel, 1972; Lacey, 1967).

Sometimes the distinction between differences in arousal and arousability are not clear. A difference in generalized arousal implies that people differ reliably in characteristic levels of activation of all systems under any circumstances, including those in which there is minimal stimulation or activity. Arousability, however, suggests that people differ primarily in response to activating stimuli rather than in an unstimulated condition. A general theory of arousability suggests that the particular kind of stimuli makes little difference in the individual differences in arousability. The personality psychophysiology literature shows that one cannot ignore the specific parameters of stimulus (or situation) response specificity in the relation between personality and psychophysiology, and this has proved to be true for sensation seeking (Zuckerman, 1990a) as well as other traits like extraversion (Stelmack, 1990).

General arousal

Cortical arousal

Sleep. Cortical arousal in any person varies during the course of the diurnal cycle from the low extreme (deep sleep) to the high produced by intense concentration, problem solving, or emotional arousal. Generally, cortical arousal is low at bedtime before sleep; if it is not, the person may suffer insomnia. The capacity to fall asleep quickly after going to bed and to spend the night in sleep is called *sleep efficiency;* it is defined as the percentage of the time in bed actually spent asleep as indicated by EEG criteria. Persons with major depressive disorders often suffer from reduced sleep efficiency.

Coursey, Buchsbaum, and Frankel (1975) tested a group of insomniacs and matched controls, both free from any other psychiatric disorders such as anxiety or depression, on the General SSS and measures of depression, repression-sensitization, and other tests. The SSS was the most discriminating of all the tests used; insomniacs tended to be low sensation seekers and sensation seeking was significantly and positively correlated with sleep efficiency over all subjects. If sensation seeking was partialed out of the multiple regression, none of the other variables could predict sleep efficiency.

Studies of sleep and EEG patterns in the laboratory have demonstrated what is called the "first-night effect." Not surprisingly, many subjects find it difficult to fall asleep on the first night in a strange laboratory setting with electrodes glued to their scalps, aware that they are being monitored and observed. Hauri and Olmstead (1989) studied the first-night effect in a group of insomniacs. One group of subjects clearly demonstrated the first-night effect with a sleep efficiency of only 61%, but another group showed a reversal of this effect with fairly efficient sleep (85% sleep efficiency) as compared with their own sleep patterns at home. The more sleep-efficient group scored higher on the SSS General and BS scales than those insomiacs showing the usual first-night effect. The results show a lack of arousal in average or higher sensation seekers in what is normally a novel and arousing setting, and a high level of arousal in low sensation seekers among insomniacs.

EEG indexes of arousal in the waking state. There are several methods of analyzing arousal from the raw EEG record. With filters, the EEG spectrum can be analyzed for relative amounts of *delta* slow waves, characteristic of deep sleep; high-amplitude *theta,* slow waves usually accompanying drowsiness or light sleep; *alpha,* a synchronized wave form of 8 to 13 cycles per second (cps), typical in a relaxed but fully awake state; and *beta,* a low-amplitude, high-frequency (more than 13 cps) desynchronized wave found during highly alert, excited states, or states of intense mental activity. Sometimes the percent of alpha alone is used as an inverse measure of arousal on the assumption that all other activity in a waking subject will be of the faster type characteristic of higher states of arousal. The frequency of waves within the alpha band provides another index of arousal. Genetic analyses show very high heritabilities for each of the spectrum bands and the frequency of alpha (Lykken, 1982).

Many studies have attempted to test Eysenck's hypothesis that extraverts are underaroused and introverts are overaroused (see Zuckerman, 1991a, pp. 235–240). The results are inconsistent and it is difficult to find the variables distinguishing studies that support, do not support, or yield results in the opposite direction to the hypothesis. Impulsivity has not been as widely studied as extraversion, but its closer connection to conditionability (H. Eysenck & Levey, 1972) suggests that it might also be related to arousal. O'Gorman and Lloyd (1987) found that a measure of narrow impulsivity (acting quickly without reflection) was related to alpha activity in relaxing, nonstimulating conditions thought to be optimal for detecting individual differences in arousal. High impulsives showed less EEG arousal during these conditions.

Since impulsivity is more highly related to sensation seeking than sociability (Zuckerman et al., 1988; Zuckerman et al., 1991), one might expect that sensation seeking would also be negatively related to arousal under resting conditions. However, EEG studies of sensation seeking have not supported this hypothesis (Cox, 1977; Golding & Richards, 1985; Passini, Watson, Dehnel, Herder, & Watkins, 1977; Watson, Jacobs, & Herder, 1979).

High sensation seekers may be sleep efficient, but this may be more indicative of what Pavlovians call the trait of "mobility," or the capacity to switch from excitatory to inhibitory states of cortical activity, rather than differences in strengths of cortical excitatory or inhibitory systems per se. There is no evidence that cortical arousal in the waking state is related to sensation seeking.

Skin conductance arousal

Skin conductance level (SCL), recorded during a period when a subject is resting and calm, has been used as a measure of tonic level of arousal. SCL is minimal during sleep and maximal during periods of high levels of stimulation or emotional arousal. Few studies have found any relationship between sensation seeking and SCL during rest periods (Zuckerman, 1990a). Zahn, Schooler, and Murphy (1986) found negative correlations between SCL during rest and the SSS General and TAS scales in females (but not in males), and Plouffe and Stelmack (1986) found a negative correlation between the SSS Total and SCL in young (but not in old) women. But Cox (1977), Feij, Orlebeke, Gazendam, and van Zuilen (1985), Neary and Zuckerman, (1976), D. Ridgeway and Hare (1981), Smith, Davidson, Smith, Goldstein, and Perlstein (1989), and Zuckerman, Simons, and Como (1988) did not find differences in SCL between high and low sensation seekers among young men or women. Svebak and Murgatroyd (1985) used the Telic Dominance scale and found that paratelic dominant subjects (sensation seekers) had lower SCLs than telic subjects even prior to stimulation. A number of studies have found differences in SCL over conditions when the person was receiving periodic stimulation from slides, tones, and other stimuli (Robinson & Zahn, 1983; Smith et al., 1986; Stelmack, Plouffe, & Falkerberg, 1983), but in these studies the SCL difference was specific to one class of stimuli and not to others and the high sensation seekers usually had higher SCLs than the low sensation seekers. The specificity of these differences suggest that they do not reflect the general level of arousal, but only the activation by a particular kind of stimulation.

Cardiac arousal

Twin studies of tonic levels of heart rate (HR) have shown heritabilities ranging from .40 to .60, about the same range as for personality measures (Boomsa & Plomin, 1986). Boomsa and Plomin noted that heritabilities were lower in resting than in stimulation conditions. Broad heritabilities for blood pressure (BP) are higher in twins, but narrow heritabilities are only around .40 (Rose, Miller, Grim, & Christian, 1979).

Some investigators have found lower HR in high sensation seekers than in lows (D. Ridgeway & Hare, 1981; T. Robinson & Zahn, 1983) but others have not (Cox, 1977; Zuckerman, Simons, & Como, 1988), and one study found higher HR for high sensation seekers (Stern, Cox, & Shahan, 1971).

Von Knorring et al. (1984) found a low but significant negative correlation between BP and sensation seeking with the systolic BP readings taken during a medical examination given to Swedish army inductees. Carrol et al. (1982) discovered that low sensation seekers who volunteered for an experiment had higher systolic BPs than high sensation seekers when the BP was taken by a physician during the subject selection period. However, when a nurse took BP readings before and after each of three experimental sessions, the differences in BPs disappeared, suggesting that the higher BP in low sensation seekers was a specific reaction to the examining physician rather than a general characteristic of lows.

Salivation

The stimulation of salivary glands by lemon juice dropped on the tongue was negatively related to extraversion in a number of studies and this finding has been interpreted as indicative of greater brain arousal in introverts than in extraverts. Deary, Ramsay, Wilson, and Riad (1988) found that stimulated salivation correlated significantly and negatively with Total SSS, E, and P scales in a group run in the morning but positively with SS and E in another small group run in the afternoon. The P scale was the only one that correlated significantly with salivation in the combined morning and afternoon group. Arousal levels are higher in the afternoon than in the morning for rate of spontaneous skin conductance changes and breathing rate (Zuckerman, Persky, & Link, 1969), and in the Deary et al. study salivation was greater in the afternoon than in the morning. Sensation-seeking state is also considerably higher at noon than in the morning (G. T. Hauty, personal communication, 1978). High sensation seekers may be less aroused than lows in the morning phase of the diurnal cycle, but their arousal increases while that of lows (and introverts) decreases in the afternoon. These hypotheses could be better tested by measuring arousal levels in the same subjects throughout the day, thereby allowing within as well as between group comparisons.

Arousability

Orienting, defensive, and startle reflexes

The orienting reflex (OR) is an indication of sensitivity or focused attention on a specific stimulus. The defensive reflex (DR), typically elicited by high intensities of stimulation, represents a preparation for physical action of a defensive nature. The startle reflex (SR), in response to strong or unanticipated stimuli, is a rapid response involving an interruption of action and a generalized flexion of muscles. The three types of reflex cannot be distinguished in the uniphasic skin conductance response (SCR), but Graham (1979) described different characteristics of these three types of reflexes in HR activity. In SCRs the nature of the response is inferred from the stimulus; stimuli of moderate intensity that are not unexpected are assumed to elicit ORs that *habituate* rapidly if the same stimulus is repeated a number of times. Presentation of a new (novel) stimulus should disinhibit the OR.

Electrodermal reactivity

Neary and Zuckerman (1976) conducted the first experiments relating electrodermal reactivity to sensation seeking. In their first experiment, male and female subjects were selected from the extremes of the distribution of scores on the General SSS. They were first presented with a simple visual stimulus consisting of a rectangle of light and the stimulus was repeated nine more times at randomly determined intervals. On the eleventh trial a new stimulus, consisting of a complex colored design, was projected and this stimulus was repeated nine more times. The mean SCRs of the high and low sensation seekers over the trials are shown in Figure 12.1.

On the first presentation of the simple stimulus, the high sensation seeking subjects had a significantly greater SCR than the low sensation seekers, but this difference disappeared completely on the second presentation of the stimulus. The two groups did not differ in reaction to the subsequent presen-

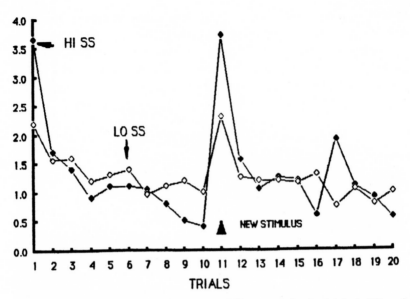

Figure 12.1. Skin conductance responses (SCRs) to a simple (trials 1–10) and a complex (trials 11–20) visual stimulus. Data from Neary & Zuckerman (1976). Figure from ''The psychophysiology of sensation seeking,'' by M. Zuckerman, 1990, *Journal of Personality, 58,* 322. Copyright 1990 by Duke University Press. Reprinted by permission.

tations of the same stimulus and habituated at the same rate from the second presentation to the 10th. On the 11th trial, when a new stimulus was presented, the high sensation seekers again showed a higher amplitude SCR than the low sensation seekers, but dropped to the level of response of the lows on the 12th trial and all subsequent trials. High and low sensation seekers differed only in response to novel visual stimuli, and not in response to repeated stimuli. Low-intensity visual stimuli do not usually elicit startle, so we can assume the SCR differences were in the strength of the orienting reflex.

In a second study using only male subjects, two auditory stimuli were added to the presentations of the visual stimuli from the previous experiment to see if the visual findings could be replicated and extended to the auditory stimulus modality. Subjects were selected on the basis of high and low scores on a measure of trait anxiety as well as sensation seeking in order to see how these two traits might interact in influencing the OR. The high sensation seekers gave stronger responses across all trials, but the response to the first presentation of the simple visual stimulus was not different in high and low sensation seekers. The response to the second novel stimulus showed a nonsignificant tendency toward a difference. High sensation seekers had a larger response than lows to the first novel auditory stimulus, but the groups did not differ on repetitive presentations (trials 2–10). The groups did not differ in response to the second novel auditory stimulus. *Trait anxiety* did not have any effect on SCRs to either visual or auditory stimuli, but subjects high on *state anxiety* gave *weaker* ORs to both of the novel auditory stimuli and one of the two novel visual stimuli. The high and low sensation-seeking groups did not differ on measures of habituation for any of the four stimulus series.

Some of the subsequent studies found some evidence that high sensation seekers had stronger electrodermal ORs than low sensation seekers to first presentations of simple auditory or visual stimuli in a series, and did not differ on subsequent repetitions of the stimuli (Feij et al., 1985; T. Robinson & Zahn, 1983; Smith et al., 1986), but other studies could not replicate these results (Cox, 1977; Plouffe & Stelmack, 1986; D. Ridgeway & Hare, 1981; Zahn et al., 1986; Zuckerman, Simons, & Como, 1988). The evidence from the study by Stelmack et al. (1983) was equivocal. Although the finding of stronger ORs to initial presentation of a visual stimulus was found for one class of stimuli (visually presented words), the difference was not significant after controlling SCR for SCL, and it was in an opposite direction for another type of visual stimuli (pictures).

Smith et al. (1986) investigated SCRs in response to tones and words, presented on sound tapes, and slides and videotapes. The words, slides, and videotapes contained two types of stimuli. The loaded stimuli were words, pictures, and video scenes with content presumed to be of interest to high sensation seekers, based on the content of items in the SSS. Neutral words and visually portrayed activities were not relevant to sensation seeking. The high sensation seekers had a stronger OR to the first presentation of the tone, confirming the results of Neary and Zuckerman (1976), but not over subsequent trials. Figure 12.2A shows the results for the first presentations of the words for loaded and neutral words separately. Both high and low sensation seekers gave stronger SCRs to loaded words than to neutral words, but the differences between responses to the two types of stimuli were greater for high than for low sensation seekers. Differences between high and low sensation seekers were greater for the loaded stimuli than for the neutral ones. Figure 12.2B shows the results for all trials. The magnitudes of response were lower, due to habituation after the first presentation, but the same significant interaction between stimulus content and sensation seeking was found across all stimuli.

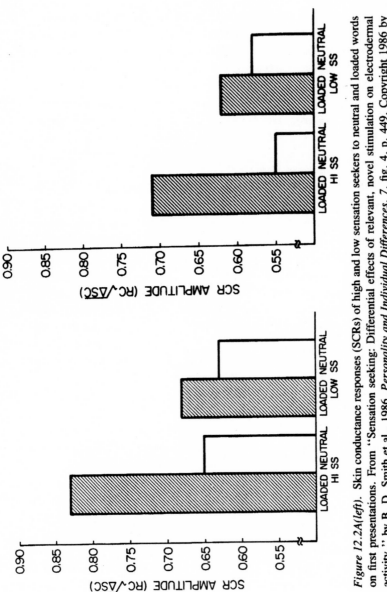

Figure 12.2A(left). Skin conductance responses (SCRs) of high and low sensation seekers to neutral and loaded words on first presentations. From "Sensation seeking: Differential effects of relevant, novel stimulation on electrodermal activity," by B. D. Smith et al., 1986, *Personality and Individual Differences, 7,* fig. 4, p. 449. Copyright 1986 by Pergamon Press. Reprinted by permission.

Figure 12.2B(right). Skin conductance responses (SCRs) of high and low sensation seekers to neutral and loaded words over all trials. From "Sensation seeking: Differential effects of relevant novel stimulation on electrodermal activity," by B. D. Smith et al., 1986, *Personality and Individual Differences, 7,* fig. 1, p. 448. Copyright 1986 by Pergamon Press. Reprinted by permission.

High sensation seekers gave stronger responses than low sensation seekers to initial presentations of the slide stimuli, regardless of content, but did not differ from lows in responses over all slides, indicating habituation of the effect after initial presentations. This result resembles that found with contentless visual stimuli in the first Neary and Zuckerman study. Responses to the video scenes showed similar effects to those of words. High sensation seekers responded much more strongly to loaded stimuli than to neutral stimuli, with less difference in the low sensation seekers and little difference between high and low sensation seekers in response to neutral stimuli.

Considering the preferences of high sensation seekers for aggressive and sexual themes in the media (Chapter 8), they should show stronger ORs to such stimuli than low sensation seekers. Smith et al. (1989) presented tape-recorded words classified as low, medium, or high in intensity of sexual and aggressive content categories. As shown in figure 12.3A, both high and low sensation seekers had stronger initial SCRs in response to high-intensity content words than to medium- and low-intensity words, but no differences between high and low sensation seekers were found for low-intensity words and differences were maximal for high-intensity words. Figure 12.3B shows that the same differences obtain for SCRs across all words in the given categories, even those beyond the first presentations.

These studies by Smith and his colleagues show that the content of stimuli is important as a determinant of differences between high and low sensation seekers on electrodermal responses. Although they replicated some of the differences in respect to neutral stimuli like tones and slides, high sensation seekers were particularly more electrodermally responsive than lows to content of interest to them, and intense sexual and aggressive stimuli. The OR has been interpreted as a measure of interest and attention to the stimulus, and sensation seekers have been defined as persons with a strong attraction to stimuli that are novel and exciting. The electrodermal OR shows that they are more aroused than lows by such stimuli, particularly when their novelty lies in their content.

Responses to neutral stimuli rarely persist beyond their initial presentation, but when novelty was maximal the high sensation seekers continued to give larger responses than lows to loaded stimuli on subsequent presentations. However, it should be noted that all the stimuli within a category were different and had some novelty value. SCR still tends to habituate to any series of stimuli of the same general character, even though each stimulus is a different one (the reader may recall reactions to an evening spent looking at someone else's travel slides). Another feature of Smith's experiments may account for his impressive results. He selected very extreme groups of high

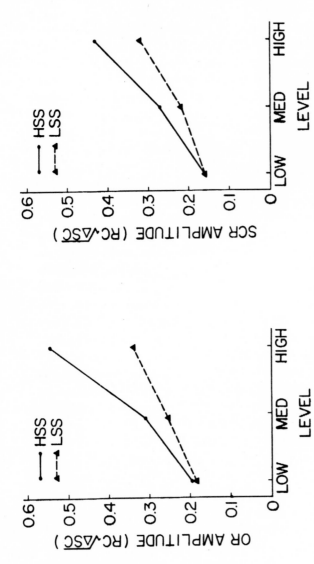

Figure 12.3A(left). Skin conductance response (SCRs) of high and low sensation seekers to low-, medium-, and high-intensity sexual and aggressive words on first presentations. From "Sensation seeking and arousal: Effects of strong stimulation on electrodermal activation and memory task performance," by B. D. Smith et al., 1989, *Personality and Individual Differences, 10,* fig. 1, p. 674. Copyright 1989 by Pergamon Press. Reprinted by permission.

Figure 12.3B(right). Skin conductance responses (SCRs) of high and low sensation seekers to low-, medium-, and high-intensity sexual and aggressive words over all words in given categories. From "Sensation seeking and arousal: Effects of strong stimulation on electrodermal activation and memory task performance," by B. D. Smith et al., 1989, *Personality and Individual Differences, 10,* fig. 3, p. 675. Copyright 1989 by Pergamon Press. Reprinted by permission.

and low sensation seekers (5%–10% at each extreme). The SCR relationship to sensation seeking is not strong. The correlation between magnitude of initial SCR and the SSS was only .28 in the Feij et al. (1985) study and .26 in the Stelmack et al. (1983) study. With correlations like these, the results in high and low group comparisons will only be significant when very extreme and/or large groups are compared.

Because those with antisocial personality disorders are high sensation seekers (Chapter 10), study of their SCRs are relevant to the relation of orienting to sensation seeking. Hare (1978) found a weak but replicable tendency for psychopathic prisoners to have lower SCLs than less psychopathic prisoners. High and low normal sensation seekers do not differ in SCL as previously discussed. SCRs in psychopaths tend to be *weaker* than those in other prisoners, particularly in younger prisoners and using more intense stimuli. But studies showing any differences have found *stronger* SCRs in high than in low normal sensation seekers, at least in response to moderate stimulus intensities.

Some subjects, even among supposedly normal groups, show no electrodermal response at all, even to the first presentation of the stimulus. These extreme nonresponders are found among groups of schizophrenics and sometimes in antisocial groups as well. Raine and Venables (1984) screened a group of 15-year-old schoolchildren for antisocial tendencies and selected anti- and prosocial groups for psychophysiological studies. Nonresponding on SCRs to a 65-decibel (dB) tone was relatively more frequent among children rated as antisocial than among prosocials. The antisocial group was divided into responders and nonresponders and these two groups were compared with the prosocial group on the SSS and measures of schizoid tendency. The antisocial responders were higher than the prosocial group on the SSS Total and Dis scores, while the nonresponder antisocials fell in between these two groups, not differing significantly from either. The nonresponder group scored higher than the other two groups on scales of schizoid tendencies. The electrodermal nonresponding type of antisocial personality, therefore, represents an atypical psychopath with asocial as well as antisocial tendencies, while the normally responsive antisocial type is more like the classical, high sensation-seeking psychopath. This result is reinforced by a study of electrodermal responders and nonresponders among college students (Simons, Losito, Rose, & MacMillan, 1983). Those who were consistently nonresponsive over two recording sessions scored lower than inconsistent nonresponders on general sensation seeking and higher on scales of schizoid tendency and perceptual aberration. Recalling that withdrawn schizophrenics

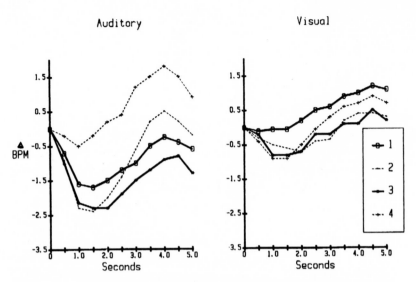

Figure 12.4. Auditory and visual stimulus intensity and heart rate response (BPM = beats per minute). From "Sensation seeking and stimulus intensity as modulators of cortical, cardiovascular, and electrodermal response: A cross-modality study," by M. Zuckerman et al., 1988, *Personality and Individual Differences, 9,* fig. 2, p. 366. Copyright 1988 by Pergamon Press. Reprinted by permission.

tend to be low sensation seekers, the results are consistent with the finding of weak electrodermal ORs in low sensation seekers.

Heart rate responses

The heart rate (HR) orienting reflex (OR) is characterized by a deceleration of HR immediately following the stimulus and lasting 2 to 4 seconds (Graham, 1979). The defensive reflex (DR) has a somewhat longer latency and consists of an increase in HR following the stimulus. The startle reflex (SR) is a short latency increase in HR, starting immediately after the stimulus. The intensity of the stimulus is an important determinant of the deceleration and acceleration tendencies of HR as seen in Figure 12.4 from the study by Zuckerman, Simons, and Como (1988). For auditory stimuli, the characteristic response to auditory tones of moderate intensity (50–80 dB) is initial deceleration of HR followed by an acceleration back to baseline. However, a 95-dB stimulus elicited an acceleration above baseline peaking about 4 seconds after the stimulus.

Orlebeke and Feij (1979) used an 80-dB tone that elicited a mixture of

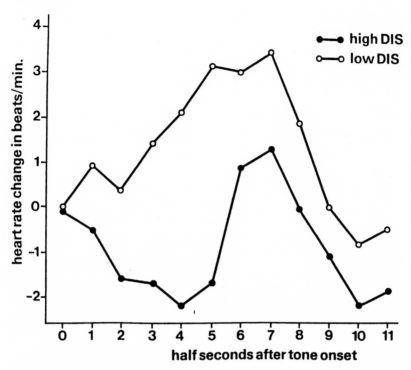

Figure 12.5. Heart rate response of high and low scorers on the Disinhibition (Dis) subscale of the Sensation Seeking Scale (SSS) to the first presentation of an 80-dB tone. From "The orienting reflex as a personality correlate," by J. F. Orlebeke & J. A. Feij, 1979. In H. D. Kimmel, E. H. van Olst, & J. F. Orlebeke (Eds.), *The orienting reflex in humans,* p. 579. Hillsdale, NJ: Erlbaum. copyright 1979 by Lawrence Erlbaum Associates. Reprinted by permission.

deceleratory and acceleratory patterns. The Dis subscale of the SSS was most strongly related to these reactions as shown in Figure 12.5. The HRs of the high Dis subjects tended to show a decelerative response in the first 2 seconds after stimulus onset. In contrast, the low Dis subjects showed an acceleratory pattern to the same tone reaching a peak about 4 seconds after stimulus onset. The differences between high and low sensation seekers persisted for only the first two trials after which both accelerative and decelerative patterns habituated. The difference in deceleration of HR indicates a stronger OR in high sensation seekers compared with lows, but the accelerative pattern could reflect either DRs or SRs.

Because of the short latency and rapid habituation of the acceleratory pattern and the use of a tone with a fast rise time (more likely to elicit startle)

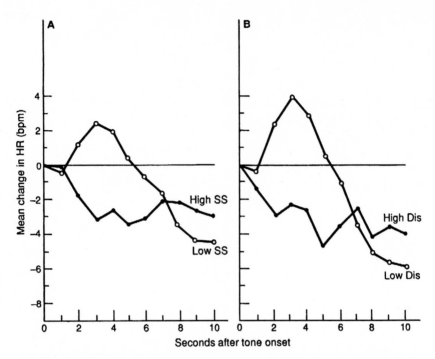

Figure 12.6. Heart rate (HR) response of high and low scorers on the General (A) and Disinhibition (B) Sensation Seeking Scales (SSS) in response to a 60-dB tone. From "Sensation seeking and psychophysiological responses to auditory stimulation," by D. Ridgeway & R. D. Hare, 1981, *Psychophysiology, 18,* 616. Copyright 1981 by Society for Psychophysiological Research. Reprinted by permission.

in the Orlebeke and Feij study, D. Ridgeway and Hare (1981) maintained that the acceleratory HR reaction of low disinhibiters was a blend of SR and DR rather than a DR difference. However, Ridgeway and Hare used a slow rise-time tone in their own study and found the same type of HR difference between high and low General SS subjects and extreme high and low Dis subjects (Figure 12.6). The low SS and Dis subjects showed an acceleratory trend to a 60-dB tone while the high SS and Dis subjects showed a deceleratory tendency to the same tone. The differences were only found on the first stimulus presentation and the rapid habituation of the acceleratory response of the low sensation seekers argues for an SR rather than a DR interpretation. A slow rise-time tone was also been used in the study by Cox (1977) who also found that in response to a 70-dB tone high sensation seekers (General scale) showed stronger HR deceleration and low sensation seekers had stronger acceleratory HR reactions.

Zuckerman, Simons, and Como (1988) examined HR reactions to tones and flashing lights across a range of stimulus intensities. Subjects were selected from the upper and lower 25% of scores on the Dis scale. In reaction to visual stimuli, high sensation seekers had more HR deceleration than low sensation seekers across all stimulus intensities, but in the responses to auditory stimuli from 50dB to 95dB the differences in deceleration and acceleration were found at different intensities of stimulation. At the lowest intensity of 50 dB most subjects showed deceleration but the high disinhibiters showed more than the lows. This difference was only significant at this intensity and it held for the first trial only. Acceleration was higher in low than in high disinhibiters across all intensities, but particularly at the highest intensity (95 dB) where more subjects showed an acceleratory pattern.

The HR results are more consistent than those for SCR in showing a stronger OR in high than in low sensation seekers, particularly those of the disinhibitory type. However, these differences, like those for the SCRs, disappear rapidly with habituation, and are only found for certain stimulus intensities. It is the interaction between novelty and intensity aspects of stimuli that produces different reactions in high and low sensation seekers.

Augmenting–reducing of the cortical evoked potential

Skin conductance and heart rate results show the effects of novelty and intensity of stimulation combined, but the early components of the cortical evoked potential (EP) primarily reflect the intensity aspect of stimulation. At 100 milliseconds (ms) after the stimulus, the stimulus has just arrived at the cortical level and little elaborate processing is possible. Novelty is primarily detected at 300 ms after the stimulus.

EPs are obtained by presenting a brief-duration stimulus like a flash of light or a tone many times and running the raw EEG record through a computer that averages the amplitudes of the EEG at a number of points time-locked to the stimulus. The averaging smooths out the irregularities of the raw EEG. The result is a wave form for a half-second (500-ms) period that reflects both the characteristics of the evoking stimulus and the responding nervous system at the site where the electrode is placed.

The complex wave forms show a remarkable degree of similarity in pairs of identical twins, compared with fraternal twins or unrelated subjects, showing a high degree of genetic determination (Buchsbaum, 1974; Lewis, Dustman, & Beck, 1972). The total amount of EP reactivity, as reflected in the perimeter of the entire wave form or the area under the curve, has been interpreted as a measure of arousability (H. Eysenck, 1967). Golding, Ashton, Marsh, and Thompson (1986) related this index in somatosensory EPs to personality dimensions including a short form of the SSS. The SSS correlated significantly and negatively with the somatosensory EP measures and the correlations were increased when the EP measures were controlled for stimulus intensity. Extraversion also correlated negatively with these measures of cortical arousability. However, most personality studies have used visual and auditory EPs, and since there is little relationship between somatosensory and other sensory evoked EPs (Buchsbaum, Haier, & Johnson, 1983), the significance of the findings is problematic.

Buchsbaum and Silverman (1968) developed a method of analyzing individual EPs over a range of stimulus intensities. Visual, auditory, or somatosensory EPs are recorded at a vertex scalp location for the active electrode and the EPs are averaged for four or five intensities of the stimulus. An amplitude-intensity slope function for a specific component of the EP is used, usually the P1 (positive peak at about 100 ms after the stimulus) to N1 (negative peak at about 140 ms poststimulus). Strong positive slopes show a cortical response that increases in direct relation to the intensity of the stimulus over the range of intensity used. Zero or negative slopes show that either there is little cortical response to increasing intensities of stimulation or that cortical response is inhibited at high intensities of stimulation. Positive slopes are called *augmenting* and zero or negative slopes are labeled *reducing*. Although this sounds like a typology, the range of augmenting and reducing is treated as a continuum and the distribution of individual values approximates a normal one (Buchsbaum et al. 1983).

The terminology for the phenomena reflects the origin of the EP method in an attempt to provide a central measure of a construct devised by Petrie (1967). Petrie said that the brains of some persons are characterized by reduction of the intensity of sensation whereas others tend to augment sensations. Reducers would be resistant to pain and "stimulus hungry" (sensation seeking) under low stimulation conditions, whereas augmenters should be intolerant of pain and have low optimal levels of stimulation. Petrie's method for assessing individual differences in augmenting–reducing was a psychophysical rather than a psychophysiological one. It involved the judgment of the width of a block of wood before and after stimulation produced by rubbing other blocks of wood. The second judgment is assumed to reflect the fate of the interpolated stimulation in the brain where it may be augmented or reduced. A debate about the reliability and construct validity of this Kinesthetic After Effect (KAE) method was published in *Behavioral and Brain Sciences* (Zuckerman, 1986a, pp. 744–754). Because Buchsbaum called the EP method by the same name as Petrie's psychophysical method, people expect them to yield comparable results. Actually they tend to yield opposite types of results so that reducers defined by the KAE (Petrie's method) could be augmenters as defined by Buchsbaum's EP method (Davis, Cowles, & Kohn, 1983). The EP method is a direct measure of the brain's reaction to intensities of stimulation, whereas the KAE is a voluntary, peripheral response with no retest reliability and a questionable relationship to the brain processes it is supposed to reflect. Another point is that most of the personality research using the EP method has been based on visual or auditory evoked potentials whereas the KAE is based on reactions to somatosensory stimulation. Somatosensory EP augmenting–reducing is not related to visual or auditory EP augmenting–reducing.

Genetic studies of EP augmenting–reducing measure show a relatively high correlation for identical twins ($r = .71$) compared with fraternal twins ($r = .09$) (Buchsbaum, 1974). The low correlation of fraternal twins might indicate a pattern of epistasis rather than additive genetic determination, but studies of siblings and offspring show correlations of about .30 that are just slightly below what would be expected from additive genetic determination.

Augmenting–reducing and sensation seeking

Buchsbaum (1971) first suggested a *positive* relationship between EP *augmenting* and sensation seeking. Zuckerman et al. (1974) tested this hypothesized relationship using the visual EP. The strongest and only significant relationship between augmenting of the EP and the SSS IV was with the Dis subscale ($r = .59$, $p < .001$). As shown in Figure 12.7, high disinhibiters showed an augmenting pattern of relationship between stimulus intensity and visual EP, whereas low disinhibiters demonstrated a reducing pattern with significant reduction at the highest intensity of stimulation.

A number of attempts at replication of this original study have been made with significant results in half of them (Zuckerman, 1990a). Hardly any two studies used the same methodology or range of stimuli; all used fewer subjects than the Zuckerman et al. (1974) study, and most used mixed groups of males and females whereas the Zuckerman et al. study was confined to males. Four of the eight attempts at replication found some significant positive relationship between visual EP augmenting and Dis or the Total SSS (Lukas, 1987; Stenberg, Rosen, & Risberg, 1988; von Knorring, 1980; Zuckerman, Simons, & Como, 1988), whereas four others found no significant relationships (Roger & Raine, 1984; Stenberg et al., 1990) and two found relationships in the opposite direction to prediction from the original study (Coursey et al., 1975; Haier, Robinson, Braden, & Williams, 1984).

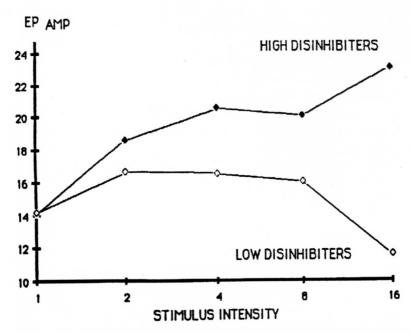

Figure 12.7. Visually evoked potentials (EPs) of high and low scorers on the Disinhibition subscale of the Sensation Seeking Scale as a function of stimulus intensity. From "Sensation seeking and cortical augmenting-reducing," by M. Zuckerman et al., 1974, *Psychophysiology, 11*, 539. Copyright 1974 by the Society for Psychophysiological Research. Reprinted by permission.

Some of the positive replications must also be qualified. Zuckerman, Simons, and Como (1988) found that high disinhibiters showed more augmenting in a group receiving a long interstimulus interval (ISI), but not in a group with a short ISI. Von Knorring (1980) used the P1N2 EP component instead of the usual PINI and had his active electrode on the occiput rather than the vertex scalp. The opposite-to-expected results in Coursey et al. (1975) and Haier et al. (1984) studies may be because they just used settings 1 to 8 on the Grass Photostimulator, whereas the Zuckerman et al. (1974; and Zuckerman, Simons, & Como, 1988) studies both used the maximum intensity at 16. In both studies the differences depended on EP responses at the 16 setting where high disinhibiters augmented and lows reduced. Haier et al. also had a marked imbalance in sexes; 10 of their 11 augmenters were females compared with 5 females and 5 males in the reducer group. The relationship between augmenting–reducing and sensation seeking in females is problematical and the higher augmenting among females than males is not consistent with the relationships of augmenting to sensation seeking, delinquency, and alcoholism where men predominate. Coursey et al. found that insomniacs, who tended to be low sensation seekers, also were visual augmenters, but the results for auditory EPs were just the reverse; the low sensation seekers were augmenters as in most other studies.

The vertex site for recording visual EPs to calculate the augmenting–reducing indexes was selected on empirical grounds showing that it gave a distribution of augmenters and reducers, whereas recordings from primary visual areas (occipital) yielded only augmenting slopes (Buchsbaum & Pfefferbaum, 1971). The vertex sits over the central sulcus, and the brain area immediately below it is regarded as a polysensory cortex. Similar sequences of components are evoked by visual, auditory, and somatosensory stimuli from this site, although latencies of components for the three modalities differ. Näätänen and Picton (1987) suggested that the generator of the modality independent N1 component is in frontal and premotor cortex and the EP is the cortical projection of a reticular process that "facilitates motor activity." Stenberg et al. (1990) recorded the visual EP from both vertex and occipital sites and calculated the balance of response between the sites. At all intensities of stimulation, extraverts had relatively stronger dominance than the lows. The authors relate the introversion–extraversion difference to Brebner and Cooper's (1974) hypothesis that introverts are "geared to inspect" and extraverts are "geared to act." In trait terms this means that introverts tend to be more reflective and cautious and extraverts tend to be more impulsive. Applying the same hypothesis to the Dis data would suggest that impulsive behavior is activated in high sensation seekers by strong stimuli.

Ten studies compared *auditory* EP augmenting–reducing and sensation seeking. The results are more consistent for the auditory than for the visual EP with 8 of 10 studies (Coursey et al., 1975; Hegerl, Prochino, Ulrich, & Muller-Oerlinghausen, 1989; Lukas & Mullins, 1985; Mullins & Lukas, 1984, 1987; Orlebeke, Kok, & Zeillemaker, 1989; Pueyo, 1990; Zuckerman, Simons, & Como, 1988) showing a significant and positive relationship between auditory EP augmenting in at least one condition with at least one of the SS scales, and two studies (Lukas & Mullins, 1983; Stenberg et al., 1988) showing no relationships. Coursey et al. (1975) reported the first study using auditory EPs. Insomniacs showed more reducing on the auditory EP than controls, and the General SSS (no subscales used) correlated positively with augmenting. Both augmenting and sensation seeking correlated positively with sleep efficiency. In the studies by Mullins and Lukas (1984) and Lukas and Mullins (1985), there were no correlations between the SSS and

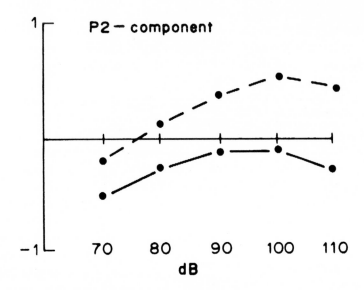

Figure 12.8. Auditory evoked potentials of high (dash line) and low (solid line) scorers on the Disinhibition subscale of the Sensation Seeking Scale as a function of stimulus intensity in passive and active listening conditions. From "Disinhibition and the processing of auditory stimulus intensity: An ERP study," by J. F. Orlebeke, A. Kok, & C. W. Zeillemaker, 1989, *Personality and Individual Differences, 10*, fig. 3, p. 449. Copyright 1989 by Pergamon Press. Reprinted by permission.

augmenting in a condition where subjects were instructed to listen passively to the tones, but there were significant correlations when subjects were required actively to attend to the tones. However, Orlebeke et al. (1989) found that Dis was related to augmenting at P200 in both passive and active conditions of listening with high disinhibiters showing a steeper slope under both conditions (Figure 12.8). At the maximum intensity (110 dB) used in any of these studies, both high and low sensation seekers showed some reducing tendency (Figure 12.8). Reducing is a protective mechanism for all persons, but the threshold for its activation seems to be raised in high compared to low sensation seekers.

Zuckerman, Simons, and Como (1988) found a relation between Dis and augmenting of the auditory EP for a group with a short ISI, but not for the group with a long ISI. The relationships between EP amplitudes (short ISI) and stimulus intensities for high and low Dis groups are shown in Figure 12.9. The high Dis group clearly augmented at 80 and 95 dB while the

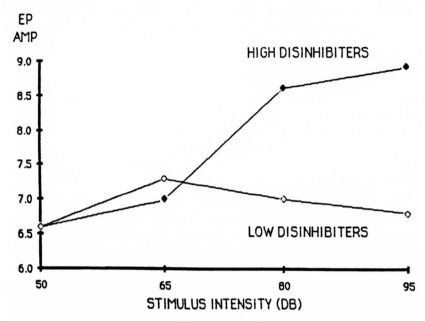

Figure 12.9. Auditory evoked potentials (EPs) of high and low scorers on the Disinhibition subscale of the Sensation Seeking Scale as a function of stimulus intensity for the short interstimulus interval condition (2 seconds). From "Sensation seeking and stimulus intensity as modulators of cortical, cardiovascular, and electrodermal response: A cross-modality study," by M. Zuckerman et al., 1988, *Personality and Individual Differences, 9,* 368. Copyright 1988 by Pergamon Press. Reprinted by permission.

low Dis group showed little augmenting at any point. The conditions were essentially passive; the subjects were merely asked to listen to the tones.

Hegerl et al. (1989) ran their subjects three times with the first and second EP runs only 20 minutes apart, and the third run 3 weeks later. They used the N1-P2 component for the auditory EP. Both high and low sensation seekers showed augmenting patterns on the first run, but the slope of the high sensation seekers (General SSS) was even steeper than that of the lows because of a markedly higher EP amplitude at the 88-dB level of stimulation. However, on subsequent runs there was no difference between high and low sensation seekers because there was a marked reduction in the slope in the highs due to the reduction of their response to the 88-dB stimulus. Although there is some evidence of reduction of EP amplitudes across sessions (Buchsbaum, 1976), other investigators have not reported a reduction within the same session. Perhaps the novelty effect of the loudest tone affected the high sensation seekers more than the lows in the first run. This adaptation effect, specific to high sensation seekers, bears further investigation.

Augmenting–reducing and impulsivity

Like sensation seeking, impulsivity has also been related to augmenting of the visual EP in humans (Barratt, Pritchard, Faulk, & Brandt, 1987; Carrillo-de-la Peña & Barratt, 1993). Sensation seeking and impulsivity are closely related at the trait level (Chapter 3). Expressed emotionality (EE) is a concept that has been used in characterizing the relatives of schizophrenic patients. A high degree of EE means that these relatives tend to express negative emotions critical of a recovering schizophrenic. Since schizophrenics are sensitive to criticism and negative feelings, a high level of EE in their relatives at home is associated with an increased rate of recurrence of symptoms. Low EE relatives have an easier, more positive, and less critical relationship with the patient. Hegerl, Priebe, Wildgrube, and Müller-Oerlinghausen (1990) found that low EE nonbiologically related relatives (spouses) exhibit a more positive slope (augmenting) than high EE relatives in the auditory EP (N1-P2). They suggest that low EE is "related to a more open and impulsive way of dealing with interpersonal problems, preventing the accumulation of interpersonal tensions" (p. 112).

Augmenting–reducing and psychopathology

Augmenting of the EP provides another biological connection between sensation seeking and bipolar disorder (the MAO connection was described in Chapter 11). Bipolar disorders are characterized by EP augmenting (Buchsbaum, Landau, Murphy, & Goodwin, 1973; Buchsbaum, Post, & Bunney, 1977). The augmenting is more prominent in the manic phase of the disorder and can change to reducing during the depressive phase (von Knorring, 1978). Lithium has been successfully used in preventing manic and depressive swings in bipolar disorders. Lithium reduces activity in brain neurons by replacing sodium in the neuron and stabilizing the potassium sodium balance. It also tends to reduce catecholamine activity. Lithium changes augmenting patterns to reducing ones in bipolar disorders (Buchsbaum, Goodwin, Murphy, & Borge, 1971), and bipolars who are augmenters before lithium treatment show a better response to lithium than those who are already reducers. Augmenting–reducing, therefore, seems to be a good psychophysiological index for whatever it is in the brain of the bipolar disorder that produces the high activity, euphoria, and impulsivity characteristic of mania. In more controlled form, these same traits characterize normal high sensation seekers.

Haier, Buchsbaum, Murphy, Gottesman, and Coursey (1980) proposed a model for vulnerability to psychopathology that combines both MAO and EP augmenting–reducing as markers. Low MAO/augmenting individuals are described as high sensation seekers who lack protection (reducing) against sensory overload. High MAO/reducers are described as low sensation seekers with strong sensory inhibition. Both of these groups are regarded as unbalanced in the need for sensation as against the capacity to deal with overload or underload, and therefore vulnerable to depression and other forms of psychopathology. The remaining two combinations of MAO and augmenting are balanced and therefore should not be vulnerable to psychopathology.

Haier et al. (1980) interviewed and diagnosed a group of students who were classified into four groups on the basis of MAO and EP data. As they predicted, affective disorders were more frequent (52%) in the low MAO-augmenting and high MAO-reducing groups than in the other two groups where the diagnoses were made in only 6% of the cases. A follow-up of these cases showed that 67% of the imbalanced groups and only 18% of the other 2 groups had episodes of major depression or hypomania in the year and a half after the initial studies.

Augmenting is also found to be characteristic in other disinhibitory disorders including alcoholism (von Knorring, 1976), delinquency (Silverman, Buchsbaum, & Stierlin, 1973), and criminality (Carrillo-de-la-Peña & Barratt, 1993). Alcoholics are more likely to reduce than normal controls when given alcohol during sensory overload. Acute schizophrenics tend to be reducers, and those among them who are reducers have a better prognosis than those who are augmenters, suggesting that the reducing function has a protective function (Landau, Buchsbaum, Carpenter, Strauss, & Sacks, 1975). Augmenting tends to be more prevalent in chronic than in acute schizophrenia.

Sensation seeking has been associated with another psychophysiological measure that is a marker for schizophrenia. Smooth pursuit eye-tracking impairment has been found in about 50%–90% of schizophrenics and only about 7% of normals. Eye tracking is under genetic control, does not change with improvement in the clinical state of schizophrenics, and is not impaired by antipsychotic medications. Siever et al. (1982) identified a group of low-accuracy or borderline trackers in a nonpsychiatric population of college students and compared them to accurate trackers. Those with impaired pursuit eye tracking scored lower on the SSS, reported fewer heterosexual contacts, scored higher on the MMPI social introversion scale, and had a poorer self-concept that controls with normal eye tracking.

Augmenting–reducing and performance

EP augmenting–reducing is, on logical grounds, the best method for assessing the Pavlovian construct, *Strength of the Nervous System* (Zuckerman, 1987c). According to Pavlov, the strength of the nervous system meant the ability of cortical cells to work under conditions of intense or prolonged stimulation. At high intensities of stimulation the weak nervous system is likely to show a reduction of function called *transmarginal inhibition*. Pavlov defined these cortical reactions by the effects of stimulation on reflexive or conditioned reflexive responses. The EP reducing effect directly measures cortical inhibition at high intensities of stimulation; EP augmenters may therefore be regarded as persons with a strong nervous system and EP reducers as those with a weak nervous system. The behavioral predictions are that those with strong nervous systems should be able to perform more efficiently than weak nervous system types under high work loads and distracting stressors, since cortical inhibition should reduce performance efficiency.

Lukas and his colleagues have investigated the relationship between visual EP augmenting–reducing in military subjects and performance with different task loads and under distraction conditions (Lukas & Mullins, 1985, 1988). Errors increased as the visual monitoring task became more difficult and noise distraction and a competing task were introduced. Reducers made more errors, especially at the higher work loads and with distraction. Certain jobs such as controlling air traffic and piloting jet fighters require high performance under stress, characteristic of strong nervous systems. In fact, Lukas's experimental task resembles the job of air traffic controllers (high sensation seekers as noted in Chapter 6). Lukas, Monty, Dominessy, Malkin, and Oatman (1990) tested a group of army helicopter pilots and compared them with male college students on visual EP augmenting–reducing. Almost all of the pilots (17 of 18) were augmenters, whereas nearly half of the student controls (8 of 19) were reducers. They also attempted to replicate the result relating errors at high work loads with EP reducing in the pilot group. Although they found negative correlations in this group, most were not significant. The relationship may have been attenuated because there were practically no reducers in this group.

Animal models for augmenting–reducing

The P1-N1 component of the visual EP can be identified in cats and rats as well as humans (Figure 12.10; Siegel & Sisson, 1993). Hybrid cats show a range of augmenting and reducing EP patterns, just as humans do, and the behavioral correlates of the EP paradigm have been studied in cats (Hall, Rappaport, Hopkins, Griffin, & Silverman, 1970; Lukas & Siegel, 1977; Saxton, Siegel, & Lukas, 1987). Augmenter cats were more exploratory, active, and aggressive, and more likely to approach novel stimuli than reducer cats in all studies. In two of the studies the reducer cats were more passive and tended to withdraw from novel stimuli. Differences in emotionality (fear and rage) were not consistent between studies. In all three studies there was evidence that an analogue of sensation-seeking trait in humans was also associated with the augmenting and reducing EP patterns in cats.

Saxton et al. (1987) also tested their cats on two experimental paradigms: a fixed interval (FI) bar-pressing task with food as a reward, and a differential reinforcement for low rate of response (DRL) in bar pressing for food. In the latter task a failure to inhibit or modulate response rate led to a delay in reinforcement. Augmenters adapted easily to the novel test chamber, whereas reducers were slower to adjust and initially more fearful. Augmenters learned the FI task more quickly and were more proficient at responding and getting reinforced. However, reducers were better on the DRL task because they were more able to inhibit their bar pressing during times when responding was penalized for overeagerness.

Siegel, Sisson and Driscoll (1993) extended the augmenting–reducing paradigm to rats, comparing strains of roman high avoidance (RHA) and roman low avoidance (RLA) rats selectively bred from a parental Wistar strain for ability to learn to avoid punishment actively. The RLA rats tend to freeze in a shock avoidance task and therefore are slow to learn to avoid the punishment. RHA rats are more active in response to shock and learn to avoid it more rapidly. Figure 12.11 shows the EP patterns in both strains as well as the parental Wistar stock. Nearly all RLA and Wistar rats were either EP reducers or very weak augmenters, and almost all of the RHA rats were moderate to strong EP augmenters. There was little overlap between the two groups in augmenting–reducing slopes.

All members of a highly inbred strain are almost like identical twins so that strain differences on other traits can be assumed to be correlates of the strain related EP difference. RLA rats (EP reducers) are less exploratory and more fearful in the open field test, less aggressive when shocked, have little

Visual Evoked Potentials

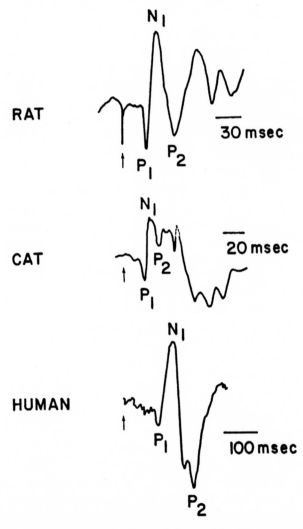

Figure 12.10. Comparisons of visually evoked potentials of humans, cats, and rats. From "Evoked field potentials – Beyond correlates of behavior: An approach to determining the neural mechanisms of behavior," by J. Siegel & D. E. Sisson, 1993. In W. Haschke, E. J. Speckman, & A. I. Roitbak (Eds.), *Slow potential changes in the brain,* p. 154. Boston, MA: Birkhäuser. Copyright 1993 by Birkhäuser. Reprinted by permission.

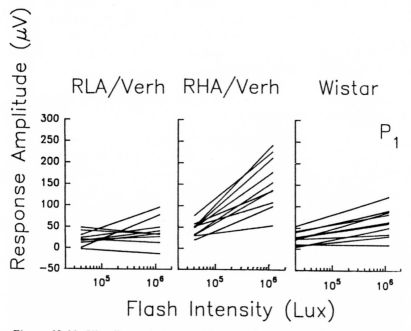

Figure 12.11. Visually evoked potentials as a function of stimulus intensity in Roman high avoidance (RHA) and Roman low avoidance (RLA) and the parental Wistar stock rats. From "Augmenting and reducing of visual evoked potentials in Roman High- and Low-avoidance rats," by J. Siegel, P. Driscoll, D. F. Sisson, 1993, *Physiology and Behavior, 54,* 707–711. Reprinted by permission.

tolerance for barbiturates and little taste for alcohol, are more maternal toward their pups, and show more serotonergic and hypothalamic and pituitary hormonal stress response than RHA rats. The RHA rats (EP augmenters) are more exploratory and more aggressive like augmenting cats. They are also less emotional, have higher tolerance for barbiturates and a taste for alcohol, are less nuturing toward their pups, and less stress responsive. The RHA rats are less responsive to weak-intensity stimulation and more responsive to strong-intensity stimulation in "reward centers" of the lateral hypothalamus. In many respects the RHA rat resembles the human high sensation-seeking and antisocial personalities. The self-stimulation data suggest a biological basis for the need for high intensities of stimulation in human sensation seekers.

The comparison of animal behavior with human traits is fraught with the dangers of anthropomorphism. But the finding of a common biological correlate, like MAO or augmenting–reducing, for similar forms of animal and human behavior reinforces the connection, even if it does not conclusively prove it. The traits suggested by the behavior of augmenting cats resemble sensation seeking, in exploration and tendency to approach rather than withdraw from novel stimuli, and impulsivity, in the lack of restraint in a situation requiring inhibition of reward-directed response.

Neural and biochemical bases of augmenting–reducing

Lukas and Siegal (1977) attempted to find the locus of the separation of augmenters and reducers in the brain. The individual differences in cats appeared only at the cortical level, suggesting that the inhibitory process in reducers occurs at the cortical rather than the subcortical levels. However, the neural mechanism is still unknown.

MAO, which has been related to sensation seeking (Chapter 11), is also low in augmenters of the visual EP in patient groups (Buchsbaum et al., 1973; von Knorring & Perris, 1981). Reducers tend to have high MAO levels. Similar results were found in students showing some evidence of mild affective disorders but not in more normal students (Haier et al., 1980). Exactly how MAO affects the augmenting–reducing phenomenon is not known but it is likely to be through one of the monoamine systems that it regulates. Visual EP augmenters among patients had lower CSF levels of 5-HIAA (the serotonin metabolite), HVA (the dopamine metabolite), and endorphins (endogenous opiate-like regulators) (von Knorring & Perris, 1981). They also found lower levels of DBH in augmenters and this was the enzyme negatively related to sensation seeking in some studies (Chapter 11). Experimental studies of the effects of brain-infused neurotransmitters or their blockers in cats are needed to see the effects on EP augmenting–reducing. Von Knorring and Johansson (1980) gave zimelidine, a selective inhibiter of serotonin uptake, to humans and effected a reduction in the amplitude-intensity slope of the P1-N1 component, suggesting that serotonin may affect the sensory-motor centers of the brain in an inhibitory fashion. This would be consistent with the role of this neurotransmitter in behavioral inhibition (Chapter 11).

Spinal motorneuronal excitability

Almost all arousal theories are based on central nervous system or autonomic nervous system arousal or both. However, it is possible that personality differences are based on more general properties of neuronal conduction that would include peripheral sensory or motor neurons as well as those in the

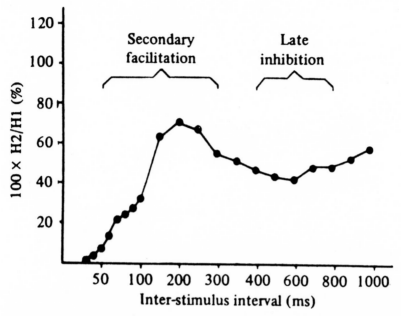

Figure 12.12. Average H-Reflex recovery curve for normals. From "Descriptive studies of the H-reflex recovery curves in psychiatric patients," by J. Metz, D. J. Goode, & H. Y. Meltzer, 1980, *Psychological Medicine, 10,* fig. 1, p. 543. Copyright 1980 by Cambridge University Press.

brain. The Hoffman reflex (H-Reflex) is evoked in a set of leg muscles by stimulation of the posterior tibial nerve. When the tibial nerve is stimulated twice within a short space of time, the second elicited reflex is usually smaller than the first, the difference in amplitude depending on the interstimulus interval (ISI). The *recovery curve* is defined by plotting the ratio of the second reflex (H2) to the first as a function of the ISI. Figure 12.12 shows an average H-reflex recovery curve for normals. The first phase called *secondary facilitation* reaches a peak at about 200 ms, at which time the second reflex is mostly recovered from inhibition, and is then followed by a late inhibition phase. The recovery curve in normals is both reliable and stable (Metz, Goode, & Meltzer, 1980), indicating that it could be a biological trait related to personality differences.

Pivik, Stelmack, and Bylsma (1988) stimulated the posterior tibial nerve in the leg and recorded muscle potentials in subjects who had been given the EPQ and the SSS V. Only the Dis subscale of the SSS and the E scale of the EPQ were related to the reflex recovery function. There were no differences between low and high sensation seekers or introverts and extraverts on

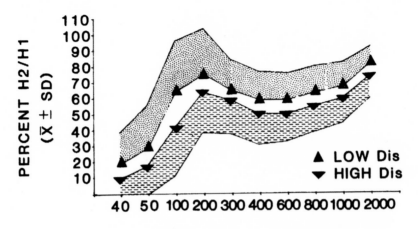

Figure 12.13. H-Reflex recovery curves for high and low scorers on the Disinhibition (Dis) subscale of the Sensation Seeking Scale. Note the absence of overlap in mean values across interstimulus intervals and the greater mean differences associated with secondary facilitation (100–300 ms.). From "Personality and individual differences in spinal motoneuronal excitability," by R. T. Pivik, R. M. Stelmack, & F. W. Bylsma, *Psychophysiology, 25*, fig. 3, p. 20. Copyright 1988 by Society for Psychophysiological Research. Reprinted by permission.

threshold measures of sensitivity to stimulus intensity or for latency of direct motor or reflex measures. However, high scorers on the Dis scale and extraverts showed less reflex recovery than those scoring low on Dis or E (introverts). The results for the Dis scale are shown in Figure 12.13. The low Dis subjects exhibited greater reflex recovery across the entire reflex recovery function, and the differences were specifically significant at the 50-ms and 100-ms ISIs, within the period of secondary facilitation.

Pivik et al. associate a reduction in motoneuronal excitability with the deficits in refined motor control and superior performance in tests requiring gross motor activity typical of extraverts. They suggest that the need for activity in high sensation seekers may be more important than the need for novel or intense stimulation. Although this hypothesis is interesting, there are many aspects of the behavior and interests of sensation seekers that are not explainable by a mere need for activity. For instance, why are those who engage in sports like parachuting and hang gliding, which require little overt physical activity, so much higher in sensation seeking than physical education students, gymnasts, runners, and others whose sports demand high levels of activity (Chapter 6)? It is true that sensation seekers react to the deprivation of sensation with increased restlessness (Zuckerman et al., 1966), but given a high level of varying stimulation in a situation of confinement, they are more content and happy than low sensation seekers (Zuckerman et al., 1968).

But Pivik et al. also propose an interesting biological hypothesis. Decreased motorneuronal excitability, as indexed by recovery function, has been associated with increased dopaminergic activity. Parkinsonism patients, with a damaged and depleted nigrostriatal dopamine system, show earlier and higher peaks of secondary facilitation than normals as do chronic schizophrenics (Metz et al., 1980). Metz et al. suggest that "dopamine is inhibitory to the facilitation portion of the recovery curve: a deficiency of dopamine produces an elevation of the curve, an excess is associated with a lowered recovery curve" (p. 546). Since high disinhibiters showed a lower curve than low disinhibiters, this could indicate that disinhibition is positively associated with dopaminergic activity. The low levels of type B MAO in high sensation seekers (Chapter 12) led to the hypothesis (Zuckerman, 1979a) that dopaminergic activity was elevated in high sensation seekers.

However, dopamine may not be the only neurotransmitter affecting recovery of the H-reflex. Metz et al. (1980) found that the antidepressant drug fluoxetine, which potentiates serotonin function by blocking serotonin reuptake, produced higher levels of secondary facilitation in the H-reflex. Perhaps disinhibition and extraversion are related to the balance between activity in dopamine and serotonin systems rather than just one or the other.

Summary

Freud's *constancy principle* (Breuer & Freud, 1895/1937) proposed individual differences in an optimal level of "intracerebral tonic excitement" at which level "the brain is accessible to all external stimuli." He suggested that differences in characteristic levels of cortical arousal might be related to a trait of personality he called "vivaciousness" (not unlike extraversion and activity). The concept of *brain accessibility* may be useful in describing the psychophysiological characteristics that differentiate high and low sensation seekers.

The brain of the high sensation seeker is more accessible to stimuli that are intense and novel than the brain of the low sensation seeker. This difference is not based on tonic levels of cortical arousal, but on arousability in response to certain types of stimuli. In response to intense stimuli the cortex of the high sensation seeker is activated whereas that of the low sensation seeker shows inhibition or reduction of arousal. While protecting low sensation seekers from overstimulation, the reducing mechanism may make them inefficient in cognitive function during stressful overload situations.

Tonic levels of skin conductance, heart rate, and blood pressure were lower in high sensation seekers in a few studies, but the finding is often limited to one sex (generally females) or is found only under special conditions. More studies simply find no relationship between these peripheral indicators of arousal and sensation seeking in either sex.

There is no consistent evidence that sensation seekers are underaroused and seek novel stimulation in order to increase arousal to optimal levels. But novel stimuli have ready access to the brain of high sensation seekers, as indicated by their strong electrodermal or HR deceleratory orienting responses to the initial presentations of stimuli. Low sensation seekers, however, respond to novelty in general, and threatening themes in particular, with defensive or startle types of cardiac responses. Their brains are not accessible to such stimuli and the type of arousal they exhibit is associated with inhibition and avoidance.

The orienting reflex is a psychophysiological strategy aimed at maximizing and clarifying information input by a shifting of attentional resources to the newest stimulus on the scene. Stimuli representing challenges to survival and stimuli associated with food or sexual pleasure may have the strongest claim on attention. Both positive and negative stimuli may elicit orienting, but intense, threatening, or merely novel and unanticipated stimuli may elicit defensive physiological reactions that are incompatible with accurate stimulus evaluation. There is no predicting the direction of the behavior after the orienting reaction occurs because the information obtained may lead to approach, withdrawal, or immobility. But since the orienting reflex is a reflexive attempt to maximize information, inherited strong OR tendencies are more likely to be associated with approach than withdrawal traits.

In order to further maximize information, sense organs must be brought nearer to the object. The male dog sees and smells something interesting, a strange dog. But is it a receptive female or a combative male? Only by bringing his olfactory receptors closer can he determine which it is, so he approaches closer, and at some risk if the latter possibility is the correct one. Another type of dog with less tolerance for ambiguity looks away and backs off growling with his heart steadily accelerating. The association between the strength of the OR stimulated by novel stimuli and sensation seeking may represent information-processing strategies that are associated with approach–withdrawal tendencies.

The psychophysiological reaction to novelty seems to be related to the broadest kind of sensation seeking as defined by General or Total SSS scores. Accessibility to novel or ambiguous stimuli may be the psychophysiological equivalent of the "big-five" trait of openness to experience (Costa & McCrae, 1985). But those psychophysiological reactions that depend on intensity alone or intensity plus novelty, such as EP augmenting or reducing and HR deceleration or acceleration, are more closely related to disinhibition than to any of the other SSS factors. Dis was also the only one of the four SSS factors related to recovery of the spinal motorneuronal H-reflex, possibly an indication of the strength of dopaminergic activity. Some of these variables, such as augmenting–reducing, are related to manic-depressive disorder in a direction that is consistent with their common correlate in the Dis scale.

Some of the psychophysiological reactions like the orienting and defensive reflexes represent different strategies for processing information. Do high and low sensation seekers differ in actual information processing, including sensation, perception, learning, memory, cognitive mechanisms, creativity, and general intelligence? The next chapter describes the research in these areas.

13

Information processing, cognitive styles, intelligence, and creativity

This chapter will examine the evidence that high and low sensation seekers differ in fundamental mechanisms of information processing, including attention, conditioning, more complex types of learning, memory, cognitive abilities and styles, intelligence, and creativity. If such differences exist, to what extent are they dependent on the novelty, complexity, or content of the materials being processed? Given the preferences of high and low sensation seekers described in previous chapters, and their psychophysiological reactivity to novelty (described in Chapter 12), one would expect that these qualities of tasks or stimuli would interact with differences in basic mechanisms. The special boredom susceptibility to monotonous or predictable stimulation must also be considered in judging differences in task performance. Although high sensation seekers may show strong attention in response to novel stimuli or tasks, their attention, arousal, and consequent performance would be expected to deteriorate in repetitive or unchallenging tasks.

Attention

The qualities of stimuli that attract and hold attention are the same as those determining the interests of sensation seekers in music, media, and art (Chapter 8). These qualities also determine the strength of the orienting reflex, discussed in Chapter 12. Since sensation seekers were shown to have stronger orienting reflexes to first (novel) presentations of stimuli, one would predict a stronger focused attention mechanism for them than for low sensation seekers. It was postulated that the high sensation seeker has a psychobiological trait that might be called *brain accessibility*, or openness to novel and/or intense stimuli. However, extrapolating from the orienting reflex experiments and the boredom susceptibility subtrait of sensation seeking, one would not expect the attention advantage to be maintained over repeated trials where the novelty of the task or stimuli is diminished. High sensation seekers would be expected to be good in focused and divided attention but poor in sustained attention.

High sensation seekers report that they often engage in other activities while watching television, including reading, conversing with someone present or on the telephone, engaging in handicraft work, or "cuddling" with a girl- or boyfriend (Rowland et al., 1989). High sensation seekers seem to divide their attention between two activities, although it is not certain how effective they are in either the focal or secondary activities. Low sensation seekers avoid distraction, suggesting that they may find it difficult to concentrate on a focal activity when there is competition for their attention from some other activity.

M. Martin (1985) interpreted the Embedded Figures Test (EFT; Witkin, Oltman, Raskin, & Karp, 1971) as a measure of focused attention. The task requires the subject to distinguish a simple figure embedded in a more complex design. The subject must ignore the distractions of the lines and areas of the overall design and focus attention on the embedded figure. The test has been interpreted as a personality style called *field independence* (*vs. field dependence*) or *psychological differentiation*. Most previous studies have found sensation seeking to be related to the trait of field independence as measured by the EFT and other methods (Baker, 1988; Cohen, Dingemans, Lesnick-Oberstein, & van der Vlugt, 1983; Zuckerman et al., 1964; Zuckerman & Link, 1968). M. Martin (1985) also found that high sensation seekers were better able than lows to pick out quickly the simple figure embedded in the complex one and she interpreted this as a superiority of the highs in focused attention. However, she found that high sensation seekers were inferior to lows on a task requiring concurrent signal detection and reading.

The dichotic listening task is more specifically designed to measure focused and divided attention. Subjects listen to different stimuli presented separately to each ear. In a focused attention condition they are asked to repeat or "shadow" the stimuli coming in one ear while ignoring the stimuli coming into the other ear. Divided attention is assessed by instructing subjects to attend to both channels for target stimuli, or by including a simultaneous secondary task extraneous to the auditory one. Ball and Zuckerman (1992) used this task to assess attention in high and low sensation seekers. Subjects were administered a sequence of tasks: (1) shadowing only; (2) shadowing with an extraneous light detection task; (3) identifying specific target words in both channels. On some of the trials in the dichotic listening task (4) the target words were paired with sensation-seeking relevant words in the other channel.

Figure 13.1 shows the results in terms of errors in shadowing. The high

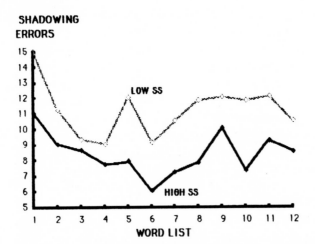

Figure 13.1. Errors in shadowing during different trial conditions. From "Sensation seeking and selective attention: Focused and divided attention on a dichotic listening task," by S. A. Ball & M. Zuckerman, 1992, *Journal of Personality and Social Psychology, 63*, 828. Copyright American Psychological Association, 1992.

sensation seekers began with a near-significant advantage on the first trial of the simple shadowing task, but this advantage narrowed on subsequent trials (2–4). On trial 5 when the distracting light detection task was introduced, the task performance of low sensation seekers was disrupted whereas the highs were relatively unaffected by the distracting task, and the difference between highs and lows was significant for the first two trials of this task (5–6). There were no significant differences in accuracy of signal detection on the divided attention task. An expected right ear advantage (left hemisphere dominance) was found for all subjects, but, as in the study by Cohen and Merckleback (1987), the relative difference was not related to sensation seeking.

High sensation seekers were able to establish a focus of attention on the attended channel earlier than low sensation seekers and were able to maintain the focus in the face of a distracting task. The low sensation seekers' performance was clearly disrupted by the distracting task. The performance of the high sensation seekers on the distracting task itself was not inferior to that of the lows, as indicated by reaction times to the light. Thus there was no trade-off of their stronger attention to the focal task with performance on the peripheral task. They also did not differ from the low sensation seekers on the divided-attention task.

The expectation that high sensation seekers would be more distracted than the lows by competing words of interest in the opposite channel was not borne out. The shadowing or recall of words was not related to sensation seeking. Barbee, Hammock, and Richardson (1987) also found that the intensity of visually presented words did not interact with sensation seeking level in memory for words. They did find that low sensation-seeking females remembered more words of all kinds than other groups, but no such interaction of gender and sensation seeking was found in the Ball and Zuckerman study. Unlike the electrodermal orienting studies (Smith et al., 1986) in which the content of word stimuli had a marked effect on orienting, the results of Ball and Zuckerman indicate a pure attention effect for novel stimuli and a strong ability of high sensation seekers to maintain a focused attention in the face of competing attention demands from a secondary task. It is the low sensation seekers who find it difficult to "chew gum and walk at the same time," to use the example provided by President Lyndon Johnson in describing Representative Gerald Ford.

As has been found with the orienting reflex, the superiority of high sensation seekers on the first shadowing trial quickly disappeared over further trials in the Ball and Zuckerman study. Because sensation seekers are susceptible to boredom, their performance on vigilance tasks calling for sustained attention would be expected to deteriorate with repetition of the performance. A study by Waag (1971), described by Thackray and Touchstone (1980), found that performance on a simple visual monitoring task was directly related to Cognitive Structure and Order scales from the Personality Research Form. These two PRF scales are inversely related to sensation seeking. Persons who like order and organization and dislike uncertainty and change did well on vigilance tests. Based on these results, Thackray and Touchstone expected that sensation-seeking scales should be inversely related to performance on a task requiring sustained attention. However, the task they used was a simulated air traffic display in which signals represented sudden changes in altitude of targets. This kind of task may have had more intrinsic interest than the usual kind of vigilance task. Comparing subjects who showed marked performance decrements over time with those who showed little decrement, they found that the high decrement group scored higher on PRF Impulsivity, but *lower* on the ES subscale of the SSS. No differences were found on General and BS scales of the SSS or with the Cognitive Structure and Change scales from the PRF. The unexpected direction of the relation to experience seeking may have more to do with the specific type of task that may have more interest for high experience seekers. Real air traffic controllers are high sensation seekers (Musolino & Hershenson, 1977) so there must be something in the work task that sustains their need for variety of experience.

Smith et al. (1989) contrasted the performance of high and low sensation seekers on a less interesting type of vigilance task. There were no significant differences between these high and low sensation seekers on hit rates, false alarm rates, or mean reaction times on the vigilance task. However, the task only lasted 10 minutes and it is possible that vigilance of a longer duration may reveal the expected deterioration in the performance of high sensation seekers.

Attention Disorder–Hyperactive children are often characterized as sensation seekers. Their incapacity for focused attention in the classroom situation is one of their major symptoms. Zentall and Meyer (1987) investigated the performance of hyperactive and control children in an auditory vigilance task. They found that under the usual conditions requiring sustained attention to a single task the hyperactives made more impulsive errors and engaged in more irrelevant activity than the controls. However, when they were allowed to press a lever to view slides while monitoring the auditory signals in the vigilance task, their performance in the vigilance task was as good as that of the controls. Performance in a decoding task also improved in the active condition and they talked and moved around less in that condition. The results support the idea that the problems of attention and hyperactivity stem from underarousal in what is for them an understimulation condition. If we extend these findings to adult sensation seekers we may surmise that their reports of engaging in two activities simultaneously represent an attempt to maintain an optimal level of stimulation and prevent deterioration of information acquisition by boredom.

Shaw and Giambra (1991) studied the performance of college students with histories of hyperactivity during childhood, using a vigilance task. Sensation seeking was significantly related to reported characteristics of hyperactivity during childhood, and to spontaneous task-unrelated thoughts (TUTS) during the procedure, but not to actual performance on the vigilance task. Since TUTS were related to performance, particularly to false alarms, these results suggest that high sensation seekers were able to maintain normal performance levels despite the distractions from their own spontaneous thoughts. This is another indication that potential distractors may actually serve to maintain performance on a primary task in high sensation seekers, presumably by keeping them sufficiently aroused and interested.

Sensory sensitivity and tolerance

The original conception of sensation seeking was based on the optimal level of stimulation (OLS) construct (Zuckerman, 1969a; Zuckerman et al., 1964).

The primary motive underlying the trait of sensation seeking was assumed to be the regulation of stimulation, but more specifically *stimulus intensity.* Many of the original items written for form I of the SSS referred to reactions to intense stimulation, but only a few of these items survived the subsequent scale refinements. Novelty appeared to be a more salient characteristic of stimulation than intensity in the emerging construct of sensation seeking. In fact, intensity was not even included as one of the stimulation needs defining the trait of sensation seeking in the first volume (Zuckerman, 1979a).

However, the relation of sensation seeking to augmenting–reducing of the cortical evoked potential (Chapter 12) suggested the importance of differences in stimulus regulation. The problem was that, with the evoked potential (EP) method, high sensation seekers (disinhibiters in particular) appeared to be augmenters while lows were reducers. The theory developed by Petrie (1967) was largely based on a psychophysical size judgment called the Kinesthetic Affect-Effect (KAE). According to the theory, high sensation seekers should be reducers and lows are likely to be augmenters. Reducers supposedly need stronger stimulation and augmenters seek reduced stimulation because of the typical reactivities of their nervous systems. Thresholds for auditory or pain sensation, and tolerance for high intensities of these sensations have also been used to measure the augmenting–reducing tendency. Several questionnaires (described in Chapter 3) have been developed to measure these stimulus regulation traits including Vando's (1974) Reducing–Augmenting scale, K. White's (1984) Sensitivity scale, Mehrabian's (1978) Stimulus Screening scale, Kohn's (1987) Reactivity scale, and Strelau's (1983) Strength of Excitation scale. Some of these scales are correlated with the SSS, but none of them have been validated against the EP cortical criteria and few have shown any relationship with the KAE criteria. Even when found, the relationship between questionnaires and the KAE has been quite minimal (Zuckerman, 1986a). This could be due to the poor retest reliability of the KAE although internal reliabilities are satisfactory (Mishara, 1986). However the KAE is not supposed to be a state test, but a measure of a stable trait, so that internal reliability on a single occasion is not enough. Perhaps because of these problems with the KAE, many investigators have turned to measures of sensory thresholds and pain tolerance to assess stimulus regulation.

According to Petrie's (1967) concept of augmenting–reducing and Strelau's (1983) theory of reactivity, augmenters should have low thresholds or *sensitivity* to sensory stimulation, and less tolerance for high intensities of stimulation than reducers. Studies reviewed in the last volume (Zuckerman, 1979a) yielded inconsistent results, with some tendencies toward high auditory thresholds and greater tolerance for high intensities of auditory stimulation in high sensation seekers. The latter finding is consistent with the high sensation seeker's taste for rock music (Litle & Zuckerman, 1986).

Goldman, Kohn, and Hunt (1983) correlated the General and Dis SSS, the Vando Reducer–Augmenter scale, and a measure of the Absolute Auditory Threshold (AAT). Most of the sensory items in the RAS refer to preferences for loud music as opposed to soft music. A previous study of AAT and sensation seeking found a substantial and significant positive correlation with only one SSS, Disinhibition (Kish, Frankel, Masters, & Berry, 1976); high disinhibiters had higher auditory thresholds. In the Goldman et al. study, the Vando RAS scale correlated highly with the General SSS ($r = .59$), but only the General SSS correlated significantly with auditory thresholds ($r = .45$). It is rather surprising that the RAS measure, designed specifically around the augmenting–reducing construct and containing a special group of auditory preference items, did not correlate with auditory thresholds, whereas the SSS, which contains few such items, did so. Davis et al. (1984) found no relation between the RAS and the KAE measure of augmenting–reducing.

Evidence from previous studies (Zuckerman, 1979a) also showed greater tolerance for high auditory stimulation and high preferred levels of stimulation in high sensation seekers, although the findings were weak, and sometimes confined to one sex or one SSS subscale. The RAS also correlates with preferred levels of loudness when listening to music, although the results are confined to the music preference factor within the scale (Kohn, 1987).

Given the evidence that high sensation seekers qualify as "reducers" using the sensory threshold and tolerance criteria, how can we explain their classification as "augmenters" by the cortical EP measures? Davis et al. (1983) resolved this "paradox" by proposing that the KAE measures sensitivity to stimulation at the low end of the intensity spectrum, whereas the EP augmenting method measures tolerance for high intensities of stimulation. Since the reactivity theory suggests an inverse relationship between sensitivity and pain tolerance, we would expect to find opposite results using the two methods for defining augmenting–reducing. The problem with this is that the KAE and the AER have both shown relationships with pain tolerance in some studies. However, those with the EP method have used somesthetic stimulation for both the EP and pain measurements, and somesthetic augmenting–reducing does not correlate with visual or auditory augmenting–reducing, the types related to sensation seeking. This may be the nub of the augmenting–reducing quandry, a lack of cross modality generalizability for a construct that seems to demand it. Perhaps, we should stop using "augmenting–reducing" as a personality construct and describe the phenomena in terms of the actual experimental validity for the techniques and their relationships with broader established dimensions of personality.

Perceptual satiation

Reversible figures have been used to assess an interesting quality termed *perceptual satiation*. A reversible figure is one in which the foreground–background relationship is unstable and tends to reverse spontaneously as one stares at the figure; one sees first one figure as foreground and then the other. Neary and Zuckerman (1976, data not included in report) found that high sensation seekers experienced more reversals than low sensation seekers on three reversible figures, vase profile, old woman–young woman, and Necker cube. Schalling, Åsberg, and Edman (1985) reported more frequent fluctuations of the Necker cube in psychopathic criminals and in normal controls scoring high on scales of Impulsivity and Monotony Avoidance (sensation seeking), and low on a scale of Socialization. Hallman, Klinteberg, and Oreland (1990) found a high rate of reversals of the Necker cube (twice the rate of controls) in a group of Swedish Air Force pilots also characterized by high Sensation Seeking, Monotony Avoidance, Impulsivity, and EPQ E and P scores. In some of these Swedish studies a high rate of figure reversals was associated with low levels of the enzyme MAO. Low levels of MAO have been associated rather consistently with sensation seeking (Chapter 11). A high rate of reversals has also been associated with frontal lobe lesions (Cohen, 1959).

Learning and performance

Classical conditioning

The eyelid conditioning paradigm has been extensively used in the study of extraversion, anxiety, and impulsivity (Zuckerman, 1991a). H. Eysenck and Levey (1972) showed that it was the impulsivity factor in the extraversion scale that was involved in the findings of differences between introverts and extraverts in eyelid conditioning. After finding that an overall impulsivity measure devised by S. Eysenck and Eysenck (1978) did not predict conditioning, Frcka and Martin (1987) decided to factor analyze the impulsivity scales to see what particular kind of impulsivity might be related to eyelid conditioning. They found three factors among the items. The IMP 1 factor consisted of items describing acting quickly without much forethought or planning; it is impulsivity in the narrow sense. IMP 2 contained items which were nearly all adapted from the Disinhibition and Boredom Susceptibility subscales of the SSS. IMP 3 was the Venturesomeness scale, which consists of items adapted from or resembling those in the Thrill and Adventure Seeking subscale of the SSS. Thus their impulsivity factors 2 and 3 actually represent different aspects of the sensation-seeking scales and their results with these factors provide us with information on conditioning and sensation seeking.

The IMP 1 factor was related to conditionability. Persons high in narrow impulsivity were poor conditioners; they started to show conditioned responses later than low impulsives and their conditioned responses were of lower amplitude than those of low impulsives. Venturesomeness (Thrill and Adventure Seeking in the SSS) affected the linear trend of CR amplitude over trials in interaction with UCS intensity. Low Venturesome subjects showed a greater increase in CR amplitude over trials using a low intensity stimulus, but high venturesome subjects showed a greater increase in CR amplitude using a high intensity UCS. In other words, high thrill seekers conditioned better under high-intensity conditions and low thrill seekers showed more progressive conditioning using low-intensity stimulation. H. Eysenck and Levey (1972) noted similar results for the impulsivity component of extraversion as a function of UCS intensity.

The Imp 2 measure, corresponding to the disinhibition and boredom susceptibility types of sensation seeking, was not related to any of the measures of conditioning. This result was surprising because it is the disinhibition component of sensation seeking that is most highly related to augmenting of the evoked potential and heart rate deceleration versus acceleration; both EP augmenting–reducing and HR acceleration–deceleration represent an intensity effect of stimulation. Interaction effects between Disinhibition and stimulus intensity had been expected rather than the one actually found with Venturesomeness.

Instrumental conditioning

Biofeedback is a form of instrumental conditioning in which a subject learns to control some physiological function by getting perceptible feedback of the function. Stern et al. (1981) exposed high and low sensation seekers to HR feedback and no feedback conditions with instructions to increase their HRs in one condition and decrease them in another. The provision of feedback facilitated both types of learning, but high sensation seekers were better at increasing HR, whereas low sensation seekers were more effective at decreasing HR. High sensation seekers showed more anxiety on a state affect test when using feedback to decrease their HR, whereas low sensation seekers showed an increase in anxiety when increasing their HRs. Conversely, the high sensation seekers showed a decrease in anxiety (toward pleasant affect) in the HR increase condition whereas low sensation seekers decreased in anxiety during the HR decrease condition. The results suggest that increases in cardiac arousal are positively reinforcing for high sensation seekers but aversive for low sensation seekers. This could explain why sensation seekers like to gamble and engage in risky sports that typically raise HRs during anticipatory periods (Anderson & Brown, 1984). The gambler is reinforced by increases in arousal regardless of outcomes.

Ball and Zuckerman (1990) compared high and low sensation seekers in learning concepts using instrumental reward and punishment following correct and incorrect choices. Scales for generalized reward and punishment expectancies (GRAPES) were also used as predictors. On the first concept learning task, prior to a shift in the rewarded attribute, the high sensation seekers were more effective than the lows in learning (trials to criterion). Subjects with low generalized expectancies of punishment also learned better than those with high expectancies of punishment. The SSS Total score correlated negatively with the generalized expectancy of punishment scale. One might attribute the faster learning of the high sensation seekers to their lack of punishment expectancy, except for the fact that subjects high on neuroticism learned faster than stables and neuroticism correlated positively with punishment expectancy. Intelligence was controlled in the analyses without effect on the personality results.

Kish (1967; Kish & Ball, 1968) reported two experiments on word learning by the method of serial anticipation. The subjects in one study were schizophrenics and in the other study they were alcoholics. In both groups of patients the higher sensation seekers made fewer errors and took fewer trials to reach criterion. In the alcoholics the correlations between learning and sensation seeking were still significant after controlling for age and education. Later Kish reported that he was unable to replicate the result in college students. Probably sensation seekers in the clinical groups represented patients who were more alert and more attentive to the learning task. Schizophrenics tend to be low sensation seekers, particularly those who are withdrawn (Chapter 10). Capacity for focused attention is essential in any learning task.

Memory

Smith et al. (1989) tested subjects' recall for neutral words and for low-, medium-, and high-intensity sexual and violent words presented in the auditory mode. During the initial presentation of these words, high sensation seekers had shown stronger skin conductance orienting reactions than low sensation seekers to the high-intensity words but not to the low-intensity ones. Assuming arousal is related to recall, one would expect that high sensation seekers would recall more of the high- and perhaps medium-intensity words, but would not differ from low sensation seekers in recall of low-intensity words. The actual recall performance is shown in Figure 13.2.

High sensation seekers recalled more words than low sensation seekers over all intensities. As expected, the highs recalled more of the high-intensity words than the lows. Unexpectedly, they also recalled more of the low-intensity words. Whereas the low sensation seekers showed a linear relationship between recall and word intensity, the high sensation seekers had a quadratic pattern. No personality differences were found for neutral words suggesting no general memory difference between high and low sensation seekers, but only a difference related to reaction to the content of the words and their effects on arousal during learning exposures.

Barbee et al. (1987) also examined the memory effects of intensity and pleasantness–unpleasantness of words presented visually. The content of the prerated words was not described and presumably they were of diverse meanings. Low sensation seekers recalled more words than highs, but this difference was largely due to the low sensation-seeking females who recalled more words than all other groups. There were no interactions between sensation seeking and valence or intensity of words. The differences between results from this study and the one by Smith et al. may be in the mode of presentation, or the specific sexual and aggressive content of the words in the previous experiment. These words were selected to be of particular interest to sensation seekers. The auditory presentation of words probably has a stronger arousal effect than visual presentation. Barbee et al. suggest that their task may have been boring to many subjects and, if that is so, it might account for the superior performance of low sensation seekers. Low sensation-seeking females may be particularly compliant.

Shaw and Brown (1990) studied a group of attentional deficit–hyperactive (ADH) children with above average intelligence in comparison with a control group of normal children of equivalent intelligence. The ADH children were significantly higher on a sensation-seeking questionnaire for children designed by the authors. On a test of memory for objects, the ADH subjects

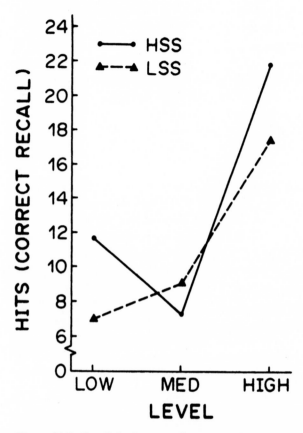

Figure 13.2. Recall for low-, medium-, and high-intensity words by high and low sensation seekers. From "Sensation seeking and arousal: Effects of strong stimulation on electrodermal activation and memory task performance," by B. D. Smith et al., 1989, *Personality and Individual Differences, 10,* fig. 6, p. 676. Copyright 1989 by Pergamon Press. Reprinted by permission.

recalled fewer focally presented objects than the controls but did not differ from controls in memory for peripherally presented objects, which they had been instructed to ignore. The authors interpreted the results as indicating that the ADH children were distracted by the peripheral objects and allowed their attention to wander in defiance of instructions. The ADH children subsequently solved more anagrams, which could have been due to a priming effect of the previous memory task because the words in the anagrams represented the peripheral objects. Similarly, the ADH children showed a superior use of incidental information in memory for placements of animals in backgrounds when they had been instructed to remember just the names of the animals. The experiment showed that the deficits of ADH children stem from their broad scanning style. When memory for incidental information is required or provides useful cues for subsequent tasks, they show superiority to the normal children. This study did not directly compare these differences to sensation seeking per se, but it would not be surprising if this component of the ADH personality is related to the same cognitive styles.

Laterality of information processing

Shaw and Brown (1990) found striking differences between their high sensation-seeking ADH children and the control group in laterality: 15 of 16 controls were strongly right-handed in contrast to only 7 of the 16 ADH children. More ADH children also showed atypical eye dominance. But Cohen and Merkelback (1987) and Ball and Zuckerman (1992) found no difference between high and low sensation seekers in ear dominance in the dichotic listening test. Braverman and Farley (1978) presented both text and pictures in pictorial form and found that retention of verbal and pictorial information were correlated in high but not in low sensation seekers. This could suggest that there is a stronger connection between right brain (pictorial) and left brain (semantic) processing in the high sensation seeker or that high sensation seekers use an encoding process that translates pictorial information into verbal units, as suggested by the authors.

Cognitive abilities and styles

Intelligence and academic performance

Table 13.1 shows the correlations between SSS scores and intelligence as measured by the Wechsler Adult Intelligence Scale (WAIS) or Scholastic Aptitude (SAT) in samples of high school and college students, delinquents, and former drug abusers. Total or General SSS shows low but significant correlation with full scale WAIS IQ and SAT total (verbal and quantitative) scores in all but one of the five samples with correlations ranging between .19 and .33. The subscale showing the most consistent correlation with intelligence is Boredom Susceptibility with only one of the five correlations falling below .20, and three of the five reaching significant levels.

Only one of the correlations was negative, the one between disinhibition

Table 13.1. *Correlations between Wechsler Adult Intelligence Scale (WAIS) Full Scale IQ and Scholastic Aptitude (SAT) and Sensation Seeking Scale (SSS)*

SSS	WAIS FS-IQ			SAT-Total (verbal + quantitative)[d]	
	High school students[a] (n = 138)	Drug abusers[b] (n = 80)	Juvenile delinquents[c] (n = 34)	College males (n = 200)	College females (n = 200)
General/Total	.22*	.29**	.33	.19*	.19*
TAS	.11	.38**	.00	.13	.16*
ES	.34**	.21*	.14	.18**	.02
Dis	.19*	.11	.38*	−.07	−.14*
BS	.21*	.23*	.32	.20**	.10

Note: TAS = Thrill and Adventure Seeking; ES = Experience Seeking; Dis = Disinhibition; BS = Boredom Susceptibility.
[a] Buchsbaum & Murphy, personal communication, 1974.
[b] Carrol & Zuckerman (1977).
[c] Cohen et al. (1983).
[d] Pemberton, personal communication, 1970.
*p < .05.
**p < .01.
Source: Adapted from table 8.2, p. 234, from *Sensation seeking: Beyond the optimal level of arousal,* by M. Zuckerman, 1979. Hillsdale, NJ: Erlbaum. Copyright 1979 by Lawrence Erlbaum Associates. Reprinted by permission.

and SAT score in the female college group tested by Pemberton. Disinhibition also correlated negatively with grades in females as well as in males. But experience seeking, which correlated positively with intelligence in males, also correlated negatively with grades. During the time these students were tested in the early 1970s drug use was rampant and the sexual revolution had arrived in Delaware. Experience seeking and disinhibition correlated with both sexual experience and drug use in data collected at the university during the same period. It is not unlikely that the grades of the sensation seeking first year students, even the more intelligent experience-seeking ones, were suffering because of their extracurricular interests.

During the same period Anderson (1973) studied the relationship between sensation seeking and academic ability and performance in a Canadian high school. High sensation-seeking students (General and Boredom Susceptibility scales) had higher academic ability, as indexed by an academic aptitude test; but those who were high on disinhibition had lower academic achievement and those who scored high on experience seeking had more class absences.

Sensation seekers, particularly experience seekers, in college populations tend to be somewhat more intelligent than low sensation seekers, but their "openness to experience" is not limited to academic studies and their boredom susceptibility may make drugs, sex, and parties more attractive than tedious studies.

Cognitive styles

Intelligence has been associated with speed of mental processing, even using fairly simple or choice reaction times. But on many intellectual tasks there is a trade-off between speed and accuracy. Given the close association between sensation seeking and impulsivity, high sensation seekers might be expected to favor speed at the expense of accuracy.

The Matching Familiar Figures Test (MFFT; Kagan, 1966) provides a test of cognitive impulsivity in terms of the trade-off between speed and accuracy. Cohen et al. (1983) correlated this test with the SSS in several samples. The General SSS correlated negatively with errors in three of the five samples, but these correlations became insignificant when controlled for education, age, and intelligence. There was no correlation with latency of response. Thus, there is no evidence that high sensation seekers are cognitively impulsive in their reactions. An interesting footnote is that high sensation seekers have faster decision times in choosing between the forced choices in the SSS items themselves (Rogers, 1987). In this case, however, there is no explicit set for accuracy although subjects are requested to give honest answers and not to dwell too long on the questions.

Necka (1991) compared high and low sensation seekers on a choice reaction time test. One stimulus, an arrow with an "N" in it, required the subject to push a joystick in the direction of the arrow. This was termed the "normal" condition. A second letter required the subject to push the joystick in the opposite direction to the arrow (called the "abnormal condition"). A third letter signaled the subject to push the response stick in a perpendicular direction; this was called a "superabnormal" condition. Reaction times lengthened going from the normal to the superabnormal conditions since the abnormal and superabnormal required more nonhabitual responses. High sensation-seeking subjects were faster in reactions overall. The highs did not differ from lows in accuracy during the normal and abnormal conditions, but they made fewer errors in reaction than the lows during the abnormal condition. In this study there was no trade-off between speed and accuracy for the high sensation seekers. They were both faster than and as accurate as lows in response, and even more accurate in the most complicated condition.

Category breadth

Broad categorizers tolerate diversity in their constructs and tend to be "over-inclusive" (Zuckerman, 1979a). Several studies using Pettigrew's (1958) category width test showed a relationship between category width and sensation seeking in males, but only one of four studies found a significant relationship in women.

Cognitive complexity–simplicity

In order to include more instances in a construct, one must be able to entertain more complex constructs. In Chapter 8 studies were described that showed that high sensation seekers tended to prefer complex visual stimuli, whereas low sensation seekers preferred simpler stimuli. Domangue (1984) extended these findings to the cognitive realm, using a structured form of Kelly's Role Construct Repertory test. She measured the extent to which subjects used a variety of concepts in describing their friends. High sensation seekers showed greater cognitive complexity in interpersonal description. There is also the possibility that their friends really do represent a greater variation of traits than those of low sensation seekers.

Originality and creativity

Divergent thinking, curiosity, and a tolerance for complexity and ambiguity are traits involved in creativity. Creativity by definition involves new and original solutions to problems. Studies described in the previous volume on sensation seeking (Zuckerman, 1979a) showed that sensation seeking was directly related to various tests of cognitive innovation, variety, and originality. A recent study by Okamoto and Takari (1992) found a substantial correlation ($r = .54$) between a Japanese translation of the SSS and the Picture Creation test of creativity. McCrae (1987) correlated performance tests of divergent thinking (associational fluency, expressional fluency, ideational fluency, word fluency, and obvious and remote consequences) with various personality scales including the SSS form V. The SS Total score was significantly correlated with the total score of the divergent thinking tasks. Because the ES subscale of the SSS is the one primarily related to the Openness to

Experience scale of the NEO (Chapter 3), and to preferences for complexity (Chapter 8), it would be expected to have a much higher relationship to divergent thinking than the other SS scales. But McCrae's results show nearly equal and significant correlations between divergent thinking and all of the SS subscales. Divergent thinking is apparently a general characteristic of sensation seeking rather than a specific characteristic of the experience-seeking subtype.

Paranormal beliefs and experiences

Davis, Peterson, and Farley (1973) found a moderate correlation between belief in psychic phenomena in males and a weaker but significant correlation in female college students. However, these subjects were all enrolled in a special class in creativity and this was during the early 1970s when there was a general interest in odd beliefs. Given the openness of sensation seekers to novel experience and their interest in altered states of consciousness produced by drugs or psychological techniques, it would not be surprising to find a predilection for unusual beliefs among them. More recent studies, however, have found little correlation between sensation seeking and beliefs in para-normal phenomena, including witchcraft, spiritualism, and extraterrestrials on earth (Glicksohn, 1990; Tobacyk & Milford, 1983). However, Kumar et al. (1993) and Tobacyk and Milford (1983) have found some weak relation-ships between sensation seeking and a belief in psi phenomena, like mental telepathy and psychokinesis. Sensation seekers also tend to report having "paranormal" experiences and states of altered consciousness. Glickson (1991) also found that subjects scoring high on the ES scale of the SSS reported more "altered states of consciousness" in a homogeneous, invariant sensory environment (a visual *Ganzfeld* with constant white noise) than low experience seekers. The primary reason that sensation seekers tend to use hallucinogenic drugs is to have such experiences. High sensation seekers do not tend to be spiritual or religious, but they are often attracted to ideas that are outside the realm of normal science and experiences that are far outside the boundaries of day-to-day experiences.

Summary

Sensation seekers have a strong capacity to focus attention on a stimulus or task. Unlike low sensation seekers, their performance does not suffer when competing stimuli or extraneous tasks are introduced. In some instances a distraction or unusual challenge in the primary task may enhance their performance or at least counteract the influence of habituation and boredom. Presumably, they are able to shift attention rapidly between the primary and secondary tasks. A perceptual analogue of this is found in their rapid rate of alternation between reversible figures.

The theories of sensitivity and reactivity are based on the idea of individual differences in nervous system response to different intensities of stimulation. There is some evidence that high sensation seekers are less sensitive at the low end of the intensity continuum and more tolerant of high-intensity stimulation. However, these findings are largely confined to the auditory dimension. Cross-modality consistency in stimulus regulation traits is rarely found and this is a limitation to the constructs.

Although impulsivity seems to be related to classical conditioning (eyelid reflex), the associated trait of sensation seeking is not. However, high sensation seekers tend to learn faster than lows with instrumental conditioning of certain kinds. They also seem to benefit more from peripheral cues not directly associated with the immediate learning task. Memory for such cues as well as for high-intensity words is better than in low sensation seekers. It is as if the high sensation seeker has a broad scanning style that takes in much more information than is contained in the immediate focus of the task. Learning and memory in high sensation seekers depend on the challenge or interest in the task. When there is a low level of challenge, their performance may drop below the level of low sensation seekers, but when challenge is great, their performance is better than that of low sensation seekers.

There are low but significant correlations between general intelligence and sensation seeking. The need for change in experience and the capacity to be bored by repetition are the elements of sensation seeking associated with intelligence. Despite the low positive correlation with intelligence, sensation seeking is either not correlated with grades or in the case of disinhibition or experience seeking is negatively related to academic achievement. The likely answer to this paradox is that sensation seeking needs are usually not met in the classroom learning situation, but instead find expression in extracurricular activities. The brighter sensation seekers can often alternate between the two kinds of activities without much loss of efficiency in learning. Academic achievement in the less gifted sensation seeker probably suffers as a consequence of the competition between the classroom and the barroom.

Cognitive styles associated with sensation seeking include a tendency for broad cognitive generalization and a tendency to use more complex cognitive categories in contrast to the use of a narrower range of simpler constructs in the lows. This may be one reason why low sensation seekers tend to be more dogmatic, conservative, and religious than high sensation seekers. Openness to new experience is a requisite for creativity in any field. Sensation seekers tend to be original and innovative in open-ended problem solving, whereas low sensation seekers tend to be too rigid and unimaginative. Their openness and readiness to include many kinds of diverse phenomena under broad constructs may also explain why high sensation seekers are so ready to accept unusual ideas and certain kinds of belief in paranormal phenomena outside the boundaries of both conventional religion and science. Like Hamlet, they say: "There are more things between heaven and earth, Horatio, Than are dreamt of in your philosophy" (Shakespeare, *Hamlet*, act 1, scene 5).

14

New theoretical models

Biology is truly a realm of limitless possibilities; we have the most surprising revelations to expect from it, and cannot conjecture what answers it will offer in some decades to the questions we have put to it. Perhaps they may be such as to overthrow the whole artificial structure of [psychological] hypotheses.

—S. Freud (1920/1958)

The first sensation-seeking scale was developed more than 30 years ago with the narrow validity goal of predicting responses to a specific experimental situation: sensory deprivation. The scale was based on the theoretical premise of the existence of consistent individual differences in optimal levels of stimulation and cortical arousal. Research on the scale (SSS II) was soon extended into other areas far beyond the initial aims for the scale. It was soon apparent that sensation seeking was not just another ad hoc trait measure, but was central to a basic dimension of personality and predictive of a wide variety of life experiences, behaviors, preferences, and attitudes. Recent factor analyses of the subscales of the SSS, together with many other scales, have shown that sensation seeking, together with impulsivity and lack of socialization, constitutes part of the core of Hans and Sybil Eysenck's (1976) *P dimension* of personality in the three-factor model and is strongly related to the *conscientiousness* trait in Costa and McCrae's (1985) five-factor model.

The research on sensory deprivation conducted in the 1960s and the first factor analyses of the SSS items convinced us that the essence of the trait was a need for changing, novel, and complex sensations and experiences. More recently, intensity has been added to the list of characteristics of sensations sought by sensation seekers, although this attribute of sensation may be more specific to the subtrait of disinhibition than to general experience seeking. High disinhibiters seem to have an insensitivity to weak stimulation and a high tolerance for strong visual and auditory stimuli.

The willingness to take physical and social risks in order to have arousing experiences was a corollary of the postulated trait, but not an essential aspect of the trait. Sensation seekers enjoy many kinds of experiences, as in music, art, and the media, that are not at all risky. When they do take risks, it is generally not the point of the activity and they seek to minimize the risk. They are more likely to have more varied sexual experience, for instance, but are not more likely to avoid the use of condoms. Male sensation seekers are more likely to drive fast but are not more likely to avoid using their seat belts. Mountain climbers and parachutists are high sensation seekers, but they take full advantage of any safety equipment and check their gear carefully before climbing or jumping. They do not consider what they are doing as very risky because they are confident in their own abilities and equipment. Drug users do not attempt to see how much of the drug they can ingest without overdosing. Of course, when impulsivity is combined with sensation seeking there may be an insensitivity to the risk and a lack of planning. But even nonimpulsive sensation seekers sometimes miscalculate the risks with fatal consequences.

There are two notable exceptions to the generalization that risk is not the primary source of positive arousal for sensation seekers. Pathological gamblers only enjoy gambling when the risk is high in terms of the sums of money bet. Certain types of antisocial personalities seem to derive their excitement from taking unnecessary risks when commiting crimes.

Low sensation seekers are not generally anxious or neurotic; their risk aversion is based on conservative attitudes. They simply do not see the sense or reward in the experiences engaged in by high sensation seekers. Low sensation seekers do have a tendency to see more risk in such situations and anticipate they would feel anxious rather than elated if they were to enter into these situations, but they are not necessarily anxious in everyday social situations. Sensation seeking and social anxiety or neuroticism are separate and independent traits. Sensation seeking is not the mere absence of anxiety.

The only thing constant in the life of high sensation seekers is change. They change activities, sexual and marital partners, and drugs, just as they switch from one channel to another if compelled to watch television for any length of time. What is the source of their need for varied and novel stimulation and their boredom susceptibility and restlessness when exposed to constant and predictable stimulation?

Psychophysiology

A clue to the basis of the trait in arousability comes from experiments on the strength and persistence of the orienting reflex (OR). When they are first exposed to a stimulus they show a strong OR compared with low sensation seekers, indicating a high degree of focused attention. But when the stimulus is presented a second or third time their response weakens and is no greater than that of low sensation seekers, unless the stimulus is of some special significance or interest to them. Sexual stimuli, for instance, may maintain their stronger ORs over more exposures. In contrast, the low sensation seeker is less aroused by the first presentation of the novel stimulus but shows a more gradual decline in responsivity over trials. If a strong reactivity to novelty is part of the genetically determined aspect of sensation seeking, then the optimal level of arousal may be set by the characteristic level of arousal reached in response to a novel stimulus. Anything less arousing may be regarded as bland or "boring." Repetition of stimulation produces an unconditioned inhibition or "habituation." Introduction of a novel stimulus *disinhibits* response to a previous habituated stimulus. High sensation seekers may seek novelty in order to renew their levels of arousal, just as a smoker takes another puff from a cigarette in order to send a new dose of nicotine to the brain as arousal from the previous dose subsides. This kind of explanation in terms of an optimal level of cortical arousal was compatible with the earlier theories of sensation seeking but not with certain findings that led "beyond the optimal level of arousal."

The brain of the high sensation seeker may be more accessible to novel or intense stimuli. There is a natural cortical protection again overstimulation as reflected in the reduction of cortical arousal in response to very intense stimulation. Fainting can result when pain is sharp and sudden. The strength of the inhibitory process can be assessed by the method of augmenting–reducing of cortical evoked potentials in response to an extended range of stimuli. This research has shown that the disinhibiter type of sensation seeker continues to show an augmented cortical evoked potential at levels of stimulation where the low disinhibiter shows reduced cortical potentials. Augmenting is positively associated with the appetite and tolerance for intense stimuli. The augmenting reaction represents a natural psychophysiological reaction to increases in intensity of stimulation. It is the reducing inhibitory reaction that demands a more basic explanation in the form of the pharmacology of the neural systems involved.

The dorsal ascending noradrenergic system originating in the locus coeruleus has direct pathways to all parts of the cerebral cortex and serves a general arousal function. It is especially responsive to novel signals of uncertain significance. Tonic CSF levels of norepinephrine are lower in high sensation seekers than in low sensation seekers. Low norepinephrine levels in the brain may be associated with states of boredom and sensation seekers are highly susceptible to boredom. Novel *and* intense stimuli provide a phasic activation of the noradrenergic system bringing the high sensation seekers closer to their optimal levels of catecholamine system arousal, as shown in Figure 14.1. But arousal produced by a stimulus is transient and

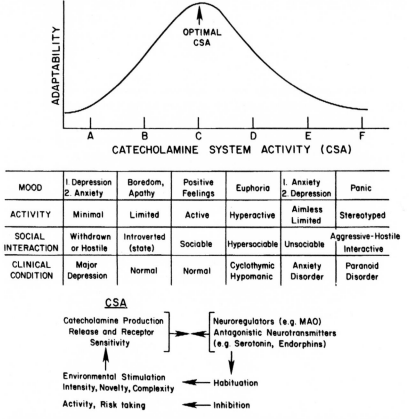

Figure 14.1. Levels of catecholamine systems activity (CSA) and associated mood, activity, social interaction, and psychopathology. From "Sensation seeking: A comparative approach to a human trait," by M. Zuckerman, 1984, *Behavioral and Brain Sciences, 7,* fig. 6, p. 431. Copyright 1984 by Cambridge University Press.

the sensation seeker needs to search for new stimuli to reininstitute the state of heightened arousal.

Inhaling cigarette smoke also produces transient states of arousal that are under the control of the smoker. After inhaling the smoke the nicotine quickly moves from the lungs to the brain. When arousal begins to decline, the smoker takes another "drag" on the cigarette. In a similar manner the high sensation seekers must find another novel stimulus to renew their arousal peaks. When stimulation ceases or becomes constant, catecholamine system arousal quickly declines.

Inhibitory processes, such as habituation and satiation, reduce arousal. Whereas repetition of stimuli reduces arousal, novel stimuli disinhibit response to a habituated stimulus. Familiar stimuli in a new context also disinhibit response. Stimulant drugs counteract the effects of inhibition. Disinhibition constitutes one of the major subtypes of sensation seeking. The term *disinhibition* refers to disinhibition of behavior, but it also has a physiological connotation. High disinhibiters are distinguished from lows by a stronger heart rate orientation reaction to novel stimuli but with rapid habituation when stimuli are repeated. Disinhibiters are also characterized by the capacity of the cortex to respond to intense stimuli that elicit cortical inhibition in low disinhibiters. But are the responses to novelty and intensity qualities of stimuli distinctive or related? Correlations between HR-orienting and cortical augmenting reactions or between defensive and reducing responses are low, but there is some relationship (Zuckerman, Simons, & Como, 1988). The fact that both types of reactions are related to the sensation-seeking subscale of Disinhibition suggests that they may represent different aspects of a common biological mechanism.

Gonadal hormones

Gonadal hormones affect personality in both direct and indirect ways. Prenatal gonadal hormones affect the developing brain of the fetus. Girls exposed to excessive testosterone during the fetal period exhibit more typically masculine patterns of play after birth. Compared with girls of their own age and their own female siblings, they tend to prefer "rough-and-tumble" play to "dolls" and "house" (Ehrhardt et al., 1968). Similar gender reversed play effects have been found in boys exposed to estrogen during the prenatal period. It is often assumed that differences in play behavior and interests prior to puberty are entirely a function of socialization. The biological environment of the womb, however, is part of the nonshared environment for siblings, other than twins. Interestingly, genetic studies of masculinity–femininity, as a test measured trait, show hardly any heritability and, unlike most other personality traits, some influence of shared environment (Zuckerman, 1991a).

Sex differences in the Thrill and Adventure Seeking and Disinhibition subscales of the SSS could be due to differences in gonadal hormones. Gonadal hormones in males are related to sensation seeking, particularly disinhibition, and testosterone is related to masculinity (on the Bem scale)

(Daitzman & Zuckerman, 1980). Furthermore, gonadal hormones in males correlate negatively with socialization and self-control. Disinhibition is itself correlated with asocial tendencies and lack of behavioral control.

A more direct influence of gonadal hormones is seen in sexual behavior. Testosterone correlates positively with variety and number of sexual partners in young, single males, and with reported sexual gratification, sexual responsivity during intercourse, and frequency of intercourse in married women (Persky et al., 1982). Sexual experience, of course, represents a major mode of sensation seeking (Chapter 7).

Gonadal hormones can themselves be influenced by immediate experiences, increased by sexual stimulation and lowered by stress, an example of the "chicken-or-egg" quandry. However, measures of gonadal hormones are reliable when measured in the same individuals at the same time of day so they do have the characteristics of traits, even if they are influenced by intense stimulation and subject to normal diurnal variation.

Gonadal hormones probably play a role in the development of sensation seeking from childhood to adult life. Testoserone peaks in males during late adolescence at the same time as sensation-seeking trait peaks. Both sensation seeking and testosterone decline gradually in males from that peak to old age. Some part of the decline in sensation seeking could be accounted for by diminished testosterone. Aggressiveness in men and criminality in psychopaths also decline with age. Perhaps, the general conservatism and reduced risk taking characteristic of older persons are due as much to changes in their biology as to the cumulation of acquired wisdom.

Gonadal hormones increase arousal by lowering MAO levels in the brain. Thus, the decline of sensation seeking with age could also be due to the increased level of MAO in the brain and decreased dopamine levels as well as to the direct effects of gonadal hormones on brain. The decrease in dopamine in the brain may be, in part, a function of the catabolic reactions of increased levels of type B MAO in the dopamine neuron. Dopamine function is important in sexual arousability and may be also important in sensation seeking as well as impulsivity and sociability.

Monoamines and their regulators

The serotonin metabolite 5-HIAA and the enzymes MAO and DBH are elevated in cortical EP reducers and a selective inhibitor of serotonin uptake increases EP augmenting (von Knorring & Johansson, 1980). The latter finding suggests that serotonin may be a neurochemical basis of disinhibition.

Serotonin seems to serve a general behavioral inhibitory function as indicated by the results of both animal experiments and human clinical studies. Although no direct relationship has been found between sensation seeking and the serotonin metabolite 5-HIAA, 5-HIAA is negatively related to the P scale, the marker for the broad dimension (ImpUSS) of which sensation seeking is one component. The serotonergic system may be responsible for the tendency of low sensation seekers to deliberate about possible risks and consequences of an activity. The high sensation seeker acts impulsively without thought of negative outcomes. In this respect the high sensation seeker resembles the psychopath, the difference being that psychopaths have little concern for others as well as themselves, whereas the high sensation seekers may consider the possibility of harm to others if not to themselves.

Low MAO is another biological characteristic of EP augmenters, high sensation seekers, impulsives, delinquents, and drug users. MAO is regarded by some as a direct marker for the serotonergic system, because it is localized in heavily serotonergic areas of the brain. However, the type B MAO, found in platelets is found primarily in dopamine containing neurons in the primate brain. High levels of MAO are associated with lower levels of activity and sociability as well as sensation seeking. Perhaps a low level of MAO deregulates the dopamine systems associated with activity in the pursuit of reward. Unstable catecholamine activity is a characteristic of bipolar disorders, and there are many trait, behavioral and biological links between bipolar disorder and sensation seeking. Perhaps sensation seekers have a dopamine system that is alternatively over- or underactive, depending on current levels of activity and stimulation. The high sensation seekers might seek intense or novel stimulation, or drugs that directly activate the dopaminergic systems.

Figure 14.2 shows a psychopharmacological model for the broad P-Imp-USS trait. P-ImpUSS involves three behavioral mechanisms: strong approach and weak inhibition and arousal mechanisms. The mesolimbic dopamine system, extending from the ventral tegmental area to the nucleus accumbens through the medial forebrain bundle and lateral hypothalamus and ascending to frontal cortex, is the basis of the approach mechanism and its orientation to potential rewards in the environment. The nigrostriatal dopamine pathways to the basal ganglia are involved in the motivated initiation of behavior and the impetus for motor activity in general. The serotonergic system originating in the raphé nucleus and eventually reaching limbic and cortical areas and descending pathways from the frontal cortex may mediate behavioral inhibition and emotional regulation. The noradrenergic dorsal tegmental bundle originating in the locus coeruleus influences cortical arousal through ascending pathways and stimulates peripheral autonomic arousal through de-

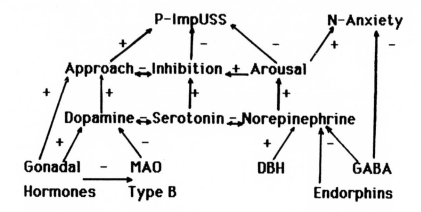

Figure 14.2. A psychopharmacological model for Impulsive Unsocialized Sensation Seeking (ImpUSS) and Neuroticism-Anxiety (N-Anxiety) with underlying behavioral and physiological mechanisms (Approach, Inhibition, and Arousal) and neurotransmitters, enzymes, and hormones involved. MAO = monoamine oxidase, DBH = dopamine-beta-hydroxylase, GABA = gamma-aminobutyric acid. Interactions between behavioral and biochemical factors indicated (+) for agonistic and (−) for antagonistic actions. Single-headed arrows indicate the hypothesized direction of influence; double-headed arrows indicate a two-way interaction between the factors.

scending pathways from limbic centers. Arousal from this system is one component of anxiety; the others are the influences of GABA, endorphins, and the enzyme DBH, which is involved in the production of norepinephrine from dopamine.

All of these neurotransmitters, enzymes, and hormones influence the strength of the three behavioral mechanisms involved in P-ImpUSS and therefore should be related to the trait as well. P-ImpUSS should be related to a strong dopaminergic system (or a deregulated one), and weak or unreactive serotonergic and noradrenergic systems. (When we say that a system is weak or strong or reactive or underreactive, there is no presumption of the specific neural mechanisms involved. It could be the production of the neurotransmitter, or the enzymes controlling production, the sensitivity or number of postsynaptic receptors, the sensitivity of presynaptic receptors regulating production through a negative feedback system, the catabolism mechanism as regulated by enzymes like MAO, or other factors. Any or all of these factors could contribute to the differences in activity or reactivity of a neurotransmitter system.)

Different combinations of the three monoamines could result in the same net behavioral result in different persons and this could attenuate the correlational results with any one neurotransmitter or its metabolite. The three monoamines interact at the cellular level as well. Thus far, correlational results with transmitters or metabolites in the cerebrospinal fluid support the hypothesis of a weak noradrenergic system in high sensation seekers and reduced serotonergic activity in unsocialized or impulsively violent persons. High testosterone and low MAO and DBH levels and endorphins have been found to be characteristic of sensation seekers in some studies. Experimental results using dopamine precursors and blockers also link sensation seeking and impulsivity to active or reactive dopamine systems. The model is a complex, involving interactions at the biochemical and behavioral levels as well as between them. But as Crick (1988, pp. 138–139) so aptly put it:

What is found in biology is *mechanisms,* mechanisms built with chemical components and that are modified by other, later mechanisms added to the earlier ones. While Occam's razor is a useful tool in the physical sciences, it can be a very dangerous implement in biological research. . . . To produce a really good biological theory one must try to see through the clutter produced by evolution to the basic mechanisms lying beneath them, realizing that they are likely to be overlaid by other secondary mechanisms. What seems to physicists to be a hopelessly complicated process may have been what nature found simplist, because nature could only build on what was there.

Development

Recent work in behavioral genetics suggests the importance of genotype–environment correlation in comparison with genotype–environment interaction. The latter refers to independent effects of the environment on tendencies stemming from the genotype. The former (genotype–environment correlation) proposes that the phenotype influenced by the genotype is selectively responsive to the environment, choosing from activities and associates that are congruent with the genotype. It might be said that the genotype is "self-actualizing" through the phenotype.

Let us use the enzyme MAO as an example. MAO is highly heritable and its behavioral effects are seen quite early in life (Sostek et al., 1981). Infants low in MAO are more active than high MAO infants in the first three days of life. Later they may become the spontaneous children who approach novel stimuli and persons. High MAO children may be more tentative when confronted with novel situations or people and less adaptable to changes in routine. As the child matures, the characteristic reactions to novelty may become more apparent in risk-taking, sensation-seeking kinds of behaviors.

If parents are high sensations seekers themselves they are likely to encourage sensation-seeking exploration in their children (with appropriate risk management), but if they are low sensation seekers they may be frightened by potential risks and attempt to discourage sensation seeking in their children. Their success will depend on the strength of the genetic disposition in the child. Recently, ImpSS in college students was related to their account of relationships with their parents using standardized scales measuring parental love, punishment, and control (Zuckerman, Kraft, & Cummings, 1993). Paternal punishment was significantly correlated with ImpSS in two different samples. If we assume the accuracy of the children's reports of parental behavior, how should such results be interpreted? It seems more plausible that the father's punishment was a response to a rebellious, impulsive, sensation-seeking child than that punishment somehow produces sensation seeking. Judging from the correlation, a father's punishment is not very effective in suppressing impulsive sensation-seeking tendencies.

Children who are of moderate or average sensation-seeking disposition will be the most influenced by parental modeling and reinforcement. Those who are extremely high in the disposition can be best guided by diversion into safe expressions of the trait and activities that provide high stimulation at minimal risk rather than punishing any manifestation of the trait. Those who are extremely low in the disposition can be gently encouraged and gradually desensitized to overcome their natural cautiousness. Wise parents respect the natural temperament of their children and work with what they have been given. Both the extreme environmentalist and the extreme nativist may have difficulty if their children are not what they would like them to be, but the environmentalists overestimate and the nativists underestimate their potential influence on their children.

The lack of shared environmental influence in the genetical analyses of sensation seeking suggests that peer influences may be more influential than parental ones. While one cannot select one's parents, there is more choice among friends and peers. The high sensation seeker will be drawn to adventurous and disinhibited peers, and the low sensation seeker will be more attracted to conforming and conservative groups. Role models among teachers and other authority figures may have a more immediate effect on the low sensation seekers, but possibly a delayed effect on high sensation seekers depending on their abilities and reinforcements in school. Once one has chosen a peer group, that group, particularly its leaders, will model and reinforce the behavioral expectations for the group. Later, the selection of a marital partner is strongly influenced by the sensation-seeking traits of that partner.

The sensation seeker learns new forms of expression for that need, whether in sports, sex, social expressions, drugs, or crime. In the low sensation-seeking groups, sensation-seeking forms of behavior are discouraged. Socioeconomic aspects of environment determine the range of possible sensation-seeking expressions. In the middle- or upper-class environments, there is a greater range of sensation-seeking possibilities available in sports, cars, and travel, whereas possibilities in the lower-class environments may be limited to sex, drugs, gambling, and crime. Good education could open the possibilities for experience-seeking types in any class, but in the lower socioeconomic classes education is likely to be focused on the pragmatics of job preparation rather than the challenges of cognitive complexity. Early environmental opportunities may influence whether one becomes a business entrepreneur or a drug dealer, a professional artist or a graffiti artist, an Olympic skier or a criminal. We are aware of the conspicuous exceptions like the upper-class drug dealer and the lower-class athlete or artist, but the vast majority will find expressions of sensation seeking from those typical of the culture in which they develop. Low sensation seekers will usually find it easier to adapt since there are always niches for the conformist in any culture, particularly in institutions like school or church.

Social learning

Social learning and biological determination are often regarded as opposite and incompatible explanations of behavior, but they are not, as was pointed out in the discussion of genotype–environment correlation. Just as humans are "biologically prepared" to learn certain types of fears, (such as fear of snakes, heights, or fire) individuals are probably biologically disposed to "learn" to be aggressive, sociable, or sensation seeking. But within our species individual variation in biology may also predispose learning of particular kinds of behavior. The genetic code is written on the "tabula rasa" and therefore the slate is not really blank.

Risk takers are attracted to peers seen as equally adventurous (Horvath & Zuckerman, 1993). High sensation seekers tend to date and marry other high sensation seekers and lows tend to marry lows. Both peer attraction and assortative mating illustrate the genotype–environment correlation. Observational learning is guided by observed outcomes (Bandura, 1986). Although sensation seekers may be attracted to groups or individuals because of anticipated rewards, they may learn from observed negative outcomes for others in the group or may experience such outcomes themselves. Children growing up in a home where alcohol or drugs are abused may learn to imitate that behavior if the outcomes they observe are relatively benign, but they may also shun the behaviors if they associate them with unpleasant consequences for themselves or others. If personal experience with risky behavior is lacking, the person may seek information about outcomes from general sources. In this case the strength of the sensation-seeking disposition might result in the person attending more closely to reported reward outcomes and ignoring punishment outcomes. Often there are two conflicting messages: "Just say no" from parents and authorities and "Try it, you'll like it" from peers and media models. Biological predispositions may determine which message prevails.

Sensation seekers show a tendency to attend more strongly to stimuli relevant to their interests and needs (Smith et al., 1986). Donohew et al. (1991) have used this selectivity to design television messages against drug use that will appeal to high sensation seekers (who are the primary ones at risk for drug abuse). The fact that a much smaller proportion of high male sensation seekers is smoking in the 1980s as compared with the 1970s (Zuckerman et al., 1990) suggests that they can process risk information and turn from one expression of sensation seeking to another (but unfortunately not always a healthier one). Where once society only offered war as a thrill and adventure-seeking activity for young men, a variety of activities, described in this book, can provide the physical sensations and excitement that attract men to war.

Most sociobiology is an essentially untestable metaphor. Although the evolutionary premises concerning natural selection are reasonable, there is no way to look back to the Pleistocence era to observe the "natural" behavior patterns of our species and to know their adaptive significance at that time. Some of the problems faced then are not now applicable or are drastically changed by the different circumstances of urban society, mobility, and technology. Unless one can equate a trip to the supermarket with "foraging," and the fight with colleagues for research space with "territoriality," we are just dealing with metaphors. Metaphors have their use in science if they lead to testable hypotheses, but to test a sociobiological metaphor one needs very broad cross-cultural sampling to establish universality. The variety .of social behavior observed in different cultures by anthropologists is remarkable and suggests that there are any number of solutions to a particular environmental challenge, and the one selected at a given time may change within a generation to a new one, but not through biological selection.

In this sociobiological sense, the high sensation seeker is a hunter and the low sensation seeker is a farmer. Hunters are positively excited by change, danger, and the variety and unpredictability of the hunt. They need a strong capacity to focus attention on the prey while remaining alert to other factors like the direction of the wind and the movements of other hunters. Farmers, in contrast, depend on stability of the environment (rainfall, sun, and other seasonal regularities of climate). Plants grow slowly and require patience and tedious kinds of labor to insure their survival. Great religions arose in order to exert control over the unpredictability of the natural environment by placating sometimes irrational gods. The sensation seeker–hunter types, with their susceptibility to boredom, became a liability except in times of war. Many societies evolved a class of professional soldiers to accommodate the high sensation-seeking types.

Overview

Sensation seeking is part of a broader trait called impulsive-sensation seeking (Zuckerman et al., 1988; Zuckerman et al., 1991). Underlying ImpSS, as well as extraversion, is a mechanism that might be called *approach*. The trait has obvious adaptive significance. In obtaining food or mates, or competing with others for these goals, the animal or human must leave the shelter of its burrow, nest, or cave, and approach animate or inanimate objects in a potentially dangerous environment.

Sensation seeking represents the optimistic tendency to approach novel stimuli and explore the environment. Impulsivity is a style of rapid decision making in deciding to approach. Sociability is the tendency to approach social objects, whether familiar or strangers. All three of these traits are involved in the general approach disposition. Persons low on the trait tend to withdraw under circumstances where the stimuli are too novel, or the anticipated outcome is too uncertain. Because unfamiliar persons pose a particular kind of uncertainty, low ImpSS types also tend to be shy or unsocial as well as low in impulsivity and sensation seeking.

All three components of approach – sensation seeking, impulsivity, and sociability – have a genetic basis accounting for from 40% to 60% of the variance in the phenomenal traits. The model suggests that underlying the trait at the biological level are the monoamine neurotransmitters and the gonadal hormones. Dopamine in the nigrostriatal system energizes active exploration of the social and physical environment, and in the mesolimbic system it provides the positive arousal and reward associated with novel and intense stimulation. Low levels of MAO in high sensation seekers, sociables, and impulsives are indicators of an active or deregulated dopaminergic system. Norepinephine in the dorsal tegmental bundle originating in the locus coeruleus provides the arousal associated with novel and intense stimuli and amplifies the reaction to such stimuli. It also accounts for the enhanced capacity for focused attention without significant loss of attention to nonfocal stimuli found in the high sensation seeker. Serotonin in the pathway originating in the medial raphé nucleus is involved in the inhibition of behavior in the presence of novel or potentially threatening stimuli. Its behavioral function is neither approach or withdrawal but immobility or indecisiveness. The interactions of these three monoamines, as well as the enzymes like DBH and MAO that regulate their production and catabolism, and the concentration and sensitivity of receptors involved in their regulation, are determinants of the broad approach tendency and the specific sensation-seeking aspect of it.

Testosterone has been primarily associated with sexual drive and aggressiveness, but research suggests that it is also involved in other personality traits like sensation seeking, impulsivity, social dominance, and sociability. Testosterone may interact with the dopamine system through its effect on type B MAO, the enzyme that regulates dopamine through its catabolic action. Both testosterone and dopamine are involved in the type of sensation seeking (disinhibition) that seeks excitement through other people. A deficit of dopamine in the reward centers of the nucleus accumbens and the medial forebrain bundle limits natural euphoria, positive emotions, and probably the tendency to engage in activities that normally produce these. In a person chronically low in dopamine, there may be a natural kind of anhedonia and asociality, but in a person who has been hedonically driven, a deficit in the transmitter would lead to compensatory activity in search of stimulation that would activate the dopaminergic systems. Most drugs of abuse produce euphoria through activation of the mesolimbic dopamine system: stimulant drugs at the nucleus accumbens and opiates at the ventral tegmental end of the medial forebrain bundle (Bozarth, 1987). High sensation seekers are attracted to drugs of both types. Does this indicate a deficit in their dopaminergic function or a special sensitivity to this kind of biological reward? Opiates also act more directly on specialized opiate receptors in the brain. Does this indicate a deficit in the endogenous opiates (endorphins) in high sensation seekers (Zuckerman, 1986b)? Another possibility is a special sensitivity to dopaminergic agonists produced by inefficient metabolism (MAO), production, or concentrations and sensitivities of receptors. The actual involvements of dopamine and the other monoamines and the endorphins in the trait are hard to predict at this point. Most of the evidence is derived from comparative studies of the behavioral functions in other species (Zuckerman,

1984a). Correlational data in humans, except for that on MAO, are sparse and often inconclusive, relating sometimes to sensation seeking, and other times to extraversion or psychoticism. If more biological psychiatrists included personality measures in their studies of abnormal populations and controls, we might be able to evaluate the hypotheses better.

Freud's (1923) final classification of "instincts" (more like "drives" in the modern sense) included two supraordinate types: life and death instincts. Life instincts, such as hunger and sex, were those which caused increases of tension, the reductions of which were pleasurable (Freud could not seem to conceive of an increase in tension as pleasurable). These instincts were described as "disturbers of the peace." The death instinct was said to work less ostentatiously toward the goal of death (total stimulus reduction), or at least constancy of stimulation at a low intensity. In a metaphorical sense, Freud could have been describing the two extremes of the normal dimension of sensation seeking. Sensation seeking is not an "instinct," but a drive with genetical-biological bases and various learned forms of expression.

Dopamine could be regarded as the substance of the "life instinct." Its absence results in a "living death," sans activity, sans desire, sans interest, sans joy, sans sensation seeking. Conversely, overactivity of the system can produce an unrelenting and eventually exhausting mania. An optimal level of catecholamine system activity (Zuckerman, 1984a) is maintained by the balance between genetically determined characteristics of the systems and the sensation-seeking or -reducing behavioral activities of the individual that alter the levels of activity in the systems. Dopamine is the drive mechanism and the serotonin is the brakes of the approach mechanism.

More than 70 years ago Freud predicted that biology would produce some surprising answers to the questions of human motivation and personality, as noted at the beginning of this chapter. Followers of Freud ignored this admonition and interpreted his views as pure social determinism, whereas for him they were only a temporizing expedient awaiting the development of the neurosciences. Findings in the neurosciences will not negate psychological hypotheses; they will simply place them in a psychobiological context. The genotype and biological phenotypes have been the "ghosts" in the mental structures postulated by personality and cognitive theorists. But they are not ghosts. They are very tangible neurons and chemicals that we share with our animal cousins and our hominid ancestors. A complete theory of any personality trait will have to explore and not exorcise them.

Appendix A:

Sensation Seeking Scale – form V (SSS-V)

Interest and preference test

Directions: Each of the items below contains two choices A and B. Please indicate which of the choices most describes your likes or the way you feel. In some cases you may find items in which both choices describe your likes or feelings. Please choose the one which better describes your likes or feelings. In some cases you may find items in which you do not like either choice. In these cases mark the choice you dislike least. Do not leave any items blank. It is important you respond to all items with only one choice, A or B. We are interested only in your likes or feelings, not in how others feel about these things or how one is supposed to feel. There are no right or wrong answers as in other kinds of tests. Be frank and give your honest appraisal of yourself.

1. A. I like "wild" uninhibited parties.
   B. I prefer quiet parties with good conversation.
2. A. There are some movies I enjoy seeing a second or even third time.
   B. I can't stand watching a movie that I've seen before.
3. A. I often wish I could be a mountain climber.
   B. I can't understand people who risk their necks climbing mountains.
4. A. I dislike all body odors.
   B. I like some of the earthy body smells.
5. A. I get bored seeing the same old faces.
   B. I like the comfortable familiarity of everyday friends.
6. A. I like to explore a strange city or section of town by myself, even if it means getting lost.
   B. I prefer a guide when I am in a place I don't know well.
7. A. I dislike people who do or say things just to shock or upset others.
   B. When you can predict almost everything a person will do and say he or she must be a bore.

8. A. I usually don't enjoy a movie or play where I can predict what will happen in advance.

   B. I don't mind watching a movie or play where I can predict what will happen in advance.

9. A. I have tried marijuana or would like to.

   B. I would never smoke marijuana.

10. A. I would not like to try any drug which might produce strange and dangerous effects on me.

    B. I would like to try some of the drugs that produce hallucinations.

11. A. A sensible person avoids activities that are dangerous.

    B. I sometimes like to do things that are a little frightening.

12. A. I dislike "swingers" (people who are uninhibited and free about sex).

    B. I enjoy the company of real "swingers."

13. A. I find that stimulants make me uncomfortable.

    B. I often like to get high (drinking liquor or smoking marijuana).

14. A. I like to try new foods that I have never tasted before.

    B. I order the dishes with which I am familiar so as to avoid disappointment and unpleasantness.

15. A. I enjoy looking at home movies, videos, or travel slides.

    B. Looking at someone's home movies, videos, or travel slides bores me tremendously.

16. A. I would like to take up the sport of water skiing.

    B. I would not like to take up water skiing.

17. A. I would like to try surfboard riding.

    B. I would not like to try surfboard riding.

18. A. I would like to take off on a trip with no preplanned or definite routes, or timetable.

    B. When I go on a trip I like to plan my route and timetable fairly carefully.

19. A. I prefer the "down to earth" kinds of people as friends.

    B. I would like to make friends in some of the "far-out" groups like artists or "punks."

20. A. I would not like to learn to fly an airplane.

    B. I would like to learn to fly an airplane.

21. A. I prefer the surface of the water to the depths.

    B. I would like to go scuba diving.

22. A. I would like to meet some persons who are homosexual (men or women).

    B. I stay away from anyone I suspect of being "gay" or "lesbian."

23. A. I would like to try parachute jumping.

B. I would never want to try jumping out of a plane, with or without a parachute.

24. A. I prefer friends who are excitingly unpredictable.

B. I prefer friends who are reliable and predictable.

25. A. I am not interested in experience for its own sake.

B. I like to have new and exciting experiences and sensations even if they are a little frightening, unconventional, or illegal.

26. A. The essence of good art is in its clarity, symmetry of form, and harmony of colors.

B. I often find beauty in the "clashing" colors and irregular forms of modern paintings.

27. A. I enjoy spending time in the familiar surroundings of home.

B. I get very restless if I have to stay around home for any length of time.

28. A. I like to dive off the high board.

B. I don't like the feeling I get standing on the high board (or I don't go near it at all).

29. A. I like to date persons who are physically exciting.

B. I like to date persons who share my values.

30. A. Heavy drinking usually ruins a party because some people get loud and boisterous.

B. Keeping the drinks full is the key to a good party.

31. A. The worst social sin is to be rude.

B. The worst social sin is to be a bore.

32. A. A person should have considerable sexual experience before marriage.

B. It's better if two married persons begin their sexual experience with each other.

33. A. Even if I had the money, I would not care to associate with flighty rich persons in the "jet set."

B. I could conceive of myself seeking pleasures around the world with the "jet set."

34. A. I like people who are sharp and witty even if they do sometimes insult others.

B. I dislike people who have their fun at the expense of hurting the feelings of others.

35. A. There is altogether too much portrayal of sex in movies.

B. I enjoy watching many of the "sexy" scenes in movies.

36. A. I feel best after taking a couple of drinks.

B. Something is wrong with people who need liquor to feel good.

37. A. People should dress according to some standard of taste, neatness, and style.

    B. People should dress in individual ways even if the effects are sometimes strange.

38. A. Sailing long distances in small sailing crafts is foolhardy.

    B. I would like to sail a long distance in a small but seaworthy sailing craft.

39. A. I have no patience with dull or boring persons.

    B. I find something interesting in almost every person I talk to.

40. A. Skiing down a high mountain slope is a good way to end up on crutches.

    B. I think I would enjoy the sensations of skiing very fast down a high mountain slope.

END OF TEST

Note. Some of the items have been slightly modified from the original version of form V in order to explain outmoded colloquial or slang terms like *swingers,* to use terms more relevant to current times such as *videos* with home movies and substituting *punks* for *hippies,* to remove currently offensive terms like *queer* and substitute prevalent terms like *gay,* and to make the items more inclusive as in substituting *persons* for *members of the opposite sex* in item 29 referring to dating preferences. These should probably make no differences in item response characteristics but the author would appreciate any new information from item analyses.

Appendix B

Appendix B. *Scoring key for SSS form V*

	No. items				Keyed items					
TAS	10	3A	11B	16A	17A	20B	21B	23A	28A	38B	40B
ES	10	4B	6A	9A	10B	14A	18A	19B	22A	26B	37B
Dis	10	1A	12B	13B	25B	29A	30B	32A	33B	35B	36A
BS	10	2B	5A	7B	8A	15B	24A	27B	31B	34A	39A
Total[a]	40	1A	2B	3A	4B	5A	6A	7B	8A	9A	10B
		11B	12B	13B	14A	15B	16A	17A	18A	19B	20B
		21B	22A	23A	24A	25B	26B	27B	28A	29A	30B
		31B	32A	33B	34A	35B	36A	37B	38B	39A	40B

[a] The Total score may also be obtained by summing the four subscale scores but it may be desirable to also score the 40 items and check with the sum of the subscales.

Appendix C

Appendix C. *T-score conversions for subscales of SSS form V*

Raw score	TAS		ES		Dis		BS		Raw score
	Male	Female	Male	Female	Male	Female	Male	Female	
10	60	63	72	72	66	68	81	82	10
9	56	59	67	67	62	64	76	77	9
8	51	55	63	63	57	60	71	73	8
7	47	51	59	58	53	56	66	68	7
6	42	48	54	54	49	52	61	63	6
5	37	44	50	50	45	48	56	59	5
4	33	40	45	45	41	44	51	54	4
3	28	36	41	40	37	40	46	49	3
2	24	33	37	35	33	36	41	45	2
1	19	29	32	31	29	32	36	40	1
0	14	25	28	26	25	28	31	35	0

Note: Based on means and standard deviations for Personality Psychology students at the University of Delaware, 1986–1992; $n = 410$ males, 807 females.

Appendix D

Appendix D. *T-score conversions for Total score of SSS form V*

Raw score	Male	Female	Raw score	Male	Female
40	83	79	20	45	49
39	81	77	19	43	48
38	79	76	18	41	46
37	77	74	17	39	45
36	75	73	16	37	44
35	73	71	15	35	42
34	71	70	14	34	41
33	69	69	13	32	39
32	68	67	12	30	38
31	66	66	11	28	36
30	64	64	10	26	35
29	62	63	9	24	33
28	60	61	8	22	32
27	58	60	7	20	30
26	56	58	6	18	29
25	54	57	5	17	27
24	52	55	4	15	26
23	51	54	3	13	24
22	49	52	2	11	23
21	47	51	1	9	21
			0	7	20

Note: Based on means and standard deviations for Personality Psychology students at the University of Delaware; $n = 410$ males, 807 females.

Appendix E

Activities schedule (SSS form VI)

Part I – experience

Below you will find a list of many different kinds of activities. Please indicate whether you have actually engaged in this activity or not. Answer all items using one of the following options: A. I have never done this; B. I have done this once; C. I have done this more than once. Please mark only one response for each of the items: A, B, or C. Please answer all of the items. Please be frank and honest in answering these items. There are no right or wrong answers. We are only interested in your experiences, not in how others might regard these activities. Your responses are entirely confidential.

 1. Climbing steep mountains.
 2. Reading books about explicit sex.
 3. Running in a marathon.
 4. Traveling around with a spontaneous, uninhibited, fun-loving group.
 5. Going to a "wild," uninhibited party.
 6. Walking a tightrope.
 7. Being in the company of people who are very casual about sex, and who sometimes switch partners.
 8. Being "disrespectful" to a teacher or employer.
 9. Taking an unknown drug.
10. Shocking older persons just for the fun of it.
11. Swimming the English Channel.
12. Having sex in public (where others were doing the same thing).
13. Parachute jumping.
14. Having premarital sexual relations.
15. Flying an airplane.
16. Getting "high" in the company of other people.
17. Doing something illegal, but enjoyable.
18. Scuba diving.

19. Horseback riding at a gallop.
20. Sailing long distances.
21. Swimming alone far out from shore.
22. Having a sexual relationship with someone you just met and may not see again.
23. Climbing Mount Everest.
24. Skiing down high mountain slopes.
25. Sacrificing safety to speed when driving a car.
26. Doing something very unconventional.
27. Trying cocaine.
28. Exploring caves.
29. Discussing your sex life with friends.
30. Hunting lions and tigers.
31. Going to an "X-rated" movie which shows open sexual activity.
32. Getting drunk deliberately.
33. Living with someone of the opposite sex in a temporary arrangement.
34. Trying the drug LSD.
35. "Doing what feels good," regardless of the consequences.
36. Racing cars.
37. Riding a motorcycle.
38. Enjoying "wild" or unusual sexual fantasies.
39. Backpacking in Europe.
40. Hitchhiking.
41. Traveling in Antarctica.
42. Going to a party where there is heavy drinking.
43. Associating with friends who are excitingly unpredictable.
44. Going to a large rock concert.
45. Taking a trip to the moon.
46. Going out with someone just because you find them physically exciting.
47. Doing something dangerous because someone dared you to.
48. Doing unconventional things even if they are a little frightening.
49. Refusing to follow an order from a parent or employer.
50. Snorkeling over a reef.
51. Backpacking in the wilderness (in U.S.A.).
52. Having sex with more than one person on the same day.
53. Traveling up the Amazon.
54. Stealing something when you knew you wouldn't be caught.
55. Doing "crazy" things just to see the effects on others.
56. Using illegal drugs (other than marijuana).
57. Surviving alone on an island for a week.

58. Nude swimming in the company of persons of both sexes.
59. Seducing someone you wanted to sleep with.
60. Taking a long-odds bet rather than a sure bet if you had the chance to make a lot of money.
61. Using marijuana.
62. "Picking up" someone of the opposite sex.
63. Gambling for high stakes.
64. Going alone to a "singles bar."

Part II beginning with item 65 is on the following page. Be sure you read the new instructions for this part.

Part II-intentions for the future

Below you will find a list of many different kinds of activities. Please indicate whether you would like to engage in this activity *in the future regardless of whether or not you have engaged in the activity in the past.* Answer all items using one of the following options: IN THE FUTURE:
A. I have no desire to do this; B. I have thought of doing this, but probably will not do it; C. I have thought of doing this and will do it if I have the chance. Please mark only one response for each of the items: A, B, or C. Answer all of the items. Be frank.
65. Climbing steep mountains.
66. Reading books about explicit sex.
67. Running in a marathon.
68. Traveling around with a spontaneous, uninhibited, fun-loving group.
69. Going to a "wild," uninhibited party.
70. Walking a tightrope.
71. Being in the company of people who are very casual about sex, and who sometimes switch partners.
72. Being "disrespectful" to a teacher or employer.
73. Taking an unknown drug.
74. Shocking older persons just for the fun of it.
75. Swimming the English Channel.
76. Having sex in public (where others were doing the same thing).
77. Parachute jumping.
78. Having premarital sexual relations.
79. Flying an airplane.
80. Getting "high" in the company of other people.
81. Doing something illegal, but enjoyable.
82. Scuba diving.
83. Horseback riding at a gallop.
84. Sailing long distances.
85. Swimming far out from shore.
86. Having a sexual relationship with someone you just met and may not see again.
87. Climbing Mount Everest.
88. Skiing down high mountain slopes.
89. Sacrificing safety to speed when driving a car.
90. Doing something very unconventional.
91. Trying cocaine.

92. Exploring caves.
93. Discussing your sex life with friends.
94. Hunting lions or tigers.
95. Going to an "X-rated" movie which shows open sexual activity.
96. Getting drunk deliberately.
97. Living with someone of the opposite sex in a temporary arrangement.
98. Trying the drug LSD.
99. "Doing what feels good," regardless of the consequences.
100. Racing cars.
101. Riding a motorcycle.
102. Enjoying "wild" or unusual sexual fantasies.
103. Backpacking in Europe.
104. Hitchhiking.
105. Traveling in Antarctica.
106. Going to a party where there is heavy drinking.
107. Associating with friends who are excitingly unpredictable.
108. Going to a large rock concert.
109. Taking a trip to the moon.
110. Going out with someone just because you find them physically exciting.
111. Doing something dangerous because someone dared you to.
112. Doing unconventional things even if they are a little frightening.
113. Refusing to follow an order from a parent or employer.
114. Snorkeling over a reef.
115. Backpacking in the wilderness (U.S.A.).
116. Having sex with more than one person on the same day.
117. Traveling up the Amazon.
118. Stealing something when you knew you wouldn't be caught.
119. Doing "crazy" things just to see the effect on others.
120. Using illegal drugs (other than marijuana).
121. Surviving alone on an island for a week.
122. Nude swimming in the company of other persons of both sexes.
123. Seducing someone you wanted to sleep with.
124. Taking a long-odds bet rather than a sure bet if you had the chance to make a lot of money.
125. Using marijuana.
126. "Picking up" someone of the opposite sex.
127. Gambling for high stakes.
128. Going alone to a "singles bar."

END OF TEST

Appendix F

Scoring keys for SSS form VI

Infrequency (7 items): 11, 23, 30, 41, 45, 53, 57

Experience – Thrill and Adventure Seeking (E-TAS) (15 items): 1, 3, 6, 13, 15, 18, 19, 20, 21, 24, 28, 36, 39, 50, 51

Experience – Disinhibition (E-Dis) (42 items): 2, 4, 5, 7, 8, 9, 10, 12, 14, 16, 17, 22, 25, 26, 27, 29, 31, 32, 33, 34, 35, 37, 38, 40, 42, 43, 44, 46, 47, 48, 49, 52, 54, 55, 56, 58, 59, 60, 61, 62, 63, 64

Intention – Thrill and Adventure Seeking (I-TAS) (22 items): 65, 67, 70, 75, 77, 79, 82, 83, 84, 85, 87, 88, 92, 94, 100, 103, 105, 109, 114, 115, 117, 121

Intention – Disinhibition (I-Dis) (42 items): 66, 68, 69, 71, 72, 73, 74, 76, 78, 80, 81, 86, 89, 90, 91, 93, 95, 96, 97, 98, 99, 101, 102, 104, 106, 107, 108, 110, 111, 112, 113, 116, 118, 119, 120, 122, 123, 124, 125, 126, 127, 128

Scoring: In scoring either Experience or Intention scales each response is weighted as follows: A = 1, B = 2, C = 3. All of the weighted responses for each of the four subscales are summed and the total constitutes the raw score for that scale.

The Infrequency measure is just scored to determine individual test-taking validity. It does not have sufficient reliability to be regarded as a scale. A score of anything greater than 7 (one on each item) occurs in less than 5% of the college population. Any report of experience in these items (B or C response) raises the question of not understanding the instructions, carelessness, or negativism toward the test. If it was an isolated response, it may not invalidate the other scales. If it was due to a general misunderstanding of instructions, the test may have to be readministered or the results discarded. In a rare case a subject may have actually traveled up the Amazon or in Antarctica.

Appendix G

Appendix G. *Means, standard deviations (SD), and t tests between males and females on SSS form VI*

| Scales | Males ($n = 74$) | | Females ($n = 192$) | | |
	Mean	SD	Mean	SD	t
E-TAS	22.45	4.77	20.32	3.74	3.82**
E-Dis	93.59	16.77	83.68	14.00	4.89**
I-TAS	45.22	9.32	41.30	8.87	3.18*
I-Dis	98.05	18.76	87.96	16.23	4.35**

*$p < .01$.
**$p < .001$.

Appendix H

Appendix H. *Standard (T) scores for SSS form VI scales*

T scores	E-TAS M	E-TAS F	E-Dis M	E-Dis F	I-TAS M	I-TAS F	I-Dis M	I-Dis F	T scores
94	43	37							94
92	42	36							92
90	42	35							90
88	41	35							88
86	40	34							86
84	39	33							84
82	38	32							82
80	37	32		126					80
78	36	31		123		66			78
76	35	30		120		64			76
74	34	29		117		63		127	74
72	33	29		114	66	61		124	72
70	32	28	127	112	64	59		120	70
68	31	27	124	109	62	57		117	68
66	30	26	120	106	60	55	128	114	66
64	29	26	117	103	58	54	124	111	64
62	28	25	114	100	56	52	121	107	62
60	27	24	110	98	54	50	117	104	60
58	26	23	107	95	53	48	113	101	58
56	25	23	104	92	51	47	109	98	56
54	24	22	100	89	49	45	106	94	54
52	23	21	97	86	47	43	102	91	52
50	22	20	94	84	45	41	98	88	50
48	22	20	90	81	43	40	94	85	48
46	21	19	87	78	41	38	91	81	46
44	20	18	84	75	40	36	87	78	44
42	19	17	80	72	38	34	83	75	42
40	18	17	77	70	36	32	79	72	40
38	17	16	73	67	34	31	76	68	38
36	16	15	70	64	32	29	72	65	36
34	15		67	61	30	27	68	62	34
32			63	54	28	25	64	59	32
30			60	51	27	24	61	56	30
28			57	49	25	22	57	52	28
26			53	46	23		53	49	26
24			50	43	21		49	46	24
22			47	40			46	43	22
20			43				42	39	20
18			40						18

Appendix I

Translations of the sensation seeking scales

Arabic

M. A. Torki (1993) translated the SSS form VI into Arabic and gave it to 102 male and 152 female undergraduate Kuwaiti students. Alpha reliabilities of E-Dis, I-TAS, and I-Dis scales were high, ranging from .86 to .92 for males and females. E-TAS alpha was fair for males (.77) but low for females (.45). Kuwaiti males scored significantly higher than females on E-TAS, E-Dis, and I-Dis, but the means were about the same on I-TAS. Means for Kuwaitis were lower than those for U.S. students on the scales. The author notes that some of the items, particularly the Dis ones, are more suitable to Western culture.

Address: Dr. Mostafa A. Torki, Kuwait University, P. O. Box 23558, 13096 Safat, Kuwait.

Chinese

Yuching (1988, in Chinese) translated the SSS form V into Chinese and gave the translated scales to 516 persons divided among five age groups and five occupations. He also compared high and low sensation seekers among 18 undergraduates on the Kinesthetic Figural After-Effects, and reported that the high sensation seeker is a reducer on this task.

Address: Zhang Yuching, Psychology Dept., Beijing University, Beijing PR, China.

Dutch

Feij, van Zuilen, and Gazendam (1982) constructed a Dutch version of the SSS, starting with a translation of the items from SSS form IV. They separated the forced-choice alternatives in the original form and converted them into Likert-type items with a weighted scoring system depending on degree of agreement or disagreement with each item. The item responses were factor analyzed and the original four dimensions of sensation seeking were found in the Dutch sample. Reasonably high internal reliabilities were found for all four subscales in both men and women ranging from .72 to .82. Men scored higher than women on Total, TAS, and Dis scales. Validity studies concerning sleep, smoking and other characteristics are presented in the published manual for the test (Feij & van Zuilen, 1984).

Address: Dr. J. A. Feij, Group on Work and Organizational Psychology, Faculty of Psychology, Free University, De Boelelaan 1081, HV Amsterdam, the Netherlands.

Finnish

S. Eysenck and Haapasalo (1989) translated the SSS form V and gave it to 501 male and 448 female Finnish subjects, ages 18–70, randomly selected from the national register. The item responses were factor analyzed separately for men and women. Factors were highly alike in men and women for TAS (.99) and ES (.93) but showed less resemblance in Dis (.87) and BS (.71). New scales were composed with 13 items for TAS, 7 for ES, 10 for Dis, and 6 for BS, and 36 items for Total score. Internal (alpha) reliabilities for revised scales were quite good for Total score (.85–.87), TAS (.85), fair for Dis (.76), but poor for ES (.56–61) and BS (.37–.44), probably because of the abbreviated length of these revised scales. All subscales except BS were highly intercorrelated. Males scored higher than females on TAS and Dis as in other studies.

Address: Dr. S. B. G. Eysenck, Institute of Psychiatry, De Crespigny Park, Denmark Hill, London, SE 5 8AF, England, and J. Haapasalo, Turk Central Prison, Turku, Finland.

French

Carton, Jouvent, and Widlöcher (1992) translated SSS form IV into French and gave it to 102 subjects from 15 to 62 years of age. The General scale was highly correlated with age ($r = -.53$). Men scored higher than women on the TAS and Dis scales. Factor analyses and scale revisions are being planned.

Address: Mlle S. Carton, INSERM U 302, Psychopathologie et psychopharmacologie des comportments hôpital de la Salpetrière, 47, boulevard de l'Hôpital, 75651, Paris Cedex 13, France.

German

Andressen (1986, article in German) translated SSS form V into German and gave it to 233 normal subjects of both sexes. Examined reliabilities of the original and revised form V scales and correlated them with 54 new, very specific kinds of sensation-seeking scales. Internal (alpha) reliabilities of the original scales were: TAS .87, ES .74, Dis .77, and BS .40. For the revised scales they were: TAS .85, ES .83, Dis .80, and BS .71. Concludes that the SSS covers only a very limited domain of the highly differentiated kinds of sensation seeking.

Address: Dr. B. Andressen, Psychiatrische Universitatsklinic Hamburg, Hamburg, Germany.

Hebrew

Birenbaum (1986); Birenbaum and Montag (1984) translated the SSS form V into Hebrew. A nonmetric multidimensional scaling technique located 35 of 40 items on the scales designated.

Address: Dr. M. Birenbaum, Tel Aviv University, Ramat-Aviv, Israel.

Italian

Magaro, Smith, Cionini, and Velicogna (1979) translated the General scale from SSS form IV into Italian and factor analyzed the test along with other scales.

Address: Prof. Peter Megaro, Dept. of Psychology, Ohio State University, Columbus, Ohio.

Japanese

Terasaki (1987, in Japanese) translated SSS form IV into Japanese and factor analyzed the items recovering the four factors plus a fifth one involving marijuana use and sex. He refactored the four factors. The items on the TAS were very consistent with the American version, but items on the remaining scales were somewhat different from the original. Internal consistency for the total score was .75 for males and .65 for females. Subscales reliabilities were low for TAS, ES, and Dis ranging from .56 to .67 for males and .47 to .61 for females. BS showed even poorer reliability (.29). Three-month retest reliabilities were .87 for males and .65 for females.

Address: Dr. M. Terasaki, Dept. of Psychology, Kwansei Gakuin University, Nishinomiya, Hyogo 662, Japan.

Norwegian

Pederson, Clausen, and Lavik (1989) developed a revised and shortened form of the SSS form V to be used with persons aged 15 and older. All items dealing with interest in drugs were eliminated along with others deemed to be inappropriate. The final version is an 18-item scale with TAS, ES, and Dis scales but no BS scale. As in other analyses, BS proved to be too weak a factor. Most of the Dis items reflect an interest in sex.

Address: Dr. W. Pederson, Dept. of Psychiatry, University of Oslo, Oslo, Norway.

Oriyan (an Indian dialect)

Mahanta (1983) attempted to translate SSS items into a form compatible with Indian culture. While traces of the original SSS items can be seen in some of the new items, it is not certain how well the scale would relate to the original SSS. The forced-choice format was retained and 15 items were finally used. Of the 15 items, 14 correlated with the total score but the size of the correlations is not given.

Address: J. Mahanta, Institute of Criminology and Forensic Science, New Delhi, India.

Polish

Oleszkiewicz (1982, 1985) translated the SSS form IV into Polish. Inappropriate items for the Polish population were removed and the scale was subjected to analysis using item total correlations. The final form of the inventory includes 68 items, with the four original subscales plus an additional scale assessing seeking of intellectual stimulation. Retest reliability (Gen scale?) for a 3-week interval was .88 for females and .85 for males.

Address: Dr. Zofia Oleszkiewicz-Zsurzs, Dept. of Psychology, University of Warsaw, Poland.

Spanish

Adult Version. Perez and Torrubia (1986) translated the SSS V into Spanish. Internal (alpha) reliabilities for the Total score were .82 for men and .77 for women. Reliabilities for the subscales for men ranged from .62 to .78 and for women from .52 to .72. As usual, the lowest reliabilities were for the BS and ES scales. High retest reliabilities were reported for Total score for 10 days (men, .90; women, .92) and 5 weeks (men, .88; women .87). Men scored significantly higher than women on every scale but ES.

Children's Version. Perez, Ortet, Pla, and Simo (1986) constructed a Spanish SSS for children, ages 11 to 15 years. The SSS V was used as a model but some new items were written and older ones revised in wording for the four subscales and a Lie scale. Factor analysis was used to select 10 items each for TAS, Dis, ES, BS, and Lie scales. Of the 40 items used in the new SS subscales, 24 are from the adult SSS. One-month retest reliabilities ranged from .64 to .83 for Total score and TAS, ES, and Dis subscales. As usual the reliability of BS was lower (.56–.58). Boys scored significantly higher than girls on Total score and all subscales except TAS. The largest difference was on Dis. In a group of 15- and 16-year-olds given the child and adult forms, the correlations between the Total scores were as high as the reliabilities of these scales (.80–.86). TAS correlations were even higher (.9), but ES, Dis, and BS correlations ranged from .52 to .76.

Address: Dr. J. Perez, Dept. of Medical Psychology, Faculty of Medicine, Autonomous University of Barcelona, Bellaterra, Catalonia, Spain.

Swedish

Children's Version. Björck-Akesson (1990) developed a Swedish SSS designed for children between the ages of 12 and 15. Most of the items from the SSS forms IV and V were changed and adapted for children. All items pertaining to drugs, drinking, or sex were eliminated. On the basis of an exploratory factor analysis, four subscales were constructed. The final form of the test consists of a 62-item forced-choice version containing 22 items similar to those in the SSS form IV (mostly TAS items). The scales are: Thrill and Adventure Seeking (15 items), New Experience Seeking (15 items), Activity [social (like Dis)] (14 items), Outgoingness [unconventionality] (12 items). No BS scale was constructed because the results of the factor analysis could not define such a factor.

Appendix J

Sensation Seeking and Anxiety States scales (SSAST)

Directions: The following statement describes various moods and feelings. Please read each statement and indicate on the 1 to 5 scale the degree to which the statement describes how you feel NOW, at this time.* Use the following scale in answering each item.

(1) Not at all, (2) Slightly, (3) Somewhat, (4) Definitely, (5) Very much

1. I feel interested
2. I feel afraid
3. I feel thoughtful
4. I feel elated
5. I feel secure
6. I feel desperate
7. I feel adventurous
8. I feel pleased
9. I feel steady
10. I feel lucky
11. I feel upset
12. I feel loving
13. I feel daring
14. I feel contented
15. I feel nervous
16. I feel enthusiastic
17. I feel amused
18. I feel frightened

19. I feel imaginative
20. I feel tense
21. I feel confident
22. I feel shaky
23. I feel pleasant
24. I feel zany
25. I feel calm
26. I feel curious
27. I feel fearful
28. I feel cooperative
29. I feel cheerful
30. I feel terrified
31. I feel mischievous
32. I feel joyful
33. I feel panicky
34. I feel playful
35. I feel happy
36. I feel worried

*The time set in the instructions may be altered to fit the experiment or study, e.g., "Today," "During the time __," "While you were __," etc., instead of "Now." If this is done, the wording of the items must be changed from "I feel" to "I felt." Experiments with other state tests have shown that there is little change with time periods of up to 1 day, but beyond that trait aspects begin to influence response and norms may change. This form should not be used as a trait measure in place of the questionnaire forms.

Scoring

Sensation Seeking State (15 items) Weighted score 1 to 5 for each item.

   items: 1, 4, 7, 8, 10, 13, 16, 17, 19, 21, 24, 26, 28, 32, 34

Anxiety State (15 items) Weighted score 1 to 5 for all items except items 5, 9, 14, and 25 which are scored in the reverse direction (i.e., $1 = 5$, $2 = 4$, $3 = 3$, $4 = 2$, $1 = 5$). *items:* 2, 5, 6, 9, 11, 14, 15, 18, 20, 22, 25, 27, 30, 33, 36

   Total the weighted scores for each of the scales (range = 15–75).

Means and standard deviations for college students (86 males, 102 females) on a neutral occasion:

   Sensation Seeking State: Males $M = 39.5$, $SD = 10.7$; Females $M = 39.6$, $SD = 10.2$.

   Anxiety State: Males $M = 25.3$, $SD = 7.3$; Females $M = 25.9$, $SD = 9.3$

References

Adolfsson, R., Gottfries, C. G., Oreland, L., Roos, B. E., & Winblad, B. (1978). Monoamine oxidase activity and serotonergic turnover in human brain. *Progress in Neuropsychopharmacology, 2,* 225–230.

Adorno, T. W., Frenkel-Brunswick, E., Levinson, D. J., & Sanford, R. N. (1950). *The authoritarian personality.* New York: Harper.

Ahern, F. M., Johnson, R. C., Wilson, J. R., McClearn, G. E., & Vandenberg, S. G. (1982). Family resemblance in personality. *Behavior Genetics, 12,* 261–280.

Allcock, C. C., & Grace, D. M. (1988). Pathological gamblers are neither impulsive nor sensation-seekers. *Australian and New Zealand Journal of Psychiatry, 22,* 307–311.

Allen, J. G. (1976). Correlates of emotional styles. *Journal of Consulting and Clinical Psychology, 44,* 678.

Allen, J. G., & Hamsher, J. H. (1974). The development and validation of a test of emotional styles. *Journal of Consulting and Clinical Psychology, 42,* 663–668.

Allport, G. W. (1937). *Personality: A psychological interpretation.* New York: Holt.

Allport, G. W., & Odbert, H. S. (1936). Trait names: A psycholexical study. *Psychological Monographs, 47* (Whole No. 211).

Anderson, G., & Brown, R. I. (1984). Real and laboratory gambling, sensation seeking and arousal. *British Journal of Psychology, 75,* 401–410.

Anderson, R. E. (1973). *Relationship between sensation seeking and academic achievement, school attendance, academic ability, and alcohol use.* Unpublished master's thesis, University of Alberta.

Andresen, B. (1986). Experience seeking motives: I. A psychometric reanalysis of Zuckerman's SSS-V within the context of the development of the MISAP-II. *Zeitschrift für Differentielle und Diagnostische Psychologie, 7,* 177–203.

Andrucci, G. L., Archer, R. P., Pancoast, D. L., & Gordon, R. A. (1989). The relationship of MMPI and sensation seeking scales to adolescent drug use. *Journal of Personality Assessment, 53,* 253–266.

Apt, C., & Hurlbert, D. F. (1992). The female sensation seeker and marital sexuality. *Journal of Sex and Marital Therapy, 18,* 315–324.

Apter, M. J. (1982). *The experience of motivation: The theory of psychological reversals.* London: Academic Press.

Arnett, J. (1991). Still crazy after all these years: Reckless behavior among young adults aged 23–27. *Personality and Individual Differences, 12,* 1305–1313.

Arque, J. M., Beltri, R., & Torrubia, R. (1988). Personality, bioelectric profile, and platelet monoamine oxidase activity in psychophysiological disorders: Headaches, insomnia, and loss of consciousness due to neurocirculatory dystonia. *Psychiatry and Psychobiology, 3,* 263–267.

Arque, J. M., Segura, R., & Torrubia, R. (1987). Correlation of thyroxine and thyroid-stimulating hormone with personality measurements: A study in psychosomatic patients and healthy subjects. *Neuropsychobiology, 18,* 127–133.

Arque, J. M., & Torrubia, R. (1987). Alcohol and tobacco consumption, platelet monoamine oxidase activity, and personality variables. *Psiquis Revista de Psiquiatria, Psicologia y Psicosomatica, 8,* 43–47.

Arque, J. M., & Torrubia, B. (1988). Personality, bioelectric profile and platelet monoamine oxidase activity in psychophysiological disorders: headaches, insomnia, and loss of consciousness due to neurocirculatory dystonia. *Psychiatry and Psychobiology, 3,* 263–267.

Arque, J. M., Unzeta, M., & Torrubia, R. (1988). Neurotransmitter systems and personality measurements: A study in psychosomatic patients and healthy subjects. *Neuropsychobiology, 19,* 149–157.

Aston-Jones, G., & Bloom, F. E. (1981). Norepinephrine-containing Locus Coeruleus neurons in behaving rats exhibit pronounced responses to non-noxious environmental stimuli. *Journal of Neuroscience, 8,* 887–890.

Azima, H., & Cramer-Azima, F. J. (1956). Effects of partial isolation in mentally disturbed individuals. *Diseases of the Nervous System, 17,* 117–122.

Babbitt, T., Rowland, G. L., & Franken, R. E. (1990a). Sensation seeking and participation in aerobic exercise classes. *Personality and Individual Differences, 11,* 181–183.

Babbitt, T., Rowland, G. L., & Franken, R. E. (1990b). Sensation seeking: Preoccupation with diet and exercise regimes. *Personality and Individual Differences, 11,* 759–761.

Back, K. W. (1981). Social networks and psychological conditions in diet preferences: Gourmets and vegetarians. *Basic and Applied Social Psychology, 2,* 1–9.

Bailey, K. G. (1987). *Human paleopsychology: Applications to aggression.* Hillsdale, NJ: Erlbaum.

Bailey, K. G., Burns, D. S., & Bazan, L. C. (1982). A method for measuring "primitive" and "advanced" elements in pleasures and aversions. *Journal of Personality Assessment, 46,* 639–646.

Bain, A. (1859/1875). *The emotions and the will* (3rd ed.). London: Longmans Green.

Baird, J. G. (1981). The brighter side of deviance: Implications from a study of need for uniqueness and sensation-seeking. *Psychological Reports, 49,* 1007–1008.

Baker, A. H. (1988). Sensation seeking and field independence. *Psychology, A Journal of Human Behavior, 25,* 44–49.

Ball, I. L., Farnill, D., & Wangeman, J. F. (1983). Factorial invariance across sex of the form V of the Sensation Seeking Scale. *Journal of Personality and Social Psychology, 45,* 1156–1159.

Ball, I. L., Farnill, D., & Wangeman, J. F. (1984). Sex and age differences in sensation seeking: Some national comparisons. *British Journal of Psychology, 75,* 257–265.

Ball, S. A., & Zuckerman, M. (1990). Sensation seeking, Eysenck's personality dimensions and reinforcement sensitivity in concept formation. *Personality and Individual Differences, 11,* 343–345.

Ball, S. A., & Zuckerman, M. (1992). Sensation seeking and selective attention: Focused and divided attention on a dichotic listening task. *Journal of Personality and Social Psychology, 63,* 825–831.

Ballenger, J. C., Post, R. M., Jimerson, D. C., Lake, C. R., Murphy, D. L., Zuckerman, M., & Cronin, C. (1983). Biochemical correlates of personality traits in normals: An exploratory study. *Personality and Individual Differences, 4,* 615–625.

Bandura, A. (1986). *Social foundations of thought and action: A social cognitive theory.* Englewood Cliffs, NJ: Prentice-Hall.

Barbee, A., Hammock, G., & Richardson, D. (1987). Are sensation seekers attracted to intense or positive stimuli? The importance of "sensation" to research on sensation seeking. *Personality and Individual Differences, 8,* 441–443.

Barratt, E. S., & Patton, J. H. (1983). Impulsivity: Cognitive, behavioral, and psychophysiological correlates. In M. Zuckerman (Ed.), *Biological bases of sensation seeking, impulsivity, and anxiety* (pp. 77–116). Hillsdale, NJ: Erlbaum.

Barratt, E. S., Pritchard, W. S., Faulk, D. M., & Brandt, M. E. (1987). The relationship between impulsiveness subtraits, trait anxiety, and visual N100-augmenting–reducing: A topographic analysis. *Personality and Individual Differences, 8,* 43–51.

Bates, M. E., Labourie, E. W., & White, H. R. (1985). *A longitudinal study of sensation seeking needs and drug use.* Paper presented at the Annual Convention of the American Psychological Association (93rd) Los Angeles, CA, August 23–27. Available from EDRS reproduction services (MF01/PC02).

Beck, A. T. (1967). *Depression: Clinical, experimental and theoretical aspects.* New York: Paul B. Boeber.

Bem, S. (1974). The measurement of psychological androgyny. *Journal of Consulting and Clinical Psychology, 42,* 155–162.

Bench, C. J., Prue, G. W., Lammertsma, A. A., Cremer, J. C., Luthra, S. R., Turton, D., Dolan, R. J., Kettler, R., Dingemanse, J., Da Prada, M., Biziere, K., McClelland, G. R., Jamieson, V. L., Wood, N. D., & Franchowiak, R. S. (1991). Measurement of human cerebral monoamine oxidase type B (MAO-B) activity with positron emission tomography (PET): A dose ranging study with the reversible inhibitor Ro 19-6327. *European Journal of Clinical Pharmacology, 40,* 169–173.

Berg-Cross, L., Berg-Cross, G., & McGeehan, D. (1979). Experience and personality differences among breast- and bottle-feeding mothers. *Psychology of Women Quarterly 3,* 344–356.

Berlyne, D. E. (1960). *Conflict, arousal, and curiosity.* New York: McGraw-Hill.

Berlyne, D. E. (1967). Arousal and reinforcement. In D. Levine (Ed.), *Nebraska Symposium on Motivation* (Vol. 15), pp. 1–110. Lincoln: University of Nebraska Press.

Berlyne, D. E. (1971). *Aesthetics and psychobiology.* New York: Appleton-Century-Crofts.

Berlyne, D. E., & Madsen, K. B. (1973). *Pleasure, reward, preference: Their nature, determinants and role in behavior.* New York: Academic Press.

Berman, T., & Paisley, T. (1984). Personality in assaultive and non-assaultive juvenile male offenders. *Psychological Reports, 54,* 527–530.

Berzins, J., Dove, J., & Ross, W. (1972). Cross-validational studies of the personality correlates of the A-B therapist "type" distinction among professionals and nonprofessionals. *Journal of Consulting and Clinical Psychology, 39,* 388–395.

Biersner, R. J., & LaRocco, J. M. (1983). Personality characteristics of US Navy divers. *Journal of Occupational Psychology, 56,* 329–334.

Birenbaum, M. (1986). On the construct validity of the Sensation Seeking Scale in a non-English speaking culture. *Personality and Individual Differences, 7,* 431–434.

Birenbaum, M., & Montag, I. (1986). Patterns of relationship between the 16PF and

Zuckerman's Sensation Seeking Scale. *Multivariate Experimental Clinical Research, 8,* 165–173.

Birenbaum, M., & Montag, I. (1987). On the replicability of the factorial structure of the Sensation Seeking Scale. *Personality and Individual Differences, 8,* 403–408.

Björk-Åkesson, E. (1990). *Measuring sensation seeking.* Göteborg Studies in Educational Sciences, 75. Göteborg, Sweden: Acta Universitatis Gothoburgensis.

Blackburn, R. (1969). Sensation seeking, impulsivity, and psychopathic personality. *Journal of Consulting and Clinical Psychology, 33,* 571–574.

Blackburn, R. (1978). Electrodermal and cardiovascular correlates of psychopathy. In R. D. Hare & D. Schalling (Eds.), *Psychopathic behavior: Approaches to research* (pp. 157–164). New York: Wiley.

Blackburn, R. (1987). Two scales for the assessment of personality disorder in antisocial populations. *Personality and Individual Differences, 8,* 81–93.

Blaszczynski, A. P., McConaghy, N., & Frankova, A. (1990). Boredom Proneness in an impulse control disorder. *Psychological Reports, 67,* 35–42.

Blaszczynski, A. P., McConaghy, N., & Frankova, A. (1991). Control versus abstinence in the treatment of pathological gambling: A two to nine year follow-up. *British Journal of Addiction, 86,* 299–306.

Blaszczynski, A. P., Wilson, A. C., & McConaghy, N. (1986). Sensation seeking and pathological gambling. *British Journal of Addiction, 81,* 113–117.

Blaszczynski, A. P., Winter, S. W., & McConaghy, N. (1986). Plasma endorphin levels in pathological gambling. *Journal of Gambling Behavior, 2,* 3–14.

Block, J. H., & Block, J. (1980). The role of ego-control and ego-resiliency in the organization of behavior. In W. A. Collins (Ed.), *Development of cognition, affect, and social relations: The Minnesota Symposia on Child Psychology* (Vol. 13, pp. 39–101). Hillsdale, NJ: Erlbaum.

Bone, R. N., Montgomery, D. D., & McAllister, D. S. (1973). *The relationship between sensation seeking, sex, family size, and birth order.* Unpublished manuscript.

Boomsa, D. I., & Plomin, R. (1986). Heart rate and behavior of twins. *Merrill Palmer Quarterly, 32,* 141–151.

Bouchard, T. J., Lykken, D. T., McGue, M., Segal, N. L., & Tellegen, A. (1990). Sources of human psychological differences: The Minnesota study of twins reared apart. *Science, 250,* 223–228.

Bouter, L. M., Knipschild, P. G., Feij, J. A., & Volovics, A. (1988). Sensation seeking and injury risk in downhill skiing. *Personality and Individual Differences, 9,* 667–673.

Bozarth, M. A. (1987). Ventral tegmental reward system. In J. Engel, L. Oreland, B. Pernov, S. Rössner, & L. A. Pelhorn (Eds.), *Brain reward systems and abuse* (pp. 1–17). New York: Raven Press.

Bradley, R., & Redfering, D. L. (1978). Drug abuses in the military: Correlates of successful rehabilitation. *Journal of Clinical Psychology, 34,* 233–237.

Brain, P. F. (1983). Pituitary-gonadal influences on social aggression. In B. B. Svare (Ed.), *Hormones and aggressive behavior* (pp. 1–26). New York: Erlbaum.

Brand, C. (1981). Personality and political attitudes. In R. Lynn (Ed.), *Dimensions of Personality: Papers in honour of H. J. Eysenck* (pp. 7–38). Oxford: Pergamon.

Braverman, M. T., & Farley, F. H. (1978). Arousal and cognition: The stimulation-seeking motive and structural effects in the comprehension of film. *Educational Communication and Technology, 26,* 321–327.

Brebner, J., & Cooper, C. (1974). The effect of a low rate of regular signals upon the reaction time of introverts and extraverts. *Journal of Research in Personality, 8,* 263–276.

Breivik, G. (1991a). *Personality and sensation seeking in risk sport: A summary.* Unpublished data.

Breivik, G. (1991b). *Sensation seeking among Norwegian prisoners.* Unpublished abstract.

Breuer, J., & Freud, S. (1895/1937). *Studies in hysteria* (A. A. Brill, translator). New York: Nervous and Mental Disease Publishing, 1937.

Brill, N. Q., Crumpton, E., & Grayson, H. M. (1971). Personality factors in marihuana use. *Archives of General Psychiatry, 24,* 163–165.

Brimer, E., & Levine, F. M. (1983). Stimulus seeking behavior in hyperactive and nonhyperactive children. *Journal of Abnormal Child Psychology, 11,* 131–139.

Broen, W. E., Jr. (1968). *Schizophrenia, research and theory.* New York: Academic Press.

Brown, L. T., Ruder, V. G., Ruder, J. H., & Young, S. D. (1974). Stimulation seeking and the change seeker index. *Journal of Consulting and Clinical Psychology, 42,* 311.

Brown, R. I. (1986). Arousal and sensation seeking components in the general explanation of gambling and gambling addictions. *International Journal of the Addictions, 21,* 1001–1016.

Brownfield, C. A. (1966). Optimal stimulation levels of normal and disturbed subjects in sensory deprivation. *Psychologia, 9,* 27–38.

Buchsbaum, M. S. (1971). Neural events and the psychophysical law. *Science, 172,* 502.

Buchsbaum, M. S. (1974). Average evoked response and stimulus intensity in identical and fraternal twins. *Physiological Psychology, 2,* 365–370.

Buchsbaum, M. S. (1976). Self-regulation of stimulus intensity: Augmenting–reducing and the average evoked response. In G. E. Schwartz & D. Shapiro (Eds.), *Consciousness and self-regulation* (pp. 101–135). New York: Plenum.

Buchsbaum, M. S., Goodwin, F. K., Murphy, D. L., & Borge, G. (1971). AER in affective disorders. *American Journal of Psychiatry, 128,* 19–25.

Buchsbaum, M. S., Haier, R. J., & Johnson, J. (1983). Augmenting and reducing: Individual differences in evoked potentials. In A. Gale & J. A. Edwards (Eds.), *Physiological correlates of human behavior* (Vol. 3, pp. 120–138). London: Academic Press.

Buchsbaum, M. S., Landau, S., Murphy, D. L., & Goodwin, F. K. (1973). Average evoked response in bipolar and unipolar affective disorders: Relationships to sex, age of onset, and monoamine oxidase. *Biological Psychiatry, 7,* 199–212.

Buchsbaum, M. S., Muscettola, G., & Goodwin, F. K. (1981). Urinary MHPG, stress response, personality factors and somatosensory evoked potentials in normal subjects and patients with major affective disorders. *Neuropsychobiology, 7,* 212–224.

Buchsbaum, M. S., & Pfefferbaum, A. (1971). Individual differences in stimulus-intensity response. *Psychophysiology, 8,* 600–611.

Buchsbaum, M. S., Post, R. M., & Bunney, W. E., Jr. (1977). AER in a rapidly cycling manic-depressive patient. *Biological Psychiatry, 12,* 83–99.

Buchsbaum, M. S., & Silverman, J. (1968). Stimulus intensity control and the cortical evoked response. *Psychosomatic Medicine, 30,* 12–22.

Buss, A. H., & Plomin, R. (1975). *A temperament theory of personality development.* New York: Wiley.

Buss, A. H., & Plomin, R. (1984). *Temperament: Early developing personality traits.* Hillsdale, NJ: Erlbaum.

Buss, D. M., Abbott, M., Angleitner, A., et al. (1990). International preferences in selecting mates: A study of 37 cultures. *Journal of Cross-Cultural Psychology, 21,* 5–47.

Butler, R. A., & Alexander, H. M. (1955). Patterns of visual exploratory behavior in monkeys. *Journal of Comparative and Physiological Psychology, 48,* 247–249.

Cacioppo, J. T., & Petty, R. E. (1982). The need for cognition. *Journal of Personality and Social Psychology, 42,* 116–131.

Calhoon, L. L. (1988). Explorations in the biochemistry of sensation seeking. *Personality Individual Differences, 9,* 941–949.

Calhoon, L. L. (1991). Sensation seeking, exercise, and dopamine beta hydroxylase. *Personality and Individual Differences, 12,* 903–907.

Campbell, J. B., & Palus, J. P. (1987). *Intercorrelations and correlates of impulsivity measures.* Paper presented at meeting of the Eastern Psychological Association, April.

Cappella, J. N., & Green, J. O. (1984). The effects of distance and individual differences in arousability on nonverbal involvement: A test of discrepancy arousal theory. *Journal of Nonverbal Behavior, 8,* 259–286.

Caputo, P. (1977). *Rumor of war.* New York: Ballantine Books.

Carlson, L. D., & Lester, D. (1980). Thrill seeking in police officers. *Psychological Reports, 47,* 1102.

Carpenter, D. W. (1992). *Addictive behaviors of recovering alcoholics.* Paper presented at the meeting of the Eastern Psychological Association, Boston, MA, April.

Carrigan, P. M. (1960). Extraversion–introversion as a dimension of personality: A reappraisal. *Psychological Bulletin, 57,* 329–360.

Carrillo-de-la-Peña, M. T., & Barratt, E. S. (1993). Impulsivity and ERP augmenting/reducing. *Personality and Individual Differences, 15,* 25–32.

Carrol, E. N., & Zuckerman, M. (1977). Psychopathology and sensation seeking in "downers," "speeders," and "trippers": A study of the relationships between personality and drug choice. *International Journal of the Addictions, 12,* 591–601.

Carrol, E. N., Zuckerman, M., & Vogel, W. H. (1982). A test of the optimal level of arousal theory of sensation seeking. *Journal of Personality and Social Psychology, 42,* 572–575.

Carton, S., Jouvent, R., Bungener, C., & Widlöcher, D. (1992). Sensation seeking and depressive mood. *Personality and Individual Differences, 7,* 843–849.

Carton, S., Jouvent, R., & Widlöcher, D. (1992). Cross-cultural validity of the Sensation Seeking Scale. Development of a French abbreviated form. *European Psychiatry, 7,* 225–234.

Cattell, R. B. (1950). *Personality: A systematic, theoretical, and factual study.* New York: McGraw-Hill.

Cattell, R. B., & Luborsky, L. B. (1947). Personality factors in response to humor. *Journal of Abnormal and Social Psychology, 42,* 402–421.

Cellini, H. R., & Lorenz, J. R. (1983). Job club training with unemployed offenders. *Federal Probation, 46,* 46–50.

Chapman, L. J., Chapman, J. P., & Raulin, M. L. (1976). Scales for physical and social anhedonia. *Journal of Abnormal Psychology, 85,* 374–382.

Clarke, A., & Innes, J. M. (1983). Sensation seeking motivation and social-support moderators of the life stress/illness relationship: Some contradictory and confirmatory evidence. *Personality and Individual Differences, 4,* 547–550.

Cleckley, H. (1976). *The mask of sanity* (5th ed.). St. Louis, MO: Mosby.

Clement, R., & Jonah, B. A. (1984). Field dependence, sensation seeking and driving behaviour. *Personality and Individual Differences, 5,* 87–93.

Cloninger, C. R., Sigvardsson, S., & Bohman, M. (1988). Childhood personality predicts alcohol abuse in young adults. *Alcoholism: Clinical and Experimental Research, 12,* 494–505.

Cohen, L. (1959). Perception of reversible figures after brain injury. *Archives of Neurology and Psychiatry, 81,* 765–775.

Cohen, L. H. (1982). Life change and the sensation seeking motive. *Personality and Individual Differences, 3,* 221–222.

Cohen, L., Dingemans, P. M. A. J., Lesnik-Oberstein, M., & van der Vlugt, H. (1983). *Report of findings with the sensation seeking scale in Holland.* Poster presented at the meeting of the American Psychological Association, Anaheim, CA, August 26.

Cohen, L., & Merkelbach, H. (1987). Dichotic listening in relation to dysphoria, sensation seeking, and other personality characteristics. *Perceptual and Motor Skills, 64,* 471–477.

Connolly, P. M. (1981). *An exploratory study of adults engaging in high-risk sport of skiing.* Unpublished master's thesis, Rutgers University.

Cooley, E. J., & Keesey, J. C. (1981). Moderator variables in life stress and illness relationship. *Journal of Human Stress, 7,* 35–40.

Corulla, W. J. (1988). A further psychometric investigation of the Sensation Seeking Scale form-V and its relationship to the EPQ-R and the I.7 Impulsiveness Questionnaire. *Personality and Individual Differences, 9,* 277–287.

Corulla, W. J. (1989). The relationship between the Strelau Temperament Inventory, Sensation Seeking and Eysenck's dimensional system of personality. *Personality and Individual Differences, 10,* 161–173.

Costa, P. T., Jr., & McCrae, R. R. (1985). *The NEO Personality Inventory Manual.* Odessa, FL: Assessment Resources.

Costa, P. T., Jr., & McCrae, R. R. (1988). Personality in adulthood: A six year longitudinal study of self reports and spouse ratings on the NEO personality inventory. *Journal of Personality and Social Psychology, 54,* 853–863.

Costa, P. T., Jr., & McCrae, R. R. (1992). *NEO-PI-R: Revised NEO Personality Inventory (NEO-PI-R).* Odessa, FL: Psychological Assessment Resources.

Costa, P. T., Jr., McCrae, R. R., & Dye, D. A. (1990). *Facet scales for agreeableness and conscientiousness: A revision of the NEO Personality Inventory.* Unpublished manuscript.

Coursey, R. D., Buchsbaum, M. S., & Frankel, B. L. (1975). Personality measures and evoked responses in chronic insomniacs. *Journal of Abnormal Psychology, 84,* 239–249.

Coursey, R. D., Buchsbaum, M. S., & Murphy, D. L. (1979). Platelet MAO activity and evoked potentials in the identification of subjects biologically at risk for psychiatric disorders. *British Journal of Psychiatry, 134,* 372–381.

Cox, D. N. (1977). *Psychophysiological correlates of sensation seeking and socialization during reduced stimulation.* Unpublished doctoral dissertation, University of British Columbia.

Craig, R. J. (1982). Personality characteristics of heroin addicts: Review of empirical research 1976–1979. *International Journal of the Addictions, 17,* 227–248.

Craig, R. J. (1986). The personality structure of heroin addicts. *National Institute on Drug Abuse Research Monograph Series,* Monograph 74, 25–36.

Crick, F. (1988). *What mad pursuit: A personal view of scientific discovery.* New York: Basic Books.

Cronin, C. (1991). Sensation seeking among mountain climbers. *Personality and Individual Differences, 12*, 653–654.

Cronin, C., & Zuckerman, M. (1992). Sensation seeking and bipolar affective disorder. *Personality and Individual Differences, 13*, 385–387.

Crow, T. J. (1977). Neurotransmitter related pathways: The structure and function of central monoamine neurons. In A. N. Davidson (Ed.), *Biochemical correlates of brain structure and function* (pp. 137–174). New York: Academic Press.

Crowne, I. P., & Marlowe, D. (1960). A new scale of social desirability independent of psychopathology. *Journal of Consulting Psychology, 24*, 349–354.

Custer, R., & Milt, H. (1985). *When luck runs out.* New York: Facts on File.

Dabbs, J. M., Jr., Hopper, C. H., & Jurkovic, G. J. (1990). Testosterone and personality among college students and military veterans. *Personality and Individual Differences, 11*, 1263–1269.

Dahlback, O. (1990). Criminality and risk taking. *Personality and Individual Differences, 11*, 265–272.

Daitzman, R. J. (1979). *Recognition of sensation seekers from facial photos.* Unpublished study.

Daitzman, R. J., & Tumilty, T. M. (1974). Support for an activation–regulation deficit in schizophrenia: Implications for treatment. *Newsletter for Research in Mental Health and Behavioral Science, 16*, 31–35.

Daitzman, R. J., & Zuckerman, M. (1980). Disinhibitory sensation seeking, personality, and gonadal hormones. *Personality and Individual Differences, 1*, 103–110.

Daitzman, R. J., Zuckerman, M., Sammelwitz, P., & Ganjam, V. (1978). Sensation seeking and gonadal hormones. *Journal of Biosocial Science, 10*, 401–408.

Daum, I., Hehl, F. J., & Schugens, M. M. (1988). Construct validity and personality correllates of the Strelau Temperament Inventory. *European Journal of Personality, 2*, 205–216.

Davidson, L. M., & Baum, A. (1986). Chronic stress and posttraumatic stress disorders. *Journal of Consulting and Clinical Psychology, 54*, 303–308.

Davis, C., Cowles, M., & Kohn, P. (1983). Strength of the nervous system and augmenting–reducing. Paradox lost. *Personality and Individual Differences, 4*, 491–498.

Davis, C., Cowles, M., & Kohn, P. (1984). Behavioural and physiological aspects of the augmenting–reducing dimension. *Personality and Individual Differences, 5*, 683–691.

Davis, G. A., Peterson, J. M., & Farley, F. H. (1973). Attitudes, motivation, sensation seeking and belief in ESP as predictors of real creative behavior. *Journal of Creative Behavior, 8*, 31–39.

Day, H. (1968). Curiosity in school achievement. *Journal of Educational Psychology, 59*, 33–43.

Deary, I. J., Ramsay, H., Wilson, J. A., & Riad, M. (1988). Stimulated salivation: Correlations with personality and time of day effects. *Personality and Individual Differences, 9*, 903–909.

Deckers, L., & Ruch, W. (1992). Sensation seeking and the Situational Humour Response Questionnaire (SHRQ): Its relationship in American and German samples. *Personality and Individual Differences, 13*, 1051–1054.

Deforest, F. D., & Johnson, L. S. (1981). Modification of stimulation seeking behavior in psychopaths using hypnotic imagery conditioning. *American Journal of Clinical Hypnosis, 23*, 184–194.

DeFries, J. C., Gervais, M. C., & Thomas, E. A. (1978). Responses to 30 generations of selection for open-field activity in laboratory mice. *Behavior Genetics, 8*, 3–13.

deWit, H., Uhlenhuth, E. H., & Johanson, C. E. (1986). Individual differences in the reinforcing and subjective aspects of amphetamine and diazepam. *Drug and Alcohol Dependence, 16,* 341–360.

Diagnostic and Statistical Manual of the Mental Disorders (DSM-III). (1987). Washington, DC: American Psychiatric Association.

Dickerson, M. G. (1979). FI schedules and persistence at gambling in the UK betting office. *Journal of Applied Behavior Analysis, 12,* 315–323.

Dickerson, M. G., Hinchy, J., & Fabre, J. (1987). Chasing and sensation seeking in off-course gamblers. *British Journal of Addiction, 82,* 673–680.

Diener, E., Larsen, R. J., Levine, S., & Emmons, R. E. (1985). Intensity and frequency: Dimensions underlying positive and negative affect. *Journal of Personality and Social Psychology, 48,* 1253–1265.

Ditunno, P. L., & McCauley, C. (1985). Sensation-seeking behavior and the incidence of spinal cord injury. *Archives of Physical Medicine and Rehabilitation, 66,* 152–155.

Domangue, B. B. (1984). Sensation seeking and cognitive complexity. *Perceptual and Motor Skills, 59,* 749–750.

Donaldson, S. (1989). Similarity in sensation-seeking, sexual satisfaction and contentment in relationship in heterosexual couples. *Psychological Reports, 64,* 405–406.

Donnelly, E. F., Murphy, D. L., Waldman, I. N., Buchsbaum, M. S., & Coursey, R. D. (1979). Psychological characteristics corresponding to low versus high platelet monoamine oxidase activity. *Biological Psychiatry, 14,* 375–383.

Donohew, L., Helm, D. M., Lawrence, P., & Shatzer, M. J. (1990). Sensation seeking, marijuana use, and responses to prevention messages. In R. R. Watson (Ed.), *Drug and alcohol abuse prevention* (pp. 73–93). Towata, NJ: Humana Press.

Donohew, L., Lorch, E., & Palmgreen, P. (1991). Sensation seeking and targeting of televised anti-drug PSA's. In L. Donohew, H. E. Sypher, & W. Bulkoski (Ed.), *Persuasive communication and drug abuse prevention* (pp. 209–226). Hillsdale, NJ: Erlbaum.

Donovan, D. M., & Marlatt, G. A. (1982). Personality subtypes among driving-while-intoxicated offenders: Relationship to drinking behavior and driving risk. *Journal of Consulting and Clinical Psychology, 50,* 241–249.

Donovan, D. M., Queisser, H. R., Salzberg, P. M., & Umlauf, R. L. (1985). Intoxicated and bad drivers: Subgroups within the same population of high-risk men drivers. *Journal of Studies on Alcohol, 46,* 375–382.

Donovan, D. M., Queisser, H. R., Umlauf, R. L., & Salzberg, P. M. (1986). Personality subtypes among driving while-intoxicated offenders: Follow-up of subsequent driving records. *Journal of Consulting and Clinical Psychology, 54,* 563–565.

Douglass, F. M., & Khavari, K. A. (1978). The drug use index: A measure of the extent of polydrug use. *International Journal of the Addictions, 13,* 981–993.

Dragutinovich, S. (1987a). Australian factorial confirmation of Vando's Reducer–Augmenter Scale. *Personality and Individual Differences, 8,* 489–497.

Dragutinovich, S. (1987b). Stimulus intensity reducers: Are they sensation seekers, extraverts, and strong nervous types? *Personality and Individual Differences, 8,* 693–704.

Duffy, E. (1951). The concept of energy mobilization. *Psychological Review, 58,* 30–40.

Duffy, E. (1972). Activation. In N. S. Greenfield & R. A. Sternback (Eds.), *Handbook of psychophysiology.* New York: Holt, Rinehart, & Winston.

Edwards, E. (1984). *The interrelationship between sensation-seeking and horror movie interest and attendance.* Unpublished doctoral dissertation, University of Tennessee.

Ehrhardt, A., Epstein, K., & Money, J. (1968). Fetal androgens and female gender identity in the early treated adrenogenital symptom. *Johns Hopkins Medical Journal, 122,* 160–167.

Eisenman, R. (1987). Creativity, birth order, and risk-taking. *Bulletin of the Psychonomic Society, 25,* 87–88.

Eisenman, R., Grossman, J. C., & Goldstein, R. (1980). Undergraduate marijuana use as related to internal sensation novelty seeking and openness to experience. *Journal of Clinical Psychology, 36,* 1013–1019.

Elliot, G. E., Edelman, A. M., & Berger, P. A. (1977). Indoleamines and other neuroregulators. In J. D. Barchas, P. A. Berger, R. D. Ciaranello, & G. R. Elliot (Eds.), *Psychopharmacology: From theory to practice* (pp. 33–50). New York: Oxford University Press.

Emmons, R. A. (1981). Relationship between narcissism and sensation seeking. *Psychological Reports, 48,* 247–250.

Emmons, T. D., & Webb, W. W. (1974). Subjective correlates of emotional responsivity and stimulation seeking in psychopaths, normals, and acting-out neurotics. *Journal of Consulting and Clinical Psychology, 42,* 620–625.

Engel, B. T. (1972). Response specificity. In N. S. Greenfield & R. A. Sternback (Eds.), *Handbook of psychophysiology* (pp. 571–576). New York: Holt, Rinehart, & Winston.

English, G. E., & Jones, R. E. (1972). *Sensation seeking in hospitalized drug addicts.* Paper presented at the meeting of the Southeastern Psychological Association, Atlanta, GA, April.

Epstein, S. (1970). Anxiety, reality and schizophrenia. *Schizophrenia, 2,* 11–35.

Exline, R. V., Ellyson, S. L., & Long, B. (1975). Visual behavior as an aspect of power role relationships. In P. Pliner, L. Kranes, & T. Aloway (Eds.), *Nonverbal communication of aggression* (pp. 21–52). New York: Plenum.

Eysenck, H. J. (1957). *The dynamics of anxiety and hysteria.* New York: Praeger.

Eysenck, H. J. (1967). *The biological basis of personality.* Springfield, IL: Charles C. Thomas.

Eysenck, H. J. (1983). A biometrical–genetical analysis of impulsive and sensation seeking behavior. In M. Zuckerman (Eds.), *Biological bases of sensation seeking, impulsivity, and anxiety* (pp. 1–36). Hillsdale, NJ: Erlbaum.

Eysenck, H. J. (1984). The comparative approach in personality study. *Behavioral and Brain Sciences, 7,* 440–441.

Eysenck, H. J. (1990). Genetic and environmental contributions to individual differences: Three major dimensions of personality. *Journal of Personality, 58,* 245–261.

Eysenck, H. J., & Eysenck, M. W. (1985). *Personality and individual differences: A natural science approach.* New York: Plenum.

Eysenck, H. J., & Eysenck, S. B. G. (1976). *Psychoticism as a dimension of personality.* London: Hodder & Stoughton.

Eysenck, H. J., & Levey, A. (1972). Conditioning, introversion–extraversion and the strength of the nervous system. In V. D. Nebylitsyn & J. A. Gray (Eds.), *Biological bases of individual behavior* (pp. 206–220). New York: Academic Press.

Eysenck, H. J., Nias, D. K., & Cox, D. N. (1982). Sport and personality. *Advances in Behaviour Research and Therapy, 4,* 1–56.

Eysenck, S. B. G., Easting, G., & Pearson, P. R. (1984). Age norms for impulsiveness, venturesomeness and empathy in children. *Personality and Individual Differences, 5*, 315–321.

Eysenck, S. B. G., & Eysenck, H. J. (1963). On the dual nature of extraversion. *British Journal of Social and Clinical Psychology, 2*, 46–55.

Eysenck, S. B. G., & Eysenck, H. J. (1977). The place of impulsiveness in a dimensional system of personality description. *British Journal of Social and Clinical Psychology, 16*, 57–68.

Eysenck, S. B. G., & Eysenck, H. J. (1978). Impulsiveness and venturesomeness: Their position in a dimensional system of personality description. *Psychological Reports, 43*, 1247–1255.

Eysenck, S. B. G., Eysenck, H. J., & Barrett, P. (1985). A revised version of the psychoticism scale. *Personality and Individual Differences, 6*, 21–29.

Eysenck, S. B. G., & Haapasalo, J. (1989). Cross-cultural comparisons of personality: Finland and England. *Personality and Individual Differences, 10*, 121–125.

Eysenck, S. B. G., Pearson, P. R., Easting, G., & Allsopp, J. F. (1985). Age norms for impulsiveness, venturesomeness, and empathy in adults. *Personality and Individual Differences, 6*, 613–619.

Eysenck, S. B. G., & Zuckerman, M. (1978). The relationship between sensation seeking and Eysenck's dimensions of personality. *British Journal of Psychology, 69*, 483–487.

Faravelli, C., Degl'Innocenti, B., Sessarego, A., & Cabras, P. L. (1987). Personality features of patients with panic anxiety. *New Trends in Experimental and Clinical Psychiatry, 3*, 13–23.

Farley, F. H. (1967). Social desirability and dimensionality in the sensation seeking scale. *Acta Psychologica, 26*, 89–96.

Farley, F. H. (1973). *Implications for a theory of delinquency*. Paper presented at *The sensation seeking motive*, a symposium at the meeting of the American Psychological Association, Montreal, Canada. August.

Farley, F. H. (1981). Basic process individual differences: A biologically based theory of individualization for cognitive, affective, and creative outcomes. In F. H. Farley & N. J. Gordon (Eds.), *Psychology and education: The state of the union*. Berkeley, CA: McCutchon Publishing.

Farley, F. H., & Cox, S. O. (1971). Stimulus-seeking motivation in adolescents as a function of age and sex. *Adolescence, 6*, 207–218.

Farley, F. H., & Davis, S. A. (1977). Arousal, personality, and assortative mating in marriage. *Journal of Sex and Marital Therapy, 3*, 122–127.

Farley, F. H., & Dionne, M. T. (1972). Value orientations of sensation seekers. *Perceptual and Motor Skills, 34*, 509–510.

Farley, F. H., & Farley, S. V. (1967). Extraversion and stimulus seeking motivation. *Journal of Consulting Psychology, 31*, 215–216.

Farley, F. H., & Farley, S. V. (1972). Stimulus seeking motivation and delinquent behavior among institutionalized delinquent girls. *Journal of Consulting and Clinical Psychology, 39*, 140–147.

Farley, F. H., & Mueller, C. B. (1978). Arousal, personality, and assortative mating in marriage: Generalizability and cross-cultural factors. *Journal of Sex and Marital Therapy, 4*, 50–53.

Farmer, R., & Sundberg, N. D. (1986). Boredom proneness: The development of a new scale. *Journal of Personality Assessment, 50*, 4–17.

Farnill, D., & Ball, I. L. (1982). Sensation seeking and intention to donate blood. *Psychological Reports, 51*, 126.

Feij, J. A., Doorn, C. D., van Kampen, D., van den Berg, P. T., & Resing, W. C. M. (1992). Sensation seeking and social support as moderators of the relationship between life events and physical illness. In J. A. M. Winnubst & S. Maes (Eds.), *Life styles, stress and health: New developments in health psychology.* Leiden: Leiden University Press.

Feij, J. A., Orlebeke, J. F., Gazendam, A., & van Zuilen, R. (1985). Sensation seeking: Measurement and psychophysiological correlates. In J. Strelau, F. H. Farley, & A. Gale (Eds.), *Biological bases of personality and behavior* (Vol. 1, pp. 195–210). Washington, DC: Hemisphere.

Feij, J. A., & van Zuilen, R. W. (1984). *SBL Handleiding: Spanningsbehoeftiligst.* Lisse, the Netherlands: Swets & Zeitlinger, B. V.

Feij, J. A., van Zuilen, R. W., & Gazendam, A. (1982). The development of a Dutch sensation seeking questionnaire: The Spanningsbehoeftelijst. *Gedrag-Tijdschrift-voor-Psychologie, 10,* 364–383.

Ficher, I. V., Zuckerman, M., & Neeb, M. (1981). Marital compatibility in sensation seeking as a factor of marital adjustment. *Journal of Sex and Marital Therapy, 7,* 60–69.

Ficher, I. V., Zuckerman, M., & Steinberg, M. (1988). Sensation seeking congruence in couples as a determinant of marital adjustment: A partial replication and extension. *Journal of Clinical Psychology, 44,* 803–809.

File, S. E., & Hyde, J. R. G. (1978). Can social interaction be used to measure anxiety? *British Journal of Pharmacology, 62,* 19–24.

Fisher, S. (1973). *The female orgasm.* New York: Basic Books.

Fiske, D. W., & Maddi, S. R. (1961). *Functions of varied experience.* Homewood, IL: Dorsey Press.

Fletcher, R., & Dowell, L. (1971). Selected personality characteristics of high school athletes and nonathletes. *Journal of Psychology, 77,* 39–41.

Flynn, J. R. (1987). Massive IQ gains in 14 nations. What IQ tests really measure. *Psychological Bulletin, 101,* 171–191.

Forney, M. A., Ripley, W. K., & Forney, P. D. (1988). A profile and prediction study of problem drinking among first-year medical students. *International Journal of the Addictions, 23,* 767–779.

Forsyth, G., & Hundleby, John, D. (1987). Personality and situation as determinants of desire to drink in young adults. *International Journal of the Addictions, 22,* 653–669.

Fowler, C. J., von Knorring, L., & Oreland, L. (1980). Platelet monoamine oxidase activity in sensation seekers. *Psychiatry Research, 3,* 273–279.

Franken, R. E., Gibson, K. J., & Mohan, P. (1990). Sensation seeking and disclosure to close and casual friends. *Personality and Individual Differences, 11,* 829–832.

Franken, R. E., Gibson, K. J., & Rowland, G. L. (1989). Sensation seeking and feelings about the forced-choice format. *Personality and Individual Differences, 10,* 337–339.

Franken, R. E., Gibson, K. J., & Rowland, G. L. (1992). Sensation seeking and the tendency to view the world as threatening. *Personality and Individual Differences, 13,* 31–38.

Franken, R. E., & Rowland, G. L. (1990). Sensation seeking and fantasy. *Personality and Individual Differences, 11,* 191–193.

Frcka, G., & Martin, I. (1987). Is there– or is there not– an influence of impulsiveness on classical eyelid conditioning? *Personality and Individual Differences, 8,* 241–252.

Freixanet, M. G. I. (1991). Personality profile of subjects engaged in high physical risk sports. *Personality and Individual Differences, 12,* 1087–1093.

Freud, S. (1905). *Wit and its relation to the unconscious.* Vienna: Deutiscke.

Freud, S. (1915/1957). Instincts and their vicissitudes. In J. Strachey (Ed.), *The standard edition of the complete psychological works* (Vol. 44, pp. 104–140). London: Hogarth Press.

Freud, S. (1920/1955). Beyond the pleasure principle. In J. Strachey (Ed.), *The standard edition of the complete psychological works* (Vol. 18, pp. 7–64). London: Hogarth Press.

Freud, S. (1923). *The Ego and the Id.* London: Hogarth Press.

Freud, S. (1928/1961). Dostoevsky and parricide. In J. Strachey (Ed.), *The standard edition of the complete psychological works of Sigmund Freud* (Vol. 21, 175–196). London: Hogarth Press.

Freud, S. (1930/1961). Civilization and its discontents. In J. Strachey (Ed.), *The standard edition of the complete psychological works* (Vol. 21, pp. 59–145). London: Hogarth Press.

Frith, C. D. (1971). Smoking behavior and its relation to the smoker's immediate experience. *British Journal of Social and Clinical Psychology, 10,* 73–78.

Fulker, D. W., Eysenck, S. B. G., & Zuckerman, M. (1980). A genetic and environmental analysis of sensation seeking. *Journal of Research in Personality, 14,* 261–281.

Furnham, A. F. (1984). Extraversion, sensation seeking, stimulus screening and Type "A" behaviour pattern: The relationship between measures of arousal. *Personality and Individual Differences, 5,* 133–140.

Furnham, A. F., & Bunyan, M. (1988). Personality and art preferences. *European Journal of Personality, 2,* 67–74.

Furnham, A. F., & Saipe, J. (1993). Personality correlates of convicted drivers. *Personality and Individual Differences, 14,* 329–336.

Gale, A., Kingsley, E., Brookes, S., & Smith, D. (1978). Cortical arousal and social intimacy in the human female under different conditions of eye contact. *Behavioural Processes, 3,* 271–275.

Galizio, M., Gerstenhaber, L., & Friedensen, F. (1985). Correlates of sensation seeking in alcoholics. *International Journal of the Addictions, 20,* 1479–1493.

Galizio, M., Rosenthal, D., & Stein, F. (1983). Sensation seeking, reinforcement and student drug use. *Addictive Behaviors, 8,* 243–252.

Galizio, M., & Stein, F. (1983). Sensation seeking and drug choice. *International Journal of the Addictions, 18,* 1039–1048.

Gangstead, S. W., & Simpson, J. A. (1990). Toward an evolutionary history of female sociosexual variation. *Journal of Personality, 58,* 69–96.

Garlington, W. K., & Shimona, H. E. (1964). The Change Seeker Index: A measure of the need for variable sensory input. *Psychological Reports, 14,* 919–924.

Gerbing, D. W., Ahadi, S. A., & Patton, J. H. (1987). Toward a conceptualization of impulsivity: Components across the behavioral and self-report domains. *Multivariate and Behavioral Research, 22,* 357–379.

Giambra, L. M. (1977). Adult male daydreaming across the life-span: A replication; further analyses and tentative norms based upon retrospective reports. *International Journal of Aging and Human Development, 8,* 197–228.

Giambra, L. M., Camp, C. J., & Grodsky, A. (1992). Curiosity and stimulation seeking across the adult life span: Cross-sectional and seven-year longitudinal findings. *Psychology and Aging, 7,* 150–157.

Gibson, K. J., Franken, R. E., & Rowland, G. L. (1989). Sensation seeking and marital adjustment. *Journal of Sex and Marital Therapy, 15,* 57–61.

Gilliland, K. (1985). The temperament inventory: relationship to theoretically similar western personality dimensions and construct validity. In J. Strelau, F. H. Farley, & A. Gale (Eds.), *The biological bases of personality and behavior* (pp. 161–170). Washington, DC: Hemisphere.

Ginsberg, N., & Pollack-Fels, S. (1991). Headache and sensation seeking. *Psychological Reports, 68,* 615–619.

Glascow, M. R., Cartier, A. M., & Wilson, G. D. (1985). Conservatism, sensation seeking and music preferences. *Personality and Individual Differences, 6,* 395–396.

Glicksohn, J. (1990). Belief in the paranoid and subjective paranormal experience. *Personality and Individual Differences, 11,* 675–683.

Golding, J. F., Ashton, C. H., Marsh, V. R., & Thompson, J. W. (1986). Early and late SEPs, the later the potential the greater the relevance to personality. *Personality and Individual Differences, 7,* 787–794.

Golding, J. F., & Cornish, A. M. (1987). Personality and life-style in medical students: Psychopharmacological aspects. *Psychology and Health, 1,* 287–301.

Golding, J. F., Harpur, T., & Brent-Smith, H. (1983). Personality, drinking and drug-taking correlates of cigarette-smoking. *Personality and Individual Differences, 4,* 703–706.

Golding, J. F., & Richards, M. (1985). EEG spectral analysis, visual evoked potential and photic driving correlates of personality and memory. *Personality and Individual Differences, 6,* 67–76.

Goldman, D., Kohn, P. M., & Hunt, R. W. (1983). Sensation seeking, augmenting-reducing and absolute auditory threshold: A strength-of-the-nervous-system perspective. *Journal of Personality and Social Psychology, 45,* 405–411.

Goma, M., & Grau, P. P. (1989). *Personality in antisocial and normative subjects showing disinhibitory behavior.* Paper presented at the fourth meeting of the International Society for the Study of Individual Differences, Heidelberg, Germany, June 22–25.

Goma, M., Perez, J., & Torrubia, R. (1988). Personality variables in antisocial and prosocial disinhibitory behavior. In T. E. Moffitt & S. A. Mednick (Eds.), *Biological contributions to crime causation* (pp. 211–222). Dordrecht, the Netherlands: Martinus Nijhoff.

Goodall, J. (1986). *The chimpanzees of Gombe.* Cambridge, MA: Belknap/Harvard University Press.

Goreman, B. S., & Wesman, A. E. (1974). The relationships of cognitive styles and moods. *Journal of Clinical Psychology, 30,* 18–36.

Graham, F. K. (1979). Distinguishing among orienting, defensive, and startle reflexes. In H. D. Kimmel, E. H. van Olst, & J. F. Orlebeke (Eds.) *The orienting reflex in humans* (pp. 137–167). Hillsdale, NJ: Erlbaum.

Grant, S. J., Aston-Jones, G., & Redmond, E. (1988). Responses of primate locus coeruleus neurons to simple and complex sensory stimuli. *Brain Research Bulletin, 21,* 401–410.

Gray, J. A. (1964). Strength of the nervous system and levels of arousal. In J. A. Gray (Ed.), *Pavlov's Typology.* (pp. 289–364). New York: Macmillan.

Gray, J. A. (1973). Causal theories of personality and how to test them. In J. R. Royce (Ed.), *Multivariate analysis and psychological theory* (pp. 409–463). New York: Academic Press.

Gray, J. A. (1982). *The neuropsychology of anxiety: An enquiry into the functions of the septohippocampal system.* New York: Oxford University Press.

Gray, J. A. (1987). The neuropsychology of emotion and personality. In S. M. Stahl, S. D. Iverson, & E. C. Goodman (Eds.), *Cognitive neurochemistry* (pp. 171–190). Oxford: Oxford University Press.

Guilford, J. P. (1975). Factors and factors of personality. *Psychological Bulletin, 82,* 802–811.

Gundersheim, J. (1987). Sensation seeking in male and female athletes and nonathletes. *International Journal of Sport Psychology, 18,* 87–99.

Haapasalo, J. (1990). Sensation seeking and Eysenck's personality dimensions in an offender population. *Personality and Individual Differences, 11,* 81–84.

Haidt, J., McCauley, C., & Rozin, P. (1992). *A scale to measure disgust sensitivity.* Unpublished manuscript.

Haier, R. J., Buchsbaum, M. S., Murphy, D. L., Gottesman, I. I., & Coursey, R. D. (1980). Psychiatric vulnerability, monoamine oxidase, and the average evoked potential. *Archives of General Psychiatry, 37,* 340–345.

Haier, R. J., Robinson, D. L., Braden, W., & Williams, D. (1984). Evoked potential augmenting–reducing and personality differences. *Personality and Individual Differences, 5,* 293–301.

Hall, R. A., Rappaport, M., Hopkins, H. K., Griffin, R. B., & Silverman, J. (1970). Evoked response and behavior in cats. *Science, 170,* 998–1000.

Hallman, J., Klinteberg, B., Oreland, L., Wirsen, A., Levander, S. E., & Schalling, D. (1990). *Personality, neuropsychological and biochemical characteristics of air force pilots.* Unpublished manuscript.

Hallman, J., von Knorring, A. L., von Knorring, L., & Oreland, L. (1990). Clinical characteristics of female alcoholics with low platelet monoamine oxidase activity. *Alcoholism: Clinical and Experimental Research, 14,* 227–231.

Hamilton, J. A., Haier, R. J., & Buchsbaum, M. S. (1984). Intrinsic enjoyment and boredom coping scales: Validation with personality evoked potential and attention measures. *Personality and Individual Differences, 5,* 183–193.

Hare, R. D. (1978). Electrodermal and cardiovascular correlates of psychopathy. In R. D. Hare & D. Schalling (Eds.), *Psychopathic behaviour: Approaches to research* (pp. 107–143). New York: Wiley.

Hare, R. D., & Cox, D. N. (1978). Clinical and empirical conceptions of psychopathy and the selection of subjects for research. In R. D. Hare & D. Schalling (Eds.), *Psychopathic Behavior: Approaches to research* (pp. 1–22). New York: Wiley.

Harlow, H. F. (1953a). Mice, monkeys, men and motives. *Psychological Review, 60,* 23–32.

Harlow, H. F. (1953b). Motivation as a factor in the acquisition of new responses. In *Nebraska Symposium on Motivation* (Vol. 1, pp. 24–49). Lincoln: Univ. of Nebraska Press.

Harlow, W. V., & Brown, K. C. (1990). *The role of risk-tolerance in the asset allocation process: A new perspective.* Charlottesville, VA: Research foundation of the Institute of Chartered Financial Analysts.

Harpur, T. J., Hakistan, A. R., & Hare, R. D. (1988). Factor structure of the Psychopathy Check List. *Journal of Consulting and Clinical Psychology, 56,* 741–747.

Harpur, T. J., Hare, R. D., & Hakstian, R. (1989). Two-factor conceptualization of psychopathy: Construct validity and assessment implications. *Psychological Assessment: Journal of Consulting and Clinical Psychology, 1,* 6–17.

Harris, A. (1959). Sensory deprivation in schizophrenia. *Journal of Mental Science, 105,* 235–237.

Harrison, R. H., & Nichols, J. S. (1984). The effect of presenting novel and familiar word pairs on the stimulus-seeking behavior of schizophrenics and normals. *Journal of Psychology, 118,* 179–188.

Hartman, M. K., & Rawson, H. E. (1992). Differences in and correlates of sensation seeking in male and female athletes and non-athletes. *Personality and Individual Differences, 13*, 805–812.

Hartmann, H. (1964). *Essays on ego psychology: Selected problems in psychoanalytic theory.* New York: International Universities Press.

Hauri, P. J., & Olmstead, E. M. (1989). Reverse first night effect in insomnia. *Sleep, 12*, 97–105.

Hayes, M. E. (1988). *A motivational model of gambling behavior.* Unpublished master's thesis, Connecticut State University.

Hebb, D. O. (1946). The nature of fear. *Psychological Review, 53*, 259–276.

Hebb, D. O. (1949). *The organization of behavior.* New York: Wiley.

Hebb, D. O. (1955). Drives and the CNS (conceptual nervous system). *Psychological Review, 62*, 243–254.

Hegerl, U., Priebe, S., Wildgrube, C., & Müller-Oerlinghausen, B. (1990). Expressed emotion and auditory evoked potentials. *Psychiatry, 53*, 108–114.

Hegerl, U., Prochno, I., Ulrich, G., & Muller-Oerlinghausen, B. (1989). Sensation seeking and auditory evoked potentials. *Biological Psychiatry, 25*, 179–190.

Hehl, F. J., & Ruch, W. (1985). The location of sense of humor within comprehensive personality spaces: An exploratory study. *Personality and Individual Differences, 6*, 703–715.

Heino, A., van der Molen, H. H., & Wilde, G. J. S. (1992). *Risk-homeostatic processes in car-following behaviour: Individual differences in car-following and perceived risk.* Traffic Research Center monograph VK 92-02. Groningen, the Netherlands: University of Groningen Press.

Hendrick, C., & Hendrick, S. S. (1986). A theory and method of love. *Journal of Personality and Social Psychology, 50*, 392–402.

Hendrick, C., & Hendrick, S. S. (1988). Lovers wear rose colored glasses. *Journal of Social and Personal Relationships, 5*, 161–183.

Hendrick, S. S., & Hendrick, C. (1987a). Love and sexual attitudes, self-disclosure and sensation seeking. *Journal of Social and Personal Relationships, 4*, 281–297.

Hendrick, S. S., & Hendrick, C. (1987b). Multidimensionality of sexual attitudes. *Journal of Sex Research, 23*, 502–526.

Heyman, S. R., & Rose, K. G. (1979). Psychological variables affecting SCUBA performance. In C. H. Nadeau, W. R. Halliwell, K. M. Newell, & G. C. Roberts (Eds.), *Psychology of motor behavior and sport–1979* (pp. 180–188). Champaign, IL: Human Kinetics Press.

Hirschowitz, R., & Nell, V. (1983). The relationship between need for power and the life style of South African journalists. *Journal of Social Psychology, 121*, 297–304.

Hobfoll, S. E., Rom, T., & Segal, B. (1989). Sensation seeking, anxiety, and risk-taking in the Israeli context. In S. Epstein (Ed.), *Drugs and alcohol use: Issues and facts* (pp. 53–59). New York: Plenum.

Hocking, J., & Robertson, M. (1969). The sensation seeking scale as a predictor of need for stimulation during sensory restriction. *Journal of Consulting and Clinical Psychology, 33*, 367–369.

Horvath, P., & Zuckerman, M. (1993). Sensation seeking, risk appraisal, and risky behavior. *Personality and Individual Differences, 14*, 41–52.

Howard, K. (1961). A test of stimulus-seeking behavior. *Perceptual and Motor Skills, 13*, 416.

Huba, G. J., Newcomb, M. D., & Bentler, P. M. (1981). Comparison of canonical correlation and interbattery factor analysis on sensation seeking and drug use domains. *Applied Psychological Measurement, 5*, 291–306.

Hull, C. L. (1943). *Principles of behavior.* New York: Appleton.

Hymbaugh, K., & Garrett, J. (1974). Sensation seeking among skydivers. *Perceptual and Motor Skills, 38,* 118.

Innes, J. M., & Clarke, A. (1986). Social and personal factors in occupational stress in the emergency services. In J. Sheppard (Ed.), *Advances in behavioral medicine* (Vol. 3, pp. 249–256). Sydney, Australia: Cumberland College of Health Services.

Irey, P. A. (1974). *Personality dimensions of crisis interveners vs. academic psychologists, traditional clinicians and paraprofessionals.* Unpublished doctoral dissertation, Southern Illinois University.

Jackson, D. N. (1974). *Personality Research Form Manual.* Goshen, NY: Research Psychologists Press.

Jackson, D. N. (1976). *Manual, Jackson Personality Inventory.* Goshen, NY: Research Psychologists Press.

Jacobs, K. W., & Koeppel, J. C. (1974). Psychological correlates of the mobility decision. *Bulletin of the Psychonomic Society, 3,* 330–332.

Jaffe, L. T., & Archer, R. P. (1987). The prediction of drug use among college students from MMPI, MCMI, and sensation seeking scales. *Journal of Personality Assessment, 51,* 243–253.

Jansen, A., Klaver, J., Merckelbach, H., & van den Hout, M. A. (1989). Restrained eaters are rapidly habituating sensation seekers. *Behaviour Research and Therapy, 27,* 247–252.

Jimerson, D. C., Nurnberger, J. I., Jr., Post, R. M., Gershon, E. S., & Kopin, I. J. (1981). Plasma MHPG in rapid cyclers and healthy twins. *Archives of General Psychiatry, 38,* 1287–1290.

Jinks, L., & Fulker, D. W. (1970). Comparison of the biometrical, genetical, MAVA, and the classical approaches to the analysis of human behavior. *Psychological Bulletin, 73,* 311–349.

Jobe, J. B., Holgate, S. H., & Sorapansky, T. A. (1983). Risk taking as motivation for volunteering for a hazardous experiment. *Journal of Personality, 51,* 95–107.

Johansson, F. (1982). Differences in serum cortisol concentrations in organic and psychogenic chronic pain syndromes. *Journal of Psychosomatic Research, 26,* 351–358.

Johansson, F., Almay, B. G. L., von Knorring, L., Terrenius, L., & Astrom (1979). Personality traits in chronic patients related to endorphin levels in cerebrospinal fluid. *Psychiatry Research, 1,* 231–239.

Johnson, J. H., Sarason, I. G., & Siegel, J. M. (1979). Arousal seeking as a moderator of life stress. *Perceptual and Motor Skills, 49,* 665–666.

Johnson, V., & White, H. R. (1989). An investigation of factors related to intoxicated driving behaviors among youth. *Journal of Studies on Alcohol, 50,* 320–330.

Jones, A. (1969). Stimulus-seeking behavior. In J. P. Zubek (Ed.), *Sensory deprivation: Fifteen years of research* (pp. 167–206). New York: Appleton-Century-Crofts.

Jones, M. C. (1968). Personality correlates and antecedents of drinking patterns in adult males. *Journal of Consulting and Clinical Psychology, 32,* 2–12.

Jones, M. C. (1971). Personality antecedents and correlates of drinking patterns in women. *Journal of Consulting and Clinical Psychology, 36,* 61–69.

Jönsson, L. E., Anggard, E., & Gunne, L. M. (1971). Blockade of intravenous amphetamine euphoria in man. *Clinical Pharmacology and Therapeutics, 12,* 889–896.

Jöreskog, K. G., & Sörbom, D. (1988). *LISREL 7: A guide to the program and applications.* Chicago: SPSS.

Jorgensen, R. S., & Johnson, J. H. (1990). Contributors to the appraisal of major life changes: Gender, perceived controllability, sensation seeking, strain and social support. *Journal of Applied Psychology, 20,* 1123–1138.

Kaestner, E., Rosen, L., & Apel, P. (1977). Patterns of drug abuse: Relationships with ethnicity, sensation seeking, and anxiety. *Journal of Consulting and Clinical Psychology, 45,* 462–468.

Kafry, D. (1982). Sensation seeking of young children. *Personality and Individual Differences, 3,* 161–166.

Kagan, J. (1966). Reflection–impulsivity: The generality and dynamics of conceptual tempo. *Journal of Abnormal Psychology, 71,* 17–24.

Kagan, J., Rosman, B. L., Day, D., Albert, J., & Phillips, W. (1964). Information processing in the child: Significance of analytic and reflective attitudes. *Psychological Monographs, 78* (Whole No. 578).

Karoly, P. (1975). Comparison of "psychological styles" in delinquent and nondelinquent females. *Psychological Reports, 36,* 567–570.

Kern, M. F., Kenkel, M. B., Templer, D. I., & Newell, T. G. (1986). Drug preference as a function of arousal and stimulus screening. *International Journal of the Addictions, 21,* 255–265.

Kerr, J. H., & Svebak, S. (1989). Motivational aspects of preference for and participation in "risk" and "safe" sports. *Personality and Individual Differences, 10,* 797–800.

Khavari, K. A., Humes, M., & Mabry, E. (1977). Personality correlates of hallucinogen use. *Journal of Abnormal Psychology, 86,* 172–178.

Kilpatrick, D. G., McAlhany, D., McCurdy, L., Shaw, D. L., & Roitzsch, J. C. (1982). Aging, alcoholism, anxiety, and sensation seeking: An exploratory investigation. *Addictive Behaviors, 7,* 97–100.

Kilpatrick, D. G., Sutker, P. B., & Smith, A. D. (1976). Deviant drug and alcohol use: The role of anxiety, sensation seeking, and other personality variables. In M. Zuckerman & C. D. Spielberger (Eds.), *Emotions and anxiety: New concepts, methods, and applications* (pp. 247–278). Hillsdale, NJ: Erlbaum.

Kinsey, A. C., Pomeroy, W. B., Martin, C. E., & Gebhard, P. H. (1953). *Sexual behavior in the human female.* Philadelphia: Saunders.

Kish, G. B. (1966). Studies of sensory reinforcement. In W. K. Honig (Ed.), *Operant behavior.* Englewood Cliffs, NJ: Prentice-Hall.

Kish, G. B. (1967). *Stimulus seeking and learning.* Unpublished manuscript.

Kish, G. B. (1970a). Reduced cognitive innovation and stimulus-seeking in chronic schizophrenics. *Journal of Clinical Psychology, 26,* 170–174.

Kish, G. B. (1970b). Correlates of active–passive food preferences: Failure to confirm a relationship with alcoholism. *Perceptual and Motor Skills, 31,* 839–847.

Kish, G. B. (1971). CPI correlates of stimulus seeking in male alcoholics. *Journal of Clinical Psychology, 27,* 251–253.

Kish, G. B. (1973). *A two-factor theory of sensation seeking.* Paper presented at *The sensation seeking motive,* a symposium at the meeting of the American Psychological Association, Montreal, Canada, August.

Kish, G. B., & Ball, M. E. (1968). *Effects of individual differences in stimulus-seeking upon learning rate in schizophrenics.* Unpublished manuscript.

Kish, G. B., & Busse, W. (1968). Correlates of stimulus seeking: Age, education, intelligence and aptitudes. *Journal of Consulting and Clinical Psychology, 32,* 633–637.

Kish, G. B., & Donnenwerth, G. V. (1969). Interests and stimulus seeking. *Journal of Counseling Psychology, 16,* 551–556.

Kish, G. B., & Donnenwerth, G. V. (1972). Sex differences in the correlates of stimulus seeking. *Journal of Consulting and Clinical Psychology, 38,* 42–49.

Kish, G. B., Frankel, A., Masters, J. J., & Berry, R. A. (1976). Augmenting–reducing and sensation seeking: A test of Sales' hypothesis. *Journal of Clinical Psychology, 32,* 302–305.

Klinteberg, B., Oreland, L., Hallman, J., Wirsen, A., Levander, S. E., & Schalling, D. (1991). Exploring the connections between platelet monoamine oxidase (MAO) activity and behavior: Relationships with performance in neuropsychological tasks. *Neuropsychobiology, 23,* 188–196.

Klinteberg, B., Schalling, D., Edman, G., Oreland, L., & Åsberg, M. (1985). Personality correlates of monoamine oxidase (MAO) activity in female and male subjects. *Neuropsychobiology, 18,* 89–96.

Knott, V. J. (1988). Dynamic EEG changes during cigarette smoking. *Neuropsychobiology, 19,* 54–60.

Kohn, P. M. (1987). Issues in the measurement of arousability. In J. Strelau & H. J. Eysenck (Eds.), *Personality dimensions and arousal* (pp. 233–250). New York: Plenum.

Kohn, P. M., & Annis, H. M. (1978). Personality and social factors in adolescent marijuana use: A path-analytic study. *Journal of Consulting and Clinical Psychology, 46,* 366–367.

Kohn, P. M., Barnes, G. E., & Hoffman, F. M. (1979). Drug-use history and experience seeking among male correctional inmates. *Journal of Consulting and Clinical Psychology, 47,* 708–715.

Kohn, P. M., Hunt, R. W., Cowles, M. P., & Davis, C. A. (1986). Factor structure and construct validity of the Vando Reducer–Augmenter Scale. *Personality and Individual Differences, 7,* 57–64.

Kohn, P. M., Hunt, R. W., Davis, C. A., & Cowles, M. P. (1982). Volunteering in principle, volunteering in fact, and experience seeking. *Psychological Record, 32,* 205–213.

Kohn, P. M., Hunt, R. W., & Hoffman, F. M. (1982). Aspects of experience seeking. *Canadian Journal of Behavioural Science, 14,* 13–23.

Kreuz, L. E., & Rose, R. M. (1972). Assessment of aggressive behavior and plasma testosterone in a young criminal population. *Psychosomatic Medicine, 34,* 321–332.

Kuhlberg, G. E., & Franco, E. A. (1976). A-B as a measure of external sensation-seeking. *Journal of Clinical Psychology, 32,* 572–576.

Kulcsár, Z., Kutor, L., & Arató, M. (1984). Sensation seeking, its biochemical correlates, and its relation to vestibulo-ocular functions. In H. Bonarius, G. van Heck, & N. Smid (Eds.), *Personality psychology in Europe: Theoretical and empirical developments* (pp. 327–346). Lisse, the Netherlands: Swets & Zeitlinger.

Kulcsár, Z., Nabrady, M., & Kutor, L. (1986). Sensation seeking and vestibulo-ocular functions in prepubertal children. *Magyar-Pszichologiai-Szemle, 43,* 199–215.

Kuley, N. B., & Jacobs, D. F. (1988). The relationship between dissociative-like experiences and sensation seeking among social and problem gamblers. *Journal of Gambling Behavior, 4,* 197–207.

Kumar, V. K., Pekala, R. J., & Cummings, J. (1993). Sensation seeking, drug use, and reported paranormal beliefs and experiences. *Personality and Individual Differences, 14,* 685–691.

Kuperman, S., Kramer, J., & Loney, J. (1988). Enzyme activity and behavior in hyperactive children grown up. *Biological Psychiatry, 24,* 375–383.

Kurtz, J. P., & Zuckerman, M. (1978). Race and sex differences on the Sensation Seeking Scales. *Psychological Reports, 43,* 529–530.

Kusyszyn, I., & Rutter, R. (1985). Personality characteristics of male heavy gamblers, light gamblers, nongamblers, and lottery players. *Journal of Gambling Behavior, 1,* 59–64.

Lacey, J. I. (1967). Somatic response patterns and stress: Some revisions of activation theory. In M. H. Apley & R. Trumbell (Eds.), *Issues in research* (pp. 14–22). New York: Appleton.

Lambert, W., & Levy, L. H. (1972). Sensation-seeking and short-term isolation. *Journal of Personality and Social Psychology, 24,* 46–52.

Landau, S. G., Buchsbaum, M. S., Carpenter, W., Strauss, J., & Sacks, M. (1975). Schizophrenia and stimulus intensity control. *Archives of General Psychiatry, 32,* 1239–1245.

Landeweerd, J. A., Urlings, I. J. M., & DeJong, A. H. J. (1990). Risk taking tendency among construction workers. *Journal of Occupational Accidents, 11,* 183–196.

Langer, E. J. (1975). The illusion of control. *Journal of Personality and Social Psychology, 32,* 311–328.

Leckman, J. F., Gershon, E. S., Nichols, A. S., & Murphy, D. L. (1977). Reduced MAO activity in first degree relatives or individuals with bipolar affective disorders. *Archives of General Psychiatry, 34,* 601–606.

Lerner, P., Goodman, F. K., van Kammen, D. P., Post, R. M., Major, L. K., Ballenger, J. C., & Lovenberg, W. D. (1978). Dopamine-beta-hydroxylase in the cerebrospinal fluid of psychiatric patients. *Biological Psychiatry, 13,* 685–694.

Lesieur, H. R., Blume, S. B., & Zoppa, M. (1986). Alcoholism, drug abuse, and gambling. *Alcoholism: Clinical and Experimental Research, 10,* 33–38.

Lesnik-Oberstein, M., & Cohen, L. (1984). Cognitive style, sensation seeking, and assortative mating. *Journal of Personality and Social Psychology, 46,* 112–117.

Levin, B. H., & Brown, W. E. (1975). Susceptibility to boredom of jailers and law enforcement officers. *Psychological Reports, 36,* 190.

Lewis, E. G., Dustman, R. E., & Beck, E. C. (1972). Evoked response similarity in monozygotic, dizygotic and unrelated individuals: A comparative study. *Electroencephalography and Clinical Neurology, 23,* 309–316.

Lindner, R. M. (1958). The psychodynamics of gambling. *Annals of the American Academy of Political and Social Science, 269,* 93–107.

Lindsley, D. B. (1961). Common factors in sensory deprivation, sensory distortion and sensory overload. In P. Solomon, P. E. Kubzansky, P. H. Leiderman, J. H. Mendelson, R. Trumbull, & D. Wexler (Eds.), *Sensory deprivation* (pp. 174–194). Cambridge, MA: Harvard University Press.

Litle, P. (1986). *Effects of a stressful movie and music on mood and physiological arousal in relation to sensation seeking.* Unpublished doctoral dissertation University of Delaware.

Litle, P., & Zuckerman, M. (1986). Sensation seeking and music preferences. *Personality and Individual Differences, 4,* 575–578.

Loehlin, J. C. (1992). *Genes and environment in personality development.* Newbury Park, CA: Sage Publications.

Logue, A. W., & Smith, M. E. (1986). Predictors of food preferences in adults. *Appetite, 7,* 109–125.

Loo, R. (1979). Role of primary personality factors in the perception of traffic signs and driver violations and accidents. *Accident Analysis and Prevention, 11,* 125–127.

Looft, W. R., & Baranowski, M. D. (1971). Analysis of five measures of sensation seeking and preference for complexity. *Journal of General Psychology, 85,* 307–313.

Loper, R. G., Kammeier, M. L., & Hoffman, H. (1973). MMPI characteristics of college males who later became alcoholics. *Journal of Abnormal Psychology, 82,* 159–162.

Lukas, J. H. (1987). Visual evoked potential augmenting–reducing and personality: The vertex augmenter is a sensation seeker. *Personality and Individual Differences, 8,* 385–395.

Lukas, J. H., Monty, R. A., Dominessy, M. E., Milkin, F. J., & Oatman, L. C. (1990). Workload, target acquisition and piloting performance: Psychological and physiological predictors. *Proceedings of the Army Science Conference*

Lukas, J. H., & Mullins, L. F. (1983). Auditory augmenting–reducing and sensation seeking. *Psychophysiology, 20,* 457 (Abstract).

Lukas, J. H., & Mullins, L. F. (1985). Auditory augmenters are sensation seekers and perform better under high work loads. *Psychophysiology, 22,* 580–581 (Abstract).

Lukas, J. H., & Mullins, L. F. (1988). Evoked potential technique for predicting performance under high mental workloads. *Proceedings of the Army Science Conference, 2,* 203–215.

Lukas, J. H., & Siegel, J. (1977). Cortical mechanisms that augment or reduce evoked potentials in cats. *Science, 196,* 73–75.

Lykken, D. T. (1982). Research with twins: The concept of emergenesis. *Psychophysiology, 25,* 4–15.

Lynn, R. (1990). The role of nutrition in secular increases in intelligence. *Personality and Individual Differences, 11,* 273–285.

MacAndrew, C. (1979). On the possibility of the psychometric detection of persons who are prone to the abuse of alcohol and other substances. *Addictive Behaviors, 4,* 11–20.

Madsen, D. B., Das, A. K., Bogen, I., & Grossman, E. E. (1987). A short sensation seeking scale. *Psychological Reports, 60,* 1179–1184.

Magaro, P. A., & Smith, P. (1981). The personality of clinical types: An empirically derived taxonomy. *Journal of Clinical Psychology, 37,* 796–809.

Magaro, P. A., Smith, P., Cionini, L., & Velicogna, F. (1979). Sensation seeking in Italy and the United States. *Journal of Social Psychology, 109,* 159–165.

Mahanta, J. (1983). The development of a sensation-seeking scale in Oriya: A preliminary attempt. *Psychological Studies, 28,* 1–3.

Major, L. F., Lerner, P., Goodwin, F. K., Ballenger, J. C., Brown, G. L., & Lorenberg, W. (1980). Dopamine-beta-hydroxylase in CSF. *Archives of General Psychiatry, 37,* 307–310.

Major, L. F., & Murphy, D. L. (1978). Platelet and plasma amine oxidase activity in alcoholic individuals. *British Journal of Psychiatry, 132,* 548–554.

Malatesta, V. J., Sutker, P. B., & Treiber, F. A. (1981). Sensation seeking and chronic public drunkenness. *Journal of Consulting and Clinical Psychology, 49,* 292–294.

Mangelsdorf, A. D., & Zuckerman, M. (1975). Habituation to scenes of violence. *Psychophysiology, 12,* 124–129.

Mann, R. E., Vingilis, E. R., Anglin, L., Suuriali, H., Poudrier, L. M., & Vaga, K. (1987). Long-term follow-up of convicted drunken drivers. In P. C. Noordzij & R. Roszbach (Eds.), *Alcohol, drugs, and traffic safety* (pp. 545–548). Amsterdam: Elsevier.

Martin, M. (1985). Individual differences in sensation seeking and attentional ability. *Personality and Individual Differences, 6,* 637–639.

Martin, N. G., Eaves, L. J., & Fulker, D. W. (1979). The genetical relationship of impulsiveness and sensation seeking to Eysenck's personality dimensions. *Acta Genetica Medica Gemellol, 28,* 197–210.

Maslow, A. H. (1954). *Motivation and personality.* New York: Harper.

Mattson, A., Schalling, D., Olweus, D., Low, H., & Svensson, J. (1980). Plasma testosterone, aggressive behavior, and personality dimensions in young male delinquents. *Journal of the American Academy of Child Psychiatry, 19,* 476–490.

McAuliffe, W. F., Rohman, M., & Wechsler, H. (1984). Alcohol, substance use, and other risk factors of impairment in a sample of physicians in training. *Advances in Alcohol and Substance Abuse, 4,* 67–87.

McCann, S. C., Mueller, C. W., Hays, P. A., Scheuler, A. D., & Marsella, A. J. (1990). The relationship between sensation seeking and anhedonia. *Personality and Individual Differences, 11,* 77–79.

McClearn, G. E. (1959). Genetics of mouse behavior in novel situations. *Journal of Comparative and Physiological Psychology, 52,* 62–67.

McClelland, D. C., Atkinson, J. W., Clark, R. A., & Lowell, E. L. (1953). *The achievement motive.* New York: Appleton-Century-Crofts.

McCrae, R. R. (1987). Creativity, divergent thinking and openness to experience. *Journal of Personality and Social Psychology, 52,* 1258–1265.

McCrae, R. R., & Costa, P. T., Jr. (1985). Openness to experience. In R. Hogan & W. H. Jones (Eds.), *Perspectives in personality* (Vol. 1, pp. 145–172). Greenwich, CT: JAI Press.

McCrae, R. R., & Costa, P. T., Jr. (1987). Validity of the five-factor model of personality across instruments and observers. *Journal of Personality and Social Psychology, 52,* 81–90.

McCrae, R. R., & Costa, P. T., Jr. (in press). Conceptions and correlates of openness to experience. In R. Hogan, J. A. Johnson, & S. R. Briggs (Eds.), *Handbook of personality psychology.* New York: Academic Press.

McCutcheon, L. (1981). Running and sensation seeking. *Footnotes* (publication of Road Runners Club of America), *9,* 8.

McDougall, W. (1923). *Outline of psychology.* New York: Scribners.

McGhie, A., & Chapman, J. S. (1961). Disorders of attention and perception in early schizophrenia. *British Journal of Medical Psychology, 34,* 103–116.

McNeal, E. T. (1986). Antidepressants and biochemical theories of depression. *Psychological Bulletin, 99,* 361–374.

McReynolds, P. (1963). Reactions to novel and familiar stimuli as a function of schizophrenic withdrawal. *Perceptual and Motor Skills, 16,* 847–850.

Mednick, S. A. (1958). A learning theory approach to research in schizophrenia. *Psychological Bulletin, 55,* 316–327.

Meehl, P. E. (1962). Schizotaxia, schizotypy, schizophrenia. *American Psychologist, 17,* 827–838.

Mehrabian, A. (1975). Affiliation as a function of attitude discrepancy with another and arousal-seeking tendency. *Journal of Personality, 43,* 582–590.

Mehrabian, A. (1978). Characteristic individual reactions of preferred and unpreferred environments. *Journal of Personality, 46,* 718–731.

Meier, S. T., & Schmeck, R. R. (1985). The burned-out college student: A descriptive profile. *Journal of College Student Personnel, 26,* 63–69.

Mellstrom, M., Jr., Cicala, G. A., & Zuckerman, M. (1976). General versus specific trait anxiety measures in the prediction of fear of snakes, heights, and darkness. *Journal of Consulting Psychology, 44,* 83–91.

Metz, J., Goode, D. J., & Meltzer, H. Y. (1980). Descriptive studies of the H-reflex recovery curves in psychiatric patients. *Psychological Medicine, 10,* 541–548.

Miller, I., & Magaro, P. (1977). Toward a theory of personality style: Measurement and reliability. *Journal of Clinical Psychology, 33,* 460–466.

Mishara, B. L. (1986). The myth of aftereffect's unreliability. *Behavioral and Brain Sciences, 9,* 747–748.

Montag, I., & Birenbaum, M. (1986). Psychopathological factors and sensation seeking. *Journal of Research in Personality, 20,* 338–348.

Mookherjee, H. N. (1986). Comparison of some personality characteristics of male problem drinkers in rural Tennessee. *Journal of Alcohol and Drug Education, 31,* 23–28.

Moorman, P. P., deCocq van Delwijnen, H., van Wessel, K., & Bauer, H. (1989). *Personality characteristics of drug addicts in the Netherlands* (Leiden Psychological Reports LPR-PP02-89). Dept. of Psychology, Leiden University, the Netherlands.

Morgan, W. P. (1980). The trait psychology controversy. *Research Quarterly for Exercise and Sport, 51,* 50–76.

Moruzzi, G., & Magoun, H. W. (1949). Brain stem reticular formation and activation of the EEG. *EEG Clinical Neurophysiology, 1,* 455–473.

Mullins, L. F., & Lukas, J. H. (1984). Auditory augmenters are sensation seekers if they attend the stimuli. *Psychophysiology, 21,* 589 (Abstract).

Mullins, L. F., & Lukas, J. H. (1987). *Brain potentials and personality: A new look at stress susceptibility* (Technical memorandum 20-87). U.S. Army Human Engineering Laboratory, Aberdeen Proving Ground, Aberdeen, MD.

Murgatroyd, S. (1985). The nature of telic dominance. In M. J. Apter, D. Fontana, & S. Murgatroyd (Eds.), *Reversal theory applications and development* (pp. 20–41). Cardiff, Wales: University College Cardiff Press.

Murgatroyd, S., Rushton, C., Apter, M. J., & Ray, C. (1978). The development of the Telic dominance scale. *Journal of Personality Assessment, 42,* 519–528.

Murphy, D. L., Aulakh, C. S., Garrick, N. A., & Sunderland, T. (1987). Monoamine oxidase inhibitors as antidepressants: Implications for the mechanism of action of antidepressants and the psychobiology of the affective disorders and some related disorders. In H. Y. Meltzer (Ed.), *Psychopharmacology: the third generation of progress* (pp. 545–552). New York: Raven Press.

Murphy, D. L., Belmaker, R. H., Buchsbaum, M. S., Martin, N. F., Ciaranello, R., & Wyatt, R. J. (1977). Biogenic amine related enzymes and personality variations in normals. *Psychological Medicine, 7,* 149–157.

Murphy, D. L., & Weiss, R. (1972). Reduced monoamine oxidase activity in blood platelets from bipolar depressed patients. *American Journal of Psychiatry, 128,* 1351–1357.

Murphy, D. L., Wright, C., Buchsbaum, M. S., Nichols, A., Costa, J. L., & Wyatt, R. J. (1976). Platelet and plasma amine oxidase activity in 680 normals: Sex and age differences and stability over time. *Biochemical Medicine, 16,* 254–265.

Murray, H. A. (1938). *Explorations in personality.* New York: Oxford University Press.

Muscettola, G., Potter, W. Z., Pickar, D., & Goodwin, F. K. (1984). Urinary-3-

methoxy-4-hydroxyphenylglycol and major affective disorders. *Archives of General Psychiatry, 41*, 337–342.

Musolino, R. F., & Hershenson, D. B. (1977). Avocational sensation seeking in high and low risk taking occupations. *Journal of Vocational Behavior, 10*, 358–365.

Myers, T. I., & Eisner, E. J. (1974). *An experimental evaluation of the effects of karate and meditation* (Report No. 42800/P-391X-1-29). Washington, DC: American Institutes for Research.

Näätänen, R., & Picton, T. (1987). The N1 wave of the human electric and magnetic response to sound: A review and an analysis of the component structure. *Psychophysiology, 24*, 375–425.

Nadler, L. B. (1985). The epidemiology of pathological gambling: Critique of existing research and alternative strategies. *Journal of Gambling Behavior, 1*, 35–50.

Neary, R. S. (1975). *The development and validation of a state measure of sensation seeking*. Unpublished doctoral dissertation, University of Delaware.

Neary, R. S., & Zuckerman, M. (1976). Sensation seeking, trait and state anxiety, and the electrodermal orienting reflex. *Psychophysiology, 13*, 205–211.

Necka, E. (1991). *Traits, states, and dealing with novelty.* Paper presented at the fifth meeting of the International Society for the Study of Individual Differences, Oxford, England, July 22–26.

Nerviano, J. (1976). Common personality problems among alcoholic males: A multivariate study. *Journal of Consulting and Clinical Psychology, 44*, 104–110.

Netter, P., & Rammsayer, T. (1989). Serotoninergic effects on sensory and motor responses in extraverts and introverts. *International Clinical Psychopharmacology, 4* (Suppl. 1), 21–26.

Netter, P., & Rammsayer, T. (1991). Reactivity to dopaminergic drugs and aggression related personality traits. *Personality and Individual Differences, 12*, 1009–1017.

Newcomb, M. D., & McGee, L. (1991). The influence of sensation seeking on general and specific problem behaviors from adolescence to young adulthood. *Journal of Personality and Social Psychology, 61*, 614–628.

Nurnberger, J. I., Jr., Hamovit, J., Hibbs, E. D., Pellegrini, D., Guroff, J. J., Maxwell, M. E., Smith, A., & Gershon, E. S. (1988). A high-risk study of primary affective disorder: Selection of subjects, initial assessment, and 1- to 2-year follow-up. In D. L. Dunner, E. S. Gershon, & J. E. Barrett (Eds.), *Relatives at risk for mental disorder* (pp. 161–177). New York: Raven Press.

O'Carroll, R. E. (1984). Androgen administration to hypogonadal and eugonadal men: Effects on measures of sensation seeking, personality and spatial ability. *Personality and Individual Differences, 5*, 595–598.

O'Connor, K. (1980). Individual differences in situational preferences among smokers. *Personality and Individual Differences, 1*, 249–257.

O'Connor, K. (1982). Individual differences in the effect of smoking on frontal-central distribution of the CNV: Some observations on smokers' control of attentional behavior. *Personality and Individual Differences, 3*, 271–285.

O'Gorman, J. G., & Lloyd, J. E. M. (1987). Extraversion, impulsiveness, and EEG alpha activity. *Personality and Individual Differences, 8*, 169–174.

Okamoto, K., & Tokari, E. (1992). Structure of creativity measurements and their correlations with sensation seeking and need for uniqueness. *Japanese Journal of Experimental Social Psychology, 31*, 203–210.

Olds, J., & Milner, P. (1954). Positive reinforcement produced by electrical stimulation of septal area and other regions of the rat brain. *Journal of Comparative and Physiological Psychology, 47*, 419–427.

Oleszkiewicz, Z. Z. (1982). Demand for stimulation and vocational preferences. *Polish Psychological Bulletin, 13,* 185–195.

Oleszkiewicz, Z. Z. (1985). Adaptation of M. Zuckerman's Sensation Seeking Scale for Polish conditions. *Przeglad-Psychologiczny, 28,* 1123–1128.

Olson, K. R., & Camp, C. J. (1984). Factor analysis of curiosity measures in adults. *Psychological Reports, 54,* 491–497.

Olson, K. R., Camp, C. J., & Fuller, D. (1984). Curiosity and the need for cognition. *Psychological Reports, 54,* 71–74.

O'Neil, P. M., Giacinto, J. P., Waid, L. R., Roitzsch, J. C., Miller, W. C., & Kilpatrick, D. G. (1983). Behavioral, psychological, and historical correlates of MacAndrew scale scores among male alcoholics. *Journal of Behavioral Assessment, 5,* 261–273.

Ono, A., & Murayama, K. (1986). Stimulation seeking and selective attention in juvenile delinquents. *Memoirs of Osaka Kyoiku University,* Ser. IV, Vol. *35,* No. 1, pp. 33–41.

Oreland, L., Hallman, J., von Knorring, L. V., & Edman, G. (1988). Studies on monoamine oxidase in relation to alcohol abuse. In K. Kuriyama, A. Takeda, & H. Ishii (Eds.), *Biomedical and social aspects of alcohol and alcoholism* (pp. 207–210). New York: Elsevier Science Publishers, Biomedical Division.

Oreland, L., Wilberg, A., & Fowler, C. J. (1981). Monoamine oxidase activity as related to monoamine oxidase activity and monoaminergic function in the brain. In B. Angrist (Ed.), *Recent advances in neuropsychopharmacology* (Vol. 31). Oxford: Pergamon.

Orlebeke, J. F., & Feij, J. A. (1979). The orienting reflex as a personality correlate. In E. H. van Olst & J. F. Orlebeke (Eds.), *The orienting reflex in humans* (pp. 567–585). Hillsdale, NJ: Erlbaum.

Orlebeke, J. F., Kok, A., & Zeillemaker, C. W. (1989). Disinhibition and the processing of auditory stimulus intensity: An ERP study. *Personality and Individual Differences, 10,* 445–451.

Orr, S. P., Claiborn, J. M., Altman, B., Forgue, D. F., deJong, J. B., Pitman, R. K., & Herz, L. R. (1990). Psychometric profile of posttraumatic stress disorder, anxious, and healthy Vietnam veterans: Correlations with psychophysiologic responses. *Journal of Consulting and Clinical Psychology, 58,* 329–335.

Osborne, J. W., & Farley, F. H. (1970). The relationship between aesthetic preference and visual complexity in abstract art. *Psychonomic Science, 19,* 69–70.

Otis, L. P. (1984). Factors influencing the willingness to taste unusual foods. *Psychological Reports, 54,* 739–745.

Oxenstierna, G., Edman, G., Iselius, L., Oreland, L., Ross, S. B., & Sedvall, G. (1986). Concentrations of monoamine metabolites in the cerebrospinal fluid of twins and unrelated individuals: A genetic study. *Journal of Psychiatric Research, 20,* 19–20.

Pandey, G. N., Fawcett, J., Gibbons, R., Clark, D. C., & Davis, J. M. (1988). Platelet monoamine oxidase in alcoholism. *Biological Psychiatry, 24,* 15–24.

Panksepp, J. (1982). Toward a general psychobiological theory of emotions. *Behavioral and Brain Sciences, 5,* 407–422.

Passini, F. T., Watson, C. G., Dehnel, L., Herder, J., & Watkins, B. (1977). Alpha wave feedback training therapy in alcoholics. *Journal of Clinical Psychology, 33,* 292–299.

Patrick, A., Zuckerman, M., & Masterson, F. (1974). An extension of the trait-state distinction from affects to motive measures. *Psychological Reports, 34,* 1251–1258.

Pavlov, I. (1927/1960). *Conditioned reflexes: An investigation of the physiological activity of the cerebral cortex* (G. V. Anrep, Ed.). New York: Dover Publications.

Payne, R. W., Matussek, P., & George, E. I. (1959). An experimental study of schizophrenic thought disorder. *Journal of Mental Science, 105*, 627–652.

Pearson, P. H. (1970). Relationships between global and specific measures of sensation seeking. *Journal of Consulting and Clinical Psychology, 34*, 199–204.

Pearson, P. R., Francis, L. J., & Lightbown, T. J. (1986). Impulsivity and religiosity. *Personality and Individual Differences, 7*, 89–94.

Pearson, P. R., & Sheffield, B. F. (1975). Social attitude correlates of sensation seeking in psychiatric patients. *Perceptual and Motor Skills, 40*, 482.

Pederson, S. L., & Magaro, P. A. (1982). Personality styles and psychopathy. *Journal of Clinical Psychology, 38*, 320–324.

Pederson, W., Clausen, S. E., & Lavik, N. J. (1989). Patterns of drug use and sensation seeking among adolescents in Norway. *Acta Psychiatrica Scandinavica, 79*, 386–390.

Pemberton, W. A. (1971). *Further dimensions of sensation seeking.* Paper presented at the meeting of the Delaware Psychological Association, Newark, DE, May.

Penney, R. K., & Reinehr, R. C. (1966). Development of a stimulus-variation seeking scale for adults. *Psychological Reports, 18*, 631–638.

Perez, J., Ortet, G., Pla, S., & Simo, S. (1986). A junior Sensation Seeking Scale. *Personality and Individual Differences, 7*, 915–918.

Perez, J., & Torrubia, R. (1985). Sensation seeking and antisocial behaviour in a student sample. *Personality and Individual Differences, 6*, 401–403.

Perez, J., & Torrubia, R. (1986). Reliability and validity of the Spanish version of the Sensation Seeking Scale (form V). *Revista Latinoamericana de Psicologia, 18*, 7–22.

Perone, M., Dewaard, R. J., & Baron, A. (1979). Satisfaction with real and simulated jobs in relation to personality variables and drug use. *Journal of Applied Psychology, 64*, 660–668.

Perris, C., Jacobssen, L., Oreland, L., Perris, H., & Ross, S. B. (1980). Enzymes related to biogenic amine metabolism and personality characteristics in depressed patients. *Acta Psychiatrica Scandinavica, 61*, 477–484.

Persky, H., Dreisbach, L., Miller, W. R., O'Brien, C. P., Khan, M. A., Lief, H. I., Charney, N., & Straus, D. (1982). The relation of plasma androgen levels to sexual behaviors and attitudes of women. *Psychosomatic Medicine, 44*, 305–319.

Petrie, A. (1967). *Individuality in pain and suffering.* Chicago: University of Chicago Press.

Pettigrew, T. F. (1958). The measurements and correlates of category width as a cognitive variable. *Journal of Personality, 26*, 532–544.

Piet, S. (1987). What motivates stunt men? *Motivation and Emotion, 11*, 195–213.

Pilkington, C. J., Richardson, D. R., & Utley, M. E. (1988). Is conflict stimulating? Sensation seekers responses to interpersonal conflict. *Personality and Social Psychology Bulletin, 14*, 596–603.

Pivik, R. T., Stelmack, R. M., & Bylsma, F. W. (1988). Personality and individual differences in spinal motoneuronal excitability. *Psychophysiology, 25*, 16–24.

Platt, J. J., & Labate, C. (1976). *Heroin addiction: Theory, research, and treatment.* New York: Wiley.

Plomin, R., & Bergeman, C. S. (1991). The nature of nurture: Genetic influences on "environmental" measures. *Behavioral and Brain Sciences, 14*, 373–427.

Plomin, R., Lichenstein, P., Pederson, N., McClearn, G. E., & Nesselroade, J. R. (1990). Genetic influence on life events during the last half of the life span. *Psychology and Aging, 5,* 25–30.

Plouffe, L., & Stelmack, R. M. (1986). Sensation seeking and the electrodermal orienting response in young and elderly females. *Personality and Individual Differences, 7,* 119–120.

Popper, K. R. (1979). *Objective knowledge: An evolutionary approach.* Oxford: Clarendon.

Post, R. M., Jimerson, D. C., Ballenger, J. C., Lake, C. R., Uhde, T. W., & Goodwin, F. K. (1984). Cerebrospinal fluid norepinephrine and its metabolites in manic-depressive illness. In R. M. Post & J. C. Ballenger (Eds.), *Neurobiology of mood disorders* (pp. 539–553). Baltimore: Williams & Wilkins.

Potgieter, J., & Bisschoff, F. (1990). Sensation seeking among medium and low risk sports. *Perceptual and Motor Skills, 71,* 1203–1206.

Pueyo, A. A. (1990). Búsqueda de sensaciones y el fenómeno *augmenting–reducing* en potenciales evocados auditivos. *Annuario de Psicologia, 46,* 23–37.

Quay, H. C. (1965). Psychopathic personality as pathological stimulation seeking. *American Journal of Psychiatry, 122,* 180–183.

Raine, A., & Venables, P. H. (1984). Electrodermal, nonresponding, antisocial behavior, and schizoid tendencies in adolescents. *Psychophysiology, 21,* 424–433.

Randhawa, B. S., deLacey, P. R., & Saklofske, D. H. (1986). Personality and behavioural measures: Gender, age, and race contrasts in an Australian setting. *International Journal of Psychology, 21,* 389–402.

Rapaport, D. (1960). On the psychoanalytic theory of motivation. In M. R. Jones (Ed.), *Nebraska Symposium on Motivation* (Vol. 8, pp. 173–247). Lincoln: University of Nebraska Press.

Raskin, R. N., & Hall, C. S. (1979). A Narcissistic Personality Inventory. *Psychological Reports, 45,* 590.

Rathus, S. A. (1973). A 30 item schedule for assessing assertive behavior. *Behavior Therapy, 4,* 398–406.

Ratliff, K. G., & Burkhart, B. R. (1984). Sex differences in motivations for and effects of drinking among college students. *Journal of Studies on Alcohol, 45,* 26–32.

Redmond, D. E., Jr. (1977). Alterations in the function of the nucleus locus coeruleus: A possible model for studies of anxiety. In I. Hanin & E. Usdin (Eds.), *Animal models in psychiatry and neurology* (pp. 293–305). New York: Pergamon.

Redmond, D. E., Jr., Murphy, D. L., & Baulu, J. (1979). Platelet monoamine oxidase activity correlates with social affiliative and agonistic behaviors in normal rhesus monkeys. *Psychosomatic Medicine, 41,* 87–100.

Reist, C., Haier, R. J., DeMet, E., & Cicz-DeMet, A. (1990). Platelet MAO activity in personality disorders and normal controls. *Psychiatry Research, 30,* 221–227.

Reitman, E. E., & Cleveland, S. E. (1964). Changes in body image following sensory deprivation in schizophrenic and control groups. *Journal of Abnormal and Social Psychology, 68,* 168–176.

Richardson, D. R., Medvin, N., & Hammock, G. (1988). Love styles, relationship experience, and sensation seeking: A test of validity. *Personality and Individual Differences, 9,* 645–651.

Ridgeway, D., & Hare, R. D. (1981). Sensation seeking and psychophysiological responses to auditory stimulation. *Psychophysiology, 18,* 613–618.

Ridgeway, D., & Russell, J. A. (1980). Reliability and validity of the Sensation Seeking Scale: Psychometric problems in form V. *Journal of Consulting and Clinical Psychology, 48,* 662–664.

Robins, L. N. (1966). *Deviant children growing up: A sociological and psychiatric study of sociopathic personality.* Baltimore: Williams & Wilkins.

Robinson, D. S., Davis, J. M., Nies, A., Revaris, C. L., & Sylvester, D. (1971). Relationship of sex and aging to monoamine oxidase activity of human brain, plasma, and platelets. *Archives of General Psychiatry, 24,* 536–539.

Robinson, D. W. (1985). Stress seeking: Selected behavioral characteristics of elite rock climbers. *Journal of Sport Psychology, 7,* 400–404.

Robinson, T. N., Jr., & Zahn, T. P. (1983). Sensation seeking, state anxiety and cardiac and EDR orienting reactions. *Psychophysiology, 20,* 465 (Abstract).

Rogeness, G. A., Hernandez, J. M., Macedo, C. A., Mitchell, E. L., Amrung, S. A., & Harris, W. R. (1984). Clinical characteristics of emotionally disturbed boys with very low activities of dopamine-β-hydroxlase. *Journal of the American Academy of Child Psychiatry, 23,* 203–208.

Roger, D. B., & Raine, A. (1984). Stimulus intensity control and personality: A research note. *Current Psychological Researach and Reviews, 3,* 43–47.

Rogers, T. B. (1987). Evidence for sensation seeking behaviour during assessment of the trait: A note on the construct validity of the measurement operation. *Personality and Individual Differences, 8,* 957–959.

Rokeach, M. (1960). *The open and closed mind: Investigations into the nature of belief systems and personality.* New York: Basic Books.

Rose, R. J., Miller, J. Z., Grim, C. E., & Christian, J. C. (1979). Aggregation of blood pressures in the families of identical twins. *American Journal of Epidemiology, 109,* 503–511.

Rosenhan, D. L. (1973). On being sane in insane places. *Science, 179,* 250–258.

Routtenberg, A. (1968). The two-arousal hypothesis: Reticular formation and limbic system. *Psychological Review, 75,* 51–81.

Rowland, G. L., Fouts, G., & Heatherton, T. (1989). Television viewing and sensation seeking: Uses, preferences and attitudes. *Personality and Individual Differences, 10,* 1003–1006.

Rowland, G. L., & Franken, R. E. (1986). The four dimensions of sensation seeking: A confirmatory factor analysis. *Personality and Individual Differences, 7,* 237–240.

Rowland, G. L., Franken, R. E., & Harrison, K. (1986). Sensation seeking and participating in sporting activities. *Journal of Sport Psychology, 8,* 212–220.

Rowland, G. L., Franken, R. E., Williams, S. E., & Heatherton, T. (1988). The perception of sensation seeking in familiar and unfamiliar others. *Personality and Individual Differences, 9,* 237–241.

Rowland, G. L., & Heatherton, T. (1987). Social norms for the desirability of sensation seeking. *Personality and Individual Differences, 8,* 753–755.

Roy, A., Adinoff, B., Roehrich, L., Lamparski, D., Custer, R., Lorenz, V., Barbaccia, M., Guidotti, A., Costa, E., & Linnoila, M. (1988). Pathological gambling: A psychobiological study. *Archives of General Psychiatry, 45,* 369–373.

Royce, J. R. (1984). The concept of sensation seeking and the structure of personality. *Behavioral and Brain Sciences, 7,* 448–449.

Rozin, P., & Fallon, A. E. (1987). A perspective on disgust. *Psychological Review, 94,* 23–41.

Rubin, Z. (1970). Measurement of romantic love. *Journal of Personality and Social Psychology, 16,* 265–273.

Ruch, W. (1988). Sensation seeking and the enjoyment of structure and content of humor: Stability of findings across four samples. *Personality and Individual Differences, 9,* 861–871.

Ruch, W. (1992). Assessment of appreciation of humor: Studies with the 3 WD Humor Test. In C. D. Spielberger & J. N. Butcher (Eds.), *Advances in personality assessment* (Vol. 9, pp. 27–75). Hillsdale, NJ: Erlbaum.

Ruch, W., Angleitner, A., & Strelau, J. (1991). The Strelau Temperament Inventory–Revised (STI-R): Validity studies. *European Journal of Personality, 5,* 287–308.

Ruch, W., & Hehl, F. J. (1986). Conservatism as a predictory of response to humor – II. The location of sense of humor in a comprehensive attitude space. *Personality and Individual Differences, 7,* 861–874.

Ruch, W., & Hehl, F. J. (1988). Attitudes to sex, sexual behaviour and enjoyment of humor. *Personality and Individual Differences, 9,* 983–994.

Ruch, W., McGhee, T. E., & Hehl, F. J. (in press). Age differences in the enjoyment of incongruity resolution and nonsense humor during adulthood. *Psychology and Aging.*

Rushton, J. P. (1988). Race differences in behaviour: A review and evolutionary analysis. *Personality and Individual Differences, 9,* 1009–1024.

Russo, M. F., Lakey, B. B., Christ, M. A. G., Frick, P. J., McBurnett, K., Walker, J. L., Loeber, R., Stouthhamer-Loeber, M., & Green, S. (1991). Preliminary development of a sensation seeking scale for children. *Personality and Individual Differences, 12,* 399–405.

Russo, M. F., Stokes, G. S., Lahey, B. B., Christ, M. A. G., McBurnett, K., Loeber, R., Stouthamer-Loeber, M., & Green, S. M. (1993). A sensation seeking scale in children: Further refinement and psychometric development. *Journal of Psychopathology and Behavioral Assessment, 15,* 69–86.

Sacks, O. (1983). *Awakenings.* New York: E. P. Dutton.

Salkind, N. J. (1981). Stimulation seeking and hyperactivity in young children. *Journal of Pediatric Psychology, 6,* 97–102.

Satinder, K. P., & Black, A. (1984). Cannibis use and sensation seeking orientation. *Journal of Psychology, 116,* 101–105.

Satterfield, J. H. (1987). Childhood diagnostic and neurophysiological predictors of teenage arrest rates: An eight year prospective study. In S. A. Mednick, T. E. Moffitt, & S. A. Stack (Eds.), *The causes of crime: New biological approaches* (pp. 146–167). Cambridge: Cambridge University Press.

Saxton, P. M., Siegel, J., Lukas, J. H. (1987). Visual evoked potential augmenting/reducing slopes in cats – 2. Correlations with behavior. *Personality and Individual Differences, 8,* 511–519.

Schaffer, H. R. (1971). *The growth of sociability.* Baltimore: Penguin Books.

Schalling, D., Åsberg, M., & Edman, G. (1984). *Personality and CSF monoamine metabolites.* Department of Psychiatry and Psychology, Karolinska Hospital and the Department of Psychology, University of Stockholm, Sweden. Preliminary manuscript.

Schalling, D., Åsberg, M., & Edman, G. (1985). *Personality and neurochemical risk factors for disinhibitory psychopathology.* Paper presented at IV World Congress of Psychiatry, Philadelphia, Sept. 8–13.

Schalling, D., Åsberg, M., Edman, G., & Oreland, L. (1987). Markers for vulnerability to psychopathology: Temperament traits associated with platelet MAO activity. *Acta Psychiatrica Scandinavica, 76,* 172–182.

Schalling, D., Åsberg, M., Oreland, L., Askanas, I., Pfannsschmidt, W., Tiberg, B., & Edman, G. (1981). *Impulsive and platelet MAO activity in two groups of normal male subjects.* Unpublished manuscript.

Schalling, D., Edman, G., & Åsberg, M. (1983). Impulsive cognitive style and the inability to tolerate boredom. In M. Zuckerman (Ed.), *Biological bases of sen-*

sation seeking, impulsivity, and anxiety (pp. 123–145). Hillsdale, NJ: Erlbaum.

Schalling, D., Edman, G., Åsberg, M., & Oreland, L. (1988). Platelet MAO activity associated with impulsivity and aggressivity. *Personality and Individual Differences, 9*, 597–605.

Schiendel, J. (1964). Psychological differences between athletes and nonparticipants in athletics at three educational levels. *Research Quarterly, 36*, 52–67.

Schierman, M. J., & Rowland, G. L. (1985). Sensation seeking and selection of entertainment. *Personality and Individual Differences, 6*, 599–603.

Schildkraut, J. J., Orsulak, P. J., Schatzberg, A. F., & Rosenbaum, A. H. (1984). Urinary MHPG in affective disorders. In R. M. Post & J. C. Ballenger (Eds.), *Neurobiology of mood disorders* (pp. 519–528). Baltimore: Williams & Wilkins.

Schlosberg, H. (1954). Three dimensions of emotion. *Psychological Review, 61*, 81–88.

Schmitz, P. G. (1985). Sociocultural and personality differences in the dimension of the open and closed mind. In *Authoritarianism and dogmatism* (Part 2, pp. 348–364). Chapel Hill: The High School Journal, University of North Carolina Press.

Schneirla, T. C. (1959). An evolutionary and developmental theory of biphasic processes underlying approach and withdrawal. In M. R. Jones (Ed.), *Nebraska Symposium on Motivation* (Vol. 7, pp. 1–42). Lincoln: University of Nebraska Press.

Schooler, C., Zahn, T. P., Murphy, D. L., & Buchsbaum, M. S. (1978). Psychological correlates of monoamine oxidase activity in normals. *Journal of Nervous and Mental Disease, 166*, 177–186.

Schumaker, J. F., Groth-Marnat, G., Small, L., & Macaruso, P. A. (1986). Sensation seeking in a female bulimic population. *Psychological Reports, 59*, 1151–1154.

Schwarz, R. M., Burkhart, B. R., & Green, S. B. (1978). Turning on or turning off: Sensation seeking or tension reduction as motivational determinants of alcohol use. *Journal of Consulting and Clinical Psychology, 46*, 1144–1145.

Schwarz, R. M., Burkhart, B. R., & Green, S. B. (1982). Sensation seeking and anxiety as factors in social drinking by men. *Journal of Studies on Alcohol, 43*, 1108–1114.

Sciortino, J. J., Huston, J. H., & Spencer, R. W. (1987). Perceived risk and the precautionary demand for money. *Journal of Economic Psychology, 8*, 339–346.

Segal, B. S., Huba, G. J., & Singer, J. F. (1980). *Drugs, daydreaming and personality: Study of college youth*. Hillsdale, NJ: Erlbaum.

Segal, B., & Singer, J. L. (1976). Daydreaming, drug and alcohol use in college students: A factor analytic study. *Addictive Behaviors, 1*, 227–235.

Shaw, G. A., & Brown, G. (1990). Laterality and creativity concommitants of attention problems. *Developmental Neuropsychology, 6*, 39–57.

Shaw, G. A., & Giambra, L. (1993). Task-unrelated thoug 1ts of college students diagnosed as hyperactive in childhood. *Developmental Neuropsychology, 9*, 17–30.

Shekim, W. O., Bylund, D. B., Frankel, F., Alexson, J., Corcoran, C. M., McAllister, J. M., & Ray-Prenger, C. (1990). Platelet alpha adrenergic receptor binding to 3H2-yohimbine and personality variations in normals. *Psychiatry Research, 32*, 125–134.

Shekim, W. O., Bylund, D. B., Frankel, F., Alexson, J., Jones, S. B., Blue, L.

D., Kirby, J., & Corchoran, C. (1989). Platelet MAO activity and personality variations in normals. *Psychiatry Research, 27,* 81–88.

Shoham, S. G., Askenasy, J. J., Rahav, G., Chard, F., & Addi, A. (1989). Personality correlates of violent prisoners. *Personality and Individual Differences, 10,* 137–145.

Shostrom, E. L. (1966). *Manual for the Personal Orientation Inventory.* San Diego: Educational and Industrial Testing Service.

Sidle, A., Acker, M., & McReynolds, P. (1963). Stimulus-seeking behavior in schizophrenics and nonschizophrenics. *Perceptual and Motor Skills, 17,* 811–816.

Sieber, M., & Angst, J. (1977). *Zur Persoenlichkeit von Drogen- Alkohol- und Zigarettenkonsumenten.* Unpublished manuscript.

Siegel, J., & Sisson, D. F. (1993). Evoked field potentials – beyond correlates of behavior: An approach to determining the neural mechanisms of behavior. In W. Haschke, E. J. Speckman, & A. I. Roitbak (Eds.), *Slow potential changes in the brain* (pp. 151–165). Boston: Birkhäuser.

Siegel, J., Sisson, D. F., & Driscoll, P. (1993). Augmenting and reducing of visual evoked potentials in Roman High- and Low-avoidance rats. *Physiology and Behavior, 54,* 707–711.

Siegel, J. M., Johnson, J. H., & Sarason, I. G. (1979). Mood states and the reporting of life changes. *Journal of Psychosomatic Research, 23,* 103–108.

Siever, L. J., Haier, R. J., Coursey, R. D., Sostek, A. J., Murphy, D. L., Holzman, P. S., & Buchsbaum, M. S. (1982). Smooth pursuit eye tracking impairment. *Archives of General Psychiatry, 39,* 1001–1005.

Silverman, J., Buchsbaum, M. S., & Stierlin, H. (1973). Sex differences in perceptual differentiation and stimulus intensity control. *Journal of Personality and Social Psychology, 25,* 309–318.

Simmel, E. C. (1984). Sensation seeking: Exploration of empty spaces or novel stimuli? *Behavioral and Brain Sciences, 3,* 449–450.

Simo, S., & Perez, J. (1991). Sensation seeking and antisocial behavior in a junior high school sample. *Personality and Individual Differences, 12,* 965–966.

Simons, R. F., Losito, B. D., Rose, S. C., & MacMillan III, F. W. (1983). Electrodermal nonresponding among college undergraduates: Temporal stability, situational specificity, and relationship to heart rate change. *Psychophysiology, 20,* 498–506.

Simpson, D. D., & Sells, S. B. (1982). Effectiveness of treatment for drug abuse: An overview of the DARP research program. *Advances in Alcohol and Substance Abuse, 2,* 7–29.

Singer, J. L., & Antrobus, J. S. (1972). Daydreaming, imaginal processes, and personality: A normative study. In P. Sheehan (Ed.), *The function and nature of imagery.* New York: Academic Press.

Skinner, B. F. (1953). *Science and human behavior.* New York: Free Press.

Skolnick, N. J., & Zuckerman, M. (1979). Personality changes in drug abusers: A comparison of therapeutic community and prison groups. *Journal of Consulting and Clinical Psychology, 47,* 768–770.

Smith, B. D., Davidson, R. A., Smith, D. L., Goldstein, H., & Perlstein, W. (1989). Sensation seeking and arousal: Effects of strong stimulation on electrodermal activation and memory task performance. *Personality and Individual Differences, 10,* 671–679.

Smith, B. D., Perlstein, W. M., Davidson, R. A., & Michael, K. (1986). Sensation seeking: Differential effects of relevant, novel stimulation on electrodermal activity. *Personality and Individual Differences, 7,* 445–452.

Smith, R. E., Johnson, J. H., & Sarason, I. G. (1978). Life change, the sensation seeking motive, and psychological distress. *Journal of Consulting and Clinical Psychology, 46,* 348–349.

Smith, R. E., Ptacek, J. T., & Smoll, F. L. (1992). Sensation seeking, stress and adolescent injuries: A test of stress buffering, risk-taking, and coping skills hypotheses. *Journal of Personality and Social Psychology, 62,* 1016–1024.

Snyder, C. R., & Fromkin, H. L. (1977). Abnormality as a positive characteristic: The development and validation of a scale measuring need for uniqueness. *Journal of Abnormal Psychology, 86,* 518–527.

Sostek, A. J., Sostek, A. M., Murphy, D. L., Martin, E. B., & Born, W. S. (1981). Cord blood amine oxidase activities relate to arousal and motor functioning in human newborns. *Life Sciences, 28,* 2561–2568.

Sparks, G. (1984). *The development of a scale to assess cognitive responses to frightening mass media.* Paper presented at the annual meeting of the International Communication Association, San Francisco.

Spotts, J. V., & Shontz, F. C. (1984). Correlates of sensation seeking by heavy, chronic drug users. *Perceptual and Motor Skills, 58,* 427–435.

Spotts, J. V., & Shontz, F. C. (1986). Drugs and personality: Dependence of findings on method. *American Journal of Drug and Alcohol Abuse, 12,* 355–382.

Stacy, A. W., Newcomb, M. D., & Bentler, P. M. (1991). Personality, problem drinking, and drunk driving: Mediating, moderating, and direct-effect models. *Journal of Personality and Social Psychology, 60,* 795–811.

Stanton, H. E. (1976). Hypnosis and encounter group volunteers: A validational study of the Sensation Seeking Scale. *Journal of Consulting and Clinical Psychology, 44,* 692.

Stein, L. (1978). Catecholamines and opioid peptides. In M. A. Lipton, D. Mascio, & K. F. Killam (Eds.), *Psychopharmacology: A generation of progress* (pp. 569–581). New York: Raven Press.

Stellar, J. R., & Stellar, E. (1985). *The neurobiology of motivation and reward.* New York: Springer-Verlag.

Stelmack, R. M. (1990). Biological bases of extraversion: Psychophysiological evidence. *Journal of Personality, 58,* 293–311.

Stelmack, R. M., Plouffe, L., & Falkenberg, W. (1983). Extraversion, sensation seeking and electrodermal response. *Personality and Individual Differences, 4,* 607–614.

Stenberg, G., Rosen, I., & Risberg, J. (1988). Personality and augmenting/reducing and visual and auditory evoked potentials. *Personality and Individual Differences, 9,* 571–579.

Stenberg, G., Rosen, I., & Risberg, J. (1990). Attention and personality in augmenting/reducing of visual evoked potentials. *Personality and Individual Differences, 11,* 1243–1254.

Stern, G. S., Cox, J., & Shahan, D. (1981). Feedback in pulse rate change and divergent affective reactions for high and low sensation seekers. *Biofeedback and Self Regulation, 6,* 315–326.

Stewart, C. H., & Hemsley, D. R. (1984). Personality factors in the taking of criminal risks. *Personality and Individual Differences, 5,* 119–122.

Stillman, R. C., Wyatt, R. J., Murphy, D. L., & Rauscher, F. P. (1978). Low platelet monoamine oxidase activity and chronic marijuana use. *Life Sciences, 23,* 1577–1582.

Stoner, S., & Bandy, M. A. (1977). Personality traits of females who participate in intercollegiate competition and nonparticipants. *Perceptual and Motor Skills, 45,* 332–334.

Straub, W. F. (1982). Sensation seeking among high and low-risk male athletes. *Journal of Sport Psychology, 4,* 246–253.

Strelau, J. (1983). *Temperament, personality, activity.* London: Academic Press.

Strelau, J., Angleitner, A., & Ruch, W. (1989). Strelau Temperament Inventory (STI): General review and studies based on German samples. In C. D. Spielberger & J. N. Butcher (Eds.), *Advances in personality assessment* (Vol. 8, pp. 187–241). Hillsdale, NJ: Erlbaum.

Sturgis, E. T., Calhoun, K. S., & Best, C. L. (1979). Correlates of assertive behavior in alcoholics. *Addictive Behaviors, 4,* 193–197.

Sutker, P. B., & Allain, A. N. (1983). Behavior and personality assessment in men labeled adaptive psychopaths. *Journal of Behavioral Assessment, 5,* 65–79.

Sutker, P. B., Archer, R. P., & Allain, A. N. (1978). Drug abuse patterns, personality characteristics, and relationships with sex, race, and sensation seeking. *Journal of Consulting and Clinical Psychology, 46,* 1374–1378.

Svebak, S., & Kerr, J. (1989). The role of impulsivity in preference for sports. *Personality and Individual Differences, 10,* 51–58.

Svebak, S., & Murgatroyd, S. (1985). Metamotivational dominance: A multimethod validation of reversal theory constructs. *Journal of Personality and Social Psychology, 48,* 107–116.

Symons, D. (1979). *The evolution of human sexuality.* New York: Oxford University Press.

Tamborini, R., & Stiff, J. (1987). Predictors of horror film attendance and appeal: An analysis of the audience for frightening films. *Communication Research, 14,* 415–436.

Tamborini, R., Stiff, J., & Zillman, D. (1987). Preference for graphic horror featuring male versus female victimization. *Human Communication Research, 13,* 529–552.

Teichman, M., Barnea, Z., & Rahav, G. (1989a). Sensation seeking, state and trait anxiety, and depressive mood in adolescent substance users. *International Journal of the Addictions, 24,* 87–89.

Teichman, M., Barnea, Z., & Rahav, G. (1989b). Personality and substance abuse: A longitudinal study. *British Journal of Addiction, 84,* 181–190.

Tellegen, A., Lykken, D. T., Bouchard, T. J., Wilcox, K., Segal, N., & Rich, A. (1988). Personality similarity in twins reared together and apart. *Journal of Personality and Social Psychology, 54,* 1031–1039.

Terasaki, M., & Imada, S. (1988). Sensation seeking and food preferences. *Personality and Individual Differences, 9,* 87–93.

Terasaki, M., Shiomi, K., Kishimoto, Y., & Hiraoka, K. (1987). A Japanese version of the sensation seeking scale. *Japanese Journal of Psychology, 58,* 42–48.

Thackray, R., & Touchstone, R. (1980). An exploratory investigation of various assessment instruments as correlates of complex visual monitoring performance. *FAA Office of Aviation Medicine Reports* (FAA-AM-80-17) October.

Thomas, A., & Chess, S. (1977). *Temperament and development.* New York: Bruner/Mazel.

Thomas, A., Chess, S., Birch, H. G., Hertzig, M. E., & Korn, S. (1964). *Behavioral individuality in early childhood.* New York: New York University Press.

Thorne, G. L. (1971). The Sensation Seeking Scale with deviant populations. *Journal of Consulting and Clinical Psychology, 37,* 106–110.

Thornquist, M. H. (1993). *Psychopathy, passive-avoidance learning and basic dimensions of personality.* Unpublished doctoral dissertation, University of Delaware.

Thornquist, M. H., Zuckerman, M., & Exline, R. V. (1991). Loving, liking, looking and sensation seeking in unmarried college couples. *Personality and Individual Differences, 12,* 1283–1292.

Thornton, B., Ryckman, R. M., & Gold, J. A. (1981). Sensation seeking as a determinant of interpersonal attraction toward similar and dissimilar others. *Journal of Mind and Body, 2,* 85–91.

Tobacyk, J. J., & Milford, G. (1983). Belief in paranormal phenomena: Assessment instrument development and implications for personality functioning. *Journal of Personality and Social Psychology, 44,* 1029–1037.

Tobacyk, J. J., Myers, H., & Bailey, L. (1981). Field-dependence, sensation seeking and preference for paintings. *Journal of Personality Assessment, 45,* 270–277.

Tobacyk, J. J., & Thomas, C. (1980). Correlations of masculinity and femininity to sensation seeking. *Psychological Reports, 47,* 1339–1343.

Tolman, E. C. (1926). The nature of the fundamental drives. *Journal of Abnormal Psychology, 20,* 349–358.

Tolman, E. C. (1932). *Purposive behavior in animals and men.* New York: Century.

Torki, M. A. (1993). Sex differences in sensation seeking in Kuwait. *Personality and Individual Differences, 14,* 861–863.

Trice, A. D., & Ogden, E. P. (1986). Informed consent: I. The institutional nonliability clause as a liability in recruiting research subjects. *Journal of Social Behavior and Personality, 1,* 391–396.

Tumilty, T. N., & Daitzman, R. (1977). *Locus of control and sensation seeking among schizophrenics: Extensions and replication.* Unpublished manuscript.

Turner, C. W., Ford, M. H., West, D. W., & Meible, A. W. (1986). *Genetic influences on testosterone, hostility, and type A behavior in adult male twins.* Paper presented at a meeting of the Eastern Psychological Association, Washington, DC, August.

Tyrer, P., Casey, P., & Gall, J. (1983). Relationship between neurosis and personality disorder. *British Journal of Psychiatry, 142,* 404–408.

Umapathy, A., & Suvarna, B. J. (1988). A comparative study of sensation seeking among working journalists and non-journalists. *Indian Journal of Applied Psychology, 25,* 7–12.

Umberkoman-Wiita, B., Vogel, W. H., & Wiita, P. J. (1981). Some biochemical and behavioral (sensation seeking) correlates in healthy adults. *Research Communications in Psychiatry and Behavior, 6,* 303–316.

Van Court, M., & Bean, F. D. (1985). Intelligence and fertility in the United States. *Intelligence, 9,* 23–32.

Van den Berg, P. T., & Feij, J. A. (1988). De ontwikkeling van een selectierersie van de spansingsbehoeftelijst (SBL-s). *Nederlands Tydschrift voor de Psychologie, 43,* 328–343.

Van den Berg, P. T., & Feij, J. A. (1991). Selection and work redesign in an attempt to retain information technology professionals. In H. Schuler & W. Stehle (Eds.), *Eignungsdiagnostik in Forschung und Praxis: Psychologische Information für Auswahl, Beratung und Föderung von Mitarbeitern* (pp. 350–353). Stuttgart: Verlag für Angewandte Psychologie.

Vando, A. (1974). The development of the R-A scale: A paper-and-pencil measure of pain tolerance scale. *Personality and Social Psychology Bulletin, 1,* 28–29.

Velten, E. (1967). A laboratory test for induction of mood states. *Behavior Research and Theory, 6,* 473–482.

Venables, P. H. (1964). Input dysfunction in schizophrenia. In B. A. Maher (Ed.), *Progress in experimental personality research* (Vol. 1, pp. 1–47). New York: Academic Press.

Victor, H. R., Grossman, J. C., & Eisenman, R. (1973). Openness to experience and marijuana use in high school students. *Journal of Consulting and Clinical Psychology, 41,* 78–85.

Virkkunen, M. (1985). Urinary free cortisol secretion in habitually violent offenders. *Acta Psychiatrica Scandinavica, 72,* 40–44.

von Knorring, L. (1976). Visual averaged-evoked responses in patients suffering from alcoholism. *Neuropsychobiology, 3,* 233–238.

von Knorring, L. (1978). Visual evoked responses in patients with bipolar affective disorders. *Neuropsychobiology, 4,* 314–320.

von Knorring, L. (1980). Visual averaged evoked responses and platelet monoamine oxidase in patients suffering from alcoholism. In H. Begleiter (Ed.), *Biological effects of alcohol* (pp. 619–660). New York: Plenum.

von Knorring, L., Almay, B. G. L., & Johansson, F. (1987). Personality traits in patients with idiopathic pain disorder. *Acta Psychiatrica Scandinavica, 76,* 490–498.

von Knorring, L., & Johansson, F. (1980). Changes in the augmenter–reducer tendency and in pain measures as a result of treatment with a serotonin reuptake inhibitor: Zimelidine. *Neuropsychobiology, 6,* 313–318.

von Knorring, L., & Oreland, L. (1985). Personality traits and platelet monoamine oxidase in tobacco smokers. *Psychological Medicine, 15,* 327–334.

von Knorring, L., Oreland, L., & von Knorring, A. L. (1987). Personality traits and platelet MAO activity in alcohol and drug abusing teenage boys. *Acta Psychiatrica Scandinavica, 75,* 307–314.

von Knorring, L., Oreland, L., & Winblad, B. (1984). Personality traits related to monoamine oxidase activity in platelets. *Psychiatry Research, 12,* 11–26.

von Knorring, L., Palm, U., & Andersson, H. E. (1985). Relationship between treatment outcome and subtype of alcoholism in men. *Journal of Studies in Alcohol, 46,* 388–391.

von Knorring, L., & Perris, C. (1981). Biochemistry of the augmenting–reducing response in visual evoked potentials. *Neuropsychobiology, 7,* 1–8.

Waag, W. L. (1971). *The prediction of individual differences in monitoring performance.* Unpublished doctoral dissertation, Texas Technical Univesity.

Wallbank, J. (1985). Antisocial and prosocial behavior among contemporary Robin Hoods. *Personality and Individual Differences, 6,* 11–19.

Walsh, R. N., & Cummins, R. A. (1976). The open-field test: A critical review. *Psychological Bulletin, 83,* 482–504.

Ward, P. B., Catts, S., Norman, T. R., & Burrows, G. D. (1987). Low platelet monoamine oxidase and sensation seeking in males: An established relationship? *Acta Psychiatrica Scandinavica, 75,* 86–90.

Wasson, A. S. (1981). Susceptibility to boredom and deviant behavior at school. *Psychological Reports, 48,* 901–902.

Waters, C. W. (1974). Multidimensional measures of novelty experiencing, sensation seeking and ability: Correlational analysis for male and female college samples. *Psychological Reports, 34,* 43–46.

Waters, C. W., & Pincus, S. (1976). Sex of respondent, respondent's sex role concept and responses on the Sensation Seeking Scale. *Psychological Reports, 39,* 749–750.

Waters, L. K., & Kirk, W. E. (1968). Stimulus seeking motivation and risk-taking behavior in a gambling situation. *Education and Psychological Measurement, 28,* 549–55.

Watson, C. G. (1972). Relationships of anhedonia to learning under various contingencies. *Journal of Abnormal Psychology, 80,* 43–48.

Watson, C. G., Anderson, R., & Schulte, D. (1977). Responses of high- and low-emotional deficit patients to exciting, grating and neutral stimuli. *Journal of Clinical Psychology, 33,* 552–554.

Watson, C. G., & Jacobs, L. (1977). Evidence for a dual factor concept of psycho-pathological emotional deficit: Anhedonia and sensation seeking. *Journal of Clinical Psychology, 33,* 384–389.

Watson, C. G., Jacobs, L., & Herder, J. (1979). Correlates of alpha, beta, and theta wave production. *Journal of Clinical Psychology, 35,* 364–369.

Weinstein, M. (1978). Changes in drug usage and associated personality traits among college students. *International Journal of the Addictions, 13,* 683–688.

Welsh, G. S. (1959). *Preliminary manual for the Welsh Figure Preference Test.* Palo Alto, CA: Consulting Psychologists Press.

Wheeler, J., & Kilmann, P. R. (1983). Comarital sexual behavior: Individual and relationship variables. *Archives of Sexual Behavior, 12,* 295–306.

Whimbey, A. E., & Denenberg, V. H. (1967). Two independent behavioral dimensions in open-field performance. *Journal of Comparative and Physiological Psychology, 63,* 500–504.

White, H. R., & Johnson, V. (1988). Risk taking as a predictor of adolescent sexual activity and use of contraception. *Journal of Addiction Research, 3,* 317–331.

White, H. R., LaBouvie, E. W., & Bates, M. E. (1985). The relationship between sensation seeking and delinquency: A longitudinal analysis. *Journal of Research in Crime and Delinquency, 22,* 197–211.

White, K. D. (1984). *Nervous system sensitivity and the Strelau Temperament Inventory: Australian findings.* Unpublished manuscript, cited in Dragutinovich, 1987b, p. 704.

Williams, S., Ryckman, R. M., Gold, J. A., & Lenney, E. (1982). The effects of sensation seeking and misattribution of arousal on attraction toward similar or dissimilar strangers. *Journal of Research in Personality, 16,* 217–226.

Wilson, G. D., & Patterson, J. R. (1968). A new measure of conservatism. *British Journal of Social and Clinical Psychology, 7,* 264–269.

Winchie, D. B., & Carment, D. W. (1988). Intention to migrate: A psychological analysis. *Journal of Applied Social Psychology, 18,* 727–736.

Winblad, B., Gottfries, C. G., Oreland, L., & Wiberg, A. (1979). Monoamine oxidase in platelets and brains of non-psychiatric and non-neurological geriatric patients. *Medical Biology, 57,* 129–132.

Windholz, G. (1970). Dissatisfaction and sensation seeking as related to frequency of daydreaming reported by male subjects. *Perceptual and Motor Skills, 30,* 892–894.

Windle, M., Barnes, G. M., & Welte, J. (1989). Causal models of adolescent substance use: An examination of gender differences using distribution-free estimators. *Journal of Personality and Social Psychology, 56,* 132–142.

Witkin, H. A., Oltman, P. K., Raskin, E., & Karp, S. A. (1971). *A manual for the Embedded Figures Test.* Palo Alto, CA: Consulting Psychologists Press.

Wolf, A. W., Schubert, D. S. P., Patterson, M. B., Grande, T. P., Brocco, K. J., & Pendleton, L. (1988). Associations among major psychiatric disorders. *Journal of Consulting and Clinical Psychology, 66,* 292–294.

Wolowitz, H. M. (1964). Food preferences as an index of orality. *Journal of Abnormal and Social Psychology, 69,* 650–654.

Wundt, W. M. (1893). *Grundzuge der physiologischen Psychologie.* Leipzig: Engelman.

Yerkes, R. M., & Dodson, J. D. (1908). The relation of strength of stimulus to rapidity of habit-formation. *Journal of Comparative and Neurological Psychology*, *18*, 459–482.

Young, P. T. (1936). *Motivation of behavior*. New York: Wiley.

Young, P. T. (1948). Appetite, palatability, and the feeding habit: A critical review. *Psychological Bulletin*, *45*, 289–320.

Young, W. F., Laws, E. R., Sharbeough, F. W., & Weinshilboum, R. M. (1986). Human monoamine oxidase. *Archives of General Psychiatry*, *43*, 604–609.

Yuching, Z. (1988). Some experimental research on sensation seeking. *Journal of Psychology*, *3*, 20–24. (In Chinese)

Zahn, T. P., Schooler, C., & Murphy, D. L. (1986). Autonomic correlates of sensation seeking and monoamine oxidase activity: Using confirmatory factor analysis on psychophysiological data. *Psychophysiology*, *23*, 521–531.

Zaleski, Z. (1984a). Sensation seeking and risk-taking behaviour. *Personality and Individual Differences*, *5*, 607–608.

Zaleski, Z. (1984b). Sensation seeking and preference for emotional visual stimuli. *Personality and Individual Differences*, *5*, 609–611.

Zentall, S. S., & Meyer, M. J., (1987). Self-regulation of stimulation for ADD-H children during reading and vigilance task performance. *Journal of Abnormal Child Psychology*, *15*, 519–536.

Zentall, S. S., & Zentall, T. R. (1983). Optimal stimulation: A model of disordered activity and performance in normal and deviant children. *Psychological Bulletin*, *94*, 446–471.

Zuckerman, M. (1960). The development of an Affect Adjective Check List for the measurement of anxiety. *Journal of Consulting and Clinical Psychology*, *24*, 457–462.

Zuckerman, M. (1969). Theoretical formulations. In J. P. Zubek (Ed.), *Sensory deprivation: Fifteen years of research* (pp. 407–432). New York: Appleton-Century.

Zuckerman, M. (1971a). Dimensions of sensation seeking. *Journal of Consulting and Clinical Psychology*, *36*, 45–52.

Zuckerman, M. (1971b). Physiological measures of sexual arousal in the human. *Psychological Bulletin*, *75*, 297–329.

Zuckerman, M. (1974). The sensation seeking motive. In B. A. Maher (Ed.), *Progress in experimental personality research* (Vol. 7, pp. 79–148). New York: Academic Press.

Zuckerman, M., (1976a). Sensation seeking and anxiety, traits and states, as determinants of behavior in novel situations. In I. G. Sarason & C. D. Spielberger (Eds.), *Stress and anxiety* (Vol. 3, pp. 141–170). Washington, DC: Hemisphere.

Zuckerman, M. (1976b). General and situation-specific traits and states: New approaches to assessment of anxiety and other constructs. In M. Zuckerman & C. D. Spielberger (Eds.), *Emotions and anxiety: New concepts, methods, and applications* (pp. 133–174). New York: Wiley.

Zuckerman, M. (1976c). Research on pornography. In W. W. Oaks, G. A. Melchiode, & I. Ficher (Eds.), *Sex and the life cycle* (pp. 147–161). New York: Grune & Stratton.

Zuckerman, M. (1978). Sensation seeking. In H. London & J. Exner (Eds.), *Dimensions of personality* (pp. 487–559). New York: Wiley.

Zuckerman, M. (1979a). *Sensation seeking: Beyond the optimal level of arousal*. Hillsdale, NJ: Erlbaum.

Zuckerman, M. (1979b). Traits, states, situations and uncertainty. *Journal of Behavioral Assessment*, *1*, 43–54.

Zuckerman, M. (1979c). Sensation seeking and risk taking. In C. E. Izard (Ed.),

Emotions in personality and psychopathology (pp. 163–197). New York: Plenum.

Zuckerman, M. (1983a). The distinction between trait and state scales is *not* arbitrary. Comment on Allen and Pokay's "On the arbitrary distinction between traits and states." *Journal of Personality and Social Psychology, 44,* 1083–1086.

Zuckerman, M. (1983b). A biological theory of sensation seeking. In M. Zuckerman (Ed.), *Biological bases of sensation seeking, impulsivity and anxiety* (pp. 37–76). Hillsdale, NJ: Erlbaum.

Zuckerman, M. (1983c). Sensation seeking and sports. *Personality and Individual Differences, 4,* 285–292.

Zuckerman, M. (1983d). Sensation seeking: The initial motive for drug abuse. In E. H. Gottheil, K. A. Druley, T. E. Skoloda, & H. M. Waxman (Eds.), *Etiological aspects of alcohol and drug abuse* (pp. 202–220). Springfield, IL: Charles C. Thomas.

Zuckerman, M. (1983e). Sexual arousal in the human: Love, chemistry, or conditioning? In A. Gale & J. A. Edwards (Eds.), *Physiological correlates of human behavior: Vol. 1. Basic issues* (pp. 299–326). London: Academic Press.

Zuckerman, M. (1983f). *Biological bases of sensation seeking, impulsivity and anxiety.* Hillsdale, NJ: Erlbaum.

Zuckerman, M. (1984a). Sensation seeking: A comparative approach to a human trait. *Behavioral and Brain Sciences, 7,* 413–471.

Zuckerman, M. (1984b). Experience and desire: A new format for sensation seeking scales. *Journal of Behavioral Assessment, 6,* 101–114.

Zuckerman, M. (1984c). *Preliminary manual for form VI of the Sensation Seeking Scale (SSSVI).* Unpublished manuscript.

Zuckerman, M. (1985). Sensation seeking, mania, and monoamines. *Neuropsychobiology, 13,* 121–128.

Zuckerman, M. (1986a). Sensation seeking and augmenting–reducing: Evoked potentials and/or kinesthetic figural aftereffects? *Behavioral and Brain Sciences, 9,* 749–754.

Zuckerman, M. (1986b). Sensation seeking and the endogenous deficit theory of drug abuse. *National Institute on Drug Abuse Research Monograph Series, 74,* 59–70.

Zuckerman, M. (1987a). Biological connection between sensation seeking and drug abuse. In J. Engle, L. Oreland, D. H. Ingvar, B. Pernow, S. Rössner, & L. A. Pellborn (Eds.), *Brain reward systems and abuse* (pp. 165–176). New York: Raven Press.

Zuckerman, M. (1987b). Is sensation seeking a predisposing trait for alcoholism? In E. Gottheil, K. A. Druley, S. Pashkey, & S. P. Weinstein (Eds.), *Stress and addiction* (pp. 283–301). New York: Bruner/Mazel.

Zuckerman, M. (1987c). A critical look at three arousal constructs in personality theories: Optimal levels of arousal, strength of the nervous system, and sensitivities to signals of reward and punishment. In J. Strelau & H. J. Eysenck (Eds.), *Personality dimensions and arousal* (pp. 217–231). New York: Plenum.

Zuckerman, M. (1988a). Behavior and biology: Research on sensation seeking and reactions to the media. In L. Donohew, H. E. Sypher, & E. T. Higgens (Eds.), *Communication, social cognition and affect* (pp. 173–194). Hillsdale, NJ: Erlbaum.

Zuckerman, M. (1988b). Sensation seeking, risk taking and health. In M. P. Janisse (Ed.), *Individual differences, stress and health* (pp. 72–88). New York: Springer-Verlag.

Zuckerman, M. (1990a). The psychophysiology of sensation seeking. *Journal of Personality, 58*, 313–345.

Zuckerman, M. (1990b). Some dubious premises in research and theory on racial differences: Scientific, social, and ethical issues. *American Psychologist, 45*, 1297–1303.

Zuckerman, M. (1991a). *Psychobiology of personality*. Cambridge: Cambridge University Press.

Zuckerman, M. (1991b). One person's stress is another person's pleasure. In C. D. Spielberger, I. G. Sarason, Z. Kulcsár, & G. L. Van Heck (Eds.), *Stress and emotion* (Vol. 14, pp. 31–45). Washington, DC: Hemisphere.

Zuckerman, M. (1993). Out of sensory deprivation and into sensation seeking: A personal and scientific journey. In G. C. Brannigan & M. R. Merrins (Eds.) *The undaunted psychologist: Adventures in research* (pp. 45–57). Philadelphia: Temple University Press.

Zuckerman, M. (1994a). An alternative five factor model for personality. In C. F. Halverson, G. A. Kohnstamm, & R. P. Martin (Eds.), *The developing structure of temperament and personality from infancy to adulthood*. Hillsdale, NJ: Erlbaum.

Zuckerman, M. (1994b). Sensation seeking and impulsivity: A marriage of traits made in biology? In W. McCown, J. Johnson, & M. Shure (Eds.), *The impulsive client: Theory, research and treatment* (pp. 69–89). Washington, DC: American Psychological Association.

Zuckerman, M., Ball, S., & Black, J. (1990). Influences of sensation seeking, gender, risk appraisal, and situational motivation on smoking. *Addictive Behaviors, 15*, 209–220.

Zuckerman, M., Ballenger, J. C., & Post, R. M. (1984). The neurobiology of some dimensions of personality. In J. R. Smythies & R. J. Bradley (Eds.), *International review of neurobiology* (Vol. 25, pp. 391–436). New York: Academic Press.

Zuckerman, M., Bone, R. N., Neary, R., Mangelsdorf, D., & Brustman, B. (1972). What is the sensation seeker? Personality trait and experience correlates of the Sensation Seeking Scales. *Journal of Consulting and Clinical Psychology, 39*, 308–321.

Zuckerman, M., Buchsbaum, M. S., & Murphy, D. L. (1980). Sensation seeking and its biological correlates. *Psychological Bulletin, 88*, 187–214.

Zuckerman, M., & Como, P. (1983). Sensation seeking and arousal systems. *Personality and Individual Differences, 4*, 381–386.

Zuckerman, M., Eysenck, S. B. G., & Eysenck, H. J. (1978). Sensation seeking in England and America: Cross-cultural, age, and sex comparisons. *Journal of Consulting and Clinical Psychology, 46*, 139–149.

Zuckerman, M., Kolin, I., Price, L., & Zoob, I. (1964). Development of a sensation seeking scale. *Journal of Consulting Psychology, 28*, 477–482.

Zuckerman, M., Kraft, M., & Cummings, J. (1993). Relationships between basic personality traits and reported parental behavior. Unpublished data.

Zuckerman, M., & Kuhlman, D. M. (1978). *Sensation seeking and risk taking in response to hypothetical situations*. Paper presented at the meeting of the International Association of Applied Psychology, Munich, August.

Zuckerman, M., Kuhlman, D. M., & Camac, C. (1988). What lies beyond E and N? Factor analyses of scales believed to measure basic dimensions of personality. *Journal of Personality and Social Psychology, 54*, 96–107.

Zuckerman, M., Kuhlman, D. M., Joireman, J., Teta, P., & Kraft, M. (1993). A comparison of three structural models for personality: The big three, the big five and the alternative five. *Journal of Personality and Social Psychology, 65,* 757–768.

Zuckerman, M., Kuhlman, D. M., Thornquist, M., & Kiers, H. (1991). Five (or three) robust questionnaire scale factors of personality without culture. *Personality and Individual Differences, 12,* 929–941.

Zuckerman, M., & Link, K. (1968). Construct validity for the Sensation Seeking Scale. *Journal of Consulting and Clinical Psychology, 32,* 420–426.

Zuckerman, M., & Litle, P. (1986). Personality and curiosity about morbid and sexual events. *Personality and Individual Differences, 7,* 49–56.

Zuckerman, M., & Lubin, B. (1965). *Test manual for the Multiple Affect Adjective Check List (MAACL).* San Diego: Educational and Industrial Testing Service.

Zuckerman, M., & Lubin, B. (1985). *Manual for the MAACL-R: The Multiple Affect Adjective Check List-Revised.* San Diego: Educational and Industrial Testing Service.

Zuckerman, M., Murtaugh, T. T., & Siegel, J. (1974). Sensation seeking and cortical augmenting–reducing. *Psychophysiology, 11,* 535–542.

Zuckerman, M., & Myers, P. L. (1983). Sensation seeking in homosexual and heterosexual males. *Archives of Sexual Behavior, 12,* 347–356.

Zuckerman, M., Neary, R. S., & Brustman, B. A. (1970). Sensation-seeking scale correlates in experience (smoking, drugs, alcohol, "hallucinations" and sex) and preference for complexity (designs). *Proceedings of the 78th Annual Convention of the American Psychological Association* (pp. 317–318). Washington, DC: American Psychological Association.

Zuckerman, M., & Neeb, M. (1979). Sensation seeking and psychopathology. *Psychiatry Research, 1,* 255–264.

Zuckerman, M., & Neeb, M. (1980). Demographic influences in sensation seeking and expressions of sensation seeking in religion, smoking, and driving habits. *Personality and Individual Differences, 1,* 197–206.

Zuckerman, M., Persky, H., Hopkins, T. R., Murtaugh, T., Basu, G. K., & Schilling, M. (1966). Comparison of stress effects of perceptual and social isolation. *Archives of General Psychiatry, 14,* 356–365.

Zuckerman, M., Persky, H., & Link, K. E. (1969). The influence of set and diurnal factors on autonomic responses to sensory deprivation. *Psychophysiology, 5,* 612–624.

Zuckerman, M., Persky, H., Link, K. E., & Basu, G. K. (1968). Experimental and subject factors determining responses to sensory deprivation, social isolation and confinement. *Journal of Abnormal Psychology, 73,* 183–194.

Zuckerman, M., Schultz, D. P., & Hopkins, T. R. (1967). Sensation seeking and volunteering for sensory deprivation and hypnosis experiments. *Journal of Consulting Psychology, 31,* 358–363.

Zuckerman, M., Simons, R. F., & Como, P. G. (1988). Sensation seeking and stimulus intensity as modulators of cortical, cardiovascular, and electrodermal response: A cross-modality study. *Personality and Individual Differences, 9,* 361–372.

Zuckerman, M., Sola, S., Masterson, J., & Angelone, J. V. (1975). MMPI patterns in drug abusers before and after treatment in therapeutic communities. *Journal of Consulting and Clinical Psychology, 43,* 286–296.

Zuckerman, M., & Teta, P. (1988). *Development of a non-forced choice version of the Sensation Seeking Scale.* Unpublished manuscript.

Zuckerman, M., Tushup, R., & Finner, S. (1976). Sexual attitudes and experience:

Attitude and personality correlations and changes produced by a course in sexuality. *Journal of Consulting and Clinical Psychology, 44,* 7–19.

Zuckerman, M., Ulrich, R. S., & McLaughlin, J. (1993). Sensation seeking and reactions to nature paintings. *Personality and Individual Differences, 15,* 563–576.

Zureick, J. L., & Meltzer, H. Y. (1988). Platelet MAO activity in hallucinating and paranoid schizophrenics: A review and meta-analysis. *Biological Psychiatry, 24,* 63–78.

Author index

Subject index

Printed in the United States
R1733800004B/R17338PG37413LVSX00005B/2}